TREATIES IN MOTION

The law of treaties is in constant motion, understood not only as locomotion, but also as motion through time and as change. Thus, kinesis and stasis, two sides of the same concept of 'motion', are the central themes of *Treaties in Motion*.

The concept of motion adopted in this book is based on the philosophy of Aristotle. He identified six types of motion: creation (genesis), increase (auxesis), diminution (meiosis), alteration (alloiosis), destruction (phthora), and change of place (kata topon metabole), which has been amended by the authors to change in space-time (kata topon kai chronon metavole) to reflect our modern scientific understanding of time as a dimension through which motion and change occurs.

Each chapter's analysis proceeds by focusing on a specific area of a treaty's 'life-cycle', where each type of motion shines through and is described through three different frames of reference: treaties, the Vienna Convention of the Law of Treaties, and customary law.

MALGOSIA FITZMAURICE is Professor of International Law at the School of Law, Queen Mary University of London and an associate member of the Institut de Droit International. She has delivered lectures at The Hague Academy of International Law, was involved in a multi stakeholder project funded by the EU Commission on environmental crime, is Editor in Chief of International Community Law Review journal (ICLR) and Queen Mary Studies in International Law, and has advised as expert on law of treaties.

PANOS MERKOURIS is Professor at the University of Groningen. In 2017 he was awarded the prestigious ERC Starting Grant for his 5-year project TRICI-Law (The Rules of Interpretation of Customary International Law). He has written extensively on law of treaties and on interpretation, has been cited in international reports and cases, and has advised as expert on these issues.

CAMBRIDGE STUDIES IN INTERNATIONAL AND COMPARATIVE LAW: 149

Established in 1946, this series produces high quality, reflective and innovative scholarship in the field of public international law. It publishes works on international law that are of a theoretical, historical, cross-disciplinary or doctrinal nature. The series also welcomes books providing insights from private international law, comparative law and transnational studies which inform international legal thought and practice more generally.

The series seeks to publish views from diverse legal traditions and perspectives, and of any geographical origin. In this respect it invites studies offering regional perspectives on core *problématiques* of international law, and in the same vein, it appreciates contrasts and debates between diverging approaches. Accordingly, books offering new or less orthodox perspectives are very much welcome. Works of a generalist character are greatly valued and the series is also open to studies on specific areas, institutions or problems. Translations of the most outstanding works published in other languages are also considered.

After seventy years, Cambridge Studies in International and Comparative Law sets the standard for international legal scholarship and will continue to define the discipline as it evolves in the years to come.

A list of books in the series can be found at the end of this volume.

TREATIES IN MOTION

The Evolution of Treaties from Formation to Termination

MALGOSIA FITZMAURICE
Queen Mary University of London
PANOS MERKOURIS
University of Groningen

CAMBRIDGE
UNIVERSITY PRESS

CAMBRIDGE
UNIVERSITY PRESS

University Printing House, Cambridge CB2 8BS, United Kingdom

One Liberty Plaza, 20th Floor, New York, NY 10006, USA

477 Williamstown Road, Port Melbourne, VIC 3207, Australia

314–321, 3rd Floor, Plot 3, Splendor Forum, Jasola District Centre, New Delhi – 110025, India

79 Anson Road, #06–04/06, Singapore 079906

Cambridge University Press is part of the University of Cambridge.

It furthers the University's mission by disseminating knowledge in the pursuit of education, learning, and research at the highest international levels of excellence.

www.cambridge.org
Information on this title: www.cambridge.org/9781108495882
DOI: 10.1017/9781108863407

First published 2020

A catalogue record for this publication is available from the British Library.

Library of Congress Cataloging-in-Publication Data
Names: Fitzmaurice, Malgosia, 1957– author. | Merkouris, Panos, author.
Title: Treaties in motion : the evolution of treaties from formation to termination / Malgosia Fitzmaurice, Queen Mary, University of London; Panos Merkouris, University of Groningen
Description: Cambridge, United Kingdom ; New York, NY, USA : Cambridge University Press, 2020. | Series: Cambridge studies in international and comparative law | Includes bibliographical references and index.
Identifiers: LCCN 2019057481 (print) | LCCN 2019057482 (ebook) | ISBN 9781108495882 (hardback) | ISBN 9781108797924 (paperback) | ISBN 9781108863407 (epub)
Subjects: LCSH: Treaties.
Classification: LCC KZ1301 .F58 2020 (print) | LCC KZ1301 (ebook) | DDC 341.3/7–dc23
LC record available at https://lccn.loc.gov/2019057481
LC ebook record available at https://lccn.loc.gov/2019057482

ISBN 978-1-108-49588-2 Hardback

CONTENTS

FIGURES

TABLES

ACKNOWLEDGEMENTS

The authors would like to thank Professor Olufemi Elias, Professor Roucounas, Professor Pazartzis, Professor Gormley, Dr Joanna Gomula (Lauterpacht Centre for International Law), Dr de Hoogh, Dr Papastavridis, Dr Gourgourinis, and Dr Tsampi for their thoughts, criticisms, and comments on various ideas presented in this book, and draft versions of the chapters.

The book is a collaborative effort between the authors. The initial ideas for Chapters 2, 3, and 5 are attributed to Professor Malgosia Fitzmaurice and for Chapters 1, 4, 6, and 7 to Professor Merkouris. The charts, tables and empirical data analysis in Chapter 5 were created by a team led by Professor Merkouris, and special thanks go to Konrad Turnbull for his invaluable assistance. We would also like to thank Ms Fortuna and Mr Zuidema for their assistance with the table in Chapter 4, and Ms Rydberg, Ms Mileva, and Dr Longobardo for their editorial assistance.

Chapter 4 was research conducted in the context of the project 'The Rules of Interpretation of Customary International Law' ('TRICI-Law'). This project has received funding from the European Research Council (ERC) under the European Union's Horizon 2020 Research and Innovation Programme (Grant Agreement No. 759728).

Finally, we would also like to thank the editors of the Cambridge Series in International and Comparative Law, Professor Larissa van den Herik and Professor Jean d' Aspremont, as well as Tom Randall and Gemma Smith from Cambridge University Press, for seeing the merit in our book proposal and for their helpful comments throughout the publication process.

LIST OF ABBREVIATIONS

A/M/R	Amendment/Modification/Revision
Add	Addendum
AFDI	*Annuaire Français de Droit International*
AG	Advocate-General
AIA/s	Autonomous Institutional Arrangement/s
AIDI	*Annuaire de l'Institut de Droit International*
AJIL	*American Journal of International Law*
App No/s	Application Number/s
ARIEL	*Austrian Review of International and European Law*
ARSIWA	Articles on Responsibility of States for Internationally Wrongful Acts
art/s	article/s
ASDI	*Annuaire Suisse de Droit International*
ASEAN	Association of Southeast Asian Nations
AYBIL	*Australian Yearbook of International Law*
BAA	British Airport Authority
BerkJIntlL	*Berkeley Journal of International Law*
Bern Convention	Convention on the Conservation of European Wildlife and Natural Habitats
BFSP	British and Foreign State Papers
BIICL	British Institute of International and Comparative Law
BIT	Bilateral Investment Treaty
BSAP	Baltic Sea Action Plan
BYIL	*British Yearbook of International Law*
CalWInt'lLJ	*California Western International Law Journal*
CEDAW	Convention on the Elimination of All Forms of Discrimination against Women
cf	*conferatur*
Ch/s	Chapter/s
CIL	Customary International Law
CILJ	*Cambridge International Law Journal*
CITES	Convention on International Trade in Endangered Species of Wild Fauna and Flora

CJEU	Court of Justice of the European Union
CJICL	*Cambridge Journal of International and Comparative Law*
Climate L	*Climate Law*
CLJ	*Cambridge Law Journal*
CMLR	*Common Market Law Review*
CMP	Conference of the Parties Serving as the Meeting of the Parties to the Kyoto Protocol
ColumJTransnat'lL	*Columbia Journal of Transnational Law*
COP	Conference of the Parties
COW	Committee of the Whole
CSC	Convention for Safe Containers
CSIH	Court of Session, Inner House
CSOH	Court of Session, Outer House
CTS	Consolidated Treaty Series
CUP	Cambridge University Press
DePaul LR	*DePaul Law Review*
Doc	Document
DOC	2002 China–ASEAN Declaration on the Conduct of Parties in the South China Sea
EBRD	European Bank for Reconstruction and Development
EC	European Communities
ECHR	European Convention on Human Rights
ECLI	European Case Law Identifier
ECmmHR	European Commission of Human Rights
ECOSOC	United Nations Economic and Social Council
ECOWAS	Economic Community of West African States
ECR	*European Court Reports*
ECtHR	European Court of Human Rights
ed/s	editor/s
eg	*exempli gratia*
EIF	Entry into force
EJIL	*European Journal of International Law*
ELR	*European Law Review*
EP&L	*Environmental Policy and Law*
et al	*et alii* / and others
EU	European Union
EuConst	*European Constitutional Law Review*
EurJLegStud	*European Journal of Legal Studies*
EWHC	High Court of Justice of England and Wales
FCO	Foreign and Commonwealth Office
ff	folio / and the following

fn/s	footnote/s
FoundPhys	Foundations of Physics
FRG	Federal Republic of Germany
FXO	Foreign Exchange Office
FYROM	Former Yugoslav Republic of Macedonia
GC	Grand Chamber
GeoIntlEnvtlLRev	*Georgetown International Environmental Law Review*
GYIL	*German Yearbook of International Law*
HELCOM	Baltic Marine Environment Protection Commission (Helsinki Commission)
HILJ	*Harvard International Law Journal*
HistMath	*Historia Mathematica*
HLR	*Harvard Law Review*
HRCttee	Human Rights Committee
HRLJ	*Human Rights Law Journal*
HYIL	*Hague Yearbook of International Law*
IACtHR	Inter-American Court of Human Rights
IACtHR Series	*Inter-American Court of Human Rights Series*
ibid	*ibidem*
ICAO	International Civil Aviation Organisation
ICC	International Criminal Court
ICCPR	International Covenant on Civil and Political Rights
ICESCR	International Covenant on Economic, Social and Cultural Rights
ICJ	International Court of Justice
ICJ Rep	*International Court of Justice Reports*
ICLQ	*International and Comparative Law Quarterly*
ICLR	*International Community Law Review*
ICRW	International Convention for the Regulation of Whaling
ICSID	International Centre for Settlement of Investment Disputes
IDI	Institut de Droit International
ie	*id est*
IGO/s	Inter-Governmental Organisation/s
IHRR	*International Human Rights Reports*
IJECL	*International Journal of Estuarine and Coastal Law*
IJIL	*Indian Journal of International Law*
ILA	International Law Association
ILC	International Law Commission
ILM	*International Legal Materials*
ILO	International Labour Organisation
ILR	*International Law Reports*

IMO	International Maritime Organisation
Inc	Incorporated
Int'lJConstL	*International Journal of Constitutional Law*
INTELSAT	International Telecommunications Satellite Organisation
IOLR	*International Organisations Law Review*
IPES	Istituto per l'Edilizia sociale della Provincia autonoma di Bolzano
Iran-USCTR	*Iran–US Claims Tribunal Reports*
ITLOS	International Tribunal for the Law of the Sea
ITLOS Rep	*International Tribunal for the Law of the Sea Reports*
ITU	International Telecommunications Union
IWC	International Whaling Commission
JDI	*Journal du Droit International*
JEL	*Journal of Environmental Law*
JIDS	*Journal of International Dispute Settlement*
JILIR	*Journal of International Law and International Relations*
JLA	*Journal of Legal Analysis*
JMarL&Com	*Journal of Maritime Law and Commerce*
JPhil	*Journal of Philosophy*
KLJ	*King's Law Journal*
LCIA	London Court of International Arbitration
LGDJ	Librairie générale de droit et de jurisprudence
LJIL	*Leiden Journal of International Law*
LNTS	*League of Nations Treaty Series*
London Convention	London Convention on the Prevention of the Pollution from Dumping of Wastes and Other Matter
LRTAP	Long-Range Transboundary Air Pollution
Ltd	Limited
MAPS	Mitigation Actions Plans and Scenarios
MARPOL Convention	International Convention for the Prevention of Pollution from Ships
McGill LJ	*McGill Law Journal*
MEA/s	Multilateral Environmental Agreement/s
MEPC	Marine Environment Protection Committee
MichJInt'lL	*Michigan Journal of International Law*
MichLRev	*Michigan Law Review*
MOP	Meeting of the Parties
MOU	Memorandum of Understanding
MPEPIL	*Max Planck Encyclopaedia of Public International Law*
MSC	Maritime Safety Committee
MUP	Manchester University Press

NAFO	Northwest Atlantic Fisheries Organisation
NCJInt'lL & ComReg	*North Carolina Journal of International Law and Commercial Regulation*
NCP/s	Non-Compliance Procedure/s
NDC	Nationally Determined Contribution
NEAFC	North East Atlantic Fishery Commission
NILR	*Netherlands International Law Review*
NJIL	*Nordic Journal of International Law*
no/s	number/s
NYIL	*Netherlands Yearbook of International Law*
OAS	Organisation of American States
OECD	Organisation for Economic Co-operation and Development
OSPAR Convention	Convention for the Protection of the Marine Environment of the North-East Atlantic
OUP	Oxford University Press
PacPhilosQ	*Pacific Philosophical Quarterly*
para/s	paragraph/s
PCA	Permanent Court of Arbitration
PCIJ	Permanent Court of International Justice
PCIJ Rep	*Permanent Court of International Justice Reports*
Philos&PhenomenolRes	*Philosophy and Phenomenological Research*
PRC	People's Republic of China
QuestInt'lL	*Questions of International Law*
RdC	*Recueil des Cours de l'Academie de Droit International de la Haye*
RECIEL	*Review of European Community and International Environmental Law*
Rev	revised
RGDIP	*Revue Générale de Droit International Public*
RHD	*Revue historique de droit français et étranger*
RHDI	*Revue Hellénique de Droit International*
RivDirInternaz	*Rivista di Diritto Internazionale*
RTDE	*Revue Trimestrielle de Droit Europeen*
SCC	Stockholm Chamber of Commerce
Sect/s	Section/s
Sn	*Sine nomine*/without a name
SOLAS	International Convention for the Safety of Life at Sea
SRFC	Sub-Regional Fisheries Commission
SSRN	Social Sciences Research Network
TA/NO	Tacit Acceptance/No Objection
TA/RO	Tacit Acceptance/Regular Objection

TA/SO	Tacit Acceptance/Strong Objection
TA/WO	Tacit Acceptance/Weak Objection
TEU	Treaty of the European Union
TFEU	Treaty on the Functioning of the European Union
THRR	*Tydskrif vir Hedendaagse Romeins-Hollandse Reg (Journal for Contemporary Roman-Dutch Law)*
TIR	Transport International Routier
tr	translation
UIllLRev	*University of Illinois Law Review*
UK	United Kingdom
UKHL	United Kingdom House of Lords
UN	United Nations
UNCED	United Nations Conference on Environment and Development
UNCITRAL	United Nations Commission on International Trade Law
UNEP	United Nations Environment Programme
UNFCCC	United Nations Framework Convention on Climate Change
UNGA	United Nations General Assembly
UNODC	United Nations Office on Drugs and Crime
UNRIAA	United Nations *Review of International Arbitral Awards*
UNSG	United Nations Secretary General
UNTS	*United Nations Treaty Series*
US/USA	United States of America
v	*versus*
VaLRev	*Virginia Law Review*
VCLT	Vienna Convention on the Law of Treaties
Vol/s	Volume/s
WAMU	West African Monetary Union
WHO	World Health Organisation
WMO	World Meteorological Organisation
WTO	World Trade Organisation
YBILC	*Yearbook of the International Law Commission*
YEL	*Yearbook of European Law*
ZaöRV	*Zeitschrift für ausländisches öffentliches Recht und Völkerrecht*
ZOffR	*Zeitschrift für öffentliches Recht*

TABLE OF CASES

International Court of Justice

Permanent Court of International Justice

International Tribunal on the Law of the Sea

Court of Justice of the European Union

Iran–US Claims Tribunal

Arbitration

European Court of Human Rights & European Commission of Human Rights

Inter-American Court of Human Rights

UN Human Rights Treaty Bodies

International Criminal Court

WTO Dispute Settlement Bodies

Other Cases

TABLE OF TREATIES

Multilateral Treaties

Bilateral Treaties

1

Motion as a Notion

1.1 Introduction

Law, and international law in particular, sits at the oscillation point between competing forces; stability and change, rest and motion.[1] According to Ackermann and Fenrich, '[l]aw ought to be steady as a rock and reliable in times of uncertainty, while simultaneously adaptable to shifting needs and emerging challenges'.[2] This tug of war between stability and change is revelatory of the fact that international law is a dynamic system that, on the one hand, needs to accommodate for the fundamental need for stability and predictability as the quintessential building blocks of any legal system, but, on the other hand, must also by necessity stay relevant by adapting to the 'requirements of international life',[3] as the International Court of Justice (ICJ) put it, which do not refer only to changes in law but also to changes in fact, historic events, changing morals, and leaps in science, technology, and morals. The competing forces of motion and rest are the two main drivers of the international legal system, and not just of that. As more poetically put by Emerson, '[m]otion or change, and identity or rest, are the first and second secrets of nature: Motion and Rest. The whole code of her laws may be written on the thumbnail, or the signet of a ring'.[4]

[1] See M Ambrus and R Wessel, 'Between Pragmatism and Predictability: Temporariness in International Law' (2014) 45 NYIL 3, and all articles in that volume.

[2] T Ackermann and K Fenrich, 'Motion and Rest: International Law's Responsiveness towards Terrorism, Mass Surveillance, and Self-Defence' (2017) 77 ZaöRV 745, 746.

[3] *Reparation for Injuries Suffered in the Service of the United Nations* (Advisory Opinion) [1949] ICJ Rep 174, 178.

[4] RW Emerson, 'Nature' in J Slater, AR Ferguson and JF Carr (eds), *Collected Works of Ralph Waldo Emerson, Vol III: Essays* (Belknap Press/Harvard University Press 1983) 105. More than two millennia earlier, Aristotle had said something quite similar when he proposed that nature (but nature as an attribute of objects) is an inner principle of *kinesis* (change/motion) and of being at rest (Aristotle, *Physics* II:1, 192b20–3).

1.2 The Force That Set Things in Motion

The idea for *Treaties in Motion* resulted from an observed bias in international authorship to examine treaties in a relatively static and fragmented way; for instance, through the lens either of the Vienna Convention on the Law of Treaties' (VCLT)[5] structure, or of a particular VCLT provision (eg Articles 31–33 VCLT on interpretation), or of its application in a specialised regime. Treaties are the connecting bridge between the two constant competing interests of, on the one hand, stability of international relations and, on the other hand, ensuring the adaptability/dynamism of the international legal system. The concept of time, so critical in the functioning of treaties, is implied in the classical aphorism that treaties are 'living instruments'.[6] However, this concept of treaties being living instruments has been inextricably linked to evolutive/dynamic interpretation.[7] That is not *eo ipso* incorrect. However, to relegate the concept of time and change with respect to treaties only to the process of interpretation is a somewhat gross oversimplification. Treaties, as any rule of international law, are in a constant state of motion. As in nature no object is ever in a condition of absolute *stasis* (even when it is motionless), the same is true for treaties. Treaties, the 'treaty on treaties' (as the VCLT is sometimes referred to), and the customary law on treaties constantly evolve, change, and adapt. This process is not a compartmentalised one. It does not affect only treaties or only their interpretation. This 'motion' of treaties is ubiquitous. It affects treaties even before their coming into existence (*in statu nascendi*) up until and including their termination. Furthermore, the aforementioned motion affects not just treaties but also the rules on which these treaties are based (ie treaty law based either on the VCLT or customary international law). The VCLT itself also partakes of this motion in two ways. First, its content also

[5] 1969 Vienna Convention on the Law of Treaties (adopted 23 May 1969, entered into force 27 January 1980) 1155 UNTS 331.

[6] *Vo v France* [GC] ECtHR, App No 53924/00 (8 July 2004) [82]; *Tyrer v UK*, ECtHR, App No 5856/72 (25 April 1978) [31]; *Loizidou v Turkey (Preliminary Objections)* [GC] ECtHR, App No 15318/89 (23 March 1995) [71]; *RR v Poland*, ECtHR, App No 27617/04 (26 May 2011) [186]; *EB v France* [GC] ECtHR, App No 43546/02 (22 January 2008) [92].

[7] G Nolte (ed), *Treaties and Subsequent Practice* (OUP 2013); R Gardiner, *Treaty Interpretation* (2nd edn, OUP 2015); E Bjorge, *The Evolutionary Interpretation of Treaties* (OUP 2014); D Moeckli and ND White, 'Treaties as "Living Instruments"' in MJ Bowman and D Kritsiotis (eds), *Conceptual and Contextual Perspectives on the Modern Law of Treaties* (CUP 2018) 136–70. See also analysis in Chapter 4 of the present book.

changes through time, and second it has found its way into and affected the content of several 'special regimes' in international law.

From the aforementioned, it is evident that the notion of motion is critical to our analytical perspective. It is necessary, therefore, to elaborate on our understanding of motion and the manner in which it influences the structure of this book.

1.3 Notion of Motion

The concept of motion was central to ancient Greek philosophy. So much so, in fact, that some of the arguments proposed on whether motion is something real or merely an illusion were and continue to be debated even today. Zeno of Elea, for instance, is famous for proposing a number of paradoxes in which he attempted to prove the illusion of motion, in defence of the teachings of his mentor, Parmenides of Elea, who had famously argued that there is no motion at all. Zeno's most famous paradoxes of motion are three: (i) *the bisection paradox*;[8] (ii) *Achilles's race against a tortoise*;[9] and (iii) *the (non)-moving arrow paradox.*[10]

[8] Aristotle, *Physics* VI:9, 239b10; according to this paradox, which is very similar to the *Achilles' paradox*, one can never traverse a specific distance, eg walk from one end of the room to the other. The reason is quite simple, according to Zeno. In order to achieve that goal, one would have to walk half the distance of the room. Once that was accomplished, out of the remaining distance, half would have to be traversed as well. After that, the half of the remaining distance, and so on and so forth *ad infinitum*. Since there is an infinite number of halfway points, and since no mortal human being can perform infinite tasks in a finite amount of time, then clearly motion is impossible and what we perceive as motion is an illusion.

[9] ibid 239b15; in this paradox, Zeno asks his audience to imagine that Achilles is racing against a tortoise. Because Achilles is famous for his speed (after all Homer used the adjective 'swift-footed' to describe him in the *Iliad*) he offers the tortoise stadium-odds, ie the tortoise will start the race being one stadium (a stadium, or *stadion*, in ancient Greece was a unit of length, equivalent to roughly 175 meters) ahead of Achilles. As soon the signal is given, both Achilles and the tortoise start racing. However, in Zeno's view, no matter how fast Achilles is he will never be able to overtake the tortoise. The reason is quite simple. As soon as Achilles covers the distance of one *stadion* the tortoise will have moved x distance. Achilles will then cover that distance as well within a short amount of time. But by that point the tortoise will have moved a, smaller granted but existing nonetheless, y distance, and so on and so forth. Achilles will always be trailing slightly behind the tortoise.

[10] According to this thought experiment by Zeno, an arrow is at rest if it occupies a place equal to itself. However, even a moving arrow at any given instance will occupy a particular place in space. Consequently, the arrow will always be at a state of rest, as it will always occupy a particular place, neither moving into that place nor out of that place. Consequently, there is no motion occurring and the arrow is always at rest.

Paying homage to these paradoxes, the authors of the present book, inspired by Marcel Duchamp's *Nude Descending a Staircase No 2*, where a person is depicted in the various stages of descending a staircase all at the same time, selected the image that features as the cover of the present book. This not only alludes to Zeno's paradoxes of motion but also to various attempts at their refutation, as well as to more recent theoretical views on the matter of time and change, as will be analysed next and in Sections 1.4–1.5.

Many have grappled with finding ways to resolve Zeno's paradoxes, or proving them to be pseudo-paradoxes. Diogenes the Cynic famously attempted to refute Zeno's paradoxes of motion in the simplest possible fashion. After listening to them, he simply stood up and walked,[11] which led to the phrase *solvitur ambulando* being coined. Aristotle's own attempt at refutation is a precursor of Georg Cantor's mathematical refutation several centuries later, and distinguishes between actual infinity and potential infinity.[12] Bertrand Russell and several other philosophers believed that Zeno's paradoxes on motion have been solved, at least mathematically,[13] by the transfinite arithmetic invented by Cantor.[14] The motion paradoxes emerge from several unsubstantiated presumptions, such as that humans are incapable of performing 'supertasks', ie infinitely many acts performed in a finite interval of time,[15] that all infinite series are of the same nature, or that since an infinite set consists of infinite elements its sum will tend to

[11] Simplicius, *On Aristotle's Physics* 1012.22 (Bloomsbury 1997).

[12] Aristotle, *Physics* VIII:17, 263a15; Aristotle, *Physics* VI:9, 239b5.

[13] R Sorensen, *A Brief History of the Paradox: Philosophy and the Labyrinths of the Mind* (OUP 2003) 54.

[14] G Cantor, *Contributions to the Founding of the Theory of Transfinite Numbers* (Ph Jourdain tr, Dover Publications 1951); J Ferreirós, '"What Fermented in Me for Years": Cantor's Discovery of Transfinite Numbers' (1995) 22 HistMath 33.

[15] On the position that it is impossible for human beings to perform 'supertasks', see: M Black, 'Achilles and the Tortoise' (1951) 11/5 Analysis 91; J Gwiazda, 'A Proof of the Impossibility of Completing Infinitely Many Tasks' (2012) 93 PacPhilosQ 1–7. *Contra,* see: JF Thomson, 'Tasks and Super-Tasks' (1954) 15 Analysis 1, who provides a criticism of supertasks and offers the famous Thompson's lamp thought experiment. Generally, on supertasks, see: JD Norton, 'A Quantum Mechanical Supertask' (1999) 29/8 FoundPhys 1265; P Benacerraf, 'Tasks, Super-Tasks, and the Modern Eleatics' (1962) 59 JPhil 765–84; A Grünbaum, 'Modern Science and Zeno's Paradoxes of Motion' in WC Samon (ed), *Zeno's Paradoxes* (Bobbs-Merrill 1970) 200–50; J Earman and JD Norton, 'Infinite Pains: The Trouble with Supertasks' in A Morton and S Stich (eds), *Paul Benacerraf: The Philosopher and His Critics* (Blackwell 1996) 231–61.

infinity. However, as has been demonstrated by set theory, this is far from the case, since not all infinities are equal.[16]

Despite the continuous claims that Zeno's paradoxes of motion have been refuted, every now and then there is another additional refutation or another venue of inquiry (mathematical, physical or philosophical) that is deemed worthy to explore. As Alfred North Whitehead insightfully remarked: 'To be refuted in every century after you have written is the acme of triumph ... No one ever touched Zeno without refuting him, and every century thinks it worthwhile to refute him'.[17] This goes to show how critical the inquiry into the very nature of motion has been and remains, not only in philosophy but in other sciences as well, including the legal science.

As mentioned, Aristotle made one of the early attempts at refutation of Zeno's claim that motion is an illusion. This should come as no surprise, as the father of science had dealt in one of his treatises with the topic of motion. It is precisely Aristotle's typology of motion that has influenced the structure and focus of the present book and therefore it is helpful to reproduce it in full. In his *Categories,* Aristotle, unlike Zeno, not only accepts motion (*kinesis*) but typologises it in six categories and provides an analysis of the interactions and differences between these six groups. Those six categories are: generation (*genesis*), destruction (*phthora*), increase (*auxesis*), diminution (*meiosis*), alteration (*alloiosis*), and change of place (*kata topon metabole*). In more detail:

> **XIV – Of Motion**
> There are six sorts of movement: generation, destruction, increase, diminution, alteration, and change of place.
>
> It is evident in all but one case that all these sorts of movement are distinct each from each. Generation is distinct from destruction, increase and change of place from diminution, and so on. But in the case of alteration it may be argued that the process necessarily implies one or another of the other five sorts of motion. This is not true, for we may say that all affections, or nearly all, produce in us an alteration which is distinct from all other sorts of motion, for that which is affected need not suffer either increase or diminution or any of the other sorts of motion. Thus,

16 In the present case, we are dealing with a convergent series, ie an infinite series whose sequence of its partial sums tends to a limit. By 'limit' what is meant is that the partial sums of that divergent series become ever closer to a given number. In the case of Zeno's paradoxes, the infinite series is in the form of: $s_n = 1/2 + 1/4 + 1/8 \ldots$ The closer n gets to infinite the sum of the series, (s_n) tends to 1.

17 AN Whitehead, *Essays in Science and Philosophy* (Philosophical Library 1948) 114.

alteration is a distinct sort of motion; for, if it were not, the thing altered would not only be altered, but would forthwith necessarily suffer increase or diminution or some one of the other sorts of motion in addition; which as a matter of fact is not the case. Similarly, that which was undergoing the process of increase or was subject to some other sort of motion would, if alteration were not a distinct form of motion, necessarily be subject to alteration also. But there are some things which undergo increase but yet not alteration. The square, for instance, if a gnomon is applied to it, undergoes increase but not alteration, and so it is with all other figures of this sort. Alteration and increase, therefore, are distinct.

Speaking generally, rest is the contrary of motion. But the different forms of motion have their own contraries in other forms; thus, destruction is the contrary of generation, diminution of increase, rest in a place or change of place. As for this last, change in the reverse direction would seem to be most truly its contrary; thus, motion upwards is the contrary of motion downwards, and vice versa.

In the case of that sort of motion which yet remains, of those that have been enumerated, it is not easy to state what is its contrary. It appears to have no contrary, unless one should define the contrary here also either as 'rest in its quality' or as 'change in the direction of the contrary quality', just as we defined the contrary of change of place either as rest in a place or as change in the reverse direction. For a thing is altered when change of quality takes place; therefore, either rest in its quality or change in the direction of the contrary may be called the contrary of this qualitative form of motion. In this way, becoming white is the contrary of becoming black; there is alteration in the contrary direction, since a change of a qualitative nature takes place.[18]

[18] Aristotle, *Categories*, ch XIV; the original text is as follows: '§ 14. Κινήσεως δέ ἐστιν εἴδη ἕξ· γένεσις, φθορά, αὔξησις, μείωσις, ἀλλοίωσις, κατὰ τόπον μεταβολή.

Αἱ μὲν οὖν ἄλλαι κινήσεις φανερὸν ὅτι ἕτεραι ἀλλήλων εἰσίν· οὐ γάρ ἐστιν ἡ γένεσις φθορὰ οὐδέ γε ἡ αὔξησις μείωσις οὐδὲ ἡ κατὰ τόπον μεταβολή, ὡσαύτως δὲ καὶ αἱ ἄλλαι· ἐπὶ δὲ τῆς ἀλλοιώσεως ἔχει τινὰ ἀπορίαν, μήποτε ἀναγκαῖον ᾖ τὸ ἀλλοιούμενον κατά τινα τῶν λοιπῶν κινήσεων ἀλλοιοῦσθαι.

Τοῦτο δὲ οὐκ ἀληθές ἐστιν· σχεδὸν γὰρ κατὰ πάντα τὰ πάθη ἢ τὰ πλεῖστα ἀλλοιοῦσθαι συμβέβηκεν ἡμῖν οὐδεμιᾶς τῶν ἄλλων κινήσεων κοινωνοῦσιν· οὔτε γὰρ αὔξεσθαι ἀναγκαῖον τὸ κατὰ πάθος κινούμενον οὔτε μειοῦσθαι, ὡσαύτως δὲ καὶ ἐπὶ τῶν ἄλλων, ὥσθ' ἑτέρα ἂν εἴη παρὰ τὰς ἄλλας κινήσεις ἡ ἀλλοίωσις· εἰ γὰρ ἦν ἡ αὐτή, ἔδει τὸ ἀλλοιούμενον εὐθὺς καὶ αὔξεσθαι ἢ μειοῦσθαι ἤ τινα τῶν ἄλλων ἀκολουθεῖν κινήσεων· ἀλλ' οὐκ ἀνάγκη.

Ὡσαύτως δὲ καὶ τὸ αὐξόμενον ἤ τινα ἄλλην κίνησιν κινούμενον ἀλλοιοῦσθαι· ἀλλ' ἔστι τινὰ αὐξανόμενα ἃ οὐκ ἀλλοιοῦται· οἷον τὸ τετράγωνον γνώμονος περιτεθέντος ηὔξηται μέν, ἀλλοιότερον δὲ οὐδὲν γεγένηται· ὡσαύτως δὲ καὶ ἐπὶ τῶν ἄλλων τῶν τοιούτων.

Ὥσθ' ἕτεραι ἂν εἴησαν αἱ κινήσεις ἀλλήλων.

[15b.1-32] Ἔστι δὲ ἁπλῶς μὲν κίνησις ἠρεμίᾳ ἐναντίον· ταῖς δὲ καθ' ἕκαστα, γενέσει μὲν φθορά, αὐξήσει δὲ μείωσις· τῇ δὲ κατὰ τόπον μεταβολῇ ἡ κατὰ τόπον ἠρεμία μάλιστα ἔοικεν ἀντικεῖσθαι, καὶ εἰ ἄρα ἡ εἰς τὸν ἐναντίον τόπον μεταβολή, οἷον τῇ κάτωθεν ἡ ἄνω, τῇ ἄνωθεν ἡ κάτω.

It is these six types of motion that have informed the structure and focus of this book. It is interesting to note that Aristotle's approach to motion is important for a number of other reasons as well, most importantly because it highlights the interconnectedness between motion, identity, change, and time, to which we shall turn our attention now.

1.4 Motion as Change

The word used by Aristotle for motion is *kinesis*. This term has a wider meaning than simply 'locomotion'. It refers to that, but it also refers to change.[19] And this is neither the only point where the connection between motion and change is made, nor where its critical role is highlighted. Nature, according to Aristotle, is an inner principle of *kinesis* (change/motion) and of being at rest.[20] Natures as inner principles of change/motion and rest are contrasted with active powers or potentialities (*dunameis*), which are external principles of change and being at rest,[21] operative on the corresponding internal passive capacities or potentialities (*dunameis* again).[22]

Even today the connection between motion and change is evident. According to the Oxford Dictionary, 'motion' is the 'action or process of moving or being moved'.[23] This is not extremely helpful as far as definitions go. If we then turn to the definition of 'move', then we get 'change the place, position, or state of',[24] which goes to show that motion

Τῇ δὲ λοιπῇ τῶν ἀποδοθεισῶν κινήσεων οὐ ῥᾴδιον ἀποδοῦναι τί ποτέ ἐστιν ἐναντίον, ἔοικε δὲ οὐδὲν εἶναι αὐτῇ ἐναντίον, εἰ μή τις καὶ ἐπὶ ταύτης τὴν κατὰ τὸ ποιὸν ἠρεμίαν ἀντιθείη ἢ τὴν εἰς τὸ ἐναντίον τοῦ ποιοῦ μεταβολήν, καθάπερ καὶ ἐπὶ τῆς κατὰ τόπον μεταβολῆς τὴν κατὰ τόπον ἠρεμίαν ἢ τὴν εἰς τὸ ἐναντίον τόπον μεταβολήν, —ἔστι γὰρ ἡ ἀλλοίωσις μεταβολὴ κατὰ τὸ ποιόν·— ὥστε ἀντίκειται τῇ κατὰ τὸ ποιὸν κινήσει ἡ κατὰ τὸ ποιὸν ἠρεμία ἢ ἡ εἰς τὸ ἐναντίον τοῦ ποιοῦ μεταβολή, οἷον τὸ λευκὸν γίγνεσθαι τῷ μέλαν γίγνεσθαι· ἀλλοιοῦται γὰρ εἰς τὰ ἐναντία τοῦ ποιοῦ μεταβολῆς γιγνομένης'.

19 B Russell, *The History of Western Philosophy* (Simon & Schuster 1967) 205. The atomists held that all change was in reality the motion of atoms into new configurations, a concept that would start unfolding itself in the seventeenth century, especially in the work of René Descartes, and reach its full potential much later; N Huggett and C Hoefer, 'Absolute and Relational Theories of Space and Motion' (*Stanford Encyclopedia of Philosophy*, 22 January 2015) accessed 20 September 2019.

20 Aristotle, *Physics* II:1, 192b20–3.

21 Aristotle, *Metaphysics* IX:8, 1049b5–10.

22 ibid IX:1, 1046a11–3. This echoes the debate surrounding the basis of evolutive interpretation, especially whether it can be attributed to the nature of the treaty. We shall return to this point in Chapter 4 on Interpretation.

23 'Motion' (*Oxford Dictionaries* 2018) accessed 20 September 2019.

24 'Move' (*Oxford Dictionaries*, 2018) accessed 20 September 2019.

and change are concepts inextricably linked on multiple levels. Critical to the idea of motion is the manifestation of change either to the position or to the state of being of the object examined.

Unsurprisingly, change as a manifestation of motion was tackled extensively in ancient Greek philosophy. Zeno's mentor, Parmenides of Elea, was famous for arguing that everything is one and nothing changes.[25] Heraclitus of Ephesus, on the other hand, took the completely opposite view,[26] believing that 'everything changes/moves/flows and nothing stands still'.[27] In the philosophy of Heraclitus, change is a foundational block. One of his most famous quotes is 'δὶς ἐς τὸν αὐτὸν ποταμὸν οὐκ ἂν ἐμβαίης', which translates to 'the same person cannot enter the same river twice'. Here, Heraclitus touches on the paradox of change and of identity. According to him, the moment a person enters a river at a particular instance in time, that river will consist of a certain volume of water, and that volume of certain very specific atoms of hydrogen and oxygen. If after a few minutes the same person attempts to enter the allegedly 'same' river, they would be entering a completely different river, or so Heraclitus posits. The droplets of water covering you during your first immersion have long moved on with the flow of the river. The second time around, you are entering a river that is both qualitatively and quantitatively different.[28]

This *Heraclitus's river paradox* is one of a string of similar paradoxes,[29] such as *Theseus's ship paradox*[30] or *Chrysippus's*

[25] Russell, *The History of Western Philosophy* 48–52. Parmenides's views were expounded in his poem *On Nature*, which has survived only in *fragmenta*.

[26] Although Parmenides would not accept this, because since all is One and indivisible, there can be no opposition.

[27] 'πάντα ρεῖ καὶ οὐδὲν μένει'; Plato, *Cratylus* 402a.

[28] Various solutions have been offered and theories developed as a direct result of the ongoing discussion on how to reconcile this paradox with our everyday experience of time, change and identity; see in more detail Section 1.4.

[29] A favourite tool of ancient Greek and Roman philosophers in order to highlight either the pitfalls of our own preconceptions or the limits of our quest for true knowledge. For instance, Agrippa held that true knowledge is unobtainable, as any logical argument would inexorably lead to one of the three following logical dead-ends: (i) an *argumentum ad absurdum*, ie an argument leading to a paradoxical/absurd conclusion; (ii) an *argumentum ad infinitum*, an argument that ends up in an eternal, self-perpetuating circular argument; or (iii) an axiomatic argument, ie an argument which is based on a statement that can be neither proven or disproven. This is known as *Agrippa's trilemma*. For an overview of the trilemma and modern responses to it, see PD Klein, 'Contemporary Responses to Agrippa's Trilemma' in J Greco (ed), *The Oxford Handbook of Skepticism* (OUP 2008) 484–503.

[30] Plutarch, *Theseus* ch 23:1. According to this paradox, Theseus has devoted to the gods the ship that he used on his quest to slay the Minotaur. However, due to the passage of time, several wooden planks of the ship need to be replaced at regular intervals. This process is

paradox.[31] A detailed analysis of these paradoxes falls outside the scope of this book, nonetheless all have as a common denominator the aforementioned notion of motion as change. In addition to this and in the context of the aforementioned philosophical musing on motion, motion as change is also strongly connected with the passage of time, which brings us to an additional manifestation of motion.

1.5 Motion through Time

So, is time a concept clearly distinct from motion and change? Absolutely not, either according to ancient Greek philosophers or to more modern scientific minds in physics. 'Time, [Aristotle] says, is motion that admits of numeration[32] . . . There always has been motion, and there always will be; for there cannot be time without motion'.[33]

repeated over and over, to the extent that none of the original planks survives. The question is at which point (if any) did the ship stop being his old ship and become a new one due to the replacement of rotten planks to the extent that the entire ship ended up being comprised of entirely new pieces of wood. Thomas Hobbes posited a modern variant of this paradox. In the previous example, another ship is built in a different location, and every time *Theseus's ship* needs new planks, those are taken from that second ship, and the planks from *Theseus's ship* are used in that second ship. Gradually, the new ship would consist entirely of the original planks of *Theseus's ship.* In that case, which of the two ships would be the true *Theseus's ship*, the one in the original place, or the one in the second location? And if a change happened, at what point in time did it happen? Or alternatively, do we at any point end up with a situation where we have two *Theseus's ships* existing at the same time? Th Hobbes, *Elements of Philosophy – The First Section, Concerning Body* (R and W Leybourn 1656) ch XI, sect 7, 100. See also H Deutsch, 'Relative Identity' (*Stanford Encyclopedia of Philosophy*, 17 August 2018) accessed 20 September 2019.

31 Philo, *De aeternitate mundi* IX:48–51. Chrysippus, a third-century BC Stoic philosopher, posited the following paradox, which is similar to Hobbes's variant of *Theseus's ship.* We have two men: Dion and Theon. The only difference between these two men is that Theon consists of Dion minus his left foot. Chyrsippus asks the following question: If a situation occurs where Dion's left foot is amputated, then does this affect the relationship between Theon and Dion? Do they remain two distinct entities that simply occupy the same space, or do we only have one entity? If the latter is the case, which entity has survived? Has Dion ceased to exist and been subsumed by Theon, or has the reverse taken place, ie Theon being subsumed by the now-amputee Dion? For an in-depth analysis of this paradox, see MB Burke, 'Dion and Theon: An Essentialist Solution to an Ancient Puzzle' (1994) 91 JPhil 129–39; WR Carter, 'Dion's Left Foot (and the Price of Burkean Economy)' (1997) 57 Philos&PhenomenolRes 371–9.

32 Although for why this is the case, he does not offer an explanation.

33 Russell, *The History of Western Philosophy* 206; see also, U Coope, 'Why Does Aristotle Say That There Is No Time without Change?' (2001) 101 Proceedings of the Aristotelian Society 359–67.

Physics as well have demonstrated that time is but another dimension through which we can move,[34] and Einstein's special and general relativity highlighted the interconnection between motion in the 3-D space and time.[35] It is this very modern understanding of time as another dimension, additional to the three dimensions of space, and through which objects move that led the authors of this book to reconceptualise one of the six types of motion that Aristotle had identified, specifically altering the change of place type of motion (*kata topon metabole*) to change of place and time (*kata topon kai chronon metavole*).[36] This type of motion permeates the entirety of *Treaties in Motion*.

The conceptualisation of time as a dimension spilled over from the realm of physics into that of philosophy as well. The link between time, change, and motion has led to the emergence of a number of philosophical schools that offer theories trying to explicate these phenomena. The two most prominent schools of thought on the matter are *endurantism* (endurance theory) and *perdurantism* (perdurance theory). The critical difference between these two schools is the answers they provide as to how things persist, how they change through time, and whether objects have only spatial or also temporal parts.[37] Since time and temporal parts is a *differentia specifica* between endurantism and perdurantism, the former school of thought is often referred to as three-dimensionalism (3D-ism), whereas the latter as four-dimensionalism (4D-ism).[38]

[34] Albeit, and as long as the speed of light holds as the maximum speed that can be achieved in our universe, only in one direction. This is known as 'time's arrow' a phrase coined by A Eddington, *The Nature of the Physical World* (CUP 1928) 68–9. Eddington and Neumann were of the view that time has an intrinsic arrow that points in the direction of entropy change, ie heat dissipation; *contra* C Callender, *What Makes Time Special?* (OUP 2017) 21, who argues that the arrow of time is not a feature of time itself, but only of the 'local asymmetries in material processes'. The reason why Callender focuses on asymmetry is because asymmetry is the feature that gives time its alleged directionality. See also P Horwich, *Asymmetries in Time* (MIT Press 1987) 38, who claims that 'the current empirical evidence indicates that time itself is intrinsically symmetric'.

[35] A Einstein et al, *The Principle of Relativity* (W Perrett and GB Jeffery tr, Dover Books 1952); H Minkowski, 'Space and Time' as reprinted and translated in A Einstein and FA Davis (eds), *The Principle of Relativity* (Dover Publications 1952) 73–91; CH Hinton, 'What Is the Fourth Dimension?' in CH Hinton (ed), *Scientific Romances No 1* (Swan Schonneschein & Co 1884) 1–32.

[36] See in this chapter, Section 1.7.

[37] S Haslanger, 'Persistence through Time' in MJ Loux and DW Zimmerman (eds), *The Oxford Handbook of Metaphysics* (OUP 2005) 315–54.

[38] Because, as we shall see, in perdurantism time considerations and the temporal nature of objects are predominant.

According to endurantism, things have only spatial elements/parts and are 'wholly present whenever they exist'.[39] Although this theory is not without its merits, one glaring problem occurs when it tries to account for change.[40] Sorensen provides an insightful account on how a strict application of endurantism may run into a multitude of problems, not the least of which is *Leibniz's Law of Identity*.[41]

> The Heracliteans did have a logical argument for the universality of change. If *x* is identical to *y* and *x* has property *F*, then *y* has property *F* [indiscernibility of identicals] ... If Socrates when ill is identical to the man who recovered, then every property possessed by the ill Socrates is possessed by the recovered Socrates. But then the healthy Socrates would still be ill. What appears to be a single individual, Socrates enduring through time is actually a succession of individuals. The Heracliteans conclude that our ordinary use of *identical* is loose talk founded on mere resemblance. Socrates before and after his illness are only identical in the way that distinct grains of salt are identical.[42]

This is not to say that these criticisms have led to a debunking of endurantsim as a theory of identity and change through time. Endurantists have hit back at these inconsistencies by proposing a wide variety of theories such as presentism,[43] temporal-relationism,[44] and adverbialism,[45] none of which, however, is completely immune to incongruencies and inconsistencies.

39 K Hawley, 'Temporal Parts' (*Stanford Encyclopedia of Philosophy*, 5 October 2015) accessed 20 September 2019.

40 More commonly referred to as the problem of 'temporary intrinsics'; A Gallois, 'Identity over Time' (*Stanford Encyclopedia of Philosophy*, 6 October 2016) accessed 20 September 2019 [2.3].

41 Leibniz's Law of Identity is an ontological principle which can be expressed in two different ways. In the first way, Leibniz's Law of Identity posits that if two objects are one and the same, they will have the exact same properties ('indiscernibility of identicals'). However, the converse is also true, ie that if two objects have all the same properties they are one and the same ('identity of indescernibles'); Gallois 'Identity over Time' [1]; P Forrest, 'The Identity of Indiscernibles' (*Stanford Encyclopedia of Philosophy*, 15 August 2010) accessed 20 September 2019. Here, we concern ourselves with the first version of Leibniz's law of identity.

42 Sorensen, *A Brief History of the Paradox* 77.

43 The view that only objects in the present exist. Everything in the past and the future does not exist; Hawley, 'Temporal Parts' [2].

44 The view that 'objects change by standing in different relations to different times' (ibid).

45 The view that time and change is simply a way of expressing the manner in which an object possesses a particular property. For instance, in the aforementioned ill *versus* healthy Socrates example: If Socrates is ill in the morning and healthy in the afternoon,

Perdurantism, in turn, pays more focus on time than does endurantism. According to this theory, things have not only spatial parts but also temporal parts.[46] Unlike what endurantists posit, ie that an object at any given moment is wholly present, perdurantists hold that this is not true. According to them, an object persists as a unit throughout the fourth dimension, ie time. Objects are to be seen as 'space-time worms', wriggling though the fourth dimension.[47] This means that an object at any given 'time-slice'[48] is only partially present.

A third set of theories has also emerged that tries to borrow the best features of endurantism and perdurantism, most notable amongst these being *exdurantism*, also known as 'stage theory'. Similar to perdurantism and contrary to endurantism, in exdurantism objects also have temporal parts,[49] which are known as 'stages'. However, unlike perdurantism, in exdurantism, an object is entirely present 'at momentary regions that lack temporal extension',[50] and persists through time by exduring, ie 'by standing in temporal *counterpart* relations to later and earlier object stages'.[51] Whereas perdurantism views an object as a continuity, as a 'space-time worm', exdurantism views the object as a compilation of the sum of 'time-slices' or 'stages', where the object exists wholly in each and every one of them.[52]

Irrespective of which of the above theories on motion through time, identity, and change one may find more convincing, it is undeniable that this type of motion is essential when examining how objects have changed or remained the same throughout time, and in a book such as this where identity and change through time is a focal analytical point, it goes without saying that the aforementioned considerations will emerge time and time again throughout all the Chapters.

then Socrates possesses the ill property in a morning way, and the healthy property in an afternoon way (ibid).

46 ibid [2].

47 Hawley, 'Temporal Parts' [2]; Sorensen, *A Brief History of the Paradox* 77 and 143.

48 ie at a particular temporal point or period.

49 In this sense, it is closer to perdurantism and falls under the general rubric of 4D-ism.

50 Y Balashov, 'Persistence' in E Callender (ed), *The Oxford Handbook of Philosophy of Time* (OUP 2011) 14.

51 Balashov, 'Persistence' 14.

52 An example that is often provided in order to explain exdurantism is the film roll of a movie. If the film roll is played at a high enough speed, in order to trigger the persistence of vision in an individual's eye, then all we see is a continuous image. However, if it is slowed down enough, then we can see each and every still frame. In the same manner, exdurantism posits that objects are the sum of an infinite amount of such still images, called 'stages'.

1.6 Motion Dependent on Frames of Reference

Apart from the obvious connection between motion, change, and time, another observation that springs from the previous analysis and from the very definitions of motion as related to change[53] is that motion inherently presupposes a particular frame of reference. In order for a change/motion to occur, one must compare two things: the object/variable that is being observed, and the object/variable compared to which that change/motion has occurred. Consequently, motion is inherently and inextricably dependent on comparing two things on the basis of a particular frame of reference. But what is that frame of reference? Compared to what is the object moving? These questions might sound trivial, 'for surely what is usually meant by saying that something is moving is that it is moving *relative* to something, often tacitly understood between speakers'.[54] Still, however, that does not answer the question of what is this frame of reference, and more importantly what is its nature, ie is it an absolute or a relative one?

Since Descartes, Isaac Newton, and Gottfried Leibniz, philosophers have struggled to comprehend the three tightly interconnected concepts of space, time, and motion. The dispute has often taken the form of a tug of war between *absolute* conceptions of space, time, and motion, and *relational* ones. Whereas Descartes subscribed to 'relational motion', viewing motion as motion of bodies relative to one another, not a literal change of space,[55] Newton proposed instead that true motion is 'motion relative to a temporally enduring, rigid, 3-D Euclidean space, which he dubbed "absolute space"'.[56] Although, Leibniz's writings reveal a somewhat convoluted and constantly shifting view of the author on motion,[57] in his *Correspondence* with Samuel Clarke, Leibniz, while discussing the relativity of motion, which he calls the 'equivalence of hypotheses' about the states of motion of bodies, describes his understanding of space as it

[53] See Oxford Dictionary definitions of 'motion' and 'move'.

[54] Huggett and Hoefer, 'Absolute and Relational Theories' [1].

[55] R Descartes, *Principles of Philosophy* (RP Miller and VR Miller tr, Kluwer 1983) Book II:13 and II:24–5.

[56] In *De Gravitatione*, Newton rejected the traditional philosophical categories of substance and attribute as suitable characterisations for space. In his view, 'absolute space' was neither a substance as it lacked causal power and an independent existence, nor an attribute as it would exist even in a vacuum. Thus, in Newton's view space was something of a 'pseudo-substance'.

[57] GA Hartz and JA Cover, 'Space and Time in the Leibnizian Metaphysic' (1988) 22 Noûs 493–519.

being 'something merely relative, as time is, . . . an order of coexistences, as time is an order of successions'.[58] Ernst Mach, in turn, criticised Newton's postulate of absolute space 'as a metaphysical leap that is neither justified by actual experiments, nor methodologically sound'. These remarks gave birth to what Albert Einstein referred to as 'Mach's Principle', which is based on a relational conception of space, time, and motion.[59] Einstein's Special Theory of Relativity, but most importantly his General Theory of Relativity was a genuine conceptual leap forward. Almost all physicists in the latter half of the nineteenth century worked under the assumption that a privileged reference frame of 'rest' (ie an inertial frame of reference) existed. General relativity shattered this misconception, proving that there are no privileged inertial frames of reference. Any description of motion would depend on the selected (agreed upon) frame of reference, or simply put, on the frame of reference of the observer.

1.7 Motion in *Treaties in Motion*

Based on the previous discussion, *Treaties in Motion* draws inspiration from Aristotle's typology of 'motion', and supplements it with our modern understanding of: (i) time as dimension where motion can occur, thus amending Aristotle's sixth type of motion from 'change in place' to 'change in space-time'; and (ii) the non-existence of a preferred inertial frame of reference, thus proceeding in each chapter's analysis by hopping between three different frames of reference, ie treaties, VCLT, and customary law on treaties.

Motion is examined on two levels. First, on an examination of motion itself, which has occurred in this introductory chapter, and second on an examination of how motion can be described with respect to three main sets of objects and their respective interactions. In the case of treaties, this concept of motion would encompass three main 'object-states': (i) the emergence of a treaty, ie when specific non-treaty elements move towards each other and coalesce into a treaty document; (ii) the continued existence of a treaty through time. In this case, the notion of 'motion' would cover situations where a treaty changes either through evolutive

58 GW Leibniz, *The Leibniz-Clarke Correspondence: With extracts from Newton's 'Principia' and 'Optiks'* (edited with introduction and notes by HG Alexander, MUP 1998) Letter 3, sect 4.

59 Huggett and Hoefer, 'Absolute and Relational Theories' [8.1].

interpretation, or amendment/modification/revision (A/M/R); and (iii) the withdrawal from or termination of a treaty. This would describe the situation where the motion of a treaty is halted either temporarily or permanently.

For the purposes of completeness, the aforementioned motion will also be examined with respect to three sets of rules that will function as 'frames of reference', and whose motion[60] and their interaction will be critical to our analysis:

(i) treaties. This first category is pretty self-explanatory. Since this book will be devoted to an explanation of the motion of treaties, the latter should be at the centre of analysis. However, within this category particular emphasis will be given to 'special regimes' and examine whether a distinct or 'special' kind of motion can be identified with respect to these regimes;
(ii) the VCLT. The same considerations as with the first category apply to the VCLT but with a further twist; the VCLT, in and of itself is a treaty, so it falls within the set of objects to be examined and can itself be subject to motion. However, by virtue of it also providing the rules which govern treaties, it functions as an external force as well, that is exerted to treaties and affects their motion;
(iii) finally, the customary law on treaties. This is also subject to change, albeit in a different fashion than that of treaties. However, its own motion also exerts force that affects the motion of all treaties, including the VCLT.

Furthermore, since the aforementioned sets of rules interact with each other, any analysis of their motion would be incomplete without examining their possible interactions. During said interactions one set of rules exerts force to the others and vice versa.[61] The rule's own motion would be affected by the rules of the other categories.

It is evident from the previous description that the analytical approach adopted, as well as our understanding of motion, offers a much broader, more accurate, and more holistic description of the phenomenon of treaties and its law, revealing hidden potential areas of analysis and

[60] When viewed as a set of rules, rather than an agreed upon inertial frame of reference.

[61] This fits well with the general theme of this book, as this two-way influential interaction echoes Newton's Third Law of Motion, ie that 'for every action there is an equal and opposite reaction'. In the extreme scenario, where the 'motion' would be at directly opposite directions, then this would describe the situation of 'normative conflict'.

interaction through a perspective that so far has remained unexplored. Consequently, *Treaties in Motion* fills this lacuna by examining the motion of treaties. It will do so by focusing on five particular areas where the aforementioned motion is most prominent, and which correspond to the types of motion suggested by Aristotle: creation (*genesis*), increase (*auxesis*), diminution (*meiosis*), alteration (*alloiosis*), destruction (*phthora*), and change of place (*kata topon metabole*, which has been amended as stated above to change of place and time [*kata topon kai chronon metavole*]).[62]

- *Genesis:* The formation of the treaty (ie what is a treaty)
- *Genesis & Alloiosis:* The issue of consent to be bound (ie who can negotiate a treaty, how can consent to be bound be given)
- *Auxesis & Meiosis:* The interpretation of the treaty (eg evolutive/ dynamic interpretation, principle of contemporaneity, subsequent agreements and practice, and the fallacy of the 'immutability' of rules of interpretation)
- *Alloiosis:* The amendment/modification of the treaty (eg various approaches to amendment and modification, from unanimity to percentage-based amendment/modification, 'opting-out'/'tacit acceptance' procedures, COP/MOP decisions, and the problematic distinction between interpretation and modification)
- *Phthora*: The unilateral withdrawal from a treaty (which from the frame of reference of the withdrawing party can be considered as the death of a treaty, and from the frame of reference of the other parties as partial *phthora*) or the termination of a treaty (eg material breach, fundamental change of circumstances, supervening impossibility of performance, as well as some other debatable grounds that may or may not still exist in customary international law, such as obsolescence, desuetude, and some that are not grounds for termination *per se* but feature prominently in such discussions, such as *exceptio non adimpleti contractus*).

In this manner, the authors provide a unique 'from cradle to grave' examination of the phenomenon of treaties in motion. Instead of attempting the usual static/ 'picture-frame' like examination of treaties, *Treaties in Motion* attempts to promote the understanding of how and why treaties (and treaty law rules) have or may change in time, and how

[62] The last category of motion permeates all chapters as the various sets of rules are examined in order to reveal the degree of change through time.

this process is not one solely connected to interpretation, but is endemic to the notion of treaties from their inception to their termination.

Inspired by this analytical lens *Treaty in Motion* consists of the following chapters. Chapter 1 offers a framework for the authors' understanding of 'motion' and the fact that Aristotle's six types of motion are reflected in the chapters. Chapter 2 deals with the *genesis* of the treaty. The motion of treaties is evident from the very start. What constitutes a treaty is a matter that despite the deceptively simple definition of Article 2(1)(a) VCLT,[63] continues to change even as we speak. From whether verbal treaties are possible (although not covered by the VCLT)[64] and their connection to unilateral acts creating international obligations,[65] to whether a particular set of documents could be qualified as a treaty. With respect to the latter, several have been the cases that have been brought before international courts and tribunals on this exact issue, ie whether Minutes, Declarations, or Communiqués amounted to a treaty.[66] Matters are made even more complex when the manner and the person who can express a State's consent to be bound is also thrown into the crucible, as was done for instance, in *Land and Maritime Boundary between Cameroon and Nigeria*,[67] and *Bay of Bengal (Bangladesh/Myanmar)*.[68] These cases also raised the critical issue of the practical effect of the exception of Article 46 VCLT, which is the only provision that provides for invocation of a national law provision as justification for failure to perform a treaty. Finally, apart from these issues and how they affect the modern understanding of the notion of 'treaty', this book also examines the process of simplified agreements, which has emerged through diplomatic practice in order,

[63] '"Treaty" means an international agreement concluded between States in written form and governed by international law, whether embodied in a single instrument or in two or more related instruments and whatever its particular designation'.

[64] See for instance, the Ihlen Declaration.

[65] VR Cedeño, 'Fourth Report on Unilateral Acts of States' (30 May 2001) UN Doc A/CN.4/519, reproduced in [2001/II – Part One] YBILC 115–36.

[66] *Aegean Sea Continental Shelf (Greece v Turkey)* (Jurisdiction) [1978] ICJ Rep 3 [96]; *Maritime Delimitation and Territorial Questions between Qatar and Bahrain (Qatar v Bahrain)* (Jurisdiction and Admissibility) [1994] ICJ Rep 112 [23–30]; *Dispute Concerning Delimitation of the Maritime Boundary between Bangladesh and Myanmar in the Bay of Bengal (Bangladesh/Myanmar)* (Judgment) [2012] ITLOS Rep 4 [92–4]; *Land and Maritime Boundary between Cameroon and Nigeria (Cameroon v Nigeria: Equatorial Guinea Intervening)* (Judgment) [2002] ICJ Rep 303 [263–5].

[67] *Land and Maritime Boundary between Cameroon and Nigeria* [263–5].

[68] *Bay of Bengal (Bangladesh/Myanmar)* [92–4].

as the term denotes, to simplify and expedite the processes of expression of consent to be bound and entry into force of certain treaties.

Chapter 3 deals with consent to be bound, as an area of treaty law which in and of itself is pervasive through multiple 'object-states' of the treaty and by consequence can describe multiple types of motion. Until very recently, the question of the consent to be bound was considered by many scholars a rather uninteresting – if not outright staid – part of the law of treaties. Nothing could be further from the truth. There are very few areas of the law of treaties which would show such a robust motion as consent to be bound. Consent to be bound is evident not only in the formative stages of a treaty, ie its *genesis*, but also in the regime of reservations and that of amendment and modification (where depending on the consent given, we can observe *auxesis*, *meiosis*, or even *alloiosis* of the treaty). With respect to reservations to treaties, these also belong to the general area of the expression of the consent to be bound. It is an incontrovertible fact, acknowledged by States and scholars, that reservations to treaties are part and parcel of the whole procedure of giving consent. Although the faculty of making reservations has its own place in the 1969 VCLT and does not form part of Article 11 VCLT, in practical terms it belongs to a widely conceived process of the expression of the consent to be bound by a treaty. Therefore, reservations to treaties are discussed in this chapter as well, together with other classical and more modern forms of consent to be bound.

Chapter 4 deals with the question of interpretation. This is the area where most literature, including some by the authors of this book, has focused. Of course, a complete examination of the entirety of the rules of interpretation falls outside the aim and scope of the present book.[69] For this reason, only the areas which most exemplify the motion treaties are a target for analysis. Based on these considerations, and having gone through a brief analysis of the relevant drafting history of the VCLT, the tug of war between the principle of contemporaneity and evolutive/dynamic interpretation (corresponding to considerations on *meiosis* and *auxesis* types of motion)[70] is examined, ie whether

[69] See for such a book, Gardiner, *Treaty Interpretation*; U Linderfalk, *On the Interpretation of Treaties* (Springer 2007).

[70] G Fitzmaurice, 'The Law and Procedure of the International Court of Justice, 1951–4: Treaty Interpretation and Other Points' (1957) 33 BYIL 203, 212; H Thirlway, 'The Law and Procedure of the International Court of Justice 1960–1989: Part Two' (1991) 62 BYIL 1, 57.

the terms of a treaty should be understood as they stood at the time of the conclusion of the treaty or at the time of the interpretation of the treaty (*kata chronon metavole*). Various theories have been proposed in support of either approach, ie that any solution should be based on the intention of the parties,[71] on the object and purpose of the treaty,[72] or on the 'generic' nature of the terms employed.[73] Furthermore, evolutive interpretation has become something of a default position with respect to human rights treaties, and it is argued that the same should be with respect to environmental treaties and constituent instruments of international organisations.[74] Irrespective of whether these theories are correct or not, these debates demonstrate that this is an areas where the motion of treaties is quite pronounced.

Finally, an area that is often neglected is that the rules of interpretation can themselves also be the subject of change.[75] For instance, the International Law Commission's (ILC) work on subsequent agreements and practice clearly demonstrates this fact and the pervasiveness of motion in this area.[76] Even the original title of the ILC's work, ie 'Treaties over Time', is a nod to the temporal and normative motion of treaties. This chapter critically deconstructs the argument in favour of the immutability (and immovability) of the rules of interpretation, and drawing from the conclusions on evolutive interpretation, demonstrates how this motion as change through time (*kata chronon metavole*) has important theoretical and practical implications in the manner in which we approach interpretation of treaties both new and old.

71 P Merkouris, *Article 31(3)(c) VCLT and the Principle of Systemic Integration: Normative Shadows in Plato's Cave* (Brill/Martinus Nijhoff 2015) 138-43.

72 ibid 143–7.

73 ibid 147–52.

74 For an analysis and criticism of these theories, see ibid 144–7.

75 Merkouris, *Article 31(3)(c) VCLT*; P Merkouris, '(Inter)temporal Considerations in the Interpretative Process of the VCLT: Do Treaties Endure, Perdure or Exdure?' (2014) 45 NYIL 121; U Linderfalk, 'The Application of International Legal Norms over Time: The Second Branch of Intertemporal Law' (2011) 58/2 NILR 147.

76 G Nolte, 'First Report on Subsequent Agreements and Subsequent Practice in Relation to Treaty Interpretation' (19 March 2013) UN Doc A/CN.4/660; G Nolte, 'Second Report on Subsequent Agreements and Subsequent Practice in Relation to the Interpretation of Treaties' (26 March 2014) UN Doc A/CN.4/671; G Nolte, 'Third Report on Subsequent Agreements and Subsequent Practice in Relation to the Interpretation of Treaties' (7 April 2015) UN Doc A/CN.4/683; G Nolte, 'Fourth Report on Subsequent Agreements and Subsequent Practice in Relation to the Interpretation of Treaties' (7 March 2016) UN Doc A/CN.4/694; G Nolte, 'Fifth Report on Subsequent Agreements and Subsequent Practice in Relation to the Interpretation of Treaties' (28 February 2018) UN Doc A/CN.4/715.

Another area where the motion of treaties is evident is that of amendment/modification, and this is the focal point of analysis in Chapter 5. In one frame of reference, motion is extremely visible by virtue of the fact that amendment/modification deals with the change of rights and obligations contained within a treaty (depending on the change this could amount to an *auxesis, meiosis,* or if the change amounts to an alteration to the very nature of treaty even *alloiosis*). However, this is not the only frame of reference, where motion is pervasive. Even when negotiating the Draft Articles of the VCLT, the members of the ILC has serious misgivings as to whether the constantly changing and wildly diverse practice with respect to amendment/modification lent that topic to codification in draft articles.[77] Matters were further muddled as the dividing line between interpretation and modification was,[78] and still remains,[79] unclear. Despite the inclusion of certain 'residual'[80] articles in the VCLT current State practice clearly demonstrates that this is an area where everything is in a constant state of flux. Most notable examples are the 'opting out'/'tacit acceptance' procedures (most common in the International Maritime Organisation (IMO) Conventions)[81] and the more recent COP/MOP decisions. With respect to the latter, there is an ongoing heated debate as to whether these decisions are/can be binding and on what legal basis.[82]

This chapter concludes with a quantitative analysis of the existing amendment/modification provisions in treaties that have been published in the *League of Nations Treaty Series* and the *United Nations Treaty*

[77] M Fitzmaurice and P Merkouris, 'Re-Shaping Treaties while Balancing Interests of Stability and Change: Trends in the Amendment/Modification/Revision of Treaties' (2015) 20/1 ARIEL 41.

[78] Fitzmaurice and Merkouris, 'Re-Shaping Treaties'.

[79] Nolte, 'Third Report'.

[80] ILC, 'Report of the International Law Commission on the Work of Its Eighteenth Session' (4 May–19 July 1966) UN Doc A/6309/Rev.l, reproduced in [1966/II] YBILC 172, Commentary to Arts 35–6, 232–3 [2], [7]; H Waldock, 'Third Report on the Law of Treaties' (3 March, 9 June, 12 June, and 7 July 1964) UN Doc A/CN.4/167 and Add.1–3, reproduced in [1964/II] YBILC 5, 50 [10–1].

[81] See M Fitzmaurice and P Merkouris, 'Uniformity versus Specialization (1): The Quest for a Uniform Law of Inter-State Treaties' in C Tams, A Tzanakopoulos, and A Zimmermann (eds), *Research Handbook on the Law of Treaties* (Edward Elgar 2014) 341.

[82] Fitzmaurice and Merkouris 'Uniformity versus Specialization'; M Fitzmaurice and D Costelloe, 'Lawmaking by Treaty: Conclusion of Treaties and the Evolution of Treaty Regimes in Practice' in C Brölmann and Y Radi (eds), *Research Handbook on the Theory and Practice of International Lawmaking* (Edward Elgar 2016) 111–32.

Series (LNTS and UNTS, respectively). By typologising these provisions, we present some interesting results as to how this area of treaty law has evolved (moved) and what practical solutions/patterns of motion seem to be emerging and whether these are dependent on the specific time period, the number of parties, and the particular area of law.

The final substantive chapter examines the circumstances under which a treaty can be withdrawn from or terminated. If a treaty provides in and of itself an expiry date, this would be a straightforward process. However, most treaties are drafted with a view to apply for an undetermined period of time. Both these scenarios, ie withdrawal and termination, amount to *phthora*, and the degree will depend on the particular frame of reference. From the frame of reference of the withdrawing party, withdrawal can be considered as the death of a treaty (*phthora stricto sensu*), whereas from the frame of reference of the other parties, withdrawal can be viewed as partial *phthora*. The issue of withdrawal from a treaty recently stole the spotlight with the Brexit situation, and it is this real-life example that will be used as a case study to examine motion in the context of withdrawal (and even withdrawal of the withdrawal) from a treaty.

This is not the only situation where motion as *phthora* is clearly visible. What complicates matters is when anomalous situations emerge where termination or suspension may be required. The most characteristic examples of such grounds, which also reflect the motion of treaties, are supervening impossibility of performance, fundamental change of circumstances, and material breach. Despite the fact that fundamental change of circumstances has only rarely been upheld in international courts and tribunals[83] (material breach even less),[84] the international jurisprudence where these grounds have been recognised as reflecting customary international law will shed light as to their gradual clarification.

However, this chapter examines not only the existing grounds of termination/suspension under the VCLT (*intra*-VCLT grounds) but also certain grounds that despite not being included in the VCLT have been argued to provide additional, customary law-based grounds for termination/suspension (*praeter*-VCLT grounds). The most notable of these are

[83] *Case C-162/96 – A Racke GmbH & Co v Hauptzollamt Mainz* [1998] ECR I-03655.

[84] Usually, it is only its customary status that is recognised, but no material breach is held to have occurred; *Application of the Interim Accord of 13 September 1995 (FYROM v Greece)* [2011] (Judgment) ICJ Rep 644 [118–9], [162–3] (hereinafter *FYROM v Greece*).

obsolescence, *desuetude*[85] and *exceptio non adimpleti contractus* (also known as *inadimplenti non est adimplendum*).[86]

In the final section of the chapter, the 'relative motion' of both *praeter-* and *intra-*VCLT grounds for termination is examined. What is shown is that all these grounds move not only with respect to their own content/change 'frame of reference', but also with respect (i) to one another, ie when there are unclear and shifting borders between two or more grounds (such as those between material breach and *exceptio inadimpleti contractus*), and (ii) to other sets of rules of international law, such as State responsibility. This latter is especially pronounced in the case of material breach the connection of which with countermeasures is still a topic of consternation for academics and practitioners alike. In this manner, *Treaties in Motion* provides a complete picture as to whether the grounds for termination/suspension of a treaty have moved since the drafting of the VCLT and how this may affect the current VCLT regime.

Chapter 7, the final chapter, examines the findings from the preceding chapters to demonstrate what conclusions can be drawn regarding the motion of treaties, and the interaction between treaties, the VCLT, and the customary law on treaties.

85 *Nuclear Tests (Australia v France)* [1974] ICJ Rep 253, Joint Dissenting Opinion of Judges Onyeama, Dillard, Jiménez de Aréchaga and Sir Humphrey Waldock [53]; G Fitzmaurice, 'Second Report on the Law of Treaties', (15 March 1957) UN Doc A/CN.4/107, reproduced in [1957/II] YBILC 16, 31; R Kolb, 'La désuétude en droit international public' (2007) 111/3 RGDIP 577; A Vamvoukos, *Termination of Treaties in International Law: the Doctrines of* Rebus sic Stantibus *and* Desuetude (Clarendon Press 1985).

86 *FYROM v Greece* [115–7], [161], Separate Opinion of Judge Simma and Dissenting Opinion of Judge *ad hoc* Roucounas.

2

Treaty *Genesis*

Concept of a Treaty in International Law, Including Its Formation and Motion

2.1 Introduction

Questions as to what constitutes a treaty and consent to be bound[1] are connected to the first type of motion, ie *genesis*. They illustrate rather unambiguously the notion of treaty and the evolution ('motion') of the provisions of the VCLT. The present chapter examines State practice and the case law of international and national judicial bodies that contribute to the development and further understanding of these notions (and motions), both being of great importance to the formation of a treaty.[2]

The impression that the definition of 'treaty' contained in the 1969 VCLT is simple and uncomplicated is simply illusory. Article 1(1)(a) VCLT defines a 'treaty' as 'an international agreement concluded between the States in written form and governed by international law, which is embodied in a single instrument or in two or more related instruments and whatever its designation'. The existence of vast case law debating what constitutes a treaty is proof that the question of definition of treaty remains one of the most taxing and unresolved problems in the relations between States and in the practice of international courts and tribunals. Indeed, the evolution of the notion of treaty in international law has mostly arisen on the basis of the jurisprudence of various international and national courts, and this is a continuous and robust process, adding new elements to the definition of what constitutes a treaty.

The inherent problems concerning uncertainties of what may be a treaty were already observed in 1962 in the *South West Africa* cases by Judge Jessup, whose comments on the nature of a treaty are prophetic.

[1] Consent to be bound and its connection to motion will be analysed in Chapter 3.

[2] The ideas presented in this chapter are inspired by and are an evolved and updated version of M Fitzmaurice, 'The Identification and Character of Treaties and Treaty Obligations between States in International Law' (2002) 73/1 BYIL 141–85.

He stated that 'the notion that there is a clear and ordinary meaning of the treaty is a mirage' and that a treaty is distinguished from other instruments if 'a State has given a promise or an undertaking from which flow international legal rights and duties'.[3] Therefore, the perplexing question of what constitutes a treaty is not only theoretical but also deeply practical, and is of fundamental importance for State practice.[4]

One of the difficulties in the identification of a treaty is the expansion and constant evolution of comparatively new areas of international law, such as environmental law, which has led to the development of novel regulatory regimes and techniques, such as umbrella and framework treaties, which only set out the general obligations of States, often in a very vague and imprecise manner, thus encouraging the misperception and misinterpretation that such regimes and the treaties on which they rest are of an entirely soft law character and thus do not create binding obligations under international law. Soft law provisions may eventually become binding, either through their influence on the formation of customary international law or through their eventual elevation to, or incorporation into, a binding treaty; and they are often, but not always, intended to do so.

Some of these treaties, such as the Paris Agreement on Climate Change, contain legal obligations, which are vague and woolly. However, their legal character is different from such classical soft law documents as various non-binding declarations. Such treaties, or some of their provisions, evidence the 'motion' in respect to international legal norms from a clearly defined dichotomy between binding treaties and non-binding soft law instruments to a grey area of norms which are, for want of a better formulation, 'less binding'.

Conversely, there are also agreements, which in their entirety may sensibly be characterised as examples of soft law that include however sets of fairly precise – strictly speaking non-legal – obligations. There is also notable confusion between instruments such as Memoranda of Understanding (MOUs) and treaties, and there is no hard and fast rule as to their division and distinction in order to precisely discern the legal character of an instrument in question.

[3] *South West Africa Cases (Ethiopia v South Africa; Liberia v South Africa)* (Preliminary Objections) [1962] ICJ Rep 402, Separate Opinion of Judge Jessup. See also GJH van Hoof, *Rethinking the Sources of International Law* (Kluwer Law and Taxation Publishers 1983) 117.

[4] Cf, J de Arechaga, 'International Law in the Past Third Century' (1978/I) 159 RdC 35.

An MOU and a treaty are neither necessarily coextensive nor mutually exclusive; a particular instance of MOU may very well be a treaty within the strictures of treaty law, but not all MOUs amount to treaties or automatically are parts of existing treaties *per se*. In that sense, it is best to understand MOU as a term of art. Moreover, MOUs are not expressly mentioned in the provisions of the 1969 VCLT; therefore, the legal analysis of the provisions of MOUs is developed entirely through the practice of States and the case law of international courts and tribunals.

Relying on the pure form or title of an instrument can be misleading and deceptive; therefore, a thorough examination of the legal content of an instrument in question must be conducted, as demonstrated by the recent *Maritime Delimitation in the Indian Ocean* case before the ICJ, in which the Court performed an in-depth analysis of the legal character of a contested instrument as to whether it was a treaty or merely a non-binding MOU.[5] The jurisprudence of the ICJ in the context of the analysis of what is a treaty has chiefly evolved in relation to the question of whether the instrument in question suffices in establishing jurisdiction. However, even in such cases, the Court has made several observations concerning the character of treaties in general, and also regarding the definition of the term 'treaty'; its jurisprudence includes the *Aegean Sea Continental Shelf*[6] and the *Maritime Delimitation and Territorial Questions between Qatar and Bahrain*[7] cases.

In principle, treaty obligations comprise such legal obligations that arise directly by operation of the principle of *pacta sunt servanda*. This fundamental notion of international law, and of the law of treaties more specifically, demands that agreements must be honoured by parties to them, and that such agreements ought to be upheld by law; this is without doubt one of the 'general principles of law' contemplated by Article 38(1)(c) of the ICJ Statute. Therefore, the problem of what instrument gives rise to legally binding obligation within the definition of the 1969 VCLT is extremely relevant in order to identify which instruments are subject to the principle of *pacta sunt servanda* (ie a principle that treaties be observed). Such a question is of particular

[5] *Maritime Delimitation in the Indian Ocean (Somalia v Kenya)* (Preliminary Objections) [2017] ICJ Rep 3.

[6] See *Aegean Sea Continental Shelf (Greece v Turkey)* (Judgment) [1978] ICJ Rep 3.

[7] See *Maritime Delimitation and Territorial Questions between Qatar and Bahrain (Qatar v Bahrain)* (Jurisdiction and Admissibility) [1994] ICJ Rep 112.

importance in relation to soft law instruments and even more so to MOUs, whose language often very closely resembles that of a binding treaty and given that obligations contained therein are often treated by States as binding.

There are various sources in international law that generate legal obligations. It was explained in the 2001 ILC Commentary to the Articles on Responsibility of States for Internationally Wrongful Acts (ARSIWA), which states that 'international obligations may be established by a customary rule of international law, by a treaty or by general principles applicable within the international legal order. States may assume international obligations by a unilateral act', and also that 'these various grounds of obligations interact with each other'.[8] What is more, international courts and tribunals in several cases have confirmed that an international obligation can be derived from a variety of sources. In the *Rainbow Warrior* arbitration, the arbitral tribunal made the following statement: 'any violation by a State of any obligation, of whatever origin, gives rise to State responsibility and consequently, to the duty of reparation'.[9] In the *Gabčikovo–Nagymaros* case, the ICJ stated that it is 'well-established that, when a State has committed an internationally wrongful act, its international responsibility is likely to be involved whatever the nature of the obligation it has failed to respect'.[10]

There is a fundamental difference between municipal and international legal orders regarding the existence of certain legal tools to distinguish, in the case of municipal law, what is a contract and, in the case of international law, what is a treaty. Municipal/national legal orders invariably contain normative frameworks – eg, the law of contract or obligations or whatever the relevant terms in municipal legal systems – in

[8] ILC, 'Draft Articles on Responsibility of States for Internationally Wrongful Acts with Commentaries' (23 April–1 June and 2 July–10 August 2001) UN Doc A/56/10, Commentary to Art 12, [3–4], reproduced in [2001/II – Part Two] YBILC 31, 55 (ARSIWA with Commentaries). On the interaction between treaties and customary international law, see Sir M Wood, 'Third Report on Identification of Customary International Law' (27 March 2015) UN Doc A/CN.4/682, 16–30. See also: ILA Committee on Formation of Customary (General) International Law, 'Final Report of the Committee: Statement of Principles Applicable to the Formation of General Customary International Law' (*ILA*, 2000) <https://ila.vettoreweb.com/Storage/Download.aspx?DbStorageId=1107&StorageFileGuid=e6663317-c7ca-4fff-a6e8-1cc2423756bf> accessed 20 September 2019; R Higgins, *Problems and Process: International Law and How We Use It* (OUP 1994) 32–88.

[9] *Rainbow Warrior Arbitration (New Zealand v France)* (1990) 20 UNRIAA 215, 251.

[10] *Case Concerning Gabcikovo–Nagymaros Project (Hungary/Slovakia)* (Judgment) [1997] ICJ Rep 38 [47].

which often only particular express and defined types of contract may be valid and upheld. This is primarily based on the Roman system of law in which such normative distinctions were of fundamental legal importance and is to varying degrees the basis to various civil law systems, including French law. Both civil and common law systems have evolved to contain precise and fairly well-defined substantive rules on the formation of legally binding agreements through, amongst other things, the concept of *offer* and *acceptance* (including the concept of *consideration* – ie, that a synallagmatic relationship exists between the parties – in common law). The respective provisions in both systems of law promote the necessity for certainty in the subject matter of contracts. For instance, in French law, this is expressed in the form of the requirement of an *objet;* and in common law in the concept of contracts, or clauses in contracts, being void of uncertainty.

No such precise analytical toolkit exists in international law. The role of the intention of the parties as a comparable analytical tool is quite controversial, as one is likely to conclude based on the international case law. Determining the normative character of an international instrument – that is to say, whether it is legally binding or not – on the criterion of the intention of the parties is, no doubt, in part a legacy of the seemingly voluntarist origins and character of international law. It can be said that a modern approach to the intention of the parties should be analysed from the objective point of view based on the apparent or external factors and facts, rather than as an insight into the subjective state of mind of the parties. In deciding these issues of *fact*, international law does in fact take into account, albeit indirectly, some of the factors referred to in connection with the national systems, such as certainty of the subject matter. It has to be emphasised, however, that such similarities can be illusory or even misleading and the objective test applied to the subjective intention of the parties can be illusive, if not purely fictional, as international law gives rise to a greater problem of proof than do more specific and precise tests in national legal systems. Therefore, it is important to bear in mind some fundamental differences between legal systems operating on the international and on the national planes that are relevant to the distinction between binding and non-binding international agreements.

The first difference is the relative importance in international relations of structured, relatively formal, and often continuous relations between States, which take many forms, ranging from relations between their respective government departments, through diplomatic relations, to meetings of Heads of State, some of which are not intended in themselves to have – and do not ordinarily and automatically have – specific legal consequences. A second factor operating at the international level is, in the absence of any international legislative body, recourse to agreements to achieve objectives, which at the national level would generally be achieved through legislation. This has given rise, among other things, to the growing importance of international instruments that are negotiated and drafted in ways virtually indistinguishable from binding treaty instruments, such as MOUs, but which are not intended to be, and are not, legally binding. The other type of non-binding instruments belongs to the so-called soft law category. A third difference, of a more practical nature, is the sheer difficulty and expense of negotiating and concluding international agreements, especially at the multilateral level. This is an additional element in the preference of States for informal non-binding agreements and the use of soft law approaches to State cooperation.

2.2 Definition of a Treaty in the 1969 VCLT

2.2.1 Introduction

It is perhaps impossible to consider any aspect of the law of treaties without reference to the Vienna Convention on the Law of Treaties (VCLT), which, broadly speaking and for the most part, has codified international law on the subject of the conclusion, interpretation, and termination of treaties. In relation to the subject of the present chapter, however, the 1969 VCLT is only of limited assistance. The definition of a treaty as 'an international agreement concluded between States in written form and governed by international law, whether embodied in a single instrument or in two or more related instruments and whatever its particular designation', whilst it lays down a number of positive formal rules as to what constitutes a treaty, is essentially silent with respect to the substantive issue as to which 'agreements' meet the positive formal requirements set out in the 1969 VCLT and are to be upheld by international law, and which not. It simply refers to 'international agreement' but gives no further indication of what the content of that term is.

As shall be discussed in this section, the formal notion of treaty has arguably moved and evolved though the practice of States and the jurisprudence of international courts and tribunals beyond the succinct definition in the 1969 VCLT. The questions concerning the notion of treaty have come up frequently before international courts and tribunals and their case law has contributed to the notion of a treaty in respect of further understanding of what constitutes a treaty in international law through analysing its components, filling in gaps, and further developing the basic definition. As it has turned out, even the apparently clear formal definition of 'treaty' in the 1969 VCLT has proved to give rise to controversy, given the conflicting views and lack of a common understanding amongst States.

2.2.2 'Legal Obligation' and 'Governed by International Law'

This section briefly presents the journey of the International Law Commission (ILC) to reach the succinct definition that eventually found its way in the text of the 1969 VCLT. The records of the ILC deliberations evidence robust and exhaustive debates pertaining to each and every element of the definition that, in its final form, reflects the compromise between the ILC members. The question of *intention* was debated but it did not result in its inclusion in the definition.

Brierly, in his 'First Report on the Law of Treaties', merely mentioned the problem of the establishment of a relationship under international law.[11] Lauterpacht, while not proposing a comprehensive definition of the term 'treaty', sought to include as elements thereof the creation of legal obligations, and the entering by the parties into undertakings of a legal character. This legal obligation was the element that singled out a treaty from a political instrument. This line of reasoning was shared by Fitzmaurice, who had at the time presented several drafts, all of which referred to the creation of 'legal obligations' or the establishment of a 'relationship' governed by international law. In his first draft, however, Fitzmaurice added the requirement of the intention to create international obligations and the intention to establish a relationship under international law. Once established, treaties would automatically be governed by international law. Article 1(2) of the Expository Draft Code presented in 1959 to the General Assembly contained only the phrase 'governed by international law' – as opposed to other instruments which are governed by domestic law – even when they regulate matters of international character. The main problem with the definition of the treaty in the VCLT is its substantive aspect, namely, the indication that a treaty creates an internationally binding

[11] JL Brierly, 'First Report on the Law of Treaties' (14 April 1950) UN Doc A/CN.4/23, Art 1(a), reproduced in [1950/II] YBILC 222, 226.

obligation and thus is distinguished from non-binding agreements of a political or a moral nature.

In this event, in order to reflect the substantive element of a treaty, the phrase 'international agreement governed by international law' was decided upon. This phrase is meant to imply that in order to constitute a treaty, an agreement must be legally binding in international law and create legally binding rights and obligations: it is not enough that it falls within the ambit of international law or that international law be applicable to it. In other words, for an agreement to constitute a treaty, not only must international law[12] be applicable to it, but international law must also designate the agreement as one that is legally binding on the parties (as opposed to an agreement that relies on the good will alone of its parties for its fulfilment). Even on this basis, there remains a further crucial element in establishing a comprehensive definition of what may constitute a treaty – namely, the distinction between legally binding agreements and other agreements or arrangements between States.

What is more, there are numerous agreements between States and other subjects of international law that are regulated by the national law of one of the parties, or by some other legal system – be it regional or thematic – that has been selected by the parties.[13] Such examples are energy trade contracts and lease of land and buildings. It is also possible for non-State parties to enter into an agreement governed by international law, either on its own or as a supplement to the application of national laws, such as in the case of State-investor investment contracts.[14]

From the point of view of agreements between States and other entities, the *Anglo–Iranian Oil Company* case is an interesting precedent.[15] The Iranian government granted a concession in 1933 to the Anglo–Iranian Oil Company for a period of sixty years. Article 22 of the concession agreement provided that all disputes relating to the concession were to be submitted to arbitration. The procedure to be followed was that of the Permanent Court of International Justice (PCIJ), and it was stated that awards were to be based on the juridical principles

[12] As opposed to any other legal system.

[13] F Berman and D Bentley, 'Treaties and Other International Instruments – I General Definition, Treaty Formalities' in Sir I Roberts (ed), *Satow's Diplomatic Practice* (7th edn, OUP 2017) 599 [31.2].

[14] ibid 602 [31.6].

[15] *Anglo–Iranian Oil Company (UK v Iran)* (Preliminary Objections) [1952] ICJ Rep 20, 93.

contained in Article 38 of the Statute of the PCIJ. By Article 21 of the concession agreement it was agreed that performance of the agreement would be based on principles of mutual good will and good faith, as well as on the reasonable interpretation of the agreement. The Government of Iran also agreed that the Concession shall not be annulled, and the terms shall not be altered either by general or special legislation in the future, or by administrative measures or any other executive acts whatsoever.

On 15 and 20 March 1951, the Iranian Majlis (Parliament) and Senate passed a law nationalising the oil industry in Iran. The British Government, exercising its right of diplomatic protection, submitted an Application to the ICJ on the basis of the Optional Clause Declarations made by itself and Iran. The case raised difficult issues in relation to jurisdiction. The Iranian Optional Clause Declaration referred to disputes arising in regard to situations or facts relating directly or indirectly to the application of treaties or conventions accepted by Iran and subsequent to the ratification of that declaration. The question, thus, was whether the concession in question belonged to the category of such treaties or conventions. The argument submitted by the British government was based on the involvement of the League of Nations in the cancellation of an earlier concession in 1932 by the Iranian government. The matter was submitted to the League of Nations. In 1933, the League of Nations Rapporteur submitted his report on the matter to the League Council, together with the text of a new concession which replaced the earlier concession, and declared that 'the dispute between His Majesty's Government in the UK and the Imperial Government of Persia is now finally settled'. Since the representatives of both countries were satisfied with the outcome, the matter was removed from the agenda of the Council. Crucially, the Government of the UK argued before the ICJ that, as a result of these proceedings, the Government of Iran undertook certain treaty obligations in relation to the UK. The government of the UK claimed that due to these obligations, the agreement signed by the Iranian government and the Anglo–Iranian Oil Company 'has a double character, the character of being at once a concessionary contract between the Iranian Government and the Company and a treaty between the two Governments'.[16] The ICJ rejected UK's argument as to the double character of the agreement, stating that:

[16] ibid 112.

> The Court cannot accept the view that that the contract signed by the Iranian Government and the Anglo–Persian Oil Company has a double character. It is nothing more than a concessionary contract between a Government and a foreign corporation. The United Kingdom is not a party to the contract; there is no privity of the contract between the Government of Iran and the Government of the United Kingdom. Under the contract the Iranian Government cannot claim from the United Kingdom Government any rights which it may claim from the company, nor can it be called upon to perform towards the United Kingdom Government any obligations which it is bound to perform towards the Company. The document bearing the signatures of the representatives of the Iranian Government and the Company has a single purpose: the purpose of regulating the relations between that Government and the Company in regard to the concession. It does not regulate in any way the relations between the two Governments.[17]

2.2.3 Form and Substance of the Treaty in Their Infinite Variety

2.2.3.1 Preliminary Remarks

Both the form and substance are elements of a treaty that can be said to be of fundamental importance in relation to the question of what constitutes a treaty in international law. The form and substance of a treaty are contentious questions of fact that are much debated, as demonstrated by significant international litigation.[18] This is undoubtedly the most intellectually stimulating aspect of the evolution of the notion of treaty and exemplifies the development of the succinct definition contained in the 1969 VCLT. It must be said at the outset that numerous decisions of international courts and tribunals have not provided a definitive definition of both the necessary form and substance of a treaty and controversy remains, despite certain general pronouncements on this matter.

The drafting history of the 1969 VCLT indicates that the ILC treated the notion of 'treaty' as a generic term and suggested that 'an extraordinarily varied nomenclature has developed which serves to confuse the question of classifying international agreements', adding that 'there is no exclusive or systematic use of nomenclature for particular types of transaction'.[19]

[17] ibid.

[18] Including on the problem of the jurisdictional basis of international courts and tribunals.

[19] ILC 'Draft Articles on the Law of Treaties with Commentaries' (4 May–19 July 1966) UN Doc A/CN.4/191, reproduced in [1966/II] YBILC 187, 188, Commentary to Art 2 [3].

The VCLT does not prefer or specify a particular written form for an international agreement to constitute a treaty. Certain problems were addressed by the ILC's Rapporteurs. For instance, the first Rapporteur, Brierly, explained that the requirement for treaties to be recorded in 'writing' was fulfilled by 'typewriting and printing and, indeed, any other permanent method of recording'. Similarly, the number of documents in which an agreement is contained has no influence on its legal character. The main problem that divided the ILC was the normative character of so-called exchanges of notes and/or letters, which are intended to acquire legal force upon mutual exchange. Brierly was of the view that instruments of this kind should be covered,[20] and despite doubts raised in the ILC, later drafts did include exchanges of notes and letters within the definition of a treaty. For example, the 1962 ILC Draft Articles referred to treaties concluded in simplified form, which, the Commission explained, included exchanges of notes, exchanges of letters, agreed minutes, memoranda of agreement, joint declarations, and 'any other document concluded by any similar procedure'.[21]

Eventually, due to inherent difficulties connected with defining treaties in 'simplified form', the ILC abandoned a general definition of simplified agreements. Only very general conclusions may be drawn from the designation of an instrument or its subject matter. There is a wide range of terms employed, including covenant, agreed minutes, charter, *notes verbales*, MOU, convention, and agreement.[22]

The designation as a 'treaty' is often encountered in international agreements of a particularly significant character, eg the 1949 North Atlantic Treaty.[23] Treaties between States and governments are less

[20] Brierly, 'First Report on the Law of Treaties' Art 1(b), 229.

[21] Sir H Waldock, 'First Report on the Law of Treaties' (26 March 1962) UN Doc A/CN.4/144 and Add.1, Art l(b), reproduced in [1962/II] YBILC 28, 33. It must be noted that the inclusion of this group of treaties influenced the drafting of the article on presentation of full powers, which provided that the production of full powers will be dispensed with for treaties in simplified form, unless they are requested by other negotiating States (see Art 4(1)(b) of the Draft).

[22] See DP Myers, 'The Names and Scope of Treaties' (1957) 51 AJIL 574. On names of treaties, see F Berman and D Bentley, 'Treaties and Other International Instruments – II Most Common Forms: Treaty/Convention/Agreement/Protocol' in Sir I Roberts (ed), *Satow's Diplomatic Practice* (7th edn, OUP 2017) 608–15 [32.1–22]; F Berman and D Bentley, 'Treaties and Other International Instruments – III Pact, Act, *Modus Vivendi*, Declaration, Exchange of Notes, Memorandum of Understanding' in Sir I Roberts (ed), *Satow's Diplomatic Practice* (7th edn, OUP 2017) 616–27 [33.1–26].

[23] 1949 North Atlantic Treaty (adopted 4 April 1949, entered into force 24 August 1949) 34 UNTS 243.

formal than those between Heads of State. The term 'convention' is usually used for a multilateral instrument of a law-making character – eg, the Hague Conventions and the VCLT.[24] The term 'agreement' is the most commonly used designation for a treaty. It is used both in a generic and a restrictive manner. 'In a generic sense it covers any meeting of minds-in this case the minds of two or more international persons . . . a distinction must be drawn between agreement intended to have an obligatory character and agreements not intended to be legally binding'.[25] 'In its restricted sense, the term *agreement* [is] intended to be binding, but usually of less formal or significant nature that a treaty or convention'.[26] Treaties termed *agreements* are sometimes concluded between government departments between two or more States.[27]

The term 'protocol' usually refers to a single instrument that amends or supplements an earlier agreement. It may be used in a versatile way. It may mean an instrument that is ancillary to a treaty or convention, although concluded simultaneously (eg protocols are annexed to accession treaties to the EU in 2003). Certain particular matters are regulated by protocols to conventions, such as the right to petition the ECtHR, or for regulating compulsory dispute settlement provisions (eg the compulsory settlement of disputes provided in the Optional Protocol to the Vienna Convention on Diplomatic and Consular Relations).[28] Some protocols prolong the life of a treaty that is nearing expiry; other types regulate some particular areas (such as the 1968 Protocol Concerning the Demarcation and Marking of the Argentine–Uruguayan Boundary Line on the River Uruguay).[29] However, modern practice most frequently uses the term 'protocol' for an instrument subsidiary to a treaty or convention[30] – eg the 1987 Montreal Protocol on Substances

[24] Berman and Bentley, 'Treaties and Other International Instruments – II' 608–12 [32.1–10].

[25] ibid 612 [32.11].

[26] ibid.

[27] ibid 612 [32.13].

[28] 1961 Optional Protocol to the Vienna Convention on Diplomatic Relations Concerning the Compulsory Settlement of Disputes (adopted 18 April 1961, entered into force 24 June 1964) 500 UNTS 241.

[29] 1985 Vienna Convention for the Protection of the Ozone Layer (adopted 22 March 1985, entered into force 22 September 1988) 1513 UNTS 293.

[30] Berman and Bentley, 'Treaties and Other International Instruments – II' 613–5 [32.14–22].

That Deplete the Ozone Layer[31] to the 1985 Vienna Convention on Protection of the Ozone Layer.[32,33] Protocols may also expand or add to existing treaties, such as to the 1949 Geneva Conventions. Lastly, in its secondary sense, a protocol may mean the minutes (a record) of the conference on the conclusion of an international instrument.[34] In general, the term 'pact' has been used for a solemn international agreement – eg 1928 Kellogg–Briand Pact,[35] 1945 Pact of the League of Arab States.[36]

The term *modus vivendi* is usually a temporary or provisional agreement, intended to be replaced by one of a more permanent or detailed character. However, the term *modus vivendi* is not frequently employed, but rather the terms 'temporary agreement' or 'interim agreement' are preferred.[37] Exchange of notes in contemporary practice is the most frequent means for formally recording the agreement of two governments on all kinds of transactions. It takes the form of an ordinary exchange of correspondence, consisting of two 'notes', namely, the initiating note and the accepting note.[38]

2.2.3.2 Form and Substance of a Treaty before International Courts and Tribunals

This section analyses the jurisprudence of international courts and tribunals on what constitutes a treaty. This question will be considered with regard to, both the *substance* – ie, the content of the instrument – and the *form* of an instrument in question.

2.2.3.2.1 Substance of the Instrument International courts and tribunals have dealt in numerous cases with the question of determination of the legal character of an instrument and whether it is a treaty in

[31] 1987 Montreal Protocol on Substances That Deplete the Ozone Layer (adopted 16 September 1987, entered into force 1 January 1989) 1522 UNTS 3.
[32] 1985 Vienna Convention for the Protection of the Ozone Layer (adopted 22 March 1985, entered into force 22 September 1988) 1513 UNTS 293.
[33] Both instruments are independent international treaties.
[34] Berman and Bentley, 'Treaties and Other International Instruments – II' 614 [32.18].
[35] 1928 General Treaty for the Renunciation of War as an Instrument of National Policy (Kellogg–Briand Pact) (adopted 27 August 1928, entered into force 25 July 1929) 94 LNTS 57.
[36] 1945 Pact of the League of Arab States (adopted 22 March 1945, entered into force 10 May 1945) 70 UNTS 237.
[37] Berman and Bentley, 'Treaties and Other International Instruments – III' 617–8 [33.5–6].
[38] ibid 616–23 [32.14–9].

international law. Often, the very jurisdiction itself of courts and tribunals depended on such a determination. The instruments analysed by courts and tribunals have spanned across very different forms, including minutes, joint communiqués, and MOUs. The question of the variety of forms was also considered by the arbitral tribunal in the 2015 *South China Sea Arbitration (Philippines v China).*[39] This is an instructive award, as the arbitral tribunal examined both the form and the content of the instrument in question. The tribunal acknowledged that a treaty may assume a variety of forms and that the form is 'not decisive of its status as an agreement establishing legal obligations between the parties'.[40] It stated as follows:

> The form or designation of an instrument is thus not decisive of its status as an agreement establishing legal obligations between the parties. The Tribunal observes that [the China–ASEAN Declaration on the Conduct of Parties in the South China Sea of 4 November 2002] shares some hallmarks of an international treaty. It is a formal document with a preamble, it is signed by the foreign ministers of China and the ASEAN States, and the signatory States are described in the DOC as 'Parties'. However, with respect to its terms, the DOC contains many instances of the signatory States simply 'reaffirming' existing obligations [...] The only instance where the DOC uses the word 'agree' is in paragraph 10 where the signatory States "agree to work, on the basis of consensus, towards the eventual attainment" of a Code of Conduct. This language is not consistent with the creation of new obligations but rather restates existing obligations pending agreement on a Code that eventually would set out new obligations ... On the other hand, some of the terms used in the DOC are suggestive of the existence of an agreement.[41]

Having examined the terms of the instrument, the arbitral tribunal came to the conclusion that

> it becomes apparent to this Tribunal that the DOC was not intended to be a legally binding agreement with respect to dispute resolution. The purpose and circumstances surrounding the DOC's adoption reinforce the Tribunal's understanding that the DOC was not intended to create legal rights and obligations. Descriptions from contemporaneous documents leading up to and surrounding the adoption of the DOC amply demonstrate that the DOC was not intended by its drafters to be a legally binding

[39] *South China Sea Arbitration (Philippines v China)* (Jurisdiction and Admissibility) (2015) PCA Case No 2013-19 [214–5].
[40] ibid [214].
[41] ibid.

> document, but rather an aspirational political document . . . The Parties' subsequent conduct further confirms that the DOC is not a binding agreement. In this respect, the Tribunal notes the Parties' continuing efforts over a decade after the DOC was signed to agree upon a Code of Conduct. The Tribunal also observes that in recent years, at least before the arbitration commenced, several Chinese officials described the DOC as a 'political' document.[42]

In the 1978 *Aegean Sea Continental Shelf* case, the question was whether the Brussels Joint Communiqué issued by Greece and Turkey amounted to an agreement in international law embodying the intention of both parties to the dispute to submit disputes to the ICJ.[43] The document bore no signatures, nor was it initialed. According to the Turkish government, it did not constitute an agreement under international law, and accordingly had not been ratified, 'at least on the part of Turkey'.[44] The Greek government maintained that the joint communiqué did constitute an agreement. According to the Greek government, '[i]t is necessary, and it is sufficient, for the communiqué to include – in addition to customary forms, protestations of friendship, recital of major principles and declarations of intent – provisions of a treaty nature'.[45] During the oral proceedings before the ICJ, Greece submitted that the joint communiqué was 'a modern ritual which has acquired full status in international practice'. The ICJ noted that treaties assume a multitude of forms. The ICJ declined the jurisdiction in that case by stating that the joint communiqué did not contain an agreement binding upon either State to accept the unilateral referral of the dispute to the Court. It stated: 'It does not settle the question simply to refer to the form – a communiqué – in which that act or transaction is embodied. On the contrary, in determining what was indeed the nature of the act or transaction embodied in the Brussels Communiqué, the Court must have regard above all to its actual terms and to particular circumstances in which it was drawn up'.[46]

In the 1994 *Maritime Delimitation and Territorial Questions between Qatar and Bahrain* case, the ICJ had to decide on the legal character of two instruments upon which Bahrain filed a case against Qatar: namely, (i) the two sets of exchange of letters concluded in December 1987

[42] ibid [217].

[43] L Gross, 'The Dispute between Greece and Turkey Concerning the Continental Shelf in the Aegean' (1977) 71 AJIL 31.

[44] *Aegean Sea Continental Shelf* [95].

[45] ibid.

[46] ibid [96].

between Qatar and Saudi Arabia, and between Bahrain and Saudi Arabia; and (ii) a set of minutes signed by the Foreign Ministers of Qatar and Bahrain in December 1990, on the occasion of the meeting of the Cooperation Council of Arab States of the Gulf. Again, the question arose whether the instruments in question constituted treaties and thus gave rise to legal obligations, and whether there was a consequent basis for the ICJ to establish its jurisdiction in that dispute. This case also illustrates the role that rules of interpretation play in determining whether an instrument constitutes a treaty. An important element of the dispute was the agreement of both parties that the 1987 exchange of letters constituted an international agreement with binding force in their mutual relations. According to Bahrain, however, the 1990 Minutes were only a simple record of negotiations, and, therefore, did not constitute an international agreement and, thus, could not serve as the basis for the Court's jurisdiction. Again, the ICJ observed that international agreements may assume a variety of forms and have many denominations. It adopted the same approach as it had in the *Aegean Sea Continental Shelf* case, finding it necessary to analyse the actual terms and particular circumstances in which the alleged agreement had been drawn up. Having considered all the facts of the case, the Court decided that the two sets of exchange of letters and the 1990 Minutes were indeed international agreements creating rights and obligations for the parties. The Court decided that by the terms of those agreements the parties had undertaken to submit to the Court the entire dispute between them, as provided for by the text proposed by Bahrain to Qatar on 26 October 1990, accepted by Qatar in December 1990, and referred to in the 1990 Minutes as the 'Bahrain formula'. In paragraph 25 of its judgment, the Court laid down the elements of an international undertaking that constitutes a treaty. According to the Court,

> contrary to the contentions of Bahrain, the Minutes are not a simple record of a meeting, similar to those drawn up within the Tripartite Committee; they do not merely give an account of discussions and summarize points of agreement and disagreement. They enumerate the commitments to which Parties have consented. They thus create rights and obligations in international law for the Parties. They constitute an international agreement.[47]

[47] *Maritime Delimitation and Territorial Questions between Qatar and Bahrain* (1994 Jurisdiction and Admissibility) [25].

As has been observed, the word 'thus' in that paragraph is of great importance, because it is the link between 'commitments to which the Parties have consented', on the one hand, and the creation of 'rights and obligations in international law' on the other.[48] The Court's ruling may be interpreted as indicating that the consent to commitments is of fundamental importance for the creation of a treaty under international law.

In the 2012 judgment of the International Tribunal for the Law of the Sea (ITLOS) in the *Bay of Bengal (Bangladesh/Myanmar)* case,[49] the legal character of minutes was again at issue. In relation to the legal character of these minutes, Bangladesh argued that their terms are 'clear and unambiguous' and '[t]heir ordinary meaning is that a boundary has been agreed'.[50] In this case, ITLOS, having examined the two sets of agreed minutes in question, proceeded in an entirely different manner than did the ICJ reaching the opposite conclusion. There are fundamental differences in reasoning relating to essentially very similar sets of documents. The ICJ was firmly of the view that the agreed minutes in question had created rights and obligations for States and thus constituted an international agreement. The ITLOS, having analysed two sets of fairly detailed and precise agreed minutes dating from 1974 and 2008, was of the view they were nothing more than a record of two meetings. Such disparities in decisions regarding very similar cases must cause uncertainty and tension in inter-State relations. Myanmar argued that the 'ordinary language' indicates that the 1974 Agreed Minutes 'were never intended to constitute a legally binding agreement'. In particular, the opening words in paragraph 1 of these Minutes state that they 'are clearly the language of a record of a meeting, not of a legally binding agreement'.[51] Myanmar further argued that the circumstances in which the 1974 Agreed Minutes and 2008 Agreed Minutes were concluded 'confirm that the Minutes were no more than an *ad hoc* conditional understanding, reached at an initial stage of the negotiations, which never ripened into a binding agreement between the two negotiating sides'.[52] Having analysed the agreed minutes, ITLOS came to the conclusion that in

[48] J Klabbers, *The Concept of Treaty in International Law* (Kluwer Law International 1996) 366–7.
[49] *Bay of Bengal (Bangladesh/Myanmar)* [72] ff.
[50] ibid [72].
[51] ibid [76].
[52] ibid [78].

international practice there is a possibility that agreed minutes may constitute an agreement and in this respect relied on, *inter alia,* the *Maritime Delimitation and Territorial Questions between Qatar and Bahrain* case. The tribunal observed that:

> the terms of the 1974 Agreed Minutes confirm that these Minutes are a record of a conditional understanding reached during the course of negotiations, and not an agreement within the meaning of article 15 of the Convention. This is supported by the language of these Minutes, in particular, in light of the condition expressly contained therein that the delimitation of the territorial sea boundary was to be part of a comprehensive maritime boundary treaty. The Tribunal notes that the circumstances in which the 1974 Agreed Minutes were adopted do not suggest that they were intended to create legal obligations or embodied commitments of a binding nature. From the beginning of the discussions Myanmar made it clear that it did not intend to enter into a separate agreement on the delimitation of territorial sea and that it wanted a comprehensive agreement covering the territorial sea, the exclusive economic zone and the continental shelf.[53]

Additionally, the tribunal added that issues of delimitation are of a sensitive nature.[54] It may be derived from this statement that perhaps extra caution is due in according binding force to instruments that may be determinative of such sensitive and critical matters as is definitive territorial delimitation.

The issue of what is a treaty was also considered by the ICJ more recently in the 2017 *Maritime Delimitation in the Indian Ocean* case. The question of the legal status of an MOU between the parties arose. The Minister for Foreign Affairs of the Government of Kenya and the Minister for National Planning and International Cooperation of the Transitional Federal Government of Somalia signed an instrument entitled 'Memorandum of Understanding between the Government of the Republic of Kenya and the Transitional Federal Government of the Somali Republic to Grant to Each Other No Objection in Respect of Submissions on the Outer Limits of the Continental Shelf beyond 200 Nautical Miles to the Commission on the Limits of the Continental Shelf'. This MOU was registered with the UN Secretary-General according to Article 102 of the UN Charter. The Court stated that the MOU is a written document in which Somalia and Kenya recorded their

[53] ibid [93–4].
[54] ibid [96].

agreement on certain points governed by international law.[55] Regarding the content of the MOU, the Court interpreted its substantive provisions – in particular, the sixth paragraph of the MOU – in accordance with Articles 31 and 32 of the VCLT, ie the VCLT rules pertaining to treaty interpretation. The Court decided that the MOU was not intended to establish a procedure for the settlement of the maritime boundary dispute between the parties;[56] however it concluded that the MOU was a treaty. As the Court stated, the MOU was 'a written document, in which Somalia and Kenya record their agreement on certain points governed by international law' and the 'inclusion of a provision addressing the entry into force of the MOU is indicative of the instrument's binding character'.[57]

The MOU was executed by Ministers who, in accordance with Article 7 of the VCLT, are assumed to be capable of binding their States 'by virtue of their functions and without having to produce full powers'.[58] Even if that were not the case, the Prime Minister of the Somali Transitional government had signed a document affording the Minister full powers.[59] The MOU also stated that it was to enter into force upon signature,[60] which was further proof that the MOU was considered to be of a binding nature. The national law of Somalia,[61] which 'made the President's authority to sign binding international agreements conditional upon subsequent ratification by Parliament', could not be invoked for the purposes of arguing that such ratification had not taken place due to Articles 27 and 46 of the VCLT.[62] Following a similar line of reasoning as in *Land and Maritime Boundary between Cameroon and Nigeria,* the Court found that it would be too odious of an obligation to require that Kenya should have been aware of any constitutional impediment to the exercise of full powers by the Minister. After all, Article 46 requires that any violation of a provision of a State's internal law, regarding competence to conclude treaties, must be *manifest* in order to invalidate its consent.

[55] *Maritime Delimitation in the Indian Ocean* [42].
[56] ibid [105].
[57] ibid [42].
[58] ibid [43].
[59] ibid.
[60] ibid [45].
[61] Specifically, the Transitional Federal Charter of the Somali Republic, applicable between 2004 and 2012.
[62] *Maritime Delimitation in the Indian Ocean* [39].

Interestingly, although the Court concluded that the MOU was binding, it did not 'prescribe a method of dispute settlement'.[63] The MOU, therefore, was not an agreement '"to have recourse to some other method or methods of settlement" within the meaning of Kenya's reservation to its Article 36, paragraph 2, declaration, and consequently this case [did] not, by virtue of the MOU, fall outside the scope of Kenya's consent to the Court's jurisdiction'.[64]

The question of creating legally binding obligations through a communication alleged to be an international agreement has arisen in relation to the Communication of 16 March 2016 to the European Parliament, the European Council, and the Council entitled 'Next Operational Steps in EU–Turkey Cooperation in the Field of Migration'. The European Commission stated that, on 7 March 2016, the '[European Union] leaders [had] warmly welcomed the additional proposals made by Turkey and agreed to work with Turkey on the basis of a set of six principles', that 'the President of the European Council [had been] requested to take forward these proposals and work out the details with Turkey before the March European Council' and that 'this Communication [sets] out how the six principles should be taken forward, delivering on the full potential for [EU–Turkey] cooperation while respecting European and international law'.[65] This communication was the subject of proceedings before the Court of Justice of the European Union (CJEU). NF, an asylum seeker national of Pakistan, relied on the communication being a treaty within the meaning of Article 2 of the 1969 VCLT and of Article 218 of the Treaty on the Functioning of the European Union (TFEU).[66] In its replies of 18 November 2016 to the Court's questions, the European Council explained, *inter alia*, 'that, to the best of its knowledge, no agreement or treaty in the sense of Article 218 TFEU or Article 2(1)(a) of the VCLT had been concluded between the EU and Turkey'. The EU–Turkey statement, as published by means of Press Release No 144/16, was, it submitted, merely 'the fruit of an international dialogue between the member States and [the Republic of] Turkey and – in the light of its content and of the intention of its authors – [was] not intended to

[63] ibid [106].

[64] ibid.

[65] *Case T-192/16 – NF v Council* (Order) [2017] ECLI:EU:T:2017:128 [5].

[66] 2007 Consolidated Version of the Treaty on the Functioning of the European Union (adopted 13 December 2007, entered into force 1 December 2009) OJ C 115 (9 May 2008) 45.

produce legally binding effects nor constitute an agreement or a treaty'.[67] In fact, according to the Council, the use of the term 'EU' had no bearing at all on the determination whether this act was an EU act or an act of the Heads of State of its members, since it appeared only in a press release that used simplified language in order to inform a wide audience. In its view, 'the term "EU" must be understood *in this journalistic context* as referring to the Heads of State or Government of the Member States of the European Union'.[68]

The CJEU found that the instrument in question had not been concluded by the European Council; had it been, that could indicate that the Communication was an international treaty by which the European Council sought to conclude, on behalf of the European Union, an agreement with the Republic of Turkey on 18 March 2016.[69] However, the Court found that the expression 'Members of the European Council' and the term 'EU', contained in the EU–Turkey statement as published by means of Press Release No 144/16, must be understood as references to the Heads of State or Government of the European Union not the European Council.[70] Therefore the Court concluded that

> [i]t follows from all of the foregoing considerations that, independently of whether it constitutes, as maintained by the European Council, the Council [of the European Union], and the Commission, a political statement or, on the contrary, as the applicant submits, a measure capable of producing binding legal effects, the EU–Turkey statement, as published by means of Press Release No 144/16, cannot be regarded as a measure adopted by the European Council, or, moreover, by any other institution, body, office or agency of the European Union, or as revealing the existence of such a measure that corresponds to the contested measure. For the sake of completeness, with regard to the reference in the EU–Turkey statement to the fact that 'the EU and [the Republic of] Turkey agreed on . . . additional action points', the Court considers that, even supposing that an international agreement could have been informally concluded during the meeting of 18 March 2016, which has been denied by the European Council, the Council and the Commission in the present case, that agreement would have been an agreement concluded by the Heads of State or Government of the Member States of the European Union and the Turkish Prime Minister.[71]

[67] *Case T-192/16 – NF v Council* [27].
[68] ibid [58] (emphasis added).
[69] ibid [46].
[70] ibid [69].
[71] ibid [71–2].

Finally, the most recent Judgment of the Court of 1 October 2018 in the *Obligation to Negotiate Access to the Pacific Ocean* case[72] deserves attention since it raises the question whether several joint memoranda and declarations and unilateral acts between Chile and Bolivia constituted a treaty. To answer this question, the Court relied on its previous jurisprudence such as the *Maritime Delimitation and Territorial Questions between Qatar and Bahrain* case, *Aegean Sea Continental Shelf* case, and *Nuclear Tests* cases, according to which it is necessary to assess whether States wanted to create legal obligations, on the basis of their intentions as resulting from an objective test. The Court stated that

> [t]he Court notes that Chile's declarations and other unilateral acts on which Bolivia relies are expressed, not in terms of undertaking a legal obligation, but of willingness to enter into negotiations on the issue of Bolivia's sovereign access to the Pacific Ocean. For instance, Chile declared that it was willing 'to seek that Bolivia acquire its own outlet to the sea' and 'to give an ear to any Bolivian proposal aimed at solving its landlocked condition' . . . On another occasion, Chile stated its 'unchanging purpose of studying, together with that brother country, within the framework of a frank and friendly negotiation, the obstacles that limit Bolivia's development on account of its landlocked condition' . . . The wording of these texts does not suggest that Chile has undertaken a legal obligation to negotiate Bolivia's sovereign access to the Pacific Ocean.[73]

The Court applied a very strict test and based its analysis on the text of the instrument in question:

> The Court notes that the Declaration of Charaña is a document that was signed by the Presidents of Bolivia and Chile which could be characterized as a treaty if the Parties had expressed an intention to be bound by that instrument or if such an intention could be otherwise inferred. However, the overall language of the Declaration rather indicates that it has the nature of a political document which stresses the 'atmosphere of fraternity and cordiality' and 'the spirit of solidarity' between the two States, who in the final clause decide to 'normalize' their diplomatic relations. The wording of the Declaration does not convey the existence or the confirmation of an obligation to negotiate Bolivia's sovereign access to the Pacific Ocean. The engagement 'to continue the dialogue, at different levels, in order to search for formulas to solve the vital issues that both countries face, such as the landlocked situation that affects Bolivia', cannot constitute a legal commitment to negotiate Bolivia's sovereign access to the sea,

[72] *Obligation to Negotiate Access to the Pacific Ocean (Bolivia v Chile)* (Merits) [2018] ICJ Rep 507.

[73] ibid [147].

> which is not even specifically mentioned. While the Ministers for Foreign Affairs of the Parties noted in their Joint Declaration of 10 June 1977 that 'negotiations have been engaged aiming at finding an effective solution that allows Bolivia to access the Pacific Ocean freely and with sovereignty', they did not go beyond reaffirming 'the need of continuing with the negotiations' and did not refer to any obligation to negotiate. Based on this evidence, an obligation for Chile to negotiate cannot be inferred from the Declaration of Charaña.[74]

Accordingly, notwithstanding the fact that the Declaration was signed by the Presidents of Chile and Bolivia, it was not considered binding.[75] The Court went on to stress that '[w]ith regard to the circumstances of Chile's declarations and statements, ... there is no evidence of an intention on the part of Chile to assume an obligation to negotiate. The Court therefore concludes that an obligation to negotiate Bolivia's sovereign access to the sea cannot rest on any of Chile's unilateral acts referred to by Bolivia'.[76]

Finally, the Court also confirmed the validity of oral and tacit agreements, by noting that

> according to customary international law, as reflected in Article 3 of the Vienna Convention, 'agreements not in written form' may also have 'legal force'. Irrespective of the form that agreements may take, they require an intention of the parties to be bound by legal obligations. This applies also to tacit agreements. In this respect, the Court recalls that '[e]vidence of a tacit legal agreement must be compelling'.[77]

2.2.3.2.2 Form (Who Can Bind the State): The Question of Domestic Law In the *Land and Maritime Boundary between Cameroon and Nigeria* case[78] two declarations – namely, the Yaoundé and Maroua Declarations relating the delimitation – due to their adoption procedure were held to be binding international law instruments. Nigeria argued that the declarations were not binding, as they were adopted contrary to Nigerian constitutional rules. It argued that the Head of State of Nigeria had no powers to bind the State, as according to the domestic law of

74 ibid [126].
75 ibid [147].
76 ibid [148].
77 ibid [97] citing *Territorial and Maritime Dispute between Nicaragua and Honduras in the Caribbean Sea (Nicaragua v Honduras)* (Judgment) [2007] ICJ Rep 659 [253].
78 *Land and Maritime Boundary between Cameroon and Nigeria (Cameroon v Nigeria: Equatorial Guinea Intervening)* [2002] ICJ Rep 303.

Nigeria only the Military Council could do it. In this respect, the ICJ invoked Article 46 VCLT, which only allows the invocation of such an argument against the validity of treaties when the domestic rules are of *fundamental importance.* This is not the case as 'a limitation of a Head of State's capacity' in this respect is not manifest in the sense of Article 46(2) VCLT unless at least properly publicised. This is particularly so because the Head of State belongs to the group of persons who, in accordance with Article 7(2) VCLT, '[i]n virtue of their functions and without having to produce full powers' are considered as representing their State'.[79]

Likewise, the ICJ stated that the argument of Nigeria that Cameroon knew or ought to have known that the Head of State of Nigeria did not have powers to legally bind Nigeria without consulting the Nigerian Government is unfounded. There is no general obligation for States to keep themselves informed of the legislative and constitutional intricacies and developments in the constitutional settings of other States that are relevant to their international relations.[80] The Court also observed that there are other indications that both States treated both Declarations as binding, such as the insertion of the correction in the Maroua Declaration that 'in so acting they treated the Declaration as valid and applicable, and that Nigeria does not claim to have contested its validity or applicability prior to 1997'.[81] The Court stated that in those circumstances both Declarations must be considered binding under international law and as establishing legal obligations for Nigeria.[82]

This case can be compared to the *Bay of Bengal (Bangladesh/Myanmar)* case, in which Myanmar argued that members of its delegation to the negotiations in November 1974 lacked authority to enter into binding commitments on behalf of their Government to conclude a legally binding treaty. The head of the Burmese delegation, Commodore Hlaing, a naval officer, could not be considered as representing Myanmar for the purpose of expressing its consent to be bound by a treaty, as he was not one of those holders of high-ranking office as defined in Article 7(2) VCLT. Myanmar also argued that Article 7(2) of the VCLT does not apply in this case since Commodore Hlaing did not have full powers

[79] ibid [265].
[80] ibid [266].
[81] ibid [267].
[82] ibid [268].

issued by the Government of Myanmar and there were no circumstances to suggest that it was the intention of Myanmar and Bangladesh to dispense with full powers. In the view of Myanmar, under Article 8 VCLT, an act by a person who cannot be considered as representing a State for the purposes of concluding a treaty is without legal effect unless afterwards confirmed by that State.[83]

ITLOS in the *Bay of Bengal (Bangladesh/Myanmar)* case also stressed that the fact that both parties not having submitted the instrument in question – namely, the agreed minutes – to their domestic constitutional procedures in regard to the conclusion of treaties was an indication that the agreed minutes were not to be considered legally binding.[84] That said, according to Article 46 VCLT, however, a State may not invoke the fact that its consent to be bound by a treaty violates a provision of its internal law regarding competence to conclude treaties as in itself invalidating its consent, unless that violation was *manifest* and concerned a rule of its internal law of *fundamental* importance. This was confirmed by the ICJ in the *Land and Maritime Boundary between Cameroon and Nigeria* case.[85] Again, there seems to be a divergence of approach between the ICJ and ITLOS on this point.

In the *Maritime Delimitation in the Indian Ocean* case, the ICJ first analysed the power to enter into an agreement by the Somalian Minister for National Planning and International Cooperation and whether the signature can be a final expression of consent to be bound. Relying on the full powers of the Minister, signed by the Prime Minister of the Transitional Federal Government of Somalia, and the clear statement in the MOU, namely that 'this Memorandum of Understanding shall enter into force upon its signature', the Court came to the conclusion that the Minister had indeed the power to bind the State upon signature, and did not require the ratification provided for by Somalian law.[86] The Court also relied on Article 7 VCLT, and stated as follows:

> The Court recalls that, under international law, as codified in Article 7 of the Vienna Convention, by virtue of their functions and without having to produce full powers, Heads of State, Heads of Government and Ministers for Foreign Affairs are considered as representing their State for the

[83] *Bay of Bengal (Bangladesh/Myanmar)* [833].
[84] ibid [97].
[85] ibid [265].
[86] Thus relying on the *Land and Maritime Boundary between Cameroon and Nigeria* case.

> purpose of performing all acts relating to the conclusion of a treaty. These State representatives, under international law, may also duly authorize other officials to adopt, on behalf of a State, the text of a treaty or to express the consent of the State to be bound by a treaty.[87]

In the 2018 *Obligation to Negotiate Access to the Pacific Ocean* case, the Court analysed the Charaña Declaration, which was signed by the Presidents of Bolivia and Peru. The Court affirmed that it could have been a treaty, if the parties had expressed an intention to be bound by that instrument or if such an intention could be inferred; however, the wording on the instrument indicated that it was a political instrument only.[88] This judgment can be compared with the one in the *Land and Maritime Boundary between Cameroon and Nigeria* case, where the Court reached the conclusion about the legal character of the two disputed declarations as treaties because of their being signed by the President of Nigeria, which binds the State according to Article 7 VCLT; in this latter case, the Court did not analyse the substance of these declarations but inferred their binding character from the procedural element of the role of the President in consent to be bound. Moreover, it should be recalled that in the *Maritime Delimitation and Territorial Questions between Qatar and Bahrain* case, the Court, in paragraphs 23 and 27, not only had not inferred the legal character of the minutes in question based on the intention of the parties but it also stated that the Court must have regard *above all to the actual terms and circumstances of the instrument.* Therefore, it may be said that that the *Obligation to Negotiate Access to the Pacific Ocean* case in many ways departs somewhat from the previous practice of the Court in defining what constitutes a treaty in international law.

2.2.3.2.3 'Curious Case' of Mr Ihlen Another interesting example in connection to the discussion of the plasticity of the notion of treaty is the so-called Ihlen Declaration. This has been the subject of many studies in international law and has frequently been given as an example of a unilateral declaration creating international obligations. In the view of the authors of this study, this is a declaration of a hybrid character, given that an element of bilateral dealings was also involved. However, it is also interesting from the point of view of the role of a Minister of Foreign Affairs binding a State through his/her statements.

[87] *Maritime Delimitation in the Indian Ocean* [43].

[88] *Obligation to Negotiate Access to the Pacific Ocean* [146–7].

The *Legal Status of Eastern Greenland* case[89] shows clearly the limitations of the VCLT definition in the face of multifaceted sources of international legal obligations – in that case, obligations created by unilateral acts. The act in question was the so-called Ihlen Declaration. On 14 July 1919, the Danish Minister accredited in Norway, in a conversation with the Norwegian Minister of Foreign Affairs, Nils Claus Ihlen, stated that Denmark would not object to any claim to Spitsbergen which Norway might submit at the Peace Conference, if Norway were not to oppose the Danish claim at the same conference to the whole of Greenland. In another conversation on 22 July 1919, Ihlen stated that 'the plans of the Royal [Danish] Government respecting Danish sovereignty over the whole of Greenland . . . would meet with no difficulties on the part of Norway'. These were words recorded by Ihlen in the form of minutes, and submitted to his Government, ie Norway. One of the questions before the Court was the legal character of the Ihlen Declaration: was it simply a unilateral declaration, or a hybrid instrument combining the features of an agreement with those of a unilateral declaration? The Court's judgment did not fully address any of these questions. It focused rather on the binding nature of an international obligation, regardless of its source. The Court said that it 'considers it beyond all dispute that a reply of this nature given by the Minister for Foreign Affairs on behalf of his Government in response to a request by the diplomatic representative of a foreign Power, in regard to a question falling within his province, is binding upon the country to which the Minister belongs'.[90]

The Court, having taken into consideration all circumstances, concluded that it was 'unable to regard the Ihlen Declaration of 22 July 1919 otherwise than as unconditional and definitive', since

> [i]t was so understood by the Norwegian Minister for Foreign Affairs when he told the Danish Minister at Christiania (ie, modern-day Oslo) on 7 November 1919, that 'it was a pleasure to Norway to recognize Danish sovereignty over Greenland'. It was also in the same sense that the Danish Minister at Christiania had understood the Ihlen Declaration, when he informed the Danish Minister for Foreign Affairs on 22 July 1919, that Mr Ihlen had told him 'that the plans of the Royal Government in regard to the sovereignty of Denmark over the whole Greenland would not encounter any difficulties on the part of Norway.[91]

[89] *Legal Status of Eastern Greenland (Denmark v Norway)* (Judgment) PCIJ Rep Series A/B No 53.

[90] ibid 71.

[91] ibid 72–3.

Eventually, the Court found that it followed that 'as a result of the undertaking involved in the Ihlen Declaration of 22 July 1919, Norway is under an obligation to refrain from contesting Danish sovereignty over Greenland as a whole, and *a fortiori* to refrain from occupying a part of Greenland'.[92]

Perhaps the most interesting aspect of the analysis was the Court's indication that interdependence of mutual obligations might not necessarily create a bilateral engagement. The Court stated that

> [i]t is clear from the relevant Danish documents which preceded the Danish Minister's demarche at Christiania on July 14th 1919, that the Danish attitude in the Spitsbergen question and the Norwegian attitude in the Greenland question were regarded in Denmark as interdependent, and this interdependence appears to be reflected also in Ihlen's minutes of the interview. Even if this interdependence – which, in view of the affirmative reply of the Norwegian Government, in whose name the Minister for Foreign Affairs was speaking, would have created a bilateral engagement – is not held to have been established, it can hardly be denied that what Denmark was asking of Norway ('not to make any difficulties in the settlement of the [Greenland] question') was equivalent to what she was indicating her readiness to concede in the Spitsbergen question (to refrain from opposing 'the wishes of Norway in regard to the settlement of this question'). What Denmark desired to obtain from Norway was that the latter should do nothing to obstruct the Danish plans in regard to Greenland. The declaration which the Minister for Foreign Affairs gave on July 22nd, 1919, on behalf of the Norwegian Government, was definitely affirmative: 'I told the Danish Minister to-day that the Norwegian Government would not make any difficulty in the settlement of this question'.[93]

The Court appears to have based its decision as to the binding nature of the declaration in part on the formal legal ground of the inherent power of Ministers of Foreign Affairs to bind States by virtue of their statements, as now codified in Article 7 VCLT.[94] The Court emphasised that

[92] ibid 73.

[93] ibid 70–1.

[94] Of special interest is VCLT Art 7(2), according to which '[i]n virtue of their functions and without having to produce full powers, the following are considered as representing their State:

> (a) Heads of State, Heads of Government and Ministers for Foreign Affairs, for the purpose of performing all acts relating to conclusion of a treaty;
> (b) heads of diplomatic missions, for the purpose of adopting the text of a treaty between the accrediting State and the State to which they are accredited;
> (c) representatives accredited by States to an international conference or to an organ of an international organisation or one of its organs, for the purpose of adopting the text of a treaty in that conference, organisation or organ'.

the position of the Minister for Foreign Affairs who had made a statement binding his government was sufficient to create an obligation for such a State, even without it having been an 'interdependent' commitment. The Court held that it resulted in 'an undertaking' on the part of the Norwegian Government, its content being to refrain from opposing Denmark asserting its sovereignty over the whole of Greenland, but without constituting a direct acknowledgement of Danish sovereignty, and to refrain from occupying any part of Greenland. The Court thus characterised the Ihlen Declaration as a unilateral statement of a purely verbal nature that had legal implications for the *inter se* relations between Denmark and Norway.

However, this was perhaps an oversimplification, dictated no doubt by the exigencies of the case. It is difficult not to acknowledge some force in the position of the Danish government, which claimed that in this case there existed, if not a treaty, then at least two interdependent engagements in the form of two unilateral acts. The understanding of the Danish government was that the statements made by the Danish representative and the Norwegian Minister for Foreign Affairs were 'interdependent'. Thus, establishing a so-called *do ut des* reciprocal contractual recognition of Norwegian interests in Spitsbergen by Denmark and recognition of Danish interests in Greenland by Norway. Although not satisfactory, if viewed in terms of a hard and fast, consistent, and universal definition, it may be said that the Ihlen Declaration was a hybrid – in terms of its normative character – instrument where unilateral and bilateral obligations were inextricably interlocked. Very instructive from this point of view was the opinion of Judge Anzilotti, who stated that

> [t]he dispute is one between Denmark and Norway regarding the sovereignty over a territory in Eastern Greenland. Denmark's position formed the subject of a request addressed by the Danish Government to the Norwegian Government in July 1919, and of a declaration on the part of the latter Government accepted by the Danish Government. Accordingly, in my view, the first thing to be done was to decide whether this constituted a valid agreement between two governments; if so, the rule to be applied for the solution of the dispute should first and foremost have been sought in this agreement.[95]

Later, he continued:

> The outcome of all this is therefore an agreement, concluded between the Danish Minister, on behalf of the Danish Government, and the

[95] *Legal Status of Eastern Greenland*, Dissenting Opinion of Judge Anzilotti 76.

> Norwegian Minister for Foreign Affairs, on behalf of the Norwegian Government, by means of purely verbal declarations. The validity of this agreement has been questioned, having regard, in the first place, to its verbal form, and to the competence of the Minister of Foreign Affairs. As regards the form, it should be noted, to begin with, that as both Parties are agreed as to the existence and tenor of these declarations, the question of proof does not arise. Moreover, there does not seem to be any rule of international law requiring that agreements of this kind must necessarily be in writing, in order to be valid.[96]

It has to be noted that the question of the role of the Head of State in binding a State also arose in the aforementioned *Land and Maritime Boundary between Cameroon and Nigeria* case. Nigeria invoked Article 7(2) VCLT, and argued that Cameroon, according to an objective test based on the provisions of the VCLT, either knew or ought to have known that the Head of State of Nigeria lacked the power to make legally binding commitments on the part of the State of Nigeria without referring the matter first to the Government of Nigeria – at the time exercised by the Supreme Military Council. According to Nigeria, Article 7(2) VCLT refers solely to the way in which a person's function as a State's representative is established and does not deal with the extent of that person's powers when exercising that representative function. Cameroon also submitted that, according to Article 7(2) VCLT, as a matter of international law a Head of State is ordinarily considered as representing a State for the purpose of expressing consent to be bound by a treaty.[97]

The Court rejected the Nigerian contention that Article 7(2) VCLT is solely concerned with the way that a person's function as a State's representative is established, and that it does not deal with the extent of that person's authority when exercising the representative functions.

2.2.3.2.4 Role of the Intention of the Parties One of the crucial elements in distinguishing between formal and informal instruments is the element of the 'role the intention' – that is to say, whether parties to a treaty intended to be bound by it or not. The case law of international courts and tribunals is inconclusive on this issue.

The element of intention of the parties has at least three different functions in treaty law:

[96] ibid 91.

[97] *Land and Maritime Boundary between Cameroon and Nigeria* [260].

- The first is its role as one of the elements of the concept of the treaty, which distinguishes binding instruments from non-binding ones;
- the second is its role within the canons of treaty interpretation, as suggested by, for example, Sir Hersch Lauterpacht[98] and Lord McNair;[99] and
- the third is its role in determinations on the expression of the will of the parties to a dispute to subject themselves to adjudication or not. To some extent there is some overlap with the second function, as intention may be used in interpreting the 'agreement' between the parties to ascertain the existence and the scope of the will of parties to submit to the adjudicative scope of an international court or tribunal.

In the *Maritime Delimitation and Territorial Questions between Qatar and Bahrain* case, Bahrain advanced an argument resting on intention, claiming that the signatories had never intended to conclude an internationally binding agreement. The Foreign Minister of Bahrain had stated that by signing the Minutes in 1990 he had never intended to commit Bahrain to a legally binding agreement, and that, according to the Constitution of Bahrain, treaties affecting the territory of a State may only come into effect after their positive enactment as a law in the domestic legal order. Thus, having been aware of these strict requirements, he could not have legally bound his State, and had only treated the signing of the minutes – the instrument in question – as a political statement. The Court refused to investigate further the intentions of the representatives of the two governments, affirming that '[t]he Court does not find it necessary to consider what might have been the intentions of the Foreign Minister of Bahrain or, for that matter, those of the Foreign Minister of Qatar'.[100]

98 H Lauterpacht, 'Restrictive Interpretation and the Principle of Effectiveness of Treaties' (1949) 26 BYIL 73. Sir Lauterpacht held a strong view on this matter: 'The intention of the parties – express or implied – is the law. Any consideration – of effectiveness or otherwise – which tend to transform the ascertainable intention of the parties into a factor of secondary importance are inimical to the true purpose of interpretation'.

99 Cf, Lord A McNair, *The Law of Treaties* (Clarendon Press 1961) 366: 'Many references are to be found … to the primary necessity of giving effect to the "plain terms" of a treaty, or construing words according to their "general and ordinary meaning" or their natural signification and so forth and of not seeking *aliunde* for a meaning "when the terms are clear". But this so-called rule of interpretation like any others is merely a starting point, a *prima facie* guide, and cannot be allowed to obstruct the essential quest in the application of treaties, namely to search for the real intention of the contracting parties in using the language employed by them'.

100 *Maritime Delimitation and Territorial Questions between Qatar and Bahrain* (1994 Jurisdiction and Admissibility) [27].

The Court found that in this particular case the objective evidence was clear enough not to necessitate recourse to any further means, such as the *travaux préparatoires*. Their Governments accepted the commitments, some of which were to be given immediate application. Having signed such a text, the Foreign Minister of Bahrain was not in a position to say that he intended to subscribe only to a 'statement recording a political understanding', and not to an international agreement.[101] That finding was confirmed in the 1995 *Maritime Delimitation and Territorial Questions between Qatar and Bahrain* case.[102]

According to Klabbers,

> [t]he *Qatar v Bahrain* decision is important for two reasons. First, it unequivocally makes clear that any commitment is a legal commitment. Second, it establishes something of a methodology for ascertaining the true nature of an international instrument: first and foremost are its actual terms. If the text of an instrument allows the ascertainment of commitments, then it is a legal text and the discussion is effectively closed. It is only where the text itself is ambiguous that recourse to other indicators appears justified.[103]

Klabbers applies this statement to the general concept of a treaty. However, the 1995 ICJ judgment may be interpreted in a different way. It may be argued that the Court applied this only to the issue at hand, namely the establishment of its jurisdiction. Support for this claim may be found in the Dissenting Opinion of Judge Schwebel, who was strongly critical of the findings of the Court but referred only to the issue of the Court's jurisdiction. He stated that

> [i]n the jurisprudence of this Court, jurisdiction may be conferred upon it only by the common intention of both parties to the case ... But if that common intention is lacking, if the intention to submit to the Court's jurisdiction is that of one but not both parties, the Court is without jurisdiction to decide the merits of the dispute.[104]

[101] ibid.

[102] See *Maritime Delimitation and Territorial Questions between Qatar and Bahrain (Qatar v Bahrain)* (Jurisdiction and Admissibility) [1995] ICJ Rep 6. The judgment was not without controversy. In particular, it was subject to severe criticism by Judge Schwebel, who emphasised the failure of the Court to take into account *travaux préparatoires* to ascertain the true intention of the parties (ibid, Dissenting Opinion of Judge Schwebel 25–39).

[103] Klabbers, *The Concept of Treaty* 215.

[104] *Maritime Delimitation and Territorial Questions between Qatar and Bahrain* (1995 Jurisdiction and Admissibility), Dissenting Opinion of Judge Schwebel 27–8.

The necessity to establish the intention of the parties to submit to the Court's jurisdiction has always been maintained by the Court. In the *Aegean Sea Continental Shelf* case, the Court said that '[r]egard must be paid to the intention of the Greek Government at the time when it deposited its instrument of accession to the General Act; and it was with that jurisprudence in mind that the Court asked the Greek Government to furnish any available evidence of explanations of the instrument of accession given at that time'.[105] In any event, it could be said that the Court, having examined the content of the legal obligation included in the instrument in question, decided that it laid down very clearly the parties' rights and obligations, and, therefore, had constituted an agreement, the existence of which could be stated without the necessity of recourse to establishing the intentions of the parties through other means.

However, in the *Bay of Bengal (Bangladesh/Myanmar)* case, the ITLOS relied to some extent on the intention of the parties. In that case, the ITLOS affirmed that

> the circumstances in which the 1974 Agreed Minutes were adopted do not suggest that they were intended to create legal obligations or embodied commitments of a binding nature. From the beginning of the discussions Myanmar made it clear that it did not intend to enter into a separate agreement on the delimitation of territorial sea and that it wanted a comprehensive agreement covering the territorial sea, the exclusive economic zone and the continental shelf.[106]

Similarly, the Arbitral Tribunal in the *Philippines v China* case stressed the importance of the intention of the parties to establish rights and obligations. 'To constitute a binding agreement, an instrument must evince a clear intention to establish rights and obligations between the parties. Such clear intention is determined by reference to the instrument's actual terms and the particular circumstances of its adoption. The subsequent conduct of the parties to an instrument may also assist in determining its nature'.[107]

Therefore, in contrast to the ICJ's *Maritime Delimitation and Territorial Questions between Qatar and Bahrain* case, ITLOS and the *Philippines v China* Arbitral Tribunal deemed it necessary to look beyond the

[105] *Aegean Sea Continental Shelf* [69]. It was also confirmed by the Court, eg, in the *Fisheries Jurisdiction* case *(Spain v Canada)* (Jurisdiction) [1998] ICJ Rep 432 [49].

[106] *Bay of Bengal (Bangladesh/Myanmar)* [93].

[107] *South China Sea Arbitration* [213].

objective aspects of the documents/instruments in question, and to examine what may have been the intention of the parties through other lines of inquiry.

These decisions illustrate some inconsistencies in international arbitration and adjudication, as well as the complexities surrounding the function of parties' *intention* in the law of treaties in general. There seems to be quite a bit of back-and-forth motion as to the relevance of the intentions of the parties in the determination of the existence of a treaty, and in the view of these authors, this question is still one awaiting resolution.

2.2.4 *Registration of the Treaty (Article 102 of the UN Charter)*

There is a certain degree of conviction between States that, according to Article 102 of the UN Charter, the fact of the registration of a document with the United Nations (UN) is a clear indication of its binding character as a treaty. At any rate, in many cases in which international courts and tribunals have dealt with defining the normative character of the instrument in international law, ie whether it is legally binding or not, States, in order to substantiate their argument, have pleaded that there is a presumption that an instrument is not a treaty if not registered with the UN.[108] Such a presumption, however, is not in accordance with the jurisprudence of the ICJ. The ICJ rather unambiguously clarified in the *Maritime Delimitation and Territorial Questions between Qatar and Bahrain* case that

> [t]he Court observed that an international agreement or treaty that has not been registered with the Secretariat of the United Nations may not, according to the provisions of Article 102 of the Charter, be invoked by the parties before any organ of the United Nations. Non-registration or late registration, on the other hand, does not have any consequence for the actual validity of the agreement, which remains no less binding upon the parties. The Court therefore cannot infer from the fact that Qatar did not apply for registration of the 1990 Minutes until six months after they were signed that Qatar considered, in December 1990, that those Minutes did not constitute an international agreement. The same conclusion follows as regards the non-registration of the text with the General Secretariat of the Arab League. Nor is there anything in the material before the Court which would justify deducing from any disregard by

[108] Cf, *inter alia*, the *Bay of Bengal (Bangladesh/Myanmar)* [86–7]; *Maritime Delimitation in the Indian Ocean* [39 ff].

> Qatar of its constitutional rules relating to the conclusion of treaties that it did not intend to conclude, and did not consider that it had concluded, an instrument of that kind; nor could any such intention, even if shown to exist, prevail over the actual terms of the instrument in question. Accordingly, Bahrain's argument on these points also cannot be accepted.[109]

2.2.5 *Conclusions*

The question as to what constitutes a 'treaty' is one of the most daunting problems in international law, given the implications that uncertainty surely has for the stability of treaty relations and international relations more generally. There is no hard-and-fast formula that States can follow without any doubt and with full certainty. The succinct and somewhat enigmatic definition in the 1969 VCLT has featured in many decisions by international courts and tribunals, which moved it forward by further clarifying and developing it. However, these decisions have arguably not resulted in an unequivocal and firm definition of what constitutes a treaty in international law. It remains a puzzle. We can only attempt to extrapolate, to a certain limited extent, from the case law certain indications, originating from different angles, pointing at what may constitute a treaty in international law. Certain conclusions that may be drawn are as follows:

(i) The form of an instrument is not an indicator of a legal character of an instrument – it can be any instrument, of a variety of terms accorded to it, such as, *inter alia*, joint communiqué, MOU, exchange of notes and letters, minutes, protocol, declaration, statement, and so on. The form can be expressed in 'its infinite variety.[110]

(ii) The (non)-registration of an instrument according to Article 102 of the UN Charter is not determinative of the instrument's normative character.

(iii) The substance/contents of the instrument in question may be determinative, given that the indication of a legal character of an instrument is (a) 'actual terms and to particular circumstances in which it was drawn up';[111] and (b) the enumeration of the commitments to which parties have consented and therefore the creation of rights and obligations in international law for the parties.[112]

109 *Maritime Delimitation and Territorial Questions between Qatar and Bahrain* (1994 Jurisdiction and Admissibility) [29].

110 Cf, *Aegean Sea Continental Shelf.*

111 ibid.

112 Cf, *Maritime Delimitation and Territorial Questions between Qatar and Bahrain.*

(iv) the subsequent conduct of the parties to an instrument[113] may also have implications for the normative character of an instrument in question. Subsequent conduct of the parties to the treaty should be distinguished from the 'actual terms' of a treaty and also the 'particular circumstances'. In essence, subsequent practice is an interpretative tool, included in Article 31(3)(b) of the VCLT.[114] The role of subsequent practice in treaty interpretation, at least within the remit of the VCLT, has to fulfill certain, rather stringent, conditions to be part and parcel of the interpretative process. It can only be considered when all relevant parties to the treaty engage in common conduct in the application of the treaty and when such an action is conducted willfully and with awareness or belief of the consequences of their actions. Such strict conditions on the role of subsequent practice were set out in the *Kasikili/Sedudu Island* case.[115] However, it is still unclear whether such an approach to the notion of subsequent practice will be followed in case of its function as a constituent element of a definition of 'treaty'.

(iv) The signing of a treaty by the Head of State, Prime Minister, or a Foreign Minister or some other authorised persons is ordinarily binding on a State in international law, under Article 7 VCLT, and a State cannot argue to the contrary.[116]

(v) International case law appears to indicate that both the *substance/content* and the *form* of the instrument in question are to be taken into consideration in determining the normative character of an instrument and whether it constitutes a treaty under international law. In the majority of cases, quite sensibly, *substance* takes precedence over *form*. There is, however, a real dearth of common indicators in international practice. The difficulty of formulating a

[113] Cf, *South China Sea Arbitration*.

[114] Subsequent practice is one of the subject areas of the current work of the ILC, which elected Professor Georg Nolte as Special Rapporteur on this topic. Subsequent practice within the ILC is analysed from the point of view of its role in treaty interpretation. See G Nolte (ed), *Treaties and Subsequent Practice* (OUP 2013).

[115] See *Kasikili/Sedudu Island (Botswana/Namibia)* (Judgment) [1999] ICJ Rep 1045. See also L Crema, 'Subsequent Agreements Practice and Subsequent Practice within and Outside the Vienna Convention' in G Nolte (ed), *Treaties and Subsequent Practice* (OUP 2013) 17.

[116] Cf, *Land and Maritime Boundary between Cameroon and Nigeria; Maritime Delimitation in the Indian Ocean; Legal Status of Eastern Greenland.*

firm uniform definition of 'treaty' – and consequently the reliance on the frequently inconsistent pronouncements of international courts and tribunals, the reasoning of which is not in many cases entirely convincing – contributes to uncertainty for States regarding their international obligations.

2.3 Memoranda of Understanding

International relations call for numerous arrangements and understandings between States, which may be recorded in ways which, in terms of formality, fall short of what is generally considered as constituting a treaty.[117] Such arrangements, and the documents in which they are recorded, have been referred to variously as, for example, 'gentlemen's agreements', 'memoranda of understanding' or 'informal instruments'. The reasons for this preference, and the uses which these agreements serve, as well as the non-legal effects they may have, lie rather in the purview of the diplomat or political scientist than of the lawyer. The issues that are, strictly speaking, relevant to the lawyer, are, firstly, how to distinguish those arrangements which do constitute legally binding agreements from those which do not; and, secondly, whether, notwithstanding that the arrangements themselves are not directly binding on the parties, they may have some secondary or indirect legal effect.[118]

Such an arrangement may, nevertheless, constitute a legally binding agreement if the parties to it so desire.[119] However, for a number of

[117] RR Baxter, 'International Law in Her Infinite Variety' (1980) 29 ICLQ 549–66; O Schachter, 'The Twilight Existence of Nonbinding International Agreements' (1977) 71 AJIL 296; F Roessler, 'Law, De Facto Agreements and Declarations of Principle in International Economic Relations' (1978) 21 GYIL 27–59; C Lipson, 'Why Are Some International Agreements Informal?' (1991) 45 International Organisation 495–538; F Münch, 'Comments on the 1968 Draft Convention on the Law of Treaties' (1969) 29 ZaöRV 1–11; PM Eiseman, 'Le gentlemen's agreement comme source du droit international' (1979) 106 JDI 326–48; Klabbers, *The Concept of Treaty* 121–56.

[118] The only possible legal effect of non-binding agreements would seem to arise by way of estoppel and in relation to the doctrine of good faith. Discussion of these difficult doctrines is beyond the scope of this chapter, but see A Aust, 'The Theory and Practice of Informal International Instruments' (1986) 35 ICLQ 807–12; and A Aust, *Modern Treaty Law and Practice* (3rd edn, CUP 2013) 28–54.

[119] ILC 'Draft Articles on the Law of Treaties with Commentaries' (4 May–19 July 1966) UN Doc A/CN.4/191, Commentary to Draft Article 2, reproduced in [1966/II] YBILC 187, 188–90. In its 1966 Draft Articles on the Law of Treaties with Commentaries the ILC, explained that 'very many instruments in daily use such as an "agreed minutes" or a "memorandum of understanding", could not appropriately be called formal instruments,

reasons, States in practice frequently prefer that such arrangements between them do not give rise to legal rights and obligations enforceable under international law. As it was said, '[m]odern practice is replete with cases in which governments reach an agreement which they record in writing, but deliberately chose not male legally binding'.[120]

As cited by Berman and Bentley, the FCO Guidance defines the MOU in the following way: 'An MOU records international "commitments" but in a form and with wording which expresses the intention that it is not legally binding'.[121] It may be presumed that the conclusion of the MOU is a way of avoiding its publication in the UNTS or registration in accordance with Article 102 UN Charter. Such MOUs frequently deal with very sensitive matters for a State, such as defense, nuclear technology, and intelligence cooperation. Another reason may be the wish of not submitting the MOU for a formal national approval before the Parliament. It may be that the States wish to base an agreement on good faith rather than resort to a formal claim in cases of a breach.[122] In the UK practice of MOUs, there is FXO guidance on the terminology. The standard nomenclature in MOUs is for examples as follows: 'governments' or 'participants' not 'parties', 'provisions' not 'terms', and 'will' not 'shall'. Additionally, MOUs 'come into operation' or 'effect' whilst treaties come 'into force'. MOUs, and the Exchange of Notes conforming them, record the 'understanding' not their 'agreement'. As Berman and Bentley say, '[i]f this terminology is followed, it will generally be plain that the intention is not to create legally binding rights and obligations'.[123] The most important question is whether such instruments create obligations or commitments of any kind. It may be said the commitments established by MOUs are rather of a political than legal character. The questions of good faith and reputation are equally involved. Examples of some MOUs are evidence of a serious matter they deal with, such as the 1994 Budapest Memorandum (between the UK, US, and Russia), confirming their commitment towards the independence and sovereignty and the existing borders of Ukraine in return for the commitment of Ukraine to eliminate all nuclear weapons from its territory. The

but they are undoubtedly agreements subject to the law of treaties. A general convention on the law of treaties must cover all such agreements...' (ibid 188 [1]).

120 Berman and Bentley, 'Treaties and Other International Instruments – III' 623.

121 ibid.

122 ibid 624.

123 ibid.

subsequent annexation of Crimea by Russia was met with condemnation. A pertinent question is what the consequences of such MOUs are, considering that they do not have a legally binding effect. It is suggested that such commitments rely on good faith, which 'may have the effect of that State is legally precluded from going back on commitments made in an MOU where the other State has acted in reliance on them'.[124] As Berman and Bentley admit, however, this law is still evolving.

In the end, the conclusion on the debate on the various character of legal instruments is best captured by Sir Robert Jennings and Sir Arthur Watts:

> It follows that in order to determine the character of an international instrument, the content of the obligation therein must be scrutinized, on a case-by-case basis. It is, thus, impossible (and indeed not even in accordance with State practice) to assume an all-encompassing view that all international instruments are binding. Once again it has to be reaffirmed that the designation of an instrument cannot serve as an indicator as to the nature of the legal obligation therein. The following view reflects the position adopted by the Court: '[t]he fact that the interested State is the judge of the existence of the obligation is, although otherwise of considerable importance, not of decisive relevance for the determination of the legal character of the instrument'.[125]

The previous analysed case law clearly evidences difficulties attached to clear-cut and definitive differentiation between binding international instruments ad classically non-binding MOUs. One such an example is the *Maritime Delimitation in the Indian Ocean* case. There are numerous examples of international arbitrations where the problem of a legal nature of an international instrument was disputed and debated. For example, the arbitration case concerning Heathrow Airport Charges was focused on this issue.[126] The subject of the dispute was the MOU between the US and the UK concluded in 6 April 1983 (US–UK MOU). This US–UK MOU was a follow up to an Agreement between the US and the UK concerning Air Services signed at Bermuda on 23 July 1977 (Bermuda Agreement). The object and purpose of the Bermuda Agreement was to ensure that the charges for the use of airports on the designated air

[124] ibid 627.

[125] RY Jennings and AD Watts (eds), *Oppenheim's International Law* (9th edn, Longman 1996) 1202.

[126] *US–UK Arbitration Concerning Heathrow Airport User Charges* (1992-4) 26 UNRIAA 1–359. The case is analysed by Y Nakanishi, 'Defining Boundaries of Legally Binding Treaties – A Study of Different State Practice in Treaty-Making' (2018) 20 ICLR 169.

carrier or carriers of the contracting parties will not be higher than those imposed on national carriers. However, the British Airport Authority (BAA) intended to increase user charges in November 1979, resulting in a great dissatisfaction of US carriers. This led to the conclusion of the Settlement Agreement and the US–UK MOU in 1983. The dispute did not end, as the BAA continued to charge the US carriers more, which resulted in the arbitration. The legal character of the MOU was debated. The US considered that the US–UK MOU was intended to be legally binding and, as such, it claimed that 'the language of the MOU was in places imperative' in giving effect to the obligations created in the MOU.[127] On the other hand, the UK contended that the US–UK MOU 'could not be regarded as a source of independent and free-standing legal obligations, both parties to the MOU clearly expected and anticipated that the "understandings" embodied in it would be honoured'.[128] The US–UK MOU referred to 'understandings' and not to 'agreements'.[129] Therefore, the tribunal concluded that 'the MOU constitutes consensual subsequent practice of the Parties' and that 'it clearly stopped short of accepting any duty to use its best efforts to ensure that the views were respected'. It noted that 'the MOU is therefore available to the tribunal as a potentially important aid to interpretation but is not a source of

[127] The following provision of the US–UK MOU is relevant in terms of the US claim of UK's obligations in relation to the structure of charges at Heathrow: '5. Both Governments acknowledge in principle that an acceptable system of peak charges reflecting airport costs might be constructed in appropriate circumstances. Further, both Governments welcome the arrangements agreed upon by the BAA and the airlines for a collaborative review of peak charges. The USG has expressed a number of concerns about the BAA's peak pricing practices. In particular, the USG believes that (1) all traffic should bear at least some capital costs; (2) all traffic should bear its share of operating costs; (3) peak periods, where established at any airport, should encompass all periods of comparable activity at that airport; and (4) no peak charge should be assessed with respect to any service or facility unless a charge is also assessed for such service or facility during off-peak periods. HMG sees force in the last three of these views and will commend them to the BAA, as well as drawing all the USG concerns to the attention of the BAA so that they may be taken into account in their collaborative review of peak pricing'. (*US–UK Arbitration Concerning Heathrow Airport User Charges* 334–5, cited by Nakanishi, 'Defining Boundaries' 177–8, fn 35).

[128] *US-UK Arbitration Concerning Heathrow Airport User Charges* 131.

[129] For example, see paragraph 6 of the US-UK MOU, according to which: '6. The undersigned, being duly authorized by their respective Governments, hereby confirm that the foregoing correctly represents the understandings of the two Governments in this matter and that these understandings will take effect if on or before 12 April 1983 Action 1980 A No 4127 and 1980 P No 4245 are discontinued as contemplated by the Settlement' (ibid 335, cited in Nakanishi, 'Defining Boundaries' 178).

independent legal rights and duties capable of enforcement in the present Arbitration'.[130]

2.4 Unilateral Acts of States

2.4.1 Introduction

Unilateral acts of States are included in this Chapter as they may also be a source of international obligations of States and although they do not belong to the realm of the law of treaties, frequently rules and processes specific to the law of treaties are applied to them and comparisons are made. There is a wealth of literature on the subject of unilateral acts and this chapter deals with unilateral acts to the extent of their similarities and differences with the regime of the law of treaties.[131] The legal regime of unilateral acts of States was also analysed by the ILC.[132] The 1974 Judgment of the ICJ in the *Nuclear Tests* cases has clarified that a declaration, written or verbal, made by an official of a State, within certain very strict conditions, might give rise to a binding legal obligation, binding on the community of States.[133] As was observed, notwithstanding the legal questions concerning normative validity of such acts, States have relied on them in international practice and they appear in various, divergent forms.[134] The legal character of unilateral acts is the most frequently debated issue in relation to whether they constitute a 'new' source of international law within the context of Article 38 of the ICJ Statute and

[130] *US–UK Arbitration Concerning Heathrow Airport User Charges* 131, cited in Nakanishi, 'Defining Boundaries' 178.

[131] See eg C Goodman, '*Acta Sunt Servanda*? A Regime for Regulating Unilateral Acts of States at International Law' (2006) 25 AYBIL 3; E Kassoti, *The Juridical Nature of Unilateral Acts of States in International Law* (Brill/Martinus Nijhoff 2015); P Saganek, *Unilateral Acts of States in Public International Law* (Brill/Martinus Nijhoff 2015).

[132] See ILC, 'Guiding Principles Applicable to Unilateral Declarations of States Capable of Creating Legal Obligations, with Commentaries Thereto' [2006/II – Part Two] YBILC 161 (hereinafter, ILC, 'Guiding Principles Applicable to Unilateral Declarations of States with Commentaries').

[133] *Nuclear Tests (New Zealand v France)* (Judgment) [1974] ICJ Rep 457; *Nuclear Tests (Australia v France)* (Judgment) [1974] ICJ Rep 253. There were, however, views expressed in literature that unilateral acts do not categorically create any legal obligations in international law. See eg A Kiss, 'Les actes unilatéraux dans la pratique française du droit international' (1961) 65 RGDIP 31; R Quadri, 'Cours général de droit international public' (1964/III) 113 RdC 370.

[134] See Goodman, '*Acta Sunt Servanda*?'.

whether they have a binding force.[135] However, it is fair to say that their normative status as a 'new' source of international law has not been definitively settled. The authors of this book are of the view that under very strict conditions, unilateral acts of States can originate international obligations.

2.4.2 Unilateral Acts: Their Content and Form and the Law of Treaties

The ILC has defined a 'unilateral act' as 'an unequivocal expression of will, which is formulated by a State with the intention of producing legal effects in relation to one or more other States or international organizations, and which is known to that State or international organization'.[136] The complex legal nature of unilateral acts or declarations is well exemplified by the Ihlen Declaration, which was discussed earlier. There, several and often contradictory views were expressed. The PCIJ stated that Mr Ihlen's Declaration was without any doubt binding on Norway. A view expressed in this chapter was that the declaration was a result of an exchange of promises in a bilateral context. However, a contrasting view can be expressed that in fact this declaration has produced legal effects by itself, 'and thus falls within the definition of an autonomous Unilateral Act'.[137]

The element of intention, which is quite pronounced in the realm of unilateral declarations, distinguishes them to a certain extent from treaties. However, as it was observed in this chapter, the role of the intention of the parties is not at all clear even within the treaty context. A unilateral declaration is binding if 'clearly intended to have that effect, and held out . . . as an instrument on which others may rely and under which the declarant purports to assume such obligations'.[138] In the *Nuclear Tests* case, the Court stated:

[135] The relevant literature is vast and Kassoti presents a useful overview of the existing approaches, ie deniers of the normative value of unilateral declarations (such as A Rubin, 'The International Legal Effects of Unilateral Declarations' (1977) 71 AJIL 1; H Thirlway, 'The Sources of International Law' in M Evans (ed), *International Law* (4th edn, OUP 2014) 95. Believers in the normative force of unilateral declarations are M Virally, 'The Sources of International Law' in M Sorensen (ed), *Manual of Public International Law* (Macmillan 1968) 1564; Kassoti, *The Juridical Nature* 23–6.

[136] VR Cedeño, 'Third Report on Unilateral Acts of States' (17 February 2000) UN Doc A/CN.4/505, Art 1.

[137] Goodman, '*Acta Sunt Servanda*?' 49.

[138] G Fitzmaurice, 'The Law and Procedure of the International Court of Justice, 1951–4: Treaty Interpretation and Other Treaty Points' (1957) 33 BYIL 203, 230.

> When it is the intention of the State making the declaration that it should become bound according to its terms, that intention confers on the declaration the character of a legal undertaking, the State being thenceforth legally required to follow a course of conduct consistent with the declaration. An undertaking of this kind, if given publicly and with an intent to be bound, even though not made within the context of international negotiations, is binding.[139]

The element of intention distinguished them from non-binding obligations.[140] The intention of State is termed 'the subjective element'.[141] The 'objective element' is said to be included in the phrase that unilateral declarations are to be 'considered within the general framework of the security of international intercourse, and the confidence and trust, which are so essential in the relations of States. It is from the actual substance of these statements and the circumstances attending their making, that the legal implications of these acts must be deduced'.[142] The objective standard

> whereby the decisive intent is not that of the French authorities but that deducible from good faith, trust, confidence, and the circumstances in which the declarations were made. It is thus necessary to decide whether it is the *real* or the *declared* intention that is to govern interpretation of a unilateral act: whether construction of the declarant's intent is to be made on a *subjective* or *objective* basis.[143]

Importantly, the Court stated in this case that 'when States make statements by which their freedom of action is to be limited, a restrictive interpretation is to be called for'.[144] Similarly to the law of treaties, as stated in the *Aegean Sea Continental Shelf* case, the ICJ emphasised the significance of circumstances in which such a unilateral act takes place. This is one of the factors assessing the intentions of the States making unilateral acts.[145] The relationship with the law of treaties is evidenced by the applicability of the rules concerning the invalidity of treaties to

139 *Nuclear Tests (Australia v France)* [43].
140 M Koskenniemi, *From Apology to Utopia: The Structure of International Legal Argument* (CUP 1989) 307.
141 Goodman, '*Acta Sunt Servanda*?' 56.
142 *Nuclear Tests (Australia v France)* [43].
143 Goodman, '*Acta Sunt Servanda*?' 56.
144 *Nuclear Tests (Australia v France)* [44].
145 See *Frontier Dispute (Burkina Faso/Republic of Mali)* (Judgment) [1986] ICJ Rep 554 [40].

unilateral acts of States.[146] One of the most fundamental differences between unilateral acts and the law of treaties is the lack of reciprocal obligations. As the ICJ held in the *Nuclear Tests* case, nothing in the nature of a *quid pro quo*, reply or reaction, is necessary for a unilateral declaration to take effect.[147] As Goodman correctly states, 'a strict unilateral declaration rests on the intention of the declarant, not on "any subsequent acceptance" and thus consent adds nothing to the obligatory force of the act'.[148] The element of certainty in treaty relations between States, which is enshrined in Article 26 VCLT (*pacta sunt servanda*), which is based on good faith and fundamental to the law of treaties, is also applicable to unilateral acts of States. That was acknowledged by the Special Rapporteur for unilateral acts of States (*acta sunt servanda).* The procedural element of the binding force on the State making the unilateral declaration, ie what organ can bind the State, is also analogous to the law of treaties. In both the *Legal Status of Eastern Greenland* and *Nuclear Tests* cases, the PCIJ and the ICJ stated in an unequivocal way that persons that are now enumerated in Article 7 VCLT, ie Head of State, Prime Minister, and the Minister for Foreign Affairs, bind a State through their statements, without exception. The Court has noted that in order to determine the legal effect of a statement by a person representing the State, one must 'examine its actual content as well as the circumstances in which it was made'.[149]

In 2006, the ILC completed a set of Guiding Principles on Unilateral Acts (Special Rapporteur Mr Cedeño).[150] They consist of ten Guiding Principles applicable to unilateral declarations of States capable of creating legal obligations. These principles refer to definitions, interpretation, capacity of States to formulate unilateral acts, forms, and addressees of the act. The Principles rely on the *Nuclear Tests* cases. For example, Principle 1 defines 'unilateral declarations' as acts 'publicly made and manifesting the will to be bound may have the legal effect of creating legal obligation'. The ILC also stated that the form is of no importance and does not affect the value of the declaration. However, the work of the Commission on unilateral acts was subject to a great disagreement, even

[146] See Goodman, '*Acta Sunt Servanda*?' 58.

[147] *Nuclear Tests (Australia v France)* [43].

[148] Goodman, '*Acta Sunt Servanda*?' 61.

[149] *Armed Activities on the Territory of the Congo (New Application: 2002) (Democratic Republic of the Congo v Rwanda)* (Jurisdiction and Admissibility) [2006] ICJ Rep 6 [49].

[150] ILC, 'Guiding Principles Applicable to Unilateral Declarations of States with Commentaries'.

between the members of the ILC, and has also been the subject of harsh criticism.

There are also several critical comments voiced by scholars. For example, it is argued that the Principles do not make any differentiation between unilateral juridical and political acts, that they fail to define the elements of unilateralism, and that there is a lack of differentiation between unilateral acts and estoppel.[151]

Finally, the rare issue of the legal nature of unilateral acts of States has been debated by the Court in the *Bolivia v Chile* case.[152] Bolivia argued that Chile's obligation to negotiate Bolivia's sovereign access to the Pacific Ocean is also based on a number of Chile's declarations and other unilateral acts: 'It is well established in international law that written and oral declarations made by representatives of States, which evidence a clear intention to accept obligations vis-à-vis another State may generate legal effects, without requiring reciprocal undertakings from that other State' (para 140). Bolivia, in its analysis of the unilateral acts in question, relied on the findings of the ICJ in the *Nuclear Tests* cases. Therefore, it stressed the public character of these declarations and the intention on the part of Chile, as well the clear and specific object of these acts. Chile on its side stated that 'the burden on the State seeking to prove of a binding obligation based on a unilateral statement is a heavy one' (para 144).

The Court did not accept the arguments submitted by Bolivia and concluded: 'The Court notes that Chile's declarations and other unilateral acts on which Bolivia relies are expressed, not in terms of undertaking a legal obligation, but of willingness to enter into negotiations on the issue of Bolivia's sovereign access to the Pacific Ocean' (para 147). 'With regard to the circumstances of Chile's declarations and statements, the Court further observes that there is no evidence of an intention on the part of Chile to assume an obligation to negotiate. The Court therefore concludes that an obligation to negotiate Bolivia's sovereign access to the sea cannot rest on any of Chile's unilateral acts referred to by Bolivia' (para 148).

151 See on this E Kassoti, *The Juridical nature of Unilateral Acts of States in International Law* (Brill/Nijhoff 2015) 51–77. See also on unilateral acts of States, P Saganek, *Unilateral Acts of States in Public International Law* (Brill/Nijhoff 2015).

152 *Obligation to Negotiate Access to Pacific Ocean* [140 ff].

This section was limited to dealing with similarities and differences between the law of treaties and unilateral acts of States. It may be said that many existing similarities, both concerning substantive and procedural aspects, are only very superficial. The main point of difference is the manner in which international obligations are being made within the context of treaties and unilateral acts of States. In relation to the law of treaties, there is an element of reciprocity (*quid quo pro*), whilst unilateral acts of States are lacking this and an international obligation is formed on the basis of a law-making statement, which is subject to many strict conditions in order to be able to generate an international obligation. There is no doubt that unilateral acts of States are not treaties and that a fast and clear division line can be drawn between these two sources of international obligations.

The recent case law of the Court has evidenced that the reliance on unilateral acts of States to prove a binding in international law obligation is a difficult task that cannot be treated lightly. Rather, this is an exception, which has been stated by the Court in a consistent manner.

2.5 Soft Law

'Soft law' is the result of the diversified relationships between States. As has been said, the 'subtlety of the processes by which contemporary international law can be created is no longer adequately captured by reference to the orthodox categories of custom and treaty'.[153]

According to Dupuy,[154] it was Lord McNair who coined the term 'soft law'. There are many proponents of the view that there are some kinds of 'arrangements' or 'undertakings' constituting 'soft', 'fragile', or 'weak' law that are generally complied with, but which are free from the pressures of the principle of *pacta sunt servanda*, as well as from the rules of customary international law. Perhaps not surprisingly, many of these undertakings are drawn up under the auspices of international organisations. These arrangements are made intentionally ambiguous by their drafters, and as it has been observed, this results in a corresponding

[153] See A Boyle, 'Some Reflections on Relationship of Treaties and Soft Law' in V Gowlland-Debbas (ed), *Multilateral Treaty-Making: Current Status of Challenges to and Reforms Needed in International Legislative Process* (Springer 2000) 25.

[154] R-J Dupuy, 'Declaratory Law and Programmatory Law; From Revolutionary Custom to "Soft Law"' in RJ Akkerman, PJ van Krieken and C Pannenborg (eds), *Declarations on Principles: A Quest for Universal Peace, Liber Amicorum Discipulorumque Professor dr BVA Roling* (Sijthoff 1979) 252.

lack of clarity in the way they are discussed or written about. The ambiguity of such 'arrangements' or 'undertakings' is widely admitted in doctrine and is reflected in the way they are discussed or written about. The ambiguity of such arrangements or undertakings is widely admitted in doctrine.[155] Sir Robert Jennings observed that the same provisions are used as evidence by opposing parties before international tribunals in support of their conflicting claims, since each party can give ambiguous provisions its own slant.[156] He points out that the tests applicable to ascertaining the existence of a norm of customary law or a treaty are irrelevant since much of the new 'law' is not custom, and 'it is recent, it is innovatory, it involves topical political decisions, and it is often the focus of contention'.[157] Since soft law instruments are, thus, highly susceptible to varying interpretations, they provide for their drafters a great deal of freedom in arguing their way out of compliance with such instruments. It may be said that 'soft law' may occur in any circumstance where States wish to accord significance to something agreed on but which is plainly intended to amount to less than an expression of intention to be bound by it.[158]

Supporters of the concept of 'soft law' believe that, with its flexible character, it is a helpful technique in situations where States want to act collectively, but at the same time 'do not want to fetter their freedom of action'.[159] Examples of soft law can be found especially in environmental law. International economic soft law is also common.[160] In fact, it was first used in this field of law, in particular in dealing with economic issues that were thought to be within the sovereign power of States.[161] The nature of soft law was perfect for uses such as combining collective regulations and restraint in economic dealings with flexibility and freedom to maneuver as, and when, changed circumstances required. International economic relations had to accommodate almost irreconcilable

[155] Baxter, 'International Law in Her Infinite Variety' 556–7.

[156] RY Jennings, 'What Is International Law and How Do We Tell It When We See It?' (1981) 37 ASDI 59, 67.

[157] ibid.

[158] K Wellens and G Borchardt, 'Soft Law in the European Community Law' (1989) 14 ELR 267, 269.

[159] P Birnie, 'Legal Techniques of Settling Disputes: The Soft Settlement Approach' in WE Butler (ed), *Perestroika and International Law* (Martinus Nijhoff 1990) 175, 184.

[160] I Seidl-Hohenveldern, *International Economic Law* (Springer 1989) 42–5.

[161] G Schwarzenberger, 'The Principles and Standards of International Economic Law' (1966/I) 117 RdC 5, 27–9.

differences between the approaches of different legal systems and the different goals of a highly diverse and vastly enlarged international community. Thus, States were faced with the problems of achieving an agreement on universally acceptable rules and an unwillingness to undertake legal obligations. As a rule, States are willing to take legal obligations when they expect to fulfil them.[162] It may happen that States try to avoid legally binding obligations because of formal requirements necessary to creating and terminating them.[163] Other authors reject the concept of 'soft law' and claim that either law is binding or it is not law at all.[164] Many who maintain this view regard soft law as detrimental to the system of international law. Lysen, for instance, states that 'one legal rule cannot be more legal than another'.[165] Others find this approach unjustified because soft law 'has great strength as a conflict resolution device'.[166] Yet other authors deny even the existence of soft law because 'it is not supported by either State practice or judicial practice' and because 'it lacks plausible theoretical underpinnings and even justifications, and most importantly, its application falls victim to the same binary way of thinking which traditionally characterized law'.[167] The term 'soft law' is viewed by some as unfortunate since it suggests a source of law of inferior value.

162 M Bothe, 'Legal and Non-Legal Norms – A Meaningful Distinction in International Relations?' (1980) 11 NYIL 65, 91.

163 T Gruchalla-Wesierski, 'A Framework for Understanding Soft Law' (1984) 30 McGill LJ 38, 41.

164 Pr Weil, 'Towards Relative Normativity in International Law?' (1983) 77 AJIL 413, 416–7. See also J Klabbers, 'The Redundancy of Soft Law' (1996) 65 NJIL 167; R Bilder, 'Beyond Compliance: Helping Nations to Cooperate' in D Shelton (ed), *Commitment and Compliance: The Role of Non-Binding Norms in the International Legal System* (OUP 2000) 72, who argues for the redundancy of the concept of 'soft law'. He observes that the division of law into 'hard' and 'soft' leads to a confusion as to the consequences of breach of a norm of soft law, and begs the question whether the breach of a soft law norm leads to international wrongfulness ('by blurring the traditional distinction between law and non-law, such usage threatens to damage a valuable normative tool which States have long used an relied on, and, in effect, depreciate the currency of law'). See also, O Elias and CL Lim, *The Paradox of Consensualism in International Law* (Brill/Martinus Nijhoff 1998) 230–2.

165 G Lysen, 'The Joint Declaration by the EEC and the CMEA' (1989) 14 NCJInt'lL & ComReg 369, 376.

166 Birnie, 'Legal Techniques' 183.

167 M Virally, 'La distinction entre textes internationaux ayant une portée juridique dans les relations mutuelles entre leur auteurs et les textes juridiques qui en sont dépourvus' (1983) 60/I AIDI 166–257 (*rapport provisoire*) and 328–52 (*rapport définitif*).

The concept of soft law escapes the traditional rules of legal classification and attempts to explain the nature of soft law have not been entirely successful or persuasive. Some scholars believe that both legal and non-legal norms may be created within the realm of soft law instruments, while others restrict it to containing only non-legal norms.[168] Others see the term 'soft law' as referring to two things, the first being the 'soft' content (language) of instruments which are otherwise hard in nature, that is, formally binding in law (for example, treaty provisions), and the second being the 'soft' nature of certain international instruments themselves (for example, joint declarations; joint communiqués; various acts of international organisations).[169] Some other writers do not attempt to coin a definition of this phenomenon but satisfy themselves by observing that 'soft law' gives an impression that 'something is missing in the legal binding nature of law as we know it from the daily life, and even international life'.[170]

The legal effects, if any, of instruments of soft law are as unclear as those that may be attached to informal instruments. It is sometimes noted that soft law instruments may have legal effects arising from estoppel.[171] According to Virally, for instance, the principle of estoppel results from the general principle of *bona fide*, on which political obligations are based.[172] The same considerations, which apply to informal agreements in this respect, also apply to soft law instruments. In our view, however, the applicability of the principle of estoppel[173] to a non-binding instrument is doubtful. As to the general principle of good faith, from which estoppel results, its usefulness may also be considered of limited value if we adhere to the concept that it is not itself an independent legal principle. It must also be observed that the very link between estoppel and the principle of good faith is disputed by some authors.

168 J Sztucki, 'Reflections on International "Soft Law"' in J Ramberg, O Bring and S Mahmoudi (eds), *Festschrift till Lars Hjerner: Studies in International Law* (Norstedts 1990) 549–75.

169 ibid.

170 AJP Tammes, 'Soft Law', in ER Arbor (ed), *Essays on International and Comparative Law in Honour of Judge Erades* (Martinus Nijhoff 1983) 187.

171 Y van der Mensbrugghe, 'Legal Status of International North Sea Conference Declarations' (1990) 5 IJECL 15, 21.

172 M Virally, 'La distinction' 356 (*rapport définitif*): 'En conséquence, il est soumis aux obligations juridiques résultant de l'estoppel, lorsqu'il a créé les apparences d'un engagement juridique auxquelles une autre partie s'est fiée et que les conditions auxquelles le droit international subordonne l'apparition de telles obligations sont remplies'.

173 Which is an institution with specific independent legal effect, unlike good faith.

McGibbon, for example, sees estoppel as an independent ground for evaluating legal relationship, distinct from good faith.[174]

On the basis of the examination of certain international environmental law declarations relating to the cooperation between the Baltic Sea coastal States concerning environmental issues, our conclusion is that if any effects can be attributed to these soft law declarations, it is only the principle of good faith. On the basis of this principle, concerned States pledge to take all appropriate measures to comply with the contents of these declarations. But this is as far as it goes, and the principle of estoppel, to the best of our knowledge, was never even considered by States concerned. All interviewed lawyers and diplomats were in any event quite doubtful about any significant legal effects of such declarations, and treated them as an indication of certain future albeit uncertain aspirations, which indeed these non-binding declarations, were the basis on which a binding treaty, ie the 1992 Helsinki Convention, was concluded.[175]

The legal workings of soft law were analysed closely by jurists in relation to various declarations, in particular in the field of international environmental law, such as the 1972 Stockholm Declaration on Human Environment[176] and the 1992 Rio Declaration on Environment and Development.[177] The Baltic Sea, as was noted, was a subject of many Declarations.[178] In a similar fashion, there were many declarations

[174] I McGibbon, 'Estoppel in International Law' (1958) 7 ICLQ 468, 513.

[175] 1992 Helsinki Convention on the Protection of Marine Environment of the Baltic Sea (adopted 9 April 1992, entered into force 17 January 2000) 1507 UNTS 167.

[176] UNGA, 'Stockholm Declaration on the Human Environment' (15 December 1972) UN Doc A/RES/2994.

[177] UNCED, 'Rio Declaration on Environment and Development' (1992) 31 ILM 874.

[178] 1988 Ministerial Declaration on the Protection of the Marine Environment of the Baltic Sea (*Helsinki Commission*, 15 February 1988) <www.helcom.fi/Documents/About%20us/Convention%20and%20commitments/Ministerial%20declarations/MinDecl1988.pdf> accessed 20 September 2019; 1990 Baltic Sea Declaration (*Helsinki Commission*, 2–3 September 1990) <www.helcom.fi/Documents/About%20us/Convention%20and%20commitments/Ministerial%20declarations/RonnebyDecl1990.pdf> accessed 20 September 2019; 1993 Declaration on Resource Mobilisation for the Baltic Sea Joint Comprehensive Environmental Action Programme (*Helsinki Commission*, 24–25 March 1993) <www.helcom.fi/Documents/About%20us/Convention%20and%20commitments/Ministerial%20declarations/GdanskDecl1993.pdf> accessed 20 September 2019; 2001 Copenhagen Declaration on the Safety of Navigation and Emergency Capacity in the Baltic Sea Area (*Helsinki Commission*, 10 September 2001) <www.helcom.fi/Documents/About%20us/Convention%20and%20commitments/Ministerial%20declarations/Copenhagen2001.pdf> accessed 20 September 2019; 2003 Bremen Ministerial Declaration (*Helsinki Commission*, 25 June 2003) <www.helcom.fi/Documents/About%20us/Convention%20and%20com

concerning the status of the North Sea,[179] which charter was considered to be 'controversial'.[180] Indeed, they have an imprecise and ambiguous character and purpose: some are intended to supply only information, some to express agreed policy, and some attempt to set out more detailed obligations. There is, however, an interesting legal aspect of the Baltic Sea declarations. They are considered by the States parties to the Helsinki Convention as one of the elements of the legal system of international protection of the Baltic Sea, considered together with the Helsinki Convention and the recommendations of the Baltic Marine Environment Protection Commission (HELCOM), which are non-binding. Although, their character is definitely non-binding, State parties treat them as at least potentially generating certain obligations for States, in particular the recent ones, such as the 2013 Moscow Declaration, which set out several detailed obligations. At this juncture, it may be also mentioned that the most important so far Baltic Sea Action Plan (BSAP), adopted in 2007,[181] which is the most comprehensive plan for the protection of the Baltic Sea, was also adopted by the recommendation of the Ministers of the Environment of the Baltic States and for all practical purposes supplements the Helsinki Convention. The BSAP has been transposed by the Baltic Sea States in their national legal order.

The declarations, which were adopted in the context of the Baltic Sea and the North Sea environmental protection, were not registered in accordance with Article 102 UN Charter. However, at least in relation to the Baltic Sea Declarations, there is a variety of means in which the Baltic States approached them nationally. For example, in relation to the first of these declarations (the 1988 Ministerial Declaration), Sweden, Denmark and the former Federal Republic of Germany (FRG) published

mitments/Ministerial%20declarations/Bremen2003.pdf> accessed 20 September 2019; 2010 Moscow Ministerial Declaration (*Helsinki Commission*, 20 May 2010) <www.helcom.fi/Documents/About%20us/Convention%20and%20commitments/Ministerial%20declarations/HELCOM%20Moscow%20Ministerial%20Declaration%20FINAL.pdf> accessed 20 September 2019; 2013 Copenhagen Declaration Taking Further Action to Implement the Baltic Sea Action Plan-Reaching Good Environmental Status for a Healthy Baltic Sea (*Helsinki Commission*, 3 October 2013) <www.helcom.fi/Documents/Ministerial2013/Ministerial%20declaration/2013%20Copenhagen%20Ministerial%20Declaration%20w%20cover.pdf> accessed 20 September 2019.

[179] The Bremen Declaration; the London Declaration; and the North Sea Declaration.

[180] Van der Mensbrugghe, 'Legal Status' 15–22.

[181] 2007 HELCOM Baltic Sea Action Plan (*Helsinki Commission*, 15 November 2007) <www.helcom.fi/Documents/Baltic%20sea%20action%20plan/BSAP_Final.pdf> accessed 20 September 2019.

them in official journals. In the FRG, the 1988 Ministerial Declaration was in fact transposed into national legal order by way of an order of the Federal Minister of the Environment. This was followed up by the 1988 detailed ten-point plan presented by the Federal Minister of the Environment with the aim of strengthening the efforts to protect the Baltic Sea as a response to the 1988 Ministerial Declaration. The plan was quite detailed and related to the reduction of the input of nutrients from sewage treatment plants and also other hazardous substances. These reductions were explicitly mentioned in the declaration. As a further step in transposing the 1988 Declaration into national law, the FRG Parliament approved this programme, which was in direct implementation of the declaration. In Sweden, Denmark, and Finland, the declaration was incorporated in a long-term Action Plan for the Protection of the Environment and also approved by their Parliaments. In the former Soviet Union, a programme was set out based on the 1988 Declaration for the Baltic Sea region for the period up to 1996. This programme took into account five hundred of the most significant sources of pollution of the sea and provided in expenditure up to 1.5 billion roubles for the construction of the cleaning system. Furthermore, in order to implement the 1988 Ministerial Declaration, cleaning plants for municipal sewage were provided for in the main cities in the period 1992–3.[182]

On the other hand, Poland has not taken any steps to implement the declaration. The closer scrutiny of the Ministerial Declaration indicates that the language adopted by Ministers of the Environment of the Baltic States, aimed at setting out general policy-oriented goals than binding decisions. Thus, it was declared that the intention of the Ministers was to 'establish', 'intensify efforts', 'take appropriate action', 'develop methodologies', 'respect relevant recommendations', 'promote', and 'cooperate'. The declaration does not have any annexes, which most of treaties do in which more specific objectives are set out. The only section in the whole declaration which describes somewhat more specific goals refers to the general need to reduce the load of pollutants, in particular heavy metals and toxic or persistent organic substances and nutrients as soon as possible, but not later than 1995. Furthermore, it states that a reduction of 'for example' 50 per cent in such discharges would be 'desirable'. Even

[182] JJ Kolbasov, 'Pravovyje Mery Okhrany Morija ot Zagrazhenia s Sushi' (Legal Measures for the Protection of the Sea Land-Based Pollution), a paper presented at the International Conference on Ecology and Law in the Baltic Sea Region: Sources and Development, held in Riga, 1990, 9 (unpublished, on file with the authors).

the wording of these more detailed undertakings is rather vague and imprecise, and without doubt further legal acts will be required to transform these political commitments into legal obligations binding States, through national legislation, as it was done in the case of the FRG. The declaration was nothing more than a political act, which was emphatically and explicitly non-binding. Indeed, the intention of the Baltic States was to diminish the pollution load of the Baltic Sea without the use of non-legally binding instruments, at the time of the adoption of the declaration. However, considering the political climate of the adoption of the declaration, this was considered to be a highly significant step in itself and, in view of circumstances present at that time, more important than a commitment to fulfil obligations with clearly defined objectives. Thus, the declaration, as evidenced by further practice, served as a common ground for further discussions, in particular as the participating States had undertaken to report on their progress in its implementation. Finally, it was believed that the non-binding nature of the declaration would guarantee a sincerer approach in determining generally the needs of the Baltic Sea and compliance with the declaration.

As it was mentioned above, the North Sea was also a subject of many declarations, such as the 1984 Declaration of the International Conference on the Protection of the North Sea (Bremen I Declaration);[183] 2012 Bremen Declaration Adopted at the North Sea Commission (Bremen II Declaration),[184] 1987 London Declaration[185] and 1990 Hague Declaration.[186] Another question is how they compare to the Baltic Sea Declarations. The content of these declarations is quite varied. Some of them have annexes and employ quite a precise language despite the intention of the parties to make them non-binding.[187] They require specific action to be taken 'in the framework of the existing bodies,

[183] 1984 Declaration of the International Conference on the Protection of the North Sea (*OSPAR*, 1984) <www.ospar.org/site/assets/files/1239/1nsc-1984-bremen_declaration.pdf> accessed 20 September 2019.

[184] 2012 Bremen Declaration Adopted at the North Sea Commission Annual Business Meeting 20 June 2012 (*Eastern Norway Country Network*, 20 June 2012) <www.ostsam.no/wp-content/uploads/2012/06/Bremen-Declaration.pdf> accessed 20 September 2019.

[185] 1987 London Declaration, Second International Conference on the Protection of the North Sea (*Vlaams Instituut Voor de Zee*, 24–5 November 1987) <www.vliz.be/imisdocs/publications/140155.pdf> accessed 20 September 2019.

[186] 1990 Ministerial Declaration of the Third International Conference on the Protection of the North Sea (*University of Oregon*, 8 March 1990) <https://iea.uoregon.edu/treaty-text/1990-thirdnorthseadeclarationentxt> accessed 20 September 2019.

[187] Van der Memsbrugghe, 'Legal Status' 20.

conventions, and programmes'. The London Declaration, for example, contains some rather concrete provisions, such as one requiring the parties 'to take steps to minimize by no less than 65 per cent the use of marine incineration by 1 January 1991'[188] and 'phase out such operations by 31 December 1994, and to seek agreement to such a date within the Oslo Convention by 1 January 1990'.[189] It thus appears that the wording used is sufficiently well hedged in order to allow avoidance of duties without being see to violate the declaration. Thus, the declaration appears to record political decisions, which would have to be made more precise prior to their implementation for them to constitute legal obligations. However, the newest of these instruments, the Bremen II Declaration, has a very loose and imprecise language. The North Sea Commission 'calls on all stakeholders' and 'the NSC members commit themselves to further promote the idea of a strategy'.

The Bremen I Declaration and the London Declaration similarly indicate objectives, which would have to be further pursued, along the lines set out in the relevant documents. The general language used in these declarations is similar to that used by declarations pertaining to the Baltic Sea. The North Sea Environmental Ministers decided 'to confirm'; 'to ensure'; 'to accept the principle', 'to intensify measures'; 'to invite the appropriate international bodies'. The Hague Declaration is not very different from the Bremen I and London Declarations. Despite the fact that it contains fairly comprehensive set of annotations and annexes and with certain concrete aims, the legal obligations imposed by these Declarations remain vague. The Preamble to the declaration lists two main tasks of the conference that have arisen from it: to assess whether previously adopted measures will be met, and 'decide . . . which further initiatives needed to be taken'. In the context of these 'future initiatives', the declaration records participants' decision to adopt a comprehensive set of 'common actions' to reduce inputs of hazardous substances. The language used to define goals in such declarations is a mixed bag. Some are purely policy oriented,[190] while others are more specific.[191]

188 London Declaration, Art XVI(24(b).

189 ibid, Art XVI(24).

190 One of the most common expressions to define actions is 'to agree', presumably sometime in the future, that discharges of substances that are persistent, toxic, and liable to bio accumulate should, before year 2000, be reduced to levels 'that are not harmful to man and nature'.

191 The declaration noted that the desirability of achieving a significant reduction between 1985 and 1995 (of 5 per cent or more) of inputs via rivers estuaries for each substance

There is a myriad of soft law instruments and various declarations. Such an example is the 1978 Bonn Declaration on Hijacking[192] that was signed by seven industrialised countries that reached the agreement to boycott air traffic of any countries offering sanctuary for hijackers. This declaration appears to make a strong statement of intent. Under thorough analysis, however, it seems that this declaration also is non-binding in nature. The language is imprecise and weak ('intensify', 'will initiate', 'should take', 'urge') and although the goals seem to be clearly set out, the means of achieving them are not firmly spelled out.[193] The language used in this declaration suggests the non-legal type of obligation, perhaps rather of a political or moral nature.[194] This declaration was signed by the Prime Ministers of Italy, UK, and Canada, the Presidents of the United States and France, the Chancellor of the Federal Republic of Germany (FRG) and the Prime Minister of Japan). However, the language of the declaration, which is weak, imprecise, and ill-defined, is much different from the precise and very well-defined language used by treaties. Such a language is a clear indication that this instrument was meant to be non-binding.

Some authors attribute certain effects to soft law instruments. The view has been expressed that although the documents are non-binding, the parties must act in good faith when attempting to carry out such declarations by transferring them into legal instruments.[195] In the view of the authors of this book, such a statement is perhaps not fully reflected by the practice of States. The majority of non-binding declarations are not transposed into legal documents and most often they reflect the intention

specified in Annex IA, is achievable by applying the best available technology. Similar provisions were adopted in relation to substances causing a major threat to the environment, and to substantial reduction in the quantities of pesticides.

192 1978 Bonn Summit Statement on Air-Hijacking (1978) 17 ILM 1285.

193 See JJ Busutill, 'The Bonn Declaration on International Terrorism: A Non-Binding Agreement on Aircraft Hijacking' (1992) 31 ICLQ 474, 485. The declaration reads as follows: 'The Heads of State and Government concerned about the terrorism and taking of hostages, declare that their Governments will intensify their efforts to combat international terrorism. To this end, in cases where a country refuses extradition or prosecution of those who have hijacked an aircraft and/or not returned such an aircraft, the Heads of State and Government should take immediate action to cease all flights to that country. At the same time, their Governments will initiate action to halt all incoming flights from that country of from any country by airlines of the country concerned. The Heads of State and Government urge other Governments to join them in this commitment' (Canada, FRG, France, Italy, Japan, UK, US).

194 Busutill, 'The Bonn Declaration' 487.

195 Ven der Mensbrugghe, 'Legal Status' 21.

of States, which adopted such a document. There are exceptions to this practice and an example of such an exception is the 1992 Helsinki Convention on the Protection of the Marine Environment of the Baltic Sea Area. This convention was in fact derived from the Baltic Sea Declaration, which formed a base for the convention. The content of these Baltic Sea Declarations was incorporated in the Helsinki Convention, in a more precise and better-defined manner, such as rules on the reduction of hazardous waste and on the principles of mutual cooperation. The role of soft law instruments in such a process was defined by Boyle as 'significant, only because they are the first step in a process leading eventually leading to a conclusion of a multilateral treaty'.[196] Although as indicated above, the character of soft law as law or non-law is not at all clear, its main features, as to which there is some degree of consensus in the doctrine, may be summarised as follows: soft law is not binding; soft law consists of general principles but not rules; soft law is not really enforceable through dispute resolution mechanisms.[197]

Soft law fulfills a very useful role in the contemporary law-making process because it has several attractive features that makes it a useful alternative to treaties. For example, it is easier to reach an agreement in the case of a soft law instrument than a treaty, the consequences of non-compliance being less severe, if any. States may avoid the need to subject the instrument to a domestic ratification procedure and escape democratic accountability within that procedure; soft law instruments are more susceptible to amendment than treaties. The usefulness of a treaty as law-making instrument, on the other hand, may be greater in the event of new law-making. It cannot be denied, however, that the soft law instruments are a good evidence of State practice and *opinio juris* in support of customary international law.[198] Soft law instruments are not binding by themselves but may be an element in the process of formation of the uniform conviction of States that certain principles are law, such as the 1972 Stockholm Declaration, which started the process of the crystallisation of the principle of the prohibition of transboundary harm, as formulated in Principle 21 and indeed confirmed as a principle of

[196] Boyle, 'Some Reflections' 29.
[197] ibid 31–8.
[198] As stated by the ICJ in relation to the UNGA resolutions and intergovernmental declarations in eg the *Military and Paramilitary Activities in and against Nicaragua (Nicaragua v USA)* (Merits) [1986] ICJ Rep 14 [187–95]; *Legality of the Threat and Use of Nuclear Weapons* (Advisory Opinion) [1996] ICJ Rep 241 [7–73].

customary international law by the ICJ.[199] Another example is the 1992 Rio Declaration, which assists the ongoing, and in our view not yet completed, process of crystallisation of the principle of sustainable development. It has been observed that '[b]oth treaties and soft law instruments can be vehicles for focusing consensus on rules and principles, and for mobilizing a consistent, general response on the part of States'.[200] It simply depends on given circumstances which type of instrument will, fulfil a more useful role. The 1992 Rio Declaration, as Boyle notes, has gained general support precisely because it was drafted in the form of a non-binding 'soft law' instrument, containing rules that partly codify existing environmental law and set out new rules.[201]

Soft law instruments also play a versatile role in the multilateral treaty-making process. They may start a treaty-making process, in the form of non-binding guidelines, such as was the case with the Helsinki Convention;[202] they may serve as a mechanism for authoritative interpretation or amplification of the terms of a treaty; they may provide detailed rules and technical standards required for implementation; and they may be incorporated into the terms of a treaty by implied reference.[203] For example, standard-setting in the International Labour Organisation (ILO), although often effected by non-binding recommendations, is of paramount importance and encompasses a broad range of activities ranging from the actual standard setting to supervision, assistance, and promotion. According to the ILO Committee on Legal Issues, recommendations

> have the potential to supplement Conventions, thus enhancing their impact; or they may pave the way to the adoption of a new Convention through a maturing process ... [they] can also clear the way for the ratification of existing Conventions by promoting their principles either on an individual basis or through a consolidation, possibly around the

199 *Legality of the Threat and Use of Nuclear Weapons* [27].

200 Boyle, 'Some Reflections' 28.

201 ibid.

202 See J Friedrich, *International Environmental 'Soft Law': The Functions and Limits of Nonbinding Instruments in International Environmental Law and Governance* (Springer 2014) 157, according to whom: 'The adoption of a non-binding instrument is often a first step in the development of treaty law. A non-binding instrument such a resolution of an international organisation or treaty body frequently stands at the beginning of this process. Although non-binding, resolutions or declarations shape and restrain future negotiations on the issue by defining politically the principles, objectives, and negotiations'.

203 Boyle, 'Some Reflections' 30–1.

> four strategic objectives: and they may include details that would be unwieldy in a Convention but which provide additional reference points for national law and practice.[204]

The complex nature of declarations is exemplified by the 1956 Japan–Soviet Union Joint Declaration of 19 October 1956, which was the result of negotiations towards a peace treaty between Japan and the Soviet Union. Since no agreement was reached on the issue of the Northern Territories, both States concluded a joint declaration instead of a peace treaty stipulating the termination of the state of war and the resumption of diplomatic relations.[205]

The termination of the state of war is stipulated in Article 1, stating that '[t]he state of war between the Union of Soviet Socialist Republics and Japan shall cease on the date on which this Declaration enters into force'.[206] On the Northern Territories question, Article 9 stipulates

> the Union of Soviet Socialist Republics, desiring to meet the wishes of Japan and taking into consideration the interests of the Japanese State, agrees to transfer to Japan the Habomai Islands and the island of Shikotan, the actual transfer of these islands to Japan to take place after the conclusion of a Peace Treaty between the Union of Soviet Socialist Republics and Japan.

The joint declaration uses terms such as 'shall', 'agree', or 'enter into force', which are distinctive of legally binding treaties. Moreover, this joint declaration has a ratification clause, thus it was ratified by both States and registered with the UN in accordance with Article 102 UN Charter. As Nakanishi observes, '[o]bjectively, the terms, the format or the procedural aspect show that the Joint Declaration is legally binding. However, its legal nature has been questioned in the Diet, for example, in December 2016, the then-Foreign Minister Kishida reaffirmed the legal nature of the Joint Declaration saying that "I recognize that it is an international agreement and is legally binding"'.[207]

The Japan–China Joint Communiqué signed on 29 September 29, 1972, is a non-legally binding instrument. This joint communiqué

[204] ILO Committee on Legal Issues and International Labour Standards, 'Possible Improvements in the Standard – Setting Activities of the ILO: The Role of Standards in the Achievement of the ILO's Objectives' (March 2000) GB.277/LILS/2 [7] <www.ilo.org/public/english/standards/relm/gb/docs/gb277/pdf/lils-2.pdf> accessed 20 September 2019.

[205] Nakanishi, 'Defining Boundaries' 188–9.

[206] ibid 188.

[207] ibid 189.

established diplomatic relations between Japan and the People's Republic of China (PRC).[208] The joint communiqué refers to '[t]he Government of Japan and the Government of the People's Republic of China agree to establish relations of perpetual peace and friendship' or '[t]he Government of Japan and the Government of the People's Republic of China have agreed that, with a view to solidifying and developing the relations of peace and friendship between the two countries [. . .]'.[209] Nakanishi notes that the legal nature of the joint communiqué and the difference with the Japan–USSR Joint Declaration has been questioned in the Diet. In 1979, the government responded that

> the Japan–USSR Joint Declaration is a document that constitutes a legal agreement because of its content, which includes the renouncement of claims against each other. Therefore, it has come into effect following the approval by the Diet and the conclusion of the ratification procedure. On the other hand, between Japan and the PRC, . . . there is no need to conclude a peace treaty to manage the post-war process. In addition, the Japan–China Joint Communiqué does not contain any provision that require Diet approval, therefore, it was not submitted to the Diet for its approval [. . .].[210]

Finally, in April 2015, the government of Japan and the United States announced the revised Guidelines for the Japan–US Defence Cooperation, which replaced the 1997 Guidelines. They updated the general framework and policy direction for the roles and missions of the two countries. According to the Joint Statement of April 2015, the guidelines 'detail the ways and means through which the two governments continue to strengthen their ability to fulfil that commitment through seamless, robust, flexible, and effective Alliance responses while expanding bilateral cooperation across a range of other areas'.[211] Again , questions arise on its legal nature in the Diet. The then-Foreign Minister Kishida responded to such a question by explaining that the

[208] ibid.

[209] ibid.

[210] Response by Representative Yanagiya at the Budget Committee (5 February 1979) (translation by Nakanishi, ibid). Response by Representative Takashima at the Cabinet Committee (26 July 1973) (translation by Nakanishi, ibid).

[211] Security Consultative Committee, 'Joint Statement of the Security Consultative Committee – A Stronger Alliance for a Dynamic Security Environment: The New Guidelines for Japan – US Defence Cooperation' (*Ministry of Foreign Affairs of Japan*, 27 April 2015) <www.mofa.go.jp/files/000078186.pdf> accessed 20 September 2019.

> new Guidelines is a document where the intention of both, the Government of Japan and the US, is expressed. It stipulates that the Guidelines do not obligate either government to take legislative, budgetary, administrative, or other measures, nor do the Guidelines create legal rights or obligations for either government. This is clearly stipulated. Therefore, this document is not subject to Diet approval.[212]

As it was noted by Nakanishi, the disclaimer stating that it does not create legal rights or obligation, the actual terms used in the text or the procedural aspect were clear indication that the guidelines were not intended by either State to make it legally binding.[213]

There is a view, reflected in a number of publications, that soft law is possibly replacing formal treaties in setting obligations concerning various stakeholders, such as civil society, taking part in relations along the States.[214] An example of such a practice are model laws, such as the UNCITRAL Model Law, the purpose of which is to promote uniformity. According to Bantekas, this is a preferred form to the classical treaty, as it is devoid of the pressures connected to treaty-making and contributes to an active engagement of States.[215]

Finally, it may be said that soft law has led to the emergence, particularly in recent years, of a different type of 'soft' procedures of dispute avoidance mechanisms within the multilateral treaty context, which is based on assistance rather than the classical dispute resolution mechanism.

2.5.1 States' Obligations and Climate Change Treaties

Not only the legal character of soft law but also its relationship with the law of treaties is far from clear. In particular, the expansion in recent years of a certain type of treaty, for example in the field of international environmental law, which contains not only specific obligations but also vague provisions of an ambiguous nature which do not impose 'hard' or absolute obligations on States. Examples of such treaties can be found within the realm of climate change regulations, such as the 1992 United

[212] Response by Foreign Minister Kishida at the Budget Committee (3 March 2016) (translation by Nakanishi, 'Defining Boundaries' 190).

[213] ibid.

[214] RA Wessel, 'Informal International Law Making as New Form of World Legislation' (2011) 8 IOLR 253; I Bantekas, 'Uniformity in Model Laws as Subsequent Practice under Article 31 of Vienna Convention on the Law of Treaties' (2015) 20 ARIEL 147.

[215] Bantekas, 'Uniformity in Model Laws' 163.

Nations Framework Convention on Climate Change (UNFCCC)[216] and the 2015 Paris Agreement.[217] As Boyle has explained, some treaties may generate only principles but not rules, which do not have the strength of hard law. Such a treaty may be 'potentially normative, but still "soft" in character, because it articulates "principles" rather than "rules". They, however, should not be confused with "non-binding law!"'.[218] According to Boyle, the UNFCCC includes such principles, eg in Article 3.[219] He states that elements of Article 3 are drawn directly from the non-binding Rio Declaration. These principles are not only a part of the UNFCCC but

[216] 1992 United Nations Framework Convention on Climate Change (adopted 9 May 1992, entered into force 21 March 1994) 771 UNTS 107.

[217] 2015 Paris Agreement (adopted 12 December 2015, entered into force 4 November 2016) <https://treaties.un.org/doc/Publication/UNTS/No%20Volume/54113/Part/I-54113-0800000280458f37.pdf> accessed 20 September 2019.

[218] Boyle, 'Some Reflections' 32.

[219] According to Art 3:

'Principles: In their actions to achieve the objective of the Convention and to implement its provisions, the Parties shall be guided, *inter alia*, by the following: 1. The Parties should protect the climate system for the benefit of present and future generations of humankind, on the basis of equity and in accordance with their common but differentiated responsibilities and respective capabilities. Accordingly, the developed country Parties should take the lead in combating climate change and the adverse effects thereof. 2. The specific needs and special circumstances of developing country Parties, especially those that are particularly vulnerable to the adverse effects of climate change, and of those Parties, especially developing country Parties, that would have to bear a disproportionate or abnormal burden under the Convention, should be given full consideration. 3. The Parties should take precautionary measures to anticipate, prevent or minimize the causes of climate change and mitigate its adverse effects. Where there are threats of serious or irreversible damage, lack of full scientific certainty should not be used as a reason for postponing such measures, taking into account that policies and measures to deal with climate change should be cost-effective so as to ensure global benefits at the lowest possible cost. To achieve this, such policies and measures should take into account different socio-economic contexts, be comprehensive, cover all relevant sources, sinks and reservoirs of greenhouse gases and adaptation, and comprise all economic sectors. Efforts to address climate change may be carried out cooperatively by interested Parties. 4. The Parties have a right to, and should, promote sustainable development. Policies and measures to protect the climate system against human-induced change should be appropriate for the specific conditions of each Party and should be integrated with national development programmes taking into account that economic development is essential for adopting measures to address climate change. 5. The Parties should cooperate to promote a supportive and open international economic system that would lead to sustainable economic growth and development in all Parties, particularly developing country Parties, thus enabling them better to address the problems of climate change. Measures taken to combat climate change, including unilateral ones, should not constitute a means of arbitrary or unjustifiable discrimination or a disguised restriction on international trade'.

also reflect principles, which are emerging at the general level, common to environmental law in general, but which have not achieved the status of customary international law. They are couched in an aspirational manner, for instance through the use of the word 'should'. Their content is not certain and precise. They are, however, 'relevant to interpretation and implementation of the Convention as well as creating expectations relating to matters that must be considered in good faith in the negotiation of further instruments'.[220] Finally, it may be said that '[s]ustainable development, intergenerational equity, or the precautionary principle, are all more convincing seen in this sense: not as binding obligations which must be complied with, but as principles, considerations or objectives to be taken account of-they may be soft, but they still are law'.[221]

The Paris Agreement has also generated considerable debate concerning its legal character. The discussion reflects a general diversity of views on the question of what constitutes a treaty. Bodansky has identified the following questions pertaining to this issue: '(i) the legal form of the agreement itself, that is, whether it is a treaty under international law; (ii) whether individual provisions of the agreement create legal obligations; (iii) whether the provisions of the agreement are sufficiently precise that they serve to constrain States; (iv) whether the agreement can be applied by courts; (v) whether the agreement is enforceable; (vi) whether the agreement otherwise promotes accountability, for example, through systems of transparency and review; and (vii) the domestic acceptance process and legal status of the agreement'.[222] Bodansky, unlike many authors, rejects the view that justiciability and enforcement are not a necessary condition for the legal bindingness of an instrument. The bindingness of an instrument exists if a norm is created through a recognised law-making process, independent of whether or not there are any specific sanctions for violations. Bodansky further argues that enforcement does not depend on legal form, since non-legal norms can also be enforced through the application of sanctions. He is also of the view that legally binding norms can be imprecise whilst non-binding norms can have a high degree of precision.[223] The present authors agree with this statement to a certain degree noting, however, that in States'

[220] Boyle, 'Some Reflections' 33.
[221] ibid 34.
[222] D Bodansky, 'The Legal Character of the Paris Agreement' (2016) 25 RECIEL 142.
[223] ibid 143.

practice legally binding instruments are in the majority of cases characterised by more precise language than non-binding, as it was evidenced by the previously analysed various rather vague and loosely termed declarations. Bodansky, similarly to Boyle, distinguishes between various provisions of a treaty. He is of the view that 'not every provision in a treaty creates a legal obligation for individual parties' and that 'treaties often contain a mix of different types of provisions: obligations, recommendations, factual observations, statements of the parties' opinion and so forth'.[224] The same author, along with the majority of scholars, adheres to the view that the language used in an instrument reflects the type of an obligations it embodies. For example, 'shall' generally refers to a provision in a treaty which creates a binding obligation, 'should' in most instances is attached to a provision which is a recommendation. The Paris Agreement has different addressees of its norms: it refers to 'all Parties'; 'each party'; to certain groups of parties; or no party at all.[225] Admittedly, the strongest binding obligation in the Paris Agreement relates to the nationally determined contributions (NDCs).[226] Other authors, such as Voigt, are similarly of the view that the Paris Agreement creates few legally binding obligations, but they are 'crucial to its functioning and effectiveness'.[227] She also emphasises that legal obligations that apply to all parties include: NDCs such as 'preparing, communicating and maintaining nationally determined contributions every five years, pursuing domestic mitigation measures with the aim to achieve those NDCs, providing clear, transparent and understandable information on the NDCs, accounting for anthropogenic emissions and removals, and providing information, no less frequently than biennially, on a national inventory as well as on progress in implementing and achieving the NDC'.[228] Voigt defines these obligations as continuous and iterative, thus 'creating repetitive processes, in order to enhance the level of ambition and to ensure the constant and progressive engagement of Parties with the task of addressing climate change'.[229]

224 ibid 145.
225 ibid.
226 ibid 146–7.
227 Chr Voigt, 'On the Paris Agreement's Imminent Entry Into Force (Part II of II)' (*EJIL: Talk!*, 12 October 2016) <www.ejiltalk.org/on-the-paris-agreements-imminent-entering-into-force-what-are-the-consequences-of-the-paris-agreements-entering-into-force-part-ii/> accessed 20 September 2019.
228 ibid.
229 ibid.

She further opines that these obligations apply *erga omnes partes* and are the core of the agreement, ie 'the elements on which mutual trust is built' and that '[n]ot complying with them amounts to a *breach* of an international obligation' which could trigger State responsibility. Another consequence of entering into force is that this impacts on national legal systems, of which the agreement will become part. She, however, agrees that there are normative elements (parameters) of this agreement which are of less legal stringency than obligations and that they are not legally binding in the strict sense, but they influence domestic politics and laws. Through exerting such an influence, they can develop normative power. Voigt is of the view that there are several 'such *normative* parameters in the Agreement which are not legally binding *per se*, but nevertheless exert normative force', such as duty of care – as a standard of conduct, the requirement that each party's NDC will reflect its highest possible ambition[230] in a manner that reflects its responsibilities and respective capabilities.[231]

Some authors challenge the soft law obligations, which characterise the Paris Agreement (in particular its soft law mitigation commitments), as weakening the effectiveness of the agreement. Wide participation in the Paris Agreement and the approach adopted, arguably the only politically feasible one at the time, do not conceal the fact that the soft mitigation obligations represent a serious weakness of the agreement, and 'come at a cost in terms of its likely compliance and ultimate effectiveness'.[232] Its puzzling legal character prompted some scholars to assess it as a 'voluntary agreement'[233] or even a 'statement of good intentions'.[234] Rajamani analyses carefully all types of provisions contained in the Paris Agreement and concludes that they may be divided in three types: 'hard law' provisions (mitigations and finance), 'soft law' provisions (those related to hard provisions and creating good faith expectations from the parties), and non-legal provisions (which offer mutual reassurances, provide

230 Paris Agreement, Art 4(3).

231 ibid.

232 P Lawrence and D Wong, 'Soft Law in the Paris Climate Agreement: Strength or Weakness?' (2017) 26 RECIEL 277.

233 R Falk, '"Voluntary" International Law and the Paris Agreement' (*Richard Falk Wordpress*, 16 January 2016) <https://richardfalk.wordpress.com/2016/01/16/voluntary-international-law-and-the-paris-agreement/> accessed 20 September 2019.

234 A-M Slaughter, 'The Paris to Global Governance' (*Project Syndicate*, 28 December 2015) <www.project-syndicate.org/commentary/paris-agreement-model-for-global-governance-by-anne-marie-slaughter-2015-12?barrier=accessreg> accessed 20 September 2019.

context and construct narratives). She admits that there are no fast-and-clear division lines between obligations created by these norms. Rajamani perceives the Paris Agreement as an example of new law-making, a result of a complex political context characterised by discordant States and irresolvable differences between States.[235] It can be said that almost all treaties are a result of a complex political situation and hard negotiations, including the Kyoto Protocol. Therefore, it may be that a psychological element played a role in the formation of the Paris Agreement as States felt more reassured to put in essence soft law obligations into the binding form of a treaty.

It appears that some scholars, such as Wong, argue that the Paris Agreement represents a new type of a treaty, which contains soft law obligations which are binding on parties through the operation of the *pacta sunt servanda* rule. However, their terms do not impose enforceable obligations on parties, owing to a lack of imperative language, or vagueness or imprecision in the expression of the obligations.[236] Soft law obligations in the Paris Agreement were a *conditio sine qua non* in terms of consensus, and a strength of the agreement. The Paris Agreement provides in relation to all parties that their NDCs be voluntary and are housed outside the agreement. The main hard law binding obligations in relation to these key mitigation commitments, are procedural, namely submitting and updating the NDCs and certain obligations relating to transparency. Therefore, '[t]he soft, non- binding nature of the key commitment relating to the implementation of NDCs enabled agreement in Paris, as it allowed the negotiators to sidestep the thorny issue of whether developed as opposed to developing countries would need to take on a different quality and stringency of commitments'.[237]

2.5.2 *Conclusions*

The legal character of soft law thus remain ambiguous, especially if considered in the context of the problem of what constitutes a binding obligation. Political scientists who have analysed this phenomenon offer an answer to this question of how to treat legal obligations with a varied normative content included in the same instrument. The importance

[235] L Rajamani, 'The 2015 Paris Agreement: Interplay between Hard, Soft and Non-Obligations' (2016) 28 JEL 327.
[236] Lawrence and Wong, 'Soft Law' 282–3.
[237] ibid 265.

which States attach to international obligations is not exclusively conditioned by the legal nature of these obligations: '[t]he schematic distinction between those obligations that are and those that are not legally binding does not necessarily offer insight in the constraint obligations impose on States'.[238] Rather, practice in this regime makes clear that this is a much more diffuse process.

> [T]he principle of sustainable development has induced expectations as to the conduct of States, can be used to claim from other States that they adopt their policies and indeed had begun to act as a *de facto* constraint on policy-makers. This is no way dependent on its recent inclusion in the legally binding 1992 Helsinki and Paris Conventions. In the continuous assessments States make as to which of the large number of prescriptions for preventive actions are important and are complied with, the legal nature is only one of the relevant factors. The relevance of the legal nature cannot be taken for granted and can only be assessed on a case by case basis.[239]

Finally, it has been observed that soft law

> may be used deliberately solely to steer conduct in a desired direction to achieve generalized 'soft law' rather than hard goals, and this may in given cases be more effective over a long term, especially in the case of developing States. This is the case in the situations where there are uncertainties of a scientific, technological, economic or social nature, but when some immediate change of behavior is required.[240]

In our view, the nature of so-called soft law has not been fully explored. In particular, there is a confusion between completely non-binding declarations, such as those covering the Baltic Sea, and the provisions of binding treaties, such as the UNFCCC and the Paris Agreement, that according to Boyle contain soft principles that are not strictly binding obligations, but nevertheless are aspirational and constitute law at least to a certain degree. If we take this distinction further, they appear to be three types of situations: non-binding instruments; binding law; 'soft' but potentially normative principles contained in treaties that constitute, nevertheless, some law.

238 A Nollkaemper, *The Legal Regime for Transboundary Water Pollution: Between Discretion and Constraint* (Kluwer Law International 1993) 252.

239 ibid.

240 P Birnie, 'The Status of Environmental "Soft Law": Trends and Examples with Special Focus on IMO Norms', in H Ringbom (ed), *Competing Norms in the Law of Marine Environmental Protection, Focus on Ship Safety and Pollution Prevention* (Kluwer Law International 1997) 39.

According to Lowe,

> [t]he real differences between hard law and sot law lie in the processes by which the rule is articulated and in the consequences of the breach. The essential nature of normativity of hard law and of soft law is not great. In terms of strength of the expectations of compliance, there is no necessary distinction between categories of 'hard' and 'soft law', though there are, of course, great differences in relation of various norms within each category.[241]

We agree with the view expressed above that one of the most important legal problems concerning soft law are the legal consequences on non-compliance with soft law provisions. Again, we must differentiate between soft law *stricto sensu* and soft provisions (principles) contained in treaties.[242] What is relatively unexplored is the legal consequences of non-compliance with soft law principles incorporated in a treaty. The question arises as to whether such non-compliance is to be treated as a breach of an international obligation (a breach of a treaty rule), or whether there are some other, unspecified, legal consequences attached to a breach of such a soft principle contained in a treaty, which may differ from general rules applicable in instances of a breach of a hard obligation.

In our view, attaching any legal consequences to non-binding provisions does not reflect the practice of States. Non-binding instruments have no legal effects and therefore their breach is without legal consequences. The breach of a treaty provision even of a soft character is a different matter. Such a breach should be treated as a breach of a legal obligation, thus resulting in the possibility of the invocation of the rules of State responsibility. Furthermore, soft provisions could serve as guidance for the parties to a treaty,[243] or they could be couched in more imperative terms demanding concrete action, while still remaining somewhat weak as to the scope and the nature of the obligation. For example, Article 4(4)(b) of the UNFCCC states as follows: 'Parties shall communicate information on their policies and measures to review greenhouse emissions with the aim of returning individually or jointly to their 1990 emissions levels'. Although this provision uses the word 'shall',

[241] V Lowe, 'Sustainable Development and Unsustainable Arguments' in A Boyle and D Freestone (eds), *International Law and Sustainable Development: Past Achievements and Future Challenges* (OUP 1999) 30.

[242] See eg UNFCCC and the Paris Agreement.

[243] For instance, when the relevant provision employs the term 'should', eg '*x* should strive to'.

the only real obligation contained in this provision is to provide information on measures adopted by a party. Admittedly, States are not likely to litigate exclusively on the basis of a breach of a provision of such a general and soft character. We agree with Boyle that soft rules contained in treaties, however, may lay down parameters that affect the way courts decide issues.[244]

It may be said that the role and functioning of soft law is still not fully explored, and it escapes firm and clear-cut definitions, as 'it does not represent a legal concept with a clearly determinable scope and content. It is more of a catchword, symbolizing a specific form of social rules in the penumbra of international law'.[245]

It is clear that 'non-binding norms have complex and potentially large impact in the development of international law'.[246] Some issues and features concerning soft law have been already identified. There are, *inter alia,* several reasons why the use of soft law, even considering its shortcomings, may be preferable: it is more flexible and in certain circumstances there may not be a possibility to enact hard law; soft law instruments may be more of an incentive for States to participate; soft law may be a more appropriate solution than hard law, when the issues at hand and the response to them are still not yet clearly identified (due to scientific uncertainty or other causes) but there is an urgency to take some action and employing soft law allows its swifter adoption; soft law provides for more active participation of non-State actors.[247] Therefore, soft law is increasingly utilised because it responds in a more effective manner to the exigencies of the new international system.[248]

However, as it was as mentioned above, there is a distinct difficulty in defining what soft law is. It covers a multitude of international instruments, such as resolutions of international organisations, non-binding inter-State agreements, declarations etc.[249] There are great differences

[244] Boyle, 'Some Reflections' 32.

[245] D Thürer, 'Soft Law' [2009] MPEPIL 1469 [8].

[246] D Shelton, 'Introduction: Law, Non-Law and the Problems of "Soft Law"' in Shelton (ed), *Commitment and Compliance 1.*

[247] ibid 13–5. On the increased importance of soft law and of 'users' of international law, see T Treves, The Expansion of International Law: General Course on Public International Law' (2015) 398 RdC 9, chs 3–6; E Roucounas, 'The Users of International Law' in MH Arsanjani et al (eds), *Looking to the Future: Essays on International Law in Honor of W Michael Reisman* (Brill/Martinus Nijhoff 2010) 217–34.

[248] Shelton, 'Introduction: Law, Non-Law and the Problems of "Soft Law"' 13.

[249] Thürer, 'Soft Law' [3–6].

between these instruments and putting them under one *chapeau* of soft law, is to some extent an oversimplification, as each and every of these instruments has it is own legal features and legal effects. A question often asked is whether soft law is a new source of international law. Thürer, having denied such a possibility, opines that 'it seems to be more appropriate to consider soft law acts as indications of the meaning behind, or the stages in, the development of international law, rather than as international law itself'.[250] As to its legal effects, soft law is most frequently related to good faith, however 'this does not mean that somehow good faith transforms soft law into binding law. After all, the pertinent norms have been deliberately denied legal character by the parties choosing soft law as the appropriate form for a specific agreement or an otherwise specific act of practice. The principle of good faith requires relevant actors not to contradict their own conduct'.[251]

One of the most complex legal questions concerning soft law is its relationship with treaties. Hillgenberg presents an interesting suggestion, the gist of which is that the difference between treaties, and customary international law, depends on the parties' wish to construe their relationship with the exclusion of the application of treaty or customary law in relation to a breach of obligations. The consequences of a breach of such obligations are defined by the parties themselves. Such a relationship may be defined as a self-contained regime, whose legal nature depends on the parties' intentions, and has to be examined separately in each and every case. However, such an arrangement does not preclude the introduction of some of the rules of treaty law and general principles of law into that regime.[252] This very original approach still leaves the question open on how legally binding and non-legally binding norms of international law coexist in one treaty, such as in the case of the UNFCCC and the Paris Agreement, from the point of view of breaches and consequently the application of the rule *pacta sunt servanda* in such a case, which is widely assumed to cover the Paris Agreement. If we assume that such non-binding norms are excluded from the regime of the 1969 VCLT,[253] then we are faced with the question of a duality of regimes in one treaty as to what concerns the legal consequences of breach of its provisions.

250 ibid [24].
251 ibid [26].
252 H Hillgenberg, 'A Fresh Look at Soft Law' (1999) 10 EJIL 499.
253 ibid 509.

There is no doubt that '[t]he subject of soft law has always been an awkward one for international lawyers. On one hand, it is not law at all, strictly speaking … [O]n the other hand, virtually all legal scholars would agree that they are not simply politics, either'.[254] We agree with these authors that referring to soft law norms as quasi-legal is of little help in solving the question of its legal nature. As Guzman and Meyer correctly observe, such a distinction simply begs the question of what separates quasi-legal from non-legal on one hand and legal on the other hand.[255] However, soft law still awaits a satisfactory definition which would fully capture not only its versatility but also a rarely mentioned potential negative effect, ie 'soft law may maintain the fiction of a universal international law, while in reality leading to its destruction through the formulation of relative standards'.[256]

One definition does not fully reflect all intricacies of this tool. It is possible that such a definition is impossible to coin, exactly due to the multitude of forms and roles soft law assumes and its inherent ambiguity.

2.6 Reflections on the Role of Good Faith

The extensive discussion of the legal nature of the principle of good faith exceeds the framework of this chapter. However, it is necessary to include at least some consideration regarding its character, as undoubtedly it not only underlies all of the obligations stemming from treaties but also those of soft law and in particular of unilateral acts of States.[257] The type of legal consequences, if any, linked to the breach of good faith has generated a robust debate, in particular in situations where there was a lack of the accompanying 'hard' type of international obligation. The majority view is that the principle of good faith is 'a principle of interpretation or a foundation for other legal principles or norms, but it does not create in itself duties to act or abstain, ie subjective rights and obligations'.[258] For example, this approach was expressed by the ICJ in *Nicaragua v Honduras*, where the Court stated: 'The principle of good

[254] AT Guzman and TLO Meyer, 'International Soft Law' (2010) 2 JLA 171, 172.
[255] ibid.
[256] C Chinkin, 'Normative Development in International Legal System' in Shelton (ed), *Commitment and Compliance* 42.
[257] For an in–depth analysis on good faith, see R Kolb, *Good Faith in International Law* (Hart 2017).
[258] ibid 30.

faith is [...] not a source of obligation where none would otherwise exist'.[259] However, as Kolb explains, such as view is perhaps too narrow. According to Kolb, good faith operates through concretisation, ie a fast separation between 'the normativity of the concretising norms and the non-normativity of the founding principles is somewhat artificial'.[260] International courts and tribunals will refrain from stating that a State acted in bad faith. They will not rely on such an argument.[261] As Kolb states, the most frequent idea attached to the principle of good faith is one connected to the protection of legitimate expectations created and relied on by the subject.[262]

The principle of good faith operates in the majority of cases through the prism of existing intermediate principles and norms and very infrequently through a direct application on its own merit to a particular case. However, it must be emphasised that the principle of good faith constitutes a fall-back option, always remaining in the background of the obligation. Kolb also opines that good faith is normative under the limb of the possibility of its direct application as an obligation – creating norm, eg in investment law or international commercial law.[263] Good faith in the law of treaties is not limited to the *pacta sunt servanda* obligations, but also underlies other law of treaties norms, such as to pre-treaty commitments, and in cases of the termination of treaties to the principle of *rebus sic stantibus*.[264] It also plays a fundamental role in relation to unilateral acts.[265]

2.7 Conclusions

In our quest to examine the first type of motion, the genesis of a treaty, certain conclusions may be drawn.

(i) The definition of a treaty, as enshrined in the VCLT, does not reflect all the varied forms under which a treaty may appear. This is best

[259] *Border and Transboundary Armed Actions (Nicaragua v Honduras)* (Judgment) [1988] ICJ Rep 69 [105].

[260] Kolb, *Good Faith* 31.

[261] See eg *Whaling in the Antarctic (Australia v Japan: New Zealand Intervening)* (Judgment) [2014] ICJ Rep 226 [62 ff], in which the Court refused to engage in a discussion on a possible bad faith of Japan.

[262] Kolb, *Good Faith* 23.

[263] ibid 31.

[264] ibid 35 and 41–81.

[265] ibid 84–9.

illustrated by the jurisprudence of the PCIJ and the ICJ, which provides examples of some of the difficulties that may arise in connection with determining whether an instrument constitutes a treaty, notwithstanding its designation. The ICJ has never relied exclusively on the VCLT to determine the nature of an instrument, but in each and every case has focused rather on the legal content of the instrument in question.

(ii) The ILC (generally) was of the view that it is the content of the legal obligation that distinguishes a legally binding agreement from a political one.

(iii) The formal definition of a treaty, as contained in Article 2(a) VCLT, does not reflect the evolution (or motion) of multifaceted forms (both formal and substantive) of co-operation between States. The robust development of certain areas of international law, such as international environmental law, has resulted in the emergence of treaties with norms that are considered to be of less binding character than classical norms of international law. This new phenomenon has an impact on the rules of State responsibility concerning their breach, ie in case of the commission of a wrongful act. It remains unclear what the applicable law would be in this respect.

(iv) In determining the status of an instrument, the nature of the transaction, the text, and the circumstances of its conclusion must be taken into consideration, as exemplified in the *Aegean Sea Continental Shelf* and *Land and Maritime Boundary between Cameroon and Nigeria* cases.

(v) Interdependence of mutual obligations does not necessarily create a bilateral engagement, and, therefore, not all interdependent obligations are treaties.[266]

(vi) Binding treaties must enumerate commitments to which parties have consented in order to create rights and obligations in international law for the parties.[267]

However, these enumerated features of a treaty indicate only their general attributes. In practice, each and every instance of an instrument must be examined separately. The relationship between various forms of instruments in international law and their interrelationship makes providing a definition of a treaty that would be applicable to all instances a

[266] Cf, *Legal Status of Eastern Greenland.*

[267] Cf, *Maritime Delimitation and Territorial Questions between Qatar and Bahrain.*

rather elusive task. The complex nexus of bindings and non-binding norms, often included in one treaty, raises the complexity of the establishing of all-encompassing definition of a treaty. This was corroborated by rich practice of international courts and tribunals. In summation, the more precisely one attempts to define the notion of a treaty, the more one loses sight of the vastly complex interactions between and forms of instruments in the modern international legal system. Similar to Heisenberg's uncertainty principle,[268] the more precision and exhaustive enumeration we try to achieve on the content (location) of the definition of a treaty, the less information we actually have on its motion (*kinesis*). It is for this reason that the practice of States and courts and tribunals seems to be a juggling act between the two, certainty and flexibility, with a view to having some degree of knowledge of what elements constitute a treaty, but allowing breathing air for the multifariousness of State practice on the international scene, with all sort of instruments that are as a group and *ab initio* neither binding or non-binding, but whose legal bindingness has to be determined *ad hoc*, on the basis of the factual background of each individual case.

[268] The Heisenberg Uncertainty (or Indeterminacy) principle states that the position and the velocity of an object can never be both be measured exactly, at the same time. The more information one has on one of these the less certain the information on the other is.

3

Consent to Be Bound

The Force behind the Motion of Treaties

3.1 Introduction

There are very few areas of the law of treaties which would show such a robust motion as 'consent to be bound'. The developments in certain treaty regimes have brought about unexpected changes in the rather well-established and, we may even say, classical methods of expressing consent to be bound. These new motions in treaty law have ignited many scholarly debates, but have not resulted in any single, definitive resolution. The discussion is still ongoing. The question of consent to be bound is linked, at least formally, to the general question of what constitutes a treaty under international law. In our view, the definition of a treaty from the substantial and procedural points of view, ie whether an instrument is a treaty or not and who can bind the State, is related also to the issue of consent to be bound. However, as it was exemplified by the relevant and ample case law,[1] a State may find itself bound by an agreement, despite its intentions and express consent. This phenomenon is particularly visible in relation to the jurisdiction of the ICJ. The modern issue of 'consent without consent' is also related to modification or revisions of MEAs, which is dealt with in Chapter 5.

As is explored in this chapter, this debate does not only focus on legal questions, but also relates to questions of fairness and legitimacy. Moreover, the issue of reservations to treaties belongs to the general area of the expression of the consent to be bound as well. It is an incontrovertible fact, acknowledged by States and scholars, that reservations to treaties are part and parcel of the whole procedure of consent. Although the faculty of making reservations has its own place in the VCLT and does not form part of Article 11 VCLT, in practical terms it belongs to the widely conceived process of the expression of the consent to be bound by a

[1] See, for instance, *Maritime Delimitation and Territorial Questions between Qatar and Bahrain*.

treaty. Therefore, reservations to treaties are also discussed in this chapter. Reservations to treaties, in particular reservations to human rights treaties, have brought about the question of legitimacy of the practice of certain human rights courts of excising an offending reservation from the expression of consent to be bound by a State, which emanates from State sovereignty.

Until very recently, the question of consent to be bound was considered by many scholars a rather uninteresting – if not outright staid – part of the law of treaties. As already observed, nothing can be further from the truth. Some new developments have changed the traditional position on this subject. Recent surveys on consent to be bound have concentrated on the analysis on certain national practice, based on the traditional methods of consent to be bound that are enumerated in Articles 11–17 VCLT, including provisions on modification and amendment of a treaty.[2] The traditional approach to consent is fairly simple: consent is the necessary element for a State's being bound by an international agreement or by one of its provisions.[3] By contrast, under a treaty regime in which treaty norms can be developed in a way that goes beyond the plain textual provision, the legal position of a State party ultimately no longer depends on whether or not the State has expressed its consent in such a way as it did to become a party to the original instrument, or to a formal modification or amendment of the instrument.

[2] See eg the survey conducted by the Council of Europe; Council of Europe and BIICL (eds), *Treaty-Making: Expression of Consent to Be Bound by a Treaty* (Kluwer Law International 2001).

[3] Establishing whether or not a State has expressed its consent to be bound by a given treaty has legal consequences for several VCLT provisions, because under Art 2(1)(f) a 'contracting State' means a State which has consented to be bound by the treaty, whether or not the treaty has entered into force'. The ILC considered it necessary to distinguish a 'contracting State' from a 'negotiating State' and from a 'party' for the purposes of the Draft Articles on the Law of Treaties. The relevant point when describing a State as a contracting State, according to the ILC's commentaries on the draft provision, is that a State's consent to be bound exists independently of whether the treaty has entered into force. According to the ILC, the term 'party' should only be used for those States for which the treaty is in force. To be a party to a treaty, a State must validly have expressed its consent to be bound. Thus, the question whether a State is a contracting State must be answered by reference to Arts 11–17 VCLT and this has an implication for several other Articles of the VCLT. Similarly, Art 2(1)(g) provides that a 'party' for the purposes of the VCLT is a 'State which has consented to be bound by the treaty and for which the treaty is in force'. The term 'contracting State' arises in Arts 16, 17, 20, 22, 23, 40, 54, 57, 77, and 79 of the VCLT. The provisions of Part II of the VCLT, which include the relevant provisions on the means of a State's expressing its consent to be bound, apply to the amendments of an agreement between the parties, as set out in Art 39 VCLT.

It is important, in the context of consent, to distinguish between the expression of consent to be bound at the stage of the conclusion of a treaty and the idea that consent to a particular obligation arising under a treaty is a condition for a State's being internationally bound.

3.2 Classical Methods of the Consent to Be Bound and the VCLT

The law relating to the methods of expression of consent to be bound by a treaty is codified in Articles 11–17 VCLT. The role of the procedure of consent to bound is to constitute a mechanism by virtue of which a treaty becomes binding on States, or, as it was described, acquires characteristics of a 'juridical act'.[4] Article 11 VCLT enumerates the classical means of consent to be bound.[5] The essential feature of the system of consent to bound in the VCLT is its subsidiary character, ie the mode of expressing consent to be bound by a State depends entirely on States engaged in the process. States enjoy great freedom in this respect. This was confirmed by Judge Jessup in the *South West Africa* cases, according to whom the methods of consent to be bound, 'not being a formalistic system, hold States legally bound by their undertakings in a variety of circumstances'.[6] The Court in the *Temple of Preah Vihear (Preliminary Objections)* also emphasised the flexible character of consent to be bound.[7] This position is reflected by modern treaty practice concerning the form of an expression of consent, and is captured in the second limb of Article 11 VCLT. This practice is primality relevant in the bilateral context. The issue of form comes into sharper focus mainly in the context of the practice, not quite common, of States' issuing signed joint communiqués, or an exchange of signed or initialled notes, or indeed of unsigned or uninitialled *notes verbales*. In such a case, signature of the document, or the exchange of instruments constituting a treaty as envisaged in in Article 13 VCLT, typically would be sufficient to express the consent of a State to be bound. As it was analysed in Chapter 2 of this book, on the

4 A Bolintineanu, 'Expression of Consent to Be Bound by a Treaty in the Light of the 1969 Vienna Convention' (1974) 68 AJIL 672.

5 Article 11 – Means of Expressing Consent to Bound by Treaty: 'The consent of a State to be bound by a treaty may be expressed by signature, exchange of instruments constituting a treaty, ratification, acceptance, approval or accession, or by any other means if so agreed'.

6 *South West Africa Cases* (Preliminary Objections) 411.

7 *Case Concerning the Temple of Preah Vihear (Cambodia v Thailand)* (Preliminary Objections) [1961] ICJ Rep 17, 31.

basis of several judicial examples referring to the cases of the ICJ or other international courts and tribunals, such an informal way of expressing consent to be bound by a treaty frequently results in a dispute as to the legal character of such an instrument, whether it is a treaty or not.

The traditional, classical methods of consent to be bound are well known in the law of treaties, and about these methods much has already been written. This chapter, therefore, presents the general outline of legal issues.[8] The main focus is on 'other means so agreed', as provided for in Article 11 VCLT, and as developed in the recent practice of States. It is interesting to note that the majority view within the ILC was that the general rule on consent to be bound should not be included at all in the text of the VCLT. However, it was decided at the diplomatic conference, which finalised the text of the convention, that it was necessary and also useful to have such a rule, considering an extensive practice of States in this respect.[9]

There are very few issues of a theoretical nature of interest in relation to the methods of expression of consent to be bound as expounded in Article 11 VCLT. Historically, one of these issues had related to the question of the supremacy of either ratification or signature, as the means of consent to be bound. This question is at present of minimal importance, as all treaties, at least of the multilateral kind, contain a rule on the method of consent to be bound. In 1929, the PCIJ held that under certain circumstances, conventions are only binding on the basis of ratification.[10] In the past there was a certain debate – today largely moot – on the issue of the existence, or lack thereof of an 'inherent' requirement of the ratification of a treaty. The proponents of the view

[8] On this subject, see eg G Fitzmaurice, 'Do Treaties Need Ratification?' (1934) 5 BYIL 113; McNair, *The Law of Treaties* 113–37; Sir I Sinclair, *The Vienna Convention on the Law of Treaties* (2nd edn, MUP 1984) 34–50 and 131–55; H Blix, 'The Requirement of Ratification' (2000) 30 BYIL 352; J Klabbers, *The Concept of Treaty in International Law* (Kluwer Law International 1996) 72–5; F Berman and D Bentley, 'Treaties and Other International Instruments–IV Ratification, Accession, Acceptance, and Approval, Treaty Succession' in Sir I Roberts (ed), *Satow's Diplomatic Practice* (7th edn, OUP 2017) 638–9.

[9] United Nations Conference on the Law of Treaties, '1st Session – 15th Meeting of the Committee of the Whole (COW)' (5 April 1968) UN Doc A/CONF.39/C.1/SR.15 80, 83 [43]; S Nahlik, 'La Conference de Vienne sur le droit des traités: une vue d'ensemble' (1969) 15 AFDI 24, 36-8; RD Kearney and RE Dalton, 'The Treaty on Treaties' (1970) 64 AJIL 495, 508.

[10] *Case Relating to the Territorial Jurisdiction of the International Commission of the River Oder (Germany, Denmark, France, Great Britain, Czechoslovakia v Poland)* (Judgment) PCIJ Rep Series A No 23, 20.

of the 'inherent' ratification explained that the ratification was necessary unless the circumstances or the relevant treaty did not indicate an intention of its dispensation. A different view was expressed by Fitzmaurice, who took the approach of the lack of the existence of the 'inherent' necessity of ratification, which only depended on the intentions of the parties to the treaty to ratify it. According to his view, the treaty acquired binding force upon signature, as a main principle, unless otherwise indicated either by a treaty or intention of the parties. Such an intention had to be apparent.[11]

The survey of State practice conducted by the Council of Europe focused on the requirements for ratification by the States dictated by their constitutional law, a procedure which is entirely distinct from ratification as defined by Article 2 VCLT: '"ratification", "acceptance", "approval", and "accession" mean in each case the international act so named whereby a State establishes on the international plane its consent to be bound by a treaty'. This distinction in relation to the ratification procedure is frequently not upheld and these two distinct meanings of the ratification procedure, international and national (subject to a constitutional order of a State) is merged and treated as one, which is an erroneous approach.[12] Berman and Bentley confirm that 'as ratification is a technical term of international law which is popularly translated into "parliamentary ratification" is inaccurate'.[13] These authors also explain that, in principle, the ratification procedure is unconditional, ie the operative effect of ratifying cannot be conditioned upon ratification by other States. The need for a degree of reciprocity will be delivered by a treaty itself, either by providing for a minimum number of ratifications before its entry into force or by providing that the ratification of all signatories is required for its entry into force.[14]

Articles 12 and 14 VCLT attempt to cover all instances in which ratification and signature are means of consent to be bound, ie when it is explicitly indicated by a treaty and may be inferred from the intention of State parties or from some other pertinent circumstances.

Pergantis approaches Article 11 VCLT in a very diversified way: from the points of formalism, consensualism, and derivative international

[11] Fitzmaurice, 'Do Treaties Need Ratification?' 129.

[12] The example of this is the survey of the Council of Europe wherein the distinction is not upheld (see Council of Europe and BIICL (eds), *Treaty-Making* 10).

[13] Berman and Bentley, 'Treaties and Other International Instruments–IV' 631 [34.7].

[14] ibid 632 [34.10].

legislation, which he identifies as a 'remote consent'. Derivative international legislation is discussed in Chapter 5. In these authors' view, it is a method of consent to be bound which is placed under the *chapeau* of 'any other means' of Article 11 VCLT and the main question of such a means of consent to be bound is the legitimacy of this procedure. Some of the modifications of the treaty regimes in MEAs are effected by the decisions of COPs without enabling clauses in a basic treaty, such as the compliance procedure in the Basel Convention.

Therefore, there can be certain fundamental problems with the legitimacy concerning such legislative activities of COPs. Deformalisation of consent methods can take a different guise and at times it is taken too far. As it was observed, '[t]he result is a constant oscillation between the effort to deformalize the process for the expression of consent to be bound and the need to preserve a certain legal security in this field'.[15]

3.3 Modification of States' Consent through Reservations to Treaties

3.3.1 *Introductory Observations*

The question of reservation to treaties has been for a very long time one of the main points of preoccupation by international law practitioners and scholars in the field of the law of treaties. There is a vast and robust literature on this subject.[16] Therefore, the object and purpose of this section is to identify the problems of consent to be bound by a treaty in relation to reservations to treaties, rather than repeating what has been already analysed in numerous publications on this subject matter. The question of reservation to treaties is a classic example of the complex nexus of sovereignty and consensualism in a collective order.[17] However, the close scrutiny of a multilateral system characterised by reservations leads in fact to the bilateralisation of relations between States, since a formally multilateral treaty may result in a network of bilateral

[15] V Pergantis, *The Paradigm of State Consent in the Law of Treaties* (Edward Elgar 2017) 142.

[16] See eg MR Meek, 'International Law: Reservations to Multilateral Agreements' (1955) 5 DePaul LR 40; RW Edwards, 'Reservations to Treaties' (1989) 10 MichJInt'lL 362; M Milanovic and L-A Sicilianos, 'Reservations to Treaties: An Introduction' (2011) 24 EJIL 1055; A Pellet, 'Article 19 of the 1969 Vienna Convention' in O Corten and P Klein (eds), *The Vienna Conventions on the Law of Treaties – A Commentary* (OUP 2011) 405; Pergantis, *The Paradigm of State Consent* 234 ff.

[17] Pergantis, *The Paradigm of State Consent* 234.

obligations. Therefore, there is a paradoxical situation whereby the inclusion of States in a multilateral treaty process results in fact in a system of bilateral relations under the general *chapeaux* of a multilateral treaty. It may even be that States do not have any relations within the framework of a multilateral agreement, in the event of non-acceptance of the reservation and the explicit denial of any treaty relations between the reserving and accepting States.

Because of the faculty of reservations, States retain control over a treaty. At the same time, reservations enable States to participate in multilateral international agreements, without compromising their independent decision-making power. The ability of making reservations, however, is strictly connected with their legitimacy and there is the unresolved question of who is empowered to decide on that matter. This is one of certain gaps left in the reservations regime by the VCLT. Apart from invalid/impermissible reservations, other subjects that are not addressed by the VCLT are interpretative declarations and reservations to human rights treaties. Therefore, in order to close these gaps, reservations to treaties have been one of the areas of work of the ILC, with Pellet functioning as Special Rapporteur.[18]

The period between the two world wars was characterised by two main regimes of reservations to treaties: the regimes under the League of Nations and the Pan-American Union. The first of these regimes was based on the unanimity of the approval of the reservation in question; when the reservation was objected to, it had to either be withdrawn or the State was no longer considered to be a party to the treaty.[19] The second was based on a flexible principle, according to which the non-acceptance of a reservation by one party to a treaty, excluded treaty relations only between the objecting State and the reserving State. In relation to all other States, not objecting to the reservation, the objecting State was considered a party to the treaty.[20] The ground-breaking event in the practice of reservations was the well-known Advisory Opinion of the ICJ on the *Reservations to the Convention on Genocide*.[21] This opinion

[18] ILC, 'Guide to Practice on Reservations to Treaties, with Commentaries' (26 April–3 June and 4 July–12 August 2011) UN Doc A/66/10/Add.1.

[19] HW Malkin, 'Reservations to Multilateral Conventions' (1926) 7 BYIL 141.

[20] JK Peters, 'Reservations to Multilateral Treaties: How International Legal Doctrine Reflects World Vision' (1982–3) 23 HILJ 72, 80–4.

[21] *Reservations to the Convention on Genocide* (Advisory Opinion) [1951] ICJ Rep 15, 29. The Court advised that with respect to the validity of reservations under the Genocide Convention, a State which has made and maintained a reservation which has been

'represents the historical moment at which the rhetoric and reasoning of all discussion of reservations fundamentally changed'.[22] It introduced the flexible but at the same troublesome and puzzling criterion of the object and purpose. The Court introduced a distinction between the contractual and the normative conventions (*traités lois* and *traités contrats*). The main distinction between the Genocide Convention and other treaties between States was the object and purpose of this convention, which was not seeking a perfect balance of interest between States but was guided by its nature as a humanitarian convention. According to the Court, 'the high ideals which inspired the Convention provide, by virtue of the common will of the parties, the foundation and measure of all its provisions'.[23] The complexity of the application of the criterion of the object and purpose, which is reflected in the relevant provisions of the VCLT, was observed in the Joint Dissenting Opinion of Judges Guerrero, Sir Arnold McNair, Read, and Hsu Mo, who made the following statements on this criterion:

> It hinges on the expression 'if the reservation is compatible with the object and purpose of the Convention'. What is the 'object and purpose' of the Genocide Convention? To repress genocide? Of course; but is it more than that? Does it comprise any or all of the enforcement articles of the Convention? That is the heart of the matter. One has only to look at them to realize the importance of this question. As we showed at the beginning of our Opinion, these are the articles which are causing trouble.[24]

The dissenting judges expressed a valid concern relating to the subjectivity of an assessment of the compatibility of reservations with the purpose and object of the convention:

objected to by one or more of the parties to the convention but not by others, can be regarded as being a party to the convention if the reservation is compatible with the object and purpose of the convention; otherwise, that State cannot be regarded as being a party to the convention (ibid 29). As to the legal effects of opposition to reservations, the Court advised: (a) that if a party to the convention objects to a reservation which it considers to be incompatible with the object and purpose of the convention, it can consider that the reserving State is not a party to the convention; (b) that if, on the other hand, a party accepts the reservation as being compatible with the object and purpose of the convention, it can consider that the reserving State is a party to the convention (ibid 29–30).

22 Peters, 'Reservations to Multilateral Treaties' 85.

23 *Reservations to the Convention on Genocide* 23.

24 *Reservations to the Convention on Genocide*, Dissenting Opinion of Judges Guerrero, Sir Arnold McNair, Read, and Hsu Mo 44.

> as the admissibility of any reservation that has been objected to is left to subjective determination by individual States. It will only be objectively determined when the question of the compatibility of the reservation is referred to judicial decision; but this procedure, for various reasons, may never be resorted to by the parties. If and when the question is judicially determined, the result will be, according as the reservation is judicially found to be compatible or incompatible, either that the objecting State or States must, for the first time, recognize the reserving State as being also a party to the Convention, or that the reserving State ceases to be a party in relation to those other parties which have accepted the reservation. Such a state of things can only cause the utmost confusion among the interested States.[25]

As can be seen from these quotes, the dissenting judges were staunch supporters of the integrity of the convention over its universality.

3.3.2 *Regime of the Vienna Convention: Gaps and Confusion*

The outcome of the *Advisory Opinion to the Genocide Convention* has proved to be a burdensome legacy for the VCLT. The system of the criterion of the 'object and purpose' was finally adopted by the VCLT, and has proved to be as elusive and complex as the dissenting judges had foreseen, and which mostly relate to subjective and objective elements of the VCLT regime.[26] Articles 19–23 VCLT contain its system of reservations, whose many principles are laid out in Article 19 VCLT. This provision regulates reservations in the following manner: reservations are permitted unless not expressly prohibited, or prohibited only in relation to certain articles of the treaty. In cases of permitted or expressly authorised reservations, no subsequent acceptance is required. In cases of treaties with few parties and a unitary object and purpose, acceptance by all parties is required. In relation to the constituent instrument of international organisations, acceptance by a competent organ of international organisation is also required.

The criterion of the object and purpose of the treaty is of relevance when the treaty is silent on reservations, ie neither permits nor prohibits it. The acceptance by one State is required for a reservation to be established. The legal effects of reservations are as follows: modification of the provisions of the treaty to which the reservation relates to the extent of the reservation for the reserving State or international

[25] ibid.
[26] Peters, 'Reservations to Multilateral Treaties' 95.

organisation in its relations with the accepting parties; modification of those provisions to the same extent for that other party in its relations with the reserving State or international organisation. The reservation does not modify the provisions of the treaty for the other parties to the treaty *inter se*. When a State or an international organisation objecting to a reservation has not opposed the entry into force of the treaty between itself and the reserving State or organisation, the provisions to which the reservation relates do not apply as between the reserving State or organisation and the objecting State or organisation to the extent of the reservation. Reservations are thus construed on the basis of reciprocity, and the objecting State enjoys the reservations submitted by the reserving State. An innovation introduced by the VCLT to the flexibility regime is that only an express statement from the objecting State precludes treaty relationships between the opposing and reserving State. Having based the core of the reservations regime on the object and purpose criterion, VCLT has left the question of the effects of impermissible reservations and in general the practical application of such a test largely unanswered. This lacuna has given rise to two schools of thought: permissibility[27] and opposability,[28] neither of them reflecting actual practice of States. In brief, the permissibility school is of the view that a reservation incompatible with the object and purpose of the treaty is invalid from its inception and the acceptance by any State cannot cure its invalidity. The opposability school relies on a different premise, ie that the acceptance of the reservation by another contracting State is a decisive factor in determining the validity of the reservation. In practice, States in general are quite cautious in their reactions to reservations and choose to object to an offending reservation rather than to severe treaty relations with a State making such a reservation.[29]

An excellent example of State practice in relation to reservations is the 1946 International Convention for the Regulation of Whaling.[30] In the case of this convention, the reaction of States to the reservation of Iceland upon its adherence to the Whaling Convention in 2002 is very instructive.[31] According to the reservation of Iceland, 'we hereby declare that

[27] DW Bowett, 'Reservations to Non-Restricted Multilateral Treaties' (1976–7) 48 BYIL 67.

[28] JM Ruda, 'Reservation to Treaties' (1975) 146 RdC 95.

[29] The question of reservations to human rights treaties will be discussed later.

[30] 1946 International Convention for the Regulation of Whaling (adopted 2 December 1946, entered into force 10 November 1948) 161 UNTS 72.

[31] On the curious circumstances surrounding Iceland's reservation, see A Gillespie, 'Iceland's Reservation at the International Whaling Commission' (2003) 14 EJIL 977.

Iceland through this instrument adheres to the [. . .] Convention and [the 1956] Protocol with a reservation with respect to paragraph 10(e) of the Schedule attached to the Convention. The reservation forms an integral part of this instrument of adherence'.[32] In addition, Iceland made several statements accompanying the reservation, declaring, in the last one, that

> [n]otwithstanding this [reservation], the Government of Iceland will not authorise whaling for commercial purposes by Icelandic vessels before 2006 and, thereafter, will not authorise such whaling while progress is being made in negotiations within the international Whaling Commission on the revised Management Scheme. This does not apply, however, in case of the so-called moratorium in whaling for commercial purposes, contained in paragraph 10 (c) of the Schedule, not being lifted within the reasonable time after the completion of the Revised Management Scheme. Under no circumstances will whaling for commercial purposes be authorised by Iceland without a scientific basis and an effective management and enforcement scheme.[33]

There were several objections to this reservation, such as those from Sweden and the UK. However, a few States explicitly severed the treaty relationship with Iceland. Italy objected to the reservation and stated that 'Iceland, because of its reservation, may not be regarded as a party to the Convention nor a member of the IWC'. Mexico adopted the same approach: '[B]ecause of its reservation, Iceland will not be regarded as a party to the Convention, nor a member of the International Whaling Commission (IWC), insofar as Mexico is concerned'. In vast literature devoted to reservations to treaties, some authors classified the behaviour of States according to either the permissibility or opposability school.[34] However, such a test is not always possible and there are many variations for either of the schools, therefore clear and precise classifications are very difficult to make.

As already mentioned, the regime of the VCLT had left certain issues of the reservations to treaties open and the ILC undertook a project aimed at filling these gaps. Three were the the most important gaps identified in the VCLT regime: reservations to human rights treaties; interpretative declarations; and impermissible reservations.[35]

[32] Cited by Gillespie, 'Iceland's Reservation' 979.

[33] ibid.

[34] See the in-depth analysis of KL McCall-Smith, 'Severing Reservations' (2014) 63 ICLQ 599.

[35] L Sucharipa-Behrmann, 'The Legal Effects of Reservations to Multilateral Treaties' (1996) 1 ARIEL 67.

The work of the ILC on reservations was defined in the following way: 'This is where the Guide steps in, as essentially a Vienna-plus; nominally a nonbinding instrument interpreting and elaborating on the VCLT, but in fact developing it further, filling the gaps, and building upon the wealth of actual post-Vienna treaty practice'.[36] There is a wealth of publications devoted to the Guide to reservations. The question is how it has contributed to the further motion and evolution of State practice relating to reservations. The authors of this study are of the view that even if the Guide were not to be followed by States in their practice on reservations, it would have still made a significant contribution. It identified how this murky area of the law of treaties has evolved during the intervening years and what are the areas of conflict in this respect. According to the Guide, Article 19 VCLT should be regarded as laying down objective criteria for the validity of reservations. Secondly, Articles 20–23 VCLT deal with only those reservations which are objectively valid under Article 19; therefore, they do not pertain in any way to reservations which are impermissible. The Guide deals in a very decisive manner with the question of impermissible reservations. The States may object to reservations that they consider invalid, but this is merely persuasive evidence of invalidity. Consequently, objections have a real legal effect only if they are made against reservations which are objectively valid. Objections may be made for any reason whatsoever. Although the VCLT does not deal with the consequences of impermissible reservations, it may be presumed that such a reservation is null and void. The legal status of a State party to a treaty will depend on the intention of the reserving State, which has a choice – either stay on as a party to the treaty without the benefit of the invalid reservation or say that it no longer considers itself bound by the treaty. In the absence of a clearly expressed position in this regard, there is, according to the ILC, a rebuttable presumption that the reserving State intends to remain a party.[37] The question of the reservations to human rights treaties has been for a long time a subject of long debates, especially in light of the radical judicial practice of some human rights courts, such as the European Court of Human Rights (ECtHR),[38]

[36] Milanovic and Sicilianos, 'Reservations to Treaties' 1056.

[37] ibid 1058, commenting on ILC, 'Guide to Practice on Reservations to Treaties, with Commentaries' Guidelines 4.5.2, 4.3, 4.5.1, 4.5.3, 3.2.1, and 4.5.3.4.

[38] See in particular, *Temeltasch v Switzerland*, ECmmHR (5 May 1982) App No 9116/80; *Belilos v Switzerland*, ECtHR (Judgment on Merits and Just Satisfaction) (29 April 1988) App No 10328/28. See also, KL McCall-Smith, 'Reservations and the Determinative Function of the Human Rights Treaty Bodies' (2012) 54 GYIL 521.

and non-judicial bodies, such as the Human Rights Committee (HRCttee).[39] The severing of invalid reservations by these judicial and non-judicial bodies was not accepted by all governments and scholars as a welcome development, and was considered as interfering with consent to be bound, as the expression by States of their sovereignty.[40] Although there was a multitude of suggested solutions to this question, none of them has been accepted in the practice of States.[41] The same can be said with respect to the practice of the Nordic States, the so-called 'super maximum effect' objections, which were based on the principle of severing of invalid reservations.[42]

The main point at issue was the special character of human rights treaties and the powers of human rights bodies. The authors of this book fully support the views of Pellet that there should not be a special regime of reservations to human rights bodies. Nevertheless, during his work on reservations, Pellet modified to a certain extent his approach and adjusted it to include the role of monitoring bodies of human rights treaties.[43] He also analysed the practice of these bodies on reservations and termed it a 'reservation dialogue' between the monitoring body and the State that made a reservation that was likely incompatible with the

[39] *Kennedy v Trinidad and Tobago*, HRCttee (26 March 2002) UN Doc CCPR/C/67/D/845/1999; see also the views expressed in the HRCtttee's famous General Comment 24; Human Rights Committee, 'General Comment on Issues Relating to Reservations Made upon Ratification or Accession to the Covenant or the Optional Protocols Thereto, or in Relation to Declarations under Article 41 of the Covenant' (4 November 1994) UN Doc CCPR/C/21/Rev.1/Add.6.

[40] France, 'Observations by France on General Comment 24' (1997) 4 IHRR 6; UK, 'Observations by the United Kingdom on General Comment 24' (1996) 3 IHRR 261; US, 'Observations by the United States on General Comment 24' (1996) 3 IHRR 265. See also, R Baratta, 'Should Invalid Reservations to Human Rights Treaties Be Disregarded?' (2000) 11 EJIL 413.

[41] See eg suggestion of Goodman that an acceptable regime should 'include a rule of decision that favours severing an invalid reservation, that is, considering the reservation supererogatory unless it is established that the State intended otherwise'; R Goodman, 'Human Rights Treaties, Invalid Reservations, and State Consent' (2002) 96 AJIL 531, 560.

[42] J Klabbers, 'Accepting the Unacceptable? A New Nordic Approach to Reservations to Multilateral Treaties' (2000) 69 NJIL 179.

[43] According to Milanovic and Sicilianos, 'Reservations to Treaties' 1058, '[t]he Guide even acknowledges that human rights bodies have the competence to assess the validity of reservations, but that this does not empower them to do more than they otherwise could, ie, it would not suddenly make the Human Rights Committee's views binding or formally equal to a judgment of the European Court of Human Rights'.

object and purpose of the treaty, in order to suggest its withdrawal.[44] It may be also mentioned that the regime of the VCLT on reservations was in general assessed as sufficient to deal with reservations to human rights treaties. The debate regarding reservations to human rights treaties is a question which has arisen from the juxtaposing of the 'special character objective' of human rights treaties and a formalistic requirement of consent to be bound, as deriving from the free will of States, which may impose 'an imperialistic regime: whatever is proposed in the name of human rights ideals [which] should have precedence over previous (consensualist, inter-State) regimes'.[45]

However, the regime of reservations to human rights treaties is in a constant flux and evolution, which, in our view cannot be captured through strict and dogmatic provisions. Such an example are the reservations to the Genocide Convention and, in particular, to its Article IX on the procedure on settlement of disputes, which was the provision to which most States made a reservation and which does not constitute a substantive provision of the convention according to the *Congo v Rwanda* case.[46] Congo contended that Rwanda's reservation to Article IX was against the object and purpose of the convention and in conflict with a peremptory norm of general international law. The Court disagreed with Congo and noted that no such norm presently existed requiring a State to consent to the jurisdiction of the Court in order to settle a dispute relating to the Genocide Convention. Rwanda's reservation could not therefore be regarded as lacking legal effect.[47] The Court's approach was much criticised.[48] The dissenting judges observed that new trends in the area of the reservations to human rights treaties, such as the

[44] A Pellet, 'Fifteenth Report on Reservations to Treaties' (31 March, 26 May, and 31 May 2010) UN Doc A/CN.4/624 and Add.1–2; A Pellet and D Müller, 'Reservations to Human Rights Treaties: Not an Absolute Evil...' in U Fastenrath (ed), *From Bilateralism to Community Interest: Essays in Honour of Judge Bruno Simma* (OUP 2011) 531.

[45] See on this extensively, Pergantis, *The Paradigm of State Consent* 234–321 and particularly 285.

[46] *Armed Activities on the Territory of the Congo (New Application: 2002)* [68–9].

[47] Congo presented the same argument in relation to the reservation of Rwanda to Art 22 of the Convention on Racial Discrimination. The Court applied the same reasoning as in the case of the Genocide Convention (*Armed Activities on the Territory of the Congo (New Application: 2002)* [74], [77].

[48] See *Armed Activities on the Territory of the Congo (New Application: 2002)*, Joint Separate Opinion of Judges Higgins, Kooijmans, Elraby, Owada, and Simma 63.

practice of the HRCttee and the ECtHR, put in doubt the '*laissez faire* approach attributed to the International Court's Advisory Opinion of 1951'.[49] They also noted, '[i]ndeed, it is clear that the practice of the International Court itself reflects this trend for tribunals and courts themselves to pronounce on compatibility with object and purpose, when the need arises'.[50] Moreover, the dissenting judges argued that 'Article IX speaks not only of disputes over the interpretation and application of the Convention, but over the "fulfilment of the Convention". Further, the disputes that may be referred to the Court under Article IX "include those relating to the responsibility of a State for genocide". . . . [I]t is thus not self-evident that a reservation to Article IX could not be regarded as incompatible with the object and purpose of the Convention and we believe that this is a matter that the Court should revisit for further consideration'.[51]

Apart from this fundamental issue concerning reservations to treaties, there is also a host of puzzling and murky elements of the VCLT regime, such as the objections to reservations,[52] which may produce a minimum or maximum effect *vis-à-vis* other States, as well as the practice of the UN Secretary General, whose practice appears to be at odds with the rule contained in Article 20(4)(c).[53] In the Summary of Practice of the Secretary-General as Depository of Multilateral Treaties, it is explained that the Secretary-General agreed that any instrument expressing consent to be bound containing reservation may be deposited. The Secretary-General does not assume any position on the question of permissibility or the effects of reservations and to this effect it is indicated that the critical date will be the date on which, in accordance with the treaty provisions, the instrument would normally produce its effect. Each and every party is left to draw the conclusions it deems fit regarding the legal

[49] ibid [15].

[50] ibid [23].

[51] ibid [28–9].

[52] For a recent evaluation of the contemporary 'objection' regime, prompted by the objections raised by many States to Qatar's reservations to the ICCPR, see B Çali, 'Qatar's Reservations to the ICCPR: Anything New under the VCLT Sun?' (*EJIL: Talk!*, 19 September 2019) <www.ejiltalk.org/qatars-reservations-to-the-iccpr-anything-new-under-the-vclt-sun/> accessed 20 September 2019.

[53] G Gaja, 'Unruly Treaty Reservations' in R Ago (ed), *Droit international à l'heure de sa codification: études en l'honneur de Roberto Ago*, Vol 1 (Giuffrè 1987) 307, 323–4; A Pellet and D Müller, 'Reservations to Treaties: An Objection to a Reservation Is Definitely Not an Acceptance' in E Cannizzaro (ed), *The Law of Treaties Beyond the Vienna Convention* (OUP 2011) 36, 42–4.

consequences of the reservations. Therefore, as Pellet and Müller noted, the Secretary-General does not wait for the expression of at least of one acceptance,[54] but treats an instrument of ratification or accession 'in the same way as any other notification or ratification or accession'.[55]

3.4 Evolution of Consent to Be Bound in the Environmental Law Context

Articles 11–17 VCLT codify the customary rules of expression of consent to be bound. However, as Article 11 explicitly states, consent to be bound may be expressed 'by signature, exchange of instruments constituting a treaty, ratification, acceptance, approval or accession, *or by other means is so agreed*'.[56] Consequently, the methods of providing consent to be bound mentioned in Article 11 are not an exhaustive enumeration, and new forms may and have emerged.[57]

One of these, which has emerged in connection to amendment of treaties is that of 'tacit acceptance procedures', which is analysed in much more detail in Chapter 5 of this book. An alternative option is the practice of 'enabling clauses', especially in the context of multilateral environmental agreements (MEAs). According to this practice, States insert in the treaty text provisions that allow COPs/MOPs to adopt decisions that ensure the well-being and functioning of the treaty regime.[58] Depending on the instrument in question these decisions can be of varying degrees of normative forcefulness.

A characteristic example of how far these decisions can reach, even sometimes with a limited or unclear 'enabling clause', is the non-compliance procedure (NCP) of the Kyoto Protocol. According to Article 18 of that treaty, although the procedure would be sketched out in a decision of the CMP, it would produce binding effects only through the

[54] According to the VCLT, a condition for States to become parties to a treaty under Article 20(4)(c).

[55] Pellet and Müller, 'Reservations to Treaties' 43.

[56] Emphasis added.

[57] M Fitzmaurice and P Merkouris, 'Uniformity versus Specialization (1): The Quest for a Uniform Law of Inter-State Treaties' in C Tams, A Tzanakopoulos, and A Zimmermann (eds), *Research Handbook on the Law of Treaties* (Edward Elgar 2014) 341–74.

[58] M Fitzmaurice and DG Costelloe, 'Lawmaking by Treaty: Conclusion of Treaties and Evolution of Treaty Regimes in Practice' in C Brölmann and Y Radi (eds), *Research Handbook on the Theory and Practice of International Lawmaking* (Edward Elgar 2016) 111, 118–23.

amendment procedure provided in the final clauses of the Kyoto Protocol. CMP1 indeed discussed the Kyoto Protocol NCP and established it through Decision 27/CMP.1.[59] However, unlike what Article 18 required, no such amendment ever passed.[60] This may not have been an issue if the NCP was of a 'soft' nature. However, the NCP that was established through Decision 27/CMP.1 gave the Enforcement Branch power to impose sanctions in case of non-compliance. During the functioning of the Kyoto Protocol NCP, ten States submitted themselves willingly to the procedure of the Enforcement Branch.[61] Such an action would seem to indicate that for all intents and purposes State parties consider the NCP a binding one, irrespective of the fact that it was established through a process that was not specified under Article 18.

This practice of binding COP/MOP decisions is on the increase,[62] sometimes even against the express objection of State parties to a treaty regime,[63] and raises many questions regarding the legal basis of the alleged bindingness of this procedure,[64] as well as more general issues

[59] CMP1, 'Decision 27/CMP.1: Procedures and Mechanisms Relating to Compliance under the Kyoto Protocol' (9–10 December 2005) UN Doc FCCC/KP/CMP/2005/8/Add.3.

[60] Saudi Arabia had submitted an amendment proposal but it never entered into force; UNFCCC, 'Proposal from Saudi Arabia to Amend the Kyoto Protocol' (26 May 2005) UN Doc FCCC/KP/CMP/2005/2; see also, S Oberthür and R Lefeber, 'Holding Countries to Account: The Kyoto Protocol's Compliance System Revisited after Four Years of Experience' (2010) 1 Climate L 133, 151 and fn 94.

[61] Greece, Canada, Croatia, Bulgaria, Romania, Ukraine (twice), Lithuania, Slovakia, Monaco, and Kazakhstan; UNFCCC, 'Questions of Implementation' (*UNFCC*, 2019) <http://unfccc.int/kyoto_protocol/compliance/questions_of_implementation/items/5451.php> accessed 20 September 2019.

[62] For analysis and examples, see P Davies, 'Non-Compliance: A Pivotal or Secondary Function of COP Governance?' (2013) 15 ICLR 77, 81–2.

[63] UNEP, 'Decision III/1: Amendment to the Basel Convention' (28 November 1995) UN Doc UNEP/CHW.3/35. In more detail, G Ulfstein, 'Treaty Bodies and Regimes' in DB Hollis (ed), *The Oxford Guide to Treaties* (OUP 2012) 428, 437–8.

[64] T Goehring, 'Treaty-Making and Treaty Evolution' in D Bodansky, J Brunnée, and E Hey (eds), *The Oxford Handbook of International Environmental Law* (OUP 2008) 467, 491 ff; G Handl, 'International "Lawmaking" by Conferences of the Parties and Other Politically Mandated Bodies: Comment', in R Wolfrum and V Röben (eds), *Development of International Law in Treaty Making* (Springer 2005) 127; J Brunnée, 'The Kyoto Protocol: Testing Ground for Compliance Theories?' (2003) 63 ZaöRV 255; G Ulfstein and J Werksman, 'The Kyoto Compliance System: Towards Hard Enforcement' in OS Stokke, J Hovi, and G Ulfstein (eds), *Implementing the Climate Regime: International Compliance* (Earthscan 2005) 39, 57–8; J Brunnée, 'COPing with Consent: Law-Making Under Multilateral Environmental Agreements' (2002) 15 LJIL 1; R Churchill and G Ulfstein, 'Autonomous Institutional Arrangements in Multilateral Environmental Agreements: A Little-Noticed Phenomenon in International Law' (2000) 94 AJIL 623; Pr Weil,

on legitimacy.[65] Various theories have been suggested to account for the legal effects of certain of these decisions, including that: the consent has trickled down to the decisions through the enabling clauses;[66] that these decisions enjoy a quasi-binding, 'soft' or *de facto* status,[67] which Churchill and Ulfstein have coined as 'autonomous institutional arrangements';[68] or that the binding effect is a result of 'implied powers'.[69] The argument has also been made that even when the treaty itself does not authorise the COP/MOP to take binding decisions, these are still important for interpretative purposes as 'subsequent practice' of Article 31(3)(b) VCLT.[70] However, as Fitzmaurice and Costelloe point out, such decisions are more 'subsequent practice *of the treaty body*' rather than 'subsequent practice *of the parties*'.[71]

3.5 Theorising Consent in International Law

There are numerous theories concerning the importance of consent and above all its validation of legitimacy in international law. The traditional, classical approach to consent has emphasised its absolute role in

'Towards Relative Normativity in International Law' (1983) 77 AJIL 413, 421. The authors of the present book have argued that modification (not interpretation) through subsequent practice could be a potential legal basis; Fitzmaurice and Merkouris, 'Uniformity versus Specialization'.

65 D Bodansky, 'The Legitimacy of International Governance: A Coming Challenge for International Environmental Law?' (1999) 93 AJIL 596; A Wiersema, 'The New International Law-Makers? Conferences of the Parties to Multilateral Environmental Agreements' (2009) 1 MichJInt'lL 231; LK Camenzuli, 'The Development of International Environmental Law at the Multilateral Environmental Agreements: Conference of the Parties and Its Validity' <http://cmsdata.iucn.org/downloads/cel10_camenzuli.pdf> 26, accessed 20 September 2019.

66 J Brunnée, '"Reweaving" the Fabric of International Law? Patterns of Consent in Environmental Framework Agreements' in R Wolfrum and V Röben (eds), *Developments in International Law-Making* (Springer 2005) 101, 112.

67 Brunnée, '"Reweaving" the Fabric of International Law?' 111; Oberthür and Lefeber, 'Holding Countries to Account' 151–2.

68 They also conclude that '[i]n spite of their formal denomination, we nevertheless conclude that these self-governing, treaty-based AIAs [autonomous institutional arrangements] of MEAs may be considered to be IGOs, albeit of a less formal, more *ad hoc* nature than traditional IGOs'; Churchill and Ulfstein, 'Autonomous Institutional Arrangements' 625.

69 *Reparation for Injuries Suffered in the Service of the United Nations* (Advisory Opinion) [1949] ICJ Rep 174, 180; Churchill and Ulfstein, 'Autonomous Institutional Arrangements' 633–4.

70 Ulfstein, 'Treaty Bodies and Regimes' 437–41; Davies, 'Non-Compliance' 81-2.

71 Fitzmaurice and Costelloe, 'Lawmaking by Treaty' 127.

formation of obligations for States, which in broad brushstrokes means that that consent is the basis of the binding force of international law on a State. Such a view can be substantiated by the case law of the PCIJ[72] and the ICJ[73] and also the views of scholars[74].

As Guzman observed, there are three main arguments that strengthen the role of consent in international law. Consent encourages compliance with international law, it raises the legitimacy on the system, and finally it protects against harmful changes in international law.[75] The same author argues that these key roles of consent are debatable. For example, in relation to the first argument, it may be said that incomplete compliance with an important rule is better than not having the rule at all. Guzman argues that States' consent does not automatically ensure that they wish to or will comply.[76] Guzman also argues that unanimous consent does not always secure legitimacy. There is a possibility to evolve a non-consensual legitimacy system, through, for example, delegating authority to international tribunals operating with some form of consent from States so that the consent is provided in advance of a specific dispute.[77]

Similarly, Besson has analysed consent from the point of view of the validity of its legitimate authority. From the theoretical point of view, there is a paradox in international law since international law-making is riddled with reasonable disagreement and yet no State can be bound by international law without its consent.[78] According to Besson, such a paradox can be resolved based on circumstances of reasonable disagreement. This theory is based on the premise that consent is neither a criterion for validity nor a ground for its legitimate authority. It is argued that State consent is necessary neither to legal positivism nor to State

[72] *The Case of SS Lotus (France v Turkey)* (Judgment) PCIJ Rep Series A No 10, 18 ('The rules of law binding upon States . . . emanate from their own free will').

[73] *Nicaragua* (Merits) [269] ('in international law there are no rules, other than such rules as may be accepted by the States concerned, by treaty or otherwise').

[74] See eg, L Henkin, 'International Law: Politics. Values, and Functions' (1989) 216 RdC 9, 27 ('A State is not subject to any external authority unless it has voluntarily consented to such authority').

[75] A Guzman, 'The Consent Problem in International Law', Berkeley Programme in International Law and Economics, Working Paper Series (2011) 9, <https://escholarship.org/content/qt04x8x174/qt04x8x174.pdf> accessed 20 September 2019.

[76] ibid 9.

[77] ibid 12.

[78] S Besson, 'State Consent and Disagreement in International Law-Making: *Dissolving the Paradox*' (2016) 29 LJIL 289.

sovereignty. The role of democratic State consent is that of an exception to the legitimate authority of international law and therefore to its bindingness in a concrete case. Besson has dispelled some myths linked to international law-making and the consent in cases regarding customary international law and the law of treaties. She readily admits that international treaty-making is considered to be the 'epitome' of law-making by consent and hence by an 'agreement'. However, she further reasons, 'the reasonable disagreement amounts to a permanent concern of secondary rules of treaty law'.[79] Besson argues that although treaties exemplify the expression of mutual consent, this does not need to imply a complete agreement. She suggests that the best approach is to treat them as incompletely theorised agreements or at the very least as agreements to disagree, such as rules on reservations, on interpretation and on intractable treaty conflicts in the international law of treaties.[80] She correctly observes that in case of reservations, disagreements play a role within the realm of the law of treaties since reservations are only permitted providing that State parties agree to disagree, usually in a tacit manner. She also notes that reservations are never definitive and may always be withdrawn, thereby extending the consent on the whole treaty.[81] The question is what happens if the consent regards reservations which are not compatible with the treaty. She notes that the rule was that the parties usually sought to decide individually on the objections and approval of reservations, as we already noted above. From this principle, Besson draws the conclusion that State consent should always be respected even if the reservation is deemed invalid and that the issue of the bindingness of the treaty as a whole arises again. Besson refers to practice of the human rights bodies in respect to reservations, and comes to the conclusion that 'democratic State consent only amounts to an exception to the obligations arising out of international treaties on other grounds and an exception whose justification in not necessarily granted, especially in the context of imperative and core duties of international human rights law'.[82]

The rule on treaty interpretation can also serve as an example of a disagreement despite the primary consent to be bound by a treaty. The rule on interpretation, according to Besson, is rather broad and

[79] ibid 313.
[80] ibid.
[81] ibid 314.
[82] ibid.

pluralistic in in its constraints. She singles out in particular the subsequent agreements of the State parties in this context.[83]

Intractable treaty conflicts under Article 30(3) and (4) of the VCLT are a further example where disagreement plays a significant role. This article refers also to treaty conflicts[84] to which there is no remedy or a rule of conflict.[85] As Besson surmises, States 'acknowledge rather that consent may sometimes be used to disagree and not to agree completely on a given issue'.[86]

3.6 Consent to Be Bound and Classification of Treaties

The question of consent to be bound is closely related to the theoretical but also practical question of the classification of treaties as well. It has an impact on the termination of the participation in a treaty, and generally it influences the limits of changes in the treaty text, which in fact are also to some extent expressions of consent to be bound. It can be said from the outset that there are no fool-proof classifications of treaties, and that rich treaty practice defies strict frames of classifications, which would reflect in an absolute and categorical manner all possible categories of treaties. The question of the classification or typology of treaties and obligations contained therein has been extensively debated within the forum of the ILC. Since the whole discussion is outside the framework of this chapter,[87] suffice it to say that the typologies envisaged by Fitzmaurice are extensively debated, as his thought has an impact on the permutations of consent of the State parties to the treaty.

Classification of treaties has intrigued international law scholars, however, from the early days.[88] This section is mostly devoted to the modern classification of treaties and its impact on consent. As we have already observed, all classifications are imperfect. One of the first dominant classification was the well-known division between treaties of a contractual character and legislative treaties (*traités-lois*).[89] The schematic and

[83] ibid.

[84] Eg with non-identical parties.

[85] Art 30(4) and (5) VCLT.

[86] ibid. See also S Ranganathan, 'Between Philosophy and Anxiety? The Early International Law Commission, Treaty Conflict, and the Project of International Law' (2012) 83 BYIL 82, 91.

[87] On this subject, see extensively Pergantis, *The Paradigm of State Consent* 42–67.

[88] On early attempts on classification, see ibid 39–42.

[89] A subcategory can be distinguished in which the distinction can be made by focusing on *negotium*. Treaties may be classified depending on their statutory character or on their

unduly formalistic view considered that the category of contractual treaties was based on reciprocal obligations and the principle *do ut des*, while legislative treaties established general obligations aimed at the entire community of States; this view does not reflect the reality of treaty practice. If one follows the dichotomy between treaties of the contractual kind and legislative treaties, then there should be special rules governing consent to be bound in relation to such treaties, concerning their termination and suspension. It could be argued that this is reflected in the provisions concerning material breach of a treaty.[90] Such rules are formulated in a far stricter and more rigorous manner than in relation to contractual treaties, even prohibiting the termination or suspension of such treaties altogether.[91] However, in the view of the present authors, the different manner in which certain provisions are regulated concerning consent to be bound is dictated rather by the aim of the provisions protecting individual rights rather than by the law-making character of a treaty. There is, in our view, a methodological error in equating treaties which are law-making (and supposedly not based on reciprocity) and treaties which are contractual. There are no treaties which would be contractual or law-making in their entirety; they all retain some degree of reciprocity.[92] The view held by the majority of scholars that the 'special' law -making type of the agreements regulating the position of an individual is not based on reciprocity between States somewhat dismisses the fact that States are the subjects which conclude such agreements, and therefore, certain reciprocity between them has to be maintained (at least in the matters concerning consent to be bound, the entry into force and the management of the treaty, such as in relation to reservations). From the point of view of the law of treaties, States parties to such treaties remain the masters of treaties, concerning the procedural and substantive aspects of such treaties, including the scope of rights accorded by them to an individual. Therefore, the distinction between these two types of treaties appears to have little or no significance in relation to treaties.[93]

contractual character. See C Brölmann, 'Law-Making Treaties: Form and Function in International Law' (2005) 74 NJIL 383.

90 Art 60(5) VCLT, concerning the termination and suspension of humanitarian treaties.

91 A d'Amato, 'Treaties as a Source of General Rules of International Law' (1962) 3 Harvard International Law Club Bulletin 1, 15; Pergantis, *The Paradigm of State Consent.*

92 ILC, 'Report of the Commission to the General Assembly on the Work of its 49th Session' [1997/II – Part Two] YBILC 1, 47 [69].

93 See Pergantis, *The Paradigm of State Consent* 47.

The seminal typology of treaties introduced by Fitzmaurice, although revolutionary from the point of view of the introduction of the different type of obligations in his triad of treaties, has not solved the procedural aspects in the field of consent to be bound which would correspond to varied obligations contained in treaties. Fitzmaurice distinguished between treaties' obligations as 'reciprocal' or 'concessionary' obligations, on one hand, and 'integral' obligations, on the other. Multilateral treaties of the 'reciprocating type' contain a nexus of bilateralisable obligations 'providing for a mutual interchange of benefits between the parties', the 1961 Vienna Convention on Diplomatic Relations[94] being an example.[95] Multilateral treaties of the 'integral type' are those 'where the force of the obligations is self-existent, absolute and inherent for each party',[96] directed 'towards all the world rather than towards particular parties' and they 'do not lend themselves to differential application, but must be applied integrally', the Genocide Convention being an example of such a treaty.[97] These types of obligations generate different results concerning their suspension or termination. A fundamental breach of treaty obligations could lead to suspension or termination.[98] Later treaties conflicting with previous ones of the reciprocal type are not null and void.[99] Integral treaties cannot be terminated or suspended by the other parties as a result of a breach, as not dependent on the performance of other parties to the treaty.[100] Any subsequent treaty concluded by a few, not all, parties to an integral treaty and conflicting directly in substance with the earlier integral treaty will be, to the extent of the conflict, 'null and void'.[101] Fitzmaurice distinguished a third category of treaties, the so-called 'interdependent' treaties, which are based on the participation of all the parties, which is 'a condition of the obligatory force of the treaty', disarmament treaties being a prime example.[102] Such treaties could be terminated in case of a fundamental breach in their entirety by the other

[94] 1961 Vienna Convention on Diplomatic Relations (adopted 18 April 1961, entered into force 24 April 1964) 500 UNTS 95.

[95] G Fitzmaurice, 'Third Report on the Law of Treaties' (18 March 1958) UN Doc A/CN.4/115, Commentary to Art 18 [78], reproduced in [1958/II] YBILC 20, 41.

[96] ibid 28.

[97] G Fitzmaurice, 'Second Report on the Law of Treaties' (15 March 1957) UN Doc A/CN.4/107 [126], [128], reproduced in [1957/II] YBILC 16, 54–5.

[98] ibid Art 19.

[99] Fitzmaurice, 'Third Report' Art 18.

[100] Fitzmaurice, 'Second Report' Art 19(iv).

[101] Fitzmaurice, 'Third Report' Art 19.

[102] Fitzmaurice, 'Second Report' Art 29(1)(iii).

parties in case of fundamental breach. This is due to their character, which requires performance of all parties, which is dependent on equal or corresponding performances by all the other parties.[103] A later treaty which conflicts directly in substance with the earlier treaty will be, to the extent of the conflict, 'null and void'.[104]

It may be said that in the case of Fitzmaurice's typologies of the obligations, on the one hand we are faced with a loose bond created by concessionary obligations, which, on the other hand, is contrasted with the communitarian regime of integral and interdependent obligations, which creates a treaty system detached from the will of the States.[105] However, a closer scrutiny of interdependent obligations leads to the conclusion that from the point of view of consent to be bound, these obligations represent 'a radically reciprocal functioning of the treaty bond, not in the sense of bilateralisation of the treaty relations but in the sense of an indivisible unity'.[106]

It was observed that within the paradigm of interdependent obligations, reciprocity functions between a defaulting party and all other non-defaulting parties to the treaty as an indivisible whole. Therefore, such a type of obligations leads to oscillating between a strict bilateralism and a strict communitarianism, which may result in the entry into force of a treaty only upon the condition of expression of consent to be bound of all other parties; and the right to accede may be granted upon the unanimous decision of all the State parties. Similarly, withdrawal by one party may result in the termination of a treaty, and modification of a treaty may be conditioned upon unanimity of all States parties to the treaty. Such an obligation is based on a premise that the notion of an injured State relates to all States parties to a treaty.[107]

[103] ibid Art 19(1)(ii)(b).

[104] Fitzmaurice, 'Third Report' Art 19.

[105] Pergantis, *The Paradigm of State Consent* 50.

[106] ibid.

[107] ibid 50–1. To a less sophisticated degree, the subsequent attempts by the ILC regarding the classification of treaties also touched upon consent to be bound by a treaty. The typology of treaties was also debated within the ILC by Waldock. He adopted a numerical criterion (bilateral; plurilateral and multilateral treaties). Such a classification was objected to by some members of the Commission. However, the ILC came up later with an idea of 'a general multilateral treaty' (a treaty dealing with matters of a general interest to States and concerning norms of general international law). In relation to consent, it could be presumed that since such a general multilateral treaty would be binding on the community of States, consent would be unnecessary (Pergantis, *The Paradigm of State Consent* 54).

3.7 Conclusions

Motion is very evident in the area of consent to be bound. The developments in human rights law and environmental law have resulted in practice which has tried to overcome the non-bilateral character of the law of treaties, which in some cases include integral obligations. As Chinkin dramatically stated, '[t]he human rights world is very different from that envisaged by the VCLT: the latter is an empty, amoral world where States have reciprocal dealings only with other States , where there are no people hurt by States'.[108] It is a world, according to her, without NGOs and monitoring bodies.[109] Therefore, the HRCttee has attempted to free the reservations regime from the shackles of the bilateralism regime.[110] The ILC's Guidelines clearly indicate this forward motion of the reservations regime. The VCLT regime on reservations was found in the end to be sufficient to deal with reservations to human rights treaties. However, the developments in this area by human rights bodies, international human rights courts, and the ILC signal a *kinesis*, which had not been foreseen during the drafting on the VCLT. Finally, the structure of Multilateral Environmental Agreements (MEAs) is yet another example of the evolution of consent to be bound. These treaties are constructed in a way, where the treaty text lays down the fundamental rights and obligations of State parties, leaving for their respective bodies to build further layers of obligations and regulations directed at States. In conclusion, a common thread connecting all these diverse examples is that consent to be bound, a notion fundamental to the law of treaties, is in a state of constant motion.

[108] Chr Chinkin, 'Human Rights' in Bowman and Kritsiotis (eds), *Conceptual and Contextual Perspectives* 509, 511.

[109] ibid.

[110] B Simma and G Hernández, 'Legal Consequences of an Impermissible Reservation to a Human Rights Treaty: Where Do We Stand?' in Cannizzaro (ed), *The Law of Treaties Beyond the Vienna Convention* 60, 84.

4

Treaty Interpretation and Its Rules

Of Motion through Time, 'Time-Will', and 'Time-Bubbles'

4.1 Introduction

It's time that rules, time is our gambling partner on the other side of the table, and it holds all the cards of the deck in its hand.

José Saramago, *Blindness*[1]

In the previous chapters, the concept of 'motion' of treaties and of treaty law was discussed mainly within the frame of reference of changes to the 'object-state' of the rules under examination. However, motion is to be understood not only through space but also through time. Nowhere is this more evident in the law of treaties than in treaty interpretation, and it is exactly this motion through spacetime that will be the focus of this chapter. This chapter analyses the manner in which time and temporal considerations affect the substance of treaty rights and obligations, and which rules (if any) govern this particular motion of treaties. Furthermore, since motion as demonstrated by Einstein is dependent on the observer's particular frame of reference,[2] so in this chapter the analysis will move between the two critical frames of references: (i) that of the treaty being interpreted, ie whether from a substantive and interpretative point of view it remains at a state of *stasis* (contemporaneous interpretation) or whether it changes/evolves through time (evolutive interpretation) and (ii) that of the rules of interpretation, ie whether these interpretative rules are constants, immutable and perennial ones, in the system of the law of treaties or are as any other rule potentially subject to motion and change through the temporal dimension.

[1] J Saramago, *Blindness* (Harvest Books 1999) 318.

[2] See Chapter 1 of this book.

As is evident from these preliminary thoughts, in this chapter the concepts of time and motion through time, *inter alia* in the form of content (non-change), are critical in our analysis. The study of time and the changes effectuated by and through the passage of time have always been central to logic, philosophy, mathematics, and physics. Zeno's arrow paradox,[3] Heraclitus's river paradox,[4] and Theseus's ship paradox[5] are but a few examples from Antiquity that demonstrate not only the fascination of ancient philosophers with the notion of time and change, but also how tangled and multi-dimensional even the simplest thought experiments could become when tackled from the angle of time and change.

Legal science and, for our purposes, international law is no stranger to the complexities and the problems that the passage of time can produce. The principle of *tempus regit actum*, the principle of contemporaneity and inter-temporal law are but a few manifestations of the approaches that have emerged through practice in order to respond to the inherent difficulties of deciding in the present on matters of the near or far removed past. Several seminal academic works have been devoted to tackling the concept of time in international law from a variety of angles.[6]

The purpose of this chapter is to address neither the notion of 'time' in its totality nor all the temporal aspects that come in one way or another within the process of interpretation. What will be demonstrated is firstly that in legal interpretation there are well-established rules that govern the motion of treaties through time, and to present the key features of these rules.[7] Secondly, and perhaps more interestingly, what will be shown is

[3] N Huggett, 'Zeno's Paradoxes' (*Stanford Encyclopedia of Philosophy*, 15 October 2010) accessed 20 September 2019.

[4] Heraclitus as quoted in: Plato, *Cratylus* 402a (ancient Greek text and translation available at the Perseus Digital Library: <www.perseus.tufts.edu/hopper> accessed 20 September 2019).

[5] Plutarch, *Theseus* ch 23.1 (available at the Perseus Digital Library as above). An interesting variation on the theme is offered by Hobbes, *Elements of Philosophy* ch XI, s 7.

[6] S Rosenne, *The Time Factor in the Jurisdiction of the International Court of Justice* (Sythoff 1960) 11–75; AA Cançado Trindade, 'The Time Factor in the Application of the Rule of Exhaustion of Local Remedies in International Law' (1978) 61 RivDirInternaz 232–57; P Tavernier, *Recherches sur l' application dans le temps des actes et des règles en droit international public: problèmes de droit intertemporel ou de droit transitoire* (LGDJ 1979); R Higgins, 'Some Observations on the Inter-temporal Rule in International Law' in J Makarczyk (ed), *Theory of International Law at the Threshold of the 21st Century* (Kluwer Law International 1996) 173–81. For a great overview of the various theories on interpretation and the effect of time on it, see E Roucounas, *A Landscape of Contemporary Theories of International Law* (Brill/Martinus Nijhoff 2019) 600–13.

[7] Section 4.2 of this chapter (excluding Section 4.2.2.2) is an updated version of the ideas that appear in ch 2 Merkouris, *Article 31(3)(c) VCLT* ch 2.

also a form of 'double-think' that seems to be pervasive when we switch our frame of reference to the VCLT rules themselves.[8] Whereas when dealing with treaty rules judges and academics are familiar and often pay lip service to the fact that the law to be applied is the law contemporaneous to the relevant juridical fact, nonetheless in the case of interpretation and in particular the rules that govern interpretation, the notion of 'time' becomes rather 'relative'. What we mean by this is that even when interpreting treaties concluded before 1980,[9] in some cases even treaties of the nineteenth century, most have no hesitation to refer to the VCLT rules on interpretation. However, that would be methodologically appropriate, only if one of the following two propositions were valid; either the rules on interpretation are ubiquitous and immutable, or they are capable of moving backwards through time, ie of 'time-travelling'. As will be shown in Section 4.3 of this chapter, neither of the aforementioned propositions holds up to scrutiny.

4.2 Contemporaneous Interpretation v Evolutive Interpretation: Content *Stasis* v Content Motion

4.2.1 Interpretative Motion through Time: Intertemporality and Its Connection to Interpretation

Intertemporal law is a concept central to the *kata chronon metavole* of treaties. Despite this, its exact content is somewhat elusive. Judge Huber's *dictum* in the *Island of Palmas case* is the passage most often cited in connection to intertemporality:

> a juridical fact must be appreciated in the light of the law contemporary with it ... The same principle which subjects the act creative of a right to the law in force at the time the right arises, demands that the *existence of the right, in other words its continued manifestation, shall follow the conditions required by the evolution of law.*[10]

However, as Higgins rightly points out this quote has been read 'in the most remarkably extensive fashion, as providing obligatory rules

[8] With a particular emphasis to the ICJ.

[9] Year of entry into force of the VCLT.

[10] *The Island of Palmas* case *(or Miangas) (Netherlands v USA)* (1928) 2 UNRIAA 829, 845 (emphasis added).

in circumstances that it never addressed, with consequences that it never intended'.[11] This fluidity in the content and substance of inter-temporality is also reflected in the multitudinous terms associated with it. Indicatively, 'international intertemporal law',[12] 'doctrine of intertemporal law',[13] 'rule of intertemporal law',[14] 'rule of intertemporality',[15] 'intertemporal principle'[16], 'principle of intertemporal law'[17] and 'principle of the intertemporality of law'.[18]

Both legs of Huber's *dictum* concern the determination of the existence or non-existence of rights, not the determination of its content, so one could wonder if there is a connection with interpretation.[19] However, as Fitzmaurice observed, the principle of contemporaneity can be understood as a '*particular application of the doctrine of inter-temporal law [within treaty interpretation]*',[20] a view that seems to be shared by judges and academics alike.[21]

[11] R Higgins, 'Time and the Law: International Perspectives on an Old Problem' (1997) 46 ICLQ 501, 516.

[12] G Schwarzenberger, *A Manual of International Law* (3rd edn, Stevens 1952) 559; Zh Li, 'International Intertemporal Law' (2018) 48/2 CalWInt'lLJ 342.

[13] TO Elias, 'The Doctrine of Intertemporal Law' (1980) 74 AJIL 285 ff.

[14] *Land and Maritime Boundary between Cameroon and Nigeria*, Separate Opinion of Judge Al-Khasawneh [12]; *Jan de Nul NV and Dredging International NV v Egypt* (Award of 24 October 2008) ICSID Case No ARB/04/13 [132].

[15] *Anglia Auto Accessories Limited v Czech Republic* (Final Award of 10 March 2017) SCC Case No V 2014/181 [146].

[16] *Spence International Investments LLC and Others v Costa Rica* (Interim Award of 30 May 2017) ICSID Case No UNCT/13/2 [222]; *Duke Energy International Peru Investments No 1, Ltd v Peru* (Decision of the *Ad hoc* Committee of 1 March 2011) ICSID Case No ARB/03/28 [175] citing *Mondev International Ltd v USA* [70]; *Pac Rim Cayman LLC v El Salvador* (Decision on the Respondent's Jurisdictional Objections of 1 June 2012) ICSID Case No ARB/09/12 [2.79]; *ATA Construction, Industrial and Trading Company v Jordan* (Award of 12 May 2010) ICSID Case No ARB/08/2 [109].

[17] *Société Générale v Dominican Republic* (Award on Preliminary Objections to Jurisdiction of 19 September 2008) LCIA Case No UN 7927 [78]; *Case of the Serrano Cruz Sisters v El Salvador* (Merits, Reparations, and Costs) IACtHR Series C No 120 (1 March 2005) Dissenting Opinion of Judge AA Cançado Trindade [69].

[18] *MCI Power Group LC and New Turbine Incorporated v Ecuador* (Award of 26 July 2007) ICSID Case No ARB/03/6 [89].

[19] U Linderfalk, 'Doing the Right Thing for the Right Reason – Why Dynamic or Static Approaches Should Be Taken in the Interpretation of Treaties' (2008) 10 ICLR 109, 117–8.

[20] Fitzmaurice, 'The Law and Procedure of the International Court of Justice, 1951–4: Treaty Interpretation' 225 (emphasis added).

[21] *Arbitration Regarding the Iron Rhine ('Izjeren Rijn') Railway (Belgium v Netherlands)* (2005) 27 UNRIAA 35 [79]; *Caesar v Trinidad and Tobago* (Merits, Reparations, and Costs) IACtHR Series C No 123 (11 March 2005) Separate Opinion of Judge Cançado

The link between intertemporality and the process of interpretation was not for the first time observed by Judge Huber. Both Vattel and Grotius had included in their writings an analysis of the effect of time on treaties and, in fact, came down on the side of the principle of contemporaneity arguing, '[l]anguages vary incessantly, and the signification and force of words change with time. When an ancient act is to be interpreted, we should then know the common use of the terms at the time when it was written'.[22]

Despite this, and perhaps surprisingly, the connection between the interpretative process and intertemporality would again be seriously discussed in the international arena by the ILC. Although the Institut de Droit International had delved into several of its sessions in the 1950s on the law of treaties and particularly treaty interpretation, only Lauterpacht seems to have raised the issue and then again only *in passim*.[23] The ILC discussions on intertemporality were the completely opposite to the lackluster interest that the Institut had shown to the topic. Attempts to introduce explicit references to intertemporality happened along two main tracks. First, an article devoted specifically to intertemporality was proposed. Waldock in his 'Third Report' included a draft article entitled 'Inter-temporal Law', which followed closely Huber's *dictum* in *Island of Palmas*.[24] Draft Article 56(1) enshrined the principle of contemporaneity, which in Waldock's view was already customary law.[25] In his view, the reason for the principle being

Trindade [10]; M Kotzur, 'Intertemporal Law' [2008] MPEPIL 1433[11–122]; Elias, 'The Doctrine of Intertemporal Law' 301; G Fitzmaurice, 'The Law and Procedure of the International Court of Justice, 1951–4: General Principles and Sources of Law' (1953) 30 BYIL 1, 5–8; C McLachlan, 'The Principle of Systemic Integration and Article 31(3)(c) of the Vienna Convention' (2005) 54/2 ICLQ 279, 316.

22 E de Vattel, *The Law of Nations or Principles on the Law of Nature Applied to the Conduct and Affairs of Nations and Sovereigns* (GGJ and J Robinson 1793) Book II, ch XVII [272].

23 Institut de Droit International, 'De l' interprétation des traités' (1952) 44 AIDI 359, 405 (Lauterpacht). Two decades later the Institut would return again to the issue of intertemporality (not only from an interpretative perspective) and adopt a resolution, that is almost a *verbatim* reproduction of Huber's *dictum*; Institut de Droit International, 'Resolution of 11 August 1975: The Intertemporal Problem in Public International Law' (1975) 56 AIDI 536 [1], [3], [4].

24 'Article 56 – Inter-temporal law: 1. A Treaty is to be interpreted in the light of law in force at the time when the treaty was drawn up, [but] 2. Subject to paragraph 1, the *application* of a treaty shall be governed by the rules of international law in force at the time *when the treaty is applied*'. (emphasis added); Waldock, ''Third Report' 8–9.

25 As shown by the following cases to which he referred: *Grisbådarna Case (Norway v Sweden)* (1909) 11 UNRIAA 147, 159–60; *North Atlantic Coast Fisheries Case (Great*

supported by international jurisprudence was that it closest reflected the *will of the parties*.[26] Draft Article 56 was at the epicenter of a fiery debate, regarding the limits between interpretation and application,[27] the autonomy of the article with respect to the other articles on the law of treaties,[28] and the hierarchy between the subparagraphs of Draft Article 56. With respect to the latter, three were the main approaches: (i) the principle of contemporaneity was the rule and evolutive interpretation the exception;[29] (ii) evolutive interpretation was the rule and the principle of contemporaneity was the exception;[30] and (iii) that the two paragraphs of Draft Article 56 were neither in conflict nor in a hierarchical relationship, but should be applied in a complementary fashion.[31]

Britain v USA) (1910) 11 UNRIAA 167, 196; *Case Concerning Rights of Nationals of the United States of America in Morocco, (France v USA)* (Judgment) [1952] ICJ Rep 176, 189 (hereinafter *US Nationals in Morocco*).

26 Waldock, 'Third Report' 10.

27 ILC, 'Summary Record of the 728th Meeting' (21 May 1964) UN Doc A/CN.4/SR.728 [12] (Paredes). The debate on where to draw the line (if there is one) between these two concepts continues even today: Gardiner, *Treaty Interpretation* 26; C de Visscher, *Problémes d' interprétation judiciaire en droit international public* (Pedone 1963) 27–28; A Gourgourinis, 'The Distinction between Interpretation and Application of Norms in International Adjudication' (2011) 2/1 JIDS 31–57; C Lo, *Treaty Interpretation under the Vienna Convention on the Law of Treaties: A New Round for Codification* (Springer 2017) 81–97; S Sur, *L' interprétation en droit international public* (LGDJ 1974) 193; MK Yasseen, 'L' interprétation des traités d'après la Convention de Vienne sur le Droit des Traités' (1976) 151 RdC 1, 9–10; M Bos, *A Methodology of International Law* (North-Holland 1984) 112; R Kolb, *Interprétation et création du droit international: esquisses d'une herméneutique juridique moderne pour le droit international public* (Bruylant 2006); H Coing, 'Trois formes historiques du droit: glossateurs, pandectistes, école de l'exégèse' (1970) 48 RHD 531, 540–2; J Klabbers, 'Reluctant "Grundnormen": Articles 31(3)(c) and 42 of the Vienna Convention on the Law of Treaties and the Fragmentation of International Law' in M Craven, M Fitzmaurice, and M Vogiatzi (eds), *Time, History and International Law* (Martinus Nijhoff 2007) 141, 144; *Applicability of the Obligation to Arbitrate under Section 21 of the United Nations Headquarters Agreement of 26 June 1947* (Advisory Opinion) [1988] ICJ Rep 12, Separate Opinion of Judge Shahabuddeen 59.

28 ILC, 'Summary Record of the 728th Meeting' [6] (Verdross); ILC, 'Summary Record of the 729th Meeting' (22 May 1964) UN Doc A/CN.4/SR.729 [18–9] (Elias), [30–2] (de Luna), [41–4] (Tunkin), [49] (El-Erian) and [53–5] (Lachs).

29 ILC, 'Summary Record of the 728th Meeting' [12–3] (Paredes); ILC, 'Summary Record of the 729th Meeting' [31–7] (de Luna); Sixth Committee, '20th Session, Summary Record of the 843rd Meeting' (7 October 1965) UN Doc A/C.6/20/SR.843 [25] (UK).

30 ILC, 'Summary Record of the 729th Meeting' [3] (Castrén); Sixth Committee, '20th Session, Summary Record of the 845th Meeting' (11 October 1965) UN Doc A/C.6/SR.845 [41–2] (Greece).

31 ILC, 'Summary Record of the 729th Meeting' [14–5] (Rosenne), [38–40] (Briggs) and [54] (Lachs).

In all of these debates, however, what everybody agreed on was that the will of the parties was the decisive criterion for determining the rules that applied to a treaty *medio tempore*,[32] an approach that found the States in agreement as well.[33] This was, however, not enough to secure enough momentum for Draft Article 56 to be included in the adopted articles. Nonetheless, during the Vienna Conferences on the Law of Treaties, Waldock reiterated the importance of intertemporal law for the law of treaties, but acknowledged that the omission of an article devoted to intertemporal law was the tactically and politically correct choice to avoid the discussions being prolonged and weighed down by never-ending discussions on the relationship between customary law and treaty law.[34]

However, the rejected Draft Article 56 was not the only attempt to introduce a point of entry of intertemporal considerations in the VCLT. The second manner in which the doctrine almost found its way in the text of the VCLT was through the articles on treaty interpretation and more specifically Article 31(3)(c) VCLT. Article 31(3)(c) provides that account shall be taken of 'any relevant rules of international law applicable in the relations between the parties'. The question that the members of the ILC debated was which rules, from a temporal perspective, fell under this provision. Should a treaty be interpreted in the light of the rules *in force at the time of the conclusion of the treaty or in force at the time of the interpretation of a treaty*? Both approaches had their supporters.[35] In order to resolve the impasse Waldock proposed the following text: 'in the light of the rules of international law [in force at the time of its conclusion]'.[36] However, this did not have the compromissory effect

32 ILC, 'Summary Record of the 729th Meeting' [30] (de Luna); similarly ibid [24–6] (Tsuruoka); ILC, 'Summary Record of the 728th Meeting' [10–1] (de Aréchaga), [12–4] (Paredes).

33 Sixth Committee, '20th Session, Summary Record of the 850th Meeting' (13 October 1965) UN Doc A/C.6/SR.850 [40] (Kenya); Sixth Committee, 'Summary Record of the 845th Meeting' [9] (Syria).

34 United Nations Conference on the Law of Treaties, '1st Session – 33rd Meeting of the Committee of the Whole (COW)' (22 April 1968) UN Doc A/CONF.39/C.1/SR.33 177 [74].

35 In favour of the more static view, ie rules in force at the time of the conclusion of the treaty, see ILC, 'Summary Record of the 765th Meeting' (14 July 1964) UN Doc A/CN.4/SR.765 [56–9] (Yasseen), [75–6] (Pal), [80] (Chairman). In favour of the more evolutive approach, ie rules in force at the time of the interpretation of the treaty, see ibid [48–9] (Tunkin), [62] (Verdross), [63–6] (Bartoš).

36 ILC, 'Summary Record of the 769th Meeting' (17 July 1964) UN Doc A/CN.4/SR.769 [3] (Waldock).

that Waldock hoped for.[37] For this reason, Waldock in his 'Sixth Report' removed the bracketed part of the sentence.[38] In this way, the provision would be vague enough to ensure maximum flexibility,[39] while at the same time making it easier to achieve as close possible to a consensus among the ILC members.[40] This flexible approach was the one tabled for the Vienna Conference on the Law of Treaties and found most States in absolute agreement. As the Netherlands had acutely observed even before the Vienna Conference, the application of the principle of good faith was the key to resolving the complex relationship between interpretation and intertemporality. Consequently, it was best 'to leave unanswered the question whether any term should be interpreted in any specific case according to the law in force at the time or to that in force now. It would seem more correct and quite enough in itself to allow oneself to be guided solely by good faith when answering the question'.[41]

4.2.2 Principle of Contemporaneity and Evolutive Interpretation: *Stasis* or *Kinesis*?

4.2.2.1 Contemporaneous v Evolutive Interpretation

Although intertemporal considerations were not explicitly reflected in the text of the VCLT, that is not to say that they were still not part of the interpretative exercise as delineated by Articles 31–33 VCLT. Fitzmaurice in his seminal series of articles in the *British Yearbook of International Law* had attempted to streamline the interpretative process by identifying key principles. One of these was the *principle of contemporaneity*.[42]

[37] Rosenne, Briggs, Tunkin, Waldock, the Chairman, Yasseen, Amado and Verdross; ibid [16] (Rosenne), [21] (Briggs), [24] (Tunkin), [25] (Waldock), [27] (Chairman), [28] (Yasseen), [30] (Amado), [32] (Verdross).

[38] ILC, 'Summary Record of the 869th Meeting' (14 June 1966) UN Doc A/CN.4/SR.869 [59] (Waldock).

[39] ILC, 'Summary Record of the 770th Meeting' (20 July 1964) UN Doc A/CN.4/SR.770 [33] (Waldock), [34] (de Luna).

[40] (i) in favour of deletion: ILC, 'Summary Record of the 870th Meeting' (15 June 1966) UN Doc A/CN.4/SR.870 [13] (Verdross), [21] (Rosenne); ILC, 'Summary Record of the 871st Meeting' (16 June 1966) UN Doc A/CN.4/SR.871 [38] (Tsuruoka); (ii) in favour of the intention of the parties being the decisive criterion: ILC, 'Summary Record of the 870th Meeting' [10–1] (de Luna), [72–3] (de Aréchaga); ILC, 'Summary Record of the 871st Meeting' [31] El-Erian; ILC, 'Summary Record of the 872nd Meeting' [9–10] (Waldock); (iii) in favour of retention of some reference to intertemporal law, see ILC, 'Summary Record of the 870th Meeting' [58] (Ago), [89–92] (Bartoš); ILC, 'Summary Record of the 871st Meeting' [52–3] (Chairman).

[41] ILC, 'Report of the International Law Commission on the Work of Its Eighteenth Session' 323 [29] (Netherlands).

[42] Also known as '*contemporanea expositio*'; Kotzur, 'Intertemporal Law' [11].

According to this principle, '[t]he terms of a treaty must be interpreted according to the meaning which they possessed, or which would have been attributed to them, and in the light of current linguistic usage, at the time when the treaty was originally concluded'.[43] Taking the torch over this series, Thirlway built on and improved on Fitzmaurice's legacy by adding that this principle was not an irrebuttable presumption in favour of historical interpretation, but when it could 'be established that it was the intention of the parties that the meaning or scope of a term or expression used in the treaty should follow the development of the law, *the treaty must be interpreted so as to give effect to that intention*'.[44]

International courts and tribunals have for decades now applied both the principle of contemporaneity,[45] and 'evolutive/dynamic' interpretation.[46,47] depending on the facts of the case. Although evolutive

43 Fitzmaurice, 'The Law and Procedure of the International Court of Justice, 1951–4: Treaty Interpretation' 212; generally on the principle of contemporaneity: Fitzmaurice, 'The Law and Procedure of the International Court of Justice, 1951–4: General Principles' 5–8; H Thirlway, 'The Law and Procedure of the International Court of Justice 1960–1989: Supplement 2006: Part Three' (2006) 77 BYIL 1, 65 ff.

44 Thirlway, 'The Law and Procedure of the ICJ: Supplement 2006: Part Three' 57 (emphasis added). In this context, Thirlway in his earlier writings used the term '*intertemporal renvoi*' to describe situations in which the intention of the parties is deemed to have been 'to subject the legal relations created to such law as might from time to time thereafter become effective'; H Thirlway, 'The Law and Procedure of the International Court of Justice 1960–1989: Part One' (1989) 60 BYIL 1, 135.

45 *Minquiers and Ecrehos (France v UK)* (Judgment) [1953] ICJ Rep 47, 56; *US Nationals in Morocco* 189; *Aegean Sea Continental Shelf*, Dissenting Opinion of Judge de Castro 63 [4]; *Case Concerning Right of Passage over Indian Territory (Portugal v India)* (Merits) [1960] ICJ Rep 6, 37; *Case Concerning a Boundary Dispute between Argentina and Chile Concerning the Frontier Line between Boundary Post 62 and Mount Fitzroy (Argentina v Chile)* (1994) 22 UNRIAA 3 [130] (hereinafter *Laguna del Desierto*); *Kasikili/Sedudu Island* [25]; *Grisbådarna Case* 159; *North Atlantic Coast Fisheries* 196; *Western Sahara* (Advisory Opinion) [1975] ICJ Rep 12 [126]; *Case Concerning the Temple of Preah Vihear (Cambodia v Thailand)* (Merits) [1962] ICJ Rep 6, Dissenting Opinion of Judge Spender 128; *Dispute Regarding Navigational and Related Rights (Costa Rica v Nicaragua)* (Judgment) [2009] ICJ Rep 213, Separate Opinion of Judge Skotnikov [5].

46 *Legal Consequences for States of the Continued Presence of South Africa in Namibia (South West Africa) Notwithstanding Security Council Resolution 276* (Advisory Opinion) [1971] ICJ Rep 16 [53] (hereinafter *Namibia Advisory Opinion*); *Aegean Sea Continental Shelf* [77]; *Gabčíkovo-Nagymaros Project* [112]; *Case Concerning the Delimitation of Maritime Boundary between Guinea-Bissau and Senegal (Guinea Bissau v Senegal)* (1989) 20 UNRIAA 119 [80–5]; *Iron Rhine Arbitration* [79–81]; *Dispute Regarding Navigational and Related Rights*, Declaration of Guillaume [9–16]; *Tyrer v UK* [31]; *Matthews v UK* [GC] ECtHR, App No 24833/94 (18 February 1999) [39].

47 On evolutive/dynamic interpretation, see G Abi-Saab et al (eds), *Evolutionary Interpretation and International Law* (Bloomsbury 2019); M Fitzmaurice, 'Dynamic (Evolutive) Interpretation of Treaties – Part I' (2008) 21 HYIL 101–53; M Fitzmaurice, 'The Tale of Two Judges: Sir Hersch Lauterpacht and Sir Gerald Fitzmaurice – Human Rights and the

interpretation is usually connected to human rights treaties,[48,49] almost all courts and tribunals have at one point resorted to this kind of interpretation, or at least have had the option to do so.[50,51]

Interpretation of Treaties' (2008) 61 RHDI 125; M Fitzmaurice, 'Dynamic (Evolutive) Interpretation of Treaties – Part II' (2009) 22 HYIL 3; R Bernhardt, 'Evolutive Treaty Interpretation, Especially of the European Convention on Human Rights' (1999) 42 GYIL 11; G Letsas, *A Theory of Interpretation of the European Convention on Human Rights* (OUP 2007) 58–79; C Brölmann, 'Limits of the Treaty Paradigm' in M Fitzmaurice and M Craven (eds), *Interrogating the Treaty: Essays in the Contemporary Law of Treaties* (Wolf Legal Publishers 2005) 29, 34–6; Bjorge, *The Evolutionary Interpretation of Treaties*.

48 A point that we shall return to in the following sections.

49 Indicatively: *Christine Goodwin v UK* [GC] ECtHR, App No 28957/95 (11 July 2002) [74–5]; *Schalk and Kopf v Austria*, ECtHR, App No 30141/04 (24 June 2010) [93–4], [105–6]; *Vo v France* [82]; *Tyrer v UK* [31]; *Loizidou v Turkey (Preliminary Objections)* [71].

50 Indicatively: *Merrill & Ring Forestry LP v Canada* (Award of 31 March 2010) ICSID Case No UNCT/07/1 [190]; *Mondev International Ltd v USA* [116–25]; *ADF Inc v USA* [181–4], [190]; *Waste Management Inc v Mexico* (Award of 30 April 2004) ICSID Case No ARB(AF)/00/3 [93]; *GAMI Investment, Inc v Mexico* (Award of 15 November 2004) UNCITRAL <www.italaw.com/sites/default/files/case-documents/ita0353_0.pdf> [95]; *Namibia Advisory Opinion* [53]; *Aegean Sea Continental Shelf* [77]; *Gabčíkovo-Nagymaros Project* [112]; *Iron Rhine Arbitration* [79–81]; *Dispute Regarding Navigational and Related Rights*, Declaration of Guillaume [9–16]; WTO, *USA – Import Prohibition of Certain Shrimp and Shrimp Products – Report of the Appellate Body* (6 November 1998) WT/DS58/AB/R [130] and fns 110–3 (hereinafter *US-Shrimp (AB)*).

51 Evolutive interpretation is often automatically associated with human rights instruments. In Section 4.2.2.3, we shall demonstrate why this legal shortcut is theoretically and logically erroneous, despite the fact that there is indeed an observed tendency to refer to the nature of human rights instruments. Here, as well, there is a wide array of terms that have been employed: (i) 'living/growing tree': *Request for an Advisory Opinion Submitted by the Sub-Regional Fisheries Commission (SRFC)* (Advisory Opinion) [2015] ITLOS Rep 4, Separate Opinion of Judge Lucky [9–10]; (ii) 'living instruments/documents': *Application of the International Convention on the Elimination of All Forms of Racial Discrimination (Georgia v Russia)* (Preliminary Objections) [2011] ICJ Rep 70, Dissenting Opinion of Judge Cançado Trindade [5]; *Prosecutor v William Samoei Ruto and Joshua Arap Sang* (Decision on Prosecutor's Application for Witness Summonses and Resulting Request for State Party Cooperation of 17 April 2014) ICC-01/09-01/11-1274 [142]; *Judge v Canada*, HRCttee (5 August 2002) UN Doc CCPR/C/78/D/829/1998 [10.3]; *RR v Poland* [186]; *EB v France* [92]; *Hatton and Others v UK* [GC] ECtHR, App No 36022/97 (8 July 2003) Joint Dissenting Opinion of Judges Costa, Ress, Türmen, Zupančič, and Steiner [2]; *Puttaswamy and Khanna v Union of India and Others* (24 August 2017) Supreme Court of India [2017] 10 SCC 1, ILDC 2810 [151]; (iii) 'live instruments': *Yakye Axa Indigenous Community v Paraguay* [125]; *Case of the Mapiripán Massacre v Colombia* (Merits, Reparations, and Costs) IACtHR Series C No 134 (15 September 2005)[106]; (iv) instruments of the 'always speaking type': *M, Re, King v Bristow Helicopters Ltd* (28 February 2002) House of Lords (UK) [2002] UKHL 7.

Their practice is so wide and diverse that even the name given to describe this process is equally wide and diverse: 'evolutionary interpretation',[52] 'evolutive interpretation'[53] or 'dynamic interpretation'[54] have all been used either alone or in any and all imaginable combinations: 'dynamic or evolutive',[55] 'evolutive and dynamic',[56] or both these options in different parts of the judgment.[57] This would seem to indicate that there is no measurable qualitative difference amongst these terms. They are merely different adjectives used to describe essentially the same process. Helgesen, however, offers a different approach. According to him, 'evolutive' covers situations where the court or tribunal gives answers to a new issue that has not been brought before the court ever before. 'Dynamic', on the other hand, describes a situation where the court gives 'new answers to old facts'.[58] Such considerations aside, from the above it is evident that evolutive interpretation[59] is inextricably linked to both temporal motion and 'motion' as change. It is no coincidence

[52] *Whaling in the Antarctic* [31–2]; ibid, Separate Opinion of Judge Greenwood [7]; WTO, *India - Certain Measures Relating to Solar Cells and Solar Modules* (24 February 2016) WT/DS456/R [7.231], [7.233]; *The M/V 'Virginia G'* Case *(Panama/Guinea Bissau)* (Merits) [2014] ITLOS Rep 4 [187]; *Mayagna (Sumo) Awas Tingni Community v Nicaragua* [148]; *Gabčíkovo-Nagymaros Project*, Separate Opinion of Judge Bedjaoui [5]; *RosInvest Company UK Ltd v Russia* (Award on Jurisdiction of 1 October 2007) SCC Case No V079/2005 [39–40].

[53] *Jadhav Case (India v Pakistan)* (Provisional Measures) [2017] ICJ Rep 231, Separate Opinion of Judge Cançado Trindade [27]; *Daimler Financial Services AG v Argentina* (Award of 22 August 2012) ICSID Case No ARB/05/1 [267]; *Mondev International Ltd v USA* [123]; *Bámaca Velásquez v Guatemala* (Merits) IACtHR Series C No 70 (25 November 2000) Separate Opinion of Judge Cançado Trindade [37].

[54] Fitzmaurice 'Dynamic (Evolutive) Interpretation of Treaties - Part I' 101–53; Fitzmaurice 'Dynamic (Evolutive) Interpretation of Treaties - Part II' 3–31.

[55] *Caesar v Trinidad and Tobago*, Separate Opinion of Judge Cançado Trindade [10]; *The Right to Information on Consular Assistance*, Concurring Opinion of Judge Cançado Trindade [3].

[56] *Şahin and Şahin v Turkey* [GC] ECtHR, App No 13279/05 (20 October 2011) [58]; *Bayatyan v Armenia* [GC] ECtHR, App No 23459/03 (7 July 2011) [98]; *YY v Turkey*, ECtHR, App No 14793/08 (10 March 2015) [103]; *Meftah and Others v France* [GC] ECtHR, App No 32911/96 (26 July 2002) Concurring Opinion of Judge Lorenzen, Joined by Judge Hedigan.

[57] *Hirst v UK (No 2)* [GC] ECtHR, App No 74025/01 (6 October 2005) Joint Dissenting Opinion of Judges Wildhaber, Costa, Lorenzen, Kovler, and Jebens.

[58] JE Helgesen, 'What Are the Limits to the Evolutive Interpretation of the European Convention on Human Rights?' (2011) 31 HRLJ 275, 276.

[59] From this point onward, we will be using the term 'evolutive interpretation' for reasons of consistency, but also because this term is closer to the concept of motion as change, which is the central theme of our book.

that it has been characterised as the 'intertemporal dimension'[60] and the 'temporal issue'[61] in treaty interpretation.

This 'motion' is also evident in the manner in which evolutive interpretation can occur. Two are the main tracks along which evolutive interpretation can happen: 'evolution of fact' (*ouverture du texte*) and 'evolution of law' (*renvoi mobile*).[62] In evolution of fact, the rule being interpreted takes into account the changes that have occurred within the society in which the rule being interpreted produces its effects. Medical and scientific advancements,[63] societal and cultural changes,[64] moral developments,[65] and the socio-economic situation of a State (including current living conditions)[66] have all been considered as evolution of fact. In evolution of law, on the other hand, the content of the rule being interpreted changes on the basis of the current status of the surrounding legal framework, eg if any new rules have emerged that could potentially affect the scope of its content. Customary international law,[67] international treaties,[68] and even domestic law[69] all fall within the scope of

[60] *Caesar v Trinidad and Tobago*, Separate Opinion of Judge Cançado Trindade [10].

[61] Higgins, *Problems and Process* 797.

[62] Georgopoulos, 'Le droit intertemporel' 132–4; Higgins, *Problems and Process* 797.

[63] *Gabčíkovo-Nagymaros Project* [104], [107]; *Vo v France*, Dissenting Opinion of Judge Ress [5]; *Request for an Advisory Opinion Submitted by the Sub-Regional Fisheries Commission (SRFC)*, Separate Opinion of Judge Lucky [9–10]; *Puttaswamy and Khanna v Union of India and Others* [151].

[64] *The Right to Information on Consular Assistance*, Concurring Opinion of Judge Cançado Trindade [4]; *Öztürk v Germany*, Dissenting Opinion of Judge Bernhardt.

[65] *Cossey v UK*, Joint Dissenting Opinion of Judges Palm, Foighel, and Pekkanen [5].

[66] *India – Certain Measures Relating to Solar Cells and Solar Modules* [7.231–7.232]; WTO, *Argentina – Measures Relating to Trade in Goods and Services* (30 September 2015) WT/DS453/R [7.873–7.875]; *Yakye Axa Indigenous Community v Paraguay* [125]; *Gómez Paquiyauri and Others v Peru* [165]; ibid, Partly Concurring and Partly Dissenting Opinion of Judge Fogel [33]; *Mayagna (Sumo) Awas Tingni Community v Nicaragua* [146]; *Case of the 'Street Children' v Guatemala* [193]; *The Right to Information on Consular Assistance* [114]; *Tyrer v UK* [31].

[67] *Merrill & Ring Forestry LP v Canada* [190]; *Mondev International Ltd v USA* [116–25]; *ADF Inc v USA* [181–4], [190]; *Waste Management Inc v Mexico* [93]; *GAMI Investment, Inc v Mexico* [95].

[68] *Whaling in the Antarctic* [38]; ibid, Dissenting Opinion of Judge Yusuf [26]; *Jadhav Case* (Provisional Measures) Separate Opinion of Judge Cançado Trindade [27]; *Application of the International Convention on the Elimination of All Forms of Racial Discrimination*, Dissenting Opinion of Judge Cançado Trindade [172]; *Sawhoyamaxa Indigenous Community v Paraguay* [117]; *Yakye Axa Indigenous Community v Paraguay* [124–31]; *Mayagna (Sumo) Awas Tingni Community v Nicaragua* [148–9]; *Gómez Paquiyauri and others v Peru* [165–6]; *The Right to Information on Consular Assistance* [114]; *Case of the 'Street Children' v Guatemala* [193–4]; *Juridical Status and Human Rights of the Child* [24].

[69] *Öcalan v Turkey* [162–4]; *The Right to Information on Consular Assistance*, Concurring Opinion of Judge Cançado Trindade [7]; *Marckx v Belgium* [41]; *Dudgeon v UK* [60].

evolution of law and have, on occasion, been resorted to by courts and tribunals to breathe renewed life into treaty provisions.

4.2.2.2 Evolutive Interpretation and Subsequent Agreements and Practice

Recently, the ILC in its work on 'Subsequent Agreements and Subsequent Practice in the Interpretation of Treaties'[70] and the ICJ in the *Whaling in the Antarctic*[71] had to deal with the concept of intertemporalitry within the process of interpretation, ie whether a treaty should be interpreted in the light of the circumstances and the law at the time of its conclusion ('contemporaneous' or 'static' interpretation), or in the light of the circumstances and the law at the time of its application ('evolutive', 'evolutionary', or 'dynamic' interpretation) and in particular as to what it concerned subsequent agreement and practice, under both Article 31 and 32 VCLT.

With respect to subsequent practice and agreements, Nolte has cautioned that 'the possibility of influencing the fate of a treaty through the practice of its application should not, however, be overestimated'.[72] In his view, and in conformity with the holistic nature of the interpretative process, reference to subsequent agreements and practice is but one of the elements in the process of progressive encirclement that is interpretation.[73]

[70] ILC, 'Draft Conclusions on Subsequent Agreements and Subsequent Practice in Relation to the Interpretation of Treaties, with Commentaries' (30 April–1 June and 2 July–10 August 2018) UN Doc A/73/10, reproduced in [2018/II – Part Two] YBILC 11, Commentary to Draft Conclusion 8, 64 [2].

[71] The ICJ in *Whaling in the Antarctic* made some interesting observations as to the role of subsequent agreements and practice in the interpretative process, its connection and position with respect to other elements of Art 31 VCLT (in particular its relationship with and effect on 'object and purpose'), and its relation to and influence on evolutive interpretation. For a detailed analysis of this case, see M Fitzmaurice, 'The Whaling Convention and Thorny Issues of Interpretation' in M Fitzmaurice and D Tamada (eds), *Whaling in the Antarctic: Significance and Implications of the ICJ Judgment* (Brill/Martinus Nijhoff 2016) 55–138; M Fitzmaurice, 'The Practical Working of the Law of Treaties' in MD Evans (ed), *International Law* (5th edn, CUP 2019) 138, 155–8.

[72] G Nolte, 'Treaties and Their Practice – Symptoms of Their Rise or Decline' (2018) 392 RdC 205, 334; cf Y Hamamoto, 'Possible Limitations to the Role of Subsequent Agreements and Subsequent Practice – Viewed from Some State Practices' (2020) 22/1 ICLR 61–83; D Tamada, 'The Japan–South Korea Claims Agreement: Identification of Subsequent Agreements and Practice' (2020) 22/1 ICLR 107–36.

[73] Nolte, 'Treaties and Their Practice' 336. See, however, Tladi, who expressed 'concern about an apparent, almost surreptitious, attempt by the Commission to elevate subsequent agreements and subsequent practice as tools of interpretation to the same level as the more objective tools outlined in Article 31(1) of the [VCLT]'; D Tladi, 'Is the

As far as evolutive interpretation is concerned, and despite some sweeping claims to the contrary, such as the one made by the arbitral tribunal in the *Iron Rhine Arbitration* that 'note[d] a general support among the leading writers today for evolutive interpretation of treaties',[74] most authors take the view that while subsequent practice and evolutive interpretation are similar in objectives, in the sense that they allow for the development of treaties over time,[75] this is not to say that evolutive interpretation is the default setting when dealing with subsequent agreements and practice. As shown in the analysis in Section 4.2.1,[76] it is the intention of the parties which is the answer to the question. This intention is the 'cornerstone of evolutionary interpretation, ie obligations can evolve only if the parties intended that a particular term, or the treaty as a whole, have an evolutionary character'.[77] Similarly, Nolte, while referring to the *Dispute Regarding Navigational and Related Rights*, was of the view that this case was 'illustrative of the question of the relationship between the roles of practice in the narrow and in the broad sense for the interpretation of treaties, [but it did] not point to a general approach, or to a theory'.[78]

In the end, the ILC adopted Draft Conclusion 8 'Interpretation of treaty terms as capable of evolving over time: Subsequent agreements and subsequent practice under articles 31 and 32 *may assist in determining whether or not the presumed intention of the parties upon the conclusion of the treaty was to give a term used a meaning which is capable of evolving over time*'.[79]

In the view of the authors, this Draft Conclusion highlights the correct approach to deciding between static and evolutive interpretation. Instead

International Law Commission Elevating Subsequent Agreements and Subsequent Practice?' (*EJIL: Talk!*, 30 August 2018) <www.ejiltalk.org/is-the-international-law-commission-elevating-subsequent-agreements-and-subsequent-practice> accessed 20 September 2019.

[74] *Iron Rhine Arbitration* [81].

[75] I Buga, 'Subsequent Practice and Treaty Modification' in Bowman and Kritsiotis (eds), *Conceptual and Contextual Perspectives* 363, 370.

[76] And further strengthened in Section 4.2.2.

[77] J Arato, 'Subsequent Practice and Evolutive Interpretation' (2010) 9/3 Law and Practice of International Courts and Tribunals 443, 466; see also Merkouris, *Article 31(3)(c) VCLT* ch 2, and cases and authors cited therein. How one goes about establishing this intention is, of course, an even more complex question.

[78] Nolte, 'Treaties and Their Practice' 359.

[79] ILC, 'Draft Conclusions on Subsequent Agreements and Subsequent Practice, with Commentaries', Draft Conclusion 8.

of adopting any legal and mental shortcuts,[80] it correctly determines that any solution to that question will have to be decided on the basis of the facts of each case, and always by referring to the intention of the parties. According to the Commentary,

> Draft Conclusion 8 does not take a position regarding the question of the appropriateness of a more contemporaneous or a more evolutive approach to treaty interpretation in general ... The conclusion should, however, be understood as indicating the need for some caution with regard to arriving at a conclusion in a specific case whether to adopt an evolutive approach. For this purpose, Draft Conclusion 8 points to subsequent agreements and subsequent practice as means of interpretation that may provide useful indications to the interpreter for assessing, as part of the ordinary process of treaty interpretation, whether the meaning of a term is capable of evolving over time.[81]

4.2.2.3 Choosing between Static (Contemporaneous) and Evolutive Interpretation

As shown in Section 4.2.1, the VCLT drafters were well aware of the way that intertemporal considerations could encroach on the interpretative process. Instead of offering explicit and deatiled solutions, which could in the long run have led to issues of rigidity and *stasis*, they decided to exercise caution by opting for a 'flexible approach', in which the interpreter would sometimes 'draw upon the language and rules that were in existence when the interpreted treaty was concluded, and sometimes upon the language and rules existing at the time of interpretation'.[82] What is unclear, however, is on what basis the interpreter would know which of these two solutions was the appropriate one for the text being interpreted. Various methods have been proposed, but all can be categorised into three main groups that, unsurprisingly, are also reflective of the three mains schools of interpretation: (i) intention of the parties; (ii) text, and in particular the so-called 'generic terms'; and (iii) the object and purpose of the treaty. All of these have been, on occasion, relied on by courts and tribunals to offer guidance as to whether the interpreted provision has experienced a *kata chronon metavole* that has led to its

[80] On a deconstruction of these, see Section 4.2.2.3.

[81] ILC, 'Draft Conclusions on Subsequent Agreements and Subsequent Practice, with Commentaries', Commentary to Draft Conclusion 8, 67 [10].

[82] Linderfalk, 'Doing the Right Thing for the Right Reason' 113; Linderfalk, identifies three approaches to addressing intertemporal issues: (i) the categorically static approach, (ii) the categorically dynamic approach, and (iii) the flexible approach (ibid).

auxesis/meiosis, or whether its content has remained frozen in time, in a state of *stasis*.

4.2.2.3.1 Intention of the Parties This approach is generally uncontested. If the intention of the parties can be revealed to have shown a preference of a particular approach to the interpretation of the treaty to which they are parties, then as a logical corollary of the consent-based nature of international law this should be the determinative factor.[83] This is also evidenced by Fitzmaurice and Thirlway's definition of the principle of contemporaneity, which is built around the intention of the parties. Consequently, it is the will of the parties that provides the answer when deciding between a contemporaneous or evolutive interpretation, ie how change in time, law, and fact affects the interpretation of a legal rule. Bearing in mind the main philosophical approaches to time, change, and identity, ie endurantism, perdurantism and exdurantism,[84] where the existence of an object is described in terms such as 'time-slices' and 'space-time worms', it is only appropriate to refer to this intention of the parties that determines the temporal destiny of a particular term as the *'time-will' of the parties.*

4.2.2.3.2 Generic Terms' The text itself and, in particular, the linguistic characteristics of the terms being interpreted may also affect the intertemporal dimension in the interpretation of treaties. It has been argued that evolutive interpretation is linguistic in nature, that it is 'based on the linguistic usage of the term at the time of interpretation'.[85] The key concept in this school of thought is that of a term being 'generic'. If a term is of a generic nature, this may tip the scales in favour of an evolutive interpretation.[86] Courts and tribunals, while characterising a

[83] de Aréchaga, 'International Law in the Past Third of a Century' 49; Sinclair, *The Vienna Convention on the Law of Treaties* 140.

[84] See Chapter 1, Section 1.5.

[85] G Ress, 'The Interpretation of the Charter' in B Simma (ed), *The Charter of the United Nations: A Commentary* (2nd edn, OUP 2002) 13, 23. However, as Helmersen rightly points out, this is only fitting for terms that actually have the capacity to evolve linguistically, not for the rest; ST Helmersen, 'Evolutive Treaty Interpretation: Legality, Semantics and Distinctions' (2013) 6 EurJLegStud 127, 129; see also in more detail later in this section, where Helmersen's theory is analysed in more detail.

[86] *Iron Rhine Arbitration* [79–80]; *Nationality Decrees Issued in Tunis and Morocco* (Advisory Opinion) PCIJ Rep Series B No 4, 24; *Aegean Sea Continental Shelf* [74–7]; *Gabčíkovo-Nagymaros Project* [112]; *US–Shrimp (AB)* [130]; *Dispute Regarding Navigational and Related Rights* [65–7].

term as 'generic' when interpreting it, have on some occasions attempted to offer some glimpse of what makes a particular term a 'generic' one. The ICJ has opined that such terms have a content, which 'the parties expected would change through time',[87] and that its 'meaning was intended to follow the evolution of the law'.[88] Along similar lines, the arbitral tribunal in *Mondev* simply stated that such terms have an 'evolutionary potential'.[89] Unsurprisingly, all of these are not truly definitions but are rather, at best, broad descriptions of certain qualities that a generic term will have, and which most likely be evident after the fact.

Linderfalk and Helmersen have attempted, using linguistics as their base, to provide some guidance about how such a determination could potentially be accomplished *ex ante*. Linderfalk, identifies three groups of 'referring expressions':[90] (i) 'definite referring expressions', which refer to one or more specific phenomena; (ii) 'indefinite referring expressions', which refer to one or more non-specific phenomena; and (iii) 'generic referring expressions', which refer to one or more phenomena as they change in time.[91] Out of these three, the 'generic referring expressions' are the prime candidates for qualifying as generic terms that can be open to evolutive interpretation that takes into account not only the evolution of law but also the evolution of fact. The reason is that these 'generic referring expressions' are not time-bound, since 'no relationship is established between the time of the utterance and the time when the referent was assumed to exist'.[92] Helgersen using two axes, that of values and that of evolution, identifies four different groups of generic terms: (i) 'value-driven non-evolving', (ii) 'value driven evolving', (iii) 'non-value driven non-evolving', and (iv) 'non-value driven evolving'. If a term on the axis of evolution is non-evolving, ie groups (i) and (iii), then evolutive interpretation is possible within the context of the term being given a

[87] *Kasikili/Sedudu Island*, Declaration of Judge Higgins [2].

[88] *Aegean Sea Continental Shelf* [77].

[89] *Mondev International Ltd v USA* [119].

[90] 'Referring expression' is an expression used by an 'utterer' for the purpose of 'reference'. In turn, 'reference' refers to the relationship between an expression and what the expression stands for in the world at the time that it is uttered; Linderfalk, 'Doing the Right Thing for the Right Reason' 129. For other linguistic attempts, see J Wyatt, *Intertemporal Linguistics in International Law: Beyond Contemporaneous and Evolutionary Treaty Interpretation* (Hart Publishing 2019).

[91] Linderfalk, 'Doing the Right Thing for the Right Reason' 130–1.

[92] ibid 132.

special meaning under Article 31(4) VCLT. 'Value driven evolving' terms are the ones with the highest 'evolutionary potential', whereas for 'non-value driven evolving' terms there is no presumption, and their evolutive potential would have to be decided always on an *ad hoc* basis and by reference to the actual 'time-will' of the parties.[93] When applying this tool to the jurisprudence of the ICJ, Helgersen came to the conclusion that the Court is more likely to adopt an evolutive interpretation, when the term is generic and the treaty is of unlimited duration.[94]

Despite the undeniable theoretical value of Linderfalk's and Helgersen's approach, one major issue is that courts and tribunals rarely elaborate on why a particular term is characterised as 'generic' or not.[95] In most cases, they will assert it and so far, to the knowledge of the authors, no court has undertaken explicitly a linguistic exercise such as the ones described above. Furthermore, as both Linderfalk and Helgersen concede, in several cases the evolutive or non-evolutive potential of a term will rest on identifying the will of the parties, and even in the cases where there is a presumption in favour of evolutive interpretation that would always be rebuttable and exists in the first place by virtue of the fact that the parties intentionally selected that type of term as it served their intention. They chose a generic term to be included in the text of a treaty because its ability to evolve through time reflected their intention/will, or more appropriately their 'time-will'.[96]

In the *Namibia Advisory Opinion*, which is sometimes used as one example where the Court resorted to evolutive interpretation based on the 'generic' nature of the terms,[97] the text of the Opinion itself gives an indication that is is the 'time-will' of the parties that is the critical factor. 'The Parties to the Covenant [by selecting these generic terms] *must*

[93] ibid 139.

[94] ibid 135–8 using these cases as reinforcing his argument: *Dispute Regarding Navigational and Related Rights* [65–7]; *Aegean Sea Continental Shelf* [77].

[95] *Ambiente Ufficio SpA and Others v Argentina* (Decision of 8 February 2013) ICSID Case No ARB/08/9 [492]; *Siemens AG v Argentina* (Decision of 3 August 2014) ICSID Case No ARB/02/8 [114] (Respondent's Claim).

[96] *Namibia Advisory Opinion* [53]; *Aegean Sea Continental Shelf* [77]; *Dispute Regarding Navigational and Related Rights* [66] and Separate Opinion of Judge Skotnikov [6]; *Siemens AG v Argentina* [114] (Respondent's Claim). In all of these cases, the relevant judicial body although making use of 'generic terms' always comes back to the fact that the selection of such terms reflects the intention of the parties to allow these terms to evolve (ie is a reflection of the 'time-will of the parties').

[97] The exact wording of the ICJ was 'by definition evolutionary'; *Namibia Advisory Opinion* [53].

consequently be deemed to have accepted them as such [ie non-static and evolutive]'.[98] It is noteworthy that both Fitzmaurice in his Dissenting Opinion[99] and Thirlway in his writings[100] criticised the Court because they could find no evidence of this evolutive 'time-will' of the parties and stated that the Court had failed to provide any evidence of such intent.

Judge Higgins, in *Kasikili/Sedudu Island* drives this point home:

> [The aim] is *not to discover a mythical 'ordinary meaning'* ... we must never lose sight of the fact that *we are seeking to give flesh to the intention of the parties*, expressed in generalised terms in 1890. We must trace a thread back to this point of departure. *We should not*, as the Court appears at times to be doing, decide what *in abstracto* the term 'the main channel' might today mean, *by a mechanistic appreciation of relevant indicia*. Rather, our task is to decide what general idea the parties had in mind, and then make reality of that general idea through the use of contemporary knowledge.[101]

Consequently, the text is not and cannot be the sole basis for evolutive interpretation. It is merely a reflection of the true basis, ie the intention of the parties, and specifically, their 'time-will'.

4.2.2.3.3 Object and Purpose of the Treaty There is a growing trend in international jurisprudence to justify recourse to evolutive interpretation based on the nature of the text being interpreted, ie its object and purpose. This trend is most pronounced with respect to human rights treaties, environmental treaties (to a lesser degree of intensity than human rights treaties), and constituent instruments of international organisations. The underlying hypothesis is that the content of human rights treaties ,because of their particular character and of the nature of the rights they enshrine, must be bolstered and continuously be updated in order to remain relevant in the face of challenges posed by a constantly changing legal and societal environment.[102] Despite the existence of an

98 *Namibia Advisory Opinion* [53] (emphasis added).

99 ibid, Dissenting Opinion of Judge Fitzmaurice [85].

100 Thirlway, 'The Law and Procedure of the ICJ: Part One' 137; Fitzmaurice, 'The Tale of Two Judges' 125–70.

101 *Kasikili/Sedudu Island*, Declaration of Judge Higgins [3–4].

102 *Caesar v Trinidad and Tobago*, Separate Opinion of Judge Cançado Trindade [11], citing *Loizidou v Turkey (Preliminary Objections)* [75]; *'Other Treaties' Subject to the Advisory Jurisdiction of the Court (Art 64 American Convention on Human Rights)* (Advisory Opinion) IACtHR Series A No 1 (24 September 1982); *The Effect of Reservations on the Entry into Force of the American Convention on Human Rights (Arts 74 and 75)* (Advisory Opinion) IACtHR Series A No 2 (24 September 1982); *Restrictions to the*

extensive jurisprudence on the matter,[103] however, that is not to say that human rights treaties are an *automatic exception to the principle of contemporaneity*. Similar to what we saw in evolutive interpretation based on the 'generic' nature of a term, so this approach is actually also based on the 'time-will' of the parties. Higgins, once again, opens the blinds on any misconception as to the object and purpose being an automatic exception. '"[G]eneric clauses" and *human rights provisions* are not really random exceptions to a general rule . . . [but] an application of a wider principle – *intention of the parties, reflected by reference to the object and purpose* – that guides the law of treaties'.[104] Similarly, the tribunal in *RosInvest v Russia* draws attention to the fact that intention is always the underlying principle. '[Since human rights treaties] represent the very archetype of treaty instruments in which the Contracting Parties *must have intended* that the principles and concepts which they employed should be understood and applied in the light of developing social attitudes'.[105] Consequently, the object and purpose argument in favour of evolutive interpretation is simply a variation to the overall theme of the 'time-will' (ie the intention) of the parties.

The same is applicable to the argument that 'a treaty of constitutional character should be subject to different rules of interpretation to allow for the "intrinsically evolutionary nature of a constitution"'.[106] However, as with human rights treaties, sooner or later it always comes back to the acknowledgement that for the purposes of evolutive interpretation the nature of the treaty is a reflection of the intention of the parties.[107] Of

Death Penalty (Arts 4(2) and 4(4) American Convention on Human Rights) (Advisory Opinion) IACtHR Series No 3 (8 September 1983).

103 Generally, see Bjorge, *The Evolutionary Interpretation of Treaties*; Letsas, *A Theory of Interpretation of the ECHR*.

104 Higgins, 'Some Observations on the Inter-temporal Rule in International Law' 181 (emphasis added).

105 *RosInvest v Russia* [39] (emphasis added).

106 P Sands and P Klein, *Bowett's Law of International Institutions* (6th edn, Sweet & Maxwell 2009) 454, citing RY Jennings and AD Watts (eds), *Oppenheim's International Law* (9th edn, OUP 2008) 1268; *US Nationals in Morocco* 211.

107 HG Schermers and NM Blokker, *International Institutional Law: Unity with Diversity* (5th rev edn, Martinus Nijhoff 2011) [1155–6], [1347]; Sands and Klein, *Bowett's Law of International Institutions* 454; NM Blokker, 'Constituent Instruments: Creating a Genie that May Escape from the Bottle?' in JK Cogan, I Hurd and I Johnstone (eds), *The Oxford Handbook of International Organizations* (OUP 2013) 943–61; T Sato, *Evolving Constitutions of International Organizations: A Critical Analysis of the Interpretative Framework of the Constituent Instruments of International Organizations* (Kluwer Law International 1996) 150–60.

note is Brölmann's excellent analysis on the topic, who draws attention to the fact that teleological interpretation and evolutive interpretation should not be conflated with one another, and that it is actually teleological rather than evolutive interpretation that features more prominently in the interpretation of these treaties.[108] Consequently, object and purpose as well is not a completely independent basis for establishing an evolutive interpretation, but is rather a manifestation of the expressed or presumed intention of the parties. No *automatic* exception to the principle of contemporaneity can be deduced from international jurisprudence, and any exception will, once again, be determined on an *ad hoc* basis, on the facts of the case and, most importantly, on the intention of the parties.

The above analysis coupled with an examination of the *travaux préparatoires* of Article 31 VCLT in the previous sections has demonstrated that irrespective of which school of interpretation one takes as a starting point, and irrespective of which presumptions may apply, in all situations the deciding factor either directly or indirectly was and still is the 'time-will' of the parties. This 'time-will' may be identified by reference to the text of the treaty, the drafting history, the object and purpose of the treaty, and State practice, as well as other relevant treaties,[109,110] but it is that 'time-will' and nothing else that in each instance determines the balance to be struck between the principle of contemporaneity and evolutive interpretation.

4.2.2.4 Limits of Evolutive Interpretation

Evolutive interpretation is an extremely useful tool that allows a treaty moving along the axis of the fourth (temporal) dimension (*kata chronon metavole*) to also move within the meaning of two more of Aristotle's types of 'motion', ie increase (*auxesis*) and diminution (*meiosis*). A common characterisation of a treaty connected to the process of evolutive interpretation is that of a treaty being a 'living tree'. Similar

[108] C Brölmann, 'Specialized Rules of Treaty Interpretation: International Organizations' in DB Hollis (ed) *The Oxford Guide to Treaties* (OUP 2012) 507, 512–4.

[109] These could be either 'relevant rules' under Article 31(3)(c), or *in pari materia* treaties; *Daimler Financial Services AG v Argentina* [220 ff].

[110] Higgins, 'Some Observations on the Inter-temporal Rule in International Law' 180–1; Fitzmaurice, 'The Tale of Two Judges' 125–70; Yasseen, 'L' interprétation des traités' 66–7; FA Engelen, *Interpretation of Tax Treaties under International Law: A Study of Articles 31, 32, and 33 of Vienna Convention on the Law of Treaties and Their Application to Tax Treaties* (International Bureau of Fiscal Documentation 2004) 291.

to a 'living tree', a treaty also expands and grows (or in some rare cases may also wither away) in order to adapt to situations and problems that the original drafters may not have envisaged at all.

However, this need to adapt should not give us the false impression that this 'motion' is an unlimited one. On the contrary, not only are there limits (or precautions),[111] but these limits can be grouped into two main categories.

The first group of limits/precautions is the *internal* limits. These limits refer to the treaty itself and are connected to its building blocks, most of which are also evident in the interpretative process as enshrined in Articles 31–33 VCLT. As early as 1929, Lord Sankey, in *Edwards v Attorney-General for Canada,* expressed this, while harking back to the simile of treaties as 'living instruments'. He opined that although certain legal documents were 'living tree[s] capable of growth and expansion', this growth should always be 'within [the instrument's/"living tree's"] natural limits'.[112] But what exactly are these 'natural limits'?

The 'umbrella' limit of this first category is the one that states that evolutive interpretation should always observe the general interpretative rule laid down in Article 31 VCLT.[113] This has been further elaborated by a number of international courts and tribunals to refer, among others, to the text of the provision under interpretation,[114] its context,[115] and, of course, the intention of the parties.[116] Especially, with respect to this last one, although evolutive interpretation may be used to address modern challenges and, thus, better serve the object and purpose of a treaty, this at no point should lead to fictional considerations of object and purpose leading to a substitution of the actual intention of the parties. As Fitzmaurice, acting as an ECtHR judge, pointed out, '[t]he objects and purposes of a treaty are not something that exist *in abstracto*: they follow from and are closely bound up with the intentions of the parties, as

[111] This is a term used by Judge Bedjaoui in: *Gabčíkovo-Nagymaros Project*, Separate Opinion of Judge Bedjaoui [5].

[112] *Edwards v Attorney-General for Canada* (Judgment of 18 October 1929) Judicial Committee of the Imperial Privy Council [1930] AC 124, 136 per Lord Sankey.

[113] *Gabčíkovo-Nagymaros Project*, Separate Opinion of Judge Bedjaoui [5].

[114] *Al-Saadoon and Mufdhi v UK*, ECtHR, App No 61498/08 (2 March 2010) [119]; *Feldbrugge v Netherlands*, ECtHR, App No 8562/79 (29 May 1986) Joint Dissenting Opinion of Judges Ryssdal, Bindschedler-Robert, Lagergren, Matscher, Sir Evans, Bernhardt, and Gersing [24]; *Albert and Le Compte v Belgium*, ECtHR, App No 7299/75 (10 February 1983) Partly Dissenting Opinion of Judge Matscher [3].

[115] *Soering v UK*, ECtHR, App No 14038/88 (7 July 1989) [103].

[116] *Gabčíkovo-Nagymaros Project*, Separate Opinion of Judge Bedjaoui [7].

expressed in the text of the treaty, or as properly to be inferred from it, these intentions being the sole sources of those objects and purposes . . . *a fortiori* [these intentions] *may certainly not be subsequently imported under the guise of objects and purposes not thought of at the time*'.[117]

Another limit, within the first group of 'internal' ones, and which is the underlying common denominator of all the limits of that group, is that evolutive interpretation should never amount to a *de facto* revision of a treaty.[118] Any such outcome would be tantamount to the judges exercising a *pouvoir de légiférer*, which has been consistently held to fly in the face of the judicial function and the notion of the separation of powers.[119]

The ILC also raised this issue in 'Subsequent Agreement and Subsequent Practice in Relation to the Interpretation of Treaties'. Draft Conclusion 7(3) states:

> It is presumed that the parties to a treaty, by an agreement or a practice in the application of the treaty, *intend to interpret the treaty, not to amend or to modify it*. The possibility of amending or modifying a treaty by subsequent practice of the parties has not been generally recognised. The present draft conclusion is without prejudice to the rules on the amendment or modification of treaties under the Vienna Convention on the Law of Treaties and under customary international law.[120]

In this Draft Conclusion, the ILC recognises revision of a treaty as a limit to the interpretative process, and that when States aim to amend or modify the treaty they should do so either by following the treaty-specific rules on amendment and modification, or the VCLT residual ones, or customary international law, whichever set of rules is applicable to the treaty and the parties in question. However, even the ILC was aware of the fact that although the differentiation of subsequent agreements and practice relevant for interpretative purposes under Article 31(3)(a)

[117] *Case of National Union of Belgian Police v Belgium*, ECtHR, App No 4464/70 (27 October 1975) Separate Opinion of Judge Sir Gerald Fitzmaurice [9] (emphasis added).

[118] *Gabčíkovo-Nagymaros Project*, Separate Opinion of Judge Bedjaoui [5]; *Kasikili/Sedudu Island*, Declaration of Judge Higgins [2]; *Laguna del Desierto* [157]; *Claude Reyes and Others v Chile* (Merits, Reparations, and Costs) IACtHR Series C No 151 (19 September 2006) Separate Opinion of Judge Ramírez [1], [3].

[119] *Bayatyan v Armenia*, Dissenting Opinion of Judge Gyulumyan [2]; *Meftah and Others v France*, Concurring Opinion of Judge Lorenzen, Joined by Judge Hedigan; Helmersen, 'Evolutive Treaty Interpretation' 137; Thirlway, 'The Law and Procedure of the ICJ: Part One' 142; D French, 'Treaty Interpretation and the Incorporation of Extraneous Legal Rules' (2006) 55 ICLQ 281, 296–7.

[120] ILC, 'Draft Conclusions on Subsequent Agreements and Subsequent Practice, with Commentaries' Draft Conclusion 7(3) (emphasis added).

and (b) and subsequent agreements and practice leading to modification is a theoretically sound proposal, in practice the differentiation between the two groups may not always be so straightforward. According to the ILC, '[i]t may sometimes be difficult to draw a distinction between agreements of the parties under a specific treaty provision that attributes binding force to subsequent agreements, simple subsequent agreements under article 31, paragraph 3 (a), which are not binding as such, and, finally, agreements on the amendment or modification of a treaty under articles 39 to 41'.[121]

With the exception of the formal criteria set forth in Article 39 VCLT, and any other criteria that may have been included by the parties themselves in the treaty being interpreted, the ILC concluded:

> There do not seem to be any [other] formal criteria. It is clear, however, that States and international courts are generally prepared to accord parties a rather wide scope for the interpretation of a treaty by way of a subsequent agreement. This scope may even go beyond the ordinary meaning of the terms of the treaty. The recognition of this scope for the interpretation of a treaty goes hand in hand with the reluctance by States and courts to recognize that an agreement relating to the application of a treaty actually has the effect of amending or modifying the treaty. An agreement to modify a treaty is thus not excluded, but also not to be presumed.[122]

The difficulty of distinguishing between interpretation and modification by recourse to subsequent agreement and practice is further complicated by the fact that sometimes courts and tribunals simply avoid taking a position on the matter. In *Territorial Dispute (Libya/Chad)*, for instance, 'in the view of the Court, for the purposes of the present Judgment, there is no reason to *categorise it either as confirmation or as a modification of the Declaration*'.[123] In other cases, it is also unclear whether the judgment of the court was based on use of subsequent practice as an interpretative element or as a basis of treaty modification.[124] Another complicating

[121] ibid 58–9, Commentary to Draft Conclusion 7(3) [24].

[122] ibid 59, Commentary to Draft Conclusion 7(3) [24].

[123] *Territorial Dispute (Libyan Arab Jamahiriya/Chad)* (Judgment) [1994] ICJ Rep 6 [60] (emphasis added).

[124] In *Dispute Regarding Navigational and Related Rights*, for instance, the Court seems to indicate that subsequent practice of parties may lead to 'a departure from the original intent on the basis of a tacit agreement', but it is unclear whether it means that in the sense of modification or whether in the sense of departing from the original understanding of the terms by the drafters, which would fall under evolutive interpretation.

factor is that a subsequent agreement under Article 31(3)(a) can also have the effect of modifying a treaty,[125] although the ILC was, eventually, of the view that 'while there exists some support in international case law that, absent indications in the treaty to the contrary, the agreed subsequent practice of the parties theoretically may lead to modifications of a treaty, the actual occurrence of that effect is not to be presumed, and the possibility of amending or modifying a treaty by subsequent practice has not been generally recognised'.[126]

Irrespective of the difficulties surrounding distinguishing interpretation and revision/modification of a treaty, it is without question that the latter is a limit that interpretation should never cross. The interpretative process and the amendment/modification procedures abide and are goverved by different sets of rules. One should not be conflated with another. If an alteration (*alloiosis*) is to transpire for a treaty, then that should be the outcome of the clear intention of the parties to the treaty and not the interpretative outcome of the legal reasoning of a judge. Or as Dupuy forcefully summarised the whole debate: 'Memory must remain loyal and not serve to rewrite history; a treaty belongs to its authors and not to the judge'.[127]

The aforementioned limit, ie that evolutive interpretation should never lead to a revision of a treaty, is not only the connecting tissue between all the 'internal' limits but its proximity to concepts such as 'separation of powers' links it also to the second group of limits, which are the *systemic* limits. These limits refer to the entire system of international law and consist of limits that emerge as a result of ensuring logical and normative consistency throughout the entire system of international law. Two are

The matter is further complicated since the Court goes on to base its entire judgement on evolutive interpretation; *Dispute Regarding Navigational and Related Rights* [64]; see also *Temple of Preah Vihear* (Merits) 34; and criticism by R Moloo, 'When Actions Speak Louder Than Words: The Relevance of Subsequent Party Conduct to Treaty Interpretation' (2013) 31/1 BerkJIntlL 39, 78.

125 Aust, *Modern Treaty Law and Practice* 212–4 and cases cited therein.

126 ILC, 'Draft Conclusions on Subsequent Agreements and Subsequent Practice, with Commentaries' 63 [38].

127 P-M Dupuy, 'Evolutionary Interpretation of Treaties: Between Memory and Prophecy' in Cannizzaro (ed), *The Law of Treaties Beyond the Vienna Convention* 123, 129, although, citing Chief Justice Holmes, he acknowledges that when international judges seek the presumed intention of the parties 'evolutionary interpretation is not simply an exercise of memory; it tends towards prophecy'. In such a scenario, drawing the exact line where a judge crosses from the permitted boundaries of evolutive interpretation into the impermissible realm of exercising a *pouvoir de légiférer* would be a challenging task; ibid 126–7, citing OW Holmes 'The Path of the Law' 10 HLR 457, 458.

the main limits that belong in this category:[128] non-retroactivity and *jus cogens* norms.

As shown in the previous sections, the principle of non-retroactivity does not *eo ipso* conflict with intertemporal law. However, courts and tribunals have found it pertinent to underline that an evolutive interpretation should always be carried out in such a manner so as not to perfidiously lead to a violation of the principle of non-retroactivity.[129] Even more straightforward is the systemic limit relating to *jus cogens* norms.[130] Since *jus cogens* norms are norms from which no derogation is possible,[131] an interpretation that would end up with a result that would be in clear contradistinction to such a norm would be impermissible.[132] The Institut de Droit International considered this so fundamental to the interpretative process that it explicitly referred to it in its 'Resolution on Intertemporal Law': 'States and other subjects of international law shall, however, have the power to determine by common consent the temporal sphere of application of norms, ... subject to any imperative norm of international law which might restrict that power'.[133]

All the aforementioned limits are universal, ie apply to evolutive interpretation of any type of treaty by any international agent. Of course, this does not preclude that additional limits may emerge in the future[134]

[128] Or three, if one decides to categorise non-revision as a systemic limit as well.

[129] *ATA Construction, Industrial and Trading Company v Jordan* [109]; *Mondev International Ltd v USA* [70].

[130] On the attempts of the ILC to shed some light on the theory, emergence, and content of *jus cogens* norms, see D Tladi, 'First Report on *Jus Cogens*' (8 March 2016) UN Doc A/CN.4/693; D Tladi, 'Second Report on *Jus Cogens*' (16 March 2017) UN Doc A/CN.4/706; D Tladi, 'Third Report on Peremptory Norms of General International Law (*Jus Cogens*)' (12 February 2018) UN Doc A/CN.4/714; D Tladi, 'Fourth Report on Peremptory Norms of General International Law (*Jus Cogens*)' (31 January 2019) UN Doc A/CN.4/727.

[131] Art 53 VCLT; see also all four of Tladi's reports on *jus cogens*.

[132] *Application of the Convention on the Prevention and Punishment of the Crime of Genocide (Bosnia and Herzegovina v Serbia and Montenegro)* (Judgment) [2007] ICJ Rep 43, Joint Declaration of Shi and Koroma [2]; *South West Africa Cases (Second Phase) (Ethiopia v South Africa; Liberia v South Africa)* (Judgment) [1966] ICJ Rep 6, Dissenting Opinion of Judge Tanaka 293–5; E McWhinney, 'The Time Dimension in International Law, Historical Relativism and Intertemporal Law' in J Makarczyk (ed), *Essays in International Law in Honour of Judge Manfred Lachs* (Martinus Nijhoff 1984) 179, 183.

[133] Institut de Droit International, 'Resolution of 11 August 1975: The Intertemporal Problem' [3].

[134] See Sections 4.3 and 4.4 on the fallacy of the immutability of the rules of interpretation.

or that an individual treaty may be subject to additional limits. For instance, the ECtHR has introduced some limits which are, however, specific only to the sphere of the interpretation and application of the ECHR.[135] Regime-specific limits aside, all the aforementioned internal and systemic limits demonstrate that evolutive interpretation is not a *carte blanche* for judges to exercise a *pouvoir de légiférer* but rather is an important tool in their interpretative toolkit, which must, however, be used within certain boundaries, no matter how wide, and always with deference to the intention of the parties.

4.3 Motion through Time of the Rules on Interpretation

In the previous sections we examined, when dealing with the motion of treaties through the spacetime of the international legal system, the rules that govern the determination of the choice between a contemporaneous (static) and an evolutive interpretation. The conclusion was that, despite the variety of approaches and solutions adopted by academics and judicial bodies, the underlying constant was the intention of the parties, their 'time-will'.

However, our frame of reference for these sections were the treaties being interpreted. In order to present a 'holistic' picture of motion in the interpretative process, we need to switch our frame of reference to the VCLT itself, and specifically Articles 31–33 VCLT. What we show is that the manner in which rules of interpretation are being applied in the temporal dimension may be fraught with logical, methodological, and normative inconsistencies as well as with contradictory assertions that are detrimental to the rule of law of the international legal system. Often

[135] Such as the 'margin of appreciation', 'the common European standard' or 'European consensus' and, to a lesser degree, its established jurisprudence, departure from which is justified only for good reason. For 'margin of appreciation', see eg *Vo v France* [82]; *Rasmussen v Denmark*, ECtHR, App No 8777/79 (28 November 1984) [40]; *Sheffield and Horsham v UK* [GC] ECtHR, App Nos 22885/93, 23390/94 (30 July 1998) [1–4]; for 'the common European standard' or 'European consensus', see eg *Vo v France* [82] and Separate Opinion of Judge Costa, Joined by Judge Traja; *Scoppola v Italy (No 2)* [GC] ECtHR, App No 10249/03 (17 September 2009) [104]; for established jurisprudence as a relative limit, see eg *Chapman v UK* [GC] ECtHR, App No 27238/95 (18 January 2001) [70]; *Stafford v UK* [GC] ECtHR, App No 46295/99 (28 May 2002) [68]; *Inze v Austria*, ECtHR, App No 8695/79 (28 October 1987) [41]; *Vilho Eskelinen and others v Finland* [GC] ECtHR, App No 63235/00 (19 April 2007) [56]; *Micallef v Malta* [GC] ECtHR, App No 17056/06 (15 October 2009) [81]; *Airey v Ireland* [GC] ECtHR, App No 6289/73 (9 October 1979) [24]; *Goodwin v UK* [GC] ECtHR, App No 17488/90 (27 March 1996) [74].

when courts are required to interpret a treaty concluded several decades before the VCLT, they automatically presuppose that the customary rules of interpretation were and have remained the same throughout the ages. It is this practice of going back in the past to interpret a treaty, but in doing so 'looking back' to the future rules of interpretation for guidance, a kind of interpretative 'temporal solipsism', that this section aims to deconstruct.

Looking at the jurisprudence of the ICJ alone, this practice is quite widespread. In no less than 29 cases,[136] the Court has found it useful to refer to the VCLT for purposes of interpretation,[137] even though the VCLT was not applicable, because one or both of the parties were not parties to the VCLT or became parties to the VCLT after the date on which the treaty under interpretation was concluded, or the treaty was concluded before 27 January 1980 (date of entry into force of the VCLT). The relevant cases, along with relevant ratification and treaty information are reproduced in Table 4.1.

Of note is that in 19 of these 29 cases, the Court does not merely pay lip-service to the fact that the customary rules on interpretation are enshrined in the VCLT, and use the classical VCLT terms such as 'object and purpose', but actually actively refers to the text of the VCLT for interpretative purposes. In an additional two (*Maritime Delimitation in the Black Sea*, and *Alleged Violations of Sovereign Rights and Maritime Spaces in the Caribbean Sea*), the Court goes a step further, where it does not even refer to the fact that they have to apply CIL, and simply goes directly to the VCLT. This may not *per se* be problematic, as long as the rules have remained the same.

Bearing the above in mind, what we demonstrate is that one solution to the problem of using modern rules of interpretation when interpreting earlier treaties would be to argue that these rules are immutable, or at least that they have not changed in the last few centuries. However, that is not the case. Not only was the very existence of rules of interpretation hotly debated until recently, but even their content both in academic

136 Eight of these are the *Legality of Use of Force* cases.

137 In an additional one, the VCLT was referred to only by one of the parties to the dispute but not by the Court itself; *Elettronica Sicula SpA (ELSI) (USA v Italy)* (Judgment) [1989] ICJ Rep 15 [118]. The USA was not a party to the VCLT, and both the treaties being interpreted had been concluded before 1980; Treaty of Friendship, Commerce and Navigation (Italy–USA) (adopted 2 February 1948, entered into force 26 July 1949) 79 UNTS 171; Agreement Supplementing the Treaty of Friendship, Commerce and Navigation of 2 February 1948 (Italy–USA) (adopted 26 September 1951, entered into force 2 March 1961) 404 UNTS 326.

Table 4.1 *Relevant ICJ cases*

No	Case	VCLT EIF for Parties	Judgment Date	Relevant paras	Treaty being Interpreted
1	*Land, Island and Maritime Frontier Dispute (El Salvador/Honduras, Nicaragua Intervening)* (Judgment) [1992] ICJ 350	El Salvador (n/a) Honduras (EIF: 1980)	11/9/1992	[373], [376], [380]	General Peace Treaty (El Salvador – Honduras) (adopted 30 October 1980, entered into force 10 December 1980) 1310 UNTS 213
2	*Arbitral Award of 31 July 1989 (Guinea Bissau v Senegal)* (Judgment) [1991] ICJ Rep 53	Guinea-Bissau (n/a) Senegal (EIF 1986)	12/11/1991	[48]	Arbitration Agreement (Guinea-Bissau – Senegal) (adopted 12 March 1985)
3	*Territorial Dispute (Libyan Arab Jamahiriya/Chad)* (Judgment) [1994] ICJ Rep 6	Libya (EIF 2009) Chad (n/a)	3/2/ 1994	[41], [43]	Treaty of Friendship and Good Neighbourliness (France – Libya) (adopted 10 August 1955) 162 BFSP 470
4	*Maritime Delimitation between Qatar and Bahrain (Qatar v Bahrain)* (Jurisdiction and Admissibility) [1995] ICJ Rep 6	Qatar (n/a) Bahrain (n/a)	15/2/1995	[33]	Doha Minutes (Qatar – Bahrain) (adopted 25 December 1990)

Table 4.1 (*cont.*)

No	Case	VCLT EIF for Parties	Judgment Date	Relevant paras	Treaty being Interpreted
5	*Oil Platforms (Iran v USA)* (Preliminary Objections) [1996] ICJ Rep 803	Iran (n/a) USA (n/a)	12/12/1996	[23]	Treaty of Amity, Economic Relations and Consular Rights (USA – Iran) (adopted 15 August 1955, entered into force 16 June 1957) 284 UNTS 93
6	*Oil Platforms (Iran v USA)* (Counter-Claims) [2003] ICJ Rep 16	Iran (n/a) USA (n/a)	6/11/2003	[41]	Treaty of Amity, Economic Relations and Consular Rights (USA – Iran) (adopted 15 August 1955, entered into force 16 June 1957) 284 UNTS 93
7	*Application of the Convention on the Prevention and Punishment of the Crime of Genocide (Bosnia and Herzegovina v Serbia and Montenegro)* (Merits) [2007] ICJ Rep 43	Bosnia and Herzegovina (EIF 1993) Serbia and Montenegro (EIF 2001/2006)	26/2/2007	[160], [163]	Convention on the Prevention and Punishment of the Crime of Genocide (adopted 9 December 1948, entered into force 12 January 1951) 78 UNTS 277

8	*Kasikili/Sedudu Island (Botswana/Namibia)* (Judgment) [1999] ICJ Rep 1045	Bostwana (n/a) Namibia (n/a)	13/12/1999	[18], [20], [25], [48], [52], [55], [63], [73], [75], [78-9]	Anglo-German Treaty [Heligoland – Zanzibar Treaty] (adopted 1 July 1890) 51 Das Staatsarchiv, Sammlung der offiziellen Aktenstücke zur Geschichte der Gegenwart [German State Archive, Collection of Official Documents Relating to Contemporary History] 151
9	*Sovereignty over Pulau Litigan and Pulau Sipadan (Indonesia/ Malaysia)* (Judgment) [2002] ICJ Rep 625	Indonesia (n/a) Malaysia (EIF 1994)	17/12/2002	[37–8], [44], [48], [59–61]	Convention Between Great Britain and the Netherlands Defining Boundaries in Borneo (adopted 20 June 1891) 83 BFSP 42
10	*LaGrand (Germany v USA)* (Merits) [2001] ICJ Rep 466	Germany (EIF 1987) USA (n/a)	27/06/2001	[99–109]	Statute of the International Court of Justice (adopted 26 June 1945, entered into force 24 October 1945) 1 UNTS 993

Table 4.1 (*cont.*)

No	Case	VCLT EIF for Parties	Judgment Date	Relevant paras	Treaty being Interpreted
11	*Legality of Use of Force (Serbia and Montenegro v Belgium)* (Preliminary Objections) [2004] ICJ Rep 279	Serbia and Montenegro (EIF 2001/2006; [Yugoslavia EIF 1980]) Belgium (EIF 1992)	15/12/2004	[100–1]	Statute of the International Court of Justice (adopted 26 June 1945, entered into force 24 October 1945) 1 UNTS 993
12	*Legality of Use of Force (Serbia and Montenegro v Canada)* (Preliminary Objections) [2004] ICJ Rep 429	Serbia and Montenegro (EIF 2001/2006; [Yugoslavia EIF 1980]) Canada (EIF 1980)	15/12/2004	[99]	Statute of the International Court of Justice (adopted 26 June 1945, entered into force 24 October 1945) 1 UNTS 993
13	*Legality of Use of Force (Serbia and Montenegro v France)* (Preliminary Objections) [2004] ICJ Rep 575	Serbia and Montenegro (EIF 2001/2006; [Yugoslavia EIF 1980]) France (n/a)	15/12/2004	[99]	Statute of the International Court of Justice (adopted 26 June 1945, entered into force 24 October 1945) 1 UNTS 993
14	*Legality of Use of Force (Serbia and Montenegro v Germany)* (Preliminary Objections) [2004] ICJ Rep 720	Serbia and Montenegro (EIF 2001/2006; [Yugoslavia EIF 1980]) Germany (EIF 1987)	15/12/2004	[98]	Statute of the International Court of Justice (adopted 26 June 1945, entered into force 24 October 1945) 1 UNTS 993

15	*Legality of Use of Force (Serbia and Montenegro v Italy)* (Preliminary Objections) [2004] ICJ Rep 865	Serbia and Montenegro (EIF 2001/2006; [Yugoslavia EIF 1980]) Italy (EIF 1980)	15/12/2004	[99]	Statute of the International Court of Justice (adopted 26 June 1945, entered into force 24 October 1945) 1 UNTS 993
16	*Legality of Use of Force (Serbia and Montenegro v Netherlands)* (Preliminary Objections) [2004] ICJ Rep 1011	Serbia and Montenegro (EIF 2001/2006; [Yugoslavia EIF 1980]) Netherlands (EIF 1985)	15/12/2004	[99]	Statute of the International Court of Justice (adopted 26 June 1945, entered into force 24 October 1945) 1 UNTS 993
17	*Legality of Use of Force (Serbia and Montenegro v Portugal)* (Preliminary Objections) [2004] ICJ Rep 1160	Serbia and Montenegro (EIF 2001/2006; [Yugoslavia EIF 1980]) Portugal (20 EIF 04)	15/12/2004	[102]	Statute of the International Court of Justice (adopted 26 June 1945, entered into force 24 October 1945) 1 UNTS 993
18	*Legality of Use of Force (Serbia and Montenegro v UK)* (Preliminary Objections) [2004] ICJ Rep 1307	Serbia and Montenegro (EIF 2001/2006; [Yugoslavia EIF 1980]) UK (EIF 1980)	15/12/2004	[98]	Statute of the International Court of Justice (adopted 26 June 1945, entered into force 24 October 1945) 1 UNTS 993
19	*Avena and Other Mexican Nationals (Mexico v USA)* (Judgment) [2004] ICJ Rep 12	Mexico (EIF 1980) USA (n/a)	31/3/2004	[83]	Vienna Convention on Consular Relations (adopted 24 April 1963, entered into force 19 March 1967) 596 UNTS 261

Table 4.1 (*cont.*)

No	Case	VCLT EIF for Parties	Judgment Date	Relevant paras	Treaty being Interpreted
20	*Maritime Delimitation in the Black Sea (Romania v Ukraine)* (Judgment) [2009] ICJ Rep 61	Romania (n/a) Ukraine (EIF 1986)	3/2/2009	[42]	United Nations Convention on the Law of the Sea (adopted 10 December 1982, entered into force 1 November 1994) 1833 UNTS 397
21	*Dispute Regarding Navigational and Related Rights (Costa Rica v Nicaragua)* (Judgment) [2009] ICJ Rep 213	Costa Rica (EIF 1996) Nicaragua (n/a)	13/6/2009	[47]	Treaty of Limits (Costa Rica – Nicaragua – San Salvador) (adopted 15 April 1858, entered into force 26 April 1858) in TM Leonard (ed), *Encyclopedia of US-Latin American Relations* (SAGE 2012)
22	*Pulp Mills on the River Uruguay (Argentina v Uruguay)* (Judgment) [2010] ICJ Rep 14	Argentina (EIF 1980) Uruguay (EIF 1982)	20/4/2010	[55]	Statute on the River Uruguay (adopted 26 February 1975, entered into force 18 September 1976) (Argentina–Uruguay) 1295 UNTS 331

23	*Certain Questions of Mutual Assistance in Criminal Matters (Djibouti v France)* (Judgment) [2008] ICJ Rep 177	Djibouti (n/a) France (n/a)	4/6/2008	[112–3]	Treaty of Friendship and Cooperation between the French Republic and the Republic of Djibouti (adopted 27 June 1977, entered into force 31 October 1982) 1482 UNTS 195
24	*Maritime Dispute (Peru v Chile)* (Judgment) [2014] ICJ Rep 3	Peru (EIF 2000) Chile (EIF 1981)	27/1/2014	[33–4] (parties); [57–8], [65] (the Court)	Declaration on the Maritime Zones (Peru – Chile) (adopted and entered into force 18 August 1952) 1006 UNTS 323
25	*Question of the Delimitation of the Continental Shelf between Nicaragua and Colombia beyond 200 Nautical Miles from the Nicaraguan Coast (Nicaragua v Colombia)* (Preliminary Objections) [2016] ICJ Rep 100	Nicaragua (n/a) Colombia (EIF 1985)	17/3/2016	[33], [38], [44]	American Treaty on Pacific Settlement (Pact of Bogotá) (adopted 30 April 1948, entered into force 6 May 1949) OAS Treaty Series No 17 and 61

Table 4.1 (*cont.*)

No	Case	VCLT EIF for Parties	Judgment Date	Relevant paras	Treaty being Interpreted
26	*Alleged Violations of Sovereign Rights and Maritime Spaces in the Caribbean Sea (Nicaragua v Colombia)* (Preliminary Objections) [2016] ICJ Rep 3	Nicaragua (n/a) Colombia (1985)	17/3/2016	[40], [46]	American Treaty on Pacific Settlement (Pact of Bogotá) (adopted 30 April 1948, entered into force 6 May 1949) OAS Treaty Series No 17 and 61
27	*Maritime Delimitation in the Indian Ocean (Somalia v Kenya)* (Preliminary Objections) [2017] ICJ Rep 3	Somalia (n/a) Kenya (n/a)	2/2/2017	[63–4]	Memorandum of Understanding between the Government of the Republic of Kenya and the Transitional Federal Government of the Somali Republic to Grant to Each Other No-Objection in Respect of Submissions on the Outer Limits of the Continental Shelf beyond 200 Nautical Miles to the Commission on the Limits of the Continental Shelf (adopted and entered into force 7 April 2009) 70 Law of the Sea Bulletin 52

28	*Immunities and Criminal Proceedings (Equatorial Guinea v France)* (Preliminary Objections) General List No 163 [2018] ICJ 1	Equatorial Guinea (n/a) France (n/a)	6/6/2018	[91], [131]	United Nations Convention Against Transnational Organized Crime (adopted 15 November 2000, entered into force 29 September 2003) 2225 UNTS 209
29	*Jadhav Case (India v Pakistan)* (Merits) General List No 168 [2019] ICJ 1	India (n/a) Pakistan (n/a)	17/7/2019	[71], [135]	Vienna Convention on Consular Relations (adopted 24 April 1963, entered into force 19 March 1967) 596 UNTS 261

writings and international judicial practice has been and continues to be in a continuous state of flux. Apart from this empirical evidence, even logically such a claim would be systemically incoherent with the structure of the international legal system.

Once we demonstrate that the rules of interpretation are open to change, what we shall examine is whether the use of future rules for past treaties conflicts with any existing rules or principles of international law. If not, then it would simply be in the discretion of each judge to do as they pleased. What we show is that there are principles in play which set certain limits to what rules the judges can apply. This chapter concludes by identifying, based on the previous analysis, the scenarios where our 'time-travelling' rules of interpretation are allowed to traverse the arrow of time in the opposite direction and provide a set of guidelines as to what is the logically and normatively coherent manner in interpreting pre-VCLT treaties.

4.3.1 *Claim That Rules of Interpretation, Despite the Passage of Time, Are Immutable*

4.3.1.1 Very Existence of Rules of Interpretation

The claim that rules of interpretation enshrined in the VCLT are either immutable or have, at least, not undergone any significant changes throughout the centuries is one that deserves our attention. If that is the case, then the ICJ (and any interpreter, for that matter) by considering the VCLT rules would be in principle applying the rules at the time of the conclusion of a treaty, since their content has not changed at all. However, upon closer scrutiny this does not seem to hold any water. First, even the very existence of rules of interpretation was a topic that was highly debated decades before the ILC started discussing the draft articles on the law of treaties. Taylor, for instance, was of the opinion that 'it seems to be universally admitted that it is next to impossible "to prescribe any system of rules of interpretation for cases of ambiguity in written language that will really avail to guide the mind in the decision of doubt"'.[138] Yü, on the other hand, starting from the excessive multiplicity of alleged canons of construction or maxims of interpretation, was led to the conclusion that the abundance of such rules detracted from any meaningfulness that they may have, since 'a mere application of one, or a shrewd combination of two, of them may yield almost whatever

[138] H Taylor, *A Treatise on Public International Law* (Callaghan 1901) 394.

conclusion the interpreter desires'.[139] He acknowledged that one 'rule'[140] on interpretation existed and that was the discovery of the intention of the parties. In his view,

> [the] challenge [that the people that support the existence of a set of rules of interpretation face] ... is this: Can scientific results be obtained through sheer flights of imagination? That the collection of rules sponsored by some publicists are inefficacious in interpreting treaties between nations may be seen from the very fact that interpretation is eminently a practical science, and as such it has to consider extrinsic evidence and circumstances peculiar to each individual case. Moreover, the fundamental difficulty in prescribing a system of rules also lies in the imperfect nature of human language itself, through which no one can define or direct any intellectual process with perfection. How then is it to be expected that any artificial rules which are generally to govern the operations of human relationship can be of scientific value? It would appear, therefore, as futile to attempt to frame positive and fixed rules of construction as to endeavor in the same manner to set forth the mode by which judges should draw conclusions from various species of evidence.[141]

Similar views regarding the impossibility and/or undesirability of a strict set of rules on interpretation were expressed by Westlake,[142] Hyde,[143] Lawrence,[144] Fenwick,[145] Hershey,[146] Oppenheim[147]

139 T-C Yü, *The Interpretation of Treaties* (Sn 1927) 72. For example, in the *van Bokkelen* case, the tribunal provided an extensive list of alleged 'rules' of interpretation; *Charles van Bokkelen* case *(USA v Haiti)* (1888) 2 Moore International Arbitrations 1807, 1848 ff.

140 Understood in an abstract manner and not as a legal rule *per se*.

141 Yü, *The Interpretation of Treaties* 28.

142 '[The rules on interpretation laid down by publicists] are not likely to be of much practical use'; J Westlake, *International Law* (2nd edn, Sn 1910) 293.

143 Hyde was of the view that the objective of interpretation was to discover the intention of the parties, and that this effort should not be hampered by any preconceived rules, principles, or assumptions; CC Hyde, 'Concerning the Interpretation of Treaties' (1909) 3 AJIL 46, 47.

144 '[A] vast amount of misplaced energy has been expended [on trying to devise a set of rules of interpretation]', although he later on concedes to textual (ordinary and special meaning) and contextual interpretation; TJ Lawrence, *Principles of International Law* (7th edn, MacMillan 1923) 302.

145 Rules of interpretation only have an 'inchoate legal value'; CG Fenwick, *International Law* (The American Law Book Co 1924) 331.

146 Although Hershey puts down nine rules on interpretation in his writings, he makes it crystal-clear that these rules have found general acceptance but should not be considered as forming 'part of International Law proper'; AS Hershey, *The Essentials of International Public Law and Organization* (rev edn, MacMillan 1927) 445.

147 '[N]either customary nor conventional rules of International Law exist concerning the interpretation of treaties'; L Oppenheim, *International Law – Vol 1: Peace* (4th edn, Longmans 1928) 759.

and Brierly.[148] Even in the *Commentary of the Harvard Convention on the Law of Treaties*, the drafters acknowledged this problem, only to state that the rules on interpretation which were laid out in Article 19 were not iron-clad rules but rather 'guides to direct the interpreter'.[149]

One could brush aside most of these views by simply stating that they were a thing of the past, as they were all expressed prior to 1930, at a time when the rules of interpretation may have been considered still in formation. To that argument, however, two critical remarks must be raised in objection. First of all, that would have an underlying assumption that if a treaty from that period or before was to be interpreted, then it would be dubious whether any international court or tribunal could refer to the modern rules of interpretation. But this is exactly what several courts and tribunals have been doing, by interpreting pre-VCLT treaties by reference to the customary content of the rules of interpretation as enshrined in the VCLT. Secondly, this uncertainty continued well on into the 1950s and 1960s[150] and was reflected in the discussions

[148] Brierly was of the view that there 'are no technical rules in international law for the interpretation of treaties; its objective can only be to give effect to the intention of the parties as fully and fairly as possible'; JL Brierly, *The Law of Nations: An Introduction to the International Law of Peace* (Clarendon Press 1928) 168.

[149] It is worth reproducing the relevant part in full: 'It seems evident that the prescription in advance of hard and fast rules of interpretation – even though, as in the case of those proposed by Ehrlich, *they amount only to rebuttable presumptions* – contains an element of danger which is to be avoided ... If it be kept always in mind that the so-called rules of interpretation have no extraordinary sanctity or universality of application, and that in all probability they developed as neat *ex post facto* descriptions or justifications of decisions arrived at by mental processes more complicated than the mere mechanical application of rules to a text, they may serve some purpose as aids to interpretation. Where a rule is of such a nature as to suggest a line of investigation for discovering the general purpose of the parties, or where a consideration of all pertinent circumstances in a particular case results in a decision easily explained by a well-known maxim, there is probably no harm in relying on it. *It is always to be recalled, however, that the process of interpretation of treaties is, of necessity, one which is not to be confined within narrow limits by iron-clad rules; that all "rules", including those laid down in this article, are but guides to direct the interpreter toward a decision which conforms, not to preconceived standards, but to the circumstances peculiar to the particular case before him*' (emphasis added); JW Garner (Reporter), 'Codification of International Law: Part III – Law of Treaties – Draft Convention on the Law of Treaties' (1935) 29 AJIL Supp 657, 946–7 (hereinafter Harvard Draft Convention).

[150] See, for instance, McNair, who wrote that he was 'amongst those who are sceptical as to the value of those so-called rules and are sympathetic to the process of their gradual devaluation, of which indications exist. The many maxims and phrases which have crystallised out and abound in the textbooks and elsewhere are mere *prima facie* guides to the intention of the parties in a particular case'; McNair, *The Law of Treaties* 366.

of the Institut de Droit International, and during the ILC meetings on the law of treaties.

As far as the Institut de Droit International was concerned, members expressed similar doubts about the existence of technical rules on interpretation.[151] In the end, however, the Institut adopted, during the Grenada Session in 1956, a resolution on interpretation of treaties.[152] Despite this, the situation in the ILC was not radically different. Waldock, for instance, in his 'Third Report on the Law of Treaties', starts his commentary on the articles relating to interpretation of treaties by acknowledging that 'even the existence of rules of international law governing the interpretation of treaties are questions which are not free from controversy'.[153] Apart from the Special Rapporteur, other members also expressed qualms about the existence of rules of interpretation. For instance, Briggs was of the view that '[t]he canons of interpretation were not always rules of international law but, as Judge de Visscher had said, they were working hypotheses'.[154] Ruda also felt that 'at the present stage of development of international law, there did not as yet exist for States any obligatory rules on the subject of interpretation'.[155] According to him, if there were any rules that would simply be the Vattelian axiom *in claris non fit interpretatio*. He stressed that he was referring to rules binding upon States. In his view, 'if any rules existed, they were subject to considerable doubt, except for the rule in *claris non fit interpretatio*, which had been first formulated by Vattel and which meant that there could be no question of interpretation where the sense was clear and there was nothing to interpret'.

Both USA and Ghana also had their doubts, with the former when asked for comments on the draft articles suggesting that it might be better to draft the relevant articles as guidelines rather than as rules,[156] whereas the latter during the 1968 Vienna Conference on the Law of Treaties raised similar objections regarding the nature of the proposed 'rules'.[157]

151 Institut de Droit International, 'De l'interprétation des traités' (1950) 43/1 AIDI 336 ff.
152 Institut de Droit International, 'De l'interprétation des traités' (1956) 46 AIDI 359.
153 Waldock, 'Third Report' 53 [1].
154 ILC, 'Summary Record of the 765th Meeting' [9].
155 ibid [33] and similar comments in ibid [16] (de Luna).
156 Waldock, 'Sixth Report' 93.
157 The objection was raised by Ghana; United Nations Conference on the Law of Treaties, '1st Session – 31st Meeting of the Committee of the Whole (COW)' (19 April 1968) UN Doc A/CONF.39/C.1/SR.31 164 [68].

As is manifestly evident from the material presented above, the existence of binding rules of interpretation was questioned even right up to the adoption of VCLT. Even today there are authors who still object to the existence of binding rules of interpretation.[158] To argue that for every treaty ever signed and ratified there were immutable customary rules of interpretation which applied is to say the least a very generalised and superficial description of an extremely complex topic.[159]

4.3.1.2 Various Forms of Rules of Interpretation

But let us leave aside the highly debatable proposition that customary 'rules' of interpretation have existed since the inception of the international legal system. Even if one concedes the fact that customary rules (or more likely principles of interpretation) existed at the dawn of interpretation of international treaties, that still does not solve the problem of using the VCLT rules as a reflection of customary international law. There is still an insurmountable hurdle that must be overcome: the problem of the content of those customary rules/principles, at various points in history. As the argument goes, at least according to the practice of the ICJ, these customary rules have not been the subject of radical change. But is this really the case? In the previous section, some of the

[158] J d'Aspremont, 'The Multi-dimensional Process of Interpretation: Content-Determination and Law Ascertainment Distinguished' in A Bianchi, D Peat, and M Windsor (eds), *Interpretation in International Law* (OUP 2015) 111–29; J d'Aspremont, 'The Idea of "Rules" in the Sources of International Law' (2013) 84 BYIL 103; J Kammerhofer, *Uncertainty in International Law: A Kelsenian Perspective* (Routledge 2011); R Gardiner, 'Characteristics of the Vienna Convention Rules on Treaty Interpretation' in Bowman and Kritsiotis (eds), *Conceptual and Contextual Perspectives* 335–62.

[159] The authors wish to clarify at this point that, in their view, both after and prior to the VCLT there are and were customary rules on interpretation, although their content has changed and/or been clarified through time. Prior to the VCLT and the further back we go in time, these rules become less customary and more principles stemming from domestic legal systems and/or 'constructive rules', in the Anzilottian sense, ie rules that must by necessity exist otherwise the judges would be unable to execute properly their function (consider the logical absurdity of a case, where a judge did not have any rules of interpretation to fall back on); as one author has characterised them, these 'constructive rules' are essentially 'not the rules of the game but the necessary premises for the game to be played'; J Crivellaro, 'How did Anzilotti's Jurisprudential Conception Influence the Jurisprudence of the Permanent Court of International Justice?' (*Jura Gentium*, 2011) <www.juragentium.org/topics/thil/en/crivella.htm> accessed 20 September 2019; generally, on 'constructive rules', see D Anzilotti, *Cours de Droit International, Tome I* (Sirey 1929) 68 ff; G Gaja, 'Positivism and Dualism in Dionisio Anzilotti' (1992) 3 EJIL 123, 128 ff.

authors who doubted the existence of rules of interpretation also made some educated guesses about possible useful ones, as several other authors have done.[160] These are too numerous and diverse to enumerate here. However, and in order to demonstrate that this diversity is a common and repeating theme, in this section the focus is on the various codes and treaties that included rules of interpretation. What is shown is that each of these documents not only proposed different rules from one another, but also and most importantly differed from the VCLT rules. In the following analysis, various rules proposed have been distilled to their essence and described in a manner similar to the wording used by the VCLT in order for the differences to become more apparent.

In the first attempts towards codification of the international law of treaties, rules of interpretation are conspicuous by their absence. Not in the Havana Convention on Treaties[161] or in David Dudley Field's[162] or Bluntschli's Draft Code[163] or the 1927 Draft of the International Commission of American Jurists[164] do we find any rules of interpretation included. In Fiore's Draft Code, however, an extensive list of rules

[160] See, for instance, Fitzmaurice, who identified six principles of interpretation on the basis of the jurisprudence of the ICJ: (i) principle of actuality (or textuality); (ii) principle of the natural and ordinary meaning; (iii) principle of integration. Subject to those principles were: (iv) principle of effectiveness (*ut res magis valeat quam pereat*); (v) principle of subsequent practice, and (vi) principle of contemporaneity; G Fitzmaurice, 'The Law and Procedure of the International Court of Justice, 1951–4: Treaty Interpretation' 211–2; for presentations of the various principles of interpretation used in both international and domestic jurisprudence, see CC Hyde, 'Interpretation of Treaties by the Permanent Court of International Justice' (1930) 24 AJIL 1; WE Beckett, 'Decisions of the Permanent Court of International Justice on Points of Law and Procedure of General Application' (1930) 11 BYIL 1; WE Beckett, 'Les questions d' intérêt général au point de vue juridique dans la jurisprudence de la Cour permanente de justice internationale' (1932) 39 RdC 135, 261 ff; WE Beckett, 'Les questions d' intérêt général au point de vue juridique dans la jurisprudence de la Cour permanente de justice internationale (juillet 1932–juillet 1934)' (1934) 50 RdC 193; MO Hudson, *The Permanent Court of International Justice: A Treatise* (MacMillan 1934) 551–73; JB Moore, *A Digest of International Law* (Government Printing Office 1906) 249 ff; AD McNair, 'L' application et l' interprétation des traités d' aprés la jurisprudence britannique' (1933) 43 RdC 247.

[161] JW Garner (Reporter), 'Codification of International Law: Part III – Law of Treaties – Appendix 1: Convention on Treaties'(1935) 29 AJIL Supp 1205.

[162] JW Garner (Reporter), 'Codification of International Law: Part III – Law of Treaties – Appendix 2: David Dudley Field's Draft Code'(1935) 29 AJIL Supp 1207.

[163] JW Garner (Reporter), 'Codification of International Law: Part III – Law of Treaties – Appendix 3: Bluntschli's Draft Code'(1935) 29 AJIL Supp 1208.

[164] JW Garner (Reporter), 'Codification of International Law: Part III – Law of Treaties – Appendix 5: Draft of the International Commission of American Jurists' (1935) 29 AJIL Supp 1222.

referring to interpretation can be seen. First of all, Fiore adheres to the *in claris non fit interpretatio* maxim.[165] According to Fiore, when interpretation is necessary it can have one of two forms, either grammatical or logical. The former may be used to determine the meaning of vague expressions, whereas the latter is aimed at 'fix[ing] precisely the concept and extent of the reciprocal obligations assumed by the . . . parties'.[166] He then provides an extensive list of 'rules' that fall under each of these categories of interpretation. Grammatical interpretation, on the one hand, includes the following rules:

- *in claris non fit interpretatio*;
- ordinary meaning;
- contextual interpretation;
- technical ordinary meaning supersedes everyday ordinary meaning;
- in case of conflict between the ordinary meaning of a term and its meaning as clearly determined by the intention of the parties, it is the latter that shall prevail;
- in case of terms with different meanings in different languages the dominant meaning is that of the State which undertakes the relevant obligation; and
- interpretation by reference to prior and/or subsequent agreements, practice and other relevant rules.[167]

Logical interpretation, on the other hand, consists of the following rules:

- the intention of the parties is the dominant criterion (*semper autem in fide quid senseris, non quid dixeris cogitandum*);[168]
- *contra proferentem*;
- *in dubio mitius*;
- *ut res magis valeat quam pereat*;
- interpretation by reference to other 'relevant rules';

[165] JW Garner (Reporter), 'Codification of International Law: Part III – Law of Treaties – Appendix 4: Fiore's Draft Code' (1935) 29 AJIL Supp 1212 [797] (hereinafter Fiore's Draft Code).

[166] ibid [798].

[167] ibid [799–806].

[168] ibid [807]. The Latin phrase is a quote from Cicero's *De Officiis* and can be translated as: 'but in a promise, what you mean, not what you say, is always to be taken into account'; Marcus Tullius Cicero, *De Officiis* 1.40 (Latin text and translation available at the Perseus Digital Library, as above).

- contextual interpretation; and
- *travaux préparatoires* cannot be used to deviate from the meaning of the text.[169]

In addition to the foregoing, Fiore also offers some rules regarding resort to broad or restrictive interpretation. According to him, in principle when the text is clear, a broad interpretation or an interpretation by analogy should be avoided.[170] If, however, the text is ambiguous, this can be resolved through *in pari materia* interpretation.[171] Finally, provisions creating obligations or restricting rights should be interpreted restrictively.[172]

Unlike Fiore's Draft Code, a resolution on interpretation of treaties adopted by the Seventh International Conference of American States clearly demonstrated that the participating States were of the view that interpretation was governed not by 'rules' but by 'principles'.[173] In fact, Article 1 of the resolution states that 'the rules governing the interpretation of domestic law are applicable to the interpretation of international conventions'. Other interesting morsels taken from that Resolution are that:

- the intention of the parties[174] shall be sought in the preamble and the preparatory work;
- that the treaty must be interpreted in good faith;
- according to the ordinary meaning of its terms (or special meaning when that can be demonstrated);
- in context;
- by reference to subsequent agreements and practice;
- and in conformity with established rules of international law but only when the intention of the parties cannot be established clearly;[175,176]
- notably, restrictive or expansive interpretation may be resorted to only when the ordinary methods of interpretation have failed;
- *in dubio mitius* is to be resorted to when the issue is about an obligation of a State;[177] and finally

169 Fiore's Draft Code [807–14].
170 ibid [815–6].
171 ibid [816]; this interpretation is similar to Art 31(3)(c) VCLT.
172 ibid [817].
173 JW Garner (Reporter), 'Codification of International Law: Part III – Law of Treaties – Appendix 7: The Interpretation of Treaties' (1935) 29 AJIL Supp 1225 (hereinafter Conference of American States Resolution).
174 Referred to as 'will or purpose of the parties'.
175 A faint echo of Art 31(3)(c) VCLT.
176 Conference of American States Resolution, Arts 3–8.
177 ibid Art 10.

- if there is an issue of interpretation arising from the existence of equally authentic texts then the intention of the parties will be the deciding factor. If that cannot be established, then the restrictive interpretation will be the solution to be given.[178]

The commentary to the Harvard Convention, although explaining that the relevant Article 19 should be seen as including guidelines rather than strict rules, included the following: the object and purpose of the treaty, preparatory work, circumstances of conclusion, subsequent practice and agreements, and the conditions prevailing at the time interpretation is being made. But all of these are subservient to the general purpose of the treaty. Also, in case of multiple authentic texts the interpretation that best serves the object and purpose of the treaty will be opted for.[179]

Finally, the Institut de Droit International in its 1956 Resolution on 'Interpretation of Treaties' provided two articles that included various 'principles' from which the various courts and tribunals could draw inspiration. The first article includes references to interpretation based on good faith, the text, the ordinary meaning of the words (unless a special meaning was intended by the parties) in their context and in the light of principles of international law. In a supplementary and discretionary fashion, according to Article 2, recourse could also be had to other means, which include the recourse to preparatory work, subsequent practice and the purposes[180] of the treaty.[181]

Leaving aside the various ILC drafts on the articles on interpretation, which vary significantly from one another,[182] and focusing on the preceding attempts to codify the rules of interpretation, one thing becomes eminently clear. Although there are some similarities with Articles 31–33 VCLT, they are a far cry from being identical. Granted, there is reference to text, ordinary meaning, special meaning, good faith, and subsequent

[178] ibid Arts 9 and 11.

[179] Harvard Draft Convention, Art 19.

[180] Note the use of plural. For an extensive analysis of the inconsistencies, variations in the use and evolution of the terms 'object and purpose' see I Buffard and K Zemanek, 'The "Object and Purpose" of a Treaty: An Enigma?' (1998) 3/1 ARIEL 311; and for a recent foray into the purpose of 'object and purpose', see D Kritsiotis, 'The Object and Purpose of a Treaty's Object and Purpose' in Bowman and Kritsiotis (eds), *Conceptual and Contextual Perspectives* 237–302.

[181] Institut de Droit International, 'Resolution: L' interprétation des traités' (*IDI*, 1956) <www.idi-iil.org/app/uploads/2017/06/1956_grena_02_fr.pdf> accessed 20 September 2019.

[182] See the various ILC reports in YBILC between the years 1963 and 1966.

practice,[183] but the differences are much more pronounced. For instance, in some codes[184] there is reference to restrictive and expansive interpretations, which are activated when the main methods of interpretation have failed. Fiore's Draft Code starts with a reaffirmation of the *in claris non fit interpretatio* maxim, which, however, was rejected in the Vienna Conference on the Law of Treaties as being an 'obscurantist tautology'.[185]

Furthermore, the proposed rules in all the codes are peppered with references to other principles and maxims, which were not included explicitly in the VCLT, such as the *in dubio mititus* and *contra proferentem* maxims. Interestingly, Fiore's Draft Code and the Conference of American States Resolution place intention at the apex of the interpretative process and any other rule ends up yielding to it in case of conflict, an approach that was not necessarily reflected in the text of the VCLT, where textual interpretation was given not substantive but at least a temporal prominence. This deviation from the text of the VCLT is also reflected in the solutions in case of conflict between multiple authentic texts. Here we are presented with an embarrassment of solutions. Fiore's Draft Code gives precedence to the language of the State that undertakes the obligation; the Conference of American States Resolution opts for intention as the deciding factor and if that fails for a restrictive interpretation; only the Harvard Draft Convention goes for a version of the VCLT approach by opting for object and purpose as the means of resolving the ambiguity. A last example is that in the Resolution of the Institut de Droit International, where not only preparatory work but also subsequent practice, and even the object and purpose of the treaty, are categorised as supplementary means of interpretation, whose employment is entirely dependent on the discretion of the interpreter. The list of comparisons could continue to some length, but the above should suffice to prove the point that before the ILC, any attempts towards codification of the rules of interpretation of treaties were widely different from one another not only with respect to the actual rules codified but also their interplay and hierarchy. This, once again, demonstrates what a significant change in the interpretative process the VCLT was, where choices were made after long debates that were radically different from choices in earlier codes.

183 Although not in all of the attempts at codification. For instance, in the Harvard Draft Convention there is no explicit reference to ordinary meaning.

184 In Fiore's Draft Code and the Conference of American States Resolution.

185 United Nations Conference on the Law of Treaties, '1st Session – 31st Meeting COW' [38].

Consequently, on this front as well the claim that the rules of interpretation have not undergone any significant changes fails.

4.3.1.3 Interpretation of Rules of Interpretation

Having established that not only the nature of the 'rules' of interpretation (as being either rule, principles, canons, or maxims) were debated but even their content was in a constant state of flux at least until the adoption of the VCLT, one more thing remains to be proven: that the rules of interpretation are themselves also amenable to interpretation and change. If this can be demonstrated, then another critical blow will have been struck against the claim of immutability of the rules of interpretation in the pre-VCLT era, but this will also prove the possibility of change of the existing rules in the future.

Examining the interpretation of the rules of interpretation might sound somewhat self-referential and a recipe for legal and logical paradoxes, however the importance of this exercise cannot be overstated. Even the ILA Study Group on the Content and Evolution of the Rules of Interpretation in its 'Preliminary Report' of 2016 considered this topic one of fundamental importance and will be devoting its resources on establishing the process by which this interpretation has happened and continues to happen, as well as identifying divergent practices in interpretation depending on the tribunal in question.[186]

An exhaustive enumeration of the instances where such an interpretation has occurred falls outside the scope of this chapter. However, some examples that could be mentioned in order to prove the interpretability of the rules of interpretation are the clarificatory or divergent solutions that various courts and tribunals have given, when faced with questions relating to the exact scope of a rule of interpretation. Most notable amongst these are:

- International courts and tribunals often refer to a wide gamut of maxims such as *effet utile,*[187] *in dubio mitius,*[188] *expressio unius est*

[186] ILA, 'Preliminary Report of the Study Group on the Content and Evolution of the Rules of Interpretation' (*ILA*, 7-11 August 2016) <https://ila.vettoreweb.com/Storage/Download.aspx?DbStorageId=1401&StorageFileGuid=bcaa951e-ae3e-4ccb-9c80-248c98c741e3> accessed 20 September 2019, sect III.3.

[187] Also known as *ut res magis valeat quam pereat;* C Braumann and A Reinisch, '*Effet Utile*' in J Klingler, Y Parkhomenko and C Salonidis (eds), *Between the Lines of the Vienna Convention? Canons and Other Principles of Interpretation in Public International Law* (Wolters Kluwer 2018) 47–72.

[188] P Merkouris, '*In Dubio Mitius*' in ibid 259–306.

exclusio alterius,[189] *ex abundante cautela,*[190] *ejusdem generis,*[191] *contra proferentem*[192], *exceptio est strictissimae applicationis,*[193] *lex posterior* and *lex specialis,*[194] or apply comparative reasoning,[195] and logical tools (such as the rule of necessary implication[196] or *per argumentum a fortiori)*[197] in order to reach an interpretative conclusion. However, this use raises a slew of questions, which have been answered differently depending on the tribunals or author and particular time period.

Are these maxims and approaches to be considered as customary international law? If so, are they customary law on interpretation *praeter*-VCLT, or do they fall under the Articles 31(3)(c) or 32 VCLT (*intra legem*)?[198] If not, when they are used by courts and tribunals is this interpretation under Article 32 or *contra legem*? Any answer to these questions is by nature an interpretation of the VCLT rules on interpretation and one that crystallises and, in some cases, evolves the content of those rules.[199]

189 J Klingler, '*Expressio Unius Est Exclusio Altrerius*' in ibid 73–114.

190 A Macdonald, '*Ex Abundante Cautela*' in ibid 115–32.

191 Fr Baetens, '*Ejusdem Generis* and *Noscitur a Sociis*' in ibid 133–60.

192 P d'Argent, '*Contra Proferentem*' in ibid 241–58.

193 A Solomou, 'Exceptions to a Rule Must Be Narrowly Construed' in ibid 359–86.

194 D Pulkowski, '*Lex Specialis Derogat Legi Generali/Generalia Specialibus Non Derogant*' in ibid 161–96. On these maxims as conflict resolution tecnhiques see E Roucounas, 'Engagements parallèles et contradictoires' (1987/VI) 206 RdC 9, 56 ff.

195 D Peat, *Comparative Reasoning in International Courts and Tribunals* (CUP 2019). See along similar lines on the use of domestic law for interpretative purposes, R Yotova, 'Compliance with Domestic Law: An Implied Condition in Treaties Conferring Rights and Protections on Foreign Nationals and Their Property?' in Klingler, Parkhomenko, and Salonidis (eds), *Between the Lines of the Vienna Convention?* 307–31.

196 AD Mitchell and T Voon, 'The Rule of Necessary Implication' in Klingler, Parkhomenko, and Salonidis (eds), *Between the Lines of the Vienna Convention?* 331–58.

197 A Minon, '*Per Argumentum a Fortiori*' in ibid 197–210.

198 Even for widely used ones, such as effective interpretation and evolutive interpretation, there has been debate as to whether they are *intra legem* or *praeter legem;* for effective interpretation see Braumann and Reinisch, '*Effet Utile*' 47–72; for evolutive interpretation, see analysis in Chapter 4 of the present book, Section 4.2.2; see also, P Tzeng, 'The Principles of Contemporaneous and Evolutionary Interpretation' in Klinger, Parkhomenko, and Salonidis, *Between the Lines of the Vienna Convention?* 387–422; Moeckli and White, 'Treaties as "Living Instruments"' 136–70; C Djeffal, *Static and Evolutive Treaty Interpretation: A Functional Reconstruction* (CUP 2016); Bjorge, *The Evolutionary Interpretation of Treaties.*

199 For more detail, see entire volume by Klingler, Parkhomenko, and Salonidis (eds), *Between the Lines of the Vienna Convention?*

- The nature, form, and content of subsequent agreements/practice for the purpose of interpretation is also another area where jurisprudential interpretation of the rules of interpretation has occurred. Nolte's reports on this topic provide an extensive presentation of the relevant international jurisprudence revealing the multitude of complexities connected to identifying a particular act as 'subsequent agreement/ practice' and the conflicting or gradually more refined approaches in international jurisprudence on the matter.[200]
- Connected to this is also the debate on where the exact line between interpretation and modification should be drawn, an issue that was acknowledged by the ILC and Nolte in the discussions on subsequent agreements and practice and is addressed in more detail in Chapter 5.
- The exact meaning of the term 'rules' (does it apply also to treaties that have been signed but not ratified), 'parties' ('parties to the treaty' or 'parties to the dispute') and 'relevant' (how is relevance determined) of Article 31(3)(c), as well as the connection of that provision with *in pari materia* interpretation, has given rise to heated debates and extensive case law aiming to interpret the scope of this provision.[201]
- Whether a hierarchy exists between the various schools of interpretation, or between Article 31 and 32 VCLT, or even between the rules of interpretation enshrined in the VCLT and other extraneous rules/ maxis of interpretation.[202]
- The conditions under which subsequent agreements and practice can be considered as supplementary means under Article 32 VCLT. Draft Conclusion 2(4) has included subsequent practice as supplementary means of interpretation.[203]According to the ILC Commentary, the

[200] See Nolte's five Reports on Subsequent Agreements and Subsequent Practice.

[201] Merkouris, *Article 31(3)(c) VCLT* chs 1 and 2, and the case law analysed therein; see also, PF Henin, '*In Pari Materia* Interpretation in Treaty Law' in J Klingler, Y Parkhomenko, and C Salonidis (eds), *Between the Lines of the Vienna Convention?* 211–40.

[202] See various codification attempts analysed in Section 4.3.1.2; Klingler, Parkhomenko, and Salonidis (eds), *Between the Lines of the Vienna Convention?*; *Polish Postal Service in Danzig* (Advisory Opinion) PCIJ Rep Series B No 11, 39; *River Oder* 26.

[203] 'Conclusion 2 General rule and means of treaty interpretation.

1) Articles 31 and 32 of the Vienna Convention on the Law of Treaties set forth, respectively, the general rule of interpretation and the recourse to supplementary means of interpretation. These rules also apply as customary international law. 2) A treaty shall be interpreted in good faith in accordance with the ordinary meaning to be given to its terms in their context and in the light of its object and purpose, as provided in Article 31, paragraph 1.3. 3) Article 31, paragraph 3, provides, *inter alia*, that there shall be taken into account, together with the context, (a) any subsequent agreement between the

'subsequent practice' of Draft Conclusion 2(4) that does not meet the criteria set out for subsequent practice under Article 31(b), nonetheless may fall under the scope of Article 32, which includes a non-exhaustive list of supplementary means of interpretation.[204] The language used in Draft Conclusion 2(4), ie 'recourse may be had', mirrors that of Article 32 VCLT.[205] The inclusion of subsequent practice in Article 32 has resulted in many comments from scholars who have queried certain aspects of such an approach, for instance the consequence that the distinction between 'agreed subsequent practice' 'and subsequent practice in broad sense' would have in relation to the practice of international organisations. For instance, although the prevailing view is that such practice would presumably fall under Article 32, authors have questioned whether this is entirely correct, as there may be doubts whether such a practice is representative of the intention of the States at the time of the conclusion of a treaty.[206] The approach to subsequent practice as a supplementary means on interpretation, although treated with a certain degree of trepidation by publicists, has been in fact acknowledged by international courts and tribunals.[207]

- Article 32 VCLT allows for recourse to preparatory work only for purposes of confirmation or to determine the meaning in case of ambiguity or if the result of interpretation under Article 31 VCLT is manifestly absurd. This then raises the interesting question of whether preparatory work could also have a corrective function, ie correct the ordinary meaning of the text, a topic that, surprisingly, has been

parties regarding the interpretation of the treaty or the application of its provisions and (b) any subsequent practice in the application of the treaty which establishes the agreement of the parties regarding its interpretation. 4) Recourse may be had to other subsequent practice in the application of the treaty as a supplementary means of interpretation under Article 32. 5) The interpretation of a treaty consists of a single combined operation, which places appropriate emphasis on the various means of interpretation indicated, respectively, in Articles 31 and 32;

ILC, 'Draft Conclusions on Subsequent Agreements and Subsequent Practice, with Commentaries' Draft Conclusion 2.

204 ILC, 'Draft Conclusions on Subsequent Agreements and Subsequent Practice, with Commentaries' 20 [8], Commentary to Draft Conclusion 2(4).

205 ibid.

206 BL Bonafé and P Palchetti, 'Subsequent Practice in Treaty Interpretation between Article 31 and Article 32 of the Vienna Convention' (2018) 46 QuestInt'lL 1, 3.

207 *Kasikili/Sedudu Island* [49 ff]; WTO, *US – Section 110(5) of the US Copyright Act – Panel Report* (15 June 2000) WT/DS/160/R [6.55]; Moloo, 'When Actions Speak Louder than Words' 76; OK Fauchald, 'The Legal Reasoning of ICSID Tribunals – An Empirical Analysis (2008) 19 EJIL 301, 344.

examined in multiple cases, both before the ICJ and other arbitral tribunals.[208]

- Are the ILC discussions preparatory work or merely other supplementary means? In the ILC this point was raised, with members expressing diverging views as to whether they were 'other supplementary means' or *travaux préparatoires* of a 'second order'.[209]
- Can preparatory work be used against third States?[210] The jurisprudence of the ICJ has evolved on this matter. Whereas, originally, unless a party had not participated in the negotiations the preparatory work could not be used against it on the basis of the *res inter alios acta* and *pacta tertiis nec nocent nec prosunt* principles, this has changed in more recent cases, with knowledge or presumption of knowledge of the relevant documents being a sufficient ground for resorting to them.[211]

The above examples illustrate that even the VCLT rules of interpretation are open to interpretation in order to determine their content. There is already extensive jurisprudence on the matter, which continues to grow. Even more so, the interpretations given have either been consistently held, reversed in *toto* or partly modified and/or refined. The aim here is not to give a definitive answer to all the questions that were identified above, but rather to realise that the interpretability of the VCLT rules on interpretation shatters any illusion that the rules of interpretation have not undergone any changes both pre-VCLT and post-VCLT.

4.3.1.4 Logical Fallacies of the Immutability of Rules of Interpretation

Based on the analysis of the previous sections, it is evident that there is empirical evidence disproving any claim surrounding the immutability of the VCLT and customary rules on interpretation. In order to buttress

208 S Schwebel, 'May Preparatory Work Be Used to Correct Rather than Confirm the "Clear" Meaning of a Treaty Provision?' in Makarczyk and Skubiszewski (eds), *Theory of International Law at the Threshold of the 21st Century* 541–7; P Merkouris, '"Third Party" Considerations and "Corrective Interpretation" in the Interpretative Use of *Travaux Préparatoires* – Is It Fahrenheit 451 for Preparatory Work?' in M Fitzmaurice, O Elias, and P Merkouris (eds), *Treaty Interpretation and the Vienna Convention on the Law of Treaties: 30 Years On* (Martinus Nijhoff 2010) 75–98.

209 In the end, they were considered as preparatory work; ILC, 'Summary Record of the 872nd Meeting' [35]; ILC, 'Summary Record of the 873rd Meeting' [25–8], [34]; see also Merkouris, *Article 31(3)(c) VCLT* 11.

210 Merkouris, '"Third Party" Considerations and "Corrective Interpretation"'.

211 ibid.

further this conclusion, let us also examine the logical fallacies of accepting such a proposition.

It is generally accepted that the VCLT rules of international law reflect contemporary customary international law. However, customary international law emerges through State practice and *opinio juris*. What is there to prohibit States introducing and applying new rules of interpretation? This would, in combination with an *opinio juris*, lead to a modification of customary international law (or emergence of a new customary rule) which would deviate from that of the VCLT. This possibility of States agreeing to opt out of the VCLT rules of interpretation was explicitly recognised by ILC members.[212] This leads to one of the following scenarios. Either the VCLT and customary rules of interpretation would end up having a different content, or the VCLT would automatically adapt, by applying the customary law version of Article 31(3)(c)[213] and their respective contents would remain the same. However, in both scenarios change has occurred, and thus immutability despite the passage of time has been disproved.

Furthermore, by applying the *a majore ad minus* logical tool, since the possibility of emergence of future *jus cogens* norms and the modification of existing ones is generally accepted,[214] then clearly the same should apply for the possibility of emerging customary rules on interpretation.

Let us now argue *a contrario*. If the customary rules on interpretation cannot and have not changed and they have the same content as the VCLT rules, then this would mean that the VCLT rules are also immune to time and change. But, as was shown in the previous section, this is clearly not the case, as international courts and tribunals have gradually developed the content of these rules, not to mention that this approach also fails to offer a systemically coherent explanation of the possibility of opting out of the rules of interpretation.

The inescapable conclusion of accepting the immutability of the rules on interpretation would be that they are something entirely different from any kind of rules that we are accustomed to. If they are not affected

[212] ILC, 'Summary Record of the 765th Meeting' [61] (Verdross), [78] (Ago).

[213] Since the customary rules on interpretation would be considered as 'relevant rules' for the interpretation of the VCLT rules on interpretation.

[214] Art 53 VCLT; GM Danilenko, 'International *Jus Cogens*: Issues of Law-Making' (1991) 2 EJIL 42; U Linderfalk, 'The Effect of *Jus Cogens* Norms: Whoever Opened Pandora's Box, Did You Ever Think about the Consequences?' (2007) 18 EJIL 853, 854–6 and 863 ff; U Linderfalk, 'The Creation of *Jus Cogens*: Making Sense of Article 53 of the Vienna Convention' (2011) 71 ZaöRV 359.

by the passage of time and if they cannot change, then they clearly are not conventional rules, or customary rules, or principles. They would have to be a unique set of rules falling outside the classical sources with which we are familiar. However, no States or the ILC or international courts and tribunals have adopted this kind of approach. An additional problem that this kind of logic may create, especially with respect to the ICJ, would be one of applicable law. According to Article 38 of the ICJ Statute, the Court can apply treaties, customary law or general principles. But if rules of interpretation are something different, then not even the Court would be able to apply them!

The above thoughts demonstrate the paradoxes and internal inconsistencies that the acceptance of the immutability of the rules of interpretation leads to. To say that the rules of interpretation have not changed, significantly or not, throughout the centuries may be a practically alluring solution, as it ties all loose ends with a nice bow, however as has been shown above it is not supported by practice, nor by the history of the rules of interpretation of international law, and to make matters even worse is logically, normatively, and methodologically simply incorrect.

4.3.2 *Mutability of Rules of Interpretation Leads to Intertemporal Concerns*

4.3.2.1 Effect of Time on Rules of Interpretation

Having established that the rules of interpretation can be and are affected by the passage of time, the follow-up question that must be addressed is, what are the effects of the passage of time in the application of legal norms? In international law, as in any legal system, the need for stability presupposes that most rules are created with a view to apply for extended periods of time, but that also they are allowed to change. This, on the one hand, may ensure a modicum of stability but, on the other hand, can also give rise to a whole gamut of complex issues regarding the appropriate rules to be applied at a specific situation and at a particular juncture in time. In the previous sections, we examined how the principle of contemporaneity and evolutive interpretation offer the tools to achieve this feat of balance. According to the former, a treaty and its terms are to be understood as they stood at the time of the conclusion of the treaty. However, if the parties so intended, the treaty can evolve and its terms can be understood in the light of modern-day conditions. That is the basic tenet of evolutive interpretation.

In the case at hand, what is of interest for our analysis is whether the rules of interpretation, which, as was shown in the previous sections can, have and will continue to change and be refined through time, can be considered for the purpose of evolutive interpretation. Essentially, the question boils down to what elements can be taken into account in the process of evolutive interpretation. Do legal rules fall into the set of elements to be considered under evolutive interpretation or is that set restricted only to elements which qualify as facts?

As shown in Section 4.2.2.1, evolutive interpretation can refer to evolution of fact and/or evolution of law.[215] Examples of what international courts and tribunals have considered as evolution of fact are medical and scientific advancements, societal and cultural changes, the socio-economic situation of a State, and changes in morals.[216] On the other hand, evolution of law has been recognised as including customary international law, international treaties, and even domestic law.[217] Having this in mind, it is evident then that the rules of interpretation can also form part of the process of evolutive interpretation.

4.3.2.2 Scenarios (Dis)Allowing 'Time-Travelling' Rules of Interpretation

This analysis leads us inexorably to the necessity of examining the approach by international courts and tribunals in using the VCLT rules on interpretation to interpret pre-VCLT treaties.

International courts and tribunals have shown a tendency when interpreting treaties concluded several decades before the entry into force of the VCLT[218] to simply pay lip-service to the fact that the VCLT rules reflect customary international law[219] and, in some cases, even indicate that there have been no significant changes to the content of those rules under customary international law.[220] This practice has not gone

[215] Georgopoulos, 'Le droit intertemporel'132–4.

[216] See Section 4.2.2.1 of this chapter and cases cited therein.

[217] ibid.

[218] Such as: *Sovereignty over Pulau Ligitan and Pulau Sipadan (Indonesia/Malaysia)* (Judgment) [2002] ICJ Rep 625; *Case Concerning Avena and Other Mexican Nationals (Mexico v USA)* (Judgment) [2004] ICJ Rep 12; *Kasikili/Sedudu Island*. In detail, see Linderfalk, 'The Application of International Legal Norms Over Time' 163–5.

[219] *Kasikili/Sedudu Island* [8]; *Case Concerning Oil Platforms (Iran v USA)* (Merits) [2003] ICJ Rep 161 [23].

[220] *Kasikili/Sedudu Island*, Separate Opinion of Judge Oda [4].

Table 4.2 *Possible variations as to what rules of interpretation should apply to a treaty*

		Intention of the Parties Regarding Time/ 'Time-Will of the Parties'			
		Contemporaneous Interpretation		***Evolutive Interpretation***	
Rules	***Treaty***	√		√	
	Rules on Interpretation	√	X	√	X

unnoticed amongst academics,[221] although there is a begrudging admittance that any other solution 'would complicate matters considerably'.[222] However, that is immaterial as to what is the proper application of the law.

The question we are faced with then is what possible options exist with respect to this issue, and whether by process of elimination one can arrive at a solution. As mentioned above, the principle of contemporaneity provides that a treaty is to be understood as it stood at the time of its conclusion, unless the parties intended for it to follow the evolution of fact and/or law.[223] A treaty, therefore, can be interpreted either statically (contemporaneously) or evolutively. Similarly, the rules of interpretation applicable to that treaty can be either those of the time of the conclusion of the treaty or those at the time of its interpretation. This then provides us with all the possible variations, and these are expressed in Table 4.2.

Consequently, there are four possible variations:

(i) The treaty is to be interpreted statically and the rules of interpretation are those that existed at the time of the treaty's conclusion.

221 M Shaw, 'Case Concerning *Kasikili/Sedudu Island (Botswana/Namibia)*' (2000) 49 ICLQ 964, 968; D Greig, *Intertemporality and the Law of Treaties* (BIICL 2001) 113–4; H Fox, 'Article 31(3)(a) and (b) of the Vienna Convention and the *Kasikili/Sedudu Island* Case' in M Fitzmaurice, O Elias, and P Merkouris (eds), *The Issues of Treaty Interpretation and the Vienna Convention on the Law of Treaties* (Martinus Nijhoff Publishers 2010) 59, 64–5; Linderfalk, 'The Application of International Legal Norms' 163–5.

222 Shaw 'Case Concerning *Kasikili/Sedudu Island*' 968.

223 Elsewhere, Merkouris has opted for the term 'time-will' to express this intention of the parties that determines whether a treaty is to be understood as frozen in time or as a living instrument. For reasons of simplicity, we will be using that term from this point onwards to describe that form of intention; Merkouris, '(Inter)temporal Considerations' 140–52.

(ii) The treaty is to be interpreted statically but the rules of interpretation are those that exist at the time of the treaty's interpretation.
(iii) The treaty is to be interpreted evolutively and the rules of interpretation are those that exist at the time of the treaty's interpretation.
(iv) The treaty is to be interpreted evolutively but the rules of interpretation are those that existed at the time of the treaty's conclusion.

Let us take a closer look at these four possibilities. The first and the third should actually be considered one and the same. The reason is that the underlying premise for both of them is that the rules of interpretation follow the intention of the parties as to the treaty as a whole. If the treaty is meant to be interpreted contemporaneously, then so should be (ie contemporaneous to the time of conclusion of the treaty) the rules of interpretation. The same is true when the parties opt for evolutive interpretation. That same intention demands that the rules of interpretation are the ones applicable at the time of interpretation. Even if there is no explicit expression that the parties wish for those particular rules to apply, following the overall intention/'time-will' of the parties seems a reasonable choice. A separation of treaty and the rules that interpret it seems too artificial without the parties having clearly indicated their preference for such a two-level approach. Such an approach would also avoid the burdening of the courts with the obligation to identify the content of the rules of interpretation in bygone eras. However, this would happen only when the treaty was to be interpreted evolutively. For those treaties where the parties wanted the principle of contemporaneity to apply, the aforementioned task would become a necessity.

But let us examine the other two options to see if any of them can be rejected. The second option would bring about a situation where whereas the treaty remained in its own 'time-bubble' the rules of interpretation would be the modern ones. Indeed, this would be the preferred option by international courts and tribunals, as this would mean that they could rely on the VCLT rules as a reflection of present-day customary international law. However, this would seem to conflict with the principle of non-retroactivity, a well-recognised principle in international law,[224] and the principle of contemporaneity, as analysed earlier. Both these principles can be circumvented only when there is an express intention of the

[224] *The Chamizal Case (Mexico v USA)* (1911) 11 RIAA 309, 343; *Clipperton Island Arbitration (Mexico v France)* (1931) 2 RIAA 1105, 1105–11; *Ambatielos* case *(Greece v UK)* (Preliminary Objections) [1952] ICJ Rep 28, 40.

parties to that effect. In the present case, and unless such an express stipulation by the parties exists, the only intention that is apparent is either one that has opted for a static interpretation of the treaty, or no apparent intention either way, whereby the principle of contemporaneity kicks in. Consequently, this option conflicts with the basic tenets of the principles of non-retroactivity and contemporaneity and does not withstand scrutiny. The decisive criterion is the time-will of the parties.

A possible way out of this conclusion, would be to argue that even if one were to apply the contemporary of that time rules of interpretation, this would include the customary version of Article 31(3)(c). Consequently, the modern rules of interpretation could be taken into account as 'relevant rules' in order to determine the content of the earlier rules of interpretation. That way, although the court applies the earlier rules, it still ends up using their modern version. Apart from the evident *ouroboric* nature of this argument, it is entirely based on an assumption that is not supported by either doctrine or jurisprudence. First, whether in earlier eras Article 31(3)(c) existed as such in customary international law is a topic equally open to debate as the ones we examined in the previous sections. Second, Article 31(3)(c) is silent on the fact on what is the temporal stamp of the 'relevant rules', ie relevant rules applicable at the time of the conclusion of the treaty, or at the time of the interpretation of the treaty.[225] Unsurprisingly, we also end up returning to our starting point. This issue was extensively debated in the ILC, and eventually any such reference was omitted from the final text. However, it seems that even in this case the solution will be determined by the time-will of the parties; and once again we also return to our original conclusion that the time-will is the decisive criterion in each scenario that offers solutions not only with respect to the treaty as such, but also to the peripheral rules that may be used in order to ensure its application and interpretation.

The final option of using old rules of interpretation to interpret a treaty that is considered a 'living instrument' is perhaps the easiest to discard. Not only all the previous considerations regarding the single solution to the treaty and its rules of interpretation, and the 'time-will as the decisive criterion' apply here as well, but it is not supported by any case law whatsoever. This is not surprising. Consider, as we mentioned before, that

[225] Although earlier drafts, possibly influence by the ideas behind the principle of contemporaneity leaned in favour of 'at the time of the conclusion of the treaty'; see Merkouris, *Article 31(3)(c) VCLT* ch 2.

Table 4.3 *What rules of interpretation should apply to a treaty*

		Intention of the Parties Regarding Time/ 'Time-will of the Parties'			
		Contemporaneous Interpretation		***Evolutive Interpretation***	
Rules	***Treaty***	√	X	√	X
	Rules on Interpretation	√	X	√	X
		Unless the Parties Explicitly Express a Different Intention			

a 'living instrument' will be interpreted on the basis not only of evolution of fact but also of law. Consequently, using earlier rules of interpretation would rather be a (d)evolution of law, in clear contradiction to one of the two main venues through which evolutive interpretation is accomplished.

Based on this, the only logical solution is that there is a presumption of a single solution. The time-will choices that the parties make with respect to the treaty equally apply to the rules of interpretation. Of course, this should be considered a rebuttable presumption. Bearing in mind that parties can anytime they please opt out even from the existing rules of interpretation and agree amongst themselves to apply other ones of their own choosing,[226] the presumption can be reversed. But in order for this to happen the parties must explicitly demonstrate their intention for opting for one of the aforementioned discarded options or for an entirely different set of rules of interpretation.

Updating Table 4.2 to reflect the above analysis we arrive at the solution to our problem which is represented in Table 4.3.

4.4 Forward and Backward Motion through Time: Rules of Interpretation as 'Time-Travellers'

In this chapter we have examined the *auxesis* and *meiosis* that can happen to treaty provisions as a result of their *kata chronon metavole* and in the context of the process of interpretation. In Section 4.2 we focused on the two opposite spectra of motion, ie *stasis* and *kinesis,* as exemplified through contemporaneous and evolutive interpretation,

[226] Given the residual nature of the rules of the VCLT.

respectively. Going through the preparatory work of the VCLT and case law across different courts and tribunals, we identified that the intention of the parties is the driving force, which informs each and every instan einstance the choice between static and evolutive interpretation. Such a choice, however, is not without its limits, most notable amongst these being that evolutive interpretation should never reach the point where it modifies/amends the treaty text and the corresponding obligation. This would lead to an *alloiosis* of the obligation, a type of motion that goes beyond the scope of interpretation, and is more characteristic of amendment as is shown in Chapter 5.

In Section 4.3 of this chapter, we started from an observed tendency amongst international courts and tribunals to apply the VCLT rules, and the modern understanding thereof, to pre-VCLT treaties. This practice has been rationalised on the basis of the claim that the rules of interpretation have not changed significantly in the last few centuries.

In order to put this claim to the test, the following were examined: (i) whether pre-VCLT there was general agreement even as to the existence of rules of interpretation, (ii) whether pre-VCLT the content of those rules was fixed and enjoyed general approval, (iii) whether the rules of interpretation were also open to interpretation, and (iv) the logical and methodological fallacies of refusing the mutability of rules of interpretation through time. From that analysis, what emerged was that rules of interpretation not only can change but they have and will continue to do so.

This then led then to the question about when and under what conditions modern rules of interpretation can be applied to earlier treaties. This question opened the door to examining issues connected to intertemporality and the tug of war between the principle of contemporaneity and evolutive interpretation. By examining all the possible solutions and the logical and normative consistency with the existing international legal system, it was concluded that the time-will of the parties with respect to the earlier treaty will be determinative of whether the rules of interpretation of that time or of today should be applied. The only exception was when the parties explicitly made a determination on the specific set of rules of interpretation to be applied. In that case, the explicit expression of the intention of the parties supersedes any presumption on the basis of the 'time-will' relating to the treaty as a whole. This solution, of course, means that when they interpret a pre-VCLT treaty courts and tribunals may have to start identifying properly the exact content of the rules of interpretation of a particular era. But the difficulty of the situation does not bear upon the systemic coherence of our conclusions.

Returning, thus, to the concept of motion through time and the ability of the rules of interpretation to 'time-travel', the answer should be this: As in physics, any notion of 'time-travel' is connected and restricted by the speed of light, which is the cornerstone of the physical laws of our Universe, so any 'time-travel' in international law is dependent on the cornerstone of this system, ie the intention of the parties.

This intention provides all the answers to our questions. When a treaty is to be interpreted statically, then the rules of interpretation at the time of the conclusion of the treaty are to be applied. The treaty and its interpretative rules travel forward in time in a kind of 'time-bubble' to be adjudicated and applied today. When a treaty is to be interpreted evolutively, then the rules of interpretation to be applied are those as they have emerged through the passage of time. The only way to break up this connection between the treaty and its rules of interpretation is, once again, through that fundamental concept of the intention of the parties. In theory, and if the parties so will it, then modern rules of interpretation can go against the arrow of time and apply to a treaty that exists in its own 'time-bubble'. But this has to be expressly agreed on by the parties. In conclusion, rules of interpretation can indeed be 'time-travelers' but only if the parties so will it.

5

Amendment/Modification/Revision of Treaties

Motion as Change

5.1 Introduction

The present chapter aims at examining trends in amendment/modification/revision (A/M/R) practices in international law, both pre- and post-VCLT, and how these practices reflect the constant tug of war between the competing interests of the stability of international relations and the necessity to change in order to avoid stagnation. A/M/R is unique in this context, as it describes not only the motion of treaties through time but also encapsulates in itself multiple different forms of motion, as per the Aristotelean definition provided in Chapter 1. A/M/R can lead either to an increase of the obligations, regulations contained in a treaty (the equivalent of *auxesis*), or to a reduction (*meiosis*) or to such drastic alterations to key characteristics of the treaty that affect its very nature (*alloiosis*).[1]

In Section 5.2,[2] we examine the drafting history of the provisions relating to A/M/R as set out in the VCLT. We see that the distinction between those three processes, ie 'amendment', 'modification' and

[1] In some cases, the *alloiosis* can be so drastic that the Court may argue that we are dealing with an entirely new treaty (leading back to the first type of motion, *genesis*). This was the argument of the CJEU in the *Open Skies* cases, where it held that because of the multitude of amendments introduced to the previous treaties, they were no longer the same treaty but a new one (and therefore fell outside the scope of Article 351 TFEU). In the view of the present authors, this is a modern-day legal variant of the *Theseus's ship* paradox mentioned in Chapter 1, Section 1.4 and Chapter 4, Section 4.1; for the relevant cases and the reasoning of the Court, see *Case C-466/98 - Commission v UK* [2002] ECR I-9427; *Case C-467/98 - Commission v Denmark* [2002] ECR I-9519; *Case C-468/98 - Commission v Sweden* [2002] ECR I-9575; *Case C-469/98 - Commission v Finland* [2002] ECR I-9627; *Case C-471/98 - Commission v Belgium* [2002] ECR I-9681; *Case C-472/98 - Commission v Luxembourg* [2002] ECR I-9741; *Case C-475/98 - Commission v Austria* [2002] ECR I-9797; *Case C-476/98 - Commission v Germany* [2002] ECR I-9855.

[2] Sections 5.2–5.3 of this chapter are a modified version of similar sections that appeared in: Fitzmaurice and Merkouris, 'Re-shaping Treaties'. The authors express their thanks to Brill/Martinus Nijhoff.

'revision', 'may be sometimes blurred',[3] an issue that did not escape the ILC's attention either.[4] Despite this complexity, the ILC and the States later on in the Vienna Conference were of the view that a set of 'residual rules', despite the lack of consistency in practice and the debatable existence of relevant rules of customary law, was a good idea. The analysis of these debates reveals some trends as to the 'motion' of A/M/R rules pre-VCLT. In Section 5.3, we follow this motion to determine whether any new trends have emerged post-VCLT or whether pre-VCLT trends have survived the test of time (have endured a *kata chronon metavole*). Another issue examined in that section is the boundaries between interpretation and A/M/R, which was touched on also in the previous chapter, but which is again addressed here, in more detail, from the perspective of A/M/R.[5]

Finally, in Section 5.4 the A/M/R clauses of multilateral treaties are scrutinised to determine whether the trends identified in the previous sections are confirmed by the treaty-making practice of States, and/or if any additional trends emerge through that data pool. For the purposes of this empirical analysis, and since an exhaustive analysis of all multilateral treaties in existence is impossible,[6] the compromise made was to use treaties that have been published in the LNTS or the UNTS. In this manner, a statistically sufficient dataset could be consulted, including treaties 'moving' through time and ranging from the 1900s until today, that could highlight the diversity of motion of treaties across different regimes, but also help us identify some interesting patterns of correlation.

5.2 Drafting History of Article 39–41 VCLT

5.2.1 Characteristics and Definitions of Rules Relating to A/M/R

5.2.1.1 Need for A/M/R Articles in the VCLT

The Institut de Droit International in 1960, while examining the modification of multilateral treaties, came to the conclusion that it was

[3] ILC 'Draft Articles on the Law of Treaties with Commentaries' 236, Commentary to Art 38 [1].

[4] ibid; see also, ILC, 'Report of the International Law Commission on the Work of Its 66th Session' (5 May–6 June and 7 July–8 August 2014) UN Doc A/69/10, 188, Commentary to Draft Conclusion 7 [24].

[5] Another issue, the relationship between customary law and A/M/R, and more particularly whether a treaty can be modified by subsequent customary law, is only briefly touched on, as it is only tangential to our main analysis of the motion of A/M/R procedures.

[6] Since not all of them are registered.

desirable to insert into such treaties amendment provisions in order to allow them to adapt to changing circumstances and to enhance their relevance in a constantly shifting legal landscape. Despite this, the members of the Institut were rather reluctant to adopt or suggest the existence of any specific rules regarding A/M.[7]

In the ILC, there were some doubts about the possibility of distilling a ubiquitously applicable set of rules from the wide gamut of A/M/R procedures used in treaty practice[8] and some members were set against such an inclusion in the VCLT,[9] with one member even characterising the work of the ILC as 'bourgeois'.[10] The main point of those opposing the adoption of such rules was that despite the desirability of such rules, those issues were rooted in politics and diplomacy,[11] satisfactorily covered by other provisions on the law of treaties, or that any rules adopted would be prone to vagueness and abuse.[12] Despite these objections, the ILC – as evidenced by the existence of Articles 39–41 VCLT – saw the issue in a different light. Although the A/M/R of a treaty 'was a matter of diplomacy and politics, it nonetheless also had legal aspects and the ILC was more than competent to concern itself with those',[13] and those rules should be 'raised to the rank of positive rules of international law'.[14] There were a number of reasons that proved the necessity of the ILC undertaking such a task. First, the approach that A/M/R was firmly rooted in the sphere of politics and diplomacy had led to recourse to the *rebus sic stantibus* and the *inter se* principles to allow for the A/M/R of a treaty. Regrettably, the function of those principles in the context of A/M/R was manifestly sub-optimal.[15] Second, A/M/R rules would be the ideal balancing point between the competing interests

[7] Institut de Droit International, 'Modifications et terminaison des traités collectifs' (1961/I) 49 AIDI 229–91.

[8] ILC, 'Summary Record of the 747th Meeting' (17 June 1964) UN Doc A/CN.4/SR.747 [19] (Waldock); on the multifaceted nature of amendment/modification and its connection with other VCLT provisions, see H Waldock, 'Third Report on the Law of Treaties' (3 March, 9 June, 12 June, and 7 July 1964) UN Doc A/CN.4/167 and Add.1–3, reproduced in [1964] YBILC 5, 47 [1–2].

[9] ILC, 'Summary Record of the 747th Meeting' [6] (Amado), [26] (Waldock).

[10] ibid [6] (Amado).

[11] See for instance, McNair, *The Law of Treaties* 534.

[12] ILC, 'Summary Record of the 747th Meeting' [11] (Tsuruoka).

[13] ILC, 'Summary Record of the 744th Meeting' (12 June 1964) UN Doc A/CN.4/SR.744 [9] (Lachs).

[14] ibid [61] (Bartoš); also in favour, ILC, 'Summary Record of the 745th Meeting' (15 June 1964) UN Doc A/CN.4/SR.745 [4] (Yasseen), [56] (Tunkin).

[15] Waldock, 'Third Report' 48 [4].

of stability and change. They would safeguard the stability of treaties while at the same time ensuring that peaceful change could occur in order to avoid stagnation.[16] Finally, A/M/R rules would be useful for a multitude of other reasons, including the proliferation of treaties and the importance of those rules for international organistions.[17] In this context, Article 39 VCLT (then Draft Article 67) was considered rather useful to retain[18] as it was the only provision of that cluster relating to amendment and modification that applied to both bilateral and multilateral agreements.[19] Thus, such an all-encompassing scope of application would best serve one of the purposes for the adoption of A/M rules, ie to function as guidelines that would streamline the process of A/M/R of treaties.

Similarly, nobody disputed the fact that *inter se* agreements were an essential technique, and a necessary safety valve, for the adjustment of

[16] ILC, 'Summary Record of the 744th Meeting' [13–5] (Castrén); ILC, 'Summary Record of the 745th Meeting' [49] (El-Erian); ILC, 'Summary Record of the 746th Meeting' (16 June 1964) UN Doc A/CN.4/SR.746 [2] (Pal).

[17] ILC, 'Report of the International Law Commission on the Work of its Eighteenth Session' 231–2 [1].

[18] ILC, 'Summary Record of the 745th Meeting' [34] (Briggs), [54–5] (El-Erian).

[19] ILC, 'Summary Record of the 859th Meeting' (26 May 1966) UN Doc A/CN.4/SR.859 [29] (Briggs). This has to be contrasted with Art 40 VCLT, which is entitled 'Amendment of Multilateral Treaties'. This was intentional, in order to highlight the difference *ratione materiae* between Arts 39 and 40. Art 40 VCLT applies only to multilateral treaties since, as mentioned, any rule designed to apply only to amendment of bilateral treaties would be devoid of any true purpose, as this would be tantamount to a question of negotiation and agreement; ILC, 'Report of the International Law Commission on the Work of its Eighteenth Session' 233 [5].

In a similar vein, though, it was generally recognised that *inter se* agreements were essentially new instruments and different from amendments (ILC, 'Summary Record of the 746th Meeting' [7] (Lachs), [22] (Ruda), [32] (Jiménez de Aréchaga)), a point that kept creeping up was that from an effects perspective, amendment and modification may appear very similar, if not identical; ILC, 'Summary Record of the 747th Meeting' [23-4] (Waldock); ILC, 'Summary Record of the 754th Meeting' (29 June 1964) UN Doc A/CN.4/SR.754 [4] (Briggs), [22] (Lachs); United Nations Conference on the Law of Treaties, '1st Session – 37th Meeting of the Committee of the Whole (COW)' (24 April 1968) UN Doc A/CONF.39/11 203, 206-7 [39], [50–2]. In order to highlight the difference between amendment and *inter se* agreement, and to bolster the differences in requirements and effects, the Drafting Committee inserted what would become Art 40(2) VCLT so that the State parties would clarify *ab initio* their intention and it would be clear whether Art 40 or Art 41 VCLT was applicable; ILC, 'Summary Record of the 754th Meeting' [8–9] (Waldock), [24] and [74] (Briggs), [28] (de Luna), [30] (Ago), [82] (Castrén); ILC, 'Summary Record of the 764th Meeting' (13 July 1964) UN Doc A/CN.4/SR.764 [76] (Castrén), [85] (Bartoš), [88] (Yasseen), [94] (Lachs), [103–4] (de Luna). This was clearly established and inserted in the provision during the 764th meeting; ibid [29–33].

treaties to the dynamic needs of international society. Had such a technique not existed there would have been stagnation in many treaty relations. The *inter se* procedure had been the means for that necessary evolution.[20] One of the earliest examples of a treaty providing explicitly for *inter se* agreements was Article 19 of the 1883 International Convention for the Protection of Industrial Property.[21]

The importance of *inter se* agreements was not lost on the ILC. Although originally the ILC envisaged one provision for both amendment and modification, the discussion surrounding *inter se* agreements ballooned so quickly that it became blatantly obvious that they deserved an article of their own, not to mention the fact that if such an article was not adopted, then Articles 39 and 40 VCLT 'would become meaningless'.[22]

This analysis should not give the wrong impression that the A/M/R choices reflected in the VCLT rules were intended as the primary and preferred method of A/M/R. On the contrary, the diversity of the State practice on A/M/R guided the ILC to the conscious choice not to 'frame a comprehensive code of rules regarding the amendment of treaties ... [but to] include a formulation of the basic rules concerning the process of amendment'.[23] Articles 39–41 VCLT reflect the choice of the drafters that primacy should be given to the treaty text, in accordance with the *pacta sunt servanda* principle[24] and that the rules on A/M/R would be of a 'residual character'.[25]

[20] ILC, 'Summary Record of the 764th Meeting' [35] (Jiménez de Aréchaga); see also, H Lauterpacht, 'Second Report on the Law of Treaties' (8 June 1954) UN Doc A/CN.4/87 and Corr.1, reproduced in [1954/II] YBILC 123, 135–6 [6–8]; G Fitzmaurice, 'Third Report on the Law of Treaties' (18 March 1958) UN Doc A/CN.4/115, reproduced in [1958/II] YBILC 20, 43–4 [89]; Waldock, 'Third Report' 49 [7–8].

[21] 1883 International Convention for the Protection of Industrial Property (adopted 20 March 1883, entered into force 7 July 1884) 192 LNTS 4459. For recent examples of *inter se* agreements, see SA Sadat-Akhavi, *Methods of Resolving Conflicts between Treaties* (Brill 2003) 114–9; ILC Study Group, 'Report on Fragmentation of International Law: Difficulties Arising from the Diversification and Expansion of International Law, Finalized by Martti Koskenniemi' (13 April 2006) UN Doc A/CN.4/L.682 [297 ff].

[22] ILC, 'Summary Record of the 746th Meeting' [57] (Waldock).

[23] ibid.

[24] Waldock, 'Third Report' 47 [2].

[25] ibid 50 [10–1]; ILC, 'Report of the International Law Commission on the Work of Its Eighteenth Session' 231–2 [2], 233 [7]; ILC, 'Summary Record of the 744th Meeting' [62] (Bartoš); ILC, 'Summary Record of the 746th Meeting' [33] (Jiménez de Aréchaga), [54–5] (Tunkin).

5.2.1.2 Definitional Issues of A/M/R

Making a conscious choice on the 'residual character' of the VCLT rules on A/M/R was not the end of the ILC's troubles on the issue. Another major hurdle that the ILC had to surmount in order to adopt a set of rules relating to A/M/R was a definitional one. Two definitional issues can be discerned. First, State practice indicated that States tended to use the terms 'amendment', 'revision', and 'modification' rather loosely or even interchangeably.[26]

The ILC faced two possible courses of action; either to try and decipher from the practice of the League of Nations the terminology, or to adopt a set of terms and define them in an explanatory note or in the commentary.[27] Considering that most ILC members felt that there was only a difference of degree between 'amendment' and 'revision',[28] and that the distinction being so artificial should be dropped,[29] the ILC went for the second option, using only the terms 'amendment' and 'modification' and clarifying that

> [it] considered it sufficient in the present articles to speak of 'amendment' as being a term which covers both the amendment of particular provisions and a general review of the whole treaty. As to the term 'revision', the Commission recognised that it is frequently found in State practice and that it is also used in some treaties. Nevertheless, having regard to the nuances that became attached to the phrase 'revision of treaties' in the period preceding the Second World War, the Commission preferred the term 'amendment'. This term is here used to denote a formal amendment of a treaty intended to alter its provisions with respect to all the parties. The more general term 'modification' is used in [Article 41 VCLT] in connexion with an *inter se* agreement concluded between certain of the parties only, and intended to vary provisions of the treaty between themselves alone, and also in connexion with a variation of the provisions of a treaty resulting from the practice of the parties in applying it [which was included in Draft Article 38, but was eventually left out of the text of the VLCT].[30]

26 United Nations, *Final Clauses of Multilateral Treaties: Handbook* (United Nations 2003) 96.

27 ILC, 'Summary Record of the 744th Meeting' [33] (de Luna).

28 ibid [17] (Castrén); ILC, 'Summary Record of the 746th Meeting' [49] (Yasseen).

29 Waldock, 'Third Report' 48 [6]; ILC, 'Summary Record of the 746th Meeting' [10] (Rosenne), [20] (Liang), [31] (Jiménez de Aréchaga), [33] (de Luna).

30 ILC, 'Report of the International Law Commission on the Work of Its Eighteenth Session' 232 [3].

Several decades later, the UN Handbook *Final Clauses of Multilateral Treaties* offered its two cents on the issue without, however, deviating from the VCLT's drafting choices. According to the handbook, 'modification normally refers to alterations of certain provisions of a treaty only among certain parties to that treaty'.[31] The term 'revision' is not used in the VCLT, however, it does appear in several treaties and it usually refers 'to a general alteration affecting the treaty as a whole, as opposed to an amendment that partially alters some of the treaty provisions'.[32]

The second definitional issue was the normative essence of the ability of States to propose an amendment? Was it a 'right'[33] or a 'faculty'?[34] The matter became more convoluted because the choice of the term would affect corresponding obligations.[35] The ILC eventually took the Gordian knot approach. Since it was extremely debatable, it cut out from the text of Article 39 any qualifying term, be that 'right' or 'faculty'. It followed Tunkin's suggestion to use the terms 'a treaty *may* be amended', since such a noncommittal expression would help the ILC avoid all the major theoretical problems.[36]

5.2.2 Critical Issues Relating to the Process of A/M/R in the VCLT

Having made choices about the nature and definition of A/M/R, the ILC then had to turn to the actual content of the relevant cluster of provisions. An exhaustive analysis of the relevant debates is outside the scope of this volume. However, two issues are of great importance. The first one, on the specific rights and obligations of States attached to activating an A/M/R procedure, and the second one, also connected to our analysis in Section 5.4, concerning the debate on requiring adherence to the unanimity rule in one way or another.

[31] United Nations, *Final Clauses of Multilateral Treaties* 107.

[32] ibid 96.

[33] ILC, 'Summary Record of the 744th Meeting' [30] (Verdross), [78] (Bartoš), [81] (Amato).

[34] ibid [24] (Ago), [28] (Rosenne); Pal does not seem to take a position on the matter using both terms, however, it has to be noted that he used the term 'faculty' with greater frequency (ibid [68] (Pal)).

[35] ibid [74–6] (Ago); [78] (Bartoš), [82–3] (Ruda); ILC, 'Summary Record of the 745th Meeting' [13–5] (Paredes).

[36] ILC, 'Summary Record of the 744th Meeting' [85] (Tunkin).

5.2.2.1 Rights and Obligations of States during A/M/R Procedures

One of the main reasons for the adoption of Articles 39 and 40 was that, in earlier times, treaties were amended or revised by certain parties without the consultation of other parties. One of the most notorious examples of the pitfalls of the A/M/R system is the Concert of Europe, in which the major powers would conclude new treaties on the same subject matters without securing the consent of all the parties to the previous treaty. This, of course, gave rise to situations of conflicting obligations and treaties.[37]

By the 1960s, some writers had concluded that State parties do not have a 'right' to participate in discussions relating to amendment, since this was more of a 'practical rather than legal'[38] matter and that if such a rule existed, even if it prevented conflicting obligations, it 'would also be a formidable factor of stagnation'.[39] However, the vast majority of the ILC members were of a different view. According to them, State parties not only had a right to be notified of any proposal for amendment,[40] but also a right to participate in the negotiations,[41] which flowed logically from the principle of good faith[42] and struck the ideal balance between the competing interests.[43]

A side issue with respect to Article 40(2) was its limits *ratione personae.* Should the right to be notified and involved in the negotiations also extend to non-parties? The issue was hotly contested within the ILC,[44] with concerns being expressed that although there could be instances where this was desirable,[45] there was great danger that over-expanding

[37] Waldock, 'Third Report' 48 [4].

[38] EC Hoyt, *The Unanimity Rule in the Revision of Treaties: A Re-examination* (Martinus Nijhoff 1959) 250.

[39] J Leca, *Les techniques de révision des conventions internationales* (LGDJ 1961) 204 (authors' translation).

[40] ILC, 'Summary Record of the 745th Meeting' [25] (Castrén), [35] (Briggs), [43] (Yasseen), [52] (El-Erian), [68] (de Luna).

[41] ILC, 'Summary Record of the 746th Meeting' [42] (Reuter); ILC, 'Report of the International Law Commission on the Work of Its Eighteenth Session' 233 [8–9].

[42] Waldock, 'Third Report' 51 [14].

[43] ILC, 'Report of the International Law Commission on the Work of Its Eighteenth Session' 233-4 [10].

[44] ILC, 'Summary Record of the 745th Meeting' [32] (Waldock), [35] (Briggs), [43] (Yasseen), [69] (de Luna).

[45] ILC, 'Summary Record of the 875th Meeting' (22 June 1966) UN Doc A/CN.4/SR.875 [44] (Briggs).

the circle of participants in these discussions would lead to stagnation of international law. After a lot of deliberation and a final amendment proposed by the Netherlands during the Vienna Conference,[46] which struck the golden mean, Article 40(2) VCLT was adopted, giving a limited number of non-State parties certain rights regarding notification and participation in the discussions of an amendment. Conversely, the issue that arose from the rights of the State parties receiving notification of an amendment proposal was whether those States also had obligations. The ILC was of the opinion that the receiving States had an obligation of 'good faith' to give due consideration of the proposal.[47] However, putting this concept into black-letter law proved extremely difficult as it could be abused by leaving the door open to arbitrary denunciations of treaties on the pretended ground that the other party had not given 'due consideration'. For this reason, it was omitted from the final text of the VCLT.[48]

5.2.2.2 Unanimity Rule

Although it was accepted that the 'jurist recognises no immutable instruments'[49] and that A/M/R was necessary *inter alia* 'in order to minimise the danger of normative conflict',[50] the optimal method in order to ensure such changes to treaties was uncertain. During the ILC meetings, the question that the members had to tackle was whether the unanimity rule merited being included in the VCLT A/M/R provisions.

The inclusion of the unanimity rule was argued both in favour[51] and against,[52] with an interesting proposal by Rosenne suggesting that it could be restricted to treaties with a limited number of parties (the problem, however, being that this was an ill-defined category).[53]

[46] Netherlands, 'Amendment Proposal to Article 40' UN Doc A/CONF.39/C.1/L.232.

[47] ILC, 'Report of the International Law Commission on the Work of Its Eighteenth Session' 233 [6] Waldock, 'Third Report' 50 [12]; ILC, 'Summary Record of the 744th Meeting' [51] (Briggs); ILC, 'Summary Record of the 745th Meeting' [54] (El-Erian); with one ILC member, however, considering that any reference to 'good faith' would be an 'empty admonition', ibid [17] (Paredes). However, this 'good faith' obligation did not entail an obligation to negotiate, ibid [42] (Yasseen), [68] (de Luna).

[48] ILC, 'Report of the International Law Commission on the Work of Its Eighteenth Session' 233 [6].

[49] Ch Rousseau, *Principes généraux du droit international public: Tome 1* (Pedone 1944) 616.

[50] ILC, 'Summary Record of the 745th Meeting' [64] (de Luna).

[51] ILC, 'Summary Record of the 747th Meeting' [12] (Tsuruoka)

[52] ILC, 'Summary Record of the 746th Meeting' [8] (Rosenne).

[53] ibid [15] (Rosenne).

We return in Section 5.4 to this proposal, as its importance emerges more clearly there, when we examine patterns evolving from the practice relating to the A/M/R provisions included in the treaties published in the UNTS. In the end, however, and despite Rosenne's proposal, the ILC concluded that the rapid growth in the number of international treaties had rendered the unanimity rule impractical.[54] In Article 39 VCLT, the terms agreed upon were 'between the parties' and not 'between all the parties' in order to highlight the difference between amendment and termination and the shift from the unanimity rule.[55]

The unanimity rule was also discussed in connection to Article 41 VCLT. A/M/R is a multifaceted concept that has several cross-overs with other areas of the law of treaties. One such connection that was hinted at, in relation to the promotion of the unanimity rule, was with termination.[56] However, Waldock and de Luna clarified that modification should be distinguished from termination as they had different results as to the obligations of the parties.

Another way, in which the unanimity rule in connection to Article 41 was proposed was by means of an analogy with the system on reservations. During the Vienna Conference, Australia[57] and France[58] submitted amendments that echoed Fitzmaurice's typology of obligations[59] and Article 20(2) VCLT. They were based on the premise that '*inter se* agreements [were] primarily possible in the case of those multilateral treaties which operated in fact on a bilateral basis'.[60] Consequently, in the case of a restricted multilateral treaty the unanimity principle would be activated and any *inter se* agreement would require the acceptance by all State parties.

Several States opposed such an approach as it did not reflect practice and it would put too disproportionate a restraint on the ability to

54 ILC, 'Report of the International Law Commission on the Work of Its Eighteenth Session' 231–2 [1].

55 ILC, 'Summary Record of the 753rd Meeting' (26 June 1964) UN Doc A/CN.4/SR.753 [39–41], [46] (Waldock).

56 ILC, 'Summary Record of the 744th Meeting' [85] (Tunkin); ILC, 'Summary Record of the 745th Meeting' [67] (de Luna).

57 Australia, 'Amendment Proposal to Article 41' UN Doc A/CONF.39/C.1/L.237.

58 France, 'Amendment Proposal to Article 41' UN Doc A/CONF.39/C.1/L.46.

59 Reciprocal and non-reciprocal. The former subdivided into bilateral and bilateralisable, whereas the latter into interdependent and integral, Fitzmaurice, 'Third Report' 41–5 [77–94].

60 ILC, 'Summary Record of the 860th Meeting' (27 May 1966) UN Doc A/CN.4/SR.860 [66] (Tunkin), [62] (de Luna).

conclude *inter se* agreements, not to mention prejudge the content of Article 20(2) VCLT, which at that time had yet to be approved.[61] For that reason, no mention of such a limit to *inter se* agreements found its way in Article 41 VCLT. Whether the aforementioned objections to the Australian and French amendment proposals were well founded or not is a point to which we shall return in Section 5.4, when we examine State practice relating to A/M/R provisions in multilateral treaties published in the UNTS.

In summation, during both the ILC and the Vienna Conference on the Law of Treaties – despite some interesting proposals to the contrary – the solution opted for by the ILC was that the unanimity rules should take more of a residual role with respect to A/M.[62]

5.3 Trends and Issues in A/M/R of Treaties

5.3.1 Introduction

The previous section referred to the traditional ways of the amendment of a treaty, as enshrined in the VCLT, and the debate concerning the drafting of Articles 39–41 by the ILC. As was explained, not only were the rules incorporated in the VCLT meant to be of a 'residual nature' but a number of issues came up, that were either left out of the final text or the wording adopted was intentionally open-ended in order to allow for State practice to find its own way through a process of trial and error.

For instance, there are differences in the classification between such concepts of the law of treaties, as amendment, modification, and revision (the last one not having been included in the VCLT). This obscure and far-from-clear-cut classification is, however, not the only issue, either definitional or substantive, that has arisen in theory and in the practice of States. Consequently, and for the purpose of ensuring the completeness of this chapter, the most interesting and challenging ones will be brought to the attention of the reader and analysed.[63] These are:

[61] United Nations Conference on the Law of Treaties, '2nd Session – 86th Meeting of the Committee of the Whole (COW)' (11 April 1969) UN Doc A/CONF.39/11/Add.1 222, 223-4 [5–11].

[62] ILC, 'Summary Record of the 753rd Meeting' [39–41] (Waldock), [58] (de Luna).

[63] See in depth on this, A Chanaki, *L' adaptation des traités dans les temps* (Bruylant 2013); Buga, 'Subsequent Practice and Treaty Modification' 363.

(i) the tacit amendment procedure;[64]
(ii) the subsequent practice of Conferences of the Parties/Meetings of the Parties (COPs/MOPs) in MEAs;[65] and
(iii) the difference between interpretation and A/M/R of a treaty.[66]

The first two have been selected, as they are approaches to treaty A/M/R that have mainly developed through State practice and deviate from classical approaches to A/M, such as the requirement that a certain number or percentage of the member States adopt the amendment and the need for explicit provision of consent to be bound. Furthermore, whereas the former had already emerged pre-VCLT, it has evolved, in the meantime, and risen in prominence post-VCLT. The latter is a post-VCLT creature that has emerged through the decisions of COPs/MOPs of MEAs.

However, A/M/R is defined not only by the elements of which it consists, ie by the various A/M/R procedures, but also by the manner in which it is distinguished from other actions in the 'life-cycle' of the treaty. This brings us to the third issue, which although not an A/M/R procedure *per se* is equally important, as it purports to identify the demarcation line between A/M/R and interpretation. Although this problem was briefly touched on during the VCLT *travaux préparatoires*,[67] and also due to the ILC's work on the importance of subsequent agreements/practice in treaty interpretation, it has gradually been receiving a long overdue attention.

5.3.2 *Tacit Acceptance Procedure*

In general, Hathaway, Saurabh Sanghvi, and Solow distinguish

> between three regimes that allow for tacit amendments to treaties through the use of international bodies: regimes in which treaty alterations require the unanimous consent of all parties represented in the international body tasked with updating the treaty (what we will call 'consensus amendments') for example open skies agreement; regimes in which international committees or conferences can pass amendments without full consent, but in which State parties may opt out of changes

64 Also referred to as tacit acceptance procedure and 'opting-out' procedure.
65 A phenomenon noted and analysed by Nolte during his work on *Treaties over Time* in the ILC. See in detail Nolte (ed), *Treaties and Subsequent Practice* in particular 337–8.
66 See analysis *infra* in Section 5.3.5.
67 In more detail see *infra* Section 5.3.5.

('opt-out amendments');[68] and regimes in which a commission or conference creates changes, possibly without unanimous consent, that bind all parties ('binding amendments').[69]

This category includes, eg, the World Trade Organisation (WTO) and the Montreal Protocol. The WTO can amend its agreements through a Ministerial Conference. The WTO encourages the use of consensus at these conferences. It can, however, make changes if there exists a super-majority that overrules the objections of any one of the State parties. With respect to the Montreal Protocol, the situation is more complex. Its MOP can adopt either amendments regarding such matters as adding on new substances (which are subject to the classical ratification procedure) or so-called adjustments. The latter deal with the procedures pertaining to matters of lesser importance but which, nonetheless, still change the obligations of the parties to the protocol. For instance, an example of an adjustment would be a modification in the timeframe for the elimination of substances under the protocol. Parties to the protocol endeavor to adopt such adjustments by consensus, but failing that, by a two-thirds majority vote with a simple majority of both the Article 5 parties, ie developing countries with annual per capita consumption less than the quantity specified in Article 5 of the protocol, and the non-Article parties. An adjustment, thus adopted, is binding on all parties, even over the objection of the remaining parties.[70]

This section is devoted to the tacit procedure in the meaning of the second category as the most common and significant in practice. The third category is dealt with in Section 5.3.3.

5.3.2.1 Tacit Acceptance Procedure in International Treaties

The procedure of tacit acceptance ('opting-out procedure') has been known for a long time in relation to organisations such as the International Labour Organisation (ILO), the World Health Organisation (WHO), the International Telecommunications Union (ITU), the World Meteorological Organisation (WMO), the International Civil Aviation

[68] The examples of this system are treaties concluded within the IMO regime (see Sections 5.3.2.1–5.3.2.4).

[69] OA Hathaway, HN Saurabh Sanghvi and S Solow, 'Tacit Amendments' (Yale Law School, 15 November 2011) <https://law.yale.edu/system/files/documents/pdf/cglc/Tacit Amendments.pdf> accessed 20 September 2019, 10–6.

[70] The second (London 1990), fourth (Copenhagen 1992), seventh (Vienna 1995), ninth (Montreal 1997), eleventh (Beijing 1999), and nineteenth (Montreal 2007) MOP adopted such adjustments.

Organisation (ICAO), the International Maritime Organisation (IMO), and the International Whaling Commission (IWC). This procedure is not uncommon in relation to organs established by environmental treaties, such as the Consultative Meeting of the Contracting Parties established by the 1972 Convention on the Prevention of Marine Pollution by Dumping of Wastes and Other Matter (London Convention),[71] but is best known as applied by the IMO in the treaties concluded under its auspices. Within the framework of the IMO, the International Convention for the Prevention of Pollution from Ships (MARPOL)[72] and the International Convention for the Safety of Life at Sea (SOLAS)[73] were the first instruments to introduce these procedures.

This procedure, however, is not exclusive to these organisations and is also widely used in other international institutions, such as many international fisheries commissions, such as the North-East Atlantic Fishery Commission (NEAFC),[74] the Northwest Atlantic Fisheries Organisation (NAFO),[75] the Convention on International Trade in Endangered Species of Wild Fauna and Flora (CITES),[76] and the IWC.[77]

The system of 'opting-out' is a mechanism which was a precursor of the expanding phenomenon of the so-called autonomous institutional arrangements (AIAs), as described by Churchill and Ulfstein, and the increasing legislative powers of COPs/MOPs, including amendments to treaties.[78]

The procedures, which characterise the legal acts of an organisation set up under a treaty by way of involving the 'tacit acceptance' system, are: first, the acts are adopted by a majority vote, and, second, that member States can lodge an objection and, thus, avoid being bound by the act.

[71] 1972 Convention on the Prevention of Marine Pollution by Dumping of Wastes and Other Matter (adopted 29 December 1972, entered into force 30 August 1975) 1046 UNTS 120.

[72] 1973 International Convention for the Prevention of Pollution from Ships (adopted 2 November 1973, entered into force 2 October 1983) 1340 UNTS 184.

[73] 1974 International Convention for the Safety of Life at Sea (adopted 1 November 1974, entered into force 25 May 1980) 1184 UNTS 278.

[74] 1980 Convention on Future Multilateral Co-operation in North-East Atlantic Fisheries (adopted 18 November 1980, entered into force 17 March 1982) 1285 UNTS 129.

[75] 1949 International Convention for the Northwest Atlantic Fisheries (adopted 8 February 1949, entered into force 3 July 1950) 157 UNTS 158.

[76] 1973 Convention on International Trade in Endangered Species of Wild Fauna and Flora (adopted 3 March 1973, entered into force 1 July 1975) 993 UNTS 243.

[77] 1946 International Convention for the Regulation of Whaling.

[78] Churchill and Ulfstein, 'Autonomous Institutional Arrangements'. This issue is analysed in more detail *infra* in Section 5.3.3.

The essential characteristic is based on the premise that a member State is automatically bound by the act of the organisation unless it takes specific action to avoid being so bound (ie by way of 'opting-out').[79] Thus, this system encompasses in equal measure the legal problems of consent to be bound by a treaty and the law-making or at least rule-making acts of an international organisation, which may result in a treaty being amended.

5.3.2.2 Legality and *Telos* of the Tacit Acceptance Procedure

The power of the organisation to *prima facie* curb the obligation for expression of consent by the member States is rooted in the constituent treaty of the international organisation. Consequently, one might refer to a 'derivative treaty obligation',[80] ie although the organisation creates law that is directly binding on States, its *pouvoir de légiférer* is ultimately founded in the treaty establishing the organisation. In this manner, the principles of *pacta sunt servanda, pacta tertiis nec nocent nec prosunt* and of State sovereignty remain intact. This is further reinforced by the structure of the 'opting-out procedure', which allows a member State to object to the proposed amendment and thus not be bound.

The *telos* of the 'tacit acceptance procedure' is to combine the principle of State sovereignty (the right of a member State to lodge an objection) whilst at the same time, by making it politically unattractive to lodge an objection, to encourage the creation of a uniform system for all the States, which are party to the convention in question. Opinions differ as to whether the acts of international organisations operating under the tacit acceptance (opting-out) system have an independent law-making character, or constitute, in effect, an agreement analogous to an agreed amendment to the treaty between the States concerned.[81] On the one hand, the view has been expressed by some authors that such acts, having been taken by a majority vote of the organisation concerned, and

[79] On the subject, see, in particular, K Skubiszewski, 'A New Source of the Law of Nations Resolutions of International Organisations' in P Guggenheim and M Battelli (eds), *Recueil d'études de droit international en hommage à Paul Guggenheim* (Imprimerie de la Tribune de Genève 1968) 508.

[80] PC Szasz, 'International Norm-Making' in E Brown Weiss (ed), *Environmental Change and International Law: New Challenges and Dimensions* (UN University Press 1992) 41, 65.

[81] R Ago, 'Die Internationalen Organisationen und Ihre Funktionen im inneren Tätigkeitsgebiet der Staaten' in H Wehberg, W Schätzel, and H-J Schlochauer (eds), *Rechtsfragen der internationalen Organisation: Festschrift für Hans Wehberg zu seinem 70 Geburtstag* (Vittorio Klostermann 1956) 20–38; H Blix, *Treaty-Making Power* (Stevens & Sons 1960) 293–6.

becoming binding on the member States without their explicit agreement (as was traditionally always required for the formation of an international treaty), have a law-making character independent of the will of the member States.[82]

On the other hand, the view has equally been expressed that the 'tacit acceptance' procedure is no more than a system developed for the purpose of accelerating and simplifying the process of concluding a kind of international treaty, or of amending or modifying an existing treaty.[83] The procedure of tacit acceptance combines the principle of consent to be bound and at the same time encourages the creation of uniform rules applicable to all State parties to the treaty.[84]

5.3.2.3 *Raison d' Être* of the Tacit Acceptance Procedure: The IMO Example

In relation to the amendment of the treaties within the realm of the IMO, tacit acceptance was only one of the means to do so. In order to better understand the purpose of the establishment and the role of tacit acceptance as a method of amending treaties, the classical procedure of amendment of certain treaties concluded under the IMO auspices is described first.[85]

The early IMO Conventions were characterised by a complex and cumbersome procedure relating to amendments, which only came into force after a certain percentage of contracting States, usually two-thirds, had ratified them. This meant that at times more ratifications were required to amend a convention than were originally required for its entry into force, in particular in relation to conventions with multiple State parties. Such a classical amendment procedure was a source of difficulties. As Lost-Sieminska explains, one example were the amendments to the SOLAS Convention, which entered into force twelve months after the date on which the amendments were ratified by two-thirds of the contracting governments, including two-thirds of the

[82] Krz Skubiszewski, *Uchwaly Prawotworcze Organizacji Miendzynarodowych. Przeglad Zagadnien I Analiza Wstepna* (*Law-Making Resolutions of International Organisations. Survey of Problems and the Preliminary Analysis*) (Praca Wydana z Zasiłku Polskiej Akademii Nauk 1965) 69.

[83] GI Tunkin, *Theory of International Law* (WE Butler tr, Harvard University Press 1974) 106. The same view is expressed by Chanaki, *L'adaptation* 183.

[84] ibid 183.

[85] D Lost-Sieminska, 'The International Maritime Organization' in Bowman and Kritsiotis (eds), *Conceptual and Contextual Perspectives* 907, 920.

governments represented on the Maritime Safety Committee (MSC). In the early days of the SOLAS Convention, such a provision did not pose undue problems since, at the time of the adoption of the Convention, amendments required ratification by only fifteen States for their entry into force, seven of which had fleets consisting of at least one million gross tons of merchant shipping. However, the late 1960s witnessed the expansion of the number of State parties to SOLAS, which had reached 80 and the tonnage was also continuously rising due to the emergence of new States, which developed their shipping industry. Such an expansion of the number of State parties had an impact on the total number required to amend the convention, leading to instances where the acceptance of amendments took a longer time than that of the ratification of the convention itself.

The rapid advancement of technology in the shipping industry resulted in amending the SOLAS Convention six times after it entered into force in 1965. In 1974, a new convention was adopted in order to incorporate all these amendments as well as other minor changes. This new convention has been subsequently amended on numerous occasions.[86]

Complex requirements concerning amendments to the IMO Conventions resulted in long delays in bringing them into force. The tacit acceptance procedure was introduced to remedy this state of affairs. Following the examples of the ICAO, the WHO, and the other above-listed organisations, the IMO Conventions applied the tacit acceptance procedure to the amendment of provisions of a technical nature, included in the annexes and appendices of treaties. The classical amendment procedure has been retained for non-technical articles, 'which have limited practical importance'.[87]

Without tacit acceptance, it would have proved impossible to keep conventions up to date and the IMO's role as the international forum for technical issues involving shipping would have been placed in jeopardy.[88] As expected, the tacit acceptance procedure has greatly sped up the amendment process. Amendments generally enter into force within 18 to 24 months. On the contrary, the classical amendment procedure

[86] The classical amendment procedure has been used to non-technical provisions; tacit acceptance is used in relation to amendment of technical provisions (ibid 917).

[87] ibid 918.

[88] See in more detail, IMO, 'Introduction' (*IMO,* 2019) <www.imo.org/en/About/Conventions/Pages/Home.aspx> accessed 20 September 2019.

of the 1960 SOLAS Convention did not result in any of the amendments adopted between 1966 and 1973 in entering into force due to insufficient number of ratifications.[89] Due to its effectiveness, the tacit acceptance procedure has been applied in the majority of the IMO's technical conventions and also has been incorporated in other instruments such as on liability for oil pollution damage.

The advantages of tacit acceptance are numerous, in particular due to its quick, simple, and efficient modification of conventions to conform to the development of technology in shipping industry. An important element of this procedure is, as was observed, that it provides certainty about the date on which an amendment becomes effective, rather than leaving this to the timing of individual acceptances. Lost-Sieminska notes that, 'in reality, the classical amendment procedure meant that amendments would never have entered into force and, as a consequence, every State would have adopted its own national rules for shipping safety and environmental protection, inevitably leading to chaos'.[90]

Most of the amendments of technical annexes of the SOLAS Convention are 'deemed to have been accepted at the end of two years from the date on which it is communicated to Contracting Governments' unless the amendment is objected to by more than one-third of the contracting governments, or contracting governments owning not less than 50 per cent of the world's gross merchant tonnage. The MSC may vary this period by up to one year.

The MARPOL provides for an amendment to be deemed to have been accepted at the end of a period determined by the appropriate body at the time of its adoption, which period shall not be less than ten months. The entry into force of such amendments can be blocked in a similar fashion as with the SOLAS Convention, ie if they are objected to by not less than one-third of the State parties or by parties owning not less than 50 per cent of the world's gross merchant tonnage.[91] The whole procedure of adoption of amendments under the SOLAS Convention and MARPOL is very complex, due to the binary solution regarding the consideration of amendments: amendment after the consideration by the organisation (ie IMO committees consider the proposed amendment) and amendment by the COP, in which case only the parties consider the amendments.[92]

[89] Lost-Sieminska, 'The International Maritime Organization' 917.

[90] ibid 918.

[91] ibid 919.

[92] ibid.

In the IMO practice, all decisions, including the adoption of amendments, are taken by consensus. In case of a lack of consensus, both SOLAS and MARPOL provide that a two-thirds majority of the parties adopts amendments.[93] It appears that, at least within the framework of the IMO sponsored treaties, tacit acceptance is a simplified and effective method of speeding up entry into force of amendments. However, the undisputed efficiency of this method appears to be hindered by the unclear and complex relationship between the role of the Marine Environment Protection Committee (MEPC) and the parties, and the role of the MEPC and the parties *versus* the Assembly in the adoption of amendments.[94] The troubled relationship between the State parties to MARPOL and the MEPC as the body responsible for this convention is an example of the procedural difficulties regarding the decision on amendments. There are currently 171 States eligible for membership to the committee: 170 members of the organisation and one State that is a non-member of the Organisation but is a party to MARPOL. Of those States, only 75 are parties to the 1997 Protocol.[95] Such a structure clearly illustrates the difficulty regarding the situation in which the majority of the MEPC will have a different view than will the two-thirds of the parties.[96] Therefore, the main divisive problem concerning the adoption of amendments was the issue of departing from the principle of consensus and their adoption by a majority vote.[97]

Notwithstanding the internal problems concerning the adoption of the amendments to the IMO Conventions, the use of the system of tacit acceptance appears to be applied recently even more extensively than before. Such an example is the Guidelines for Ships Operating in Arctic Ice-Covered Waters that were adopted by the MSC and MEPC in 2002, ie the so-called Polar Code. The method of transposing it into 'hard' binding law was subject to much discussion. Finally, it was decided that it be will adopted through dissecting the code into various parts and attaching these in the form of annexes to the existing conventions, such as the SOLAS and the MARPOL, adopting them through the tacit acceptance procedure.[98]

93 In the SOLAS a two-thirds of the contracting governments and in the MARPOL a two-thirds majority of the parties (ibid).
94 See in depth on this aspect, ibid.
95 MARPOL Annex VI.
96 Lost-Sieminska, 'The International Maritime Organisation' 922.
97 ibid 921.
98 ibid.

To give an example, outside the IMO framework this time, in order to demonstrate that the tacit acceptance procedure is not merely a specialised tool unique to the workings of the IMO, parties may turn to the CITES. The CITES COP has adopted criteria for the consideration by its parties regarding proposals concerning amending Appendices I (species of wild fauna and flora threatened with extinction) and II (species of wild fauna and flora, which may become extinct unless a strict regulation of their trade has been enacted) of the CITES.[99] The updating of these lists is carried out under a tacit acceptance procedure.[100] Interestingly enough the possibility of 'opting-out' for the State parties is called a 'reservation' in CITES.[101]

5.3.2.4 Characterisation of the Tacit Acceptance Procedure

In the view of the authors of the present book, the legal character of the tacit acceptance ('opting-out') procedure has more recently been defined as a simplified amendment to a treaty, rather than as an expression of a unilateral act of an organisation.[102] The most notable feature of this procedure is its efficiency in the adoption of amendments. However, one of the characteristics of this method of amendment of a treaty is that it is most often used in relation to amendments of the provisions, which are of a technical nature, not in relation to provisions that set out the main rights and obligations of State parties to the treaty.

Nevertheless, such an inherently 'technical' procedure has led to some questions of a more theoretical nature, such as the issue of the exact moment of consent to be bound in tacit amendment: the moment of the voting or the moment of silence. We agree with the approach which views the silence of the State as the expression of consent to be bound.[103]

The voting concerning the adoption of the decision is not an expression of consent to be bound; it does not have a contractual character. Silence, on the other hand, is the element which triggers the legal obligation and, as it was stated, it is the source of validity for the rule. The other question, which arose from the analysis of tacit amendment, is whether it is a means of expression of consent to bound that falls under

[99] CITES, 'Resolution Conf 9.24 (Rev. CoP17)' (*CITES*, 2019) <www.cites.org/sites/default/files/document/E-Res-09-24-R17.pdf> accessed 20 September 2019.

[100] CITES Art XV(1) and (2).

[101] CITES Art XV(3).

[102] D König, 'Tacit Consent/Opting Out Procedure' [2013] MPEPIL 1478 [1–21].

[103] ibid [19].

the chapeau of 'any other means' of Article 11 VCLT or this article only enumerates active and not 'passive' ways of consent to be bound. It appears from the flexible character of Article 11 VCLT that the tacit amendment procedure does not seem to depart from the consensualist paradigm of Article 11.[104]

The theoretical questions concerning the tacit amendment procedure may have been solved to some extent. The same cannot be said about the practical implementation of this mechanism. It is interesting to note that the awkwardness of characterising the tacit acceptance procedure that we face at the international level is reflected in equal measure at the domestic level. Demonstrative of this is the fact that in certain States, such as Poland, the procedure of tacit acceptance, at least within the IMO, is treated as an amendment to a treaty, not a *sensu stricto* act of an international organisation, and thus is subject to the same procedure of internal approval (parliamentary and other) *as a formal amendment to a treaty.*[105] However, in other States, such as Croatia and Nigeria, the tacit acceptance procedure is *automatically transposed into the national legal order.*

5.3.3 *COPs/MOPs in MEAs and Amendment/Modification Thereof*

5.3.3.1 Legal Characterisation of COPs/MOPs

As was mentioned, the tacit acceptance procedure was the precursor of the so-called autonomous institutional arrangements (AIAs),[106] although the latter must be distinguished from the former as it partakes of different characteristics.[107] This connection, yet differentiation, between the tacit amendment procedure and AIAs has dictated the structure of our analysis. Consequently, having concluded our research into the tacit acceptance procedure, we will now proceed to examine the recent phenomenon concerning the extensive powers of organs of MEAs, in particular COPs/MOPs, the legal character of which has been variously

[104] Pergantis, *The Paradigm of State Consent* 122–5.

[105] Information obtained through Dorota Lost-Sieminska, the Head of the Legal Section of the IMO and Iva Parlov (expert maritime lawyer in Croatia). In Poland, originally the changes to the IMO Conventions adopted within the MEPC were subject to ratification by the Parliament *en bloc* according to Art 14 of the Law on International Treaties (Official Journal No 39, Item 443, 2002 with Amendments). Recent practice is simplified through the act of the Council of Ministers (the same statute). However, if changes are significant, the procedure of ratification will be employed.

[106] Churchill and Ulfstein, 'Autonomous Institutional Arrangements' 623–59.

[107] Hathaway, Saurabh Sanghvi and Solow, 'Tacit Amendments' 64.

termed as 'AIAs', 'managerial treaty making',[108] or simply as a diplomatic conference.[109] Notwithstanding that this subject matter has attracted a sizeable body of literature, there is still little understanding about the legal character of COPs/MOPs and the effects of their decisions on treaty regimes.[110] Nolte in his seminal work, *Treaties and Subsequent Practice*, stated that they are situated somewhere between a diplomatic conference and an international organisation.[111] They constitute useful *fora* for State parties to evolve treaty regimes and cooperate. They are treaty bodies in the sense that they are created on the basis of treaties; they are not to be equated, however, with bodies which comprise independent experts or bodies with a limited membership.[112]

> COPs are more or less periodical settings which are open to all parties of a treaty. As such, they can be seen as the continuing common venue of the parties of a treaty where authoritative interpretations in terms of the VCLT can take place. COPs represent a vehicle for the continuing and evolving expression of the will of the parties, allowing for the concretisation and adaptation of treaty provisions over time.[113]

COPs/MOPs adopt various legal acts, which may be classified as 'internal' and 'external'. The first category of acts relates to the structure and performance of COPs/MOPs themselves.[114] The second category of acts concerns decisions affecting substantive obligations of the State parties. However, although this in theory seems like a pretty straightforward distinction, practice demonstrates that it is far from a clear-cut one.[115]

108 JE Alvarez, *International Organisations as Law-Makers* (OUP 2006) 316.

109 AE Boyle, 'Saving the World? Implementation and Enforcement of International Environmental Law through International Institutions' (1991) 3 JEL 229.

110 For example: R Lefeber, 'Creative Legal Engineering' (2000) 13 LJIL 1; Churchill and Ulfstein, 'Autonomous Institutional Arrangements'; J Brunnée, 'COPing with Consent: Law-Making under Multilateral Environmental Agreements' (2002) 15 LJIL 1; J Brunnée, 'Reweaving the Fabric of International Law? Patterns of Consent in the Environmental Framework Agreements' in R Wolfrum and V Röben (eds), *Developments of International Law in Treaty-Making* (Springer 2005) 101; M Fitzmaurice, 'Consent to Be Bound – Anything New under the Sun?' (2005) 74 NJIL 483.

111 Nolte (ed), *Treaties and Subsequent Practice* 365.

112 ibid.

113 ibid.

114 Such as adoption of rules of procedure, finances, establishment of subsidiary bodies.

115 Nolte (ed), *Treaties and Subsequent Practice* 367. He gives several examples of such situations, such as the evolution of a financial mechanism as a part of the institutional architecture developed over time by the COP to the UNFCCC and the CMP to the Kyoto Protocol.

One aspect of the activities of COPs that is undisputed is that their decisions, which may result in the modification of treaty norms, do not follow the formal procedures laid down in the VCLT relating to amendment of treaties. Such modification of treaty provisions has an impact on the rights and obligations of States under the relevant treaty. Under certain MEAs, COPs enjoy interpretative or rule-creating powers; the formal VCLT criteria on the A/M of a treaty at times play a secondary role. This is particularly the case where obligations under the treaty and incumbent upon the State parties can be modified or potentially even created in a manner that does not call for the formal, VCLT-based procedures associated with A/M of a treaty. There are a number of theories attempting to explain the underlying effect of COP decisions for the development of a treaty regime in practice. These can be grouped into three categories:

(i) Theories that accord binding force to the COP/MOP decisions, deriving said binding force from the intention of the parties, ie that there is a 'trickle-down' effect of the consent given to the treaty than then infuses the COP/MOP decisions. There are several versions of this theory.
(ii) Theories which, assuming that such decisions do not have a formally binding legal effect, nevertheless attempt to find some intermediate ('soft' or 'de facto') status for such decisions.
(iii) Theories which, also assuming that the decisions do not have a formally binding character on the basis of the intention of the parties, seek to substitute an alternative basis from outside the realm of the law of treaties for their binding character.

It is fair to say that none of these theories reflect in a satisfactory manner the complexity of the legal nature of COPs/MOPs decisions.

Theories based on the law of treaties mostly refer to some form of enhanced powers that COPs/MOPs allegedly enjoy. These can include powers to extend the obligations of State parties, and, in other cases, powers to give these obligations greater precision as a result of the interpretation of a basic treaty provision. It is argued that it may be a technique used in a framework treaty, giving more precision to very general and at times vague provisions through decisions of COPs. This is undoubtedly true in the context of very general treaties such as the 1992 UN Framework Convention on Climate Change (UNFCCC). However, even MEAs with a more precisely formulated inventory of rights and obligations of State parties bestow on COPs powers of adding new functions, or modifying existing obligations, which in the practice of MEAs are at times difficult to distinguish with any great degree of certainty and precision. An example of such a blurred type of a function (a new obligation or an amendment) is the case of the Montreal Protocol's adjustment procedures in Article 2(9). This procedure regulates the modification in the scope of the parties' duties under the protocol, such as the tightening of control measures by bringing forward the phasing-out of certain substances. Decisions adopting an adjustment are as a rule adopted by consensus. However, in the case of a failure of all efforts to reach a consensus, such decisions can be adopted by a two-thirds majority vote of all parties present, voting, and representing a majority of both developed and developing countries. The decision must be communicated to the parties and then enters into force for all parties, including those that opposed the adoption, six months from the date of circulation of the communication. Decisions taken by the majority under this procedure are absolutely binding, not in a 'soft' or 'de facto' way.[116]

The second method for amending (or extending) States' obligations under a treaty in this way relies on the so-called enabling clauses in conventions or protocols thereto, which charge COPs/MOPs with the elaboration of rules in particular areas without expressly providing for the actual amendment of the convention or protocol. They may however result in the amendment/modification of State parties' obligations, as for example under the Kyoto Protocol. The Kyoto Protocol grants the COP of the UNFCCC the power under Article 17 to 'define the relevant principles, modalities, rules and guidelines, in particular for verification, reporting and accountability for emissions trading'. In the theory of international law there is no uniform view as to the binding force of these 'rules'. Ulfstein maintains that the notion of 'rules' presupposes that they have a legally binding character. The same author notes that this position is supported by the wording of Article 17, which refers to 'relevant principles, modalities, rules and guidelines', thus indicating that rules are different from non-binding 'principles' or 'guidelines'. Ulfstein's view that these 'rules' are binding is not shared by all authors. For example, Brunnée is more skeptical about the legally binding character of these 'rules'. She argues that '[g]iven the exceptional nature of COP authority to bind States, even the terms "procedures" (used in Articles 12(7) and 18) or

[116] And, of course, this raises the question of whether such a decision with new strict emission targets constitutes a new obligation, or perhaps is a modification of a previous one.

"rules" (used in Articles 3(4) and 17) do not necessarily imply COP authority to bind. Procedures or rules can be binding, but need not be'.[117]

This discussion indicates a certain degree of confusion[118] surrounding, what may be termed secondary legislation, leading to an amendment of a treaty. The lack of a precise definition of the legal character of such acts has practical effects for States, both from the point of view of State responsibility and that of the law of treaties. Since this is not a subject matter of this chapter, suffice it to say that the lack of certainty in relation to the binding force of an act (in this case 'rules') has an impact on the responsibility of a State in relation to breaches of these 'rules' which, depending on their bindingness, may or may not be a wrongful act – the most fundamental distinction in the law of State responsibility, with grave consequences for States.

The effects of such confusion could be equally serious in relation to the law of treaties. The unresolved issue in the legal character of 'the rules' (ie their binding force) has an impact on the amendments to the main treaty (in this case the Kyoto Protocol). It appears that such a binding nature of 'rules' would be left for State parties to decide. This would not be an acceptable position. It would result in an extremely patchy implementation of the Kyoto Protocol, as some of the amended 'rules' would be treated as a binding amendment by some of its parties and as non-binding by others. Such patterns of implementation could only cause chaos and have a very adverse effect on the implementation of the Kyoto Protocol.

In practice, State parties to the Kyoto Protocol treated such 'rules' rather as political guidelines than acts with a binding force. In fact, in case of far-reaching decisions, changing the nature and the scope of legal obligations, the parties to the Kyoto Protocol have recourse to a formal procedure of amendments, as envisaged in Articles 20 and 21 of the protocol. In accordance with Article 21(7) and Article 20(4), the amendment is subject to acceptance by the parties to the Kyoto Protocol. Pursuant to Article 20(4), the amendment will enter into force for those parties having accepted it on the 90th day after the date of receipt by the Depositary of an instrument of acceptance by at least three-fourths of the parties to the Kyoto Protocol. A total of 144 instruments of acceptance are required for the entry into force of the amendment. For example, such an amendment procedure was used in the case of the 2012 Doha

[117] Brunnée, 'COPing with Consent' 24.

[118] At least on the level of theory.

Amendment establishing the second commitment period of the Kyoto Protocol. Parties to the Kyoto Protocol adopted an amendment to the Kyoto Protocol by decision 1/CMP.8 in accordance with Articles 20 and 21 of the Kyoto Protocol, at the eighth session of the Conference of the Parties serving as the meeting of the parties to the Kyoto Protocol held in Doha, Qatar, in December 2012. On 21 December 2012, the amendment was circulated by the Secretary-General of the United Nations acting in his capacity as Depositary to all Parties to the Kyoto Protocol in accordance with Articles 20 and 21 of the protocol. In case of a formal amendment, the decision of COP does not by itself change the scope of the obligations of States parties to the MEA but is subject to a formal amendment procedure.

There are numerous examples of activities of COPs leading to the changing of scope of obligations of their parties. However, again there is no clear indication whether such a change can be termed an informal amendment to a treaty, or perhaps a treaty interpretation by COPs. Take for example the Convention on the Conservation of European Wildlife and Natural Habitats (Bern Convention).[119] Article 4(1) of the Bern Convention stipulates that each party must 'take appropriate and necessary legislative and administrative measures to ensure the conservation of the habitats of the wild flora and fauna species, especially those specified in Appendices I and II, and the conservation of endangered natural habitats'.

Article 4(2) provides that the parties in their planning and development policies 'shall have regard to the conservation requirements of the areas protected under the preceding paragraph, so as to avoid or minimise as far as possible any deterioration of such areas'. According to Davies, these provisions have been criticised due to their ambiguous character.[120] As a result, the Standing Committee addressed this situation. It adopted 'Recommendation No 25 (1991) on the conservation of natural areas outside protected areas proper', which calls upon parties to consider adopting a variety of measures, such as the setting up of environmental corridors and a network of nature parks to fulfill obligations under Article 4. In relation, for example, to the Convention on Trade in Endangered Species of Wild Fauna and Flora (CITES), there is a procedure of downlisting or uplisting species protected by the CITES, which

[119] 1979 Convention on the Conservation of European Wildlife and Natural Habitats (adopted 19 September 1979, entered into force 1 June 1982) 1284 UNTS 209.

[120] Davies, 'Non-compliance' 83–4.

means moving them between appendices based on the decision of the COP of the CITES, a procedure which also modifies (amends) to a certain extent obligations of the State parties, which differ under all three appendices.

The Executive Body of the Long-Range Transboundary Air Pollution (LRTAP),[121] the name for that treaty regime's COP, provided interpretations of ambiguous wording in a legally binding agreement. The 1985 Sulphur Dioxide Protocol stipulates that parties 'shall reduce their national annual sulphur emissions or their transboundary fluxes by at least 30 per cent as soon as possible and at the latest by 1993, using 1980 levels as the basis of calculation of reductions'. Four years after the protocol's adoption, the parties in the Executive Body reached a 'common understanding' that this obligation for the parties to 'reduce their national annual sulphur emissions or their transboundary fluxes by at least 30 per cent as soon as possible and at the latest by 1993' meant that 'reductions to that extent should be reached in that timeframe and the levels maintained or further reduced after being reached'. Such a decision of MEA bodies can be approached in a two-fold manner: as an evolution of treaty regimes through interpretation or as an informal amendment.

One of the most controversial 'law-making' activities of COPs is the establishment of so-called compliance mechanisms, aimed at monitoring and remedying non-compliance with obligations of States deriving from MEAs. Such mechanisms are different from settlement of dispute procedures. They are established in many MEAs. Their structure is roughly similar, comprised of a special body, equipped to deal with compliance issues and COPs acting as the highest organ, deciding on the adoption of relevant measures in cases of non-compliance. Decisions adopted by COPs establishing compliance mechanisms are perhaps not strictly binding, but they are nevertheless generally accepted by States parties to a MEA. These compliance procedures frequently result in the application of certain measures taken by COPs towards State parties as a result of non-compliance. For the most part, such regimes are set up by COPs under enabling clauses, such as, for instance, under Article 8 of the 1987 Montreal Protocol on Substances That Deplete the Ozone Layer[122]

[121] 1979 Convention on Long-Range Transboundary Air Pollution (adopted 13 November 1979, entered into force 16 March 1983) 1302 UNTS 217.

[122] 1987 Montreal Protocol on Substances that Deplete the Ozone Layer (adopted 16 September 1987, entered into force 1 January 1989) 1522 UNTS 3.

and Article 18 of the Kyoto Protocol.[123] The procedure under the Kyoto Protocol can result in onerous consequences for a State in the event of non-compliance, such as the suspension of flexibility mechanisms. One must note that Saudi Arabia protested continuously against the decision of the Kyoto Protocol CMP adopting a compliance procedure. Saudi Arabia argued that this procedure should instead be adopted on the basis of a formal amendment to the Kyoto Protocol. One must add, however, that COP decisions adopted in the event of non-compliance are not binding on State parties, although they can produce some political force. This, in turn, is not the case with respect to decisions by the Enforcement Branch of the Compliance Committee under the Kyoto Protocol, which are indeed binding. In principle, the legal character of such decisions must be investigated on a case-by-case basis because of the variety of possible COP functions and their legal effects, which escape generalisation. The only possible compliance procedure, application of which may lead to the modification of the scope of rights and obligations under the MEA, is (as it was noted) the Kyoto Protocol, and specifically only the decisions of its Enforcement Branch on suspension of flexible mechanisms in respect of a party in breach of its treaty obligations. Decisions of COPs under all other existing compliance mechanisms, adopted as a result of a breach of MEAs (no matter how harsh), are in fact only political decisions, compliance with which is of course desirable, but non-compliance with such decisions does amount to the breach of treaty obligations. Therefore, Saudi Arabia has protested against the establishment of the compliance mechanism under the Kyoto Protocol on the basis of a decision of COP instead of on a basis of a formal amendment to a treaty, because the decision of the Enforcement Branch of the Compliance Mechanism under this specific regime might have a binding effect on the scope of fundamental treaty obligations of its parties. It may be observed that in the Basel Convention, that was established by COP without any relevant treaty provision. According to Nolte, this procedure can be termed as a subsequent practice in parallel with formal amendment procedure. Article 18 provides for an amendment, but a more expedient system was preferred to that of a MOP decision.[124] Another such an example is the Basel Convention on Transboundary Movement of Hazardous Wastes (Basel Convention). In this case, the COP adopted

[123] 1997 Kyoto Protocol to the United Nations Framework Convention on Climate Change (adopted 11 December 1997, entered into force 16 February 2005) 2303 UNTS 162.

[124] Nolte (ed), *Treaties and Subsequent Practice* 355.

by consensus a decision banning the export of hazardous wastes from OECD member States to non-OECD member States. Such a decision, without a formal amendment of a convention, resulted in protests from many State parties to the convention. In 1995, an official amendment was adopted by inserting a new preambular paragraph 7 bis and a new Article 44 to the convention. This amendment has not yet entered into force.[125]

Another example concerning the Montreal Protocol is the Decision II/2 on several amendments to the protocol, which were adopted at the second MOP of the Montreal Protocol in 1990. The amendments and their entry into force is set out in Annex II to the MOP's Final Report. Article 2 of the Annex stated:

> The Amendment will enter into force on January 1, 1992, provided that at least twenty instruments of ratification, acceptance of approval of the Amendment have been deposited by States or regional economic integration organisation that are Parties to the Montreal Protocol on Substances That Deplete the Ozone Layer. In the event that this condition has not been fulfilled by that date, the Amendment shall enter into force on the ninetieth day following the date on which it has been fulfilled.[126]

According to Nolte, the MOP decision represents a subsequent practice by the parties, but which arguably goes well beyond the scope of interpretation by providing a modification of the amendment procedure set in the Vienna Convention.[127]

Both in the case of tacit amendment procedure and decisions of COPs/MOPs, there is a blurred line between an amendment to a treaty, subsequent agreement in the sense of Article 31 (3)(a) VCLT (ie the realm of treaty interpretation), and modification. As Nolte opines, the acts undertaken as a result of tacit amendment procedure are not as such a subsequent agreement in the meaning of the above article of the VCLT,

[125] ibid 357. Art 18: 'The Conference of the Parties serving as the meeting of the Parties to this Protocol shall, at its first session, approve appropriate and effective procedures and mechanisms to determine and to address cases of non-compliance with the provisions of this Protocol, including through the development of an indicative list of consequences, taking into account the cause, type, degree and frequency of non-compliance. Any procedures and mechanisms under this Article entailing binding consequences shall be adopted by means of an amendment to this Protocol'.

[126] UNEP, 'Report of the 2nd Meeting of the Parties to the Montreal Protocol on Substances That Deplete the Ozone Layer' (29 June 1990) UN Doc UNEP/OZL.Pro.2/3, Decision II/2, 11 and 25–39; Nolte (ed), *Treaties and Subsequent Practice* 354–5.

[127] Nolte (ed), *Treaties and Subsequent Practice* 355.

but they can, however, in certain aspects imply such a subsequent agreement. For example, the Consultative Meeting of Contracting Parties,[128] in 1993, adopted three amendments to Annex I by way of the tacit amendment procedure. As such, these amendments were not subsequent agreement; they could, however, imply a specific interpretation and even modification of the underlying treaty itself. The resolution upon which these amendments were adopted[129] established the agreement of the parties that the London Convention is an appropriate body to address the issue of law – the level of radioactive waste disposal into sub-bed repositories accessed from sea. This resolution expanded the definition of 'dumping' in the London Convention by deciding that disposal covers wastes channeled into or under the seabed from the sea but not from land by tunneling. According to Nolte, 'such an interpretative resolution is a clear case of a subsequent agreement which was then applied by the way of the amendments taken in tacit amendment procedure'.[130]

5.3.4 *Legitimacy of A/M/R by COPs*

Although much has been written about the legitimacy of international environmental law and the far-reaching functions of COPs, an elaborate analysis of these theories is outside the scope of this chapter. However, in view of the present authors, two such theories evidence the complexity of capturing the legitimacy of acts of COPs, ie the theory of fairness of Thomas Franck[131] and the interactional theory of Lon Fuller, as applied and analysed by Brunnée and Toop.

Bodansky commenting on legitimacy in the context of international environmental law expressed the view that although environmental law had developed 'through a consensual rather than an authoritative process' the phenomenon of authority plays an ancillary role.[132] This statement holds as well in relation to the issue of legitimacy in the case of COPs, due to their–at times–authoritarian functions and activities, influencing the behaviour of States. As was explained earlier in this chapter,

[128] Ie the COP of the 1972 London Convention on the Prevention of the Pollution from Dumping of Wastes and Other Matter (London Convention).
[129] Which preceded said amendments by three years.
[130] Nolte (ed), *Treaties and Subsequent Practice* 369.
[131] Th Franck, *Fairness in International Law and Institutions* (OUP 1995).
[132] D Bodansky, 'The Legitimacy of International Governance: A Coming Challenge for International Environmental Law' (1999) 93 AJIL 596, 604.

such authoritarian functions involve evolving the content of certain vague general principles, even of fundamental importance for the State parties (such as the fleshing out of flexible mechanisms in the Kyoto Protocol) and setting out procedures of the most significant importance for States (impacting on their behaviour, such as non-compliance mechanisms).

The question of legitimacy of actions and functions of COPs has taken a central place in discussion relating to the role of COPs. As was stated by Bernstein, '[l]egality is potentially violated when a treaty body, group of experts such as scientists empowered by a treaty … or even a representative body of State delegates, makes a decision that appears to go beyond the mandate given to them by the statute to which States consented'.[133]

The question of legitimacy can be analysed from the point of view of fairness, a theme elaborated on in Franck's seminal works. A full account of this author's theory exceeds the purpose of this chapter. However, it is worthwhile to remind oneself of the main tenets of his theory, in order to pose the question whether far-reaching obligations of States outside their jurisdiction fall within the concept of legitimacy, understood as fairness. It was emphasised by Franck that the key factor of legitimacy is fairness, which accommodates a popular belief that a system of rules, to be fair, must be firmly rooted in a framework of formal requirements about how the rules are made, interpreted, and applied.[134] The belief that a rule is legitimate reinforces the perception of its fairness and contributes to compliance. Fairness, he further explains, is the only formula which will command respect and ensure compliance.[135] The attributes of legitimacy are symbolic validation, determinacy, adherence, and coherence. The first of these, determinacy is defined by Franck as '[t]he ability of a text to convey a clear message. To appear transparent in the sense that one can see through the language of law to its essential meaning'.[136]

The perceived legitimacy of a rule also relies on the generality (coherence) of principles the rules apply. The belief of illegitimacy is rooted in the rule's lack of generality, ie its applicability only in one instance. Such rules are, as Franck observes, 'unprincipled'; 'they do not treat likes alike

[133] S Bernstein, 'Legitimacy in a Global Environmental Governance' (2005) 1 JILIR 139, 153–4.

[134] Franck, *Fairness in International Law* 7 ff.

[135] ibid 13.

[136] ibid 30.

and they therefore lack coherence'.[137] The rule is coherent '[w]hen its application treats cases alike and when the rule relates in a principled fashion to other rules in the same system. Constancy requires that a rule, whatever its content, be applied uniformly in every "similar" or "applicable" instance'.[138]

COPs amend/modify MEAs by fleshing out certain of their fundamental provisions, and formulate general, coherent, and well determined new rules, which are applicable in a repeated fashion in the practice of State parties, as it was evidenced in cases of the CITES and the Kyoto Protocol. The same reasoning applies to non-compliance procedures. Although each and every non-compliance case is different, and analysed separately by COPs, the rules of procedure and the measures to be adopted in cases of non-compliance are set out; and they are applicable to all cases. Again, it may be said, the test of fairness is fulfilled by decisions adopted by COPs in the event of non-compliance. Therefore, legitimacy perceived as fairness characterises COPs decisions.

There are attempts by theorists to explain the question of legitimacy of COPs' decisions based on the interactional theory of Fuller, transposed into the field of international environmental law by Brunnée and Toope.[139] This theory of 'internal morality' is based on avoidance of contradiction, generality, and congruence with underlying rules. Fuller's 'internal morality' is associated with the essential processes by which law is created, interpreted, and administered.[140] In this theory, legitimacy is based on cooperation and interaction between actors (the governing and governed) rooted within the social practice and conventions they created, within the context of norms and institutions they established.[141] Legitimacy is based on a 'thick' acceptance of the need for emerging norms, which is 'promoted by reference to past practice, contemporary aspirations and the deployment of reasoning by analogy'.[142]

The interactional perspective is not based on formal 'bindingness', and thus abandons the division between soft and hard law. The differentiation between legal norms and non-legal norms is effected through

137 ibid 38.

138 ibid.

139 J Brunnée and S Toope, 'International Law and Constructivism: Elements of an Interactional Theory of International Law' (2000) 19 ColumJTransnat'lL 19, 49–53; Brunnée, 'COPing with Consent' 15.

140 Brunnée and Toope, 'International Law' 56.

141 ibid.

142 ibid 66.

internal characteristics, which entail distinctive legal legitimacy and persuasiveness, requiring that rules be compatible with one another and reasonable, that official action is congruent with known rules, and that rules are transparent and relatively predictable. The degree to which these requirements are met defines the legitimacy of the norms or legal system 'and their power to promote adherence'.[143]

Brunnée describes the working of this theory:

> States (and other international actors), through their interaction, influence the scope and content of international norms and institutions. In turn, these norms and institutions furnish the context within which interaction takes place and shape the identities of the actors themselves. In other words, in this continuous process, actors come to understand themselves and their interests in light of their interaction with others and in light of the norms that frame the interaction. International law is generated as patterns of social practice emerge and increasingly influential mutual expectations and shared understandings of actors evolve.[144]

Brunnée explains that due to its characteristics, the interactional theory (without the formal division between binding and non-binding norms), depicts in a more accurate way the role of COPs as legislators as 'in an interactional account, legislation, whether at the national or international level, is never unidirectional imposition of authority'.[145] The COPs' legislating process, according to this theory, is engaged in a broader collective process, congruent with the expectations of society, and meets internal requirements. In this theory of law-making, State consent plays a secondary role.

> States may be most likely to agree to make law 'enforceable' when it has become binding in the interactional sense. Alternatively, States may be most likely to insist on formal consent where there is an insufficient foundation of shared understandings (such as when a protocol or an amendment on new substances or control measures has to be negotiated). In this context, the requirement of formal consent may in fact provide a protective mechanism that facilitates effective interactive processes by enabling States to participate, at least in principle, as equals.[146]

Brunnée analyses the question of legitimacy within the context of COPs through the prism of interactional theory. Law-makers, such as COPs,

[143] Brunnée, 'COPing with Consent' 36.
[144] ibid 34.
[145] ibid 38.
[146] ibid.

should keep the various legitimacy criteria in constant reference; the rules will gain more legitimacy (be more persuasive and influential) when there is stronger adherence to the criteria, with the participation of all actors.[147]

This short section is meant to be illustrative of the complex question of the legitimacy of the decisions of COPs. The authors of this book do not presume that there is one theory which would 'legitimise', in a persuasive and absolutely acceptable fashion, the legitimacy of COPs' functions. However, the quest for justification evidences the dilemma faced by States. Such functions of COPs reformulate the notion of consent as classically established, therefore resulting in attempts at legitimatisation.

5.3.5 *Juxtaposition of A/M/R with Interpretation*

5.3.5.1 Interconnectivity of A/M/R with Other Aspects of the 'Life-Cycle' of Treaties

During the preparatory work of the ILC, the similarities of both the characteristics of and the solutions relating to A/M/R with other aspects of the 'life-cycle' of a treaty kept coming up. There were three main areas where that interconnectivity was prominent: reservations (Article 20 VCLT), successive same subject matter treaties (Article 30 VCLT), and interpretation (Article 31 VCLT).

In more detail, when discussing the retention of the unanimity rule, Rosenne in the ILC meetings,[148] and Australia[149] and France[150] during the Vienna Conference suggested that the approach should be similar to that of reservations and in particular Article 20(2) VCLT. They were based on the premise that unanimity should be the norm in the case of treaties with a limited number of parties ('restricted multilateral treaties').[151]

With respect to normative conflict and successive treaties, the link emerged as the result of a draft article which eventually was left in its entirety on the cutting floor of the VCLT's *travaux préparatoires*. In the

[147] ibid 46.
[148] ILC, 'Summary Record of the 746th Meeting' [15] (Rosenne).
[149] Australia, 'Amendment Proposal to Article 41'.
[150] France, 'Amendment Proposal to Article 41'.
[151] This solution did not find its way into the final text of the VCLT, as several States opposed it as not reflecting State practice. See United Nations Conference on the Law of Treaties, '1st Session – 37th Meeting COW' [47–8].

discussions surrounding the form that the amending instrument should have, the possibility of instruments and methods other than 'in written form' was acknowledged. This led to Draft Article 68, which identified three venues through which a treaty could be modified: (i) through subsequent agreement (Draft Article 68(a)), (ii) through subsequent practice (Draft Article 68(b)), and (iii) through the emergence of a new customary rule (Draft Article 68(c)).[152] The ILC decided to dispense with 68(a) as it was considered superfluous since the same topic was addressed by Article 30 VCLT.[153]

5.3.5.2 A/M/R and Interpretation

The connection was more prominent with respect to interpretation. The prevailing view in literature on the subject is that, although interpretation is a distinct legal construct from amendment and modification, the legal boundaries are often blurred. Interpretation may change the meaning of the treaty but amendment and modification may result in the changing of the text of the treaty.[154] However, the risk of blurring between interpretation and modification has been at the centre of a significant debate for years, and still today some scholars voice their concerns on this blurring in relation to the most recent works of the ILC.[155]

The overlap between the two concepts can be seen even in the terminology used to describe A/M/R. For instance, as was already mentioned in Section 5.2, when attempting to determine the difference between 'amendment' and 'modification', de Luna suggested the trichotomy amendment *secundum/infra legem, praeter legem,* and *contra legem.*[156] This echoes the theories that interpretation can also be *infra legem, praeter legem,* and *contra legem.*[157]

[152] For an extensive analysis of the drafting history of Draft Article 68(c), see N Kontou, *The Termination of Treaties in Light of New Customary International Law* (Clarendon Press 1994).

[153] ILC, 'Report of the International Law Commission on the Work of Its Eighteenth Session' 236 [2]; ILC, 'Summary Record of the 866th Meeting' (9 June 1966) UN Doc A/CN.4/SR.866 [2] (Castrén), [6] (Jiménez de Aréchaga), [11] (Ago), [12] (Rosenne), [15] (Tunkin), [21] (de Luna), [25] (Briggs), [35] (Yasseen).

[154] Djeffal, *Static and Evolutive Treaty Interpretation* 15–6.

[155] For a recent work on this issue, see Tladi, 'Is the International Law Commission Elevating Subsequent Agreements and Subsequent Practice?'.

[156] ILC, 'Summary Record of the 746th Meeting' [104] (de Luna).

[157] See, generally, A Gourgourinis, *Equity and Equitable Principles in the World Trade Organization: Addressing Conflicts and Overlaps between the WTO and Other Regimes* (Routledge 2015).

But leaving similarities in terminology or effects aside, the difficulty of clearly identifying the line where interpretation turns into A/M/R was evident in the discussion surrounding the aforementioned Draft Article 68, and later on Draft Article 38. Draft Article 68(c), which provided for amendment by subsequent custom, had a fate similar to 68(a). It was also put on the chopping block for a variety of reasons: it was better left to be considered under the Draft Article on intertemporal law;[158] 'the question formed part of the general topic of the relation between customary norms and treaty norms which is too complex for it to be safe to deal only with one aspect of it in [one] article';[159] and it was irrelevant as the solution in any given situation would be provided by identifying the intention of the parties.[160] The argument relating to intertemporal law is quite interesting, because that article was also left out of the VCLT. The reasoning was that the first leg of the doctrine of intertemporal law (determining the existence of a rule) was provided for by Article 30 of the VCLT, while the second leg (determining the continued manifestation of a rule) would be covered by Article 31 of the VCLT. However, references to intertemporal law eventually were left out from Article 31 because the issue was too complex.[161] In the end, Draft Article 68(c) was omitted for being complex and superfluous as it would be dealt with under the draft article on intertemporal law. The latter, in turn, was left out for the exact same reasons, as part of it would be incorporated into Article 30 VCLT, and finally any reference to intertemporal law was once again omitted from Article 30 because of its complexity. The issue kept being passed along like a hot potato, from one article to the next and in the end got lost somewhere in the transition from one draft article to the next. Interestingly, the Institut de Droit International faced similar difficulties more recently, in 1995, when discussing a resolution on 'Problems Arising from a Succession of Codification Conventions on a Particular Subject'.

158 ILC, 'Summary Record of the 766th Meeting' (15 July 1964) UN Doc A/CN.4/SR.766 [121] (Waldock). Ironically enough, in the end, this article was also discarded. For an analysis of the drafting history of Draft Article 56, see Merkouris, *Article 31(3)(c) VCLT* ch 2.

159 ILC, 'Report of the International Law Commission on the Work of Its Eighteenth Session' 236 [2]; ILC, 'Summary Record of the 866th Meeting' [10] (Jiménez de Aréchaga), [11] (Ago), [12] (Rosenne), [20] (Tunkin), [24] (de Luna), [25] (Briggs), [41–2], [67] (Waldock), [58] (Rosenne).

160 ILC, 'Report of the International Law Commission on the Work of Its Eighteenth Session' 236 [2]; ILC, 'Summary Record of the 746th Meeting' [50] (Ago).

161 For a detailed analysis of the history of Draft Article 58, see Merkouris, *Article 31(3)(c) VCLT* ch 2.

Following the example of the ILC, it avoided making any pronouncements on the issue of modification by subsequent custom.[162] The reason being that it was too complex of an issue to be dealt with 'as an ancillary point at the end of a Conclusion [in the Resolution]'.[163]

However, unlike paragraphs (a) and (c) of Draft Article 68, paragraph (b), which provided for modification by subsequent practice, managed to survive the trial by fire of the ILC discussions and go through to the Vienna Conference on the Law of Treaties.

Despite its survival, a major concern was that 'the line may sometimes be blurred between interpretation and amendment of a treaty through subsequent practice'.[164] However, several members of the ILC felt that the two processes were distinct and should be treated in the VCLT as such.[165] The ILC acknowledged that when dealing with bilateral treaties it may be difficult to distinguish whether subsequent practice is evidence of a new agreement modifying the original treaty or an authentic interpretation of the treaty. The examples used were the *Temple of Preah Vihear* case (where practice was considered an authentic interpretation) and the *Air Transport Services Agreement* (where the treaty was considered modified by practice).[166]

5.3.5.2.1 Parties and (Non)-Essential Provisions But in multilateral treaties things are different. And at this point another critical point with respect to the function of Draft Article 68(b) emerged. Subsequent

162 Institut de Droit International, 'Problems Arising from a Succession of Codification Conventions on a Particular Subject' (1995/I) 66 AIDI 248.

163 Comments by Higgins, ibid 207.

164 ILC, 'Report of the International Law Commission Covering the Work of Its Sixteenth Session' (11 May–24 July 1964) UN Doc A/5809, 173, 198 [2]; ILC, 'Summary Record of the 766th Meeting' [122] (Waldock); ILC, 'Summary Record of the 767th Meeting' (16 July 1964) UN Doc A/CN.4/SR.767 [37] (Verdross), [39] (Waldock), [41] (Pal), [43] (Ago), [44–5] (Yasseen), [46–50] (Tunkin).

165 ILC, 'Report of the International Law Commission Covering the Work of Its Sixteenth Session' 198 [2]; ILC, 'Summary Record of the 866th Meeting' [4] (Castrén), [7–8] (Jiménez de Aréchaga), [11] (Ago), [26] (Briggs), [36] (Yasseen). Against: ILC, 'Summary Record of the 767th Meeting' [35] (Verdross), [36] (de Luna); ILC, 'Report of the International Law Commission on the Work of Its Eighteenth Session' 300 (Israel).

166 ILC, 'Report of the International Law Commission Covering the Work of Its Sixteenth Session' 198 [2]; H Waldock, 'Sixth Report on the Law of Treaties' ([11 March, 25 March, 12 April, 11 May, 17 May, 24 May, 1 June, and 14 June 1966) UN Doc A/CN.4/186 and Add. 1–7, reproduced in [1966/II] YBILC 51, 87–91 [1–15] and in particular [8]; ILC, 'Report of the International Law Commission on the Work of its Eighteenth Session' 236 [1].

practice for interpretation must establish the agreement of all the parties. It was not clear whether modification, on the other hand, especially in the cases of treaties creating bilateral or bilateralisable obligations, required the participation of all the parties, or just certain of the parties.[167] As Waldock summarised it:

> Clearly, on the plane of interpretation, *the treaty has only one correct interpretation*. But in practice it may have applications between particular parties which diverge from the interpretation and application of it by the general body of the parties. It hardly seems possible to classify such cases under the head of 'interpretation by subsequent practice' without seeming to throw overboard the essential concept of the integrity of the text of a multilateral treaty.[168]

The discussion within the ILC did not help clarify the issue, with members arguing both the expansive and restrictive interpretation of the term 'parties' with equal fervor.[169] The group against the expansive interpretation of the term 'parties' submitted that this was taking the analogy with *inter se* agreements a bit too far, since in the case of subsequent practice the safeguards of Article 41 (notification of parties) did not exist.[170] Additionally, it was difficult to establish whether the actual agreement between the parties had actually come into existence between certain of the parties.[171]

The ILC in its commentary tried to smooth over the debate by adopting the middle ground. It claimed that '[i]n formulating the rule in this way the Commission intended to indicate that the subsequent practice, even if every party might not itself have actively participated in the practice, must be such as to establish the agreement of the parties as a whole to the modification in question'.[172]

Finally, we need to mention an interesting point that Tunkin raised – whether a distinction should be drawn between essential and minor provisions. The latter being open to modification by subsequent practice,

[167] Waldock, 'Sixth Report' 90 [9].
[168] ibid (emphasis added).
[169] ILC, 'Summary Record of the 876th Meeting' (23 June 1966) UN Doc A/CN.4/SR.876 [19–64]; ILC, 'Summary Record of the 883rd Meeting' (4 July 1966) UN Doc A/ CN.4/ SR.883 [76–80].
[170] ILC, 'Summary Record of the 866th Meeting' [19] (Tunkin), [23] (de Luna), [27] (Briggs), [31] (Tsuruoka), [38] (Yasseen), [45] (El-Erian).
[171] ibid [57] (Tunkin).
[172] ILC, 'Report of the International Law Commission on the Work of Its Eighteenth Session' 236 [2].

but not the former. He was, however, the first to admit that he merely wished to raise the issue but had no ready answer to offer.[173] Waldock agreed with Tunkin, but he found it such an extremely delicate issue that 'as a draughtsman . . . [he] would shrink from the task of having to cover the points in the text of subparagraph *(b)*'.[174] The ILC, equally, selected not to delve more deeply into the topic.

5.3.5.2.2 Rejection of Draft Article 38 Having survived the discussions in the ILC, one would expect that Draft Article 38 (which, in essence was Draft Article 68(b)) would to a greater or lesser degree also survive the test of the Vienna Conference. Draft Article 38 was rejected by an overwhelming majority. Several States took the floor and expressed serious misgivings about the wisdom of including that article in the VCLT.[175] The main reasons for the rejection of this article can be summarised in the following points:

(i) it was not expedient to deal in the VCLT with such complex issues as the relationship between customary law and treaty law;[176]
(ii) the article was superfluous as it duplicated Article 31(3)(b) and other VCLT provisions;[177]
(iii) it raised grave concerns of conflict with the States' respective constitutional law;[178]
(iv) it conflicted or weakened *pacta sunt servanda*;[179]

173 ILC, 'Summary Record of the 866th Meeting' [18] (Tunkin).
174 ibid [64] (Waldock).
175 The only States that spoke in favour of Draft Article 38 were Israel, Italy, Austria, Cambodia, Switzerland, and Argentina.
176 United Nations Conference on the Law of Treaties, '1st Session – 37th Meeting COW' [57] (Finland), [58] (Japan).
177 ibid [57] (Finland), [58] (Japan), [59] (Venezuela), [62] (Vietnam), [67–8] (Spain); United Nations Conference on the Law of Treaties, '1st Session – 38th Meeting of the Committee of the Whole (COW)' (25 April 1968) UN Doc A/CONF.39/11 210 [2] (Russia), [28] (Turkey), [48] (Israel).
178 United Nations Conference on the Law of Treaties, '1st Session – 37th Meeting COW' [58] (Japan), [63] (France), [68] (Spain); United Nations Conference on the Law of Treaties, '1st Session – 38th Meeting COW' [4] (Russia), [17] (Poland), [27] (Turkey), [36] (Uruguay), [40–1] (Cuba), [43] (Philippines).
179 United Nations Conference on the Law of Treaties, '1st Session – 37th Meeting COW' [60] (Venezuela), [63] (France), [70] (Spain), [75] (Chile); United Nations Conference on the Law of Treaties, '1st Session – 38th Meeting COW' [3] (Russia), [6] (USA), [30–2] (Guinea), [38] (Tanzania), [40] (Cuba), [42] (Portugal), [47] (Netherlands), [53] (Czechoslovakia).

(vi) it was open to abuse;[180]
(vii) it would disrupt international relations, since 'if States were given the impression that any flexible attitude towards the application of a treaty was tantamount to agreement to modify the treaty, they would tend in future to become much more circumspect and rigid in their attitudes';[181]
(viii) it was unclear whether it applied only to non-essential provisions,[182] and also what was meant by 'practice' and 'parties';[183] and finally,
(ix) it was contrary to law and democracy.[184]

In a last-ditch attempt to save Draft Article 38, expert consultant Waldock tried to address the concerns raised by the States,[185] but to no avail. The amendment deleting Draft Article 38 was adopted by 53 votes to 15, with 26 abstentions.

5.3.5.3 The Difference between A/M/R and Interpretation

Although the previous analysis demonstrates the difficulties in distinguishing between A/M/R and interpretation, which among other reasons led to the eventual discarding of Draft Articles 68 and 38, this is not an impossible task. There are certain key differences which, although not a *passe partout*, can offer guidance in traversing the mercurial waters of the overlap between A/M/R and interpretation. There are two areas that must be addressed: the difference between A/M/R and evolutive interpretation, and the difference between A/M/R and interpretation by subsequent agreements/practice.

5.3.5.3.1 The Difference between A/M/R and Evolutive Interpretation

The critical difference between A/M/R and evolutive interpretation is one of limits. Gardiner rightly underscores the fact that

[180] United Nations Conference on the Law of Treaties, '1st Session – 37th Meeting COW' [61] (Vietnam).
[181] ibid [63] (France).
[182] ibid [69] (Spain).
[183] ibid [71-4] (Spain), [76–7] (Canada); United Nations Conference on the Law of Treaties, '1st Session – 38th Meeting COW' [13–6] (Poland), [18] (China), [34–5] (Uruguay), [44–6] (Netherlands), [52] (Czechoslovakia).
[184] United Nations Conference on the Law of Treaties, '1st Session – 38th Meeting COW' [21] (Colombia).
[185] ibid [55–7].

> [t]he indication that evolutive interpretation must be based on the concepts already in the treaty suggests that this has more limited potential for extending meanings than does concordant practice of the parties. Since the parties are acting collectively through their concordant practice, sovereign to make further treaty provisions, they can take interpretation further than can a person or body charged with the role of independent interpretation.[186]

The inherent difficulties of making fast and clear divisions between various types of formative changes in treaty provisions can be best exemplified by the murky relations between evolutive interpretation and subsequent practice. The classical case in this respect is the 2009 *Dispute Regarding Navigational and Related Rights* before the ICJ. According to Buga, evolutive interpretation of treaties and subsequent practice serve the same purpose: it allows treaties to develop over time and ensure the treaties survival and adaptation to current priorities. The main distinguishing feature is that in the case of evolutive interpretation, Buga explains, intention of the parties is taken into consideration in order to determine whether they meant to interpret and apply the treaty in a way that accounts for new developments, also including subsequent practice. Most often, however, such a construct of intention of the parties is a fiction, allowing modification of the treaty to suit contemporary conditions and the circumstances of application. Such an interpretation, as contrasted with subsequent practice, is bounded by the 'four corners of the treaty'. Subsequent practice 'can elucidate both the original and contemporary intentions of the parties and may also evidence the parties' agreement to remove a textual limit on the evolutionary potential of the treaty'. There are inherent difficulties in drawing firm conclusions from the text of the treaty as to the intention of the parties regarding evolutionary interpretation of its provisions, absent a direct intention. The ICJ has been known to do this on the basis of the interpretation of certain generic terms, such a 'commerce' in the *Dispute Regarding Navigational and Related Rights* case. Buga is of the view that although the meaning of the term might have changed in a significant manner since the formation of the treaty, such a reinterpretation cannot be equated with modifications, because they adhere to the original intention of the parties as embodied in the text. This statement is correct. However, as it was observed, this is to a certain extent a legal fiction. The conclusion regarding the intention of the parties about the evolutive (or not)

[186] Gardiner, *Treaty Interpretation* 275.

character of certain treaty provisions is decided in the majority of cases by an international judicial body in case of a dispute, thus stating in an arbitrary manner what was, according to this body, the intention of the parties to the treaty – a decision which is most often based on scant evidence, if any at all. Therefore, often such a construct of the intention of the parties is more illusory than evolutive.

The focus of subsequent practice is, as Buga explains, both intention of the parties at the formation of the treaty and also at the time of its application. Evolutive interpretation cannot modify the treaty provisions, as it refers only to provisions included in the treaty. Thus, its purpose is not the introduction of new concepts. She illustrates her statement by the practice of the ECtHR,[187] where, in most of the cases, evolutive interpretation of the ECHR has not modified treaty provisions. Similarly, the HRCttee in *Atasoy and Sarkut v Turkey* held that evolutive interpretation 'cannot go beyond the letter and spirit of the treaty or what the State parties initially and explicitly so intended'.[188]

Judge Bedjaoui in his Separate Opinion in the *Gabčíkovo-Nagymaros Project* case was also attuned to the fact that evolutive interpretation should not be unconstrained but should abide by certain limits or 'precautions', as he called them:

> Taken literally and in isolation, there is no telling where this statement may lead. The following precautions must be taken:
>
> - an 'evolutionary interpretation' can only apply in the observation of the general rule of interpretation laid down in Article 31 of the Vienna Convention on the Law of Treaties;
> - the 'definition' of a concept must not be confused with the 'law' applicable to that concept;
> - the 'interpretation' of a treaty must not be confused with its 'revision'.[189]

Of course, there are a number of other limits/precautions to evolutive interpretation,[190] including that evolutive interpretation should not end

[187] Such a controversial case was *Feldbrugge v Netherlands*.

[188] *Atasoy and Sarkut v Turkey*, HRCttee (29 March 2012) UN Doc CCPR/C/104/D/1853–1854/2008.

[189] *Gabčíkovo-Nagymaros Project*, Separate Opinion of Judge Bedjaoui [5].

[190] Such as *jus cogens* norms, non-retroactivity, judicial activism. For a complete list and detailed analysis, see Merkouris, '(Inter)temporal Considerations' 150–1; Merkouris, *Article 31(3)(c) VCLT* ch 2.

up becoming a revision of the treaty, ie an A/M/R.[191] However, since this is the exact point of our analysis, to consider it as one of the fundamental limits of evolutive interpretation here would be somewhat self-referential and of no practical use. However, thankfully, there are other limits/precautions that can prove more helpful for the purposes of our inquiry. In the context of distinguishing between A/M/R and evolutive interpretation, the three most critical limits/precautions are: the intention of the parties, the object and purpose of the treaty, and the text of the treaty.[192] Whereas A/M/R may go beyond these limits and alter the contours of each and every one of them, evolutive interpretation cannot. However, this issue is not as clear-cut in State practice. For example, in 2012 Austria addressed the question of interpretation *versus* modification with a preference to interpretation, as this procedure helps avoiding national procedures for treaty modification.[193]

The example of the judicial practice of the ECtHR evidences, in our view, that the line between evolutive interpretation and subsequent practice (which can modify the provisions) is not easily discerned in practice. Going back to ECtHR, the example of a far-reaching evolutive interpretation, which may be said to modify the provisions of the ECHR is the famous *Golder v UK* case. In this case, '[t]he Court not only rejected the view, defended by the United Kingdom, that lack of an explicit provision in the text constitutes a reason against granting an unenumerated right. It also stressed that the question whether to grant an unenumerated right is not a question whether we should stick to the actual text or read words into the text'.[194]

Buga admits that the interpretation of Article 8 (private life) of the ECHR by the Court as to give an effect to an 'environmental human right' is an example of the introduction of a new concept. She concludes, '[o]verall, the case law suggests that the implications of expansive evolutive interpretation can be similar to those resulting from (modification by) subsequent practice'.[195]

[191] *Gabčíkovo–Nagymaros Project*, Separate Opinion of Judge Bedjaoui; *Kasikili/Sedudu Island*, Declaration of Judge Higgins [2].

[192] Merkouris, *Article 31(3)(c) VCLT* ch 2; Merkouris, '(Inter)temporal Considerations', 150–1, and cases cited therein.

[193] G Hafner, 'Modification of Treaties by Subsequent Practice – Some Comments on Austrian Position' (2015) 20 ARIEL 175, 181.

[194] G Letsas, 'Strasbourg's Interpretive Ethic: Lessons for the International Lawyer' (2010) 21 EJIL 509, 516.

[195] I Buga, *The Modification of Treaties by Subsequent Practice* (OUP 2018) 99.

As it has been noted, the *Dispute Regarding Navigational and Related Rights* case clearly illustrates the lack of a hard-and-fast division between evolutive interpretation and subsequent practice and the way these two institutions change the treaty. The Court analysed the term '*commercio*' on the basis of evolutive interpretation, whilst Judge Skotnikov applied the test of subsequent practice. In his Separate Opinion, Judge Skotnikov noted the difficulty of ascertaining, by using the tool of contemporary evolutive interpretation, the intention of the original parties to the treaty, concerning certain terms included therein.[196] Contemporary interpretation of ideas concerning the intention of the parties at the inception of a treaty is a rather speculative exercise, which in fact may not reflect the real intention of the parties. The results concerning the application of both evolutive interpretation and subsequent practice were similar in this case by the majority of judges and Judge Skotnikov, the only difference being a slightly narrower scope of the interpretation achieved by the application of subsequent practice. Buga correctly identifies yet another (unresolved) legal question concerning subsequent practice, ie the result of modification in relation to ensuing obligations relating to parties to the treaty. She has noted that there are two different approaches: one which is based on a premise that the modified original agreement remains the basis of the obligations. The second approach is that subsequent practice results in the creation of an independent source of an obligation, thus rendering ineffective the original agreement. In fact, in relation to treaty modification by subsequent practice, there are more questions than answers and a plethora of unresolved legal issues. For example, the different types of treaty provisions, such as *jus cogens* norms or obligations *erga omnes* (and *erga omes partes*), 'set a very high bar for or altogether prohibit, derogation, including modification by subsequent practice'.[197] The aforementioned classical differentiation of norms of international law by Fitzmaurice into concessionary, integral, and interdependent also raises question of application of subsequent practice in relation to modification of parties' obligations.[198] Fitzmaurice attached to different types of treaties varied consequences of termination and suspension, such as the impossibility of termination or suspension of

[196] *Dispute Regarding Navigational and Related Rights*, Separate Opinion of Judge Skotnikov [2–10].

[197] Buga, *The Modification of Treaties* 183.

[198] For an analysis of the typology proposed by Fitzmaurice, see Fitzmaurice, 'Third Report' Commentary to Art 18 [78]; Fitzmaurice, 'Second Report' 54–5 [126], [128].

treaties of the 'integral' type in case of their breach by a party. Presumably, these different types of obligations have attached to them also different consequences in cases of subsequent practice modification, a problem which is still awaiting further research.

We agree with Buga that 'it should not be assumed lightly that subsequent practice has led to a modification of the treaty – but such effects can by no means be wholly precluded'.[199] She is correct in concluding that the threshold for practice to constitute agreement to modify a treaty will be dependent on the type and scope of the modification and the nature of the treaty and its provisions. She is also correct in observing the greatest conceptual difficulty in distinguishing between the treaty interpretation and treaty modification by subsequent practice. Such a distinction can only be approached on a case-by-case basis.

Despite such a cautious approach, there are cases of treaty modification by subsequent practice, such as eg *US/France Air Transport Services Agreement Arbitration*.[200] In this case, the US had for years operated an air route and the frequency of flights was different from that indicated in the text of the bilateral agreement. The French authorities had not objected to this practice. The arbitral tribunal concluded that the original agreement had been changed by subsequent practice and acquiescence. Therefore, France could not contest the modified treaty, as it would have been contrary to good faith, considering its previous conduct.[201] Kolb opines that the stability of the text has to be subsumed to the more fundamental continuity of the effective and uncontested conduct. Legal principles such as good faith, acquiescence, and estoppel outweigh the role of the parties' real will.[202] The practice must not be of all the parties to the treaty. It is sufficient that such a practice is regularly followed by a number of treaty parties, without objections from other parties. The practice becomes common by the aggregate of those who effectively engage in it and through the acquiescence of parties, who silently agree to it. The duty to speak out and object derives from the common treaty bond. Kolb states that it is a matter of good faith. The treaty parties engaged in a certain practice have legitimate expectations and the derived right 'to see their attitudes contested if that is the position of some other

[199] Buga, *The Modification of Treaties* 193.
[200] R Kolb, *Good Faith in International Law* (Hart 2017) 75.
[201] ibid.
[202] ibid 76.

treaty party. Through its silence, a State party to a treaty accepts new legal facts'.[203]

5.3.5.3.2 Distinction between A/M/R and Interpretation by Subsequent Agreements/Practice On the other hand, the distinction between A/M/R and interpretation under 31(3)(a) and (b) is slightly more problematic, as they both employ references to subsequent agreements or practice. So, what is the critical difference between them? Here, it will prove useful to distinguish between modification and amendment.

'Modification', in the VCLT sense, ie that of an *inter se* agreement, does not raise any issues. The reason is simple.

> 'Modification' in the Convention's sense could never be achieved purely by practice as envisaged in article 31(3)(b) because that provision is predication [sic] on agreement of *all* the parties, while modification is by the Vienna Convention's usage (Article 41, in particular) operative for only *some* of the parties.[204]

Consequently, no issue of conflation will arise between modification and interpretation by reference to subsequent agreements/practice.

Things become more complicated as to what concerns amendment. As Waldock insightfully noted:

> Subsequent practice when it is consistent and embraces all the parties would appear to be decisive of the meaning to be attached to the treaty, at any rate when it indicates that the parties consider the interpretation to be binding upon them. In these cases, subsequent practice as an element of treaty interpretation and as an element in the formation of a tacit agreement overlap and the meaning derived from the practice becomes an authentic interpretation established by agreement. Furthermore, if the interpretation adopted by the parties diverges, as sometimes happens, from the natural and ordinary meaning of the terms, there may be a blurring of the line between *interpretation* and the *amendment* of a treaty by subsequent practice.[205]

Two questions must be addressed. First, whether the distinction between interpretation and A/M/R in this context is of any practical importance, and, second, whether amendment by subsequent practice is customary international law or it is more of a concept *in statu nascendi* and thus, at

[203] ibid 78.
[204] Gardiner, *Treaty Interpretation* 267 fn 169 (emphasis in the original).
[205] Waldock, 'Third Report' [25].

least for the moment, the debate on its difference from interpretation is merely an academic exercise.

With respect to the former, Gardiner drives the point home by presenting both sides of the argument. The opinion that searching for the difference between amendment and interpretation is like waiting for Godot is based on the following two premises. The first is an effects-based one. Irrespective of whether one applies a treaty as a result of an *interpretation* reflecting the agreement of the parties or an *amendment* reflecting the agreement of the parties, the result is exactly the same. The qualification does nothing to change the application of the treaty.[206] Second, 'if one accepts that every application of a treaty is preceded, no matter for how fleeting a moment, by an act of interpretation, any subsequent practice or subsequent agreement to an amendment constituted by practice would each form a valid component of an interpretation'.[207]

However, Gardiner continues, such an aphoristic equation between interpretation and amendment fails to take into account 'the importance of treaty relations, procedural difficulties, and [the effect of] decisions of courts and tribunals'.[208] With respect to treaty relations, for instance, a procedure may be presumed to have been followed for amendments that give not only parties, but also potential parties, the opportunity to participate. As to what concerns procedural difficulties, these may arise in scenarios similar to *Pope & Talbot*, where one organ was vested with the power of interpreting a treaty, whereas another had the power to determine a dispute and characterise whether the act of the first body was indeed an interpretation or an act *ultra vires*.[209] This is also relevant as to the effect of international courts and tribunals that not only have to legally characterise certain acts, but whose judgments may echo through time. Although judgments of international courts and tribunals are in principle only binding on the parties to the proceedings, they 'have an effect comparable to precedent'.[210]

With respect to the second question, the answer is not quite clear.[211] The preparatory work of Draft Article 68 and 38, analysed in

[206] Gardiner, *Treaty Interpretation* 275.
[207] ibid.
[208] ibid.
[209] ibid 275, referring to *Pope & Talbot*.
[210] ibid.
[211] See on this Nolte, 'Treaties and Their Practice' 351 ff.

Section 5.3.5.2.2 seems to indicate that States accepted the amendment by subsequent practice as customary international law (although this was by no means a general consensus). The reason that most States objected to its inclusion to the VCLT was its complexity. International jurisprudence seems also to accept this possibility, although most relevant *dicta* are quite open ended. Case law seems to be swinging like a pendulum from outright rejection to unequivocal acceptance. Sometimes 'interpretation' is used when 'amendment' is probably (or possibly) meant and vice versa; and other times the relevant court does not explicitly say whether it considers a particular subsequent practice as interpretative or amending in nature.[212]

More recently, according to the ILC's Draft Conclusion 7:

> Possible effects of subsequent agreements and subsequent practice in interpretation:
>
> 1. Subsequent agreements and subsequent practice under Article 31, paragraph 3, contribute, in their interaction with other means of interpretation, to the clarification of the meaning of a treaty. This may result in narrowing, widening, or otherwise determining the range of possible interpretations, including any scope for the exercise of discretion which the treaty accords to the parties.
> 2. Subsequent practice under Article 32 may also contribute to the clarification of the meaning of a treaty.
> 3. *It is presumed that the parties to a treaty, by an agreement or a practice in the application of the treaty, intend to interpret the treaty, not to amend or to modify it.* The possibility of amending or modifying a treaty by subsequent practice of the parties has not been generally recognised. The present draft conclusion is without prejudice to the rules on the amendment or modification of treaties under the Vienna Convention on the Law of Treaties and under customary international law.[213]

ILC Draft Conclusion 7(3), thus, addresses the limits that recourse to subsequent agreements and practice must observe in order to remain within the boundaries of treaty interpretation, ie Article 31(a) and (b).[214]

212 In more detail, see Nolte 'Second Report' [115–66] and cases cited therein.

213 ILC, 'Report of the International Law Commission on the Work of Its 68th Session' (2 May–10 June and 4 July–12 August 2016) UN Doc A/71/10, 121, 173–80 (Commentary to Draft Conclusion 7(3)).

214 ILC, 'Draft Conclusions on Subsequent Agreements and Subsequent Practice, with Commentaries' 58–63 [21–38]; see generally, M Fitzmaurice, 'Subsequent Agreement and Subsequent Practice: Some Reflections on the International Law Commission's Draft Conclusions' (2020) 22 ICLR 14–32.

If these limits are crossed, then we may be in the realm of treaty modification, although the ILC acknowledges that the possibility of modifying a treaty by subsequent practice of the parties has not been generally recognised.[215] Nonetheless, '[i]t may sometimes be difficult to draw a distinction between agreements of the parties under a specific treaty provision that attributes binding force to subsequent agreements, simple subsequent agreements under Article 31, paragraph 3(a) which are not binding as such, and, finally, agreements on the amendment or modification of a treaty under articles 39 to 41'.[216]

International case law is equally ambivalent on this issue. The question of the modification of treaty provisions arose in the *Dispute Regarding Navigational and Related Rights* case, where the ICJ has held that 'subsequent practice of the parties, within the meaning of Article 31, paragraph 3 (b), of the Vienna Convention, can result in a departure from the original intent on the basis of a tacit agreement'.[217] However, in the judgment the ICJ relied on evolutive interpretation and not on modification. Some authors have referred to the *Temple of Preah Vihear* case[218] as an example where the Court found out that the subsequent practice of the parties deviated from the watershed line and superseded the treaty terms.[219] This pronouncement of the Court is subject to critique, ie that the Court confused interpretation with amendment.[220] Generally, doctrine has highlighted the dangers and pitfalls of adopting too broad and liberal an approach to allowing modification through subsequent practice.[221]

The ILC makes the following final comment on Draft Conclusion 7(3):

> In conclusion, while there exists some support in international case law that, absent indications in the treaty to the contrary, the agreed subsequent practice of the parties theoretically may lead to modifications of a treaty, the actual occurrence of that effect is not to be presumed, and the possibility of amending or modifying a treaty by subsequent practice has not been generally recognised.[222]

[215] ibid 63 [38].

[216] ibid 58–9 [24].

[217] *Dispute Regarding Navigational and Related Rights* [64].

[218] *Temple of Preah Vihear* (Merits) 34.

[219] ibid.

[220] Moloo, 'When Actions Speak Louder than Words' 78.

[221] M Kohen, 'Keeping Subsequent Agreements and Practice in Their Right Limits' in Nolte (ed), *Treaties and Subsequent Practice* 34, 42–3; S Murphy, 'The Relevance of Subsequent Agreement and Subsequent Practice in Interpretation of Treaties' in Nolte (ed), *Treaties and Subsequent Practice* 82, 89.

[222] ILC, 'Draft Conclusions on Subsequent Agreements and Subsequent Practice' [38].

This statement refrains from making a definite pronouncement relating to the legal question of the role of subsequent practice in the modification of treaties. It reflects correctly the judicial and State practice and the views of scholars. The statement is formulated in the negative, 'is not be presumed' and 'has not been generally recognised'. Therefore, even if such a modification through subsequent practice or agreement occurs, it should be approached as an exception, not as a rule. In such a doctrinal and jurisprudential quicksand, the ILC's approach, as reflected in Draft Conclusion 7, seems to be, if not the correct one, then definitely the most utilitarian one.

In sum, Draft Conclusion 7(3) creates a presumption in favour of interpretation, similar to the presumption against conflict that we see in situations of normative conflict.[223] In this manner, in most cases the scenario of having to qualify subsequent practice as either amending or interpreting the treaty will be avoided, ensuring the consistency and integrity of the text.[224]

5.3.6 *Subsequent Customary Law and Treaty Modification*

As it was stated in the introduction to this chapter, subsequent customary law and treaty modification will not be discussed herein. However, as a matter of good order, just a few comments will be presented to identify the questions ensuing from the interaction between subsequent customary law and treaty modification. As Buga has noted, such a process is inherently complex due to inherent difficulties with a 'two-element approach' to the formation of customary international law itself.[225] The next step, according to Buga, is the identification of its 'treaty modifying potential' by reference to its 'non-hierarchical, dynamic relation to treaty law'.[226] She is of the view, which we share, that such a modification to a treaty must be approached as an exception, very strictly, according to the general presumption against change. Therefore, the role of the intention of the parties is of the utmost importance. Subsequent customary law rules must then attain an evidentiary threshold, with a 'double consent', ie the practice must not

223 J Pauwelyn, *Conflict of Norms in Public International Law: How WTO Law Relates to Other Rules of International Law* (CUP 2003).

224 Kolb, *Good Faith* 78.

225 Buga, *The Modification of Treaties* 367.

226 ibid.

only establish the content of the customary rule but also how this customary rule has modified the pre-existing treaty rule. Treaty modification by a norm of customary international law may be effected by a 'treaty-related' or 'external' norm, which are both nearly identical in relation to treaties of almost universal participation.[227] In the first of these cases, treaty-related customary law is formed directly from the treaty-related subsequent practice of the parties. As Buga has observed, in such a case subsequent practice capable of modification is identical to practice as a constitutive element of the now customary rule. External modification results from the subsequent practice of the parties in relation to that customary norm rather than the treaty; therefore, evidence should be stricter in order to ascertain whether modification has occurred.[228]

5.4 Empirical Analysis of A/M/R Provisions in Multilateral Treaties

5.4.1 Data on A/M/R Provisions

In the previous sections we examined the 'motion' of the concept of A/M/R both by virtue of the adoption of the 'residual rules' of the VCLT and through recent and critical trends in the treaty-making practice of States, such as, for instance, through the emergence of the 'tacit acceptance' procedures and the effect of COP/MOP decisions in the increase (*auxesis*), diminution (*meiosis*) or alteration (*alloiosis*) of treaty obligations.

In order to make our analysis complete, this section will focus on whether empirical data as can be drawn from the treaty-making practice of States verifies the preliminary conclusions to which we arrived through the analysis of the drafting history of the VCLT and the scholarly debate on A/M/R. This empirical data was drawn from the treaties that have been registered in the UNTS and LNTS. At the moment of writing of this chapter there have been 55,637 treaties registered with the UN, in addition to the 4,834 ones that had been registered with the League of Nations. Of course, this is not an exhaustive list of all existing treaties, as there does exist a significant number of treaties that have not been registered yet. Some authors place this 'dark number' at approximately

[227] ibid 376.
[228] ibid 377.

25 per cent.[229] Despite this, the examination of the treaties published in the UNTS and LNTS should give a statistically significant pool of data from which to draw meaningful and verifiable trends in A/M/R practice.[230]

For the purposes of this analysis, certain guidelines have been followed in the taxonomy of the various treaties and respective A/M/R procedures, which we present here for the benefit of the reader.

(i) Whenever the terms 'amendment', 'modification', or 'revision' are used for the purposes of this research they are done so on the basis of the terms that have been actually adopted in the text of the relevant multilateral treaties, and not as an assessment of the qualitative differences between these procedures.[231] This guideline was also informed by the doctrine and practical difficulties in clearly delineating the differences between the three procedures, as was shown in Section 5.2.1.2.

(ii) The treaties analysed are only multilateral treaties (both open and closed ones). The reason for this is that amendment and modification of bilateral treaties essentially amounts to a renegotiation of the treaty.[232]

229 C Tams, 'Regulating Treaty Breaches' in Bowman and Kritsiotis (eds), *Conceptual and Contextual Perspectives* 440, citing P Reuter, *Introduction to the Law of Treaties* (J Mico and P Haggenmacher tr, 2nd edn, Routledge 1995) fn to [86].

230 The authors would like to thank Dr Tsampi and Mr Turnbull for their invaluable assistance in the research on and categorisation of the treaties and in the production of the relevant tables and charts. The authors would also like to thank the following University of Groningen students for their assistance in the research that led to the production of this database: Ruth Ifeoluwa Bolaji, Christian Plamenov Delev, Hyfa Azeez, Kyrill Ryabtsev, Sofie Ægidius, Nasya Desiria, Lara CF Silveira, Bagus Hadiredjo, Federica Fermani and Alessandra Faes.

231 See, for instance, the 1957 Interim Convention between the United States of America, Canada, Japan, and the Union of Soviet Socialist Republics on Conservation of North Pacific Fur Seals (adopted 9 February 1957, entered into force 14 October 1957) 414 UNTS 105. Art XIII(5) of this convention uses the term 'modification' when on the basis of its context (and particularly Art XIII(4), which refers to 'revision') would indicate that 'modification' is used in the sense of 'amendment' or 'revision', rather than as an *inter se* modification. Furthermore, only treaties that have used the term 'revision' or any version of it have been accounted for. The term 'review' was not counted as revision, as the authors considered that it could have multiple meanings and not necessarily be the same as revision.

232 ILC, 'Report of the International Law Commission on the Work of Its Eighteenth Session' 233 [5]; and contrast with ILC, 'Summary Record of the 859th Meeting' [29] (Briggs).

(iii) The date of adoption has been taken into account, as it is at that critical date that the parties agreed for a particular A/M/R procedure to be included in the adopted text. Entry into force dates may come much later (and are also vastly different for some of the parties). For these considerations, the adoption of the treaty date was considered to be the more consistent variable for statistical purposes.

(iv) The various amendments to a treaty have not been included in the overall tally, unless the amendment either amended the amendment procedure or introduced an entirely new one where none previously existed. There are many reasons for this. First, the amendments in their overwhelming majority would change a relatively small number of articles, while the vast majority of the treaty, including the amendment procedure, would remain intact. Second, and this flows from the first reason, if all these amendments were to be taken into account, this would skew statistically the results in a manner that would not be scientifically valid. Third, this approach is also the one that is followed by the UN Treaty Section in the publication of the UNTS. Ratifications, accessions, subsequent agreements, amendments, or treaties terminating prior treaties do not have their own registration number but are registered under the same number as the original treaty to which they are connected.

(v) If a multilateral treaty provides for different A/M/R procedures for different articles,[233] both of these procedures have been accounted for.

(vi) The original treaty may provide a specific A/M/R procedure for a protocol to it. If no such protocol exists, then this procedure has been counted as one of the multiple different A/M/R procedures that it provides. However, if such a protocol exists, then this procedure is not counted as one belonging to the original treaty, but rather as one of the protocol itself. This has been done in order to avoid 'double-counting issues', which would again skew the statistical data in the wrong direction.[234]

[233] Or, indicatively, a different procedure depending on whether it is a substantive or procedural obligation, or between different annexes, or between an annex and a protocol.

[234] If we were to count it both under the original treaty and the protocol, then we would be essentially counting twice the same A/M/R procedure.

(vii) In some cases, especially when dealing with protocols, the protocol may not have an A/M/R provision of its own. It may either directly refer back to the A/M/R provisions of the convention to which it is a protocol for the purposes of A/M/R[235] or may include an article that establishes a general connection between the protocol and the convention that also includes (albeit not explicitly) A/M/R.[236] If the original treaty to which they refer, did not have a specific provision for protocols, then this procedure is counted as also for the protocols, as it was not envisaged in the original treaty and it was clearly a separate and free choice on the part of the parties to the protocol. So, in essence, the procedure counts both for the original treaty and the protocol, as it was only later incorporated through the protocol. If, however, the provision to which they refer, was a protocol-specific provision of the original treaty, then Guideline (vi) is applied, and this procedure counts only for the protocol and not for the original treaty.

(viii) Finally, if a multilateral treaty provides for unanimity/consensus and only alternatively, if unanimity/consensus cannot be secured, for a different procedure, then we have counted these procedures under both respective categories, ie both under unanimity/consensus (as this is the initial preference of the drafters of the multilateral treaty) and under the alternative procedure (as this is what in most circumstances would be applied, and was the lowest common

[235] See, for instance: 'Article 27 – In accordance with the *provisions of article 11 of the Convention*, the Council of Ministers shall examine ... the application of the provisions ... *with a view to making amendments or adaptations*' (emphasis added); 1979 Protocol No 1 Concerning the Definition of the Concept of 'Originating Product' and Methods of Administrative Co-operation (adopted 31 October 1979, entered into force 1 January 1981) 1277 UNTS 3, Art 27; 'Article 14 – Adoption of any amendments to the articles and amendments to the annexes of the *Protocol shall be made according to the procedures established by the Articles XX and XXI of the Convention*' (emphasis added); 2002 Black Sea Biodiversity and Landscape Conservation Protocol to the Convention on the Protection of the Black Sea against Pollution (adopted 14 June 2002, entered into force 20 June 2011) <www.blacksea-commission.org/_convention-protocols-biodiversity.asp> accessed 20 September 2019, Art 14.

[236] See, for instance: 'Article 32: Relationship with the Convention – Except as otherwise provided in this Protocol, *the provisions of the Convention relating to its protocols shall apply to this Protocol*' (emphasis added); 2000 Cartagena Protocol on Biosafety to the Convention on Biological Diversity (adopted 29 January 2000, entered into force 11 September 2003) 2226 UNTS 208, Art 32.

ground that the parties were to agree upon), unless otherwise explicitly stated.[237]

5.4.2 *A/M/R Provisions in Multilateral Treaties*

The overwhelming majority of treaties published in the LNTS and the UNTS are bilateral ones. Nonetheless, out of the 60,471 treaties registered,[238] 2,919 are multilateral treaties, and it is these that will form our data pool, with which we will attempt to answer a number of questions. In the previous sections, for instance, and especially from the drafting history of the VCLT, it was evident that the drafters intended for the VCLT A/M/R provisions to be of a residual nature. What we must examine, then, is how truly residual these rules are in practice. Do the drafters of treaties consider the VCLT and the customary rules on A/M/R as a sufficiently solid basis on which to fall back on, or do they prefer to agree on specific procedures for themselves, which may vary depending on the nature of the treaty? Table 5.1 juxtaposes the multilateral treaties which have an A/M/R clause and those that do not, by time period.[239]

Out of 2,919 multilateral treaties, 1,708 contained an A/M/R provision, whereas 1,211 did not. This translates to 58.51 per cent containing an A/M/R provision and 41.49 per cent not. This would seem to give the impression that the attitude towards treaty-specific A/M/R provisions is somewhat balanced, albeit leaning towards self-regulation via inclusion of an A/M/R provision. However, what we must bear in mind is that our data pool covers treaties across twelve decades. We must examine

[237] 1994 Lusaka Agreement on Co-operative Enforcement Operations Directed at Illegal Trade in Wild Fauna and Flora (adopted 8 September 1994, entered into force 10 December 1996) 1950 UNTS 35, Art 11(3) (efforts to achieve consensus, and in case of failure adoption by a two-thirds majority); 2009 Agreement on Port State Measures to Prevent, Deter, and Eliminate Illegal, Unreported and Unregulated Fishing (adopted 22 November 2009, entered into force 5 June 2016) <https://treaties.un.org/doc/Publication/UNTS/No%20Volume/54133/Part/I-54133-080000028049aa1a.pdf> accessed 20 September 2019, Art 34(2) (efforts to achieve consensus, and in case of failure adoption by a two-thirds majority).

[238] The latest monthly statement of the UNTS is No 1 of 2019 and the latest registered treaty has been given a registration number of 55,637. Of one adds to that the 4,834 treaties that had been published in the LNTS, this gives us 60,471 treaties.

[239] In this and the following tables, we have decided to present the time periods after the entry into force of the VCLT in five-year intervals in order to give a clearer picture to the reader of the A/M/R tendencies in modern treaty practice. For the same reason, from the adoption of the VCLT to its entry into force, the given periods are ten years long, and prior to the VCLT twenty years.

Table 5.1 *Existence or non-existence of A/M/R clauses in multilateral treaties*

Year	Existence of Provision	No Provision	Total
1900–1919	6	7	13
1920–1939	130	252	382
1940–1959	322	300	622
1960–1969	331	212	543
1970–1979	315	200	515
1980–1984	91	58	149
1985–1989	94	70	164
1990–1994	126	52	178
1995–1999	91	31	122
2000–2004	89	17	106
2005–2009	69	9	78
2010–2014	32	2	34
2015–2019	12	1	13
Total	1,708	1,211	2,919

whether throughout the passage of time there has been a motion in the balance towards preference to inclusion or non-inclusion of A/M/R provisions, also taking into account watershed moments, such as the adoption of the VCLT, which might have signalled a change in the stance of the States during negotiations of multilateral treaties.

Bearing these things in mind, if we group the above treaties into two chronological periods, pre-VCLT and post-VCLT, we arrive at Table 5.2.

This data shows a significant shift in the apporach of parties to multilateral treaties as to the inclusion of A/M/R provisions. In the period up to the adoption of the VCLT, the treaties that had an A/M/R provision accounted for 50.58 per cent of the treaties, and those that did not for 49.42 per cent, as balanced as can be. However, if we then look at the period following the adoption of the treaty on treaties, the landscape is radically different. Treaties that have an A/M/R provision make up 67.62 per cent of the total number of treaties adopted during that period, whereas the non-A/M/R including treaties have dropped to 32.38 per cent, accounting just for one-third of the multilateral treaties of the period. This shows a strong shift in the preference of contracting States and organisations to provide greater legal certainty and bespoke A/M/R solutions for their treaties. It is evident that, despite the existence of the

Table 5.2 *Existence of A/M/R clauses in multilateral treaties, pre- and post-VCLT*

Year	Existence of Provision	No Provision	Total
1900–1969	789	771	1560
1970–2019	919	440	1359
Total	1,708	1,211	2,919

VCLT rules on A/M/R, States seem to increasingly feel more comfortable agreeing among themselves which A/M/R procedures are the ideal for the treaty they are negotiating.

The previous tables and charts demonstrate that States have become increasingly more prone to include references and provisions to A/M/R in multilateral treaties. However, that does not clarify, which particular procedure (or combination of procedures) States are more likely to regulate. Table 5.3 breaks down the data of Table 5.1 and illustrates whether the treaties examined included a reference to amendment, or modification, or revision, or any possible combination amongst these three different terms. A total of seven possible variations emerge and, of course, two more categories are included, an 'other'[240] and a final one for treaties where no provision is included and no mention of the possibility of A/M/R is made.

Figure 5.1a–c offers a visual representation of the preferencess of States both overall and in the pre- and post-VCLT era.

As is shown in Table 5.3 and Figure 5.1a–c, when an A/M/R reference is being made in the treaty, there is a 28.30 per cent likelihood that the relevant procedure would be one relating only to amendment. However, in fact this number currently is much higher, as shown in Figure 5.1c,

[240] For instance, some of the 'other' terms that, indicatively, have on occasion been used to denote, based on the context, A/M/R is 'variation' or 'varied'; 1997 Agreement between New Zealand, Papua New Guinea, Australia, Fiji and Vanuatu Concerning the Neutral Truce Monitoring Group for Bougainville (adopted 5–18 December 1997, entered into force 11 December 1997) 2039 UNTS 173, Art 28; 2003 Agreement between Solomon Islands, Australia, New Zealand, Fiji, Papua New Guinea, Samoa, and Tonga Concerning the Operations and Status of the Police and Armed Forces and Other Personnel Deployed to Solomon Islands to Assist in the Restoration of Law and Order and Security (adopted 24 July 2003, entered into force 24 July 2003) 2258 UNTS 231, Art 23; British Commonwealth Merchant Shipping Agreement (adopted 10 December 1931) 129 LNTS 177, Art 25.

Table 5.3 *Specific nature of A/M/R clauses (or lack thereof) in multilateral treaties*

Year	A	M	R	A+M	A+R	M+R	A+M+R	Other	No Provision	Total
1900–1919		5	1						7	13
1920–1939	15	25	37	23	2	13	3	12	252	382
1940–1959	101	73	125	12	8	1	1	1	300	622
1960–1969	119	144	30	23	15				212	543
1970–1979	159	60	35	21	35		5		200	515
1980–1984	66	2	8	5	8		2		58	149
1985–1989	62	3	12	7	10				70	164
1990–1994	90	1	11	10	12		1	1	52	178
1995–1999	60	5	13	7	5			1	31	122
2000–2004	68	2	3	7	6	1	1	1	17	106
2005–2009	49	2	1	3	14				9	78
2010–2014	26		2	2	2				2	34
2015–2019	11			1					1	13
Total	826	322	278	121	117	15	13	16	1,211	2,919

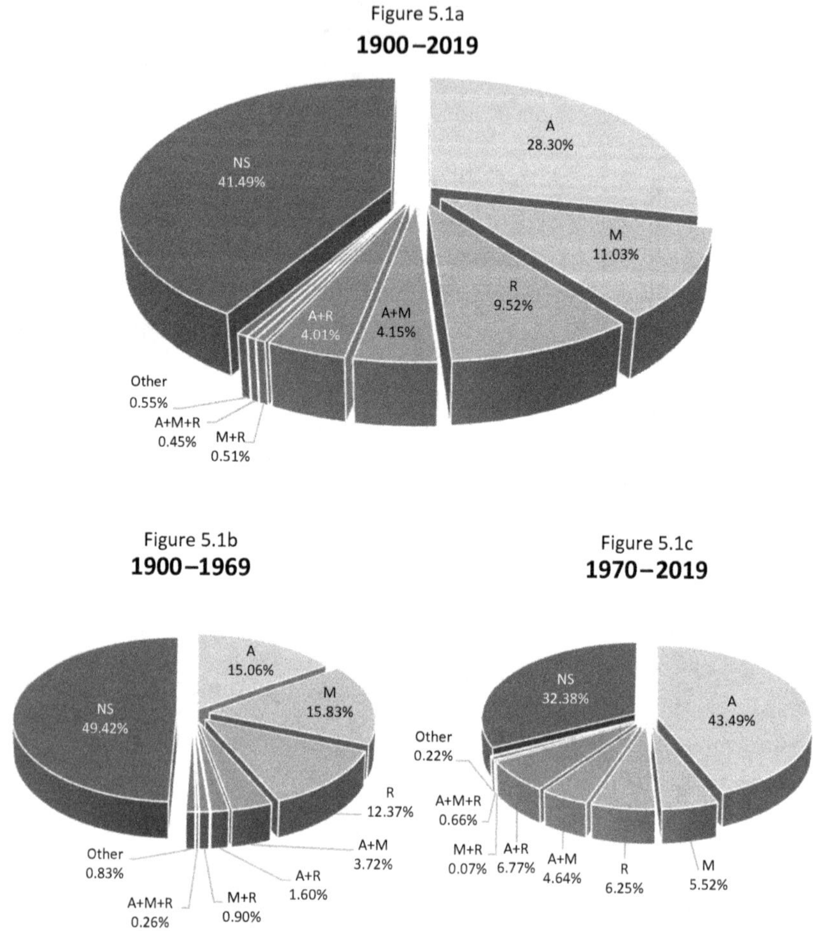

Figure 5.1(a–c) A/M/R clauses (or lack thereof) in multilateral treaties

because at the moment it stands much higher at 43.49 per cent post-VCLT. So, essentially almost one in two treaties would have an amendment procedure. This is even higher if one also adds the scenarios where references to amendment are combined with revision or modification, or all three. In such a case, the percentage rises to 55.56 per cent. By contrast, A/M/R including treaties, which only refer to modification or to revision, have shown a significant drop post-VCLT. This is no surpirse, as this dominance of 'amendment' most likely stems from the nature of this procedure (compared to the less clear-cut and way more problematic *inter se* modification avenue). This was also reflected in the ILC discussions and the final version of the A/M/R provisions included in the VCLT, which may also be partly responsible for the increase in the amendment provisions compared to modification or revision ones.

It is worth noting again that the data used for the creation of this table have been based on the actual terms that the States used and included in the text of the treaty, in accordance with Guideline (i). Of course, as shown in Section 5.2.1.2 of this chapter, there was an extensive debate in the ILC about the normative content to be attached to each of the terms, a debate that was not made any easier due to the inconsistency of State practice in employing these terms. Although the adoption of the VCLT has made things somewhat clearer, this is not to say that even today examples do not persist where States have used, for instance, the term 'revision' to refer to what theoretically would be better described as an amendment or a modification via an *inter se* agreement, and vice versa,[241] or where they have used the terms 'amendment modifying'[242] or the term 'modified' in an article titled 'amendment'.[243] For reasons of simplicity and consistency, the above table is based on the terms actually adopted by the States.

5.4.3 *Adoption and Entry into Force of Proposed A/M/Rs of Multilateral Treaties*

In the process leading to the A/M/R of a multilateral treaty there are two critical stages, the 'adoption stage' and the 'entry into force stage'.[244]

241 See above fn 231 to Guideline (i).

242 2015 Asian Infrastructure Investment Bank Articles of Agreement (adopted 29 June 2015, entered into force 25 December 2015) <https://treaties.un.org/doc/Publication/UNTS/No%20Volume/54824/Part/I-54824-08000002804e3714.pdf> accessed 20 September 2019, Art 53(2); 1990 Agreement Establishing the European Bank for Reconstruction and Development (EBRD) (adopted 29 May 1990, entered into force 28 March 1991) 1646 UNTS 97, Art 52(2). Whenever this construct has been used, we have considered it only as an amendment, and not as a modification as we were of the view that the verb 'modifying' is used in this context in an ordinary sense, ie of describing the effect that an amendment has on a provision, and not in the legal sense, ie denoting a particular type of procedure.

243 2010 Multilateral Agreement for the Establishment of an International Think Tank for Landlocked Developing Countries (adopted 24 September 2010, entered into force 6 October 2017) <https://treaties.un.org/doc/Treaties/2010/10/20101001%2002-46%20PM/X-19.pdf> accessed 20 September 2019, Art XIII(1).

244 For these two stages, the provisions considered were mainly the amendments procedures, modification and revision were considered only to the extent that information was actually given, for any of the stages. The reason is simply that modification being an *inter*

The 'adoption stage' refers to the requirements set in place by the parties in order for an amendment proposal to be discussed and voted on, for the purposes of it being adopted, and then States being allowed to, in most instances, ratify it.[245] The main variations about the adoption of an amendment to a treaty are adoption by: consensus,[246] unanimity[247] (these two terms are sometimes used interchangeably or one next to the other),[248] any other term similar to the above,[249] majority

se agreement there would be no adoption procedure, and the agreement would enter into force only between the agreeing/ratifying parties, whereas for revision, similarly the rules of procedure of the Revision Conference would be determined *ad hoc* and again the agreement would apply only between the ratifying States. For these reasons, and also to avoid any unwarranted presumptions, modification and revision provisions were not included in this calculation, unless some information was provided for either both or any of the two stages, in which case it was included in the tallying. Furthermore, in the case of several closed multilateral treaties, between a limited number of States, or a few related organisations and one or two States, often there would be either an amendment or more usually, especially pre-VCLT, a modification provision stating that the agreement 'may be modified by agreement between the parties'. Given that there was a long list of such identical treaties (especially where international organisations were involved) which all used this terminology, or variations to the effect 'between all parties', 'jointly agreed' etc, which allowed for the safe assumption that, unless an explicit other term was used (that would lead the treaty being slotted in one of the other categories), when we came across this term we categorised the treaty under unanimity for the 'adoption stage' and under ratifying/accepting/approving States for the 'entry into force stage'. If, however, 'between the parties' is not to be read that way, then the reader can simply subtract from 'unanimity' and add to 'not specified' the following number of treaties (for each of the thirteen time-periods respectively):..........................

245 For the purposes of the research in this section, 'adoption stage' includes also situations where although the treaty does not provide for an explicit adoption of the proposed A/M/R *per se*, it does provide for a body of the treaty (a Committee, Board etc) to decide to *recommend* that proposed A/M/R for ratification/acceptance/approval to the parties. If the treaty provides both for recommendation and adoption procedures, then only the adoption procedure has been accounted for.

246 2006 Southern Indian Ocean Fisheries Agreement (adopted 7 July 2006, entered into force 21 June 2012) 2835 UNTS 409, Art 21.

247 1973 Treaty Establishing the West African Monetary Union (WAMU) (adopted 14 November 1973, entered into force 22 January 1984) 1481 UNTS 21, Art 16; 1977 European Convention on the Legal Status of Migrant Workers (adopted 24 November 1977, entered into force 1 May 1983) 1496 UNTS 3, Art 33(4); 1977 Memorandum of Understanding on the Establishment of the Pacific Forum Line Limited (adopted 16 June 1977, entered into force 20 August 1978) 1137 UNTS 423, Art XIII(1).

248 See, for instance, the requirement for 'unanimity consensus' in Art 9(1) of the 1993 Revised Treaty of the Economic Community of West African States (ECOWAS) (adopted 24 July 1993, entered into force 23 August 1995) 2373 UNTS 233.

249 Eg 'common accord' or 'mutual accord', which in most likelihood would be unanimity, but since in the treaties these terms are oftentimes not explained, we have decided to include them into a separate category for this table. See, for instance: 'common consent'

(simple,[250] qualified,[251] or other)[252] with or without additional conditions; a different procedure;[253] or the treaty does not specify any adoption procedure.[254] Once an amendment has been adopted, that does not

used in the 1976 Memorandum of Understanding for a Transatlantic Balloon Programme (adopted 21 and 22 July 1976, entered into force 22 July 1976) 1207 UNTS 87, Art 10; 'common agreement' used in the 1914 International Sanitary Convention (adopted 21 April 1914, entered into force 15 January 1945) 5 LNTS 393, Art 51.

250 1984 Convention against Torture and Other Cruel, Inhuman, or Degrading Treatment or Punishment (adopted 10 December 1984, entered into force 26 June 1987) 1465 UNTS 85, Art 29(1); 1981 African Charter on Human and Peoples' Rights (adopted 27 June 1981, entered into force 21 October 1986) 1520 UNTS 217, Art 68.

251 'four-fifths' in: 1976 Agreement Establishing the International Fund for Agricultural Development (adopted 13 June 1976, entered into force 30 November 1977) 1059 UNTS 191, Art 12(a)(ii); 'three-fourths' in: 2009 Convention on the Conservation and Management of High Seas Fishery Resources in the South Pacific Ocean (adopted 14 November 2009, entered into force 24 August 2012) 2899 UNTS 211, Art 35(2);

252 See for instance, Art 57(1) of the Sixth International Tin Agreement, that requires a two-thirds majority of all Producing Members and a two-thirds majority of Consuming Members; 1981 Sixth International Tin Agreement (adopted 26 June 1981, entered into force 1 July 1982) 1282 UNTS 205. See also Arts 31 and 10(3) of the Agreement Creating the Eastern Pacific Tuna Fishing Organisation, which require for the amendment of certain provisions not only a two-thirds majority of State parties present, but also 'half plus one of Latin American Eastern Pacific Coastal States'; 1989 Agreement Creating the Eastern Pacific Tuna Fishing Organization (adopted 21 July 1989, not yet in force) <www.jus.uio.no/english/services/library/treaties/08/8-02/pacific-tuna-organization.xml> accessed 20 September 2019.

253 Sometimes the treaty may not provide information regarding the specific majority with which a decision for an amendment may be taken. It simply refers to a body (Council, Board, or Committee) that will make such a decision. If the information is not provided in other parts of the treaty or readily available from other sources, a treaty having this construction has been placed for the purposes of the 'adoption-stage' under this 'Other' category.

254 This is sometimes the case when the treaty provides that an amendment will be adopted through a revision conference or a protocol, but no indication is given as to how proposals are to be adopted in a Revision Conference. This is logical, as the procedural rules would be agreed upon at the moment of convening of said Revision Conference or protocol negotiations. See: 2000 Treaty on the Establishment of the Eurasian Economic Community (adopted 10 October 2000, entered into force 30 May 2001) 2212 UNTS 257, Art 19 (Amendment through a Protocol). Other times, the treaty simply does not make any provision for adoption at all. See, for instance, 1921 Convention and Statute on Freedom of Transit (adopted 20 April 1921, entered into force 31 October 1922) 7 LNTS 11, Art 9 (simply stating how the proposal for an amendment is to be made, but not how it will be adopted); 2002 Agreement Establishing the Caribbean Court of Justice (adopted 14 February 2001, entered into force 23 July 2002) 2255 UNTS 319, Art XXXII (1) (simply stating that the 'Agreement may be amended by the Contracting Parties'). Another significant percentage also consists of treaties that only provide for the number of State parties that are required in order for a proposal to be put on the table for discussion, or where any one State can submit a proposal, but do not provide

eo ipso mean that the amendment enters into force. This is where the second stage of 'entry into force' comes into play, and which will be discussed in more detail in Section 5.4.3.2 of this chapter. Similar to the 'adoption stage', the 'entry into force stage' and the accompanying tables have been examined through the lens of the parties for which the treaty enters into force, ie for ratifying/accepting/approving States (or organisations),[255] or for all States.[256]

5.4.3.1 Adoption

Breaking down the A/M/R clauses of multilateral treaties into specific categories depending on the adoption procedure provided for,[257] we arrive at Table 5.4.

For reasons of convenience, *ad hoc* abbreviations have been used to denote the different procedures. These are: (i) C/M (any of the possible variations between the two sets of Common/Mutual Accord/Agreement/ Consent or such similar terms); (ii) + Cond (with conditions); (iii) SM (simple majority; so SM + Cond would denote simple majority with conditions); (iv) QM (qualified majoritry); (v) NS (not specified/provided).

This table translates to Figure 5.2a–c per adoption procedure.[258]

What is interesting is that as can be seen from Tables 5.4 and 5.5, unanimity (both *stricto sensu* and *lato sensu*),[259] although not resorted to as frequently as other procedures taken in aggregate, is not entirely a thing of the past as one would originally expect, if one takes into account the difficulties that they entail with respect to the speediness with which

information for the number of State parties required for the adoption itself (or simply do not have an adoption procedure at all). In this case, these treaties have been placed under this category.

255 For reasons of simplicity, we will simply be talking about ratifying States from this point onwards.

256 With further subdivisions in these categories. Specifically, for the last category, we examine also whether States are given the option of 'opting-out' of this amendment or not and with what consequences.

257 For reasons of simplicity, the critical point was the majority that was required. No distinction was made on the basis of whether or not that majority referred to the majority of all State parties, or of the parties that had a right to participate in an organ of the treaty, or of the voting weight or any other possible option.

258 For reasons of simplicity of Figure 5.2(a–c), the variations of each majority (with and without conditions) have been counted together, eg SM accounts for simple majority procedures both with and without conditions.

259 We use this term to refer to A/M/R clauses that employ the term 'unanimity', 'consensus', or another term (such as 'common accord', 'common agreement' 'mutual agreement' 'joint agreements' etc), which in all likelihood could be equated with unanimity.

Table 5.4 *A/M/R clauses: 'Adoption Stage' – expanded version*

Year	Consensus	Unanimity	C/M	SM	SM + Cond	QM: 2/3	QM: 2/3 + Cond	QM: 3/4	QM: 3/4 + Cond	QM: Other	QM : Other + Cond	Other	NS	Total
1900–1919			3									1		4
1920–1939		58	8	18		27	2		1	1	1	3	17	136
1940–1959		106	13	19	3	39	19	1	1		2	15	42	260
1960–1969		194	2	17	10	45	17	7		9		22	46	369
1970–1979	7	143	6	14	3	59	24	23	7	7	1	24	53	371
1980–1984	9	27	5	7		20	6	10	2	1		12	11	110
1985–1989	18	21	9	9	3	24	9	9	2	1	3	7	11	126
1990–1994	40	29	19	6	1	34	10	10		3		10	15	177
1995–1999	29	28	8	8		25	1	7		4		4	8	122
2000–2004	29	20	12	6	1	23	11	8					11	121
2005–2009	18	12	8	4	2	28	5	2		1		5	8	93
2010–2014	13	6	1			12		3				3	4	42
2015–2019	4	2	1			2	4	2					1	16
Total	167	646	95	108	23	338	108	82	13	27	7	106	227	1947

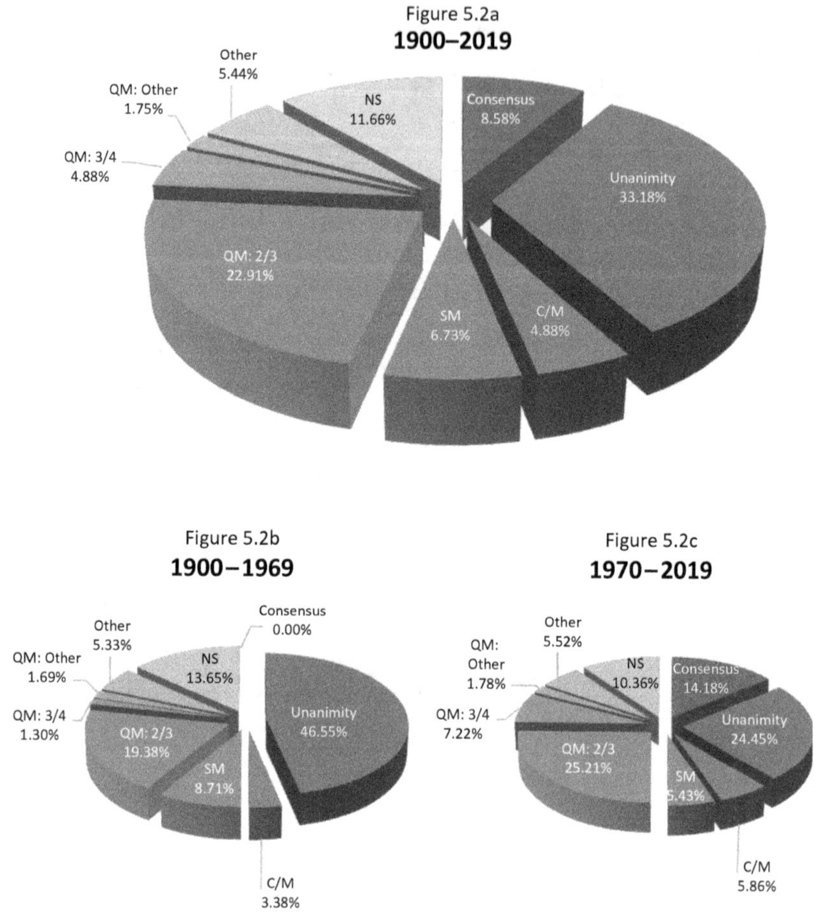

Figure 5.2(a–c) A/M/R clauses: 'Adoption Stage' – expanded version

A/M/R can enter into force, and which led to the the emergence of expedited amendment procedures, such as the 'tacit acceptance' procedure. If we compare the A/M/R clauses in multilateral treaties that require unanimity *lato sensu* and with those that provide for another procedure, we arrive at Table 5.5 and Figure 5.3a–c.

The data presented in Figure 5.3a–c would seem to indicate that both unanimity and consensus are alive and well in the 21st century. Although this may be to some degree true, there are a couple of reasons that might explain this slightly bizarre result. First, we must look again at Figure 5.2b and 5.2c that clearly shows a decrease in preference for unanimity, by

Table 5.5 *Unanimity* lato sensu, *majority voting, and other methods in A/M/R clauses*

Year	Unanimity *Lato Sensu*	Majority	Other	NS	Total
1900–1919	3		1		4
1920–1939	66	50	3	17	136
1940–1959	119	84	15	42	260
1960–1969	196	105	22	46	369
1970–1979	156	138	24	53	371
1980–1984	41	46	12	11	110
1985–1989	48	60	7	11	126
1990–1994	88	64	10	15	177
1995–1999	65	45	4	8	122
2000–2004	61	49		11	121
2005–2009	38	42	5	8	93
2010–2014	20	15	3	4	42
2015–2019	7	8		1	16
Total	908	706	106	227	1947

almost 50 per cent. What has risen post-VCLT in prominence is consensus, which formally is not identical with unanimity.

Second, the type of treaties. Several of the treaties published in the LNTS and UNTS are of a closed multilateral kind, ie with a limited number of parties. Due to the nature of these treaties, the unanimity *lato sensu* construction is most times better suited for the goals the parties aim to achieve. If one looks beyond that to truly open multilateral treaties, ratified by multiple States, then it becomes evident that unanimity *lato sensu* is more on the wane than Figure 5.3a–c may on first viewing seem to indicate.

Finally, and perhaps most importantly and connected to the first reason, our own Guidelines may be partially responsible for this high percentage. As mentioned in Guideline (viii), when a treaty provides for an 'alternative construction', then we have counted these procedures under both respective categories, ie both under consensus/unanimity and the alternative method. However, if one were to count only the second procedure, then the percentages of consensus/unanimity would drop significantly.[260]

[260] Which is a valid option, as the first one is the desired option, but the second one is the one that is as a minimum legally permissible. This downward trend is further strengthened: i) if we take into account that provisions refer to unanimity not just of

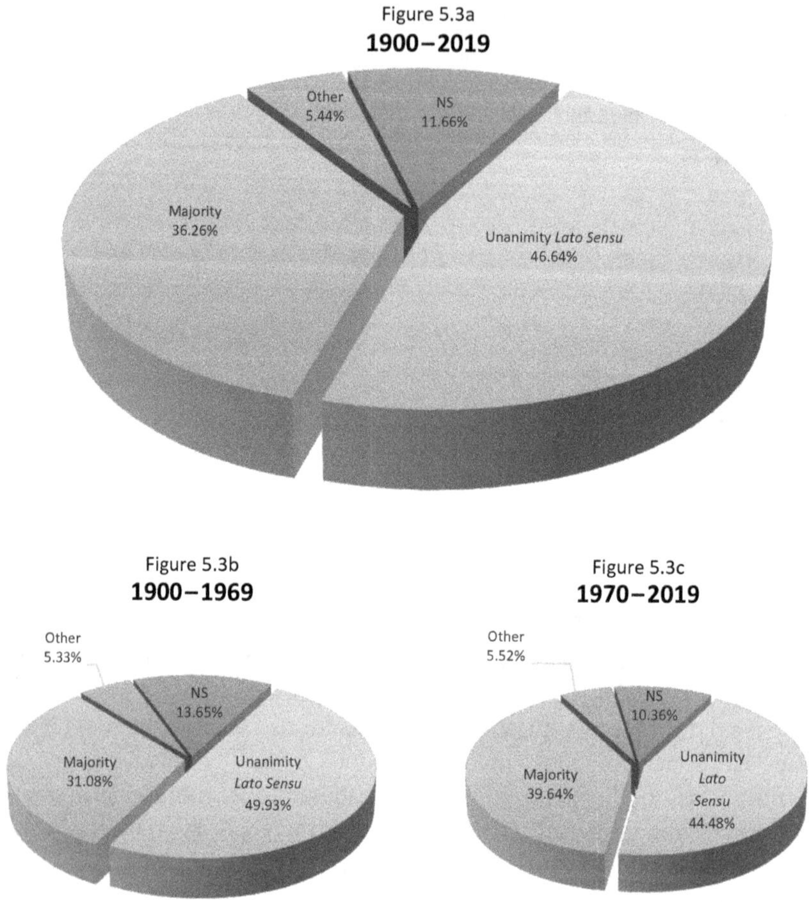

Figure 5.3(a–c) Unanimity *lato sensu*, majority voting, and other methods in A/M/R clauses

'Alternative constructions' for the adoption of A/M/Rs is a comparatively recent phenomenon. Instances of such A/M/R provisions start appearing in the 1960s and then in the form of 'unanimity or another procedure'. The 'unanimity – alternative construction' appears very few times and almost exclusively it entails a decision taken by an organ of the convention (Board, Committee) to adopt an amendment proposal or

all the parties, but also, especially post-VCLT, of a treaty body (see fn 245); and ii) if we categorise treaties with a provision allowing A/M/R by agreement 'between the parties' under 'Not Specified' and not under 'Unanimity' (see fn 244).

recommend it to the parties for their consideration.[261] It last appears in the 1980s, at least in treaties published in the UNTS and LNTS. The reason for that, in our view, is that it gave its place to the 'consensus – alternative construction',[262] which started appearing in the 1970s but became very widespread in the 1990s and is still in use. Here, we cannot but mention the 2005 Treaty on the Conservation and Sustainable Development of the Forest Ecosystems of Central Africa, which is not in force (and does not appear in the UNTS) but is somewhat unique in this context. The standard formula is consensus/unanimity as the first option and if that cannot be achieved, A/M/Rs are adopted by majority vote (simple or qualified). However, this treaty in its Article 28 takes a slightly different route by providing as the first-tier adoption procedure 'unanimity' and as an alternative one 'consensus'.[263]

More generally, the alternative construction preference could be explained as a compromise between the past tendencies of all State parties agreeing to any change to the treaty, and the more modern needs of ensuring simplified and expedited A/M/R procedures in order to breathe life in multilateral treaties and ensure that they do not become sclerotic. Taking these into account, and the fact that alternative constructions appear in no fewer than 79 instances, if we account only for the majority of last resort (and not for the desired unanimity or consensus), then we arrive at Table 5.6 and Figure 5.4a–c.

[261] See, for instance: Arts 24 and 12(6)–(7) of the 1971 Agreement on the Establishment of the 'Intersputnik' International System and Organization of Space Communications (adopted 15 November 1971, entered into force 12 July 1972) 862 UNTS 3; Art 5 and 15 of the 1964 Agreement Establishing Interim Arrangements for a Global Commercial Communications Satellite System, and Special Agreement (adopted 20 August 1964, entered into force 20 August 1964) 514 UNTS 25; Art 18 of the 1974 Convention for the Prevention of Marine Pollution from Land-Based Sources (adopted 4 June 1974, entered into force 6 May 1978) 1546 UNTS 103.

[262] See, for instance, Arts 9 and 10 of the Vienna Convention for the Protection of the Ozone Layer; Art 26(4) of the 1992 Convention on the Transboundary Effects of Industrial Accidents (adopted 17 March 1992, entered into force 19 April 2000) 2105 UNTS 457; Arts 17 and 18 of the 1991 Bamako Convention on the Ban of the Import into Africa and the Control of Transboundary Movement and Management of Hazardous Wastes within Africa (adopted 30 January 1991, entered into force 22 April 1998) 2101 UNTS 177.

[263] Which also goes to reinforce our previous statement that unanimity and consensus should not be conflated; 2005 Treaty on the Conservation and Sustainable Development of the Forest Ecosystems of Central Africa (adopted 5 February 2005, not yet in force) <www.ecolex.org/server2neu.php/libcat/docs/TRE/Full/En/TRE-154456.pdf> accessed 20 September 2019, Art 28.

Table 5.6 *A/M/R clauses: 'Adoption Stage' – alternative constructions considered*

Year	Consensus	Unanimity	C/M	SM	SM + Cond	QM: 2/3	QM: 2/3 + Cond	QM: 3/4	QM: 3/4 + Cond	QM: Other	QM : Other + Cond	Other	NS	Total
1900–1919			3									1		4
1920–1939		58	8	18		27	2		1	1	1	3	17	136
1940–1959		106	13	19	3	39	19	1	1		2	15	42	260
1960–1969		193	2	17	10	45	17	7		9		22	46	368
1970–1979	6	141	6	14	3	59	24	23	7	7	1	24	53	368
1980–1984	8	26	5	7		20	6	10	2	1		12	11	108
1985–1989	9	21	9	9	3	24	9	9	2	1	3	7	11	117
1990–1994	19	29	19	6	1	34	10	10		3		10	15	156
1995–1999	17	28	8	8		25	1	7		4		4	8	110
2000–2004	16	20	12	6	1	23	11	8					11	108
2005–2009	9	12	8	4	2	28	5	2		1		5	8	84
2010–2014	6	6	1			12		3				3	4	35
2015–2019	2	2	1			2	4	2					1	14
Total	92	642	95	108	23	338	108	82	13	27	7	106	227	1,868

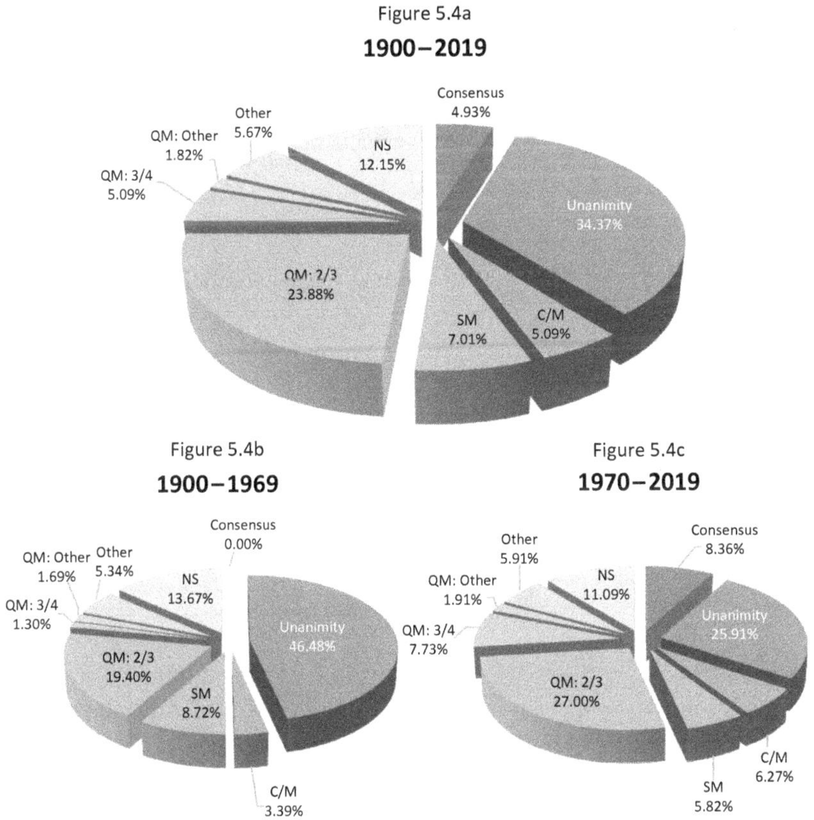

Figure 5.4(a–c) A/M/R clauses: 'Adoption Stage' – alternative constructions considered

Here it becomes evident that unanimity post-VCLT has ceased to be so dominant, but also that consensus owes much of its rise in prominence to 'alternative constructions'. Whereas in Figure 5.2c, post-VCLT consensus accounted for 14.18 per cent of the total of multilateral treaties, when 'alternative constructions' are factored in that percentage drops to 8.36 per cent. The effect is also visible when we look at the data for unanimity *lato sensu* methods of adoption, compared to other methods of adoption, as seen in Table 5.7 and Figure 5.5a–c.

This pattern, as already mentioned, diverges significantly depending on the regulatory subject or nature of the treaty, ie whether we are dealing, for instance, with an environmental treaty, a treaty setting up an international organisation or institution, or a closed multilateral

Table 5.7 *Unanimity* lato sensu, *majority voting, and other methods in A/M/R clauses – alternative constructions considered*

Year	Unanimity *Lato Sensu*	Majority	Other	NS	Total
1900–1919	3		1		4
1920–1939	66	50	3	17	136
1940–1959	119	84	15	42	260
1960–1969	195	105	22	46	368
1970–1979	153	139	23	53	368
1980–1984	39	46	12	11	108
1985–1989	39	60	7	11	117
1990–1994	67	63	11	15	156
1995–1999	53	45	4	8	110
2000–2004	48	49		11	108
2005–2009	29	42	5	8	84
2010–2014	13	15	3	4	35
2015–2019	5	8		1	14
Total	829	706	106	227	1,868

treaty. This aside, there is a growing trend at the 'adoption stage' to gradually move towards more simplified and expedited procedures that require a majority voting than the consensus or unanimity of either totality of the parties or the organ that is entrusted with adopting or recommending the proposed amendments to the parties for acceptance and approval. However, we should be careful not to attribute to majority voting characteristics that it does not intrinsically have. As Tomuschat warned: 'it would amount to a distortion of the true picture to contend that, in accepting an amendment procedure providing for majority vote, States have accepted *ex ante* the substance of any future amendments . . . [anticipatory] consent to amendments adopted by majority is . . . a pure legal fiction'.[264] It is exactly this point that we shall turn to in the next section, ie to determine how A/M/Rs enter into force for the State parties.

5.4.3.2 Entry into Force

After the 'adoption stage' of an A/M/R proposal, what follows is the 'entry into force stage'. What we examine in this stage is which parties are

[264] C Tomuschat, 'Obligations Arising for States without or against Their Will' (1993/IV) 241 RdC 195, 266.

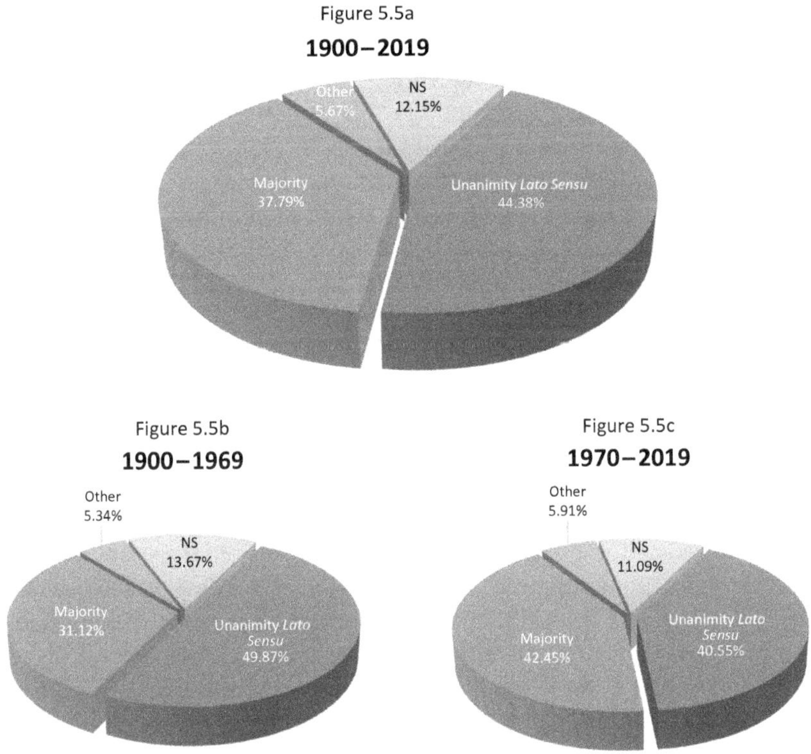

Figure 5.5(a–c) Unanimity *lato sensu*, majority voting, and other methods in A/M/R clauses – alternative constructions considered

bound by the A/M/R proposal. Is it only the ratifying/accepting/approving State parties (and/or organisations), or is it binding on all? In the latter scenario, then the follow-up question is what options, if any, are provided by the treaty for a State party to exempt itself from the application of the proposed A/M/R, ie how forceful and unavoidable that A/M/R's binding effect is for them.

The research in LNTS and UNTS-published multilateral treaties has yielded a plethora of interesting results. There are three main possibilities regarding the proposed A/M/R: (i) it enters into force only for the ratifying/accepting/approving State parties and organisations;[265] (ii) it becomes binding on all State parties, even those that have not ratified/

[265] Hereinafter and for simplicity reasons, they will be referred to simply as ratifying States.

accepted it; and (iii) the entry into force requirements and procedure are not specified in the treaty.[266]

Of import are the first two categories. With respect to the first one, the adopted A/M/R becomes binding only for the ratifying/accepting/approving State parties, but usually before it enters into force certain conditions need to be met. These conditions can be as wide and diverse as the drafters' imagination. However, the most common form is that a certain number of State parties that have deposited instruments of ratification/acceptance/approval of the adopted A/M/R needs to be reached, before the A/M/R can enter into force.[267]

In a similar fashion, and on the basis of observed patterns of convergence, the second category can also be further subdivided into multiple subcategories. What jumps out from the pool of treaties examined is that the permissibility of an objection to the adopted A/M/R, and the ensuing consequences, is a critical aspect.[268] More specifically, and similarly to the approach we followed earlier, for reasons of convenience we have characterised all these approaches as 'tacit acceptance *lato sensu*' so as to include not only 'opting-out' amendments and 'binding' amendments, but also to account for additional *sui generis* subcategories that also share the common element of State parties being bound tacitly.

In more detail, for the category 'tacit acceptance *lato sensu*' five subcategories have been identified *on the basis of the force of the objection by a State party* to an adopted (or recommended) A/M/R. The first subcategory includes treaties where adopted A/M/Rs are binding on all State parties and no objection is permitted.[269] This subcategory is one of *inexistence of objection*. The treaty does not contain a provision giving

[266] Or will be determined at a different stage by another body; see for instance, Art 31 of the 1989 Agreement Creating the Eastern Pacific Tuna Fishing Organisation. In such cases, depending on whether the VCLT is applicable or not, the 'residual rules' of the VCLT may come into play.

[267] See, for instance, the 2007 Agreement on the Conservation of Gorillas and Their Habitats (adopted 26 October 2007, entered into force 1 June 2008) 2545 UNTS 55, Art X.

[268] This is reminiscent of Hathaway, Saurabh Sanghvi, and Solow's 'opting-out' amendments and 'binding' amendments; Hathaway, Saurabh Sanghvi, and Solow, 'Tacit Amendments' 10–6.

[269] See, for instance: 1971 Agreement Relating to the International Telecommunications Satellite Organization 'INTELSAT' (adopted 20 August 1971, entered into force 12 February 1973) 1220 UNTS 21, Art XVII(e); 1979 Agreement for the Establishment of a Centre on Integrated Rural Development for Africa (adopted 21 September 1979, entered into force 16 April 1980) 1175 UNTS 369, Art XIII(1); 1996 African Nuclear Weapons-Free Zone Treaty (adopted 11 April 1996, entered into force 15 July 2009) 35 ILM 698, Art 19(3); 2013 Intergovernmental Agreement on Dry Ports (adopted 1 May 2013, entered

the option of an objection to the adopted A/M/R. We have named this procedure TA/NO ('Tacit Acceptance – No Objection').[270] TA/NO consists of two main versions: (i) where the A/M/R has been adopted by an organ of the treaty[271] and no further action is required as it immediately enters into force for all parties;[272] and (ii) where the adopted A/M/R has been ratified by a number of States, and upon reaching a specified percentage of the total number of State parties, then the A/M/R enters into force for *all parties to the treaty*.[273]

The second subcategory refers to treaties, for which the adopted A/M/R is binding on all State parties and an objection to which is permitted. Here as well, the A/M/R may become binding either directly upon adoption or pursuant to the deposit of a certain number of instruments of ratification/acceptance/approval. However, such an objection amounts to denouncement of or withdrawal from the treaty.[274] The second

into force 23 April 2016) <https://treaties.un.org/doc/Publication/UNTS/No%20Volume/53630/Part/I-53630-0800000280380a86.pdf> accessed 20 September 2019, Art 8(5).

270 From this point onwards, this and the following abbreviations will be used on the relevant tables and the main text.

271 Or upon voting by the parties.

272 2003 Convention for the Safeguarding of the Intangible Cultural Heritage (adopted 17 October 2003, entered into force 20 April 2006) 2368 UNTS 3, Art 38(5); 1993 Agreement for the Establishment of the Indian Ocean Tuna Commission (adopted 25 November 1993, entered into force 27 March 1996) 1927 UNTS 329, Art XX(4).

273 2003 Agreement for the Establishment of the Global Crop Diversity Trust (adopted 4 October 2003, entered into force 21 October 2004) 2366 UNTS 205, Art 3(2); 2014 Statute Establishing the Small Island Developing States Dock (adopted 9 July 2014, entered into force 27 September 2015) <https://treaties.un.org/doc/Publication/UNTS/No%20Volume/53471/Part/I-53471-080000028044d840.pdf> accessed 20 September 2019, Art XXI(6); 2014 Agreement on the New Development Bank (adopted 15 July 2014, entered into force 3 July 2015) <https://treaties.un.org/doc/Publication/UNTS/No%20Volume/53647/Part/I-53647-0800000280472e68.pdf> accessed 20 September 2019, Art 44(b)-(c).

274 See for instance: 1979 International Olive Oil Agreement (adopted 30 March 1979, entered into force 1 January 1981) 1219 UNTS 135, Art 47(4); 1988 Agreement on the Network of Aquaculture Centres in Asia and the Pacific (adopted 8 January 1988, entered into force 11 January 1990) 1560 UNTS 201, Art 17; 1992 Protocol to Amend the International Convention on Civil Liability for Oil Pollution Damage (adopted 27 November 1992, entered into force 30 May 1996) 1956 UNTS 255, Art 15; 2001 Convention on the Contract for the Carriage of Goods by Inland Waterway (adopted 22 June 2001, entered into force 1 April 2005) <www.ccr-zkr.org/files/conventions/cmni_en.pdf> accessed 20 September 2019, Art 37; 2002 Protocol to the Athens Convention Relating to the Carriage of Passengers and Their Luggage by Sea (adopted 1 November 2002, entered into force 23 April 2014) <https://treaties.un.org/doc/Publication/UNTS/No%20Volume/24817/A-24817-080000028053bf55.pdf> accessed 20 September 2019, Art 23(10); 2003 Agreement on the Institutionalisation of

subcategory is thus a 'weak' form of objection. The State party either remains silent and tacitly accepts the binding effect of the A/M/R,[275] or it objects, but in such a case it is forced to withdraw from or denounce the treaty.[276] This procedure is called TA/WO ('Tacit Acceptance – Weak Objection'). An argument could be made that the first two categories, TA/NO and TA/WO, are very similar, since even in the first subcategory (TA/NO) a State could possibly also denounce or withdraw from the treaty, and thus would not be bound by the amendment. However, despite the similarities, they are not identical, for two reasons. First, whether the denouncement or withdrawal would rescue the State party from the application of the A/M/R would depend on the procedure envisaged for the withdrawal/denunciation. A scenario could occur, that this procedure would take a long time, and in the meantime the A/M/R would have come into force for a limited time for the withdrawing/denouncing State party. Second, withdrawal may not even be possible. The treaty may not have a withdrawal clause, in which case Articles 56(1) and 54(b) VCLT would have to be triggered (or their customary law equivalents).[277] Consequently, a State withdrawing from the treaty will not necessarily be always an option. For these considerations, we have found it more precise to distinguish between TA/NO and TA/WO.

The third subcategory includes the treaties for which the A/M/R is binding on all State parties, but where objections are permitted. This is

the Bay of Bengal Programme as an Inter-governmental Organisation <https://iea.uoregon.edu/treaty-text/2003-bayofbengalintergovernmentalorganizationentxt> accessed 20 September 2019, Art 17.

275 Or in some cases, the State party by not accepting the A/M/R is considered to be objecting, and then either automatically or through a decision of an organ of the treaty the relevant State party is considered as having withdrawn from the treaty. These groups of situations have also been categorised as a form of TA/WO; see 1992 International Sugar Agreement (adopted 20 March 1992, entered into force 10 December 1996) 1703 UNTS 203, Art 44(2); 1993 International Cocoa Agreement (adopted 16 July 1993, entered into force provisionally on 22 February 1994) 1766 UNTS 80, Art 62(2).

276 1991 Agreement for the Establishment of the Intergovernmental Organization for Marketing Information and Co-operation Services for Fishery Products in Africa (INFOPÊCHE) (adopted 13 December 1991, entered into force 23 December 1993) 1777 UNTS 401, Art 15(2); 2000 Agreement for the Establishment of the International Organisation for the Development of Fisheries in Eastern and Central Europe (EUROFISH) (adopted 23 May 2000, entered into force 12 October 2001) 2181 UNTS 27, Art 15(1).

277 For an analysis of Arts 54 and 56 and all the issues pertaining to withdrawal from a treaty that does not have a withdrawal clause see in this book Chapter 6, Section 6.2.

the standard 'opting-out' procedure.[278] This third group, by virtue of being characterised by the 'regular' form of objection, has been designated as TA/RO ('Tacit Acceptance – Regular Objection'). The objection prevents the A/M/R from entering into force for the objecting State.

The fourth subcategory, En TA/RO, consists of two types of situations that act as a bridge between TA/RO and TA/SO (the final subcategory). In this category we have placed two types of situations: (i) where an adopted A/M/R enters into force for all State parties except for those that object, but if a certain number of State parties objects then the A/M/R does not enter into force at all[279] and (ii) where an adopted A/M/R enters into force for all State parties unless a certain number of State parties objects. However, if no such number of State parties objects, then the A/M/R enters into force for all State parties, even those that had objected.[280] Since both these categories are an enhanced version of TA/RO, as they can also block the entry into force of an A/M/R but they do not reach the level of TA/SO, they have been named En TA/RO ('Enhanced Tacit Acceptance – Regular Objection').

Finally, the fifth and final subcategory pertains to treaties where the A/M/R is binding on all State parties and objections are permitted. However, the crucial difference between this subcategory and TA/RO is that here even one objection by one State party prevents the amendment from entering into force for all State parties.[281] Thus, these treaties

[278] See for instance: 1972 International Convention for Safe Containers (CSC) (adopted 2 December 1972, entered into force 6 September 1977) 1064 UNTS 3, Arts IX(2)(c) and X(3)(4); 1976 Convention for the Protection of the Mediterranean Sea against Pollution (adopted 16 February 1976, entered into force 12 February 1978) 1102 UNTS 27, Art 17(2)(vi); 1996 Agreement on the Conservation of African-Eurasian Migratory Waterbirds (adopted 15 August 1996, entered into force 1 November 1999) 2365 UNTS 203, Arts X(5) and (6); 1997 Kyoto Protocol, Art 21(5).

[279] 1968 Convention on Road Signs and Signals (adopted 8 November 1968, entered into force 6 June 1978) 1091 UNTS 3, Art 41(2)(a); 1993 Convention on Civil Liability for Damage Resulting from Activities Dangerous to the Environment (adopted 21 June 1993, not yet in force) 32 ILM 1228, Art 30.

[280] 2001 Agreement on International Roads in the Arab Mashreq (adopted 10 May 2001, entered into force 19 October 2003) 2228 UNTS 371, Art 7(5); 2006 Intergovernmental Agreement on the Trans-Asian Railway Network (adopted 12 April 2006, entered into force 11 June 2009) 2596 UNTS 3, Art 8(7).

[281] 1970 Convention on Conduct of Fishing Operations in the North Atlantic (adopted 12 March 1970, entered into force 26 September 1976) 1051 UNTS 101, Art 11(2); 1975 Customs Convention on the International Transport of Goods under Cover of TIR Carnets (adopted 14 November 1975, entered into force 20 March 1978) 1079 UNTS 89, Art 59(4); 1978 Convention on Future Multilateral Cooperation in the Northwest Atlantic Fisheries (adopted 24 October 1978, entered into force 1 January 1979)

include provisions that allow the objection of just one State to produce the maximum effect. It prevents the entry into force of the A/M/R for any State party. Therefore, this is a 'strong' form of objection, and, consequently, the subcategory has been named TA/SO ('Tacit Acceptance – Strong Objection').

Of course, treaties can combine a number of these approaches. For instance, the 1961 Single Convention on Narcotic Drugs,[282] supplemented by the 1971 Convention on Psychotropic Substances[283] and the 1988 Convention Against Illicit Traffic in Narcotic Drugs and Psychotropic Substances,[284] are examples of such mechanisms. The drug control treaties also allow for revision through amendment and for the formal alteration of a convention article or articles. This option is provided for in Article 47 of the Single Convention, Article 30 of the 1971, and Article 31 of the 1988 Convention. Procedures for amending both the 1961 and 1971 Conventions are almost identical.[285] Procedures within all three treaties allow for even limited opposition to a proposed amendment to thwart the initiative. For both the 1961 and 1971 Conventions, if no party rejects the amendment within 18 months after circulation, then 'it shall thereupon enter into force'.[286] However, if a proposed amendment is rejected by one or more parties, the Council may follow suit in response to objections and the substantial arguments provided or decide whether a conference should be called to consider the amendment.[287] A slightly different procedure is envisaged in the 1988 Convention. If the proposed amendment is rejected by any party, then the UNSG must consult with the parties and 'if a majority so requests, bring the matter to the Council which may decide to call a conference'.[288] Therefore, 'formal mechanisms for revision exist within all

1135 UNTS 370, Art XXI(3); 2009 Convention on the Conservation and Management of the High Seas Fishery Resources in the South Pacific Ocean, Art 35(3).

282 1961 Single Convention on Narcotic Drugs (adopted 30 March 1961, entered into force 13 December 1964) 520 UNTS 151.

283 1971 Convention on Psychotropic Substances (adopted 21 February 1971, entered into force 16 August 1976) 1019 UNTS 175.

284 1988 Convention against Illicit Traffic in Narcotic Drugs and Psychotropic Substances (adopted 20 December 1988, entered into force 11 November 1990) 1582 UNTS 95.

285 DR Bewley-Taylor and M Fitzmaurice, 'The Evolution and Modernisation of Treaty Regimes' (2018) 20 ICLR 403, 411.

286 Art 47(2) and Art 30(2), respectively.

287 Bewley-Taylor and Fitzmaurice, 'The Evolution and Modernisation of Treaty Regimes' 413.

288 Art 31(2).

the treaty texts and consequently generate the impression of evolutionary capacity. Yet, in reality substantive change is difficult to achieve'.[289]

Before examining the data produced from the examination of the A/M/R provisions in multilateral treaties based on the above-described categories, special reference needs to be made to the 1981 Regional Convention on the Recognition of Studies, Certificates, Diplomas, Degrees, and Other Academic Qualifications in Higher Education in the African States. The reason is that although the VCLT rules are residual in nature, the drafters felt it necessary to provide in the conventions that '[t]he present Convention may be amended *in accordance with the principles and procedures set out in the Vienna Convention on the Law of Treaties*'.[290] A possible explanation for this is most likely that because some of the parties to the convention were not parties to the VCLT and given the whole debate on the customary or not nature of the VCLT rules on A/M/R, the drafters felt it best to explicitly state their preference. Practical considerations aside, this does not detract from the beauty of this legal nod to the VCLT's influence.

With these categories in mind, the analysis of the relevant A/M/R clauses leads us to Table 5.8 and Figure 5.6a–c.

A number of things must be pointed out in order to understand the figures of Table 5.8 and Figure 5.6a–c. What is interesting is that it seems that the relationship between the ratifying/accepting/approving States and the 'tacit acceptance *lato sensu*' methods of entry into force has remained relatively stable both pre-VCLT and post-VCLT. However, this statement must be qualified. There are two crucial reasons that seem to account for this. First, as also was the case with the 'adoption stage', a big number of the multilateral treaties published in the LNTS and UNTS are of the closed multilateral (plurilateral) type. These treaties would in the vast majority of cases provide for entry into force only for the ratifying/accepting/approving States due to the limited number of State parties and also because the adoption method also tends to be in their case, unanimity or consensus. So, this most likely accounts for the stable over-representation of ratifying/accepting/approving States both pre- and post-VCLT.

289 Bewley-Taylor and Fitzmaurice, 'The Evolution and Modernisation of Treaty Regimes' 415.

290 1981 Regional Convention on the Recognition of Studies, Certificates, Diplomas, Degrees, and Other Academic Qualifications in Higher Education in the African States (adopted 5 December 1981, entered into force 1 January 1983) 1297 UNTS 101, Art 19 (emphasis added).

Table 5.8 *A/M/R clauses: 'Entry into Force Stage'*

Year	Ratifying/Accepting/ Approving States	Tacit Acceptance *Lato Sensu*					Not Specified	Total
		TA/NO	TA/WO	TA/RO	En TA/RO	TA/SO		
1900–1919	3						1	4
1920–1939	49	31	2	1	2	1	14	100
1940–1959	127	53	14	9	5	15	24	247
1960–1969	219	53	14	7	2	13	42	350
1970–1979	187	50	9	22	16	18	37	339
1980–1984	43	27	6	4		7	13	100
1985–1989	56	21	8	6	3	3	11	108
1990–1994	96	27	9	9	2	7	14	164
1995–1999	59	24	2	7	3	9	8	112
2000–2004	76	9	3	4	9	3	5	109
2005–2009	52	6	3	6	7	2	8	84
2010–2014	25	6		1	1		2	35
2015–2019	10	2		1	1			14
Total	1,002	309	70	77	51	78	179	1,766

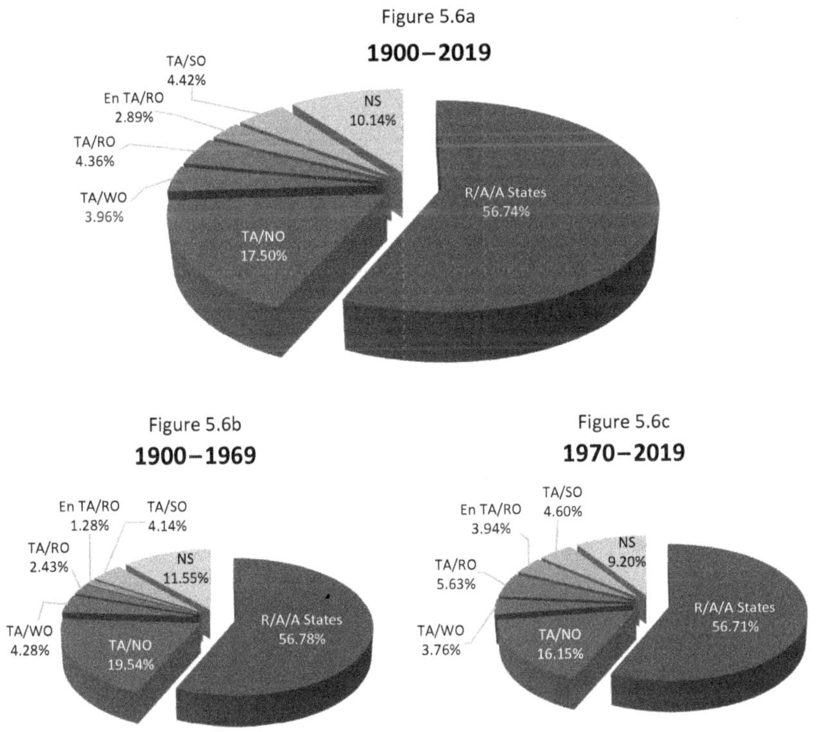

Figure 5.6(a–c) A/M/R clauses: 'Entry into Force Stage'

The second factor that must be accounted for is also the over-representation of TA/NO. The main reason for this is that groups of treaties falling under the same specialised agency (such as the Universal Postal Union) would often be renewed at regular intervals, and registered as new treaties.[291] Depending on how broad a net one wants to cast, this would account for intance for more than 50 instances pre-VCLT, and more than 20 post-VCLT.

Both these factors should mean that the figures although accurate, may allow for an over-representation of ratifying/accepting/approving States and TA/NO methods of entry into force, with a corresponding under-representation of the other 'tacit acceptance *lato sensu*' methods and

[291] See, for instance, the 1952 Agreement Concerning Subscriptions to Newspapers and Periodicals (adopted 11 July 1952, entered into force 1 July 1953) 171 UNTS 191. Agreements with the exact or near exact title and provisions were concluded and registered also in 1957, 1964, 1969, 1974, 1979, and 1984.

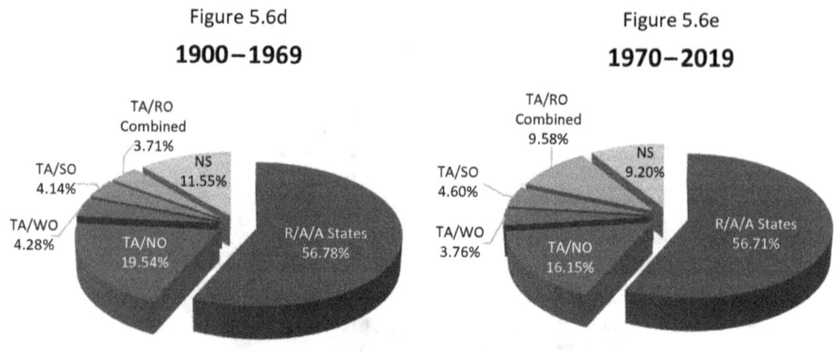

Figure 5.6(d–e) A/M/R clauses: 'Entry into Force Stage' – other TA/combined

particularly TA/RO and En TA/RO (which for illustrative purposes and due to their similarity, we have combined them in Figures 5.6d and 5.6e in one group called TA/RO Combined). If we isolate the change in those two latter categories, then we arrive at Figures 5.6d and 5.6e.

If we look at the data presented in Figures 5.6b and 5.6c, we see that TA/WO and TA/SO have remained relatively stable, TA/NO has shown a slight decrease, but TA/RO and En TA/RO in proportion to their pre-VCLT percentages have shown a dramatic increase. TA/RO pre-VCLT was 2.43 per cent, whereas post-VCLT it boasts a 5.63 per cent (an increase of 131.69 per cent). En TA/RO also went from a 1.28 per cent to a 3.94 per cent (an increase of 207.81 per cent). Combined they have gone from 3.71 per cent to a 9.58 per cent, or differenty, whereas they appeared only on 26 occasions pre-VCLT, post-VCLT they appear in 102 instances. There might be a number of reasons that can explain this. First, the increase in treaties of a technical nature, eg the IMO Conventions, that require constant updating in order to incorporate the newest and best available techniques and advances in science. TA/RO and En TA/RO are by design ideal for this type of expedited updating. Second, and connected to the first, TA/RO and En TA/RO although usually not the sole method of A/M/R, nor even the usually resorted to technique for the main provisions of the treaty, are also often a default mode of A/M/R, when the treaty distinguishes between provisions that entail and those that do not entail new obligations for the State parties (utilising TA/RO, En TA/RO, or any of the other forms of 'tacit acceptance *lato sensu*' for the latter),[292] or for annexes

[292] 1949 Agreement for the Establishment of a General Fisheries Council for the Mediterranean (adopted 6 November 1997, entered into force 29 April 2004) 126 UNTS 237,

and appendices, ie for instruments that are of a highly technical nature and that require expedited and simplified forms of A/M/R in order to stay relevant. Thus, TA/RO and En TA/RO are the linchpin that secures the continued relevance and effectiveness of numerous crucial multilateral treaties and are increasingly more relevant in modern society and treaty-making, a fact corroborated by the data presented above.

5.4.4 *Amendment of Amendment Procedures*

Before concluding, we need to mention, albeit briefly, a final subset of interesting A/M/Rs. These are the A/M/Rs that amend the amending procedure of the treaty. In several treaties, one can find explicit references to how their amendment procedures can be amended, usually either a specific procedure is provided for or it is mentioned together with other important articles, whose amendment requires a higher majority or more stringent conditions compared to the amendment procedure reserved for the other articles in that treaty.[293]

Although this may sound somewhat 'self-referential' and paradoxical, such systems have been a staple point of reference across all disciplines, from mathematics to philosophy and, of course, to law.[294] Even more than that, studying A/M/Rs that amend the amendment procedures, although not so common compared to other types of A/M/Rs, can

Art X; 2000 Agreement for the Establishment of a Commission for Controlling the Desert Locust in the Western Region (adopted 25 November 2000, entered into force 25 February 2002) 2179 UNTS 221, Art XVI; 1993 Agreement to Promote Compliance with International Conservation and Management Measures by Fishing Vessels on the High Seas (adopted 24 November 1993, entered into force 24 April 2003) 2221 UNTS 91, Art XIII(4).

293 1977 Geneva Act to the Nice Agreement Concerning the International Classification of Goods and Services for the Purposes of the Registration of Marks of June 15, 1957, as Revised at Stockholm on July 14, 1967 (adopted 13 May 1977, entered into force 6 February 1979) 1154 UNTS 89, Art 8; 1975 Fifth International Tin Agreement (adopted 21 June 1975, entered into force 14 June 1977), 1014 UNTS 43, Art 55(g); 1973 Vienna Agreement Establishing an International Classification of the Figurative Elements of Marks (adopted 12 June 1973, entered into force 9 August 1985) 1863 UNTS 317, Art 11.

294 See Sorensen, *A Brief History of the Paradox*; HLA Hart, *Essays in Jurisprudence and Philosophy* (Clarendon Press 1983); G Teubner, '"And God Laughed . . .": Indeterminacy, Self-Reference and Paradox in Law' (2011) 12 German Law Journal 376; L Goldstein, 'Four Alleged Paradoxes in Legal Reasoning' (1979) 38/2 CLJ 373; JM Rogers and RE Molzon, 'Some Lessons about the Law from Self-Referential Problems in Mathematics' (1991–2) 90 MichLRev 992; R Albert, 'Amending Constitutional Amendment Rules' (2015) 13/3 Int'lJConstL 655.

provide a concentrated insight into trends in the evolution of amendment procedures. If the State parties deemed it necessary to amend an amendment procedure, it is only reasonable to assume that there must have been a need that the A/M/R satisfies or an issue that it resolves.

- The first example of such an A/M/R, and appropriately so, is the convention that most authors tend to cite when talking about 'tacit acceptance' procedures – the SOLAS Convention. The SOLAS Convention has undergone multiple updates and revisions. The first version of the SOLAS Convention was adopted in 1914,[295] which predated the IMO, but this version never entered into force due to the outbreak of the First World War. After the creation of the IMO a Revision Conference led to the adoption of the 1960 SOLAS Convention.[296] However, its amendment procedure was deemed too slow[297] and, thus, the 1974 SOLAS Convention[298] was adopted that mainstreamed the 'tacit acceptance' procedure.[299] Since then the SOLAS Convention has been updated multiple times.[300]
- In the same area of law, another example comes from the Convention on the Prevention of Marine Pollution by Dumping of Wastes and Other Matter and Its 1978 Amendment.[301] *Stricto sensu,* the 1978 amendment did amend the amendment procedure of the original treaty. However, the changes introduced were clarificatory rather than

[295] 1914 International Convention for the Safety of Life at Sea (adopted 30 January 1914, did not enter into force) 108 BFSP 283.

[296] 1960 International Convention for the Safety of Life at Sea (adopted 17 June 1960, entered into force 26 May 1965) 536 UNTS 27, Art IX.

[297] Although Art IX of the 1960 SOLAS Convention had a 'tacit acceptance' procedure for A/M/Rs proposed through the IMO or a Revision Conference, the main procedure (Art IX(a)(i)) still was a unanimity-based procedure. To make matters even worse, even for those cases where the A/M/R could enter into force through a 'tacit acceptance' procedure, if the A/M/R was deemed of an important nature, State parties that wanted to object would cease to be parties to the Convention (this is a TA/WO example).

[298] Art VIII.

[299] Although it is not strictly speaking an amendment of an amendment procedure, as it was adopted through an entirely new treaty, nonetheless the SOLAS Conventions are considered as part of a unity.

[300] For more info, see ECOSOC, 'Activities of Other Organistions and Countries of Interest to the Working Party' (22 December 2008) UN Doc ECE/TRANS/WP.30/2009/1 [24]; I Basaran, 'The Evolution of the International Maritime Organization's Role in Shipping' (2016) 47/1 JMarL&Com 101, 104–5.

[301] Available at: <http://iea.uoregon.edu/pages/view_treaty.php?t=1978-Amendment-1972-MarinePollutionDumpingWastesOtherMatter.EN.txt&par=view_treaty_html> accessed 20 September 2019.

substantive. The amendment simply clarified that the Meeting of the Contracting Parties could decide on amendments not only of the convention, but also of the annex.

- The Constitution of the European Commission for the Control of Foot and Mouth Disease[302] is a more interesting example. Article XIV provided for adoption of amendments with a two-thirds majority. No State would be bound without expressing its consent. The 1962 amendment flipped the table completely.[303] First, it distinguished between amendments involving additional obligations for the State parties and amendments that did not. The latter enter into force immediately for all State parties upon the decision of the Council. The former, are subjected to a 'tacit acceptance' procedure with a two-year grace period. Thus, the Constitution went from a two-thirds majority to a tacit acceptance procedure in the 'blink of an amendment'.
- The International Convention for the Prevention of Pollution of the Sea by Oil[304] and its 1962 amendment,[305] is another example. They both provided for a 'tacit acceptance' procedure. However, the amendment strengthens the level of integration and the participation of international organs in the amendment procedure. Whereas in the 1954 Convention the Bureau was only involved in a 'communication facilitator' role, after the 1962 amendment both the Assembly of the Organisation and the Maritime Safety Committee are key players in the amendment procedure.
- In all the previous examples the treaties already had an amendment procedure. This was not the case[306] for the Ramsar Convention.[307] This deficiency was eventually sorted out with the 1982 Paris Protocol,[308]

[302] 1953 Constitution of the European Commission for the Control of Foot and Mouth Disease (adopted 11 December 1953, entered into force 12 June 1954) TS 47.

[303] Available at: <http://iea.uoregon.edu/pages/view_treaty.php?t=1962-Amendments-1953-EuropeanCommissionFootMouthDisease.EN.txt&par=view_treaty_html> accessed 20 September 2019.

[304] 1954 International Convention for the Prevention of Pollution of the Sea by Oil (adopted 12 May 1954, entered into force 26 July 1958) 327 UNTS 3.

[305] Available at: <http://iea.uoregon.edu/pages/view_treaty.php?t=1962-Amendment-1954-OilPollution.EN.txt&par=view_treaty_html> accessed 20 September 2019.

[306] 'Ramsar Convention: Progress Achieved' (1987) 17/5 EP&L 179, 180.

[307] 1971 Convention on Wetlands of International Importance Especially as Waterfowl Habitat (adopted 2 February 1971, entered into force 21 December 1975) 996 UNTS 245 (Ramsar Convention).

[308] 1982 Paris Protocol to Amend the Convention of 2 February 1971 on Wetlands of International Importance Especially as Waterfowl Habitat (adopted 3 December 1982,

which introduced an amendment procedure.[309] The procedure provided for an adoption by two-thirds majority and entry into force only for the ratifying States after two-thirds of State parties had deposited their instrument of ratification.[310]

- Similar to the Ramsar Convention, the International Telecommunication Convention[311] originally did not have a specific procedure on amendment of the text of the convention, apart from regulations on proposals or amendments presented during the conference. However, the Plenipotentiary Conference of the ITU in 1982 resolved that 'the provisions of the present Convention should be separated into two instruments: 1.1. A Constitution containing the provisions which are of a fundamental character, and 1.2. A Convention comprising the other provisions which by definition might require revision at periodic intervals; *[and t]hat each of these instruments should contain its own amendment procedure, it being stipulated that amendment of the Constitution shall require a special majority*'.[312] Such a provision can now be found in Article 55 of the Constitution of the ITU, which requires a special majority (two-thirds) for adoption, and enters into force for the ratifying/accepting States.[313]
- Another treaty that did not have an amendment procedure was the Convention on Conservation of Nature in the South Pacific.[314] Its 2000 amendment,[315] though, introduced one whereby an amendment would be adopted by a three-fourths majority.

entered into force 1 October 1986) 1437 UNTS 3 (Paris Protocol to the Ramsar Convention).

309 V Koester, 'The Ramsar Convention: Which Parties Are Effectively Parties to What? (and Other Legal Issues)' (2014) 44/1–2 EP&L 100.

310 Art 1 of the Paris Protocol, introducing Article 10*bis* to the Ramsar Convention. On a more detailed analysis of Ramsar's lack of amendment procedure, and the manner in which this was tackled see: MJ Bowman, 'The Multilateral Treaty Amendment Process – A Case Study' (1995) 44/3 ICLQ 540, 543–8.

311 1982 International Telecommunication Convention (adopted 6 November 1982, entered into force 1 January 1984) 1531 UNTS 1.

312 ITU, 'Resolution No 62: Basic Instruments of the Union' (1982) 1531 UNTS 493.

313 1992 Constitution and Convention of the International Telecommunication Union (adopted 22 December 1992, entered into force 1 July 1994) 1825 UNTS 330, Art 55.

314 1976 Convention on Conservation of Nature in the South Pacific (adopted 12 June 1976, entered into force 26 June 1990) 976 IEL 45.

315 Available at: <http://iea.uoregon.edu/pages/view_treaty.php?t=2000-Amendments-1976-NatureSouthPacific.EN.txt&par=view_treaty_html> accessed 20 September 2019.

Some interesting examples can also be found in amendment proposals that are either still in the process of entering into force or were outright rejected.

- In the former group, one can find a 2017 amendment proposal to the amendment procedure of the Statutes of the World Tourism Organisation. In accordance with the current text of Article 33(3) of the Statutes,[316] for adopted amendments to enter into force, two-thirds of the Member States must notify the Depositary of their approval. 'The new procedure established in the amendment to Article 33 adopted by the 22nd session of the General Assembly provides, in its third paragraph, a one-year period for the entry into force of amendments adopted by the General Assembly, not requiring for all amendments adopted by the General Assembly a two-thirds majority of Full Members ratification'.[317] But in order for this amendment to enter into force, the previous amendment requirements need to be met, ie two thirds of the Full Members notifying the Secretary-General of their approval of the amendment.[318] This, at the moment of writing, has yet to happen.
- In the latter category, we can find a proposed amendment to Article 2 of the Montreal Protocol,[319] which required consensus, compared to the two-thirds requirement of the protocol. Essentially, the proposal suggested a return to more classical unanimity *lato sensu* forms of amendment procedures. Several State parties considered this new procedure to be legally problematic and it was not followed through.

All these examples are quite diverse, and not near enough to extract statistically significant conclusions with respect to the amendment of amendment procedures. However, we can venture a few educated guesses. First, it is evident that the existence of an amendment procedure

316 1970 Statutes of the World Tourism Organisation (adopted 17–28 September 1970, entered into force 2 January 1975) 985 UNTS 339.

317 World Tourism Organisation, 'Report of the Secretary-General: Other Administrative and Statutory Matters – Status of Ratification of Amendments to the Statutes and of the 1947 Convention on the Privileges and Immunities of the Specialized Agencies' (1 October 2018) UN Doc CE/109/3(d)iii [12].

318 ibid [14].

319 UNEP, 'The Report of the Legal Drafting Group on Possible Adjustments and Amendment of the Montreal Protocol' (17 June 1999) UN Doc UNEP/OzL.Pro.11/3, 11; see also S Oberthür, 'Ozone Layer Protection at the Turn of the Century: The Eleventh Meeting of the Parties' (2000) 30/1–2 EP&L 34, 39.

is a desirable outcome, as otherwise it becomes extremely cumbersome to introduce any changes to a treaty. Take, for instance, the International Convention for the Regulation of Whaling (ICRW). Although the ICRW provides for the amendment of the schedule,[320] it has no provision for the amendment of the ICRW itself. Consequently, this can be done only through a protocol (which did happen in 1956)[321] or a new convention. Unless all parties to the ICRW sign and ratify the protocol and/or new treaty, then we end up with a fragmented system on whaling regulation. Three attempts were made in the 1970s to negotiate a new convention. These conferences were convened exactly because the ICRW lacked an amendment procedure. However, none was met with success.[322]

Second, in all the examples given the new amendment procedure either introduced an amendment procedure where none existed before or promoted either closer co-operation or more expedited forms of amendment procedure. In the case of an amendment proposal that would have turned the clock back and gone from a two-thirds majority voting to a consensus one,[323] this was simply rejected. So, it seems that amendment procedures are moving towards more multi-tiered (depending on the nature of the obligations) and more expedited approaches as they move along the temporal axis.

5.5 Conclusions

The procedures analysed in this chapter, evidence the *kinesis* inherent in the law of treaties. A 'motion' that is not only evident in the treaties themselves, as they are the ones being subjected to *alloiosis, auxesis,* or *meiosis*, partially due to their *kata chronon metavole* but is also evident from the frame of reference of the VCLT and customary law. This was clearly shown in Section 5.2 by the lengthy discussions as to the existence or not of customary rules on A/M/R, and the fiery debates within the ILC on duties and rights of States during A/M/R. It was also present in Section 5.3 where current and more 'informal' methods of

320 Art V.

321 See for instance the 1956 Protocol to the International Convention for the Regulation of Whaling (adopted 19 November 1956, entered into force 4 May 1959) 338 UNTS 366.

322 P Birnie, 'Small Cetaceans and the International Whaling Commission' (1997) 10/1 GeoIntlEnvtlLRev 1, 22; see also in more detail, P Birnie, *International Regulation of Whaling: From Conservation of Whaling to Conservation of Whales and Regulation of Whale-Watching* (Oceana Publications 1985) 549–74.

323 The amendment proposed to Art 2 of the Montreal Protocol.

A/M/R were examined,[324] with a particular focus on tacit acceptance procedures and 'autonomous institutional arrangements' as forms that emerge organically from the *kinesis* not just of international law, but of society in general.

Finally, Section 5.4 through an empirical analysis provided a bird's eye view of the shifting patterns of A/M/R in treaty-making since the beginning of the 20th century. There we identified multiple interesting patterns, such as the influence of the VCLT on the nomenclature and State preference with respect to choosing between amendment, modification, and revision; the rise of preference for majority voting at the 'adoption stage'; the increase of the role of TA/RO and En TA/RO in modern treaty-making; and the not so bizarre landscape of amendment of amendment procedures.

Behind all of our analysis on amendment procedures, the eternal and tension between stability and change, between *stasis* and *kinesis* was always palpable. What is undeniable is that A/M/R is a critical piece of the puzzle in ensuring that treaties remain viable, and relevant. To paraphrase James Madison, the amendment procedure 'guards equally against that extreme facility, which would render the [treaty] too mutable; and that extreme difficulty, which might perpetuate its discovered faults'.[325]

324 See also LR Helfer, 'Nonconsensual International Lawmaking' [2008/1] UIllLRev 71; C Tietje, 'The Changing Legal Structure of International Treaties as an Aspect of an Emerging Global Governance Architecture' (1999) 42 GYIL 26, 38–40.

325 J Madison, 'Federalist Paper No 43' in Cl Rossiter (ed), *The Federalist Papers* (New American Library 1961) 278.

6

Treaties and Their *Phthora*

Withdrawing from and Terminating/Suspending Treaties

6.1 Introduction

This chapter examines the circumstances under which a State, party to a treaty, may withdraw from that treaty or terminate or suspend it. When a State withdraws from a treaty, depending on one's frame of reference this would be equivalent to *phthora* (ie motion as destruction, from the withdrawing State's frame of reference) or partial *phtora* or *meiosis* (from the remaining State parties' frame of reference). Whereas in the case of termination or suspension of a treaty, especially in the case of supervening impossibility of performance, fundamental change of circumstances, and material breach, the emerging situation has so altered the obligations contained in the treaty that an *alloiosis* has taken place,[1] which depending on its severity may eventually lead a State to decide to use its right to bring the *phthora* of the treaty.

If all treaties provided in and of themselves an expiry date, then this would be, in most situations, a straightforward process. However, most treaties are drafted with a view to applying for an undetermined period of time, and sometimes do not even provide for the option of withdrawing

[1] Note the crucial point that Aristotle had made regarding *alloiosis* and how it is substantively distinct from other types of motion: 'But in the case of alteration it may be argued that the process necessarily implies one or other of the other five sorts of motion. This is not true, for we may say that all affections, or nearly all, produce in us an alteration which is distinct from all other sorts of motion, for that which is affected need not suffer either increase or diminution or any of the other sorts of motion. Thus, alteration is a distinct sort of motion; for, if it were not, the thing altered would not only be altered, but would forthwith necessarily suffer increase or diminution or some one of the other sorts of motion in addition; which as a matter of fact is not the case. Similarly, that which was undergoing the process of increase or was subject to some other sort of motion would, if alteration were not a distinct form of motion, necessarily be subject to alteration also. But there are some things which undergo increase but yet not alteration. The square, for instance, if a gnomon is applied to it, undergoes increase but not alteration, and so it is with all other figures of this sort. Alteration and increase, therefore, are distinct'; Aristotle, *Categories* ch XIV.

from a particular treaty regime. The second section of this chapter examines how the law of treaties evolved in respect to this very basic question. Section 6.3 then uses a recent example, connected to Brexit, to demonstrate the eternal *motion* of the law of treaties on withdrawal from a treaty. The *Wightman* case essentially posed to the Court of Justice of the European Union (CJEU) the question of whether the right to withdraw from the EU treaty should be understood as including also a right to withdraw the notification of withdrawal, ie whether the right of withdrawal should be interpreted in a way that corresponded to *auxesis* or *meiosis*, and whether the UK could reverse the arrow of the motion that had been instigated through its notification of withdrawal to the EU.

The situation is further complicated by the fact that anomalous situations can also occur where termination or suspension may be required. The most characteristic examples of such grounds, which also reflect the 'motion' of treaties, are fundamental change of circumstances and material breach. Despite the fact that fundamental change of circumstances has only rarely been upheld in international courts and tribunals[2] (material breach even less),[3] the international jurisprudence where these grounds have been recognised as reflecting customary international law sheds light on their gradual clarification. This is especially relevant for material breach, as its connection with countermeasures is still a topic of consternation for academics and practitioners alike. This is examined in Section 6.4.

However, this chapter examines not only the existing grounds of termination/suspension under the VCLT but also certain grounds that despite not being included in the VCLT have been argued to provide additional, customary law-based grounds for termination/suspension. The most notable of these are desuetude[4] and *exceptio non adimpleti contractus* (also known as *inadimplenti non est adimplendum*),[5] that are also put under the microscope in Section 6.4. With respect to the *exceptio non adimpleti contractus*, although this has been invoked as a defence for non-performance, because it is often discussed in connection to Article 60 VCLT, ie material breach, it is also analysed as it will provide useful insights as to the actual scope of grounds for termination/suspension of

[2] *Case C-162/96 – A Racke GmbH & Co v Hauptzollamt Mainz* [1998] ECR I-03655 [52–60].

[3] See Section 6.5.

[4] Fitzmaurice, 'Second Report' 31; Kolb, 'La désuétude' 577; Vamvoukos, *Termination of Treaties in International Law*.

[5] *FYROM v Greece* [115–7], [161], Separate Opinion of Judge Simma and Dissenting Opinion of Judge *ad hoc* Roucounas.

treaties. Additionally, even mere non-performance is a manifestation of *phthora* of the treaty and thus fits squarely in the analytical scope of the present chapter.

Finally, in Section 6.5 we examine two kinds of motion: (i) the motion between the afore-analysed VCLT and non-VCLT alleged grounds for termination/suspension, ie the connections, near identity, and, in some cases, suggested absorption of one ground by another; and (ii) the motion between, on the one hand, the grounds for termination/suspension, as a subset of treaty law, and, on the other hand, other sets of rules, such as State responsibility. In this manner, *Treaties in Motion* provides a complete picture about whether the grounds for termination/suspension of a treaty have moved since the drafting of the VCLT and how this may affect the current VCLT regime.

6.2 Withdrawing from a Treaty without a Withdrawal Provision

Whereas in Chapter 5 we dealt with A/M/R as the point of balance between *stasis* and *kinesis*, there are instances where the continued participation in a treaty system may be considered from the frame of reference of all parties, or of one in particular, as an onerous one. This fact alone does not *ipso facto* open the door for invocation of grounds of termination/suspension of a treaty. The death (*phthora*) of a treaty does not necessarily have to be resorted to. A logical alternative, especially where a single State party is concerned, is to consider whether there is an option of unilateral denunciation or withdrawal from a treaty. In such a scenario, the treaty would continue to live on, albeit with a reduced number of parties (*meiosis*), but would cease to produce legal obligations for the withdrawing State (*phthora* of the treaty from the frame of reference of the withdrawing State).

The relevant VCLT provision on this matter is Article 56.[6]

> A treaty which contains no provision regarding its termination and which does not provide for denunciation or withdrawal is not subject to

[6] Which according to the ICJ codifies customary international law; *Gabčíkovo-Nagymaros Project* [100]; the Court in *Gabčikovo-Nagymaros* may not have referred explicitly to Art 56 VCLT (or its customary law equivalent), but the second and third sentence in paragraph 100 seem to correspond to Art 56(1)(a) and (b), respectively, thus signaling an implicit acceptance by the Court of the customary nature of Article 56 in its entirety. For a discussion on whether State practice and the VCLT preparatory work supports this view, see T Christakis, 'Article 56' in Corten and Klein (eds), *The Vienna Conventions on the Law of Treaties* 1251–76; T Giegerich, 'Article 56' in Dörr and Schmalenbach (eds), *Vienna Convention on the Law of Treaties* 1039–60.

> denunciation or withdrawal unless: (a) it is established that the parties intended to admit the possibility of denunciation or withdrawal; or (b) a right of denunciation or withdrawal may be implied by the nature of the treaty.[7]

Article 56 VCLT, pertains to treaties that do not contain a withdrawal or termination clause. Even today, several major treaties, such as the UN Charter, the VCLT, and several core UN human rights treaties,[8] lack such provisions. Article 56 VCLT essentially tries to walk a thin line between two extremes.[9] On the one hand is 'extreme inflexibility',[10] and on the other hand is 'exaggerated flexibility',[11] which would destabilise the international legal system by allowing States to withdraw at the drop of a hat.[12] It does so by creating a *presumption against a right of denunciation or withdrawal* of States that is triggered only if two *negative conditions* are met.[13] Following the principle *onus probandi incubit actori*,[14] the onus lies with the State that claims that one of the negative conditions is applicable in the case of the treaty it wishes to withdraw from or terminate.[15]

6.2.1 *Negative or Positive Presumption*

The near unanimous adoption of Article 56 during the Vienna Conference on the Law of Treaties[16] may give the false impression about how unchallenged Article 56 was, and how much it reflected customary international law at the time.

7 VCLT, Art 56(1)(a) and (b).

8 ICCPR; 1966 International Covenant on Economic, Social and Cultural Rights (adopted 16 December 1966, entered into force 3 January 1976) 993 UNTS 3 (ICESCR); 1979 Convention on the Elimination of All Forms of Discrimination against Women (adopted 18 December 1979, entered into force 3 September 1981) 1249 UNTS 13 (CEDAW).

9 Christakis, 'Article 56' [17]; Giegerich, 'Article 56' [1–13], [24–35].

10 That would be the case of restricting the right of withdrawal of States to apply only in the anomalous cases of eg material breach, supervening impossibility of performance etc.

11 Giegerich, 'Article 56' [2].

12 This would also undermine the principle of *pacta sunt servanda*.

13 Giegerich, 'Article 56' [17]; R Plender, 'The Role of Consent in the Termination of Treaties' (1986) 57 BYIL 133, 147. However, even in the case that the presumption arises, it is still a rebuttable one (Giegerich, 'Article 56' [17]).

14 For a presentation of the use of this principle in international adjudication, see JC Witenberg, '*Onus probandi* devant les jurisdictions arbitrales' (1951) 55 RGDIP 321.

15 Aust, *Modern Treaty Law and Practice* 256; Giegerich, 'Article 56' [24].

16 95 votes in favour, 0 against, with 6 abstentions.

For instance, the negative presumption incorporated in Article 56 was debated both in the ILC and even until the very end of the Vienna Conference. Although the existence of a right of withdrawal was not generally objected to, what caused many problems was which presumption was customary law or at the very least was more reflective of the actual State practice in treaty-making.

In 1961, Giraud presented to the Institut, in his capacity as Rapporteur, a report on 'Modification and Termination of Collective Treaties', in which he supported the extremely flexible approach, which meant that 'in the absence of a provision concerning denunciation, general conventions may be denounced at any moment.[17] Giraud also clarified in that report that there could be a specific type of treaties for which this right of unilateral denunciation was not applicable; they would be truly perpetual treaties, such as peace treaties. All other treaties, including treaties of 'unlimited' or 'indefinite' duration, followed the rule expressed, ie allowing for denunciation. The reason, according to Giraud, was that even the treaties of 'unlimited'/'indefinite' duration, were not truly perpetual and, therefore, should abide by the same rules as 'temporary' or 'transitive' treaties.[18]

Fitzmaurice in his 'Second Report' stated that in the absence of a withdrawal or termination provision, the general rule was that no termination was permitted 'except by general consent'.[19] Despite the fact that Waldock may at times have given 'the impression of having yielded beneath its weight by suggesting that a tacit right of denunciation and a presumption in favour of such a right should be recognised',[20] in the end the negative presumption was the one that found its way in the draft articles that were discussed in the Vienna Conference.

Even at the very last minute during the Vienna Conference an amendment submitted jointly by Colombia, Spain, and Venezuela proposed a reversal of the presumption,[21] so that Article 56 would 'conform more closely with the practical realities and needs of contemporary

[17] E Giraud, 'Modification et terminaison des traités collectifs' (1961) 49/1 AIDI 5, 73 (author's translation. The original text goes: 'en l'absence d'une prévision concernant la dénonciation, les conventions générales peuvent être dénoncées à tout moment').

[18] ibid and fn 70.

[19] Fitzmaurice, 'Second Report' 38 [16].

[20] Christakis, 'Article 56' [11]; see also Giegerich, 'Article 56' [6].

[21] Colombia, Spain, and Venezuela, 'Amendment Proposal to Article 53' UN Doc A/CONF.39/C.1/L.307, Add.1 and 2.

international society'.[22] These oscillations aside,[23] at the end Article 56(1) VCLT, in the form of a negative presumption, was adopted almost unanimously.

6.2.2 *The Nature of the Treaty*

Whereas subparagraph (a) of Article 56(1) VCLT (the 'subjective' condition, since it is dependent on the intention of the parties) did not cause any major ripples during both the ILC and the Vienna Conference discussions,[24] the same cannot be said for subparagraph (b), which aimed at introducing an 'objective' condition, ie the 'nature' of the treaty. The reference to 'nature' in Article 56(1)(b) seems to echo Giraud's hypothesis, that there are treaties that are perpetual and others (the vast majority) which are intrinsically temporary.

Despite this, the inclusion or exclusion of the 'nature' of the treaty from the text of what would become Article 56 VCLT was hotly contested during the *travaux préparatoires* of the VCLT.[25] This is not all that surprising since the difficult balance between rigidity and flexibility that Article 56 had to strike was reflected in the positions taken by the ILC members, which were somewhat reflective also of the debates on the right presumption to be incorporated in Article 56. One group viewed unilateral withdrawal as permissible only when all the parties agreed to it (the intention exception); another held the view that unilateral withdrawal was a right, with only limited exceptions; and the third group conceded that tacit denunciation was not a right but it could be inferred from certain types of treaties.[26]

Fitzmaurice in his 'Second Report', while starting from a negative presumption, allowed for two exceptions, specifically (i) that inferences could be made as to the duration from the treaty as a whole and (ii) '[treaties] by their nature such, that any of the parties to them must

[22] United Nations Conference on the Law of Treaties, '1st Session – 58th Meeting of the Committee of the Whole (COW)' (8 May 1968) UN Doc A/CONF.39/C.1/SR.58 334, 337 [29] (Caro).

[23] And irrespective of whether an implied right of denunciation would be theoretically sound (on this see Christakis, 'Article 56' [21–6]).

[24] Ibid [12] referring to comments made by various ILC members: ILC, 'Summary Record of the 869th Meeting' [16] (Tsuruoka), [24] (Verdross), [35] (Briggs); see also Giegerich, 'Article 56' [1–13].

[25] Giegerich, 'Article 56' [30].

[26] Christakis, 'Article 56' [10 ff].

have an implied right to bring them to an end or to withdraw from them'.[27] Interestingly, both of these exceptions are manifestations of the 'nature' exception. Fitzmaurice also highlighted that the second exception only applied to treaties whose very nature imposed such an implication as a necessary characteristic of the type of obligation involved.

Along similar lines, Waldock, also in his 'Second Report', proposed a draft article (Article 17) which identified types of treaties that by their nature provided to State parties a right of unilateral denunciation.[28] Such treaties were *modus vivendi* instruments; treaties of alliance or of military cooperation; commercial or trading agreements; treaties of arbitration or judicial settlement; and constituent instruments of international organisations.[29] The inclusion of 'nature' considerations by both *Rapporteurs* (Waldock and Fitzmaurice) was criticised by the ILC members, ironically, for being both too timid and too progressive.[30]

The ILC eventually decided to omit any reference to the 'character' or 'nature' of the treaty, as its members preferred this element to be one of the supplementary means through which the intention of the parties could be determined, rather than an objective element separate from the intention of the parties.[31]

That was, however, not the end of the story. During the Vienna Conference both Cuba and the UK proposed amendments to Draft Article 53 (which eventually became Article 56 VCLT). Cuba's proposal essentially rewrote the entire article, replacing the intention of the parties with the objective element of 'nature', because it was 'contrary to all reason to regard certain types of treaties as perpetual'.[32] Any set of rules

[27] Such as treaties of alliance and commercial or trading agreements; Fitzmaurice, 'Second Report' 39 [16].

[28] H Waldock, 'Second Report on the Law of Treaties' (20 March–5 June 1963) UN Doc A/CN.4/156 and Add 1–3, reproduced in [1963/II] YBILC 36, 64, Art 17.

[29] For a detailed analysis of the 'nature' of these treaties, see Christakis, 'Article 56' [54–65]. On the other side, treaties that were not amenable to unilateral denunciation were boundary treaties, or treaties effecting a cession of territory, or a grant of rights in or over territory, treaties establishing an international regime for a particular area, territory, river, waterway, or airspace; treaties of peace, of disarmament, or for the maintenance of peace, treaties effecting a final settlement of an international dispute and human rights treaties; Waldock, 'Second Report' 64, Art 17.

[30] Depending on which of the three groups the critic belonged to.

[31] ILC 'Draft Articles on the Law of Treaties with Commentaries' 251, Commentary to Art 53 [5]; see also K Widdows, 'The Unilateral Denunciation of Treaties Containing No Denunciation Clause' (1982) 53 BYIL 83, 90 ff.

[32] United Nations Conference on the Law of Treaties, '1st Session – 58th Meeting COW' 337 [22] (Tabio).

that claimed to make a positive contribution to the progressive development of international law had to reject 'the abusive practice of perpetual treaties, which for long had helped the strong to dominate the weak'.[33]

UK's proposal was more moderate, keeping Draft Article 53 intact, but adding the 'objective' element as a second, independent of the intention of the parties, exception.[34] In the end, Cuba's proposal was narrowly rejected,[35] while the UK one was narrowly adopted.[36]

Also interesting is the fact that Article 56 employs the term 'nature'. This is the only time that this term appears in the VCLT, whereas 'character' and 'object and purpose' are much more frequent.[37] This terminological inconsistency is most likely attributable to the last minute redrafting of Article 56, as the ILC and even earlier the Institut members preferred the term 'character', possibly as a more neutral term that avoided the natural law connotations of the term 'nature'.

This tour through the negotiating history of Article 56 clearly shows that, even though the option of denunciation was not debated, the 'objective' exception[38] was hotly contested. Even Cuba, when proposing the amendment to Article 56, characterised the inclusion of the 'nature' of the treaty in the text of the article as a 'a positive contribution to the *progressive development of international law*'.[39] Since then, and although the *Gabčikovo–Nagymaros Project* case may be argued to have somewhat surreptitiously if not unintentionally recognised the customary nature of Article 56 in its entirety, doctrine overwhelmingly continues to doubt the customary character of Article 56(1)(b).[40]

33 ibid 336 [20] (Tabio).

34 UK, 'Amendment Proposal to Article 53' UN Doc A/CONF.39/C.1/L.311.

35 34 votes were cast in favour and 34 against, with 24 abstentions.

36 26 votes were cast in favour and 25 against, with 37 abstentions. According to Villiger, the large number of abstentions was due to the fact that States were worried that A would act as a destabilising force; Villiger, *Commentary on the 1969 Vienna Convention*, Commentary to Art 56 [3].

37 Five and eight times, respectively. In French, the term '*nature*' appears twice (Art 56 and Art 60(2)(c)). Surprisingly, in Art 60(5) the term is switched, once again, to '*caractère*'.

38 And to a much less intense degree the starting presumption.

39 United Nations Conference on the Law of Treaties, '1st Session – 58th Meeting COW' 336 [20] (Tabio).

40 Christakis, 'Article 56' [13], referring among others to: F Capotorti, 'L'extinction et la suspension des traités' (1971/III) 134 RdC 134, 539; J Setear, 'An Iterative Perspective on Treaties: A Synthesis of International Relations Theory and International Law' (1996) 37/1 HILJ 139, 209; and N Quoc Dinh, A Pellet, and P Daillier, *Droit International Public* (7th edn, LGDJ 2002) 307, fn 195.

Christakis points out, in this context, some logical holes in the functioning of Article 56(1)(b), which are apposite to our concept of 'motion', as they describe a situation where, by default, progressive development is theoretically impossible, thus leading to a *stasis* of the rule, if a rule exists at all.

> [Article 56(1)(b)] *exercises a sort of blackmail on custom*; either, by virtue of custom, certain categories of treaties contain an implied denunciation clause and, in those cases, [Article 56(1)(b)] is also part of customary law as it describes its existence; or custom does not include categories of treaties 'terminable by nature' and, in that case, [Article 56(1)(b)] no longer has a *raison d'être*, as the object it describes does not exist either in customary law or in treaty law. Therefore, the existence in customary law of a single category of treaties of this nature would suffice to show the customary character of [Article 56(1)(b)]. Conversely, its non-existence would render the subparagraph moot and place it in the area of uncertainty and desire. *One is faced, to some extent, by a treaty provision the survival of which is based on it having customary status. Paragraph 1(b) of Article 56 is either custom or nothing at all.*[41]

6.3 Writing on the Wall (and Its Subsequent Erasing): Withdrawal and Withdrawing the Withdrawal

In the previous section, we examined the 'motion' of the customary and VCLT rules pertaining to withdrawal from a treaty, especially in the context of treaties that did not provide for a withdrawal or termination clause. The solutions given in the VCLT, of varying degrees of codification of customary law, were far from the final word on the issue. An area which was in dire need of further clarification was whether a State having declared its intent to withdraw could revoke that notification. This was crucial not only with respect to treaties that did not have a withdrawal clause, but even to treaties that did, but did not account for this potential change in the 'motion' of the intention of the withdrawing party. This gained the spotlight, recently, with the decision of the UK to withdraw from the EU (the so-called Brexit) and the *Wightman* judgment, where the CJEU was asked to determine whether a State that has notified its intent to withdraw, could revoke said notification. In order to tackle this highly complex situation,[42] some background information is helpful.

[41] Christakis, 'Article 56' [14] (emphasis added).
[42] That, as of the moment of writing of this chapter (July 2019), is still ongoing.

6.3.1 *UK and EU: A 'Half-Hearted Relationship'*

In the much-lauded, and deservedly so, BBC series *Yes, Minister*, in the episode titled 'The Writing on the Wall', the character of Sir Humphrey, the permanent secretary for the (fictional) Department of Administrative Affairs, attempts to explains to the minister, Jim Hacker, the UK's foreign policy with respect to the EU.

> *SIR HUMPHREY:* Minister, Britain has had the same foreign policy objective for at least the last five hundred years: to create a disunited Europe. In that cause we have fought with the Dutch against the Spanish, with the Germans against the French, with the French and Italians against the Germans, and with the French against the Germans and Italians. Divide and rule, you see. Why should we change now, when it's worked so well?
>
> *HACKER:* That's all ancient history, surely?
>
> *SIR HUMPHREY:* Yes, and current policy. We had to break the whole thing [the EEC] up, so we had to get inside. We tried to break it up from the outside, but that wouldn't work. Now that we're inside we can make a complete pig's breakfast of the whole thing – set the Germans against the French, the French against the Italians, the Italians against the Dutch ... The Foreign Office is terribly pleased; it's just like old times.
>
> *HACKER:* But surely, we're all committed to the European ideal?
>
> *SIR HUMPHREY:* [chuckles] Really, Minister.
>
> *HACKER:* If not, why are we pushing for an increase in the membership?
>
> *SIR HUMPHREY:* Well, for the same reason. It's just like the United Nations; in fact, the more members it has, the more arguments it can stir up, the more futile and impotent it becomes.
>
> *HACKER:* What appalling cynicism.
>
> *SIR HUMPHREY:* Yes ... We call it diplomacy, Minister.[43]

This vintage Appleby-esque quote may be something of an oversimplification but it does reflect the 'somewhat half-hearted'[44] relationship of the UK with the EU. As Gormley points out,

[43] A Jay and J Lynn, 'Yes Minister Series, Episode Six: The Writing on the Wall: Transcript of Episode' (*Yes Minister*, 24 March 1980) <www.yes-minister.com/ymseas1b.htm> accessed 20 September 2019.

[44] LW Gormley, 'Brexit – Nevermind the Whys and Wherefores: Fog in the Channel, Continent Cut Off' (2017) 40 FordhamInt'lLJ 1175. Gormley provides an excellent and detailed account of the rocky marriage between the UK and the EU.

> [t]his goes back to the very early days, when negotiations started first on what became the European Coal and Steel Community, and history repeated itself in the negotiations leading up to what became the European Communities. That the preference for intergovernmental, rather than supranational, cooperation was a second-rate choice only gradually dawned on the British establishment, and by the time the potential suitor was ready to tie the knot, the bride was playing hard to get or at least General de Gaulle, like a parent who disapproves of a potential marriage, made it clear that the time was not yet ripe.[45]

Only in the post-de Gaulle era did France change its mind, and the UK was able, on 1 January 1973, to accede to the EC.[46] However, this was not the end of the trials and tribulations for the relationship between the EU and the UK. Just two years later, on June 1975, the UK held a referendum to gauge the public's support for UK's continued membership in the EC. The result was in favour of remaining, by roughly two-thirds of the voters (67.23 per cent).[47] The Euroscepticism revealed through this referendum, over the alleged erosion of Britain's sovereignty, was further stoked in the decades to come, and led to but also was sustained by, a kind of feedback loop effect, an increase of Eurosceptic Members of Parliament into the House of Commons.[48]

Craig provides an inspired and detailed account of the final stages that led to Brexit, in the form of 'a drama in six acts', each act being accompanied by a corresponding and relevant quote from Shakespearean plays.[49] Although, in his view, 'the origins of the referendum might be traced back to the last millennium', in the 21st century the watershed moment was then-UK Prime Minister David Cameron's 'Bloomberg Speech'.[50] In that speech, Cameron made a commitment to seek a renegotiation with the EU that would 'deliver a more flexible, adaptable and open European Union in which the interests and ambitions of all its members can be met . . . in which Britain can be comfortable and all . . .

[45] Ibid 1176; similarly, M Camps, 'Britain and the European Community 1955–1963' in R Mayne (ed), *The Recovery of Europe* (Weidenfeld & Nicholson 1970); PJG Kapteyn, PV van Themaat, *Introduction to the Law of the European Communities: from Maastricht to Amsterdam* (LW Gormley ed, 3rd edn, Kluwer Law International 1998) 17–21.

[46] 1972 Treaty of Accession of Denmark, Ireland, and the United Kingdom (adopted 22 January 1972, entered into force 1 January 1973) OJ L 73 (27 March 1972) 5.

[47] R Irving, 'The United Kingdom Referendum – June 1975' (1976) 1 ELR 3.

[48] Gormley, 'Brexit – Nevermind the Whys and Wherefores' 1178.

[49] P Craig, 'Brexit: A Drama in Six Acts' (2016) 40 ELR 447.

[50] ibid 449.

countries can thrive', and should that fail, to hold a referendum.[51] In 2015, Cameron reaffirmed the commitment to hold a referendum on the continued membership of the UK in the EU should the Conservatives be elected, which did happen.[52]

On 23 June 2016, the British citizens were asked to cast their vote on the question 'should the United Kingdom remain a member of the European Union or leave the European Union?'. 51.9 per cent of the voters cast the 'Leave' vote, while 48.1 per cent cast the 'Remain' vote. Cameron resigned and was succeeded by Theresa May as prime minister. On 29 March 2017, the UK notified the European Council of its intention to withdraw from the EU, thus triggering Article 50 of the Treaty on European Union (TEU).[53]

6.3.2 *Withdrawal Mechanism*

The original treaties of the EU (and of its earlier formative stages as EEC and EC)[54] did not contain withdrawal clauses. The possibility of States withdrawing from these treaties was highly contested in internationals scholarship.[55] This debate became moot with the changes introduced to the Treaty on European Union (TEU) through the Treaty of Lisbon,[56] one of which was the introduction of a special procedure regulating withdrawal. This is set out in Article 50 of the TEU:

[51] D Cameron, 'EU Speech at Bloomberg: Prime Minister David Cameron Discussed the Future of the European Union at Bloomberg' (*UK Government*, 23 January 2013) <www.gov.uk/government/speeches/eu-speech-at-bloomberg> accessed 20 September 2019.

[52] In more detail, see Gormley, 'Brexit – Nevermind the Whys and Wherefores' 1179.

[53] European Council, 'United Kingdom Notification under Article 50 TEU: Letter of 29 March 2017 from the Prime Minister of the United Kingdom to the President of the European Council' (29 March 2017) XT 20001/17 <http://data.consilium.europa.eu/doc/document/XT-20001-2017-INIT/en/pdf> accessed 20 September 2019.

[54] 1957 Treaty of Rome (adopted 25 March 1957, entered into force 1 January 1958) 298 UNTS 3; 1986 Single European Act (adopted 17 February 1986, entered into force 1 July 1987) 25 ILM 506; 1992 Treaty on European Union – Maastricht Treaty (adopted 7 February 1992, entered into force 1 November 1993) 31 ILM 253; 1997 Treaty of Amsterdam (adopted 2 October 1997, entered into force 1 May 1999) OJ C 340 (10 November 1997) 85; 2001 Treaty of Nice (adopted 26 February 2001, entered into force 1 February 2003) OJ C 80 (10 March 2001) 1.

[55] With people arguing both that 'leaving the European Union has always been possible' (Gormley, 'Brexit – Nevermind the Whys and Wherefores' 1178) and that 'the prevailing opinion [is that these treaties] did not allow for unilateral withdrawal' (Giegerich, 'Article 56' [21] fn 41).

[56] 2007 Treaty of Lisbon (adopted 13 December 2007, entered into force 1 December 2009) OJ C 306 (17 December 2017) 1.

1. Any Member State may decide to withdraw from the Union in accordance with its own constitutional requirements.
2. *A Member State which decides to withdraw shall notify the European Council of its intention.* In the light of the guidelines provided by the European Council, *the Union shall negotiate and conclude an agreement with that State*, setting out the arrangements for its withdrawal, taking account of the framework for its future relationship with the Union. That agreement shall be negotiated in accordance with Article 218(3) of the Treaty on the Functioning of the European Union. It shall be concluded on behalf of the Union by the Council, acting by a qualified majority, after obtaining the consent of the European Parliament.
3. *The Treaties shall cease to apply to the State in question from the date of entry into force of the withdrawal agreement or, failing that, two years after the notification referred to in paragraph 2, unless the European Council, in agreement with the Member State concerned, unanimously decides to extend this period . . .*[57]

Despite the introduction of a *lex specialis* in the TEU on withdrawal, this did not solve all problems. One critical question, most likely not given due consideration by the drafters, came to the forefront after UK's notification of withdrawal from the EU. Since that moment in time, the contours of Article 50 TEU, and in particular whether a notification of withdrawal could be revoked, became the focal point not only of academic but also of political analysis, with three main groups being formed: (i) those arguing that Article 50 TEU allowed the unilateral revocation of the notification[58] (ii) those arguing that Article 50 TEU excluded a

[57] 2007 Consolidated Version of the Treaty on the European Union (TEU) (adopted 13 December 2007, entered into force 1 December 2009) OJ C 115 (9 May 2008) 1, Art 50 (emphasis added).

[58] Craig 'Brexit: A Drama in Six Acts' 464; P Eeckhout and E Frantziou, 'Brexit and Article 50 TEU: A Constitutionalist Reading' (2017) 54/3 CMLR 695; A Sari, 'Reversing a Withdrawal Notification under Article 50 TEU: Can a Member State Change Its Mind' (2017) 42/4 ELR 451; T Tridimas, 'Article 50: An Endgame without an End?' (2016) 27 KLJ 297; S Peers, 'Can an Article 50 Notice of Withdrawal from the EU Be Unilaterally Revoked?: The Case for Unilateral Revocability of the Article 50 Notice' (*EU Law Analysis Blog*, 16 January 2018) <http://eulawanalysis.blogspot.com/2018/01/can-article-50-notice-of-withdrawal.html> accessed 20 September 2019; D Edward et al, 'In the Matter of Article 50 of the Treaty on European Union ("The Three Knights' Opinion")' (*Bindmans*, 10 February 2017) <www.bindmans.com/uploads/files/documents/Final_Article_50_Opinion_10.2.17.pdf> accessed 20 September 2019. D Sarmiento, 'Miller, Brexit and the (Maybe Not So Evil) Court of Justice' (*Verfassungsblog*, 8 November 2016) <http://verfassungsblog.de/miller-brexit-and-the-maybe-not-to-so-evil-court-of-justice/> accessed 20 September 2019.

unilateral revocation of the notification,[59] and finally (iii) those who were against unilateral revocability, but in favour of revocability *subject to the Council's approval.*[60]

6.3.3 *Wightman Petition in UK Courts*

The debate, however, did not remain bottled in academic circles but spilled over to judicial proceedings via the *Wightman* petition. On 19 December 2017, a group of seven individuals, led by Andy Wightman,[61] lodged a petition for judicial review to the Scottish Court of Session claiming that the UK could withdraw its Article 50(2) TEU notification, and requesting that the court, in accordance with Article 267 TFEU, make a reference to the CJEU. The request was denied on

[59] M Perakis, 'Does the Principle of the Autonomy of the EU Legal Order Allow for a Member State to Revoke the Notification of Its Withdrawal from the EU?' (*European Law Blog*, 31 October 2018) <http://europeanlawblog.eu/2018/10/31/does-the-principle-of-the-autonomy-of-the-eu-legal-order-allow-for-a-member-state-to-revoke-the-notification-of-its-withdrawal-from-the-eu/> accessed 20 September 2019; I Papageorgiou, 'The (Ir-) revocability of the Withdrawal Notification under Article 50 TEU' *Policy Department for Citizens' Rights and Constitutional Affairs, European Parliament*, March 2018) <www.europarl.europa.eu/RegData/etudes/IDAN/2018/596820/IPOL_IDA(2018)596820_EN.pdf> accessed 20 September 2019; P Ostendorf, 'The Withdrawal Cannot Be Withdrawn: The Irrevocability of a Withdrawal Notification under Article 50(2) TEU' (2017) 42/5 ELR 767; S Weatherill, 'Can an Article 50 Notice of Withdrawal from the EU Be Unilaterally Revoked?: Why the Withdrawal Notification under Article 50 TEU Is Not Unilaterally Revocable' (*EU Law Analysis Blog*, 16 January 2018) <http://eulawanalysis.blogspot.com/2018/01/can-article-50-notice-of-withdrawal.html> accessed 20 September 2019; M Gatti, 'The Article 50 Procedure for Withdrawal from the EU: A Well-Designed Secession Clause' (*EU Studies Association*, 6 May 2017) <www.eustudies.org/conference/papers/download/43> accessed 20 September 2019.

[60] 'Editorial Comments: Withdrawing from the Ever Closer Union?' (2016) 53/6 CMLR 1491; Georgopoulos 'The (Ir)revocability of Article 50 TEU' 4; C Hillion, 'Withdrawal under Article 50 TEU: An Integration-Friendly Process' (2018) 55/2 CMLR 29; C Hillion, 'Le retrait de l'Union européenne: Analyse juridique' (2016) RTDE 719; J Weiler, 'A Second Brexit Referendum – What Makes You Think They Will Have You Back?' (*EJIL: Talk!*, 26 November 2018) <www.ejiltalk.org/a-second-brexit-referendum-what-makes-you-think-they-will-have-you-back/#more-16684> accessed 20 September 2019; C Closa Montero, 'Is Article 50 Reversible? On Politics beyond Legal Doctrine' (*Verfassungsblog*, 4 January 2017) <https://verfassungsblog.de/is-article-50-reversible-on-politics-beyond-legal-doctrine/> accessed 20 September 2019.

[61] Wightman was a member of the Scottish Parliament. Out of the other six members of the group, one was member of the Parliament of the United Kingdom of Great Britain and Northern Ireland, two were members of the Scottish Parliament, and three were members of the European Parliament.

6 February 2018 on the basis that it was 'hypothetical and academic'.[62] This decision was appealed to the Inner House, which found 'significant problems'[63] with the Outer House's decision, and sent the case back to the Outer House.[64]

On 8 June 2018, the Lord Ordinary of the Outer House rejected the petition once more because, on the one hand, the question was a hypothetical one, and consequently the conditions for a referral under EU law, ie ascertainability of the facts and non-hypothetical nature, had not been met and, on the other hand, the matter was outside the Court's jurisdiction, as it encroached on parliamentary sovereignty.[65] The petitioners appealed, once again, and the Inner House decided on 3 October 2018 to refer the question to the CJEU. Critical in this final reversal was the fact that prior to the Inner House's judgment the UK Parliament adopted the EU Withdrawal Act,[66] which might have tipped the scales regarding the hypothetical nature of the question.[67] The Inner House, referring to the '*CILFIT* test' applicable to preliminary references and the recent jurisprudence of the CJEU,[68] came to the conclusion that the question

[62] *Andrew Wightman MSP and Others v Secretary of State for Exiting the European Union* (6 February 2018) Outer House, Court of Session (Scotland) [2018] CSOH 8 [14].

[63] *Andy Wightman MSP and Others v the Advocate General* (20 March 2018) First Division, Inner House, Court of Session (Scotland) [2018] CSIH 18 [28].

[64] ibid [34].

[65] *Andrew Wightman MSP and Others v Secretary of State for Exiting the European Union* (8 June 2018) Outer House, Court of Session (Scotland) [2018] CSOH 61 [51], [63]; see also O Garner, 'Can the United Kingdom Unilaterally Revoke Its Article 50 Notification to Withdraw from the EU? *Wightman v Secretary of State* for DexEU [2018] CSIH 62' (*European Law Blog*, 24 September 2018) <http://europeanlawblog.eu/2018/09/24/can-the-united-kingdom-unilaterally-revoke-its-article-50-notification-to-withdraw-from-the-eu-wightman-v-secretary-of-state-for-dexeu-2018-csih-62/> accessed 20 September 2019.

[66] Also, on the same day of the rendering of the judgment, Theresa May declared that withdrawal negotiations between the EU and the UK had reached an impasse.

[67] See *Andy Wightman MSP and Others v Secretary of State for Exiting the European Union* (21 September 2018) First Division, Inner House, Court of Session (Scotland) [2018] CSIH 62 [27], where the Inner House explicitly bases its reasoning on the EU Withdrawal Act: '[following the EU Withdrawal Act,] it seems neither academic nor premature to ask whether [the UK] is legally competent to revoke the notification and thus to remain in the EU'. However, see Vidmar, who argues that the EU Withdrawal Act still did not alter substantively the hypothetical nature of the question; J Vidmar, 'Unilateral Revocability in *Wightman*: Fixing Article 50 with Constitutional Tools' (2019) 15/2 EuConst 359, 363.

[68] *Andy Wightman MSP and Others v Secretary of State for Exiting the European Union* (21 September 2018) [30], [42], where Lord Carloway and Lord Menzies referred, respectively to: *Case C-304/16 – American Express Co v the Lord Commissioners of Her Majesty's Treasury* [2018] ECLI:EU:C:2018:66 [31–2]; the opinion of the Advocate-General Szpunar

was neither academic nor hypothetical because '[n]otification of withdrawal has been made . . . [and] in the absence of intervening events and perhaps in any event, [shall] take effect in about six months time'.[69]

In the end, the CJEU was asked to provide a preliminary ruling on the following question:

> Where, in accordance with Article 50 [TEU], a Member State has notified the European Council of its intention to withdraw from the European Union, does EU law permit that notice to be revoked unilaterally by the notifying Member State; and, if so, subject to what conditions and with what effect relative to the Member State remaining within the European Union?[70]

6.3.4 *Withdrawal of the Notification of Withdrawal*

This brings us to the Opinion of the advocate-general (AG) Campos Sánchez-Bordona, and the judgment of the CJEU in *Wightman v Secretary of State for Exiting the EU*.[71] Although both the Opinion of the AG and the judgment arrive at the same conclusion, there is a striking difference in the manner in which they arrive at it. Whereas the AG's Opinion is a veritable smörgåsbord of public international law and law of treaties issues, the CJEU's judgment is somewhat 'more receptive to the sovereign discretion of the withdrawing Member State',[72] but tends to be

in *Case C-327/18 – PPU, Minister for Justice and Equality v RO* (AG Opinion) [2018] ECLI:EU:C:2018:644 [32–7].

[69] *Andy Wightman MSP and Others v Secretary of State for Exiting the European Union* (21 September 2018) [31].

[70] *Case C-621/18 – Andy Wightman and Others v Secretary of State for Exiting the European Union* [2018] ECLI:EU:C:2018:999 [16] (hereinafter *Wightman* (CJEU Judgment)).

[71] S Peers, 'Brexit: You Can U-turn If You Want To. The CJEU Judgment in Wightman' (*EU Law Analysis Blog*, 10 December 2018) <http://eulawanalysis.blogspot.com/2018/12/brexit-you-can-u-turn-if-you-want-to.html> accessed 20 September 2019; S Peers, 'Revoking the Notice to Withdraw from the EU? The Opinion in Wightman' (*EU Law Analysis Blog*, 4 December 2018) <http://eulawanalysis.blogspot.com/2018/12/revoking-notice-to-withdraw-from-eu.html> accessed 20 September 2019; AS Reid, 'Scotching Brexit? Background to the Wightman Case about Reversing the Article 50 Notification Unilaterally' (*EU Law Analysis Blog*, 16 November 2018) <http://eulawanalysis.blogspot.com/2018/11/scotching-brexit-background-to-wightman.html> accessed 20 September 2019.

[72] O Garner, 'Case C-621/18, Wightman v Secretary of State for Exiting the European Union: The European Court of Justice Confirms That Article 50 Notification Can Be Unilaterally Revoked' (*European Law Blog*, 11 December 2018) <http://europeanlawblog.eu/2018/12/11/case-c-621-18-wightman-v-secretary-of-state-for-exiting-the-european-union-the-european-court-of-justice-confirms-that-article-50-notification-can-be-unilaterally-revoked/> accessed 20 September 2019.

more laconic on the critical issues of public international law, relying either mainly on the preceding analysis of the AG, or focusing its analysis on EU law and theory.

For this reason, in the following analysis we will switch between the AG's Opinion and the CJEU's judgment, depending on the discussion that best highlights the critical issues relating to the 'motion' of the rules on withdrawal from a public international law perspective.

The opinion of the AG starts with an examination of the admissibility of the question, to which the UK government had raised two objections: first, the hypothetical and theoretical nature of the question and second, that providing advisory opinions on constitutional matters falls outside the competence of the CJEU.[73] The AG rejected both grounds,[74] and along very similar lines so did the CJEU.[75] Vidmar criticises the CJEU's reasoning on admissibility as suffering from an 'element of circularity . . . or at least an absence of critical engagement with the referring court's argumentation'. According to him, the Court happily accepted the domestic court's reasoning, without substantially engaging and proving that the question was truly a non-hypothetical one.[76]

Admissibility criticisms aside, it is the AG's analysis of the question referred to the CJEU that is more interesting for the purposes of the *kinesis* of the customary and VCLT rules relating to withdrawal.[77] His opinion is grounded on three levels of analysis: (i) an analysis of the regime of withdrawal from treaties under international law,[78] (ii) the

[73] *Case C-621/18 – Andy Wightman and Others v Secretary of State for Exiting the European Union* (AG Opinion) [2018] ECLI:EU:C:2018:978 [33] (hereinafter *Wightman* (AG Opinion)).

[74] *Wightman* (AG Opinion) [37–57]; citing the Court's extensive jurisprudence on the matter, eg: *Case C-571/10 – Servet Kamberaj v IPES* [2012] ECLI:EU:C:2012:233 [41]; *Case C-617/10 – Åklagaren v Hans Åkerberg Fransson* [2013] ECLI:EU:C:2013:105 [42]; *Case C-470/12 – Pohotovosť sro v Miroslav Vašuta* [2014] ECLI:EU:C:2014:101 [29]; *Cases C-203/15 and C-698/15 – Tele2 Sverige AB v Post-och telestyrelsen and Secretary of State for the Home Department v Tom Watson and Others* [2016] ECLI:EU:C:2016:970 [130].

[75] *Wightman* (CJEU Judgment) [20–36]; also citing its case law: *Case C-62/14 – Peter Gauweiler and Others v Deutscher Bundestag* [2015] ECLI:EU:C:2015:400 [25]; *American Express Co v the Lord Commissioners of Her Majesty's Treasury* [32].

[76] Vidmar, 'Unilateral Revocability in *Wightman*' 363.

[77] For a point by point analysis of the AG's Opinion in *Wightman*, see C Brière, 'The Advocate-General Opinion in Wightman: Article 50 Notification to Withdraw from the European Union Is Unilaterally Revocable' (*European Law Blog*, 6 December 2018) <http://europeanlawblog.eu/2018/12/06/the-advocate-general-opinion-in-wightman-article-50-notification-to-withdraw-from-the-european-union-is-unilaterally-revocable/> accessed 20 September 2019.

[78] *Wightman* (AG Opinion) [63–76].

(non)-applicability of the VCLT provisions to withdrawal from the EU,[79] and (iii) the scenario of agreed revocation, which would be relevant only if the possibility of unilateral revocation was rejected.[80]

On the first level, the AG opined that although the 'international practice of unilateral withdrawal from multilateral treaties has not been very prevalent, there have been examples'.[81] There have even been cases where a State has withdrawn only to re-accede at a later point, as has been the case with respect to both the World Health Organisation (WHO) and the United Nations Educational, Scientific, and Cultural Organisation (UNESCO).[82] A more recent example is that of Bolivia withdrawing from the Single Drug Convention only to re-accede, with the benefit of a reservation.[83] But these examples refer to situations where withdrawal actually took place, and not the scenario of a 'course-correction' prior to the finalisation of withdrawal, as was the question submitted before CJEU. But even in this very specific scenario, there is some precedent in State practice.

The AG referred to four instances,[84] where such a revocation had transpired:

- the Spanish withdrawal from the League of Nations[85] in 1926. This decision was revoked in 1928, after which Spain participated in the Ninth Session of the League of Nations;[86]

[79] ibid [77–156].

[80] ibid [157–69].

[81] ibid [65]; for relevant State practice on withdrawal from treaties, see RL Helfer, 'Exiting Treaties' (2005) 91 VaLRev 1579; C Brölmann et al, 'Exiting International Organisations: A Brief Introduction' (2018) 15/2 IOLR 243.

[82] *Wightman* (AG Opinion) [66–7], as analysed in MC Dock, 'Le retrait des membres des organisations internationales de la famille des Nations Unies' (1994) 40 AFDI 106, 111 ff.

[83] The reason for the withdrawal was that Bolivia wanted an exception to the prohibition of chewing coca leaf, which is a traditional practice among its people. Bolivia had, originally, proposed an amendment to that effect, but it never came to fruition. In order, therefore, to achieve the desired result, Bolivia withdrew from the Single Drug Convention on 1 January 2012, and then applied for re-accession, but this time having made a reservation on chewing coca leaf for traditional purposes. The re-accession became effective on 10 February 2013; see Transnational Institute, 'The UN Drug Control Conventions: A Primer' (*Transnational Institute*, 24 October 2015) <www.tni.org/files/publication-downloads/primer_unconventions_24102015.pdf> accessed 20 September 2019, 14 and 18–23.

[84] *Wightman* (AG Opinion) [68–70].

[85] 1919 Covenant of the League of Nations (adopted 28 June 1919, entered into force 10 June 1920) 225 CTS 195.

[86] See on the Spanish withdrawal, DK Magliveras, 'The Withdrawal from the League of Nations Revisited' (1991) 10 Penn State International Law Review 25.

- Panama's notification of withdrawal from the Treaty Constituting the Central American Parliament and Other Political Bodies (Parlacen) on 19 August 2009;[87]
- Gambia's 2017 revocation of the 2016 notification of withdrawal from the ICC Statute;[88]
- South Africa's 2017 revocation of the 2016 notification of withdrawal from the ICC Statute, following the notification's annulment by the South African High Court.[89]

From the preceding, the AG pondered whether the aforementioned practice and the fact that Article 68 VCLT was adopted without any dissenting vote could be sufficient evidence that the revocation rule enshrined in Article 68 VCLT had achieved customary law status, only to conclude that he does not consider that to be the case.[90]

In that case, and since in the AG's view Article 68 is of dubious customary law nature and cannot be applied directly to the TEU as a VCLT provision,[91] Article 68 could not be resorted to as applicable law. However, perhaps it can be used as a 'supplementary means of interpretation' in order to determine the meaning of Article 50 TEU. Although the AG does not make this clear, simply referring to the widely diverse nature of documents that the CJEU has on occasion relied in its interpretative exercise,[92] this is the only logical option, considering that

[87] Which was reversed by virtue of a judgment of the Supreme Court of Justice of Panama: *Demanda de inconstitucionalidad contra la Ley no. 78 de 11 de diciembre de 2009* (2 February 2012) Corte Suprema de Justicia de Panamá (Pleno) (Supreme Court of Justice, Panama (Plenary session)) <https://vlex.com.pa/vid/accion-inconstitucionalidad-sala-pleno-375091942?_ga= 2.13901559.115975578.1539971406-1717765214.1539971406> accessed 19 September 2019.

[88] 1998 Rome Statute of the International Criminal Court (adopted 17 July 1998, entered into force 1 July 2002) 2187 UNTS 3.

[89] *Democratic Alliance v Minister of International Relations and Cooperation* (22 February 2017) High Court of South Africa (Gauteng Division, Pretoria), Case No 83145/2016, 3 SA 212 (GP).

[90] *Wightman* (AG Opinion) [71–6]; however, cf H Krieger, 'Article 68' in Dörr and Schmalenbach (eds), *Vienna Convention on the Law of Treaties* 1259 [3], who argues that 'as far as the basic notification requirement is concerned *there are indications for its customary international law character*' (emphasis added); see also A Tzanakopoulos, 'Article 68' in Corten and Klein (eds), *The Vienna Conventions on the Law of Treaties* 1564 [3–4].

[91] Because some EU States are not parties to the VCLT, such as France and Romania. See also Art 4 VCLT, which establishes the principle of non-retroactivity.

[92] *Wightman* (AG Opinion) [82–4].

Article 68 would not fit easily in any of the other categories of Article 31, eg it is not subsequent practice under Article 31(3)(b) as it does not reflect the intention of all the parties, nor is it a 'relevant rule' under Article 31(3)(c), since if we follow the AG's view it is not customary law, and binding only between certain of the EU member States.[93] The AG does not categorise exactly the interpretative type of Article 68, although later on he *in passim* refers to using the VCLT by analogy.[94] This judicial exercise is completely absent in the CJEU's judgment, which mainly focuses on the constitutional character of the EU treaties and the autonomy of its legal order to segue into interpretation, only referring to the VCLT *in passim* to corroborate a previously arrived at interpretative conclusion.[95]

This notwithstanding, both the AG and the CJEU rely to a greater or lesser degree on Article 68 VCLT, in combination with Articles 65 and 67 VCLT, for their interpretation. It could be questioned whether Articles 65, 67, and 68 VCLT could be taken into account, since they regulate unilateral revocation only if withdrawal occurs under Articles 65–67. According to Vidmar, it is debatable whether Article 68 applies 'to all treaties or only to those that do not contain specific withdrawal provisions'.[96] In his view, 'Article 50 TEU would appear to clearly fall under Article 54(a) Vienna Convention and thus quite possibly outside the scope of Article 68 Vienna Convention'.[97] However, given the residual nature of these articles, which was repeatedly underlined by the ILC members, such an interpretation would seem to be too restrictive and not necessarily in conformity with their gap-filling role, which would be triggered anytime a situation not envisaged by a withdrawal clause in a treaty emerged.

This intuitively leads us to the second level of the AG's analysis, where he undertakes a literal, contextual, teleological, and historical interpretation of Article 50 TEU, to conclude that the revocability of the notification of withdrawal is consistent with the objective of Article 50 and the TEU *in toto*, whereas opting for irrevocability would lead to absurd

[93] It would also possibly fail other manifestations of the 'proximity criterion'; see Merkouris, *Article 31(3)(c) VCLT*, ch 1.

[94] ibid [108]; a *per analogiam* interpretation, which also would fall under the customary law equivalent of Art 32 VCLT.

[95] *Wightman* (CJEU Judgment) [38–47] and especially [70].

[96] Vidmar, 'Unilateral Revocability in *Wightman*' 369.

[97] ibid 370.

results, such as a *de facto* expulsion of the notifying State,[98] despite the fact that it had changed its mind.[99] In the view of the authors of this book, the AG was correct in referring to Articles 31–32 VCLT as a reflection of customary law. The argument is often made that the TEU and the TFEU are *sui generis* instruments that, due to the autonomous order of the EU and their inherently unique 'nature', should be treated and interpreted more as constitutional instruments than as treaties.[100]

In this context, Vidmar criticises the CJEU for failing 'to completely assuage the treaty law/constitutional law tension inherent to Article 50'.[101] However, he also concedes that a strictly constitutional approach is not only problematic itself but also might have deleterious effects on the stability of the EU system. First and foremost, it is problematic because withdrawal from a constitutional perspective would be similar to secession. However, secession mechanisms are unusual in constitutions,[102] hence it makes much more sense to resort to classical treaty mechanisms. Second, it could have deleterious effects for the stability of the EU system because a constitutional approach would not have allowed the CJEU to make such a 'vital authoritative statement of the dual-purpose of Article 50 TEU',[103] let alone arrive at a conclusion that allows the 'subject' to change its view unilaterally. This is more akin to a classical treaty structure rather than a constitutional arrangement.[104] In any event, this discussion is *nihil novum sub sole*. Even in the 1950s and 1960s when the Institut and the ILC were discussing the rules of interpretation, the argument was often made that certain types of treaties, due

98 Which had been considered and rejected during the *travaux*. It would also be against the principles of good faith, loyal cooperation (Art 4(3) TEU), the EU's values (Art 2 TEU), and its commitment to respect the Member States' constitutional identities (Art 4(2) TEU); Eeckhout and Frantziou 'Brexit and Article 50 TEU' 714.

99 *Wightman* (AG Opinion) [90–141].

100 Papageorgiou, 'The (Ir-)revocability of the Withdrawal Notification' 15 ff.

101 Vidmar 'Unilateral Revocability in *Wightman*' 374.

102 ibid.

103 Garner 'Case C-621/18'; The dual purpose being: (i) enshrining the sovereign right of a Member State to withdraw from the European Union and (ii) establishing a procedure to enable such a withdrawal to take place in an orderly fashion; *Wightman* (CJEU Judgment) [56].

104 Although Vidmar does not completely abandon this constitutional approach, stating that from a certain point of view, '[u]nilateral revocability adds, however, to the constitutional puzzle which ensures that a State can still deliberate and change its mind on the basis of the democratic process; "secession" from the EU legal order does, after all, have far-reaching consequences for the State and EU citizens'; Vidmar, 'Unilateral Revocability in *Wightman*' 374.

to their 'unique', *sui generis* or self-contained nature, were subject to particular rules of interpretation, which were different from those that applied to the other ordinary treaties. Despite this, such arguments were consistently and summarily shut down, and the position has always been the same, rules of interpretation are the same for *all treaties*.[105]

Irrespective of one's view on the constitutional or not character of the TEU, the crux of both the Court's and the AG's interpretative analysis is that of the intention and its relevance in the withdrawal process envisaged in Article 50 TEU. According to the AG's Opinion, which was followed by the CJEU,

> Article 50(2) states that 'a Member State which decides to withdraw shall notify the European Council of its intention', thereby activating the second phase of the procedure. *The provision refers to the notification of the 'intention' to withdraw, and not to withdrawal itself*, because withdrawal may only occur after the agreement is reached or, in the absence of an agreement, after two years have elapsed.[106]

This distinction between 'withdrawal' and 'intention to withdraw' was drawn in *Minister for Justice and Equality v RO*.[107] In *Wightman* the distinction was further refined, with the AG suggesting that the intention of withdrawal is a mutable one, at least before the withdrawal becomes a fact. '*Intentions* are not definitive and may change'.[108] In a similar vein, the CJEU opined that '[a]n intention is, by its nature, neither definitive nor irrevocable'.[109] This focus on the intention of withdrawal rather than withdrawal itself has been the object of criticism. Since according to this interpretation, the 'intention of withdrawal' is the crucial element of Article 50, then 65 and 68 VCLT are not relevant, as they only refer to withdrawal but not to the 'intention of withdrawal'. 'If the intention to withdraw were a legal concept separate from the act of withdrawal itself . . . Article 50 TEU could not *prima facie* lie within the ambit of Article 68 Vienna Convention, as the latter does not deal with intentions, but only with actual withdrawal and withdrawal notifications'.[110] Furthermore, the way 'intention' is being used in *Wightman* is according to

105 Merkouris, '*In Dubio Mitius*' 271–2 and 278–89.
106 *Wightman* (AG Opinion) [99] (emphasis added).
107 *Case C-327/18 – PPU, Minister for Justice and Equality v RO* [2018] ECLI:EU:C:2018:733 [46]; see also Vidmar 'Unilateral Revocability in *Wightman*' 364–5.
108 *Wightman* (AG Opinion) [100] (emphasis in the original).
109 *Wightman* (CJEU Judgment) [49].
110 Vidmar 'Unilateral Revocability in *Wightman*' 370.

this line of criticism not in line with the ordinary meaning of the term in treaty law, corroborated by the fact that although the term 'intention' is used multiple times in the VCLT, 'on no occasion does it support the view that "intentions are not definite and may change"'.[111] This last claim, however, is debatable. Perhaps in the text of the VCLT the concept of changing intentions may not emerge with ease, however in the Vienna Conference on the Law of Treaties this concept was raised by a number of delegates. Especially, in one case, it was raised with respect to provisional application, and the change of the intention of the party prior to the entry into force of the treaty, which bears a striking similarity with the time-limits and the process of Article 50 TEU.[112]

> [Eustathiades, the delegate from Greece, said that] . . . [t]he provisions of paragraph 2, which were intended as a safety valve, could paradoxically give rise to insecurity. They raised the question *whether the intention expressed by a State that it did not wish to become a party to the treaty would be taken as final.* Actually, in a parliamentary system, it was possible for a government *to change its mind* and to express a *different intention at a later stage.* Accordingly, under the provisions of paragraph 2, a State which had accepted the provisional application of a treaty would be able to suspend that application *by expressing the intention not to become a party, although that intention need not be final.*[113]

As is evident from the above, the changing of intention was not an entirely foreign concept to the drafters of the VCLT and, thus, the reasoning of the AG and the CJEU is not in clear contradistinction with the ordinary meaning of the term 'intention'.

Having arrived at an interpretative outcome, the AG at the third level of his analysis specified certain limits to the use of this right of unilateral revocation. Amongst these, the most critical is avoiding the abuse of the right.[114] The CJEU only briefly gave a nod to this topic when addressing the concerns of the Council and the Commission,[115] but did not deem it a risk worthy of extensive analysis.

[111] ibid 367, 368.

[112] United Nations Conference on the Law of Treaties, '1st Session – 19th Meeting of the Committee of the Whole (COW)' (9 April 1968) UN Doc A/CONF.39/C.1/SR.19 97, 98 [21] (Plana), 99 [28] (Rusad); on discussions relating to Draft Article 15 'Article 15 (Obligation of a State not to frustrate the object of a treaty prior to its entry into force)'.

[113] United Nations Conference on the Law of Treaties, '2nd Session – 11th Plenary Meeting' (30 April 1969) UN Doc A/CONF.39/SR.11 35, 41 [75] (Eustathiades).

[114] *Wightman* (AG Opinion) [149–56]; for more on *abus de droit* in EU law, see A Saydé, 'Defining the Concept of Abuse of Union Law' (2014) 33/1 YEL 138.

[115] *Wightman* (CJEU Judgment) [39], [68].

According to Georgopoulos, although the AG was by and large correct in arguing that existence of a right to revocation, that is less so in the case of unilateral revocation, as it 'raises the risk of "casualisation" of the withdrawal process'.[116] In the AG's view, the scenario where the right of unilateral revocation could be abused would arise 'only when a second notification of the intention to withdraw is submitted'.[117] However, there is a small loophole in this construct. The *abus de droit* would emerge only at the moment of that second notification. But if the intention to abuse the process existed already at the moment of the first notification, or at least during the revocation of the notification, then the State could be allowed to abuse the right without any consequences, until, and even then not certainly, the second notification.[118]

6.4 Anomalous Termination/Suspension of a Treaty

In the previous section we examined how the *Wightman* case demonstrated the ongoing motion of treaty law relating to withdrawal from a treaty, and the ever-continuing process toward greater specificity. Despite the complex landscape that our short sortie in the withdrawal provisions revealed, objectively speaking, in the *Wightman* case the situation was made slightly easier by the existence of a withdrawal provision in the EU Treaties. However, as already observed, this is not always the case with respect to international treaties in force. For instance, in the *Gabčikovo-Nagymaros Project* judgment the lack of a withdrawal or denunciation provision in the 1977 Treaty inexorably led the Court to examine the possibility of termination of a treaty first by agreement of all the parties, and failing that by unilateral invocation of a ground for termination/suspension. The Court's judgment in this respect is a veritable *tour de force* of grounds of termination of treaties. If the consent (as for instance in Article 57(b) VCLT) is the pillar of the international legal system, and should be the ordinary manner of conducting oneself even in the context

116 A Georgopoulos, 'The (Ir)revocability of Article 50 TEU (C-621/18 *Wightman*): Iphigenia Must Reach the Altar' (*SSRN*, 8 December 2018) <https://papers.ssrn.com/sol3/Delivery.cfm/SSRN_ID3298401_code734328.pdf?abstractid=3298401&mirid=1> accessed 20 September 2019, 2. For similar concerns, see also R McCrea, 'Brexit II? The Legal Issues of Revoking the Notification to Leave the EU but Then Notifying to Leave Again' (*EU Law Analysis Blog*, 16 December 2018) <http://eulawanalysis.blogspot.com/2018/12/brexit-ii-legal-issues-of-revoking.html> accessed 20 September 2019.

117 *Wightman* (AG Opinion) [155].

118 On similar criticisms on the issue of *abus de droit*, see McCrea, 'Brexit II?'.

of termination/suspension, then the ways in which a treaty can be terminated/suspended starting with an invocation of a relevant ground could be, somewhat harshly, characterised as anomalous ones.

In this section, we deal with the most interesting, from the perspective of 'motion', anomalous grounds for termination/suspension of treaties.[119] This includes not only 'motion'-relevant *intra*-VCLT grounds, but also similar grounds that allegedly exist *praeter*-VCLT. In the latter category belong desuetude and *exceptio non adimpleti contractus.* The former is relevant because motion and change through time is intrinsically linked to its core of existence. Desuetude refers to abrogation from treaties by virtue of lapse of a significant amount of time.[120] *Exceptio non adimpleti contractus,*[121] on the other hand, has always had a troubled history. Strictly speaking, the *exceptio non adimpleti contractus* is not a ground for termination/suspension but rather a defence for non-performance. However, recently it has been on the receiving end of a revived interest, both in academic scholarship and international dispute settlement, as to its normative status, content, and interplay with the VCLT-permitted grounds for treaty termination/suspension, most notably material breach. It is this unclear relationship with the latter, that makes it fit within the scope of this chapter, as very motion-sensitive, not to mention that non-performance itself is a form of partial *phthora*[122] of the treaty.

The analysis of these grounds will then be followed by an examination of how the 'motion'-relevant grounds included in the VCLT, mainly impossibility of performance, fundamental change of circumstances, and material breach, have changed/moved both during and after their inclusion in the VCLT. This chapter concludes in Section 6.5 with examining the 'motion' of all these grounds with respect to an entirely

[119] It is for this reason, that not all VCLT grounds for treaty termination have been analysed. The relevance to the concept of 'motion' was determined not only by how much the content of these grounds has moved, but also by how much they have moved with respect to one another, as well as with respect to other sets of international legal rules, mainly State responsibility. This last part is the focus of Section 6.5 of this chapter. The same considerations led the authors as well to not analyse the grounds for invalidity of treaties. Not only are these grounds not so representative from the perspective of motion, but also the grounds that lead to absolute nullity of a treaty, cannot even count as *phthora* since there was no *genesis* of a treaty to begin with. No 'motion' ever took place.

[120] Although there are other elements that need to be in play as well, see Section 6.4.1.1.

[121] For reasons of simplicity, *exceptio* from this point onwards.

[122] Of a potential reversible nature.

different area of international law, ie State responsibility, in order to demonstrate that 'motion' can be understood not only as motion through time and as change of one's content but also in relation to identifying the hard, soft, or no lines at all, between different sets of legal rules, law of treaties and State responsibility.

6.4.1 Praeter-*VCLT Grounds for Treaty Termination/Suspension or Non-Performance*

6.4.1.1 Desuetude

Although Nolte recently raised the fact that treaties may be subject to desuetude or obsolescence,[123] desuetude is a concept notoriously difficult to define clearly and concisely. *Lato sensu,* we can speak of desuetude applying to customary rules as well; however, for the purpose of keeping with the theme of this book, we will focus on desuetude as an alleged ground for termination of treaties. Most attempts at circumscribing the notion of desuetude focus on two main elements, an objective and a subjective one. The objective one is the protracted non-application of the rule in question, either through abstention or divergent practice of the parties. The subjective one is that this non-application should be complemented by 'an opinion of the subjects in question that accept this state of things as being in accordance with the law, an opinion that is *usually* configured as a tacit agreement',[124] a *consuetudo abrogatoria.*[125]

[123] ILC, 'Annex A. Treaties over time in particular: Subsequent Agreement and Practice', reproduced in [2008/II – Part Two] YBILC 152, 153 [10].

[124] Kolb, 'La désuétude' 578 (author's translation, emphasis added). Although Cohen argues that the main idea behind desuetude is the termination of treaties by virtue of the passing of a considerable lapse of time during which the treaty is not applied by the treaty parties. Desuetude as focusing on the tacit accord of States 'is not the only possible understanding of desuetude and it is certainly not the traditional understanding of desuetude since post-classical Roman Law'; MG Cohen, 'Desuetude and Obsolescence of Treaties' in Cannizzaro (ed), *The Law of Treaties Beyond the Vienna Convention* 350, 351–2; see also AA Schiller, 'Custom in Classical Roman Law', (1937) 24 VaLRev 268.

[125] Kolb, 'La désuétude' 579; Vamvoukos, *Termination of Treaties in International Law* 221; G Hafner, 'L' "obsolescence" de certaines dispositions du traité autrichien de 1955' (1991) 37 AFDI 239; B Simma, 'Termination and Suspension of Treaties: Two Recent Austrian Cases' (1978) 21 GYIL 74. Cohen argues that '*[d]esuetudo* being, in a sense, the flipside of *consuetudo*, this negative practice must be coupled with an *opinio juris*, in other words, the conviction by the parties that the treaty has been extinguished'; Cohen, 'Desuetude and Obsolescence of Treaties' 352. On the identity of effects of simple inobservance of a rule and the practice contrary thereto, see: F Geny, *Méthode d' interprétation et sources en droit privé positif: Essai critique*, Vol I (LGDJ 1954) 406–7.

Depending on the author, different weight is given to each of these two elements. Although a combination of both is the standard,[126] the consensualist approach, ie the one focusing slightly more on the tacit accord (or a form of *opinio juris*) of the parties seems to be the more dominant one. This seems to be quite reasonable, since although 'we can always dread the exhumation of a mummified treaty',[127] just the lapse of a significant amount of time is by no means a guarantee that a treaty has fallen into desuetude.

Fitzmaurice in his 'Second Report', for instance, stated that 'it would be possible to point to a number of treaties centuries old, framed in archaic language, and seldom invoked in terms or referred to by the parties, which the latter nevertheless regard as being still in force and effective'.[128] In a similar vein, Judge de Castro in his Dissenting Opinion in the *Nuclear Tests* cases suggested that the non-invocation of a treaty may actually not be a sign of its desuetude but rather the opposite, a sign of its effectiveness. 'The non- invocation of a treaty may in fact be due to its efficacy in obviating disputes between the parties – and thereby constitute the best evidence of its continuance in force'.[129]

Cohen, as well, gives as an example a list of treaties concluded by France and still in force published by the French Ministry of Foreign Affairs. The earliest one 'still notified as being in force between France and Switzerland is that of 30 October 1564, concluded by Duke Emmanuel-Philibert of Savoy and the City of Bern, concerning the restitution by Bern of parts of Savoy conquered in 1536'.[130]

International jurisprudence is also no stranger to applying old treaties, as has happened in *Sovereignty over Pulau Litigan and Pulau Sipadan*, where the 1891 Convention between Great Britain and the Netherlands Defining Boundaries in Borneo was the focus;[131] *Kasikili/Sedudu Island*, where the

126 See Vamvoukos, *Termination of Treaties in International Law* 260.

127 G Scelle, 'Règles générales du droit de la paix' (1933/IV) 46 RdC 327, 418.

128 Fitzmaurice, 'Second Report' Commentary to Art 15, 48 [86]; giving the examples of British seventeenth-century treaties with Denmark, Spain, and Sweden, which were reproduced in Foreign Office, *Handbook of Commercial Treaties etc, With Foreign Powers* (4th edn, HM Stationery Office 1931).

129 *Nuclear Tests (Australia v France)* Dissenting Opinion of Judge de Castro 381 fn 1.

130 Cohen, 'Desuetude and Obsolescence of Treaties' 355 (emphasis added), referring to MF Surbiguet and P Vagogne, *Liste des traites et accords de la France en vigueur au 1er octobre 1988* (Ministère des Affaires étrangères 1988) 309.

131 *Sovereignty over Pulau Litigan and Pulau Sipadan* [37–61].

1890 Anglo-German Treaty was being applied;[132] *Dispute Regarding Navigational and Related Rights*, where the ICJ applied the 1858 Treaty of Limits;[133] *Sovereignty over Pedra Branca/Pulau Batu Puteh*, where the Court referred to the 1814 and 1824 Anglo-Dutch Treaties;[134] and the *Right of Passage*, where the Court examined the 1779 Treaty of Poona.[135]

As Kolb notes, both constitutive elements of desuetude hark back to other legal notions. The first element is reminiscent of the process of customary law formation, whereas the second one approaches a 'juridical act' which is manifested in an intention more or less instant, although tacit.[136]

Desuetude is often used interchangeably with obsolescence. Even in the ILC, the terms were either used in that manner, or were almost always mentioned together.[137] International adjudication is no different. In *Nuclear Tests* and in *Legality of Use of Force*, the representatives of France and Belgium, respectively, seemed to use these terms interchangeably.[138]

Despite the inherent difficulties in tracing the *differentia specifica* between these two concepts, Cohen argues that

> it is important to distinguish desuetude from obsolescence, which is a distinct concept. Obsolescence (either called *obsolescence* or *caducité* in French) refers to the impossibility of applying a treaty due to the disappearance of a legal situation which constituted one of its essential conditions. In contrast to Article 61 of the Vienna Convention, which deals with the *material impossibility* of performance due to the disappearance of an object indispensable for the performance of a treaty, in the case of obsolescence what is at issue is a *legal impossibility*. An example of such a scenario is found in the reference to 'Enemy States' contained in Articles 53, 106, and 107 of the United Nations Charter.[139]

132 *Kasikili/Sedudu Island* [18–20].
133 *Dispute Regarding Navigational and Related Rights* [47].
134 *Sovereignty over Pedra Branca/Pulau Batu Puteh, Middle Rocks, and South Ledge (Malaysia/Singapore)* (Judgment) [2008] ICJ Rep 12 [20–3], [81–101].
135 *Right of Passage over Indian Territory (Portugal v India)* (Merits) [1960] ICJ Rep 6, 37.
136 Kolb, 'La désuétude' 578.
137 ILC, 'Summary Record of the 847th Meeting' (9 May 1966) UN Doc A/CN.4/SR.847 [76] (Rosenne); ILC, 'Summary Record of the 848th Meeting' [15] (Waldock); ILC, 'Summary Record of the 857th Meeting' [8] Waldock); ILC, 'Summary Record of the 866th Meeting' [60] (Rosenne); ILC, 'Summary Record of the 888th Meeting' (12 July 1966) UN Doc A/CN.4/SR.888 [30] (Ago).
138 See documents cited in Cohen, 'Desuetude and Obsolescence of Treaties' fn 24.
139 Cohen, 'Desuetude and Obsolescence of Treaties' 358. For similar attempts to distinguish between desuetude and obsolescence, see Kolb, 'La désuétude' 592–3; G Le Floch, 'La désuétude en droit international public' (2007) 111/3 RGDIP 609, 624–6.

As if this were not already complicated, Kolb suggests that desuetude is often conflated with no less than eight different notions.[140] These are: obsolescence, *rebus sic stantibus*,[141] *caducité*,[142] *mort-nés* texts, *vétusté*, prescription, material impossibility of execution, and false desuetudes.[143]

The ILC may not have reached the same level of complexity as Kolb, but its members were well aware of the connection between desuetude and fundamental change of circumstances,[144] and one member (Rosenne) even alluded to a connection between desuetude and *inter se* modification.[145] Despite this complexity, during the debate within the ILC, as to whether to include desuetude as a separate ground for termination, the idea was not adverse to a number of its members.[146] Israel as well had offered its support to its inclusion.[147]

Fitzmaurice in his 'Second Report' had this to say on the concept of mutual desuetude:

> Obsolescence is sometimes ranked as a ground terminative of treaties by lapse. But although *such cases may involve circumstances* rendering it possible to invoke some other principle of law conducing to termination, *such as physical impossibility of further performance, the Rapporteur does not believe that there is any objective principle of law terminative of treaties on the mere ground of age, obsolescence, or desuetude as such.* Indeed, it would be possible to point to a number of treaties centuries old . . . still in force and effective. On the other hand, where the parties themselves, without denouncing or purporting actually to terminate the treaty, have, over a long period, conducted themselves in relation to it more or less as though it did not exist, by failing to apply or invoke it, or by other conduct evincing lack of interest in or reliance on it, it may be said that there exists what amounts to a tacit agreement of the parties, by conduct, to disregard

140 And argues that for this reason an *actum finium regundorum* would be of great practical use; Kolb, 'La désuétude' 589.

141 See in more detail Section 6.5.1.1.

142 The difference between desuetude and *caducite* is that the latter focuses on the result of the extinction, whereas the former describes the process through which particular treaty obligations become extinct; Kolb, 'La désuétude' 592. According to Scelle, when invoking desuetude 'a treaty is abrogated through a contrary negative customary rule' whereas a treaty that is destroyed through *caducité* is a treaty that is 'in contradiction with social necessity'; Scelle, 'Règles générales du droit de la paix' 630. On the difficulty distinguishing between desuetude and *caducite*, see A Goellner, *Pre-caducité, caducité et désuétude en matiere de droit international public (essai juridique)* (Rousseau 1939).

143 Kolb, 'La désuétude' 589–98; see also Le Floch, 'La désuétude' 621–6.

144 See Section 6.5.1.1.

145 ILC, 'Summary Record of the 866th Meeting' [60] (Rosenne).

146 ILC, 'Summary Record of the 847th Meeting' [76] (Rosenne, also referring to Verdross).

147 Waldock, 'Sixth Report' 75 (Israel).

> the treaty and to consider it as being at an end. In such event, however, *the basis of the termination would be the presumption of a tacit agreement of the parties* – or, alternatively, of an assent to or acceptance by each party of the non-application of the treaty by the other – and not age or desuetude as such, although the latter would be relevant factors in estimating the real attitude and intentions of the parties.[148]

Several times the members of the ILC returned again and again to the fact that desuetude was not a legally separate ground for termination, but rather the real ground for termination existed in the implied agreement / tacit consent of the parties.[149] How this implied agreement was to be proven was always a situational determination, although at one point it was suggested that even the nature/character of the treaty could offer assistance in making such a determination.[150]

An additional condition for establishing whether tacit consent exists is also that this should emerge from the acts of the State and not be merely inferred through the actions of its own citizens. In *Yuille, Shortridge & Co*, for instance, the critical issue was the argument raised by Portugal, ie that because British citizens had not used the Anglo-Portuguese Treaty of 1654,[151] the treaty had fallen into desuetude. However, the Senate of the Free City of Hamburg was of the view that the (in)action of the citizens was irrelevant for the purposes of invoking desuetude. The inaction had to be attributable to the State itself. It would have been an entirely different story if the UK itself had refused to its citizens the application of the treaty despite their requests on the basis of desuetude.[152]

Waldock's comments in ILC's 857th meeting sum up beautifully most of the key issues with respect to desuetude: (i) the terms 'obsolescence' and 'desuetude' are used interchangeably; (ii) desuetude is considered as partially covered by other provisions, such as fundamental change of circumstances[153] and the tacit agreement of the parties, as provided, for

148 Fitzmaurice, 'Second Report' Commentary to Art 15, 48 [86] (emphasis added).

149 ILC, 'Summary Record of the 857th Meeting' (24 May 1966) UN Doc A/CN.4/SR.857 [8] (Waldock), [48] (Briggs); ILC, 'Summary Record of the 876th Meeting' [94] (Waldock); ILC, 'Summary Record of the 888th Meeting' [30] (Ago); Waldock, 'Sixth Report' 76 [7].

150 Fitzmaurice, 'Second Report' Commentary to Art 15 [88].

151 1654 Treaty of Peace and Alliance between Portugal and Great Britain (adopted 10–20 July 1654, entered into force 6 July 1656) in S Whatley, *A General Collection of Treatys, Declarations of War, Manifestos, and Other Publick* [*sic*] *Papers Relating to Peace and War* Vol III (JJ and P Knapton and Others 1732) 97.

152 *Yuille, Shortridge & Co (Great Britain v Portugal)* (1861) 29 UNRIAA 57, 65.

153 This will be analysed in Section 6.5.1.1.

instance, in Article 54(b) VCLT; (iii) the question of whether desuetude is a clearly distinguishable ground for termination of treaties or not.[154] Waldock was of the view that desuetude was not a ground for termination but rather '*a factual cause of termination which had to be founded on the tacit agreement of the parties to allow the treaty to fall*'.[155] In the end, this view prevailed without much difficulty and desuetude was not included in the text of the VCLT.

International jurisprudence as well does not lend much support to the autonomy of desuetude as a ground for termination. Most of the times, courts avoid pronouncing on the issue,[156] and when they do the focus is on the need to infer from the conduct of the States a tacit accord.[157]

Kolb suggests a logical schema to try and explicate the not-so-broad use of desuetude. In his view, there are four possible scenarios: (i) a treaty rule is being abrogated through a later treaty rule; (ii) a treaty rule is being abrogated through a later customary rule; (iii) a customary rule is being abrogated by a treaty rule; and (iv) a customary rule is being abrogated by a later customary rule. Scenarios (i) and (iii) fall outside the scope of desuetude, as according to Kolb the accord must be tacit. If we have a treaty rule, then it is explicit and there is no need for resorting to desuetude.[158] Similar considerations apply to scenario (iv). Since customary law's existence is continuously based and determined by the existing practice, this scenario would not need a new negative custom to emerge, but rather the existing practice to fail to meet any more the required criteria of being widespread, representative, consistent, and uniform. This leaves desuetude with only scenario (ii) as a scope of application. In that case, Kolb posits, desuetude would be equated to a negative custom,[159] and

154 ILC, 'Summary Record of the 848th Meeting' [15] (Waldock).

155 ibid [15] (Waldock) (emphasis added); see also ILC, 'Summary Record of the 857th Meeting' (24 May 1966) UN Doc A/CN.4/SR.857 [8] (Waldock), [48] (Briggs); ILC, 'Summary Record of the 876th Meeting' [94] (Waldock); ILC, 'Summary Record of the 888th Meeting' [30] (Ago); Waldock, 'Sixth Report' 76 [7].

156 *Legality of the Use of Force (Serbia and Montenegro v Belgium)* [126]; *Aegean Sea Continental Shelf* [39]; *Aerial Incident of 10 August 1999 (Pakistan v India)* (Jurisdiction) [2000] ICJ Rep 12 [28].

157 *Yuille, Shortridge & Co* 65; *Land Sale to Alien Case (1) (Amend v Land Tirol)* (13 March 1973) Constitutional Court (Austria) Case No B 103/71, 77 ILR 433; *Amoco International Finance Corp v Iran* (14 July 1987) Iran–US Claims Tribunal, 15 Iran-USCTR 189 [97]; *Nuclear Tests (Australia v France)* Joint Dissenting Opinion of Judges Onyeama, Dillard, Jiménez de Aréchaga, and Sir Humphrey Waldock [53].

158 For scenario (i), see also Cohen, 'Desuetude and Obsolescence of Treaties' 352–3.

159 Kolb, 'La désuétude' 606–7.

thus desuetude is characterised by three cumulative elements: (i) *time*, since a significant passage of time would be required; (ii) the *negative nature of the customary rule* relating to desuetude; and (iii) the '*unidirectional non-parallelism of the sources*' which emerges from the fact that only scenario (ii) is relevant for desuetude.[160] Other authors, on the other hand, do not even concede that limited scope of application for desuetude, simply declaring that desuetude does not constitute a ground for termination of treaties that exists in general international law.[161] In any event, as shown from the previous analysis, desuetude is at the crossroads of multiple other processes, so much so in fact that it might be difficult to believe in its real autonomy.[162]

6.4.1.2 *Exceptio Inadimpleti Contractus*

In the case of obligations of a synallagmatic nature, a party may justifiably refuse to respect its obligations when the other party refuses to honour them.[163] This is the generally accepted definition of the *exceptio*.

Crawford and Olleson have argued that despite its Latin tag, the *exceptio*

> in its widest form, expressed by the maxim *inadimplenti non est adimplendum*, does not appear to have been recognised as a general principle by Roman law. Rather, it seems to have been extracted from certain specific instances, particularly the *exceptio mercis non traditae* ... It was only later that a general rule was extrapolated from these particular instances by the glossators and their followers.[164]

A detailed analysis of its roots in the interpretation of Roman law, its application in various domestic legal systems,[165] and the discussions in the ILC[166] falls outside the scope of this chapter. What we focus on in this and the following sections is certain critical elements as to the nature

[160] ibid 604–5.
[161] Cohen, 'Desuetude and Obsolescence of Treaties' 359; Vamvoukos, *Termination of Treaties in International Law* 302–3; Le Floch, 'La désuétude' 640–1.
[162] Le Floch, 'La désuétude' 640.
[163] Waldock 'Second Report' Commentary to Art 20.
[164] J Crawford and S Olleson, 'The Exception of Non-Performance: Links between the Law of Treaties and the State Responsibility' (2000) 21 AYBIL 55, 66.
[165] M Fitzmaurice, 'Angst of the *Exceptio Inadimplenti Non Est Adimplendum* in International Law' in L Bartels and F Paddeu (eds), *Exceptions in International Law* (OUP 2020) (on file with the author).
[166] M Xiouri, 'The *Exceptio Non Adimpleti Contractus* in Public International Law' (2019) 21 ICLR 56, 60–5.

and conditions of application of the *exceptio* (Section 6.4.1.2) and its point of contact with material breach (Section 6.5.1.2) and State responsibility (Section 6.5.2.2).

Fitzmaurice viewed the *exceptio* as a manifestation of reciprocity,[167] the latter being a condition in all treaties of the 'reciprocal' or 'interdependent' type.[168] The *exceptio* in its alleged individual form, and not in that which has been incorporated and circumscribed in Article 60 VCLT,[169] is a *defence*, which allows for non-performance of obligations, but does not *per se* affect the legal effect of the treaty.[170] However, international case law is not consistent on this matter, with the tribunal in *Klöckner v Cameroon*, for instance, applying the *exceptio* as a general principle and a ground for termination,[171] and the *ad hoc* committee later on not applying it but acknowledging that it had a suspensive effect.[172]

The *exceptio* has been invoked multiple times in front of courts and tribunals by the parties to the dispute; however, it has rarely been considered by those judicial bodies,[173] so very little help can be gotten

[167] In fact, 'negative reciprocity'; B Simma and CJ Tams, 'Article 60' in Corten and Klein (eds), *The Vienna Conventions on the Law of Treaties* 1351 [3].

[168] G Fitzmaurice, 'Fourth Report on the Law of Treaties' (17 March 1959) UN Doc A/CN.4/120, reproduced in [1959/II] YBILC 37, 70 [102–3].

[169] On the two versions of the *exceptio*, see J Crawford, 'Second Report on State Responsibility' UN Doc A/CN.4/498 and Add.1–4, reproduced in [1999/II – Part One] YBILC 3 [326], [329] Art 30bis; referring also to *Case Concerning the Factory at Chorzów (Germany v Poland)* (Jurisdiction) PCIJ Rep Series A No 17, 31; see also *Gabčikovo-Nagymaros Project* [107], [110].

[170] Crawford, 'Second Report' [324].

[171] *Klöckner Industrie-Anlagen GmbH and Others v Cameroon and Société Camerounaise des Engrais,* (Award of 21 October 1983) ICSID Case No. ARB/81/2 [114 ff].

[172] *Klöckner Industrie-Anlagen GmbH and Others v Cameroon and Société Camerounaise des Engrais* (Decision by the *ad hoc* Committee on the Application for Annulment of 3 May 1985) ICSID Case No ARB/81/2 [170–1]; however, we need to point out that the *exceptio* may resemble suspension but it is qualitatively different; see T Giegerich, 'Article 60' in Dörr and Schmalenbach (eds), *Vienna Convention on the Law of Treaties* 1095 [72]; in more detail, see Crawford and Olleson, 'The Exception of Non-Performance' 62–6.

[173] *Burlington Resources Inc v Ecuador* (Decision on Reconsideration and Award of 7 February 2017) ICSID Case No ARB/08/5 [55]; *Malicorp Ltd v Egypt and Others* (19 February 2015) High Court of Justice, Queen's Bench Division [2015] EWHC 361 [70]; *Compañía de Aguas del Aconquija SA and Vivendi Universal SA v Argentina* (Decision on Request for Annulment of 20 August 2007) ICSID Case No ARB/97/3 [126]; *Hulley Enterprises Ltd v Russia* (Final Award) (2014) PCA Case No AA 226 [1360]; *Yukos Universal Ltd (UK – Isle of Man) v Russia* (Final Award) (2014) PCA Case No AA 227 [1360]; *Veteran Petroleum Ltd (Cyprus) v Russia* (Final Award) (2014) PCA

from that case law as to its nature. Although international courts have been reluctant to discuss the normativity of the *exceptio*, individual judges have been somewhat more open.[174] Famous is the quote by Judge Anzilloti in his Dissenting Opinion in the *Diversion of Water from the Meuse* case where he declared that the principle *inadimplenti non est adimplendum 'is so just, so equitable, so universally recognized that it must be applied in international relations* also. In any case, it is one of these "general principles of law recognized by civilized nations" which the Court applies in virtue of Article 38 of its Statute'.[175] Many have shared Anzilloti's thoughts on the nature of the rule, as a general principle.[176]

Essentially, three are the main options as to the normative nature of the *exceptio*. Either it is a non-binding rule,[177] or a rule of customary international law,[178] or a general principle in the sense of Article 38(1)(c)

Case No AA 228 [1360]; *Eureko BV v Poland* (Partial Award of 19 August 2005) <www.italaw.com/sites/default/files/case-documents/ita0308_0.pdf> accessed 20 September 2019 [167].

174 *Namibia Advisory Opinion*, Separate Opinion of Judge de Castro 213; *Appeal Relating to the Jurisdiction of the ICAO Council*, Separate Opinion of Judge de Castro 128–9 fn 1; *Nicaragua* (Merits), Dissenting Opinion of Judge Schwebel [240], [269].

175 *The Diversion of Water from the Meuse (Netherlands v Belgium)* [1937] PCIJ Rep Series A/B No 70, Dissenting Opinion of Judge Anzilotti 50 (emphasis added).

176 Fitzmaurice, 'Fourth Report' 70 [102–3]; *Namibia Advisory Opinion*, Separate Opinion of Judge de Castro 213; *The Diversion of Water from the Meuse*, Individual Opinion of Judge Hudson 77; *Compania de Aguas del Aconquija SA and Vivendi Universal SA v Argentina* (Award of 20 August 2007) ICSID Case No ARB/97/3 [7.5.28]; *Eureko BV v Poland* [176–84]; *Sapphire International Petroleums Ltd v National Iranian Oil Company* (Arbitral Award of 15 March 1963) 35 ILR 136, 175 and 181–5; *Application of the Interim Accord (FYROM v Greece)* (Counter-Memorial of Greece) (19 January 2010) <www.icj-cij.org/files/case-related/142/16356.pdf> [8.9]; *Azurix Corp v Argentina* (Award of 14 July 2006) ICSID Case No ARB/01/12 [260]. Following this award, Argentina submitted an application for annulment, on the basis that the tribunal modified applicable law by suggesting that the *exceptio* was part of Argentine law. However, the *ad hoc* committee rejected Argentine's objection, since in its view the tribunal had used *exceptio* as a treaty standard; *Azurix Corp v Argentina* (Decision on the Application for Annulment of Argentina of 1 September 2009) ICSID Case No. ARB/01/12 [167].

177 See Crawford and Olleson, who are of the view that the *exceptio* 'has not established an independent place as a rule or principle of international law'; Crawford and Olleson, 'The Exception of Non-Performance' 73. In *Eureko BV v Poland*, the tribunal mentioned that it would not decide on the matter of whether the exception of non-performance was a maxim of interpretation or a rule of international law; *Eureko BV v Poland* [177].

178 *INA Corporation v Iran* (12 August 1985) Iran–US Claims Tribunal, 8 Iran–USCTR 373, Dissenting Opinion of Judge Ameli 434; Giegerich analyses the *exceptio* as both rule of customary law and general principle, but considers that by now it has been codified and

of the ICJ Statute,[179] which serves a gap-filling role.[180] The clear tendency is to approach *exceptio* as a general principle that has been transposed into the international legal system and may or may not have been transformed into customary law. This is not without its controversies. Leaving aside the inherent difficulties in determining what exactly a principle under Article 38(1)(c) of the Statute is,[181] 'there are *significant differences between civil and common legal systems regarding the defence of non-performance* and … in civil law regimes it is much better developed. However, … [the] *exceptio* is a principle of domestic legal regimes both in civil law and to some extent in common law regimes'.[182] Judge Simma in *FYROM v Greece* latched on this multifariousness of the *exceptio* in different domestic legal systems in order to question 'the transferability of such a concept developed in *foro domestico* to the international legal plane, respectively the amendments that it will have to undergo in order for such a general principle to play a constructive role also at the international level'.[183]

The nature of the *exceptio* is not the only thing in motion. The conditions for triggering the *exceptio* are in a constant *kinesis* as well. The generally accepted definition of the *exceptio* requires that the obligations in question that are not being performed should be 'synallagmatic' in nature,[184] but how is this term to be interpreted? The frame of reference used is Fitzmaurice's typology of obligations. According to him, treaty obligations can be categorised into two main categories, reciprocal and non-reciprocal obligations. Each group can be further subdivided in two subcategories; reciprocal (or concessionary obligations) into bilateral or bilateralisable ones, and non-reciprocal obligations into integral[185] and interdependent ones.[186] Multilateral treaties

circumscribed by Art 60 VCLT; Giegerich, 'Article 60' [72–3]; generally on the debate surrounding the nature of the *exceptio*, see Xiouri, 'The *Exceptio*' 79–83.

179 See cases and authors cited above in fn 176.

180 F Fontanelli, 'The Invocation of the Exception of Non-Performance: A Case-Study on the Role and Application of General Principles of International Law of Contractual Origin' (2012) 1 CJICL 119, 128–30; similarly, see Fitzmaurice, 'Angst of the *Exceptio*', for a good faith and Dworkinian analysis of the *exceptio*.

181 A Pellet, 'Article 38' in A Zimmermann et al (eds), *The Statute of the International Court of Justice: A Commentary* (2nd edn, OUP 2012) 731; C Bassiouni, 'Functional Approach to "General Principles of International Law"' (1989–90) 11 MichJInt'lL 768.

182 Fitzmaurice, 'Angst of the *Exceptio*'.

183 *FYROM v Greece*, Separate Opinion of Judge Simma [13].

184 *The Diversion of Water from the Meuse*, Separate Opinion of Judge Altamira 38–9.

185 Fitzmaurice, 'Second Report' Art 18 [2].

186 ibid, Art 29(1)(iii).

of the reciprocating type are those 'providing for a mutual interchange of benefits between the parties, with rights and obligations for each involving specific treatment at the hands of and towards each of the others individually'.[187] Integral multilateral are those 'where the force of the obligation is self-existent, absolute and inherent for each party'[188] directed 'towards all the world rather than towards particular parties'[189] and 'do not lend themselves to differential application, but must be applied integrally'.[190] Treaties of the interdependent kind are those where 'performance by any party is necessarily dependent on an equal or corresponding performance by all the other parties'[191] and 'the participation of all the parties is a condition of the obligatory force of the treaty'.[192]

This roadmap on obligations offered by Fitzmaurice has informed all discussions regarding the scope of what is to be considered as synallagmatic. The application of the *exceptio* to obligations that are of the reciprocating type goes without question. What is debatable is whether the *exceptio* could in principle apply to integral or interdependent treaties. Riphagen, for one, referring to the *Namibia Advisory Opinion* in his 'Preliminary Report', was of the view that the *exceptio* could be applied even in non-reciprocal obligations.[193] Yet out of the non-reciprocal obligations, integral ones are generally accepted to fall outside the scope of the *exceptio*.[194] The question that remains still unresolved is whether independent obligations are covered or not by the *exceptio*. Doctrine is split on the issue, with some leaning in favour of their inclusion in the scope of application of the *exceptio*[195] on the

187 Fitzmaurice, 'Third Report' Art 18 [2].
188 ibid, Art 19.
189 Fitzmaurice, 'Second Report' 54.
190 ibid 55.
191 ibid Art 19(1) (ii)(b).
192 ibid Art 29(1)(iii).
193 W Riphagen, 'Preliminary Report on the Content, Forms and Degrees of International Responsibility' (1 April 1980) UN Doc A/CN.4/330, reproduced in [1980/II – Part One] YBILC 107, 118 [58], referring to *Namibia Advisory Opinion*, Separate Opinion of Judge de Castro 213.
194 Fitzmaurice, 'Second Report' 31, Art 19(1)(iv); Fitzmaurice, 'Fourth Report' 70; Crawford, 'Second Report' [327]; W Riphagen, 'Seventh Report on State Responsibility' (4 March and 23 April 1986) UN Doc A/CN.4/397 and Corr.1 & 2 and Add.1 & Corr.1, reproduced in [1986/II – Part One] YBILC 1, 5 [2].
195 Fitzmaurice, 'Fourth Report' 46.

basis that interdependent obligations are characterised by a 'global reciprocity',[196] and others not.[197]

Apart from the condition that the obligations must be synallagmatic in nature, another alleged condition is that there *must be a breach*, since if there is none then this is not an issue of application of the *exceptio* but rather a retorsion.[198] However, Capitant argues that the wrongfulness of the act is not a condition for the *exceptio*, as in domestic law wrongfulness is not required.[199] A similar discussion has also occurred with respect to material breach, which again shows the connection between material breach and the *exceptio*.[200]

Finally, one more condition which the ICJ characterised as the 'minimum condition' is that the party invoking the *exceptio* must demonstrate a connection between its response and the breach, ie that the non-performance of one party must be the *actual reason* why the other party also refuses to perform.[201]

An alleged advantage of the *exceptio* over material breach and countermeasures is that the *exceptio* is not hindered by the procedural obligations that they have to abide by.[202] In *Klöckner v Cameroon*, for instance, the tribunal found that the *exceptio* can be invoked at any time, even during judicial or arbitral proceedings, without giving prior notice of default to the non-performing party.[203] In the same case, the tribunal

196 L-A Sicilianos, 'The Classification of Obligations and the Multilateral Dimension of the Relations of International Responsibility' (2002) 13/5 EJIL 1127, 1135.

197 W Riphagen, 'Sixth Report on the Content, Forms and Degrees of International Responsibility' (2 April 1985) UN Doc A/CN.4/389 and Corr.1 & Corr.2, reproduced in [1985/II – Part One] YBILC 3, Arts 8 and 11(1)(a); DW Greig, 'Reciprocity, Proportionality, and the Law of Treaties' (1994) 34 VJIL 295, 381; M Matsushita et al (eds), *The World Trade Organization: Law, Practice, and Policy* (3rd edn, OUP 2015) 62.

198 Riphagen, 'Sixth Report' 17 [22], who considers this as a measure of retorsion; see also L-A Sicilianos, *Les réactions décentralisées à l' illicite: des contre-mesures à la légitime défense* (LGDJ 1990) 39–40.

199 H Capitant, *De la cause des obligations (contrats, engagements unilatéraux, legs)* (Dalloz 1927) 282. See on this also Xiouri, 'The *Exceptio*' 70.

200 Crawford, 'Second Report' [319]; see also Section 6.4.2.3 in this chapter.

201 *FYROM v Greece* [123], [161].

202 J Crawford, 'Third Report on State Responsibility' (15 March, 15 June, 10 and 18 July, and 4 August 2000) UN Doc A/CN.4/507 and Add. 1–4 [364]; ILC, 'Summary Record of the 845th Meeting' (5 May 1966) UN Doc A/CN.4/SR.845 [26] (Reuter); see also S Forlati, 'Reactions to Non-Performance of Treaties in International Law' (2012) 25/3 LJIL 759, 768–9.

203 *Klöckner and Others v Cameroon* (Award) [116]. The lack or existence of more relaxed procedural requirements has also been raised in the context of the interaction between material breach and countermeasures. On this topic and the criticisms to it, see analysis in Section 6.5.2.2.

also implied that proportionality, although not an express condition, was implicitly built in the system of the *exceptio*.[204] Of course, such a flexibility may be open to abuse. Judge Simma in *FYROM v Greece*, cautioned against this danger. 'Absent the leash of judicial control, our principle will thus become prone to abuse'.[205] This can easily be seen by the fact that the doctrine of *exceptio* is still rather amorphous, with a number of issues not even having been touched upon in international case law, such as for instance whether the *exceptio* can also be invoked in cases of poor performance of the synallagmatic obligation.[206] Thus, recourse would have to be had to various domestic legal systems to draw inspiration from them, in an eternal *kinesis* between the domestic and the international legal system.

6.4.2 Intra-*VCLT Grounds for Treaty Termination/Suspension*

6.4.2.1 Supervening Impossibility of Performance

Supervening impossibility of performance has not received as much attention as either material breach or fundamental change of circumstances.[207] The PCIJ as well does not offer much by way of substantial consolidation of this ground for termination/suspension. Supervening impossibility of performance was argued both in the *Case Concerning the Payment in Gold of the Brazilian Federal Loans* and the *Case Concerning the Payment of Various Serbian Loans Issued in France*, but the PCIJ rejected the claims in both of these cases.[208]

The ILC as well struggled to find real life examples. The majority of the discussions revolved mainly around theoretical scenarios. This led Special Rapporteur Waldock to comment that '[n]o doubt, any of these things may happen, but none of them has so far given rise to a leading case or diplomatic incident concerning the dissolution of treaties'.[209]

204 *Klöckner and Others v Cameroon* (Award) [170].
205 *FYROM v Greece*, Separate Opinion of Judge Simma [13].
206 JC de Wet, 'Die Sogenaamde "Exceptio Non Adimpleti Contractus" in die Praktyk van Vandaag' (1945) 9/4 THRR 239, 243 ff; see also *Klöckner and Others v Cameroon* (Award) [124 ff].
207 See, more extensively, M Fitzmaurice, 'Exceptional Circumstances and Treaty Commitments' in D Hollis (ed), *The Oxford Guide to Treaties* (OUP 2012) 605.
208 *Case Concerning the Payment in Gold of the Brazilian Federal Loans (France v Brazil)* PCIJ Rep Series A No 21, 120; *Case Concerning the Payment of Various Serbian Loans Issued in France (France v Serb-Croat-Slovene State)* PCIJ Rep Series A No 20, 39–40.
209 Waldock, 'Second Report' Commentary to Art 21, 79 [5].

Despite this, a few decades later in the *Gabčikovo-Nagymaros Project* case, the ICJ had no qualms in finding Article 61 VCLT as declaratory of customary international law.[210] What is extremely pertinent is that this case moved our understanding of supervening impossibility of performance by concretising two main aspects of it, namely the 'indispensable object' and 'permanent disappearance or destruction'. The latter concept and its connection to *force majeure* will be dealt with in detail in Section 6.5.2.1.

Hungary argued that the 'essential object' of the 1977 Treaty,[211] ie 'an economic joint investment which was consistent with environmental protection and which was operated by the two contracting parties jointly', had permanently disappeared and therefore the obligations of the 1977 Treaty were impossible to perform any longer.[212]

The Court, however, was not swayed by Hungary's interpretation of the customary law equivalent of Article 61(1) VCLT,[213] an interpretation supported neither by the text of the VCLT provisions nor by the ILC's preparatory work.[214] In the Court's view, Article 61(1) VCLT regulates the *absolute* impossibility of performance. Relative impossibility falls under Article 62 VCLT.[215] Even the 'impossibility to make certain payments because of serious financial difficulties'[216] was considered not to be of an exceptional enough character to fall under Article 61.

[210] *Gabčíkovo-Nagymaros Project* [99], [102–3].

[211] 1977 Treaty between the Hungarian People's Republic and the Czechoslovak Socialist Republic Concerning the Construction and Operation of the Gabčíkovo-Nagymaros System of Locks (adopted 16 September 1977, entered into force 30 June 1978) 1109 UNTS 235.

[212] *Gabčíkovo-Nagymaros Project* [103].

[213] What is interesting is that the ICJ actually uses the term 'interpretation', although what it applied was not Art 61 VCLT, but its customary law equivalent, since due to Art 4 VCLT, and the principle of non-retroactivity the VCLT was not applicable to the 1977 Treaty (the Court also confirmed this, *Gabčíkovo-Nagymaros Project* [46], [99]). Consequently, the ICJ was interpreting a customary rule. For an extensive analysis on the theoretical validity of interpretation of customary rules and case law in support of it, see Merkouris, *Article 31(3)(c) VCLT* 231–300; P Merkouris, 'Interpreting the Customary Rules on Interpretation' (2017) 19 ICLR 126.

[214] *Gabčíkovo-Nagymaros Project* [102].

[215] ILC, 'Summary Record of the 833rd Meeting' (18 January 1966) UN Doc A/CN.4/SR.833 [9-12] (de Luna).

[216] *Gabčíkovo-Nagymaros Project* [102] referring to the United Nations Conference on the Law of Treaties, '1st Session – 62nd Meeting of the Committee of the Whole (COW)'(9 May 1968) UN Doc A/CONF.39/C.1/SR.62 361 [2], where the representative of Mexico, while explicating the reason for the Mexican amendment proposal, referred to 'the impossibility to deliver an article by a given date owing to a strike, the closing of a port or a war, or of the possibility that a rich and powerful State, faced with temporary difficulties, might be obliged to suspend its payments'.

Following this approach of the drafters of the VCLT, the Court, in turn, felt it unnecessary to determine whether a legal regime fell within the scope of 'object' of Article 61 VCLT. Although, Waldock in his 'Second Report' in Draft Article 21 gave 'permanent disappearance of a legal . . . régime' as a ground for invoking supervening impossibility of performance,[217] this disappeared in later drafts. The reason was again that the ILC when dealing with 'object' focused, once more, on exceptional cases that required the extinction of the physical object to which the treaty related.[218] Since the alleged 'object' of the 1977 Treaty had neither been destroyed nor permanently disappeared, the Court for reasons of judicial economy felt that it was unnecessary to pursue the matter any further.[219]

Although the ICJ in *Gabčíkovo-Nagymaros Project* expounded on certain elements of supervening impossibility of performance as a ground for termination/suspension, it still remains relatively underutilised in international jurisprudence.[220]

6.4.2.2 Fundamental Change of Circumstances

Article 62 VCLT deals with the notion of fundamental change of circumstances, also known as the doctrine of *rebus sic stantibus*.[221] In the discussions of the ILC it was evident that the object and purpose of this article was to strike a fair balance between stability of international relations and equity, as it would not be 'in the interest of the international

[217] Waldock 'Second Report' Art 21; '2. It shall be open to any party to call for the termination of a treaty if after its entry into force its performance shall have become impossible owing to – (b) the *complete and permanent disappearance of a legal arrangement or régime* to which the rights and obligations established by the treaty directly relate' (emphasis added).

[218] Fitzmaurice, 'Second Report' [97].

[219] *Gabčíkovo-Nagymaros Project* [103].

[220] In 2011 it was, once more, simply mentioned *in passim* in *El Paso v Argentina* but not elaborated on and not applied; *El Paso Energy International Company v Argentina* (Award of 31 October 2011) ICSID Case No. ARB/03/15 [168].

[221] On fundamental change of circumstances and *rebus sic stantibus*, see T Giegerich, 'Article 62' in Dörr and Schmalenbach (eds), *Vienna Convention on the Law of Treaties* 1143; MN Shaw and C Fournet, 'Article 62' in Corten and Klein (eds), *The Vienna Conventions on the Law of Treaties* 1411; Vamvoukos, *Termination of Treaties in International Law* 5–216; OJ Lissitzyn, 'Treaties and Changed Circumstances (*Rebus Sic Stantibus*)' (1967) 61 AJIL 895; G Haraszti, 'Treaties and the Fundamental Change of Circumstances' (1975/III) 146 RdC 1; R Müllerson, 'The ABM Treaty: Changed Circumstances, Extraordinary Events, Supreme Interests and International Law' (2005) 59 ICLQ 509.

legal and political order to petrify a treaty which has become anachronistic'.[222] As Wolfrum more recently and very succinctly, put it,

> international law proceeds from the assumption that that the establishment of continuous obligations is possible by a single original consent. The mechanism for re-establishing legitimacy if such obligation has changed over time and has thus become illegitimate is either through renunciation or withdrawal from the obligation in question or having recourse to the *clausula rebus sic stantibus.* In particular the latter is intended, within some limits, to re-adjust continuing legal obligations to the equilibrium originally envisaged by the partners.[223]

Despite agreement on the purpose that Article 62 VCLT aimed to serve, that did not translate as well to the actual content and customary nature of the rule during the ILC discussions and the Vienna Conference,[224] although modern judicial pronouncements might give a vastly different impression as to the hotly contested nature of the rule.[225]

In *Fisheries Jurisdiction (UK v Iceland)* and *Gabčikovo-Nagymaros Project,* the ICJ confirmed the customary nature of Article 62 VCLT,[226] although in both cases, in the end, it did not apply it, as the conditions for its triggering had not been met. In the time between those two cases, the Iran–US Claims Tribunal took a slightly divergent approach regarding the nature of fundamental change of circumstances, characterising it as 'a general principle of law'.[227]

Fundamental change of circumstances has actually been applied in modern adjudication by the CJEU in *Racke v Hauptzollamt Mainz.*[228] This case dealt with the suspension by the Council of Ministers of the European Communities (EC) of a Cooperation Agreement with Yugoslavia following the outbreak of hostilities in that region, and the Court found that the facts allowed for the triggering of this ground for

[222] ILC, 'Summary record of the 834th Meeting' (19 January 1966) UN Doc A/CN.4/SR.834 [77-80] (Bartoš).

[223] R Wolfrum, 'Legitimacy and International Law from a Legal Perspective: Some Introductory Considerations' in R Wolfrum and V Röben (eds), *Legitimacy in International Law* (Springer 2008) 1, 9.

[224] Giegerich, 'Article 62' [8–25].

[225] On whether Art 62 VCLT can truly be considered as customary international law both pre- and post-VCLT see: Giegerich, 'Article 62' 1143–80; Shaw and Fournet, 'Article 62' 1411–33; Vamvoukos, *Termination of Treaties in International Law* 60–151.

[226] *Gabčíkovo-Nagymaros Project* [104]; *Fisheries Jurisdiction (UK v Iceland)* [36].

[227] *Questech Inc v The Ministry of National Defence of the Islamic Republic of Iran* (25 September 1985) Iran–US Claims Tribunal, 9 Iran–USCTR 107, 122.

[228] *Racke v Hauptzollamt Mainz* [52–3].

termination and suspension.[229] The factual background of the case further complicated the matters, as hostilities by virtue of Article 73 VCLT could arguably fall outside the scope of Article 62 VCLT.[230] Nonetheless, since the Court applied customary law, this was not a major concern and it seems to suggest that, even if there might be doubts as to whether outbreak of hostilities falls within the scope of Article 62 VCLT, that is not an issue as far as the customary rule on fundamental change of circumstances is concerned.[231]

Article 62 can be triggered only if five cumulative[232] conditions are met: (i) a supervening change of circumstances, (ii) a change of fundamental character, (iii) a change not foreseen by the parties, (iv) the existence of circumstances constituting an essential basis of the consent of the parties, and (v) a radical transformation of the extent of the remaining obligations.

Hungary's claims in *Gabčikovo-Nagymaros Project* allowed the Court to expand on, or give its stamp of approval on, certain choices made by the ILC regarding these cumulative elements. For instance, the 'change' needs to be unforeseen. If a treaty, as was the case with the 1977 Treaty, includes provisions that allow for change of the kind that actually occurred, then the element of unforeseeability is not met.[233]

'Circumstances', as well, refer to *objective conditions* and not *subjective changes* in the attitudes or expectations of the parties.[234] The legal changes that Hungary claimed could potentially be such an objective condition.[235] However, since Article 62 VCLT is a residual rule that permits treaty termination/suspension as an *ultima ratio*,[236] the threshold for triggering it is quite high, and other venues would have to be exhausted before a party could resort to it.[237] In *RosInvest v Russia*, the

[229] R Rank, 'Modern War and the Validity of Treaties: A Comparative Study' (1953) 38 CLQ 321; see also AN Pronto, 'The Effect of War on Law – What Happens to Their Treaties When States Go to War?' (2013) 2 CJICL 227.

[230] AD McNair and AD Watts, *The Legal Effects of War* (4th edn, CUP 1966); *contra* Pronto, 'The Effect of War on Law' 234–5.

[231] *Racke v Hauptzollamt Mainz* [53–7].

[232] Aust, *Modern Treaty Law and Practice* 262.

[233] *Gabčíkovo-Nagymaros Project* [104].

[234] Fitzmaurice 'Second Report' 63 [170].

[235] *Gabčíkovo-Nagymaros Project* [111–3]; see also *Fisheries Jurisdiction (UK v Iceland)* (Jurisdiction) [1973] ICJ Rep 3 [32].

[236] *Gabčíkovo-Nagymaros Project* [95]; see also G Dahm, J Delbrück, and R Wolfrum, *Völkerrecht Band I/3* (2nd edn, de Gruyter 2002) 753.

[237] Giegerich, 'Article 62' [43].

claimant attempted to indirectly dilute the *ultima ratio* nature of fundamental change of circumstances by arguing that it could be taken into account as an interpretative element, thus moving 'fundamental change of circumstances' from the field of treaty termination to that of treaty interpretation. The tribunal had none of that and stressed that the VCLT 'understandably subjects [fundamental change of circumstances] to onerous and highly restrictive conditions', thus, its invocation in an interpretative context was 'misplaced'.[238]

The argument on change of the prevalent political conditions is even more difficult to make. The Court left open the possibility that such a change could fall under Article 62 VCLT, as long as those conditions were tied to the object and purpose of the treaty.[239] In doing so, it mirrored the ILC's position that a profound political transformation may qualify as a fundamental change of circumstances[240] but a mere 'change in the policies of the State or in its motives or attitude with respect to the treaty' did not.[241] The Court, in the end, was of the view that the evidence produced by Hungary did not meet the high threshold required to demonstrate that all the above conditions were met and, therefore, rejected its claims on fundamental change of circumstances.

The issue of the importance of a political or economic system, within the context of *rebus sic stantibus*, was revisited in 2013 in *Sanum Investment Ltd v Laos*. The case involved a PRC/Laos Bilateral Investment Treaty (BIT). Both States were States with planned economies, and the question was whether the extension of this BIT to a capitalist region could be considered as a fundamental change of circumstances. The PCA confirmed that this could be the case, as long as 'the treaty was based on features specific to a planned economy and irreconcilable with the liberal principles of a capitalist economy'.[242] In the case at hand, however, the PCA was unable to find such evidence and rejected the plea of fundamental change of circumstances.

238 *RosInvest v Russia* [43].
239 *Gabčíkovo–Nagymaros Project* [104].
240 Giegerich, 'Article 62' [41].
241 Waldock 'Second Report' Art 22(3).
242 *Sanum Investment Ltd v Laos* (Award on Jurisdiction of 13 December 2013) PCA Case No 2013-13 [248]. The PCA also cited in support B Stern, 'La succession d' Etats' (1996) 262 RdC 9, 170.

Finally, a recent development with respect to the doctrine of *rebus sic stantibus* comes from the PCA in *Rhine Chlorides*.[243] In Guillaume's opinion, fundamental change of circumstances has different consequences in domestic legal systems compared to international law. In domestic law, triggering the 'fundamental change of circumstances' ground can lead either to termination of the contract or revision by the adjudicator.[244] The latter option has also been 'considered, but never adopted, in the law of international contracts falling under the "*lex mercatoria*"'.[245]

The situation is radically different in public international law where the revision of a treaty by the adjudicator, as a consequence of the triggering of fundamental change of circumstances, has never been done.

> In relations between States, the *rebus sic stantibus* clause implies that where there is a fundamental change of circumstances, *the parties have a duty to negotiate, and then, if negotiations do not bear fruit, they may be allowed to withdraw* from the convention or suspend its implementation ... *Revision by the judge or arbitrator is permitted only where the Parties have granted such a power.* That is not the case here.[246]

6.4.2.3 Material Breach

Rosenne has criticised the VCLT for 'only touch[ing] the fringe' of treaty breaches.[247] One of those rare instances is Article 60 VCLT, which tackles the concept of material breach. Material breach is based on 'inverse' or 'negative reciprocity',[248] and its inclusion in the VCLT was absolutely critical as 'the drafters had to strike a balance between two conflicting interests: while, generally, they intended to promote the

243 *Case Concerning the Audit of Accounts between the Netherlands and France in Application of the Protocol of 25 September 1991 Additional to the Convention for the Protection of the Rhine from Pollution by Chlorides of 3 December 1976 (Netherlands v France)* (2004) 25 UNRIAA 267 (hereinafter *Rhine Chlorides*).

244 *Rhine Chlorides*, Declaration of Mr Gilbert Guillaume 343; With respect to 'termination of contract', Guillaume refers to 'frustration' in English law, where the contract is immediately dissolved, without the court having the power to modify it; with respect to 'revision by the adjudicator' he uses as examples the '*imprévision*' in French administrative law; the theory of '*Wegfall der Geschäftsgrundlage*'in German law; and the jurisprudence of the Swiss Federal Court.

245 ibid and the sources cited therein.

246 ibid 343–4 (emphasis added; translation taken from the unofficial translation available on the PCA website).

247 Sh Rosenne, *Breach of Treaty* (Grotius 1985) 44.

248 Tams 'Regulating Treaty Breaches' 445.

stability of treaty relations, they also had to accommodate the interest of States to free themselves, temporarily or permanently, from treaties that have lost their benefit due to a prior breach by a defaulting State'.[249]

It was also very apposite to include it in the VCLT, as its *sedes materiae* was the law of treaties. As Judge de Castro very eloquently opined, material breach is not outside the law of treaties.

> On the contrary, it is a principle which follows from the contractual nature of treaties. There is no frontier between treaties and international law; there is no frontier which leaves the content of treaties outside international law. On the contrary, it is thanks to international law that treaties have a legal significance. The rules of international law are not outside treaties, they give legal force to treaty rules. The principle *pacta sunt servanda* . . . is not *dehors* treaties; it is this principle which makes it possible to call for performance in good faith of contractual obligations. Article 60 is a complement and the sanction of the principle *pacta sunt servanda*. It is the breach of rights or obligations having their source in the agreement which lies at the root of the *exceptio non adimpleti*.[250]

Article 60 VCLT is easily one of the most complex provisions of the VCLT,[251] an adjectival description that is supported by its drafting history[252] and the wide gamut of its unresolved/debated issues.[253] To attempt to provide a meaningful overview of the intricate tapestry of permutations of the content of material breach would be an exercise in futility. For this reason, this section focuses only on certain aspects that in recent years have undergone a 'motion', in the sense of further clarification and confirmation by international jurisprudence.[254]

First and foremost, as to the nature of the rule enshrined in Article 60 VCLT, in *Gabčíkovo-Nagymaros Project* the ICJ explicitly adopted the view that Article 60 VCLT 'in many respects' is declaratory of customary international law'.[255] That wording was not accidental. The phrase

[249] Simma and Tams, 'Article 60' [3].

[250] *Appeal Relating to the Jurisdiction of the ICAO Council*, Separate Opinion of Judge de Castro 129.

[251] Capotorti, 'L'extinction et la suspension des traités' 550.

[252] Giegerich, 'Article 60' [11–45]; Sh Rosenne, *Developments in the Law of Treaties 1945–1986* (CUP 1989) 8 ff.

[253] Giegerich, 'Article 60' [1–89]; Simma and Tams, 'Article 60' [1–78]; see also in this chapter Sections 6.5.1.2 and 6.5.2.2.

[254] Despite the fact that material breach has hardly ever been applied in international case law.

[255] *Gabčíkovo-Nagymaros Project* [99]; a view that it had already expressed even in the *Namibia Advisory Opinion* [94–5].

'in many respects' clearly does not include the entirety of Article 60 VCLT but leaves the clear determination of what is and what is not, in a state of constructive ambiguity.[256]

The second important contribution of *Gabčíkovo-Nagymaros Project* was that whereas with other grounds for termination of treaties[257] a State cannot invoke the ground for termination if the situation emerged as a result of a State's own wrongful conduct,[258] Article 60 VCLT does not have a similar caveat.[259] In no uncertain terms, the ICJ took a stance on the matter that could be characterised as an *auxesis* of the rule on material breach, by specifying that it was 'a principle generally accepted ... that one Party cannot avail himself of the fact that the other has not fulfilled some obligation ... if the former Party has, by some illegal act, prevented the latter from fulfilling the obligation in question'.[260] Consequently, that principle informed the content of material breach as well, and an exception similar to that in Articles 61 and 62 VCLT should be read into Article 60 VCLT.[261] If not, then this would be tantamount to allowing States to exercise an *abus de droit*.[262]

Further 'motion' on the concept of material breach transpired just a few years ago with the Partial Award in the *Croatia/Slovenia Arbitration Agreement* case.[263] This case exemplifies in the best possible way the 'motion' of material breach, in the sense of its further development and clarification. A little background information about the case will go a long way in setting the scene for the tribunal's findings. The case emerged

256 In more detail on whether Art 60 VCLT reflects customary international law in its entirety or not, see Simma and Tams, 'Article 60' [10].

257 Such as the supervening impossibility of performance and the fundamental change of circumstances.

258 Arts 61(2)(b) and 62(2) VCLT.

259 Although in the ILC there had been members who had called for such an inclusion: ILC, 'Summary Record of the 691st Meeting' (31 May 1963) UN Doc A/CN.4/SR.691 [78] (de Luna); ILC, 'Summary Record of the 831st Meeting' (14 January 1966) UN Doc A/CN.4/SR.831 [67] (de Luna); ILC, 'Summary Record of the 693rd Meeting' (5 July 1963) UN Doc A/CN.4/SR.693 [37] (Waldock); ILC, 'Summary Record of the 832nd Meeting' (17 January 1966) UN Doc A/CN.4/SR.832 [6] (Waldock).

260 *Gabčíkovo-Nagymaros Project* [110] citing *Case Concerning the Factory at Chorzów* 31.

261 *Gabčíkovo-Nagymaros Project* [110]; similarly, Simma and Tams, 'Article 60' [60].

262 Giegerich, 'Article 60' [42].

263 *In the Matter of an Arbitration under the Arbitration Agreement between the Government of the Republic of Croatia and the Government of the Republic of Slovenia, signed on 4 November 2009 (Croatia/Slovenia)* (Partial Award) (2016) PCA Case No 2012-04 (hereinafter *Croatia/Slovenia Arbitration Agreement* (Partial Award)).

from a territorial and maritime dispute between Croatia and Slovenia, which on the basis of an Arbitration Agreement[264] was sent to the PCA. Just a few months before the rendering of the award, Serbian and Croatian newspapers published transcripts of telephone conversations between Dr Sekolec, the arbitrator appointed by Slovenia, and Ms Simona Drenik, an agent of Slovenia's legal team, where Dr Sekolec allegedly shared confidential information about the tribunal's deliberations. Soon thereafter, both resigned from the proceedings. On 30 July 2015, Croatia notified Slovenia by *note verbale* that, in its view, Slovenia had materially breached the Arbitration Agreement, and refused to participate in the proceedings further, despite the appointment by Slovenia of another arbitrator.[265]

The reconstituted tribunal had thus to tackle multiple issues relating to the alleged material breach of the Arbitration Agreement. First and foremost, it established its own jurisdiction, in conformity with the principle *Kompetenz-Kompetenz*.[266] The tribunal reaffirmed what the ICJ in the *Appeal Relating to the Jurisdiction of the ICAO Council* had found, ie that a plea of material breach and the purported termination or suspension of a treaty does not affect clauses conferring jurisdiction, since the alternative would allow States to unilaterally strip an international court's jurisdiction on the issue at hand, thus leading to an *abus de droit*.[267]

[264] 2009 Arbitration Agreement between the Government of the Republic of Slovenia and the Government of the Republic of Croatia (adopted 4 November 2009, entered into force 29 November 2010) <www.assidmer.net/doc/Arbitration_Agreement_Croatia_Slovenia.pdf> accessed 20 September 2019.

[265] For a concise general overview of the Partial Award, see M Xiouri, 'Material Breach of a Treaty: Some Remarks on the Partial Award of 30 June 2016 in the Matter of an Arbitration between Croatia and Slovenia' (2019) 8/1 CILJ 131; E Castellarin, 'La sentence partielle du 30 juin 2016 dans l' affaire du différend territorial et maritime entre la Croatie et la Slovénie' (2016) 52 AFDI 129; for the facts of the case see A Sarvarian, 'Arbitration between Croatia and Slovenia: Leaks, Wiretaps, Scandal (Part 4)' (*EJIL: Talk!*, 3 May 2016) <www.ejiltalk.org/arbitration-between-croatia-andslovenia-leaks-wiretaps-scandal-part-4/> accessed 20 September 2019.

[266] Also known as *compétence de la competence*; *Croatia/Slovenia Arbitration Agreement* (Partial Award) [148-56]. *Nottebohm Case (Liechtenstein v Guatemala)* (Preliminary Objections) [1953] ICJ Rep 111, 119.

[267] *Croatia/Slovenia Arbitration Agreement* (Partial Award) [160-2], referring to *Appeal Relating to the Jurisdiction of the ICAO Council* [16], [32]. The tribunal also based its reasoning on Art 65(4) VCLT, see *Croatia/Slovenia Arbitration Agreement* (Partial Award) [163–8].

Another highlight of the Partial Award is also that the tribunal, for the first time,[268] distinguished explicitly between the two prongs of material breach under Article 60 VCLT, which is an oft-neglected aspect of that article: 'A repudiation of the Agreement as a whole [ie Article 60(3)(a) VCLT] must be distinguished from a purported breach of any of its provisions, which may constitute a material breach under Article 60, paragraph 3, subparagraph (b) of the Vienna Convention'.[269]

'Repudiation' refers to 'all means by which a party intends to relieve itself from its obligations under the treaty'.[270] The tribunal also linked repudiation to the principle *inadimplenti non est adimplendum*[271] and seemed to indirectly confirm Fitzmaurice's views on the matter, ie that repudiation need not be explicitly stated, but can also be inferred from the conduct of the State,[272] although the tribunal does not take a position on the debate of whether both repudiation and material breach under Article 60(3)(b) VCLT need to be wrongful, or whether material breach can occur even when the breach is justified.[273]

Having not found a repudiation on the part of Slovenia, the tribunal turned to material breach in the sense of Article 60(3)(b) and examined whether Slovenia had breached a provision that was essential to the accomplishment of the Arbitration Agreement's object and purpose, ie the settlement of the dispute between the parties.[274] The tribunal stressed that that *the gravity of the breach* is not an element according

[268] *Namibia Advisory Opinion* [95]; *Appeal Relating to the Jurisdiction of the ICAO Council* [38].

[269] *Croatia/Slovenia Arbitration Agreement* (Partial Award) [213] (emphasis added); see also ibid [212].

[270] Simma and Tams, 'Article 60' [16]. For an example of repudiation, see *Namibia Advisory Opinion* [95].

[271] *Croatia/Slovenia Arbitration Agreement* (Partial Award) [213].

[272] ibid [213]; Fitzmaurice, 'Second Report' Art 30(2); according to Fitzmaurice repudiation is 'an act of outright rejection, whereby a party to a treaty declares or evidences an intention no longer to be bound by it' (ibid 69 [216]).

[273] For a detailed analysis of this quandary, see F Paddeu, *Justification and Excuse in International Law: Concept and Theory of General Defences* (CUP 2018) 74–7, who sides with the latter option.

[274] *Croatia/Slovenia Arbitration Agreement* (Partial Award) [222]; note that the tribunal focused on the object and purpose of the agreement, and not on the alleged breached provision (ibid [224–5]); on a discussion of the use by the tribunal of the term 'object and purpose' instead of the Art 60 construction of 'object *or* purpose', and of the theory and practice surrounding a treaty having multiple objects and purposes, see Xiouri, 'Material Breach of a Treaty' 139 ff.

to the letter of Article 60 (3)(b) VCLT.[275] This is an area of debate both in case law and doctrine, as there is a group that supports that gravity should be an element.[276] Following the tribunal's line of reasoning, a trivial breach of an essential provision[277] constitutes a material breach, while the converse is not true; a fundamental breach of a non-essential provision falls outside the scope of Article 60(3)(b).[278] As Paddeu comments, '[i]n short, "material" is a qualitative criterion only. Thus, even a trivial breach may be "material" if it affects an "essential provision" of the treaty'.[279]

A final point, which in the view of the authors is one of the most critical yet rather underappreciated contributions of the *Croatia/Slovenia Arbitration Agreement* case, is the fact that the tribunal discussed the potential of a material breach of an Arbitration Agreement. Although in the end it did not reach a finding of a material breach, during its deliberations at no point did the 'nature' or 'character' of the treaty as a 'procedural' treaty come into play as a factor that could affect the potentiality of the existence of a material breach or not. The tribunal implicitly confirmed that for the purposes of material breach procedural and more substantive treaties were on a level playing field. This is *per analogiam* also in line

(i) with the ILC's substitution of the term 'fundamental breach' with 'material breach', which according to the ILC's commentary was intentional and served to permit responses against breaches of provisions that are ancillary, but important. In this category, dispute settlement clauses were a prominent example;[280] and
(ii) with the ILC's tendency to avoid using the 'nature'/'character' of the treaty as deciding factor on specific choices to be made with respect

[275] *Croatia/Slovenia Arbitration Agreement* (Partial Award) [215].

[276] E Schwelb, 'Termination or Suspension of the Operation of a Treaty as a Consequence of Its Breach' (1967) 7 IJIL 309, 315; Elias, *The Modern Law of Treaties* 114; Simma and Tams, 'Article 60' [23]; Giegerich, 'Article 60' [32–3]. Case law also seems to lend some support: *Namibia Advisory Opinion* [97–100]; ibid, Separate Opinion of Judge Ammoun [8]; *Gabčíkovo-Nagymaros Project* [73].

[277] As Tams points out, an essential provision should not necessarily be equated with a provision that regulates the central purpose of the treaty; Tams 'Regulating Treaty Breaches' 447.

[278] ibid; Greig, 'Reciprocity, Proportionality, and the Law of Treaties' 342–3.; Cf, however, Waldock, 'Second Report' 76 [13].

[279] Paddeu, *Justification and Excuse in International Law* 73; see also Simma and Tams, 'Article 60' [18–9].

[280] See Tams, 'Regulating Treaty Breaches' 447, referring to ILC 'Draft Articles on the Law of Treaties with Commentaries' 255 [9]; and Waldock, 'Second Report' 75 [11].

> to the law of treaties. This is very reminiscent of the discussion surrounding the right of unilateral denunciation of or withdrawal from a treaty of Article 56 VCLT, which was analysed in Section 6.2 of this chapter. There, again, the ILC opted for not adopting different solutions on the basis of the 'character' of the treaty, and of note is that one of the treaties used as an example was arbitration or dispute settlement treaties.[281]

The previous brief discussion on recent case law demonstrates the continuous and continued 'motion' of material breach. Other critical areas where this motion is manifest are the relationships, on the one hand, between material breach and the *exceptio non adimpleti contractus* and, on the other hand, between material breach and countermeasures. However, since these describe a 'motion' that is 'relative' to another concept, they are addressed in Sections 6.5.1.2 and 6.5.2.2, respectively.

6.5 Relative 'Motion' of Grounds for Treaty Termination

In the previous sections we looked into the 'motion' of various concepts having their *sedes materiae* in the law of treaties and related to the *phthora* of treaties, either as grounds for termination/suspension or defences for non-performance (the notorious *exceptio*). This 'motion' was in the form of *kata chronon metavole*, ie how these concepts had been clarified, confirmed, augmented, or reduced through the passage of time. Of course, depending on each conclusion, that motion could also translate to *auxesis*, *meiosis*, *alloiosis*, or even *phthora*. The motion was described from the frame of reference of the concept itself, viewed as a 'time-worm'.[282] In this section, we switch our frame of reference to view motion as a more relativistic concept. Thus, motion is examined through the interaction between various concepts and sets of rules. Two main groups have been selected as most demonstrative of this 'relative motion'. On the one hand, 'relative motion' between the aforeanalysed *praeter*-VCLT rules and their *intra*-VCLT counterparts, and on the other hand, 'relative motion' between *intra*- and *praeter*-VCLT grounds with the set of rules on State responsibility. Through the examination of motion through these different frames of reference, the fluidity and constant

[281] Waldock, 'Second Report' 64, Art 17; see also Christakis, 'Article 56' [54–65].

[282] See the analysis on endurantism, perdurantism, and exdurantism in Chapter 1, Section 1.5.

motion of the grounds leading to the *phthora* of treaties is highlighted from a more systemic angle than the analysis of Sections 6.2–6.4.

6.5.1 *Relative 'Motion' of* Praeter-*VCLT Grounds to* Intra-*VCLT Grounds*

6.5.1.1 Desuetude and Fundamental Change of Circumstances

In Section 6.4.1.1 we saw how one of the main issues that affected the lack of clarity of desuetude was its proximity to a number of notions, with Kolb identifying as many as eight different neighbouring notions. Of import, for the purposes of our analysis here, are the unclear borders between desuetude and the doctrine of *rebus sic stantibus*.[283] The ILC members were well aware of the connection between desuetude and fundamental change of circumstances.[284]

According to Kolb, these two notions are distinguishable through the following three characteristics: (i) desuetude does not require a *fundamental* change of circumstances; (ii) the *cause* is different – in the case of fundamental change of circumstances, the cause of destruction (*phthora*) of the treaty is the invocation by the aggrieved party of the ground in accordance with the procedural requirements of Articles 62–65 VCLT and in the case of desuetude, the cause is the lack of practice accompanied by an *opinio non juris*; and (iii) in fundamental change of circumstances the termination is temporally localisable to a great degree of precision and acts *ex nunc*, whereas in desuetude it is more amorphous as it forms gradually through time, similarly to the process of customary law formation.[285]

That is not to say that there are not strong connections between these two notions. The lapse of a considerable amount of time, which is one of the elements of desuetude, makes all the more probable that the initial circumstances under which the treaty had originally been agreed will

[283] On the difficulty of distinguishing between these two notions, see JL Brierly, 'Some Considerations on the Obsolescence of Treaties' (1926) II Transactions of the Grotius Society 4.

[284] ILC, 'Summary Record of the 848th Meeting' [15] (Waldock); ILC 'Summary Record of the 857th Meeting' [81] (El-Erian); Waldock, 'Sixth Report' 76 [7]; see also *Land Tax Immunities case* (9 March 1927) German Reichsftnanzhof (Federal Tribunal in Revenue Matters – Germany) 4 ILR 84, 85; note, once more, the confusion in this case between desuetude and obsolescence.

[285] Kolb, 'La désuétude' 590.

have changed. Whether this change would be of a fundamental nature, that would have to be determined on a case-by-case analysis. In the opposite direction, the lack of use of treaty provisions over a significant amount of time might be in and of itself an indication that the circumstances have fundamentally changed.

Kolb points out that desuetude is essentially an informal version of the *rebus sic stantibus*. Instead of invoking that ground for termination and having to engage with the other parties to the treaty through formal procedures, the State party simply does not apply the treaty and allows a tacit accord, or a practice accompanied by an *opinio non juris* to emerge.[286]

These organic connections between desuetude and fundamental change of circumstances informed as well the ambivalence within the ILC of whether desuetude should be included as a separate ground for termination[287] or whether this was not necessary, as desuetude was already covered by other provisions, most notably that on fundamental change of circumstances.[288] In the end, the ILC decided that the inclusion of fundamental change of circumstances sufficed and that there was no need for inclusion of desuetude as well in the VCLT.[289]

Despite this, it is undeniable that '[t]here is a symbiosis between the two doctrines ... It is also possible that the change [of circumstances] gives rise to desuetude and it [in turn] is formalised through an express abrogation. The sequence is then triple (change/desuetude/accord) rather than double (change/desuetude)'.[290]

6.5.1.2 *Exceptio Inadimpleti Contractus* and Material Breach

The second set of norms that demonstrate this fluidity in the precise delimitation of their interrelationship is the one that consists of the *exceptio* and material breach. The terms describing these norms have, on occasion, been used in an interchangeable fashion by the likes of

286 Kolb, 'La désuétude' 590–1; in support, Kolb also uses as an example the minority treaties of the League of Nations after the Second World War, which have been argued to have been terminated by some authors by virtue of a fundamental change of circumstances, and by others due to desuetude (ibid).

287 ILC, 'Summary Record of the 847th Meeting' [76] (Rosenne, also referring to Verdross); Waldock, 'Sixth Report' 75 (Israel).

288 ILC, 'Summary Record of the 848th Meeting' [15] (Waldock).

289 Also, because desuetude was partially covered by other VCLT articles, such as Art 54(b), that allowed for termination through agreement by the State parties.

290 Kolb, 'La désuétude' 591 (author's translation).

Riphagen[291] and de Castro.[292] The former, in his 'Preliminary Report', after referring explicitly to Article 60 VCLT and reproducing part of it ends this by adding a parenthesis with the words *exceptio non adimpleti contractus*, signaling clearly that the *exceptio* and material breach are one and the same.[293] The latter, in *Appeal Relating to the Jurisdiction of the ICAO Council,* connects them both to *pacta sunt servanda*, as the fountain from which they emerge.

> It is not correct that the principle laid down in Article 60 of the Vienna Convention is *dehors* the Chicago Convention. On the contrary, it is a principle which follows from the contractual nature of treaties. There is no frontier between treaties and international law; there is no frontier which leaves the content of treaties outside international law. On the contrary, it is thanks to international law that treaties have a legal significance. The rules of international law are not outside treaties, they give legal force to treaty rules. The principle *pacta sunt servanda* . . . is not *dehors* treaties; it is this principle which makes it possible to call for performance in good faith of contractual obligations. Article 60 is a complement and the sanction of the principle *pacta sunt servanda.* It is the breach of rights or obligations having their source in the agreement which lies at the root of the *exceptio non adimpleti.*[294]

The crucial question, however, is whether the material breach of Article 60 VCLT and the *exceptio* have an existence independent of one another. According to Giegerich, Article 60 VCLT 'codifies and carefully circumscribes the *exceptio inadimpleti contractus*'.[295] Since it is evident that material breach and the *exceptio* are not completely unrelated, this raises the question of how much the codification of material breach in Article 60 VCLT has affected the *exceptio.* In *Oil Platforms*, the USA argued that the *exceptio* was a rule that existed independently of material breach, while Iran argued that it had been subsumed entirely by Article 60 VCLT.[296]

291 Riphagen, 'Preliminary Report' 119–20 [64–5]; ILC, 'Summary Record of the 1867th Meeting' (20 July 1984) UN Doc A/CN.4/SR.1867 [35] (Riphagen).

292 *Appeal Relating to the Jurisdiction of the ICAO Council*, Separate Opinion of Judge de Castro 129.

293 Riphagen, 'Preliminary Report'118 [58].

294 ibid.

295 Giegerich, 'Article 60' [72]; see also Simma and Tams, 'Article 60' [3]; ILC, 'Summary Record of the 1867th Meeting' [35] (Riphagen).

296 *Case Concerning Oil Platforms (Iran v USA)* (Merits) Oral Proceedings (5 March 2003) UN Doc CR 2003/18 [26.4], [26.7], [26.9] (Matthias, Counsel for the USA); ibid (3 March 2003) UN Doc CR 2003/16 [7] (Pellet, Counsel for Iran); similarly, see EU arguments in WTO, *Canada – Certain Measures Affecting the Automotive Industry – Report of the Panel* (11 February 2000) WT/DS139/R and WT/DS142/R [7.187]; for an overview of

More recently, the issue was revisited with great intensity in *FYROM v Greece*, where Greece claimed that it had complied with its obligations under the Interim Accord and that any alleged failure on its part could be justified under the *exceptio*. Greece's arguments were essentially structured around the separate existence of material breach and the *exceptio*.[297] Although Greece acknowledged that the *raison d'être* of the three notions, ie material breach, *exceptio*, and countermeasures, was the same, to address the unlawful conduct of another State, it was very clear in its view that '[t]he *exceptio inadimpleti contractus* must not be confused with the ground for suspension and termination of a treaty dealt with in Article 60 of the Vienna Convention or with countermeasures (even though the conditions for having recourse to countermeasures [were] also met). It is merely a defence against a claim of non-performance of a conventional obligation'.[298] *FYROM*, for its part, argued that the *exceptio* had no independent existence and had been codified in its entirety in Article 60 VCLT.

The Court evaded taking a position on the matter, since Greece had failed 'to establish that the conditions which it has itself asserted would be necessary for the application of the *exceptio* have been satisfied in this case'.[299] However, Judge Simma, departing from his previous writings,[300] declared in his Separate Opinion that Article 60 'is truly exhaustive, that is, totally eclipsing the earlier non-written law of the functional synallagma operating behind treaties'[301] and that'the 'pre-Vienna Convention *exceptio* ... dead ... no version of the *exceptio* has survived the codification of the law of treaties – may it rest in peace'.[302] Judge *ad hoc* Roucounas, on his part, and after a detailed examination of relevant international case law on the matter, came to the opposite conclusion that Article 60 VCLT, although codifying partly the *exceptio*, still left it room for continued relevance and application, especially due to

State practice that leans towards continued existence of the *exceptio* beyond the limits of Art 60 VCLT, see Xiouri, 'The *Exceptio*' 76–9.

297 *FYROM v Greece*, Counter-Memorial of Greece [8.6].

298 ibid; on the motion between material breach and *exceptio*, on the one hand, and countermeasures, on the other hand, see Section 6.5.2.2.

299 *FYROM v Greece* [161]; this was criticised by Simma in ibid, Separate Opinion of Judge Simma [6].

300 B Simma, 'Reflections on Article 60 of the Vienna Convention on the Law of Treaties and Its Background in General International Law', (1970) 20 ZOffR 5, 59–60.

301 *FYROM v Greece*, Separate Opinion of Judge Simma [20].

302 ibid, Separate Opinion of Judge Simma [26], [29].

the narrow scope of Article 60 VCLT, which did not offer options for States to respond to breaches that did not meet the threshold of being 'material'.[303]

Interestingly, even those that suggest that the *exceptio* has been completely overtaken by Article 60 VCLT still discuss the differences between *exceptio* and material breach. However, such a discussion, if not done merely as a theoretical exercise, makes sense only if one accepts the possibility of life for *exceptio* beyond and outside of Article 60 VCLT. If one thus accepts that the *exceptio* has not been completely subsumed in Article 60 VCLT, then how can one distinguish between *exceptio intra* and *praeter* Article 60 VCLT? There are three key differences.[304] First, material breach is a ground for termination or suspension of a treaty. The *exceptio*, on the other hand, is a defence that allows non-performance of a synallagmatic obligation corresponding to the one that is not being performed, without, however, affecting the validity and continued application of the treaty.[305] This is also one of the main arguments in favour of the continued relevance of the *exceptio* in the international legal order. As Greece argued in *FYROM v Greece*, '[i]t would be paradoxical that the victim of a treaty breach has no choice but to suspend or terminate [the treaty]'.[306] Second, Article 60 VCLT is triggered only in case of a 'material breach', whereas the *exceptio* applies to all breaches, executing a gap-filling role between material and non-material breaches,[307] and addressing thus the lacunae of Article 60 VCLT.[308] Finally, an invocation of material breach must follow the procedural requirements set in

303 ibid, Dissenting Opinion of Judge *ad hoc* Roucounas [66–7]; see along similar lines: ibid, Declaration of Judge Bennouna 709–10.

304 There are also many similarities, such as that both need to demonstrate a connection between the invoking State's response and the alleged breach (*FYROM v Greece* [123]) that they would not apply to breaches of an obligation of an 'integral' type (Crawford, 'Second Report' [327]). However, the differences are more crucial in discussing whether the two notions have any sort of independent existence.

305 Crawford, 'Second Report' [324]; *Gabčíkovo-Nagymaros Project* [106]; *FYROM v Greece*, Separate Opinion of Judge Simma [10]; ibid, Dissenting Opinion of Judge *ad hoc* Roucounas [66]; ibid, Counter-Memorial of Greece [8.2], [8.6].

306 *FYROM v Greece*, Counter-Memorial of Greece [8.11].

307 Simma, 'Reflections on Article 60' 59–60; although some authors argue that the non-material breaches would be covered by the rules on State responsibility, a point that we return in Section 6.5.2.2; D Azaria, *Treaties on Transit of Energy via Pipelines and Countermeasures* (OUP 2005) 152.

308 Greig, 'Reciprocity, Proportionality and the Law of Treaties' 320–1; see also G Hafner, 'The Drawbacks and Lacunae of the VCLT' in G Hafner et al (eds), *Völkerrecht und die Dynamik der Menschenrechte: Liber Amicorum Wolfram Karl* (2012) 421, 431.

Articles 65–67 of the VCLT. Contrarily, the *exceptio* is not subject to any such conditions.[309]

Having thus concluded our examination of the relative 'motion' of *praeter*-VCLT to *intra*-VCLT grounds for termination/suspension, we now change our frame of reference and examine the relative 'motion' of all these grounds to the secondary rules on State responsibility.

6.5.2 *Relative 'Motion' of* Intra- *and* Praeter-*VCLT Grounds to State Responsibility*

In doctrine it is argued that there is a clear distinction between the law of treaties and the law on State responsibility. This distinction can be adhered to by relying on the different objectives of these two systems – that is, on their functional separation, which guarantees their coherence.[310] A division of norms that was promoted in order to make this distinction more pronounced was that between primary and secondary norms. However, as Paddeu observes, this is a fluid distinction, adopted by the ILC as 'a heuristic devise [to] delimit the scope of its work'.[311]

This notwithstanding, certain common points of contact remain regarding the provisions on treaty termination or suspension and defences in the law of State responsibility.[312] As Agius notes,

> although each set of norms to some degree regulates the same fields and the same situations[,] the law of State responsibility is separate from the law of treaties ... nevertheless, international practice has confirmed that whenever State responsibility is incurred, the State has a right to invoke the circumstances precluding wrongfulness, as well as defences under the law of treaties ... Evidently, there is a blurred distinction between these concepts. *The conflation could stem from the overlap between the law of treaties and the law on State responsibility; the risk of confusing concepts that are linguistically close ... or a desire to cover as many defences as possible in one integrated legal defence strategy.*[313]

[309] Crawford, 'Second Report' [325].

[310] P-M Dupuy, 'Droit des traités, codification et responsabilité internationale' (1997) 43 AFDI 7, 29.

[311] Paddeu, *Justification and Excuse in International Law* 62. See also, G Gaja, 'Primary and Secondary Rules in the International Law of State Responsibility' (2014) 97 RivDirInternaz 981.

[312] F Paddeu, 'A Genealogy of *Force Majeure* in International Law' (2011) 82 BYIL 381, 467.

[313] M Agius, 'The Invocation of Necessity in International Law' (2009) 56/2 NILR 95, 112 (emphasis added).

It is these points of convergence, as extremely 'motion'-sensitive, that we examine in the last sections.

6.5.2.1 Supervening Impossibility of Performance and State Responsibility

'Motion' can also be viewed in relation to concepts that although from a strictly Aristotelian categorisation should belong to clearly delineated areas of international law nonetheless exist at least at their outer borders in a state of 'super-position', being both within and without their respective areas of law. Within the context of treaty termination, one such binary set of rules is supervening impossibility of performance and *force majeure*.

Supervening impossibility of performance under the rubric of *force majeure* was, in fact, pleaded before the PCIJ in two cases decided on the same day, the *Brazilian Federal Loans* and the *Serbian Loans* cases. In both of these cases, the PCIJ held that the economic dislocation caused by the First World War was not a good enough reason to release the debtors from their obligations to repay the loans.[314] Notably, the Court in the *Serbian Loans* case when discussing supervening impossibility of performance had given the title *force majeure* to that paragraph, and further in the same paragraph talked about 'impossibility of performance' as coterminous with *force majeure*.[315]

The PCIJ was not the only body that had difficulty distinguishing between supervening impossibility of performance and *force majeure*. The ILC, as well, when discussing how the term 'object' of Article 61 VCLT should be understood, referred to the extinction of the physical object to which the treaty related, such as the disappearance of an island owing to the subsidence in the seabed, the permanent drying up of a river, the destruction of a railway by an earthquake, or the destruction of a plant, installation, canal, lighthouse, and so on.[316] Once again, from the examples provided it is clear that a connection exists between supervening impossibility and *force majeure*.

This did not escape the attention of the members of the ILC. Fitzmaurice, for instance, in his 'Fourth Report' not only identified 'impossibility of performance' as a 'circumstance justifying non-performance',

[314] *Case Concerning the Payment in Gold of the Brazilian Federal Loans* 120; *Case Concerning the Payment of Various Serbian Loans Issued in France* 39–40.

[315] *Case Concerning the Payment of Various Serbian Loans Issued in France* 39–40.

[316] Fitzmaurice, 'Second Report' [97].

but also suggested that it is synonymous to *force majeure*.[317] Despite the ILC's best efforts to draw clear lines separating supervening impossibility of performance as a ground for termination from *force majeure* as a circumstance precluding wrongfulness, those efforts bore little fruit.[318] Admitting defeat on the matter, the ILC conceded[319] that although '[t]he *sedes materiae* of *force majeure* might therefore be said to be the question of responsibility, rather than the law of treaties … there were still some points at which the law of treaties and the question of responsibility converged, and article 61 was one of them'.[320]

Even failed attempts at the Vienna Conference on the Law of Treaties to expand the scope of Article 61 VCLT highlight the constant motion between supervening impossibility of performance and *force majeure*. Mexico had submitted a proposal that Article 61 VCLT should also cover cases of 'impossibility to make certain payments because of serious financial difficulties'.[321] Although in the end this amendment proposal was not put to vote,[322] due to not being in line with the exceptional character of Article 61 VCLT, it was noted that it might, nonetheless, fall under circumstances precluding wrongfulness.[323]

The examples given come mainly from the pre-VCLT era. That should not give the wrong impression that since then everything has settled to crystal clarity. Although, as mentioned, supervening impossibility is not the most commonly resorted to of the grounds for termination/suspension of a treaty, its unsettled relationship with *force majeure* still occupies academics and practitioners. In *Sempra Energy v Argentina*, Alvarez in his Opinion made a connection between supervening impossibility of performance and circumstances precluding wrongfulness, especially *force majeure*, in the context of discussing the 'public order/essential security'

317 Fitzmaurice, 'Fourth Report' 44, Art 14, and 64 [67].

318 United Nations Conference on the Law of Treaties, '1st Session – 62nd Meeting COW' [1–46].

319 Also, with respect to the 1986 Vienna Convention on the Law of Treaties between States and International Organizations or between International Organizations (adopted 21 March 1986, not yet in force) 25 ILM 543.

320 ILC, 'Summary Record of the 1585th Meeting' (6 May 1980) UN Doc A/CN.4/SR.1585 [8] (Reuter). See also Fitzmaurice, 'Fourth Report' [77–8].

321 United Nations Conference on the Law of Treaties, '1st Session – 62nd Meeting COW' [2].

322 The Mexican delegate withdrew it, having been satisfied by the Expert Consultant's explanations; ibid [44].

323 ibid [4–5] (Suarez), [20] (Koutikov), [27] (de Bresson), [34] (Talalaev), [43] (Waldock).

derogation clause included in a number of BITs.[324] More recently, Bodeau-Livinec and Morgan-Foster have attempted to draw hard-and-fast lines between supervening impossibility of performance and *force majeure*.[325] According to them, Article 61 VCLT 'should give rise to easier and more objective determination than *force majeure*, which is brought about by any unforeseen event in the circumstances'.[326] They agree that supervening impossibility of performance stands at the confluence of the law of treaties and of State responsibility, but are of the view that although its separation from *force majeure* may result in difficulties of application, it seems to them necessary 'to maintain the theoretical distinction that preserves the restrictive meaning of impossibility of performance in Article 61 [VCLT], insofar as admission of *force majeure* in the context of the Vienna Convention would have weakened the stability of treaties'.[327] Irrespective of how convincing the reader may find this line of argumentation, the fact remains that the motion between supervening impossibility of performance and *force majeure* was, is, and in all likelihood will remain for the foreseeable future a characteristic of this binary set of rules.

6.5.2.2 Material Breach (and *Exceptio*) and State Responsibility

Despite the fact that some international courts and tribunals have tried to paint a rosy picture of the existence of clear lines between the law of treaties and State responsibility,[328] this is a narrative that is somewhat disassociated from the reality of the situation.[329]

324 *Sempra Energy International & Camuzzi International SA v Argentina* (Opinion of José E Alvarez of 12 September 2005) ICSID Case Nos ARB/02/16 and ARB/03102 [51]; see also C Brunner, Force Majeure *and Hardship under General Contract Principles: Exemption for Non-performance in International Arbitration* (Kluwer Law International 2009).

325 P Bodeau-Livinec and J Morgan-Foster, 'Article 61' in Corten and Klein (eds), *The Vienna Conventions on the Law of Treaties* 1382.

326 ibid [29].

327 ibid [31]: 'a State having contributed to the disappearance of an object indispensable to a treaty could possible invoke *force majeure* if the situation was due to its conduct but essentially result from other factors; the wrongfulness of the act of the State thus excluded, the restriction of [Art] 61(2) [VCLT] would no longer apply to it and the grounds in [Art 61(1) VCLT] could be invoked to terminate the treaty'.

328 *Gabčíkovo–Nagymaros Project* [47].

329 *Case Concerning the Air Service Agreement of 27 March (USA v France)* (1978) 18 RIAA 417 [17–8], [81–3]; *Case Concerning the Difference between New Zealand and France Concerning the Interpretation or Application of Two Agreements, Concluded on 9 July 1986 between the Two States and Which Related to the Problems Arising from the Rainbow Warrior Affair (New Zealand v France)* (1990) 20 RIAA 215 [73–5].

Simma, for instance, observed,

> Article 60 constitutes one of the provisions [of the Vienna Convention] with regard to which – aside from the procedural shortcomings – the limited scope of the Vienna Convention on the Law of Treaties will be felt most clearly and painfully. While Article 60 and its related provisions carefully and equitably regulate the application of the reactions to breach having their *sedes materiae* in the law of treaties, any examination of the breach situation limited to an analysis of the rules of the Vienna Convention will, due to the exclusion of the similar reactions having their *sedes materiae* in the law of international responsibility, provide the observer with an incomplete picture.[330]

Although at one point it had been argued that material breach was one form of countermeasure,[331] this view has now been mostly abandoned as blurring the lines between law of treaties and State responsibility.[332] Another critical aspect of the interrelationship between material breach and countermeasures is how much Article 60 VCLT has modified or restricted a State's right to resort to countermeasures, with authors arguing both for the exclusivity of the system of Article 60 VCLT,[333] and against,[334] based on a combined reading of Articles 42(2) and 73 of the VCLT.[335] This problem is further exacerbated by the fact that the conditions of application of countermeasures are less strict than those of Article 60 VCLT; therefore, States would prefer to claim countermeasures, which are easier to establish.[336]

As Giegerich notes, '[t]he careful balancing of interests in Art 60 would be worthless if it could simply be brushed aside by resorting to the regime

[330] Simma, 'Reflections on Article 60' 83.

[331] G Abi-Saab, 'General Course of Public International Law' (1987/VII) 207 RdC 15, 463; see also, L-A Sicilianos, 'The Relationship between Reprisals and Denunciation or Suspension of a Treaty' (1993) 4 EJIL 341, 359.

[332] Crawford, 'Third Report' [324–5]; M Fitzmaurice and O Elias, *Contemporary Issues in the Law of Treaties* (Eleven International Publishing 2005) 147; Simma, 'Reflections on Article 60' 56; Sicilianos 'The Relationship between Reprisals and Denunciation' 341; MM Gomaa, *Suspension or Termination of Treaties on Grounds of Breach* (Martinus Nijhoff 1996) 44.

[333] DW Bowett, 'Treaties and State Responsibility' in D Bardonnet et al (eds), *Mélanges Virally* (Pedone 1991) 137, 139; Greig, 'Reciprocity, Proportionality, and the Law of Treaties' 356–60 and 369–82.

[334] Simma and Tams, 'Article 60' [69–73].

[335] On the parallel existence and function of countermeasures and reactions to Art 60 VCLT breaches, see *The Diversion of Water from the Meuse*, Dissenting Opinion of Judge Anzilotti 50; ibid, Individual Opinion of Judge Hudson 77–8.

[336] S Marks, 'Treaties, State Responsibility, and Remedies' (1990) 49/3 CLJ 387, 388.

of State responsibility. A good argument can thus be made for that provision's functioning as *lex specialis*. As such, it would prevent the other parties from resorting to countermeasures for the purpose of justifying their responsive non-performance of the treaty beyond what is permitted under Art 60'.[337] Along similar lines, Marks asks the question that since this 'puts into question the continued operation of the provisions of the Vienna Convention relating to the termination, suspension and invalidity of treaties ... [then i]f a State wishing to avoid its obligations under a treaty can justify breaching the treaty by reference to the full range of excuses known to the law of State responsibility, why should it pay any heed to the stricter grounds and procedures applicable under the law of treaties?'.[338]

The complexity of the relationship with State responsibility is even more pronounced in the case of the *exceptio*. Fitzmaurice viewed the *exceptio* as having its *sedes materiae* in the law of treaties.[339] Riphagen, in turn, understood the *exceptio* as a 'legal consequence of a wrongful act', highlighting thus its connection to State responsibility.[340] Simma, on the other hand, in *FYROM v Greece*, opined that 'State responsibility has *nothing to do* with the maxim *inadimlenti non est adimplendum*'.[341] It should come then as no surprise that the *exceptio* was debated during the ILC discussions both on law of treaties and State responsibility.[342] As Crawford and Olleson put it, the *exceptio* 'could be said to have fallen between the two instruments [ie the VCLT and the Articles on State Responsibility]'.[343]

The main point of contact between the *exceptio* and the law on State responsibility was circumstances precluding wrongfulness, and

337 Giegerich, 'Article 60' [75].

338 Marks, 'Treaties, State Responsibility, and Remedies' 388.

339 Fitzmaurice qualified the *exceptio* as a 'circumstance justifying non-performance'; Fitzmaurice, 'Fourth Report' 45, Art 17A; see also ILC, 'Summary Record of the 1860th Meeting' (12 July 1984) UN Doc A/CN.4/SR.1860 [33] (Reuter).

340 Riphagen, 'Preliminary Report' 116 [49]; similarly *Appeal Relating to the Jurisdiction of the ICAO Council*, Separate Opinion of Judge de Castro 127.

341 *FYROM v Greece*, Separate Opinion of Judge Simma [20] (emphasis added).

342 See for instance, W Riphagen, 'Fifth Report on the Content, Forms and Degrees of International Responsibility' (4 April 1984) UN Doc A/CN.4/380 and Corr.1, reproduced in [1984/II – Part One] YBILC 1, 3, Art 8; see also Riphagen, 'Sixth Report' 10–1, Art 8 and Commentary; see also the discussions presented in Sections 6.4.1.2 and 6.5.1.2 of this chapter.

343 Crawford and Olleson, 'The Exception of Non-Performance' 56.

countermeasures,[344] in particular.[345] When debating the law on State responsibility, the issue of the inclusion of the *exceptio*, in some shape or form, in that set of rules was a recurring theme in the ILC. Riphagen, in his 'Fourth Report', talked about reciprocity *stricto sensu* as being distinct from countermeasures.[346] However, in the end, he changed his stance on the matter by suggesting that this kind of reciprocity created a separate category of countermeasures, 'reciprocal countermeasures'.[347] This view received support from some members of the ILC, while other members disagreed, due to the practical difficulties entailed in distinguishing between reciprocal and non-reciprocal countermeasures.[348] Reuter summed up these concerns when he 'wondered where was the borderline between the concepts of reciprocity and reprisal ... There might exist a grey area between those two concepts if the principle of *exceptio non adimpleti contractus* had been adopted by the Special Rapporteur; however, that principle had been eliminated, and rightly so, if only because of its highly conventional connotations'.[349]

Although the ties of the *exceptio* with the law of treaties was seen as problematic, 'reciprocal countermeasures' were also discussed by the next Special Rapporteur Arangio-Ruiz,[350] but he also had great misgivings due to the possible problems that might arise as a result of the divide between law of treaties and the law on State responsibility.[351] Eventually, the ILC members again rejected the category of 'reciprocal countermeasures' as a distinct category for multiple reasons; not only because it would be difficult to distinguish between reciprocal and

344 On deontic, consequentialist theories on countermeasures and countermeasures as Hohfeldian liberties see Paddeu, *Justification and Excuse in International Law* 267 ff; generally, on countermeasures see ibid, ch 6.

345 Although, on occasion, other circumstances have also been discussed in connection to the *exceptio*, such as *force majeure*; *Perenco Ecuador Ltd v Ecuador* (Decision on Reexamining Issues of Jurisdiction and Liability of 12 September 2014) ICSID Case No. ARB/08/6 [424] (in this case, however, *exceptio* was discussed mainly from a domestic, Ecuadorian, perspective).

346 W Riphagen, 'Fourth Report on the Content, Forms and Degrees of International Responsibility' (14–5 April 1983) UN Doc A/CN.4/366 and Add.1 & Add.1/Corr.1, reproduced in [1983/II - Part One] YBILC 3, 17–8 [95–118].

347 Riphagen, 'Fifth Report' 3, Art 8.

348 See Xiouri, 'The *Exceptio*' 63 and sources cited in fns 44–5.

349 ILC, 'Summary Record of the 1858th Meeting' (10 July 1984) UN Doc A/CN.4/SR.1858 [31] (Reuter).

350 G Arangio-Ruiz, 'Third Report on State Responsibility' (19 July 1991) UN Doc A/CN.4/440 and Add.1, reproduced in [1991/II - Part One] YBILC 1, 9–10 [14], 13 [32].

351 ibid 14 [35].

non-reciprocal measures but also because such measures would be covered by considerations of proportionality and, thus, did not deserve special treatment.[352]

Yet, once again, with Crawford this time as Special Rapporteur, the *exceptio*'s inclusion to the articles on State responsibility was debated. Crawford was of the view that there were two versions of the *exceptio*:[353] one broader, covered by Article 60 VCLT, and one narrower that required 'a causal link between the breach of the obligation by State A and its non-performance by State B'.[354] This latter version, according to Crawford, could be included in the ARSIWA, and specifically in circumstances precluding wrongfulness.[355] The advantage of its inclusion was, according to Crawford, despite its more limited application compared to countermeasures, that the *exceptio* was not held back by the limitations associated with countermeasures. The *exceptio* 'is a more specific response to a particular breach, lacking the opprobrium often associated with countermeasures'.[356] Despite all this, in the end the *exceptio* was seen as more tied to the law of treaties and as being 'a specific feature of certain mutual or synallagmatic obligations ... [rather than] a circumstance precluding wrongfulness'.[357]

Despite this final rejection, and the non-inclusion of the *exceptio* in its narrow sense, as per Crawford, in the ARSIWA, from all the debate surrounding the *exceptio* both in the context of the law of treaties (Section 6.4.1.2 and 6.5.1.2 of this chapter) and of State responsibility, 'it would seem correct to come to the conclusion that the law of treaties contains a gateway leading into the law on State responsibility'.[358] Through this gateway various notions may carve their own path, which may not eventually be met with success and codification, but even in this they highlight the fluidity and *kinesis* that exists between two of the most fundamental building blocks of the international legal system.

352 ILC, 'Report of the International Law Commission on the Work of its 44th Session' (4 May–24 July 1992) UN Doc A/47/10, reproduced in [1992/II – Part Two] YBILC 1, 23 [151].

353 Crawford, 'Second Report' [326].

354 ibid, referring to *Case Concerning the Factory at Chorzów* 31; see also *Gabčíkovo–Nagymaros Project* [107], [110].

355 Crawford, 'Second Report' 78–83 [316–31] and in particular 87, Art 30bis.

356 ibid [323].

357 ILC, 'Draft Articles on Responsibility of States for Internationally Wrongful Acts with Commentaries' 72 [9].

358 Agius, 'The Invocation of Necessity' 113.

6.6 Conclusions

In this final substantive chapter, we started our examination by focusing on the *meiosis* and *phthora* (depending on one's frame of reference) that a treaty may be subjected to as a result of a State party withdrawing from or invoking grounds for termination/suspension of a treaty. The presentation of the debate surrounding the rules regulating the withdrawal of State from a treaty was supplemented by the recent *Wightman* case that served to highlight the continuous motion and development of treaty law in this regard.

This was then supplemented by Sections 6.4 and 6.5, where the relativity of motion was highlighted by studying the motion of the grounds for suspension/termination of a treaty not within a fictional 'objective' frame of reference, but in its proper relativistic form, ie compared to another set of rules. Section 6.4 discussed the relative motion of *intra*-VCLT grounds of termination/suspension to the *praeter*-VCLT ones. In Section 6.5, we switched again our frame of reference by now comparing the motion of the *intra*- and *praeter*-VCLT grounds of termination/suspension to another set of rules, namely the rules on State responsibility.

In this manner, we studied the points of connection and interplay between different normative regimes and understood that motion is not a mono-dimensional concept and that nothing exists in absolute clinical isolation. The main building blocks of the international legal system materialise in a web of intricate and Gordian knot connections, each moving according to its own rhythm and pace, but also in step with a tango-esque motion with other rules.

7

Concluding Remarks

Motion and its opposite, *stasis*, are central to any legal system, including that of public international law. The concept of motion, in all its wide gamut of manifestations,[1] has been and continues to be critical in intellectual, scientific, and academic discourse. Motion is ubiquitous, and although as legal scholars we continuously strive to offer definitive answers to legal answers with sometimes far-reaching implications for the society, we should not forget that the legal system that we find today is not set in stone. Rather it is the contemporary result of a continuous motion throughout several centuries, and a result that will continue to move and change as time goes by.

At the time of the writing of this book, we have just celebrated half a century since the adoption of the VCLT.[2] This 'treaty on treaties'[3] was a landmark occasion. Its importance can be seen and felt not only through the number of States that have signed and ratified it,[4] but also by the effect that it has had on international adjudication and legal discourse since its adoption. It is often referred to by courts and tribunals, even in cases when it is not directly applicable,[5] and had already become a staple point of reference even before it had entered into force.[6] This sometimes, however, may create the false impression of *stasis* and immutability, ie that the VCLT is the be-all and end-all answer to everything connected to treaty law; that it is in its entirety in absolute synchronicity with the

[1] Even that of motion seen as the passage of time viewed as a dimension; Minkowski, 'Space and Time' 73–91; Hinton, 'What Is the Fourth Dimension?' 1–32.

[2] Adopted on 23 May 1969.

[3] Kearney and Dalton, 'The Treaty on Treaties'.

[4] 116 parties at the moment of writing of these lines.

[5] *Kasikili/Sedudu Island*, Separate Opinion of Judge Oda [4].

[6] *Aegean Sea Continental Shelf* [96]; *Fisheries Jurisdiction (UK v Iceland)* [24], [36], [44]; *Appeal Relating to the Jurisdiction of the ICAO Council (India v Pakistan)* (Judgment) [1972] ICJ Rep 46 [30], [38]; *Namibia Advisory Opinion* [94], [96].

customary rules on treaty law; that it has always been so and that there is very little if any motion at all, as far as it is concerned.

However, this is far removed from the truth. If we look in the opposite direction of the arrow of time, ie the past, the VCLT was far from an easily negotiated text. It was the combined result of early codification attempts,[7] the Institut de Droit International and ILC discussions[8] and two sessions of the Vienna Conference on the Law of Treaties,[9] all of which proposed answers to treaty law issues that were of varying degrees of divergence amongst them and whose customary law nature were highly debated, or even in some cases explicitly recognised as being nothing more than progressive development of the law as it stood at the time. Although this is not an issue in and of itself, since the mandate of the ILC is a two-pronged one, ie one of codification of international law and one of progressive development,[10] it does put into question the degree to which the VCLT reflected customary law at the time of its adoption.

That is, however, not the end of our story. If we now change our frame of reference to adopt that of an 'observer', looking in the direction of the arrow of time, ie in the future,[11] the question emerges as to whether the VCLT and the customary law on treaties have since the adoption of the VCLT converged (or diverged), and also whether the VCLT has itself evolved, either in the form of clarification through interpretation, or actual change. The international political scene, case law, reports of international organisations, and academic literature all clearly show that the answer to the aforementioned question is a resounding yes. One does not have to look much further for proof than the recent UK decision to withdraw from the EU, Brexit, and the ensuing debacle on whether the notification of withdrawal from a constituent treaty of an international

[7] Such as the Havana Convention on Treaties, David Dudley Field's Draft Code, Bluntschli's Draft Code, Fiore's Draft Code, the 1927 Draft of the International Commission of American Jurists, the Resolution on Interpretation of Treaties adopted by the Seventh International Conference of American States, and the Harvard Research.

[8] See relevant Sections in Chapters 2–6 of this book, where the discussions in the Institut and the ILC on the relevant treaty issues are examined in more detail.

[9] United Nations Conference on the Law of Treaties, '1st Session'; United Nations Conference on the Law of Treaties, '2nd Session'.

[10] UNGA, 'Statute of the International Law Commission' (21 November 1947) UNGA Res 174 (II) (as amended by UNGA Res 485 (V) (12 December 1950), 984 (X) (3 December 1955), 985 (X) (3 December 1955) and 36/39 (18 November 1981)) Art 1(1).

[11] Or the present as well, depending on whether the observer is a contemporaneous or a past one, from our own frame of reference.

organisation can be withdrawn or not, which led to the *Wightman* case and a whole slew of arguments relating to treaty interpretation, treaty termination, and the customary law or not status of the procedure relating to withdrawal from a treaty. However, if we were to need further proof, one need not look any further than the work of the ILC in the last few years, which has been dominated by issues relating to change or clarification of treaty law issues[12] and/or the sources of international law and their inter-relationship.[13] This constant motion of the law of treaties is also, in some instances, reinforced by the residual nature of certain of the VCLT rules,[14] which allows States through their practice to lead to the emergence of new patterns in treaty practice and, if accompanied by the required *opinio juris*, of new customary rules on the law of treaties.[15]

The reality of law of treaties as being in a constant state of flux led to the adoption of 'motion' as the *leitmotif* of the present book. The multifariousness of the term 'motion' was well-suited to the object and purpose of the book. Motion as movement in relation to other objects, but also movement through time and a manifestation of change, was apposite to encapsulate the multi-dimensional nature of the phenomenon that we aimed to describe. In order to systematise our approach, we adopted Aristotle's six different types of 'motion' (*kinesis*), with a slight twist. In *Treaties in Motion* we examine the 'motion' of treaties, through the prism of creation (*genesis*), destruction (*phthora*), increase (*auxesis*), diminution (*meiosis*), alteration (*alloiosis*), and change of place and time (*kata topon kai chronon metavole*).[16]

12 See the ILC's work on: 'Subsequent Agreements and Subsequent Practice in Relation to Interpretation of Treaties' with Nolte as Special Rapporteur; 'Provisional Application of Treaties' with Gómez-Robledo as Special Rapporteur; 'Reservations to Treaties' with Pellet as Special Rapporteur; 'Fragmentation of International Law: Difficulties Arising from the Diversification and Expansion of International Law' with Koskenniemi as Chairman of the Study Group.

13 See the ILC's work on: 'Identification of Customary International Law' with Wood as Special Rapporteur; 'General Principles of Law' with Vázquez-Bermúdez as Special Rapporteur; 'Peremptory Norms of General International Law (*Jus cogens*)' with Tladi as Special Rapporteur.

14 As, for instance, the rules on A/M/R. In more detail, see Chapter 5.

15 ibid.

16 The twist inserted by the authors to the typology proposed by Aristotle has been in the last category, ie change in place and time (*kata topon kai chronon metavole*). Aristotle's original typology referred only to change in place (*kata topon metavole*). However, as our modern scientific understanding has evolved since the time of Aristotle to view time as a dimension as well, it was felt by the authors that the amendment of this last category was not only mandated by the philosophical (see Chapter 4) and scientific (see Chapter 1)

This also informed the selection of areas from the law of treaties on which *Treaties in Motion* focused. The areas selected were the ones where the aforementioned types of motion were most evident. Furthermore, they were also selected because they revealed that despite the fact that one particular type of motion may be somewhat more dominant than the others in a particular area of treaty law, nonetheless the precise limits between each type of motion and the others are not always so easy to precisely determine,[17] as neither are the various 'object-states' in the life-cycle of a treaty. Classical examples of this are the debate of where interpretation ends and modification begins,[18] or when a series of amendments to a treaty are so significant that what we are dealing with is essentially an entirely new treaty, as was the main theoretical underpinning of the *Open Skies* cases.[19]

Guided by these considerations Chapters 2–6 dealt with areas of treaty law where one particular type of motion was mostly evident, but which also partook of the influence of other types of motion. Chapter 2 dealt with the creation (*genesis*) of a treaty by tackling the question of what a treaty is and the surprisingly numerous instances where this issue was a critical question in international case law. Chapter 3 also dealt with *genesis* by examining consent to be bound, but also demonstrated that since consent to be bound is so integral to the whole system of treaty law, it can be identified also in situations where we have an increase (*auxesis*), diminution (*meiosis*), or even alteration (*alloiosis*) of the treaty as can happen when we are dealing with the system of reservations.

Auxesis and *meiosis* were the types of motion most evident in Chapter 4, which tackled the issue of interpretation. Here also in the context of the discussion on the tug of war between the principle of contemporaneity and evolutive interpretation the motion as change through time (*kata chronon metavole*) was most pronounced. It has to be stressed at this point that interpretation may lead to increase (*auxesis*) or diminution (*meiosis*) but never to alteration (*alloiosis*). As Aristotle very forcefully pointed out in *Categories* 'an alteration . . . is distinct from all other sorts of motion, for that which is affected need not suffer either

understanding of motion, identity, and change as notions inextricably linked to time, but also that it served perfectly the purposes of the book.

17 For a philosophical equivalent, see the *sorites* paradox of Eubulides of Miletus that arises from vague predicates.

18 Which was dealt with in Chapter 4 Section 4.2.2.2.

19 As the authors have argued in Chapter 5 Section 5.1, this string of cases is a modern-day legal variation of the *Theseus's ship* paradox.

increase or diminution or any of the other sorts of motion. Thus, alteration is a distinct sort of motion; for, if it were not, the thing altered would not only be altered, but would forthwith necessarily suffer increase or diminution or some one of the other sorts of motion in addition; which as a matter of fact is not the case ... Alteration and increase [or diminution], therefore, are distinct'.[20] Since one of the limits of interpretation is not to alter the meaning that the parties intended to give the text[21] alteration (*alloiosis*) is a motion that should never occur when interpreting. Despite this, the line between, on the one hand increase (*auxesis*) or diminution (*meiosis*), and, on the other hand, alteration (*alloiosis*) is not an easy one to draw. Although, theoretically, their distinction is not only desirable but also mandatory,[22] in practice it is much more difficult to draw a clear line, as shown recently by the ILC's difficulty in tackling this topic.[23]

This limit of interpretation segued to Chapter 5, where the amendment, modification, or revision of a treaty (A/M/R) could, depending on the nature of said A/M/R, lead to increase (*auxesis*), diminution (*meiosis*), or even alteration (*alloiosis*) of a treaty. Another bridge with other types of motion and previous chapters in *Treaties in Motion* was also the relationship between more modern types of A/M/R such as 'tacit acceptance'/'opting out' procedures, or 'autonomous institutional arrangements' and how these may have to lead us to a re-evaluation of our understanding of 'consent to be bound'.

Finally, in Chapter 6 the final type of motion, ie destruction (*phthora*), was examined within the context of treaty withdrawal and treaty termination. It has to be noted, that, once again, this type of motion is not without its connections to the other types, as, for instance, the withdrawal from a treaty depending on one's frame of reference may be destruction (*phthora*) from the frame of reference of the withdrawing State, or merely diminution (*meiosis*) or partial *phthora* from the frame of reference of the remaining State parties, which may simply see a reduction in the number of State parties.

20 Aristotle, *Categories* ch XIV [14].

21 Either interpreted contemporaneously or evolutively, depending on the treaty in question.

22 *Gabčíkovo-Nagymaros Project*, Separate Opinion of Judge Bedjaoui [5]; *Kasikili/Sedudu Island*, Declaration of Judge Higgins [2]; *Laguna del Desierto* [157]; *Claude Reyes and Others v Chile*, Separate Opinion of Judge Ramírez [1], [3].

23 ILC, 'Draft Conclusions on Subsequent Agreements and Subsequent Practice, with Commentaries' Draft Conclusion 7 and accompanying commentary.

As shown, despite the fact that in each chapter one particular type of motion was usually the dominant one, this did not preclude other types of motion entering the fray of consideration, either directly or indirectly. This underlined the interconnectedness between the various areas of treaty law and explained the transition from one area to the next. In addition to these, an underlying common thread across all chapters was also the examination of the change of treaties and treaty law through time (*kata chronon metavole*). In all chapters, we examined how reflective the VCLT rules were at the time of their adoption of customary international law and whether this situation has changed in the last 50 years. This was done, on the one part, through an examination of the preparatory work of the VCLT,[24] and, on the other part, through an evaluation of the evolution of case law and the more contemporary discussions in the ILC.

The aim of the authors throughout all the chapters of *Treaties in Motion* has been to highlight exactly that. Immutability is a false hypothesis. Treaty law and treaties are in a constant state of motion from multiple frames of reference and in all kinds of areas. This may make it harder to identify the exact content of treaty law at any given moment in the past and present and even more in the future, but it is 'in the admission of ignorance and the admission of uncertainty that there is a hope for the continuous motion of human beings in some direction that doesn't get confined, permanently blocked, as it has so many times before in various periods in the history of man'.[25] The ubiquity of this multi-dimensional and multi-faceted motion of treaties and its law should not lead us to despair at the Sisyphean task ahead of us. Motion is what keeps our legal system alive, vibrant, and responsive to the needs of our society. It is this motion that should also prompt us into action (or should we say motion) in a never-ending attempt to refine, re-evaluate, re-define, and further our understanding of the law of treaties in all its complexity. Or as much more eloquently put by Alfred Lord Tennyson, to 'strive, to seek, to find, and not to yield'.[26]

[24] As to why apart from the documents of the Vienna Conference on the Law Treaties, also the ILC discussions can be considered as preparatory work (of at least a 'second order') see ILC, 'Summary Record of the 873rd Meeting' [25] (Chairman), [27] (Tunkin), [28] (Rosenne) and [34] (El-Erian). In detail, Merkouris, *Article 31(3)(c) VCLT* 11.

[25] R Feynman, *The Meaning of It All: Thoughts of a Citizen – Scientist* (Helix Books 1998) 34.

[26] A Tennyson, *Ulysses.*

BIBLIOGRAPHY

Books and Chapters in Edited Volumes

Abi-Saab G et al (eds), *Evolutionary Interpretation and International Law* (Bloomsbury 2019)

Ago R, 'Die Internationalen Organisationen und Ihre Funktionen im inneren Tätigkeitsgebiet der Staaten' in H Wehberg, W Schätzel, and H-J Schlochauer (eds), *Rechtsfragen der internationalen Organisation: Festschrift für Hans Wehberg zu seinem 70 Geburtstag* (Vittorio Klostermann 1956) 20

Alvarez JE, *International Organisations as Law-Makers* (OUP 2006)

Anzilotti D, *Cours de Droit International, Tome I* (Sirey 1929)

Aristotle, *Categories*

Metaphysics

Physics

Aust A, *Modern Treaty Law and Practice* (3rd edn, CUP 2013)

Azaria D, *Treaties on Transit of Energy via Pipelines and Countermeasures* (OUP 2005)

Baetens F, '*Ejusdem Generis* and *Noscitur a Sociis*' in J Klingler, Y Parkhomenko, and C Salonidis (eds), *Between the Lines of the Vienna Convention?: Canons and Other Principles of Interpretation in Public International Law* (Wolters Kluwer 2018) 133

Balashov Y, 'Persistence' in E Callender (ed), *The Oxford Handbook of Philosophy of Time* (OUP 2011) 14

Berman F and D Bentley, 'Treaties and Other International Instruments – I General Definition, Treaty Formalities' in I Roberts (ed), *Satow's Diplomatic Practice* (7th edn, OUP 2017) 599

'Treaties and Other International Instruments – II Most Common Forms: Treaty/Convention/Agreement/Protocol' in I Roberts (ed), *Satow's Diplomatic Practice* (7th edn, OUP 2017) 608

'Treaties and Other International Instruments – III Pact, Act, *Modus Vivendi*, Declaration, Exchange of Notes, Memorandum of Understanding' in I Roberts (ed), *Satow's Diplomatic Practice* (7th edn, OUP 2017) 616

'Treaties and Other International Instruments – IV Ratification, Accession, Acceptance and Approval, Treaty Succession' in I Roberts (ed), *Satow's Diplomatic Practice* (7th edn, OUP 2017) 638

Bilder R, 'Beyond Compliance: Helping Nations Cooperate' in D Shelton (ed), *Commitment and Compliance: The Role of Non-Binding Norms in the International Legal System* (OUP 2003) 65

Birnie P, 'Legal Techniques of Settling Disputes: The Soft Settlement Approach' in WE Butler (ed), *Perestroika and International Law* (Martinus Nijhoff 1990) 175

International Regulation of Whaling: From Conservation of Whaling to Conservation of Whales and Regulation of Whale-Watching (Oceana Publications 1985) 549

'The Status of Environmental "Soft Law": Trends and Examples with Special Focus on IMO Norms', in H Ringbom (ed), *Competing Norms in the Law of Marine Environmental Protection, Focus on Ship Safety and Pollution Prevention* (Kluwer Law International 1997) 39

Bjorge E, *The Evolutionary Interpretation of Treaties* (OUP 2014)

Blix H, *Treaty-Making Power* (Stevens & Sons 1960)

Blokker NM, 'Constituent Instruments: Creating a Genie That May Escape from the Bottle?' in JK Cogan, I Hurd, and I Johnstone (eds), *The Oxford Handbook of International Organizations* (OUP 2013) 943

Bodeau-Livinec P and J Morgan-Foster, 'Article 61' in O Corten and P Klein (eds), *The Vienna Conventions on the Law of Treaties – A Commentary* (OUP 2011) 1382

Bos M, *A Methodology of International Law* (North-Holland 1984)

Bowett DW, 'Treaties and State Responsibility' in D Bardonnet et al (eds), *Mélanges Virally* (Pedone 1991) 137

Boyle A, 'Some Reflections on Relationship of Treaties and Soft Law' in V Gowlland-Debbas (ed), *Multilateral Treaty-Making: Current Status of Challenges to and Reforms Needed in International Legislative Process* (Springer 2000) 25

Braumann C and A Reinisch, '*Effet Utile*' in J Klingler, Y Parkhomenko, and C Salonidis (eds), *Between the Lines of the Vienna Convention?: Canons and Other Principles of Interpretation in Public International Law* (Wolters Kluwer 2018) 47

Brierly JL, *The Law of Nations: An Introduction to the International Law of Peace* (Clarendon Press 1928)

Brölmann C, 'Limits of the Treaty Paradigm' in M Fitzmaurice and M Craven (eds), *Interrogating the Treaty: Essays in the Contemporary Law of Treaties* (Wolf Legal Publishers 2005) 29

'Specialized Rules of Treaty Interpretation: International Organizations' in DB Hollis (ed) *The Oxford Guide to Treaties* (OUP 2012) 507

'Typologies and the "Essential Juridical Character" of Treaties' in MJ Bowman and D Kritsiotis (eds), *Conceptual and Contextual Perspectives on the Modern Law of Treaties* (CUP 2018) 79

Brunnée J, 'Reweaving the Fabric of International Law? Patterns of Consent in the Environmental Framework Agreements' in R Wolfrum and V Röben (eds), *Developments of International Law in Treaty-Making* (Springer 2005) 101

Brunner C, Force Majeure *and Hardship under General Contract Principles: Exemption for Non-performance in International Arbitration* (Kluwer Law International 2009)

Buga I, 'Subsequent Practice and Treaty Modification' in MJ Bowman and D Kritsiotis (eds), *Conceptual and Contextual Perspectives on the Modern Law of Treaties* (CUP 2018) 363

The Modification of Treaties by Subsequent Practice (OUP 2018)

Callender C, *What Makes Time Special?* (OUP 2017)

Camps M, 'Britain and the European Community 1955–1963' in R Mayne (ed), *The Recovery of Europe* (Weidenfeld & Nicholson 1970)

Cantor G, *Contributions to the Founding of the Theory of Transfinite Numbers* (P Jourdain tr, Dover Publications 1915)

Capitant H, *De la cause des obligations (contrats, engagements unilatéraux, legs)* (Dalloz 1927)

Chanaki A, *L' adaptation des traités dans les temps* (Bruylant 2013)

Chinkin C, 'Human Rights' in MJ Bowman and D Kritsiotis (eds), *Conceptual and Contextual Perspectives on the Modern Law of Treaties* (CUP 2018) 509

'Normative Development in International Legal System' in D Shelton (ed), *Commitment and Compliance: The Role of Non-Binding Norms in the International Legal System* (OUP 2000) 21

Christakis T, 'Article 56' in O Corten and P Klein (eds), *The Vienna Conventions on the Law of Treaties – A Commentary* (OUP 2011) 1251

Cohen MG, 'Desuetude and Obsolescence of Treaties' in E Cannizzaro (ed), *The Law of Treaties Beyond the Vienna Convention* (OUP 2011) 350

Corten O and P Klein (eds), *The Vienna Conventions on the Law of Treaties – A Commentary* (OUP 2011)

Council of Europe and BIICL (eds), *Treaty-Making: Expression of Consent to Be Bound by a Treaty* (Kluwer Law International 2001)

Crema L, 'Subsequent Agreements Practice and Subsequent Practice within and outside the Vienna Convention' in G Nolte (ed), *Treaties and Subsequent Practice* (OUP 2013) 17

d'Argent P, '*Contra Proferentem*' in J Klingler, Y Parkhomenko and C Salonidis (eds), *Between the Lines of the Vienna Convention?: Canons and Other Principles of Interpretation in Public International Law* (Wolters Kluwer 2018) 241

d'Aspremont J, 'The Multi-dimensional Process of Interpretation: Content-Determination and Law Ascertainment Distinguished' in A Bianchi, D Peat, and M Windsor (eds), *Interpretation in International Law* (OUP 2015) 111

Dahm G, J Delbrück, and R Wolfrum, *Völkerrecht Band I/3* (2nd edn, de Gruyter 2002)

de Vattel E, *The Law of Nations or Principles on the Law of Nature Applied to the Conduct and Affairs of Nations and Sovereigns* (GGJ and J Robinson 1793)

de Visscher C, *Problémes d' interprétation judiciaire en droit international public* (Pedone 1963)

Descartes R, *Principles of Philosophy* (RP Miller and VR Miller tr, Kluwer 1983)

Djeffal C, *Static and Evolutive Treaty Interpretation: A Functional Reconstruction* (CUP 2016)

Dörr O and K Schmalenbach (eds), *The Vienna Convention on the Law of Treaties: A Commentary* (2nd edn, Springer 2018)

Dupuy P-M, 'Evolutionary Interpretation of Treaties: Between Memory and Prophecy' in Cannizzaro (ed) *The Law of Treaties Beyond the Vienna Convention* (OUP 2011) 123

Dupuy R-J, 'Declaratory Law and Programmatory Law: From Revolutionary Custom to "Soft Law"' in RJ Akkerman, PJ van Krieken and Ch Pannenborg (eds), *Declarations on Principles: A Quest for Universal Peace* (Sijthoff 1979) 252

Earman J and JD Norton, 'Infinite Pains: The Trouble with Supertasks' in A Morton and S Stich (eds), *Paul Benacerraf: The Philosopher and His Critics* (Blackwell 1996) 231

Eddington A, T*he Nature of the Physical World* (CUP 1928)

Einstein A et al, *The Principle of Relativity* (W Perrett and GB Jeffery tr, Dover Books 1952)

Elias O and CL Lim, *The Paradox of Consensualism in International Law* (Brill/Martinus Nijhoff 1998)

Elias TO, *The Modern Law of Treaties* (Oceana 1974)

Emerson RW, 'Nature' in J Slater, AR Ferguson and JF Carr (eds), *Collected Works of Ralph Waldo Emerson, Vol III: Essays* (Beknap Press 1983) 105

Engelen FA, *Interpretation of Tax Treaties under International Law: A Study of Articles 31, 32, and 33 of Vienna Convention on the Law of Treaties and Their Application to Tax Treaties* (International Bureau of Fiscal Documentation 2004)

Fenwick CG, *International Law* (The American Law Book Co 1924)

Feynman R, *The Meaning of It All: Thoughts of a Citizen-Scientist* (Helix Books 1998)

Fitzmaurice M, 'Angst of the *Exceptio Inadimplenti Non Est Adimplendum* in International Law' in L Bartels and F Paddeu (eds), *Exceptions in International Law* (OUP 2020)

'Exceptional Circumstances and Treaty Commitments' in D Hollis (ed), *The Oxford Guide to Treaties* (OUP 2012) 605

'The Practical Working of the Law of Treaties' in MD Evans (ed), *International Law* (5th edn, CUP 2019) 138

'The Whaling Convention and Thorny Issues of Interpretation' in M Fitzmaurice and D Tamada (eds), *Whaling in the Antarctic: Significance and Implications of the ICJ Judgment* (Brill/Martinus Nijhoff 2016) 55

Fitzmaurice M and DG Costelloe, 'Lawmaking by Treaty: Conclusion of Treaties and Evolution of Treaty Regimes in Practice' in C Brölmann and Y Radi (eds), *Research Handbook on the Theory and Practice of International Lawmaking* (Edward Elgar 2016) 111

Fitzmaurice M and O Elias, *Contemporary Issues in the Law of Treaties* (Eleven International Publishing 2005)

Fitzmaurice M and P Merkouris, 'Uniformity versus Specialization (1): The Quest for a Uniform Law of Inter-State Treaties' in C Tams, A Tzanakopoulos, and A Zimmermann (eds), *Research Handbook on the Law of Treaties* (Edward Elgar 2014) 341

Foreign Office, *Handbook of Commercial Treaties etc, With Foreign Powers* (4th edn, HM Stationery Office 1931)

Fox H, 'Article 31(3)(a) and (b) of the Vienna Convention and the *Kasikili/Sedudu Island* Case' in M Fitzmaurice, O Elias, and P Merkouris (eds), *The Issues of Treaty Interpretation and the Vienna Convention on the Law of Treaties* (Martinus Nijhoff Publishers 2010) 59

Franck T, *Fairness in International Law and Institutions* (OUP 1995)

Friedrich J, *International Environmental "Soft Law": The Functions and Limits of Nonbinding Instruments in International Environmental Law and Governance* (Springer 2014)

Gaja G, 'Unruly Treaty Reservations' in R Ago (ed), *Droit international à l'heure de sa codification: études en l'honneur de Roberto Ago*, Vol 1 (Giuffrè 1987) 307

Gardiner R, 'Characteristics of the Vienna Convention Rules on Treaty Interpretation' in MJ Bowman and D Kritsiotis (eds), *Conceptual and Contextual Perspectives on the Modern Law of Treaties* (CUP 2018) 335

Treaty Interpretation (2nd edn, OUP 2015)

Geny F, *Méthode d' interprétation et sources en droit privé positif: Essai critique*, Vol I (LGDJ 1954)

Giegerich T, 'Article 56' in O Dörr and K Schmalenbach (eds), *Vienna Convention on the Law of Treaties: A Commentary* (2nd edn, Springer 2018) 1039

'Article 60' in O Dörr and K Schmalenbach (eds), *Vienna Convention on the Law of Treaties: A Commentary* (2nd edn, Springer 2018) 1095

'Article 62' in O Dörr and K Schmalenbach (eds), *Vienna Convention on the Law of Treaties: A Commentary* (2nd edn, Springer 2018) 1143

Goehring T, 'Treaty-Making and Treaty Evolution' in D Bodansky, J Brunnée and E Hey (eds), *The Oxford Handbook of International Environmental Law* (OUP 2008) 467

Goellner A, *Pre-caducité, caducité et désuétude en matiere de droit international public (essai juridique)* (Rousseau 1939)

Gomaa MM, *Suspension or Termination of Treaties on Grounds of Breach* (Martinus Nijhoff 1996)

Gourgourinis A, *Equity and Equitable Principles in the World Trade Organization: Addressing Conflicts and Overlaps between the WTO and Other Regimes* (Routledge 2015)

Greig D, *Intertemporality and the Law of Treaties* (BIICL 2001)

Grünbaum A, 'Modern Science and Zeno's Paradoxes of Motion' in WC Samon (ed), *Zeno's Paradoxes* (Bobbs-Merrill 1970) 200

Hafner G, 'The Drawbacks and Lacunae of the VCLT' in G Hafner et al (eds), *Völkerrecht und die Dynamik der Menschenrechte: Liber Amicorum Wolfram Karl* (2012) 421

Handl G, 'International "Lawmaking" by Conferences of the Parties and Other Politically Mandated Bodies: Comment' in R Wolfrum and V Röben (eds), *Development of International Law in Treaty-Making* (Springer 2005) 127

Hart HLA, *Essays in Jurisprudence and Philosophy* (Clarendon Press 1983)

Haslanger S, 'Persistence through Time' in MJ Loux and DW Zimmerman (eds), *The Oxford Handbook of Metaphysics* (OUP 2005) 315

Henin PF, 'In *Pari Materia* Interpretation in Treaty Law' in J Klingler, Y Parkhomenko, and C Salonidis (eds), *Between the Lines of the Vienna Convention?: Canons and Other Principles of Interpretation in Public International Law* (Wolters Kluwer 2018) 211

Hershey AS, *The Essentials of International Public Law and Organization* (rev edn, MacMillan 1927)

Higgins R, *Problems and Process: International Law and How We Use It* (OUP 1994)

'Some Observations on the Inter-temporal Rule in International Law' in J Makarczyk (ed), *Theory of International Law at the Threshold of the 21st Century* (Kluwer Law International 1996) 173

Hinton CH, 'What Is the Fourth Dimension?' in CH Hinton (ed), *Scientific Romances No 1* (W Swan Schonneschein 1884) 1

Hobbes T, *Elements of Philosophy – The First Section, Concerning Body* (R and W Leybourn 1656)

Horwich P, *Asymmetries in Time* (MIT Press 1987)

Hoyt EC, *The Unanimity Rule in the Revision of Treaties: A Re-Examination* (Martinus Nijhoff 1959)

Hudson MO, *The Permanent Court of International Justice: A Treatise* (The MacMillan Co 1934) 551

Jennings RY and AD Watts (eds), *Oppenheim's International Law* (9th edn, Longman 1996)

Oppenheim's International Law (9th edn, OUP 2008)

Kammerhofer J, *Uncertainty in International Law: A Kelsenian Perspective* (Routledge 2011)

Kapteyn PJG, PV van Themaat, *Introduction to the Law of the European Communities: From Maastricht to Amsterdam* (LW Gormley ed, 3rd edn, Kluwer Law International 1998)

Kassoti E, *The Juridical Nature of Unilateral Acts of States in International Law* (Brill/Martinus Nijhoff 2015)

Klabbers J, *The Concept of Treaty in International Law* (Kluwer Law International 1996)

'Reluctant "Grundnormen": Articles 31(3)(c) and 42 of the Vienna Convention on the Law of Treaties and the Fragmentation of International Law' in M Craven, M Fitzmaurice, and M Vogiatzi (eds), *Time, History and International Law* (Martinus Nijhoff 2007) 141

Klein PD, 'Contemporary Responses to Agrippa's Trilemma' in J Greco (ed), *The Oxford Handbook of Skepticism* (OUP 2008) 484

Klingler J, '*Expressio Unius Est Exclusio Altrerius*' in J Klingler, Y Parkhomenko, and C Salonidis (eds), *Between the Lines of the Vienna Convention?: Canons and Other Principles of Interpretation in Public International Law* (Wolters Kluwer 2018) 73

Klingler J, Y Parkhomenko, and C Salonidis (eds), *Between the Lines of the Vienna Convention?: Canons and Other Principles of Interpretation in Public International Law* (Wolters Kluwer 2018)

Kohen M, 'Keeping Subsequent Agreements and Practice in Their Right Limits' in G Nolte (ed), *Treaties and Subsequent Practice* (OUP 2013) 34

Kolb R, *Good Faith in International Law* (Hart 2017)

Interprétation et création du droit international: esquisses d'une herméneutique juridique moderne pour le droit international public (Bruylant 2006)

Kontou N, *The Termination of Treaties in Light of New Customary International Law* (Clarendon Press 1994)

Koskenniemi M, *From Apology to Utopia: The Structure of International Legal Argument* (CUP 1989)

Krieger H, 'Article 68' in O Dörr and K Schmalenbach (eds), *Vienna Convention on the Law of Treaties: A Commentary* (2nd edn, Springer 2018) 1259

Kritsiotis D, 'The Object and Purpose of a Treaty's Object and Purpose' in MJ Bowman and D Kritsiotis (eds), *Conceptual and Contextual Perspectives on the Modern Law of Treaties* (CUP 2018) 237

Lawrence TJ, *Principles of International Law* (7th edn, MacMillan 1923)

Leca J, *Les techniques de révision des conventions internationales* (LGDJ 1961)

Leibniz GW, *The Leibniz-Clarke Correspondence: With Extracts from Newton's 'Principia' and 'Optiks'* (edited with introduction and notes by HG Alexander, MUP 1977)

Letsas G, *A Theory of Interpretation of the European Convention on Human Rights* (OUP 2007)

Linderfalk U, *On the Interpretation of Treaties* (Springer 2007)

Lo C, *Treaty Interpretation under the Vienna Convention on the Law of Treaties: A New Round for Codification* (Springer 2017)

Lost-Sieminska D, 'The International Maritime Organization' in MJ Bowman and D Kritsiotis (eds), *Conceptual and Contextual Perspectives on the Modern Law of Treaties* (CUP 2018) 907

Lowe V, 'Sustainable Development and Unsustainable Arguments' in A Boyle and D Freestone (eds), *International Law and Sustainable Development: Past Achievements and Future Challenges* (OUP 1999) 19

Macdonald A, '*Ex Abundante Cautela*' in J Klingler, Y Parkhomenko, and C Salonidis (eds), *Between the Lines of the Vienna Convention?: Canons and Other Principles of Interpretation in Public International Law* (Wolters Kluwer 2018) 115

Madison J, 'Federalist Paper No 43' in Cl Rossiter (ed), *The Federalist Papers* (New American Library 1961) 278

Marcus Tullius Cicero, *De Officiis*

Matsushita M et al (eds), *The World Trade Organization: Law, Practice, and Policy* (3rd edn, OUP 2015)

McNair A, *The Law of Treaties* (Clarendon Press 1961)

McNair AD and AD Watts, *The Legal Effects of War* (4th edn, CUP 1966)

McWhinney E, 'The Time Dimension in International Law, Historical Relativism and Intertemporal Law' in J Makarczyk (ed), *Essays in International Law in Honour of Judge Manfred Lachs* (Martinus Nijhoff 1984) 179

Merkouris P, *Article 31(3)(c) VCLT and the Principle of Systemic Integration: Normative Shadows in Plato's Cave* (Brill/Martinus Nijhoff 2015)

'*In Dubio Mitius*' in J Klingler, Y Parkhomenko, and C Salonidis (eds), *Between the Lines of the Vienna Convention?: Canons and Other Principles of Interpretation in Public International Law* (Wolters Kluwer 2018) 259

'"Third Party" Considerations and "Corrective Interpretation" in the Interpretative Use of *Travaux Préparatoires* – Is It Fahrenheit 451 for Preparatory Work?' in M Fitzmaurice, O Elias, and P Merkouris (eds), *Treaty Interpretation and the Vienna Convention on the Law of Treaties: 30 Years On* (Martinus Nijhoff 2010) 75

Minkowski H, 'Space and Time' as reprinted and translated in A Einstein and FA Davis (eds), *The Principle of Relativity* (Dover Publications 1952) 73

Minon A, '*Per Argumentum a Fortiori*' in J Klingler, Y Parkhomenko, and C Salonidis (eds), *Between the Lines of the Vienna Convention?: Canons and Other Principles of Interpretation in Public International Law* (Wolters Kluwer 2018) 197

Mitchell AD and T Voon, 'The Rule of Necessary Implication' in J Klingler, Y Parkhomenko, and C Salonidis (eds), *Between the Lines of the Vienna Convention?: Canons and Other Principles of Interpretation in Public International Law* (Wolters Kluwer 2018) 331

Moeckli D and ND White, 'Treaties as "Living Instruments"' in MJ Bowman and D Kritsiotis (eds), *Conceptual and Contextual Perspectives on the Modern Law of Treaties* (CUP 2018) 136

Moore JB, *A Digest of International Law* (Government Printing Office 1906)

Murphy S, 'The Relevance of Subsequent Agreement and Subsequent Practice in Interpretation of Treaties' in G Nolte (ed), *Treaties and Subsequent Practice* (OUP 2013) 82

Newton I, *De Gravitatione*

Nollkaemper A, *The Legal Regime for Transboundary Water Pollution: Between Discretion and Constraint* (Kluwer Law International 1993) 252

Nolte G (ed), *Treaties and Subsequent Practice* (OUP 2013)

Oppenheim L, *International Law – Vol 1: Peace* (4th edn, Longmans 1928)

Paddeu F, *Justification and Excuse in International Law: Concept and Theory of General Defences* (CUP 2018)

Parmenides, *On Nature*

Pauwelyn J, *Conflict of Norms in Public International Law: How WTO Law Relates to Other Rules of International Law* (CUP 2003)

Peat D, *Comparative Reasoning in International Courts and Tribunals* (CUP 2019)

Pellet A, 'Article 19 of the 1969 Vienna Convention' in O Corten and P Klein (eds), *The Vienna Conventions on the Law of Treaties – A Commentary* (OUP 2011) 405

'Article 38' in A Zimmermann et al (eds), *The Statute of the International Court of Justice: A Commentary* (2nd edn, OUP 2012) 731

Pellet A and D Müller, 'Reservations to Human Rights Treaties: Not an Absolute Evil . . .' in U Fastenrath (ed), *From Bilateralism to Community Interest: Essays in Honour of Judge Bruno Simma* (OUP 2011) 521

'Reservations to Treaties: An Objection to a Reservation Is Definitely Not an Acceptance' in E Cannizzaro (ed), *The Law of Treaties Beyond the Vienna Convention* (OUP 2011) 37

Pergantis V, *The Paradigm of State Consent in the Law of Treaties* (Edward Elgar 2017)

Philo, *De aeternitate mundi*

Plato, *Cratylus*

Plutarch, *Theseus*

Pulkowski D, '*Lex Specialis Derogat Legi Generali/Generalia Specialibus Non Derogant*' in J Klingler, Y Parkhomenko, and C Salonidis (eds), *Between the Lines of the Vienna Convention?: Canons and Other Principles of Interpretation in Public International Law* (Wolters Kluwer 2018) 161

Quoc Dinh N, A Pellet, and P Daillier, *Droit International Public* (7th edn, LGDJ 2002)

Ress G, 'The Interpretation of the Charter' in B Simma (ed), *The Charter of the United Nations: a Commentary* (2nd edn, OUP 2002) 13

Reuter P, *Introduction to the Law of Treaties* (J Mico and P Haggenmacher tr, 2nd edn, Routledge 1995)

Rosenne S, *Breach of Treaty* (Grotius 1985)

Developments in the Law of Treaties 1945–1986 (CUP 1989)

The Time Factor in the Jurisdiction of the International Court of Justice (Sythoff 1960)

Roucounas E, *A Landscape of Contemporary Theories of International Law* (Brill/ Martinus Nijhoff 2019)

Rousseau C, *Principes généraux du droit international public: Tome 1* (Pedone 1944)

Russell B, *The History of Western Philosophy* (Simon & Schuster 1967)

Sadat-Akhavi SA, *Methods of Resolving Conflicts between Treaties* (Brill 2003)

Saganek P, *Unilateral Acts of States in Public International Law* (Brill/Martinus Nijhoff 2015)

Sands P and P Klein, *Bowett's Law of International Institutions* (6th edn, Sweet & Maxwell 2009)

Saramago J, *Blindness* (Harvest Books 1999)

Sato T, *Evolving Constitutions of International Organizations: A Critical Analysis of the Interpretative Framework of the Constituent Instruments of International Organizations* (Kluwer Law International 1996)

Schermers HG and NM Blokker, *International Institutional Law: Unity with Diversity* (5th rev edn, Martinus Nijhoff 2011)

Schwarzenberger G, *A Manual of International Law* (3rd edn, Stevens 1952)

Schwebel St, 'May Preparatory Work Be Used to Correct Rather Than Confirm the "Clear" Meaning of a Treaty Provision?' in J Makarczyk and K Skubiszewski (eds), *Theory of International Law at the Threshold of the 21st Century* (Kluwer Law International 1996) 541

Seidl-Hohenveldern I, *International Economic Law* (Springer 1989)

Shaw MN and C Fournet, 'Article 62' in O Corten and P Klein (eds), *The Vienna Conventions on the Law of Treaties – A Commentary* (OUP 2011) 1411

Shelton D, 'Introduction: Law, Non-Law and the Problems of "Soft Law"' in D Shelton (ed), *Commitment and Compliance: The Role of Non-Binding Norms in the International Legal System* (OUP 2000) 1

Sicilianos L-A, *Les réactions décentralisées à l' illicite: des contre-mesures à la légitime défense* (LGDJ 1990)

Simma B and C Tams, 'Article 60' in O Corten and P Klein (eds), *The Vienna Conventions on the Law of Treaties – A Commentary* (OUP 2011) 1351

Simma B and G Hernández, 'Legal Consequences of an Impermissible Reservation to a Human Rights Treaty: Where Do We Stand?' in E Cannizzaro (ed), *The Law of Treaties Beyond the Vienna Convention* (OUP 2011) 60

Simplicius, *On Aristotle's Physics* (Bloomsbury 1997)

Sinclair I, *The Vienna Convention on the Law of Treaties* (2nd edn, MUP 1984)

Skubiszewski K, 'A New Source of the Law of Nations Resolutions of International Organisations' in P Guggenheim and M Battelli (eds), *Recueil d'études de droit international en hommage à Paul Guggenheim* (Imprimerie de la Tribune de Genève 1968) 508

Uchwaly Prawotworcze Organizacji Miendzynarodowych. Przeglad Zagadnien I Analiza Wstepna (Law-Making Resolutions of International Organisations. Survey of Problems and the Preliminary Analysis) (Praca Wydana z Zasiłku Polskiej Akademii Nauk 1965)

Solomou A, 'Exceptions to a Rule Must Be Narrowly Construed' in J Klingler, Y Parkhomenko, and C Salonidis (eds), *Between the Lines of the Vienna Convention?: Canons and Other Principles of Interpretation in Public International Law* (Wolters Kluwer 2018) 359

Sorensen R, *A Brief History of the Paradox: Philosophy and the Labyrinths of the Mind* (OUP 2003)

Sur S, *L' interprétation en droit international public* (LGDJ 1974)

Surbiguet MF and P Vagogne, *Liste des traites et accords de la France en vigueur au 1er octobre 1988* (Ministère des Affaires étrangères 1988)

Szasz PC, 'International Norm-Making' in E Brown Weiss (ed), *Environmental Change and International Law: New Challenges and Dimensions* (UN University Press 1992) 41

Sztucki J, 'Reflections on International "Soft Law"' in J Ramberg, O Bring, and S Mahmoudi (eds), *Festschrift till Lars Hjerner: Studies in International Law* (Norstedts 1990) 549

Tammes AJP, 'Soft Law' in ER Arbor (ed), *Essays on International and Comparative Law in Honour of Judge Erades* (Martinus Nijhoff 1983) 187

Tams C, 'Regulating Treaty Breaches' in Bowman and Kritsiotis (eds), *Conceptual and Contextual Perspectives on the Modern Law of Treaties* (CUP 2018) 440

Tavernier P, *Recherches sur l' application dans le temps des actes et des règles en droit international public: problèmes de droit intertemporel ou de droit transitoire* (LGDJ 1979)

Taylor H, *A Treatise on Public International Law* (Callaghan 1901)

Tennyson A, *Ulysses*

Thirlway H, 'The Sources of International Law' in M Evans (ed), *International Law* (4th edn, OUP 2014) 95

Tunkin GI, *Theory of International Law* (WE Butler tr, Harvard University Press 1974)

Tzanakopoulos A, 'Article 68 in 56' in O Corten and P Klein (eds), *The Vienna Conventions on the Law of Treaties – A Commentary* (OUP 2011) 1564

Tzeng P, 'The Principles of Contemporaneous and Evolutionary Interpretation' in J Klingler, Y Parkhomenko, and C Salonidis (eds), *Between the Lines of the Vienna Convention?: Canons and Other Principles of Interpretation in Public International Law* (Wolters Kluwer 2018) 387

Ulfstein G, 'Treaty Bodies and Regimes' in DB Hollis (ed), *The Oxford Guide to Treaties* (OUP 2012) 428

Ulfstein G and J Werksman, 'The Kyoto Compliance System: Towards Hard Enforcement' in OS Stokke, J Hovi, and G Ulfstein (eds), *Implementing the Climate Regime: International Compliance* (Earthscan 2005) 39

United Nations, *Final Clauses of Multilateral Treaties: Handbook* (United Nations 2003)

Vamvoukos A, *Termination of Treaties in International Law: The Doctrines of* Rebus sic Stantibus *and* Desuetude (Clarendon Press 1985)

van Hoof GJH, *Rethinking the Sources of International Law* (Kluwer Law and Taxation Publishers 1983)

Villiger ME, *Commentary on the 1969 Vienna Convention on the Law of Treaties* (Brill 2009)

Virally M, 'The Sources of International Law' in M Sorensen (ed), *Manual of Public International Law* (Macmillan 1968) 1564

Westlake J, *International Law* (2nd edn, Sn 1910)

Whitehead AN, *Essays in Science and Philosophy* (Philosophical Library 1947)

Wolfrum R, 'Legitimacy and International Law from a Legal Perspective: Some Introductory Considerations' in R Wolfrum and V Röben (eds), *Legitimacy in International Law* (Springer 2008) 1

Wyatt J, *Intertemporal Linguistics in International Law: Beyond Contemporaneous and Evolutionary Treaty Interpretation* (Hart Publishing 2019)

Yotova R, 'Compliance with Domestic Law: An Implied Condition in Treaties Conferring Rights and Protections on Foreign Nationals and Their Property?' in J Klingler, Y Parkhomenko, and C Salonidis (eds), *Between the Lines of the Vienna Convention?: Canons and Other Principles of Interpretation in Public International Law* (Wolters Kluwer 2018) 307

Yü T-C, *The Interpretation of Treaties* (Sn 1927)

Articles

'Editorial Comments: Withdrawing from the Ever Closer Union?" (2016) 53/6 CMLR 1491

'Ramsar Convention: Progress Achieved' (1987) 17/5 EP&L 179

Abi-Saab G, 'General Course of Public International Law' (1987/VII) 207 RdC 15

Ackermann T and K Fenrich, 'Motion and Rest: International Law's Responsiveness towards Terrorism, Mass Surveillance, and Self-Defence' (2017) 77 ZaöRV 745

Agius M, 'The Invocation of Necessity in International Law' (2009) 56/2 NILR 95

Albert R, 'Amending Constitutional Amendment Rules' (2015) 13/3 Int'lJConstL 655

Ambrus M and R Wessel, 'Between Pragmatism and Predictability: Temporariness in International Law' (2014) 45 NYIL 3

Arato J, ''Subsequent Practice and Evolutive Interpretation' (2010) 9/3 Law and Practice of International Courts and Tribunals 443

Aust A, 'The Theory and Practice of Informal International Instruments' (1986) 35 ICLQ 787

Bantekas I, 'Uniformity in Model Laws as Subsequent Practice under Article 31 of Vienna Convention on the Law of Treaties' (2015) 20 ARIEL 145

Baratta R, 'Should Invalid Reservations to Human Rights Treaties Be Disregarded?' (2000) 11 EJIL 413

Basaran I, 'The Evolution of the International Maritime Organization's Role in Shipping' (2016) 47/1 JMarL&Com 101

Bassiouni Ch, 'Functional Approach to "General Principles of International Law"' (1989–90) 11 MichJInt'lL 768

Baxter RR, 'International Law in Her Infinite Variety' (1980) 29 ICLQ 549

Beckett WE, 'Decisions of the Permanent Court of International Justice on Points of Law and Procedure of General Application' (1930) 11 BYIL 1

'Les questions d' intérêt général au point de vue juridique dans la jurisprudence de la Cour permanente de justice internationale' (1932) 39 RdC 135

'Les questions d' intérêt général au point de vue juridique dans la jurisprudence de la Cour permanente de justice internationale (juillet 1932 – juillet 1934)' (1934) 50 RdC 193

Benacerraf P, 'Tasks, Super-Tasks, and the Modern Eleatics' (1962) 59 JPhil 765

Bernhardt R, 'Evolutive Treaty Interpretation, Especially of the European Convention on Human Rights' (1999) 42 GYIL 11

Bernstein S, 'Legitimacy in a Global Environmental Governance' (2005) 1 JILIR 139

Besson S, 'State Consent and Disagreement in International Law-Making: Dissolving the Paradox' (2016) 29 LJIL 289

Bewley-Taylor DR and M Fitzmaurice, 'The Evolution and Modernisation of Treaty Regimes' (2018) 20 ICLR 403

Birnie PW, 'Small Cetaceans and the International Whaling Commission' (1997) 10/1 GeoIntlEnvtlLRev 1

Black M, 'Achilles and the Tortoise' (1951) 11/5 Analysis 91

Blix H, 'The Requirement of Ratification' (2000) 30 BYIL 352

Bodansky D, 'The Legal Character of the Paris Agreement' (2016) 25 RECIEL 142

'The Legitimacy of International Governance: A Coming Challenge for International Environmental Law?' (1999) 93 AJIL 596

Bolintineanu A, 'Expression of Consent to Be Bound by a Treaty in the Light of the 1969 Vienna Convention' (1974) 68 AJIL 672

Bonafé BL and P Palchetti, 'Subsequent Practice in Treaty Interpretation between Article 31 and Article 32 of the Vienna Convention' (2018) 46 QuestInt'lL 1

Bothe M, 'Legal and Non-Legal Norms – A Meaningful Distinction in International Relations?' (1980) 11 NYIL 65

Bowett DW, 'Reservations to Non-Restricted Multilateral Treaties' (1976–7) 48 BYIL 67

Bowman MJ, 'The Multilateral Treaty Amendment Process – A Case Study' (1995) 44/3 ICLQ 540

Boyle AE, 'Saving the World? Implementation and Enforcement of International Environmental Law through International Institutions' (1991) 3 JEL229

Brierly JL, 'Some Considerations on the Obsolescence of Treaties' (1926) II Transactions of the Grotius Society 4

Brölmann C et al, 'Exiting International Organisations: A Brief Introduction' (2018) 15/2 IOLR 243

'Law-Making Treaties: Form and Function in International Law' (2005) 74 NJIL 383

Brunnée J, 'COPing with Consent: Law-Making under Multilateral Environmental Agreements' (2002) 15 LJIL 1

'The Kyoto Protocol: Testing Ground for Compliance Theories?' (2003) 63 ZaöRV 255

Brunnée J and S Toope, 'International Law and Constructivism: Elements of an Interactional Theory of International Law' (2000) 19 ColumJTransnat'lL 19

Buffard I and K Zemanek, 'The "Object and Purpose" of a Treaty: An Enigma?' (1998) 3/1 ARIEL 311

Burke MB, 'Dion and Theon: An Essentialist Solution to an Ancient Puzzle' (1994) 91 JPhilos 129

Busutill JJ, 'The Bonn Declaration on International Terrorism: A Non-Binding Agreement on Aircraft Hijacking' (1992) 31 ICLQ 474

Cançado Trindade AA, 'The Time Factor in the Application of the Rule of Exhaustion of Local Remedies in International Law' (1978) 61 RivDirInternaz 232

Capotorti F, 'L'extinction et la suspension des traités' (1971/III) 134 RdC 134

Carter WR, 'Dion's Left Foot (and the Price of Burkean Economy)' (1997) 57 Philos&PhenomenolRes 371

Castellarin E, 'La sentence partielle du 30 juin 2016 dans l' affaire du différend territorial et maritime entre la Croatie et la Slovénie' (2016) 52 AFDI 129

Churchill RR and G Ulfstein, 'Autonomous Institutional Arrangements in Multilateral Environmental Agreements: A Little-Noticed Phenomenon in International Law' (2000) 94 AJIL 623

Coing H, 'Trois formes historiques du droit: glossateurs, pandectistes, école de l'exégèse' (1970) 48 RHD 531, 540

Coope U, 'Why Does Aristotle Say That There Is No Time without Change?' (2001) 101 Proceedings of the Aristotelian Society 359

Craig P, 'Brexit: A Drama in Six Acts' (2016) 40 ELR 447

Crawford J and S Olleson, 'The Exception of Non-Performance: Links between the Law of Treaties and the State Responsibility' (2000) 21 AYBIL 55

Crivellaro J, 'How did Anzilotti's Jurisprudential Conception Influence the Jurisprudence of the Permanent Court of International Justice?' (*Jura Gentium*, 2011) <www.juragentium.org/topics/thil/en/crivella.htm>

d'Amato A, 'Treaties as a Source of General Rules of International Law' (1962) 3 Harvard International Law Club Bulletin 1

d'Aspremont J, 'The Idea of "Rules" in the Sources of International Law' (2013) 84 BYIL 103

Danilenko GM, 'International *Jus Cogens*: Issues of Law-Making' (1991) 2 EJIL 42

Davies P, 'Non-Compliance: A Pivotal or Secondary Function of COP Governance?' (2013) 15/1 ICLR 77

de Aréchaga EJ, 'International Law in the Past Third of a Century' (1978/I) 159 RdC 1

de Wet JC, 'Die Sogenaamde "Exceptio Non Adimpleti Contractus" in die Praktyk van Vandaag' (1945) 9/4 THRR 239

Deutsch H, 'Relative Identity' (*Stanford Encyclopedia of Philosophy*, 17 August 2018) <http://plato.stanford.edu/entries/identity-relative/>

Dock MC, 'Le retrait des membres des organisations internationales de la famille des Nations Unies' (1994) 40 AFDI 106

Dupuy P-M, 'Droit des traités, codification et responsabilité internationale' (1997) 43 AFDI 7

Edwards RW, 'Reservations to Treaties' (1989) 10 MichJInt'lL 362

Eeckhout P and E Frantziou, 'Brexit and Article 50 TEU: A Constitutionalist Reading' (2017) 54/3 CMLR 695

Eisemann PM, 'Le gentlemen's agreement comme source du droit international' (1979) 106 JDI 326

Elias TO, 'The Doctrine of Intertemporal Law' (1980) 74 AJIL 285

Fauchald OK, 'The Legal Reasoning of ICSID Tribunals – An Empirical Analysis (2008) 19 EJIL 301

Ferreirós J, '"What Fermented in Me for Years": Cantor's Discovery of Transfinite Numbers' (1995) 22 HistMath 33

Fitzmaurice G, 'Do Treaties Need Ratification?' (1934) 15 BYIL 113

'The Law and Procedure of the International Court of Justice, 1951–4: General Principles and Sources of Law' (1953) 30 BYIL 1

'The Law and Procedure of the International Court of Justice, 1951–4: Treaty Interpretation and Other Treaty Points' (1957) 33 BYIL 203

Fitzmaurice M, 'Consent to Be Bound – Anything New under the Sun?' (2005) 74 NJIL 483

'Dynamic (Evolutive) Interpretation of Treaties – Part I' (2008) 21 HYIL 101

'Dynamic (Evolutive) Interpretation of treaties – Part II' (2009) 22 HYIL 3

'Subsequent Agreement and Subsequent Practice: Some Reflections on the International Law Commission's Draft Conclusions' (2020) 22 ICLR 14

'The Identification and Character of Treaties and Treaty Obligations between States in International Law' (2002) 73/1 BYIL 141

'The Tale of Two Judges: Sir Hersch Lauterpacht and Sir Gerald Fitzmaurice – Human Rights and the Interpretation of Treaties' (2008) 61 RHDI 125

Fitzmaurice M and P Merkouris, 'Re-Shaping Treaties while Balancing Interests of Stability and Change: Trends in the Amendment/Modification/Revision of Treaties' (2015) 20/1 ARIEL 41

Fontanelli F, 'The Invocation of the Exception of Non-Performance: A Case-Study on the Role and Application of General Principles of International Law of Contractual Origin' (2012) 1 CJICL 119

Forlati S, 'Reactions to Non-Performance of Treaties in International Law' (2012) 25/3 LJIL 759

Forrest P, 'The Identity of Indiscernibles' (*Stanford Encyclopedia of Philosophy*, 15 August 2010) <http://plato.stanford.edu/entries/identity-indiscernible/>

French D, 'Treaty Interpretation and the Incorporation of Extraneous Legal Rules' (2006) 55 ICLQ 281

Gaja G, 'Positivism and Dualism in Dionisio Anzilotti' (1992) 3 EJIL 123

'Primary and Secondary Rules in the International Law of State Responsibility' (2014) 97 RivDirInternaz 981

Gallois A, 'Identity over Time' (*Stanford Encyclopedia of Philosophy*, 6 October 2016) <http://plato.stanford.edu/entries/identity-time/>

Georgopoulos Th, 'Le droit intertemporel et les dispositions conventionelles évolutives – quelle thérapie contre la vieillesse des traits?' (2004) 108/1 RGDIP 123

Gillespie A, 'Iceland's Reservation at the International Whaling Commission' (2003) 14 EJIL 977

Giraud E, 'Modification et terminaison des traités collectifs' (1961) 49/1 AIDI 5

Goldstein L, 'Four Alleged Paradoxes in Legal Reasoning' (1979) 38/2 CLJ 373

Goodman C, '*Acta Sunt Servanda*? A Regime for Regulating Unilateral Acts of States at International Law' (2006) 25 AYBIL 43

Goodman R, 'Human Rights Treaties, Invalid Reservations, and State Consent' (2002) 96 AJIL 531

Gormley LW, 'Brexit – Nevermind the Whys and Wherefores: Fog in the Channel, Continent Cut Off' (2017) 40 FordhamInt'lLJ 1175

Gourgourinis A, 'The Distinction between Interpretation and Application of Norms in International Adjudication' (2011) 2/1 JIDS 31

Greig DW, 'Reciprocity, Proportionality, and the Law of Treaties' (1994) 34 VJIL 295

Gross L, 'The Dispute between Greece and Turkey Concerning the Continental Shelf in the Aegean' (1977) 71 AJIL 31

Gruchalla-Wesierski T, 'A Framework for Understanding Soft Law' (1984) 30 McGill LJ 37

Guzman AT, '*The Consent Problem in International Law*', Berkeley Programme in International Law and Economics, Working Paper Series (2011) <https://escholarship.org/content/qt04x8x174/qt04x8x174.pdf>

Guzman AT and TLO Meyer, 'International Soft Law' (2010) 2 JLA 171

Gwiazda J, 'A Proof of the Impossibility of Completing Infinitely Many Tasks' (2012) 93 PacPhilosQ 1

Hafner G, 'L' "obsolescence" de certaines dispositions du traité autrichien de 1955' (1991) 37 AFDI 239

'Modification of Treaties by Subsequent Practice – Some Comments on the Austrian Position' (2015) 20 ARIEL 175

Hamamoto Y, 'Possible Limitations to the Role of Subsequent Agreements and Subsequent Practice – Viewed from Some State Practices' (2020) 22/1 ICLR 61

Haraszti G, 'Treaties and the Fundamental Change of Circumstances' (1975/III) 146 RdC 1

Hartz GA and JA Cover, 'Space and Time in the Leibnizian Metaphysic' (1988) 22 Noûs 493

Hawley K, 'Temporal Parts' (*Stanford Encyclopedia of Philosophy*, 5 October 2015) <http://plato.stanford.edu/entries/temporal-parts/>

Helfer LR, 'Nonconsensual International Lawmaking' (2008) 1 UIllLRev 71

Helfer RL, 'Exiting Treaties' (2005) 91 VaLRev 1579

Helgesen JE, 'What Are the Limits to the Evolutive Interpretation of the European Convention on Human Rights?' (2011) 31 HRLJ 275

Helmersen ST, 'Evolutive Treaty Interpretation: Legality, Semantics and Distinctions' (2013) 6 EurJLegStud 127

Henkin L, 'International Law: Politics, Values, and Functions' (1989) 216 RdC 9

Higgins R, 'Time and the Law: International Perspectives on an Old Problem' (1997) 46 ICLQ 501

Hillgenberg H, 'A Fresh Look at Soft Law' (1999) 10 EJIL 499

Hillion C, 'Le retrait de l'Union européenne: Analyse juridique' (2016) RTDE 719

'Withdrawal under Article 50 TEU: An Integration-Friendly Process' (2018) 55/2 CMLR 29

Holmes OW, 'The Path of the Law' 10 HLR 457

Huggett N, 'Zeno's Paradoxes' (*Stanford Encyclopedia of Philosophy*, 15 October 2010) <https://plato.stanford.edu/entries/paradox-zeno/#Arr>

Huggett N and C Hoefer, 'Absolute and Relational Theories of Space and Motion' (*Stanford Encyclopedia of Philosophy*, 22 January 2015) <https://plato.stanford.edu/entries/spacetime-theories/>

Hyde CC, 'Concerning the Interpretation of Treaties' (1909) 3 AJIL 46

'Interpretation of Treaties by the Permanent Court of International Justice' (1930) 24 AJIL 1

Irving R, 'The United Kingdom Referendum – June 1975' (1976) 1 ELR 3

Jennings RY, 'What Is International Law and How Do We Tell It When We See It?' (1981) 37 ASDI 59

Kearney RD and RE Dalton, 'The Treaty on Treaties' (1970) 64 AJIL 495

Kiss A, 'Les actes unilatéraux dans la pratique française du droit international' (1961) 65 RGDIP 317

Klabbers J, 'Accepting the Unacceptable? A New Nordic Approach to Reservations to Multilateral Treaties' (2000) 69 NJIL 179

'The Redundancy of Soft Law' (1996) 65 NJIL 167

Koester V, 'The Ramsar Convention: Which Parties Are Effectively Parties to What? (and Other Legal Issues)' (2014) 44/1–2 EP&L 100

Kolb R, 'La désuétude en droit international public' (2007) 111/3 RGDIP 577

Kolbasov JJ, 'Pravovyje Mery Okhrany Morija ot Zagrazhenia s Sushi' (Legal Measures for the Protection of the Sea Land-Based Pollution), Paper presented at the International Conference on Ecology and Law in the Baltic Sea Region: Sources and Development, held in Riga, 1990 (unpublished, on file with the authors)

König D, 'Tacit Consent / Opting Out Procedure' (2013) MPEPIL 1478

Kotzur M, 'Intertemporal Law' [2008] MPEPIL 1433

Lauterpacht H, 'Restrictive Interpretation and the Principle of Effectiveness of Treaties' (1949) 26 BYIL 73

Lawrence P and D Wong, 'Soft Law in the Paris Climate Agreement: Strength or Weakness?' (2017) 26 RECIEL 276

Le Floch G, 'La désuétude en droit international public' (2007) 111/3 RGDIP 609

Lefeber R, 'Creative Legal Engineering' (2000) 13 LJIL 1

Letsas G, 'Strasbourg's Interpretive Ethic: Lessons for the International Lawyer' (2010) 21 EJIL 509

Li Z, 'International Intertemporal Law' (2018) 48/2 CalWInt'lLJ 342

Linderfalk U, 'The Application of International Legal Norms over Time: The Second Branch of Intertemporal Law' (2011) 58/2 NILR 147

'The Creation of *Jus Cogens*: Making Sense of Article 53 of the Vienna Convention' (2011) 71 ZaöRV 359

Doing the Right Thing for the Right Reason – Why Dynamic or Static Approaches Should Be Taken in the Interpretation of Treaties' (2008) 10 ICLR 109

'The Effect of *Jus Cogens* Norms: Whoever Opened Pandora's Box, Did You Ever Think about the Consequences?' (2007) 18 EJIL 853

Lipson C, 'Why Are Some International Agreements Informal?' (1991) 45 International Organisation 495

Lissitzyn OJ, 'Treaties and Changed Circumstances (*Rebus Sic Stantibus*)' (1967) 61 AJIL 895

Lysen G, 'The Joint Declaration by the EEC and the CMEA' (1989) 14 NCJInt'lL & ComReg 369

Magliveras DK, 'The Withdrawal from the League of Nations Revisited' (1991) 10 Penn State International Law Review 25

Malkin HW, 'Reservations to Multilateral Conventions' (1926) 7 BYIL 141

Marks S, 'Treaties, State Responsibility and Remedies' (1990) 49/3 CLJ 387

McCall-Smith KL, 'Reservations and the Determinative Function of the Human Rights Treaty Bodies' (2012) 54 GYIL 521

'Severing Reservations' (2014) 63 ICLQ 599

McGibbon I, 'Estoppel in International Law' (1958) 7 ICLQ 468

McLachlan C, 'The Principle of Systemic Integration and Article 31(3)(c) of the Vienna Convention' (2005) 54/2 ICLQ 279

McNair AD, 'L' application et l' interprétation des traités d' aprés la jurisprudence britannique' (1933) 43 RdC 247

Meek MR, 'International Law: Reservations to Multilateral Agreements' (1955) 5 DePaul LR 40

Merkouris P, 'Interpreting the Customary Rules on Interpretation' (2017) 19 ICLR 126

'(Inter)temporal Considerations in the Interpretative Process of the VCLT: Do Treaties Endure, Perdure or Exdure?' (2014) 45 NYIL 121

Milanovic M and L-A Sicilianos, 'Reservations to Treaties: An Introduction' (2011) 24 EJIL 1055

Moloo R, 'When Actions Speak Louder Than Words: The Relevance of Subsequent Party Conduct to Treaty Interpretation' (2013) 31/1 BerkJIntlL 39

Müllerson R, 'The ABM Treaty: Changed Circumstances, Extraordinary Events, Supreme Interests and International Law' (2005) 59 ICLQ 509

Münch F, 'Comments on the 1968 Draft Convention on the Law of Treaties' (1969) 29 ZaöRV 1

Myers DP, 'The Names and Scope of Treaties' (1957) 51 AJIL 574

Nahlik S, 'La Conference de Vienne sur le droit des traités: une vue d'ensemble' (1969) 15 AFDI 24

Nakanishi Y, 'Defining Boundaries of Legally Binding Treaties – A Study of Different State Practice in Treaty-Making' (2018) 20 ICLR 169

Nolte G, 'Treaties and Their Practice – Symptoms of Their Rise or Decline' (2018) 392 RdC 205

Norton JD, 'A Quantum Mechanical Supertask' (1999) 29/8 FoundPhys 1265

Oberthür S, 'Ozone Layer Protection at the Turn of the Century: The Eleventh Meeting of the Parties' (2000) 30/1–2 EP&L 34

Oberthür S and R Lefeber, 'Holding Countries to Account: The Kyoto Protocol's Compliance System Revisited after Four Years of Experience' (2010) 1 Climate L 133

Ostendorf P, 'The Withdrawal Cannot Be Withdrawn: The Irrevocability of a Withdrawal Notification under Article 50(2) TEU' (2017) 42/5 ELR 767

Paddeu F, 'A Genealogy of *Force Majeure* in International Law' (2011) 82 BYIL 381

Papageorgiou I, 'The (Ir-)revocability of the Withdrawal Notification under Article 50 TEU' *Policy Department for Citizens' Rights and Constitutional Affairs, European Parliament* (March 2018) <www.europarl.europa.eu/RegData/etudes/IDAN/2018/596820/IPOL_IDA(2018)596820_EN.pdf>

Peters JK, 'Reservations to Multilateral Treaties: How International Legal Doctrine Reflects World Vision' (1982-3) 23 HILJ 71

Plender R, 'The Role of Consent in the Termination of Treaties' (1986) 57 BYIL 133

Pronto AN, 'The Effect of War on Law – What Happens to Their Treaties When States Go to War?' (2013) 2 CJICL 227

Quadri R, 'Cours général de droit international public' (1964/III) 113 RdC 237

Rajamani L, 'The 2015 Paris Agreement: Interplay between Hard, Soft and Non-Obligations' (2016) 28 JEL 337

Ranganathan S, 'Between Philosophy and Anxiety? The Early International Law Commission, Treaty Conflict and the Project of International Law' (2012) 83 BYIL 82

Rank R, 'Modern War and the Validity of Treaties: A Comparative Study' (1953) 38 CLQ 321

Roessler F, 'Law, *De Facto* Agreements and Declarations of Principle in International Economic Relations' (1978) 21 GYIL 27

Rogers JM and RE Molzon, 'Some Lessons about the Law from Self-Referential Problems in Mathematics' (1991–2) 90 MichLRev 992

Roucounas E, 'Engagements parallèles et contradictoires' (1987/VI) 206 RdC 9

'The Users of International Law' in MH Arsanjani et al (eds), Looking to the Future: Essays on International Law in Honor of W Michael Reisman (Brill/Martinus Nijhoff 2010) 217–234

Rubin A, 'The International Legal Effects of Unilateral Declarations' (1977) 71 AJIL 1

Ruda JM, 'Reservation to Treaties' (1975) 146 RdC 95

Sari A, 'Reversing a Withdrawal Notification under Article 50 TEU: Can a Member State Change Its Mind' (2017) 42/4 ELR 451

Saydé A, 'Defining the Concept of Abuse of Union Law' (2014) 33/1 YEL 138

Scelle G, 'Règles générales du droit de la paix' (1933/IV) 46 RdC 327

Schachter O, 'The Twilight Existence of Nonbinding International Agreements' (1977) 71 AJIL 296

Schiller AA, 'Custom in Classical Roman Law' (1937) 24 VaLRev 268

Schwarzenberger G, 'The Principles and Standards of International Economic Law' (1966/I) 117 RdC 5

Schwelb E, 'Termination or Suspension of the Operation of a Treaty as a Consequence of Its Breach' (1967) 7 IJIL 309

Setear J, 'An Iterative Perspective on Treaties: A Synthesis of International Relations Theory and International Law' (1996) 37/1 HILJ 139

Shaw M, 'Case Concerning *Kasikili/Sedudu Island (Botswana/Namibia)*' (2000) 49 ICLQ 964

Sicilianos L-A, 'The Classification of Obligations and the Multilateral Dimension of the Relations of International Responsibility' (2002) 13/5 EJIL 1127

'The Relationship between Reprisals and Denunciation or Suspension of a Treaty' (1993) 4 EJIL 341

Simma B, 'Reflections on Article 60 of the Vienna Convention on the Law of Treaties and Its Background in General International Law' (1970) 20 ZOffR 5

'Termination and Suspension of Treaties: Two Recent Austrian Cases' (1978) 21 GYIL 74

Stern B, 'La succession d' Etats' (1996) 262 RdC 9

Sucharipa-Behrmann L, 'The Legal Effects of Reservations to Multilateral Treaties' (1996) 1 ARIEL 67

Tamada D, 'The Japan–South Korea Claims Agreement: Identification of Subsequent Agreements and Practice' (2020) 22/1 ICLR 107

Teubner G, '"And God Laughed . . .": Indeterminacy, Self-Reference and Paradox in Law' (2011) 12 German Law Journal 376

Thirlway H, 'The Law and Procedure of the International Court of Justice 1960–1989: Part One' (1989) 60 BYIL 1

'The Law and Procedure of the International Court of Justice 1960–1989: Part Two' (1991) 62 BYIL 1

'The Law and Procedure of the International Court of Justice 1960–1989: Supplement 2006: Part Three' (2006) 77 BYIL 1

Thomson JF, 'Tasks and Super-Tasks' (1954) 15 Analysis 1

Thürer D, 'Soft Law' (2009) MPEPIL 1469

Tietje C, 'The Changing Legal Structure of International Treaties as an Aspect of an Emerging Global Governance Architecture' (1999) 42 GYIL 26

Tomuschat C, 'Obligations Arising for States without or against Their Will' (1993/IV) 241 RdC 195

Treves T, 'The Expansion of International Law: General Course on Public International Law' (2015) 398 RdC 9

Tridimas T, 'Article 50: An Endgame without an End?' (2016) 27 KLJ 297

van der Mensbrugghe Y, 'Legal Status of International North Sea Conference Declarations' (1990) 5 IJECL 15

Vidmar J, 'Unilateral Revocability in *Wightman*: Fixing Article 50 with Constitutional Tools' (2019) 15/2 EuConst 359

Weil P, 'Towards Relative Normativity in International Law' (1983) 77 AJIL 413

Wellens K and G Borchardt, 'Soft Law in the European Community Law' (1989) 14 ELR 267

Wessel RA, 'Informal International Law-Making as a New Form of World Legislation' (2011) 8 IOLR 253

Widdows K, 'The Unilateral Denunciation of Treaties Containing No Denunciation Clause' (1982) 53 BYIL 83

Wiersema A, 'The New International Law-Makers? Conferences of the Parties to Multilateral Environmental Agreements' (2009) 1 MichJInt'lL 231

Witenberg JC, '*Onus probandi* devant les jurisdictions arbitrales' (1951) 55 RGDIP 321

Xiouri M, 'Material Breach of a Treaty: Some Remarks on the Partial Award of 30 June 2016 in the Matter of an Arbitration between Croatia and Slovenia' (2019) 8/1 CILJ 131

'The *Exceptio Non Adimpleti Contractus* in Public International Law' (2019) 21 ICLR 56

Yasseen MK, 'L' interprétation des traités d'après la Convention de Vienne sur le Droit des Traités' (1976) 151 RdC 1

Unpublished/Online/Working Paper Series

Gatti M, 'The Article 50 Procedure for Withdrawal from the EU: A Well-Designed Secession Clause' (*EU Studies Association*, 6 May 2017) <,www.eustudies.org/conference/papers/download/43>

Georgopoulos A, 'The (Ir)revocability of Article 50 TEU (C-621/18 *Wightman*): Iphigenia Must Reach the Altar' (*SSRN*, 8 December 2018) <https://papers.ssrn.com/sol3/Delivery.cfm/SSRN_ID3298401_code734328.pdf?abstractid=3298401&mirid=1>

Hathaway OA, HN Saurabh Sanghvi and S Solow, 'Tacit Amendments' (*Yale Law School*, 15 November 2011) <https://law.yale.edu/system/files/documents/pdf/cglc/TacitAmendments.pdf>

International Documents

General Assembly & Security Council

UNGA, 'Statute of the International Law Commission' (21 November 1947) UNGA Res 174 (II) (as amended by UNGA Res 485 (V) (12 December 1950), 984 (X) (3 December 1955), 985 (X) (3 December 1955) and 36/39 (18 November 1981))

'Stockholm Declaration on the Human Environment' (15 December 1972) UN Doc A/RES/2994

ILC

Arangio-Ruiz G, 'Third Report on State Responsibility' (19 July 1991) UN Doc A/CN.4/440 and Add.1, reproduced in [1991/II – Part One] YBILC 1

Brierly JL, 'First Report on the Law of Treaties' (14 April 1950) UN Doc A/CN.4/23, reproduced in [1950/II] YBILC 222

Cedeño VR, 'Fourth Report on Unilateral Acts of States' (30 May 2001) UN Doc A/CN.4/519, reproduced in [2001/II – Part One] YBILC 115

'Third Report on Unilateral Acts of States' (17 February 2000) UN Doc A/CN.4/505, reproduced in [2000/II – Part One] YBILC 247

Crawford J, 'Second Report on State Responsibility' UN Doc A/CN.4/498 and Add.1–4, reproduced in [1999/II – Part One] YBILC 3

'Third Report on State Responsibility' (15 March, 15 June, 10 and 18 July, and 4 August 2000) UN Doc A/CN.4/507 and Add. 1–4

Fitzmaurice G, 'Fourth Report on the Law of Treaties' (17 March 1959) UN Doc A/CN.4/120, reproduced in [1959/II] YBILC 37

'Second Report on the Law of Treaties' (15 March 1957) UN Doc A/CN.4/107, reproduced in [1957/II] YBILC 16

'Third Report on the Law of Treaties' (18 March 1958) UN Doc A/CN.4/115, reproduced in [1958/II] YBILC 20

ILC 'Draft Articles on the Law of Treaties with Commentaries' (4 May–19 July 1966) UN Doc A/CN.4/191, reproduced in [1966/II] YBILC 187

ILC Study Group, 'Annex A. Treaties over Time in Particular: Subsequent Agreement and Practice', reproduced in [2008/II – Part Two] YBILC 152

'Draft Articles on Responsibility of States for Internationally Wrongful Acts with Commentaries' (23 April–1 June and 2 July–10 August 2001) UN Doc A/56/10, reproduced in [2001/II – Part Two] YBILC 31

'Draft Conclusions on Subsequent Agreements and Subsequent Practice in Relation to the Interpretation of Treaties, with Commentaries' (30 April–1 June and 2 July–10 August 2018) UN Doc A/73/10, reproduced in [2018/II – Part Two] YBILC 11

'Guide to Practice on Reservations to Treaties, with Commentaries' (26 April–3 June and 4 July–12 August 2011) UN Doc A/66/10/Add.1

'Guiding Principles Applicable to Unilateral Declarations of States Capable of Creating Legal Obligations, with Commentaries thereto' [2006/II – Part Two] YBILC 161

'Report of the Commission to the General Assembly on the Work of Its 49th Session' [1997/II – Part Two] YBILC 1

'Report on Fragmentation of International Law: Difficulties Arising from the Diversification and Expansion of International Law, finalised by Martti Koskenniemi' (13 April 2006) UN Doc A/CN.4/L.682

'Report of the International Law Commission Covering the Work of Its 16th Session' (11 May–24 July 1964) UN Doc A/5809

'Report of the International Law Commission on the Work of Its 18th Session' 4 May–19 July 1966) UN Doc A/6309/Rev.l, reproduced in [1966/II] YBILC 172
'Report of the International Law Commission on the Work of Its 44th Session' (4 May–24 July 1992) UN Doc A/47/10, reproduced in [1992/II – Part Two] YBILC 1
'Report of the International Law Commission on the Work of Its 66th Session' (5 May–6 June and 7 July–8 August 2014) UN Doc A/69/10
'Report of the International Law Commission on the Work of Its 68th Session' (2 May–10 June and 4 July–12 August 2016) UN Doc A/71/10
'Subsequent Agreements and Subsequent Practice in Relation to the Interpretation of Treaties: Text of the Draft Conclusions adopted by the Drafting Committee on Second Reading' (11 May 2018) UN Doc A/CN.4/L.907
'Summary Record of the 1585th Meeting' (6 May 1980) UN Doc A/CN.4/SR.1585
'Summary Record of the 691st Meeting' (31 May 1963) UN Doc A/CN.4/SR.691
'Summary Record of the 693rd Meeting' (5 July 1963) UN Doc A/CN.4/SR.693
'Summary Record of the 728th Meeting' (21 May 1964) UN Doc A/CN.4/SR.728
'Summary Record of the 729th Meeting' (22 May 1964) UN Doc A/CN.4/SR.729
'Summary Record of the 744th Meeting' (12 June 1964) UN Doc A/CN.4/SR.744
'Summary Record of the 745th Meeting' (15 June 1964) UN Doc A/CN.4/SR.745
'Summary Record of the 746th Meeting' (16 June 1964) UN Doc A/CN.4/SR.746
'Summary Record of the 747th Meeting' (17 June 1964) UN Doc A/CN.4/SR.747
'Summary Record of the 753rd Meeting' (26 June 1964) UN Doc A/CN.4/SR.753
'Summary Record of the 754th Meeting' (29 June 1964) UN Doc A/CN.4/SR.754
'Summary Record of the 764th Meeting' (13 July 1964) UN Doc A/CN.4/SR.764
'Summary Record of the 765th Meeting' (14 July 1964) UN Doc A/CN.4/SR.765
'Summary Record of the 766th Meeting' (15 July 1964) UN Doc A/CN.4/SR.766
'Summary Record of the 767th Meeting' (16 July 1964) UN Doc A/CN.4/SR.767
'Summary Record of the 769th Meeting' (17 July 1964) UN Doc A/CN.4/SR.769
'Summary Record of the 770th Meeting' (20 July 1964) UN Doc A/CN.4/SR.770
'Summary Record of the 831st Meeting' (14 January 1966) UN Doc A/CN.4/SR.831
'Summary Record of the 832nd Meeting' (17 January 1966) UN Doc A/CN.4/SR.832
'Summary Record of the 833rd Meeting' (18 January 1966) UN Doc A/CN.4/SR.833
'Summary Record of the 834th Meeting' (19 January 1966) UN Doc A/CN.4/SR.834
'Summary Record of the 845th Meeting' (5 May 1966) UN Doc A/CN.4/SR.845
'Summary Record of the 847th Meeting' (9 May 1966) UN Doc A/CN.4/SR.847
'Summary Record of the 848th Meeting' (10 May 1966) UN Doc A/CN.4/SR.848

'Summary Record of the 857th Meeting' (24 May 1966) UN Doc A/CN.4/SR.857
'Summary Record of the 859th Meeting' (26 May 1966) UN Doc A/CN.4/SR.859
'Summary Record of the 860th Meeting' (27 May 1966) UN Doc A/CN.4/SR.860
'Summary Record of the 866th Meeting' (9 June 1966) UN Doc A/CN.4/SR.866
'Summary Record of the 869th Meeting' (14 June 1966) UN Doc A/CN.4/SR.869
'Summary Record of the 870th Meeting' (15 June 1966) UN Doc A/CN.4/SR.870
'Summary Record of the 871st Meeting' (16 June 1966) UN Doc A/CN.4/SR.871
'Summary Record of the 872nd Meeting' (17 June 1966) UN Doc A/CN.4/SR.872
'Summary Record of the 873rd Meeting' (20 July 1966) UN Doc A/CN.4/SR.873
'Summary Record of the 875th Meeting' (22 June 1966) UN Doc A/CN.4/SR.875
'Summary Record of the 876th Meeting' (23 June 1966) UN Doc A/CN.4/SR.876
'Summary Record of the 883rd Meeting' (4 July 1966) UN Doc A/ CN.4/SR.883
'Summary Record of the 888th Meeting' (12 July 1966) UN Doc A/CN.4/SR.888
'Summary Record of the 1858th Meeting' (10 July 1984) UN Doc A/CN.4/SR.1858
'Summary Record of the 1860th Meeting' (12 July 1984) UN Doc A/CN.4/SR.1860
'Summary Record of the 1867th Meeting' (20 July 1984) UN Doc A/CN.4/SR.1867

Lauterpacht H, 'Second Report on the Law of Treaties' (8 June 1954) UN Doc A/CN.4/87 and Corr.1, reproduced in [1954/II] YBILC 123

Nolte G, 'Fifth Report on Subsequent Agreements and Subsequent Practice in Relation to Treaty Interpretation' (28 February 2018) UN Doc A/CN.4/715

'First Report on Subsequent Agreements and Subsequent Practice in Relation to Treaty Interpretation' (19 March 2013) UN Doc A/CN.4/660

'Fourth Report on Subsequent Agreements and Subsequent Practice in Relation to the Interpretation of Treaties' (7 March 2016) UN Doc A/CN.4/694

'Second Report on Subsequent Agreements and Subsequent Practice in Relation to the Interpretation of Treaties' (26 March 2014) UN Doc A/CN.4/671

'Third Report on Subsequent Agreements and Subsequent Practice in Relation to the Interpretation of Treaties' (7 April 2015) UN Doc A/CN.4/683

Pellet A, 'Fifteenth Report on Reservations to Treaties' (31 March, 26 May, and 31 May 2010) UN Doc A/CN.4/624 and Add.1-2

Riphagen W, 'Fifth Report on the Content, Forms and Degrees of International Responsibility' (4 April 1984) UN Doc A/CN.4/380 and Corr.1, reproduced in [1984/II – Part One] YBILC 1

'Fourth Report on the Content, Forms and Degrees of International Responsibility' (14–15 April 1983) UN Doc A/CN.4/366 and Add.1 & Add.1/Corr.1, reproduced in [1983/II – Part One] YBILC 3

'Preliminary Report on the Content, Forms and Degrees of International Responsibility' (1 April 1980) UN Doc A/CN.4/330, reproduced in [1980/II – Part One] YBILC 107

'Seventh Report on State Responsibility' (4 March and 23 April 1986) UN Doc A/CN.4/397 and Corr.1 & 2 and Add.1 & Corr.1, reproduced in [1986/II – Part One] YBILC 1

'Sixth Report on the Content, Forms and Degrees of International Responsibility' (2 April 1985) UN Doc A/CN.4/389 and Corr.1 & Corr.2, reproduced in [1985/II – Part One] YBILC 3

Waldock H, 'First Report on the Law of Treaties' (26 March 1962) UN Doc A/CN.4/144 and Add.1, reproduced in [1962/II] YBILC 28

'Second Report on the Law of Treaties' (20 March, 10 April, 30 April and 5 June 1963) UN Doc A/CN.4/156 and Add.1–3, reproduced in [1963/II] YBILC 36

'Sixth Report on the Law of Treaties' (11 March, 25 March, 12 April, 11 May, 17 May, 24 May, 1 June, and 14 June 1966) UN Doc A/CN.4/186 and Add. 1–7, reproduced in [1966/II] YBILC 51

'Third Report on the Law of Treaties' (3 March, 9 June, 12 June, and 7 July 1964) UN Doc A/CN.4/167 and Add.1–3, reproduced in [1964/II] YBILC 5

Wood M, 'Third Report on Identification of Customary International Law' (27 March 2015) UN Doc A/CN.4/682

Sixth Committee

Sixth Committee, '20th Session, Summary Record of the 843rd Meeting' (7 October 1965) UN Doc A/C.6/20/SR.843

'20th Session, Summary Record of the 845th Meeting' (11 October 1965) UN Doc A/C.6/SR.845

'20th Session, Summary Record of the 850th Meeting' (13 October 1965) UN Doc A/C.6/SR.850

ILA

ILA, 'Preliminary Report of the Study Group on the Content and Evolution of the Rules of Interpretation' (*ILA*, 7–11 August 2016) <https://ila.vettoreweb.com/Storage/Download.aspx?DbStorageId=1401&StorageFileGuid=bcaa951e-ae3e-4ccb-9c80–248c98c741e3>

ILA Committee on Formation of Customary (General) International Law, 'Final Report of the Committee: Statement of Principles Applicable to the Formation of General Customary International Law' (*ILA*, 2000) <https://ila.vettoreweb.com/Storage/Download.aspx?DbStorageId=1107&StorageFileGuid=e6663317-c7ca-4fff-a6e8–1cc2423756bf>

United Nations Conference on the Law of Treaties

Australia, 'Amendment Proposal to Article 41' UN Doc A/CONF.39/C.1/L.237

Colombia, Spain, and Venezuela, 'Amendment Proposal to Article 53' UN Doc A/CONF.39/C.1/L.307, Add.1 and 2

France, 'Amendment Proposal to Article 41' UN Doc A/CONF.39/C.1/L.46
Netherlands, 'Amendment Proposal to Article 40' UN Doc A/CONF.39/C.1/L.232
UK, 'Amendment Proposal to Article 53' UN Doc A/CONF.39/C.1/L.311
United Nations Conference on the Law of Treaties, '1st Session – 15th Meeting of the Committee of the Whole (COW)' (5 April 1968) UN Doc A/CONF.39/C.1/SR.15 80
'1st Session – 19th Meeting of the Committee of the Whole (COW)' (9 April 1968) UN Doc A/CONF.39/C.1/SR.19 97
'1st Session – 31st Meeting of the Committee of the Whole (COW)' (19 April 1968) UN Doc A/CONF.39/C.1/SR.31 164
'1st Session – 33rd Meeting of the Committee of the Whole (COW)' (22 April 1968) UN Doc A/CONF.39/C.1/SR.33 177
'1st Session – 37th Meeting of the Committee of the Whole (COW)' (24 April 1968) UN Doc A/CONF.39/11 203
'1st Session – 38th Meeting of the Committee of the Whole (COW)' (25 April 1968) UN Doc A/CONF.39/11 210
'1st Session – 58th Meeting of the Committee of the Whole (COW)' (8 May 1968) UN Doc A/CONF.39/C.1/SR.58 334
'1st Session – 62nd Meeting of the Committee of the Whole (COW)' (9 May 1968) UN Doc A/CONF.39/C.1/SR.62 361
'2nd Session – 11th Plenary Meeting' (30 April 1969) UN Doc A/CONF.39/SR.11 35
'2nd Session – 86th Meeting of the Committee of the Whole (COW)' (11 April 1969) UN Doc A/CONF.39/11/Add.1 222

Insitut de Droit International Reports

Institut de Droit International, 'De l'interprétation des traités'(1950) 43/1 AIDI 336
'De l' interprétation des traités' (1952) 44 AIDI 359
'De l'interprétation des traités'(1956) 46 AIDI 359
'Modifications et terminaison des traités collectifs' (1961/I) 49 AIDI 229
'Problems Arising from a Succession of Codification Conventions on a Particular Subject' (1995/I) 66 AIDI 248
'Resolution of 11 August 1975: The Intertemporal Problem in Public International Law' (1975) 56 AIDI 536
'Resolution: L' interprétation des traités' (*IDI*, 1956) <www.idi-iil.org/app/uploads/2017/06/1956_grena_02_fr.pdf>
Virally M, 'Rapport définitif: La distinction entre textes internationaux ayant une portée juridique dans les relations mutuelles entre leur auteurs et les textes juridiques qui en sont dépourvus' (1983) 60/I AIDI 328
'Rapport provisoire: La distinction entre textes internationaux ayant une portée juridique dans les relations mutuelles entre leur auteurs et les textes juridiques qui en sont dépourvus' (1983) 60/I AIDI 166

Other Reports

ILO Committee on Legal Issues and International Labour Standards, 'Possible Improvements in the Standard – Setting Activities of the ILO: The Role of Standards in the Achievement of the ILO's Objectives' (March 2000) GB.277/LILS/2 <www.ilo.org/public/english/standards/relm/gb/docs/gb277/pdf/lils-2.pdf>

Transnational Institute, 'The UN Drug Control Conventions: A Primer' (*Transnational Institute*, 24 October 2015) <www.tni.org/files/publication-downloads/primer_unconventions_24102015.pdf>

UNEP, 'The Report of the Legal Drafting Group on Possible Adjustments and Amendment of the Montreal Protocol' (17 June 1999) UN Doc UNEP/OzL.Pro.11/3

World Tourism Organisation, 'Report of the Secretary-General: Other Administrative and Statutory Matters – Status of Ratification of Amendments to the Statutes and of the 1947 Convention on the Privileges and Immunities of the Specialized Agencies' (1 October 2018) UN Doc CE/109/3(d)iii

Other International Documents

1978 Bonn Summit Statement on Air-Hijacking (1978) 17 ILM 1285

1984 Declaration of the International Conference on the Protection of the North Sea (*OSPAR*, 1984) <www.ospar.org/site/assets/files/1239/1nsc-1984-bremen_declaration.pdf>

1987 London Declaration, Second International Conference on the Protection of the North Sea (*Vlaams Instituut Voor de Zee*, 24–5 November 1987) <www.vliz.be/imisdocs/publications/140155.pdf>

1988 Ministerial Declaration on the Protection of the Marine Environment of the Baltic Sea (*Helsinki Commission*, 15 February 1988) <www.helcom.fi/Documents/About%20us/Convention%20and%20commitments/Ministerial%20declarations/MinDecl1988.pdf>

1990 Baltic Sea Declaration (*Helsinki Commission*, 2–3 September 1990) www.helcom.fi/Documents/About%20us/Convention%20and%20commitments/Ministerial%20declarations/RonnebyDecl1990.pdf>

1990 Ministerial Declaration of the Third International Conference on the Protection of the North Sea (*University of Oregon*, 8 March 1990) <https://iea.uoregon.edu/treaty-text/1990-thirdnorthseadeclarationentxt>

1993 Declaration on Resource Mobilisation for the Baltic Sea Joint Comprehensive Environmental Action Programme (*Helsinki Commission*, 24–25 March 1993) www.helcom.fi/Documents/About%20us/Convention%20and%20commitments/Ministerial%20declarations/GdanskDecl1993.pdf>

2001 Copenhagen Declaration on the Safety of Navigation and Emergency Capacity in the Baltic Sea Area (*Helsinki Commission*, 10 September 2001)

<www.helcom.fi/Documents/About%20us/Convention%20and%20commitments/Ministerial%20declarations/Copenhagen2001.pdf>

2003 Bremen Ministerial Declaration (*Helsinki Commission*, 25 June 2003) <www.helcom.fi/Documents/About%20us/Convention%20and%20commitments/Ministerial%20declarations/Bremen2003.pdf>

2007 HELCOM Baltic Sea Action Plan (*Helsinki Commission*, 15 November 2007) <www.helcom.fi/Documents/Baltic%20sea%20action%20plan/BSAP_Final.pdf>

2010 Moscow Ministerial Declaration (*Helsinki Commission*, 20 May 2010) <www.helcom.fi/Documents/About%20us/Convention%20and%20commitments/Ministerial%20declarations/HELCOM%20Moscow%20Ministerial%20Declaration%20FINAL.pdf>

2012 Bremen Declaration Adopted at the North Sea Commission Annual Business Meeting 20 June 2012 (*Eastern Norway Country Network*, 20 June 2012) www.ostsam.no/wp-content/uploads/2012/06/Bremen-Declaration.pdf>

2013 Copenhagen Declaration Taking Further Action to Implement the Baltic Sea Action Plan – Reaching Good Environmental Status for a Healthy Baltic Sea (*Helsinki Commission*, 3 October 2013) <www.helcom.fi/Documents/Ministerial2013/Ministerial%20declaration/2013%20Copenhagen%20Ministerial%20Declaration%20w%20cover.pdf>

CITES, 'Resolution Conf 9.24 (Rev. CoP17)' (*CITES*, 2019) <www.cites.org/sites/default/files/document/E-Res-09-24-R17.pdf>

CMP1, 'Decision 27/CMP.1: Procedures and Mechanisms Relating to Compliance under the Kyoto Protocol' (9–10 December 2005) UN Doc FCCC/KP/CMP/2005/8/Add.3

ECOSOC, 'Activities of Other Organizations and Countries of Interest to the Working Party' (22 December 2008) UN Doc ECE/TRANS/WP.30/2009/1

European Council, 'United Kingdom Notification under Article 50 TEU: Letter of 29 March 2017 from the Prime Minister of the United Kingdom to the President of the European Council' (29 March 2017) XT 20001/17 <http://data.consilium.europa.eu/doc/document/XT-20001-2017-INIT/en/pdf>

France, 'Observations by France on General Comment 24' (1997) 4 IHRR 6

Garner JW (Reporter), 'Codification of International Law: Part III – Law of Treaties – Appendix 1: Convention on Treaties'(1935) 29 AJIL Supp 1205

'Codification of International Law: Part III – Law of Treaties – Appendix 2: David Dudley Field's Draft Code'(1935) 29 AJIL Supp 1207

'Codification of International Law: Part III – Law of Treaties – Appendix 3: Bluntschli's Draft Code'(1935) 29 AJIL Supp 1208

'Codification of International Law: Part III – Law of Treaties – Appendix 4: Fiore's Draft Code' (1935) 29 AJIL Supp 1212

'Codification of International Law: Part III – Law of Treaties – Appendix 5: Draft of the International Commission of American Jurists' (1935) 29 AJIL Supp 1222

'Codification of International Law: Part III – Law of Treaties – Appendix 7: The Interpretation of Treaties' (1935) 29 AJIL Supp 1225

'Codification of International Law: Part III – Law of Treaties – Draft Convention on the Law of Treaties' (1935) 29 AJIL Supp 657

Human Rights Committee, 'General Comment on Issues Relating to Reservations Made upon Ratification or Accession to the Covenant or the Optional Protocols Thereto, or in Relation to Declarations under Article 41 of the Covenant' (4 November 1994) UN Doc CCPR/C/21/Rev.1/Add.6

ITU, 'Resolution No 62: Basic Instruments of the Union' (1982) 1531 UNTS 493

Security Consultative Committee, 'Joint Statement of the Security Consultative Committee – A Stronger Alliance for a Dynamic Security Environment: The New Guidelines for Japan–US Defence Cooperation' (*Ministry of Foreign Affairs of Japan*, 27 April 2015) www.mofa.go.jp/files/000078186.pdf>

UK, 'Observations by the United Kingdom on General Comment 24' (1996) 3 IHRR 261

UNCED, 'Rio Declaration on Environment and Development' (1992) 31 ILM 874

UNEP, 'Decision III/1: Amendment to the Basel Convention' (28 November 1995) UN Doc UNEP/CHW.3/35

'Report of the 2nd Meeting of the Parties to the Montreal Protocol on Substances That Deplete the Ozone Layer' (29 June 1990) UN Doc UNEP/OZL.Pro.2/3, Decision II/2

UNFCCC, 'Proposal from Saudi Arabia to Amend the Kyoto Protocol' (26 May 2005) UN Doc FCCC/KP/CMP/2005/2

'Questions of Implementation' (*UNFCC*, 2019) <http://unfccc.int/kyoto_protocol/compliance/questions_of_implementation/items/5451.php>

US, 'Observations by the United States on General Comment 24' (1996) 3 IHRR 265

Websites

'Motion' (*Oxford Dictionaries*, 2018) <https://en.oxforddictionaries.com/definition/motion>

'Move' (*Oxford Dictionaries*, 2018) <https://en.oxforddictionaries.com/definition/move>

Brière C, 'The Advocate-General Opinion in Wightman: Article 50 Notification to Withdraw from the European Union Is Unilaterally Revocable' (*European Law Blog*, 6 December 2018) <http://europeanlawblog.eu/2018/12/06/the-advocate-general-opinion-in-wightman-article-50-notification-to-withdraw-from-the-european-union-is-unilaterally-revocable/>

Çali B, 'Qatar's Reservations to the ICCPR: Anything New under the VCLT Sun?' (*EJIL: Talk!*, 19 September 2019) <www.ejiltalk.org/qatars-reservations-to-the-iccpr-anything-new-under-the-vclt-sun/>

Camenzuli LK, 'The Development of International Environmental Law at the Multilateral Environmental Agreements: Conference of the Parties and Its Validity' <http://cmsdata.iucn.org/downloads/cel10_camenzuli.pdf>

Cameron D, 'EU Speech at Bloomberg: Prime Minister David Cameron Discussed the Future of the European Union at Bloomberg' (*UK Government*, 23 January 2013) www.gov.uk/government/speeches/eu-speech-at-bloomberg>

Closa Montero C, 'Is Article 50 Reversible? On Politics beyond Legal Doctrine' (*Verfassungsblog*, 4 January 2017) <https://verfassungsblog.de/is-article-50-reversible-on-politics-beyond-legal-doctrine/>

Edward D et al, 'In the Matter of Article 50 of the Treaty on European Union ("The Three Knights' Opinion")' (*Bindmans*, 10 February 2017) <www.bindmans.com/uploads/files/documents/Final_Article_50_Opinion_10.2.17.pdf>

Falk R, '"Voluntary" International Law and the Paris Agreement' (*Richard Falk Wordpress*, 16 January 2016) <https://richardfalk.wordpress.com/2016/01/16/voluntary-international-law-and-the-paris-agreement/>

Garner O, 'Can the United Kingdom Unilaterally Revoke Its Article 50 Notification to Withdraw from the EU? *Wightman v Secretary of State for DexEU* [2018] CSIH 62' (*European Law Blog*, 24 September 2018) <http://europeanlawblog.eu/2018/09/24/can-the-united-kingdom-unilaterally-revoke-its-article-50-notification-to-withdraw-from-the-eu-wightman-v-secretary-of-state-for-dexeu-2018-csih-62/>

'Case C-621/18, *Wightman v Secretary of State for Exiting the European Union*: The European Court of Justice Confirms That Article 50 Notification Can Be Unilaterally Revoked' (*European Law Blog*, 11 December 2018) <http://europeanlawblog.eu/2018/12/11/case-c-621-18-wightman-v-secretary-of-state-for-exiting-the-european-union-the-european-court-of-justice-confirms-that-article-50-notification-can-be-unilaterally-revoked/>

IMO, 'Introduction' (*IMO*, 2019) <www.imo.org/en/About/Conventions/Pages/Home.aspx>

Jay A and J Lynn, 'Yes Minister Series, Episode Six: The Writing on the Wall: Transcript of Episode' (*Yes Minister*, 24 March 1980) <www.yes-minister.com/ymseas1b.htm>

McCrea R, 'Brexit II? The Legal Issues of Revoking the Notification to Leave the EU but Then Notifying to Leave Again' (*EU Law Analysis Blog*, 16 December 2018) <http://eulawanalysis.blogspot.com/2018/12/brexit-ii-legal-issues-of-revoking.html>

Peers St, 'Brexit: You Can U-turn If You Want To. The CJEU Judgment in Wightman' (*EU Law Analysis Blog*, 10 December 2018) <http://eulawanalysis.blogspot.com/2018/12/brexit-you-can-u-turn-if-you-want-to.html>

'Can an Article 50 Notice of Withdrawal from the EU Be Unilaterally Revoked?: The Case for Unilateral Revocability of the Article 50 Notice' (*EU Law*

Analysis Blog, 16 January 2018) <http://eulawanalysis.blogspot.com/2018/01/can-article-50-notice-of-withdrawal.html>

'Revoking the Notice to Withdraw from the EU? The Opinion in Wightman' (*EU Law Analysis Blog*, 4 December 2018) <http://eulawanalysis.blogspot.com/2018/12/revoking-notice-to-withdraw-from-eu.html>

Perakis M, 'Does the Principle of the Autonomy of the EU Legal Order Allow for a Member State to Revoke the Notification of Its Withdrawal from the EU?' (*European Law Blog*, 31 October 2018) <http://europeanlawblog.eu/2018/10/31/does-the-principle-of-the-autonomy-of-the-eu-legal-order-allow-for-a-member-state-to-revoke-the-notification-of-its-withdrawal-from-the-eu/>

Reid AS, 'Scotching Brexit? Background to the Wightman Case about Reversing the Article 50 Notification Unilaterally' (*EU Law Analysis Blog*, 16 November 2018) <http://eulawanalysis.blogspot.com/2018/11/scotching-brexit-background-to-wightman.html>

Sarmiento D, 'Miller, Brexit and the (Maybe Not So Evil) Court of Justice' (*Verfassungsblog*, 8 November 2016) <http://verfassungsblog.de/miller-brexit-and-the-maybe-not-to-so-evil-court-of-justice/>

Sarvarian A, 'Arbitration between Croatia and Slovenia: Leaks, Wiretaps, Scandal (Part 4)' (*EJIL: Talk!*, 3 May 2016) <www.ejiltalk.org/arbitration-between-croatia-andslovenia-leaks-wiretaps-scandal-part-4/>

Slaughter A-M, 'The Paris to Global Governance' (*Project Syndicate*, 28 December 2015) <www.project-syndicate.org/commentary/paris-agreement-model-for-global-governance-by-anne-marie-slaughter-2015-12?barrier=accessreg>

Tladi D, 'Is the International Law Commission Elevating Subsequent Agreements and Subsequent Practice?' (*EJIL: Talk!*, 30 August 2018) www.ejiltalk.org/is-the-international-law-commission-elevating-subsequent-agreements-and-subsequent-practice/>

Voigt Chr, 'On the Paris Agreement's Imminent Entry into Force (Part II of II)' (*EJIL: Talk!*, 12 October 2016) <www.ejiltalk.org/on-the-paris-agreements-imminent-entering-into-force-what-are-the-consequences-of-the-paris-agreements-entering-into-force-part-ii/>

Weatherill S, 'Can an Article 50 Notice of Withdrawal from the EU Be Unilaterally Revoked?: Why the Withdrawal Notification under Article 50 TEU Is Not Unilaterally Revocable' (*EU Law Analysis Blog*, 16 January 2018) <http://eulawanalysis.blogspot.com/2018/01/can-article-50-notice-of-withdrawal.html>

Weiler J, 'A Second Brexit Referendum – What Makes You Think They Will Have You Back?' (*EJIL: Talk!*, 26 November 2018) <www.ejiltalk.org/a-second-brexit-referendum-what-makes-you-think-they-will-have-you-back/#more-16684>

INDEX

CAMBRIDGE STUDIES IN INTERNATIONAL AND COMPARATIVE LAW

Books in the Series

149 *Treaties in Motion: The Evolution of Treaties from Formation to Termination* Edited by Malgosia Fitzmaurice and Panos Merkouris

148 *Humanitarian Disarmament: An Historical Enquiry* Treasa Dunworth

147 *Complementarity, Catalysts, Compliance: The International Criminal Court in Uganda, Kenya, and the Democratic Republic of Congo* Christian M. De Vos

146 *Cyber Operations and International Law* François Delerue

145 *Comparative Reasoning in International Courts and Tribunals* Daniel Peat

144 *Maritime Delimitation as a Judicial Process* Massimo Lando

143 *Prosecuting Sexual and Gender-Based Crimes at the International Criminal Court: Practice, Progress and Potential* Rosemary Grey

142 *Capitalism as Civilisation: A History of International Law* Ntina Tzouvala

141 *Sovereignty in China: A Genealogy of a Concept Since 1840* Adele Carrai

140 *Narratives of Hunger: Climate-Ready Seeds and International Law* Anne Saab

139 *Victim Reparation under the Ius Post Bellum: An Historical and Normative Perspective* Shavana Musa

138 *The Analogy between States and International Organizations* Fernando Lusa Bordin

137 *The Process of International Legal Reproduction: Inequality, Historiography, Resistance* Rose Parfitt

136 *State Responsibility for Breaches of Investment Contracts* Jean Ho

135 *Coalitions of the Willing and International Law: The Interplay between Formality and Informality* Alejandro Rodiles

134 *Self-Determination in Disputed Colonial Territories* Jamie Trinidad

133 *International Law as a Belief System* Jean d'Aspremont

132 *Legal Consequences of Peremptory Norms in International Law* Daniel Costelloe

131 *Third-Party Countermeasures in International Law* Martin Dawidowicz

130 *Justification and Excuse in International Law: Concept and Theory of General Defences* Federica Paddeu

129 *Exclusion from Public Space: A Comparative Constitutional Analysis* Daniel Moeckli

128 *Provisional Measures before International Courts and Tribunals* Cameron A. Miles

127 *Humanity at Sea: Maritime Migration and the Foundations of International Law* Itamar Mann

126 *Beyond Human Rights: The Legal Status of the Individual in International Law* Anne Peters

125 *The Doctrine of Odious Debt in International Law: A Restatement* Jeff King

124 *Static and Evolutive Treaty Interpretation: A Functional Reconstruction* Christian Djeffal

123 *Civil Liability in Europe for Terrorism-Related Risk* Lucas Bergkamp, Michael Faure, Monika Hinteregger and Niels Philipsen

122 *Proportionality and Deference in Investor-State Arbitration: Balancing Investment Protection and Regulatory Autonomy* Caroline Henckels

121 *International Law and Governance of Natural Resources in Conflict and Post-Conflict Situations* Daniëlla Dam-de Jong

120 *Proof of Causation in Tort Law* Sandy Steel

119 *The Formation and Identification of Rules of Customary International Law in International Investment Law* Patrick Dumberry

118 *Religious Hatred and International Law: The Prohibition of Incitement to Violence or Discrimination* Jeroen Temperman

117 *Taking Economic, Social and Cultural Rights Seriously in International Criminal Law* Evelyne Schmid

116 *Climate Change Litigation: Regulatory Pathways to Cleaner Energy* Jacqueline Peel and Hari M. Osofsky

115 *Mestizo International Law: A Global Intellectual History 1842–1933* Arnulf Becker Lorca

114 *Sugar and the Making of International Trade Law* Michael Fakhri

113 *Strategically Created Treaty Conflicts and the Politics of International Law* Surabhi Ranganathan

112 *Investment Treaty Arbitration As Public International Law: Procedural Aspects and Implications* Eric De Brabandere

111 *The New Entrants Problem in International Fisheries Law* Andrew Serdy

110 *Substantive Protection under Investment Treaties: A Legal and Economic Analysis* Jonathan Bonnitcha

109 *Popular Governance of Post-Conflict Reconstruction: The Role of International Law* Matthew Saul

108 *Evolution of International Environmental Regimes: The Case of Climate Change* Simone Schiele

107 *Judges, Law and War: The Judicial Development of International Humanitarian Law* Shane Darcy

106 *Religious Offence and Human Rights: The Implications of Defamation of Religions* Lorenz Langer

105 *Forum Shopping in International Adjudication: The Role of Preliminary Objections* Luiz Eduardo Salles

104 *Domestic Politics and International Human Rights Tribunals: The Problem of Compliance* Courtney Hillebrecht

103 *International Law and the Arctic* Michael Byers

102 *Cooperation in the Law of Transboundary Water Resources* Christina Leb

101 *Underwater Cultural Heritage and International Law* Sarah Dromgoole

100 *State Responsibility: The General Part* James Crawford

99 *The Origins of International Investment Law: Empire, Environment and the Safeguarding of Capital* Kate Miles

98 *The Crime of Aggression under the Rome Statute of the International Criminal Court* Carrie McDougall

97 *'Crimes against Peace' and International Law* Kirsten Sellars

96 *Non-Legality in International Law: Unruly Law* Fleur Johns

95 *Armed Conflict and Displacement: The Protection of Refugees and Displaced Persons under International Humanitarian Law* Mélanie Jacques

94 *Foreign Investment and the Environment in International Law* Jorge E. Viñuales

93 *The Human Rights Treaty Obligations of Peacekeepers* Kjetil Mujezinović Larsen

92 *Cyber Warfare and the Laws of War* Heather Harrison Dinniss

91 *The Right to Reparation in International Law for Victims of Armed Conflict* Christine Evans

90 *Global Public Interest in International Investment Law* Andreas Kulick

89 *State Immunity in International Law* Xiaodong Yang

88 *Reparations and Victim Support in the International Criminal Court* Conor McCarthy

87 *Reducing Genocide to Law: Definition, Meaning, and the Ultimate Crime* Payam Akhavan

86 *Decolonising International Law: Development, Economic Growth and the Politics of Universality* Sundhya Pahuja

85 *Complicity and the Law of State Responsibility* Helmut Philipp Aust

84 *State Control over Private Military and Security Companies in Armed Conflict* Hannah Tonkin

83 *'Fair and Equitable Treatment' in International Investment Law* Roland Kläger

82 *The UN and Human Rights: Who Guards the Guardians?* Guglielmo Verdirame

81 *Sovereign Defaults before International Courts and Tribunals* Michael Waibel

80 *Making the Law of the Sea: A Study in the Development of International Law* James Harrison

79 *Science and the Precautionary Principle in International Courts and Tribunals: Expert Evidence, Burden of Proof and Finality* Caroline E. Foster

78 *Transition from Illegal Regimes in International Law* Yaël Ronen

77 *Access to Asylum: International Refugee Law and the Globalisation of Migration Control* Thomas Gammeltoft-Hansen

76 *Trading Fish, Saving Fish: The Interaction between Regimes in International Law* Margaret A. Young

75 *The Individual in the International Legal System: Continuity and Change in International Law* Kate Parlett

74 *'Armed Attack' and Article 51 of the UN Charter: Evolutions in Customary Law and Practice* Tom Ruys

73 *Theatre of the Rule of Law: Transnational Legal Intervention in Theory and Practice* Stephen Humphreys

72 *Science and Risk Regulation in International Law* Jacqueline Peel

71 *The Participation of States in International Organisations: The Role of Human Rights and Democracy* Alison Duxbury

70 *Legal Personality in International Law* Roland Portmann

69 *Vicarious Liability in Tort: A Comparative Perspective* Paula Giliker

68 *The Public International Law Theory of Hans Kelsen: Believing in Universal Law* Jochen von Bernstorff

67 *Legitimacy and Legality in International Law: An Interactional Account* Jutta Brunnée and Stephen J. Toope

66 *The Concept of Non-International Armed Conflict in International Humanitarian Law* Anthony Cullen

65 *The Principle of Legality in International and Comparative Criminal Law* Kenneth S. Gallant

64 *The Challenge of Child Labour in International Law* Franziska Humbert

63 *Shipping Interdiction and the Law of the Sea* Douglas Guilfoyle

62 *International Courts and Environmental Protection* Tim Stephens

61 *Legal Principles in WTO Disputes* Andrew D. Mitchell

60 *War Crimes in Internal Armed Conflicts* Eve La Haye

59 *Humanitarian Occupation* Gregory H. Fox

58 *The International Law of Environmental Impact Assessment: Process, Substance and Integration* Neil Craik

57 *The Law and Practice of International Territorial Administration: Versailles to Iraq and Beyond* Carsten Stahn

56 *United Nations Sanctions and the Rule of Law* Jeremy Matam Farrall

55 *National Law in WTO Law: Effectiveness and Good Governance in the World Trading System* Sharif Bhuiyan

54 *Cultural Products and the World Trade Organization* Tania Voon

53 *The Threat of Force in International Law* Nikolas Stürchler

52 *Indigenous Rights and United Nations Standards: Self-Determination, Culture and Land* Alexandra Xanthaki

51 *International Refugee Law and Socio-Economic Rights: Refuge from Deprivation* Michelle Foster

50 *The Protection of Cultural Property in Armed Conflict* Roger O'Keefe

49 *Interpretation and Revision of International Boundary Decisions* Kaiyan Homi Kaikobad

48 *Multinationals and Corporate Social Responsibility: Limitations and Opportunities in International Law* Jennifer A. Zerk

47 *Judiciaries within Europe: A Comparative Review* John Bell

46 *Law in Times of Crisis: Emergency Powers in Theory and Practice* Oren Gross and Fionnuala Ní Aoláin

45 *Vessel-Source Marine Pollution: The Law and Politics of International Regulation* Alan Khee-Jin Tan

44 *Enforcing Obligations* Erga Omnes *in International Law* Christian J. Tams

43 *Non-Governmental Organisations in International Law* Anna-Karin Lindblom

42 *Democracy, Minorities and International Law* Steven Wheatley

41 *Prosecuting International Crimes: Selectivity and the International Criminal Law Regime* Robert Cryer

40 *Compensation for Personal Injury in English, German and Italian Law: A Comparative Outline* Basil Markesinis, Michael Coester, Guido Alpa and Augustus Ullstein

39 *Dispute Settlement in the UN Convention on the Law of the Sea* Natalie Klein

38 *The International Protection of Internally Displaced Persons* Catherine Phuong

37 *Imperialism, Sovereignty and the Making of International Law* Antony Anghie

35 *Necessity, Proportionality and the Use of Force by States* Judith Gardam

34 *International Legal Argument in the Permanent Court of International Justice: The Rise of the International Judiciary* Ole Spiermann

32 *Great Powers and Outlaw States: Unequal Sovereigns in the International Legal Order* Gerry Simpson

31 *Local Remedies in International Law* (second edition) Chittharanjan Felix Amerasinghe

30 *Reading Humanitarian Intervention: Human Rights and the Use of Force in International Law* Anne Orford

29 *Conflict of Norms in Public International Law: How WTO Law Relates to Other Rules of International Law* Joost Pauwelyn

27 *Transboundary Damage in International Law* Hanqin Xue

25 *European Criminal Procedures* Edited by Mireille Delmas-Marty and J. R. Spencer

24 *Accountability of Armed Opposition Groups in International Law* Liesbeth Zegveld

23 *Sharing Transboundary Resources: International Law and Optimal Resource Use* Eyal Benvenisti

22 *International Human Rights and Humanitarian Law* René Provost

21 *Remedies against International Organisations* Karel Wellens

20 *Diversity and Self-Determination in International Law* Karen Knop

19 *The Law of Internal Armed Conflict* Lindsay Moir

18 *International Commercial Arbitration and African States: Practice, Participation and Institutional Development* Amazu A. Asouzu

17 *The Enforceability of Promises in European Contract Law* James Gordley

16 *International Law in Antiquity* David J. Bederman

15 *Money Laundering: A New International Law Enforcement Model* Guy Stessens

14 *Good Faith in European Contract Law* Reinhard Zimmermann and Simon Whittaker

13 *On Civil Procedure* J. A. Jolowicz

12 *Trusts: A Comparative Study* Maurizio Lupoi and Simon Dix

11 *The Right to Property in Commonwealth Constitutions* Tom Allen

10 *International Organizations before National Courts* August Reinisch

9 *The Changing International Law of High Seas Fisheries* Francisco Orrego Vicuña

8 *Trade and the Environment: A Comparative Study of EC and US Law* Damien Geradin

7 *Unjust Enrichment: A Study of Private Law and Public Values* Hanoch Dagan

6 *Religious Liberty and International Law in Europe* Malcolm D. Evans

5 *Ethics and Authority in International Law* Alfred P. Rubin

4 *Sovereignty over Natural Resources: Balancing Rights and Duties* Nico Schrijver

3 *The Polar Regions and the Development of International Law* Donald R. Rothwell

2 *Fragmentation and the International Relations of Micro-States: Self-Determination and Statehood* Jorri C. Duursma

1 *Principles of the Institutional Law of International Organizations* C. F. Amerasinghe

www.ingramcontent.com/pod-product-compliance
Lightning Source LLC
LaVergne TN
LVHW011659200926
848484LV00004B/1003

* 9 7 8 1 1 0 8 4 9 5 8 8 2 *